Type-Logical Syntax

Type-Logical Syntax

Yusuke Kubota and Robert D. Levine

The MIT Press
Cambridge, Massachusetts
London, England

The open access edition of this book was made possible by generous funding from Arcadia—a charitable fund of Lisbet Rausing and Peter Baldwin.

ARCADIA
A charitable fund of Lisbet Rausing and Peter Baldwin

This book was set in Syntax and Times Roman by the authors. Printed and bound in the United States of America.

Library of Congress Cataloging-in-Publication Data

Names: Kubota, Yusuke, author. | Levine, Robert, 1947- author.
Title: Type-logical syntax / Yusuke Kubota, Robert D. Levine.
Description: Cambridge, Massachusetts : The MIT Press, [2016] | Includes bibliographical references and index.
Identifiers: LCCN 2020000483 | ISBN 9780262539746 (paperback)
Subjects: LCSH: Categorial grammar. | Grammar, Comparative and general–Syntax.
Classification: LCC P161 .K83 2016 | DDC 415–dc23
LC record available at https://lccn.loc.gov/2020000483

ISBN: 978-0-262-53974-6

10 9 8 7 6 5 4 3 2 1

Contents

Foreword

This book represents the culmination of a research project on which we have collaborated for close to a decade, developing a "type-logical" version of categorial grammar as a viable alternative model of natural language syntax and semantics. Our collaboration originated in our realization that some of the thorniest problems presented by the syntax-semantics interface for natural language, first in the domain of coordination and then in ellipsis, have remained problematic across a wide range of seemingly quite different theoretical frameworks for syntax. It gradually became clear to us that these problems, addressed in the following chapters, have deep connections with each other, and that their intractability reflects a foundational problem shared by these approaches—commitment to the strategy of licensing linguistic expressions via well-formedness conditions on hierarchically organized objects. Despite the fact that the strategy has become ingrained in the practice of linguistic theorizing to the point where the vast majority of researchers in the field regard it as the only conceivable approach, a look back at the early history of the field makes it clear that there never was any sense in which this hierarchical model of representation was found to be necessary, on either logical or empirical grounds, as we discuss below (and in greater detail in chapter 1).

It is by now a truism that, with the advent of generative grammar in Chomsky (1957), the middle of the twentieth century saw the emergence of a radically new view of the fundamental questions a scientific perspective on human languages should seek answers to. This turn in the field, representing as it does the full adoption of a nomological-deductive paradigm, is arguably one of the great watersheds in the history of ideas. The results of this development in the theoretical foundations of linguistics as a field include an explosive growth in both the domain of knowledge that it claims as its own and the size of the field as an academic enterprise. What is not generally recognized is that the methodological/conceptual toolkit used to implement this new approach was brought over, largely intact, from the previous taxonomic era, commonly referred to as American Structuralism. The syntactic representation of natural language stringsets that provided the basis for contemporary mainstream grammatical frameworks—derivational and monostratal alike—was a reflection, ultimately, of the analytic practice of American Structuralists, in particular, the Boasian tradition in descriptive linguistics. This tradition in turn has its roots in the challenges posed by the extreme morphological complexity of indigenous North American languages. In particular, the phrase markers that became the lingua franca of theoretical syntax build into linguistic representations an enduring hierarchical relationship among the parts of sentences, in principle allowing for the accessibility of the entire compositional history of those parts for reference in the statement of grammatical operations.

From the very outset, however, there was a genuinely alternative perspective on the fundamental architecture of grammar. Lambek (1958), building on Ajdukiewicz (1935) and Bar-Hillel (1953), outlined a very different system, one in which the well-formedness of sentences is determined not by constructing hierarchically organized objects but via proofs formally homologous to proofs of theorems in various familiar logics. In Lambek's deductive calculus, all vocabulary items are associated with syntactic types, and the complete set of such types is defined by type constructors whose behavior mirrors that of the implication connective in intuitionistic propositional logic (IPL). Specifically, Lambek's rules in his 1958 calculus, recast in so-called natural deduction format, introduce and eliminate these connectives in a fashion which mirrors the rules of implication elimination and introduction, and—just as in logical proofs—the history of the deduction is not in general uniquely recoverable from the final line of the proof. In effect, this architecture, which forms the core of more modern versions of (type-logical variants of) categorial grammar, entails that there is no internal structure to the representation of sentences, at least in its simplest form as formulated in Lambek (1958) (one of the central issues in the later extensions of this system as a theory of natural language was actually to partially reintroduce the notion of hierarchical constituency in a controlled manner).

However, as Moortgat (2014, 2) observes, "[a]t the time of their publication, these ideas did not resonate." There seem to be a couple of factors involved in the initial failure of this logical perspective on syntax pioneered by Lambek to enter contemporary theoretical debates. In the first place, Lambek's calculus embodied a level of technical rigor that few linguists at the time, or subsequently, were in a position to apply. Its fundamental character—which, as a true logic of residuation, gives it remarkable expressive power relative to its basic simplicity—made it largely inaccessible to working linguists at the time of its appearance. A second factor, at least equally important in this context, was the lack of precedence for a deductive (as opposed to an implicitly configurational) model in American linguistic practice. As noted above, the rapidly developing field of generative grammar relied on data structures which had their original applications in the working practice of the field linguists trained by Leonard Bloomfield and his students. Given this background, Lambek's approach was conceptually too alien for ordinary working linguists.

There was, however, a third contributing factor. As noted by both Pollard (1988) and van Benthem (1988a), in the first decades of theoretical syntax, the inadequacy of phrase structure grammars as accounts of natural languages was, in Pollard's (1988, 392) words, "an article of faith." Combined with the strong suspicion that pure Lambek systems had exactly the weak generative capacity of context-free grammars, researchers in the field saw little incentive to explore what was, supposedly, a notational variant of an inadequate syntactic framework. It was not until the early 1980s that research in Generalized Phrase Structure Grammar was able to demonstrate that the standard arguments against phrase structure grammars failed empirically, despite the fact that repeated efforts to adduce such data typically overlooked counterexamples and/or critical semantic factors bearing on the interpretation of the evidence.[1] Moreover, phenomena which most severely challenged phrase structure–based grammatical frameworks—so-called nonconstituent coordination and ellipsis—were not widely studied, nor their difficulties fully appreciated, until decades after Lambek's early papers. The first detailed transformational treatment of coordination, Dougherty (1970, 1971), spanning nearly one hundred pages in the journal *Language*, did not once mention any constructions in which apparent nonconstituents were conjoined, while major syntax textbooks have occasionally cited coordination as a standard test for constituency (e.g., Baker 1978; Radford 1981). Ellipsis phenomena such as sluicing and pseudogapping, while recognized as anomalies, did not attract the kind of attention that was paid to *wh* extraction or to passive, raising, and control constructions until much later in the development of grammatical theory.

Interest in categorial grammar was thus largely confined, up until the early 1980s, to work on the borders of metalogic and the theory of formal languages. The major work on categorial grammar during this period—Bar-Hillel et al. (1960), Cohen (1967), Zielonka (1978), among a few others—mostly focused on purely formal aspects such as generative capacity.[2] When the (psycho)linguistically attractive aspects of categorial grammar began to be exploited for empirical applications a quarter of a century after Lambek's 1958 paper, it was a somewhat different version which did not make use of the proof-theoretic architecture of Lambek's original system. Nonetheless, this version of categorial grammar, now known as Combinatory Categorial Grammar (CCG), was

---

1. See Pullum and Gazdar (1982) for details. Pullum (1985) provides an entertaining critique of one such effort, representative of the kinds of arguments that were made at the time in response to claims that natural languages were indeed context-free.

2. Despite much earlier conjecture and important partial results, the complete proof of weak equivalence of the Lambek calculus and context-free phrase structure grammars was not established until the appearance of Pentus (1993).

applied to some of the most difficult syntactic problems under discussion at the time. In particular, it was shown by Steedman (1985) and Dowty (1988) that varieties of "nonconstituent coordination" that could only find phrase structure–based solutions involving considerable arbitrary stipulation receive elegant and simple accounts with essentially no extra machinery in categorial grammar by exploiting an architecture that de-emphasizes the notion of hierarchical constituency (it was shown later [cf. Morrill 1994; Carpenter 1997] that these empirical results carry over straightforwardly to the original Lambek system).

During the past two decades, there has been further work showcasing the insights obtainable from the logic-based approach (see, e.g., Moortgat 1988; Morrill 1994; Bernardi 2002; Jäger 2005). Our goal in this book is to further extend this line of research and demonstrate that Type-Logical Categorial Grammar (TLCG) is a strong candidate for the optimal theory of the compositional syntax-semantics interface for natural languages.[3] For this purpose, we propose a new version of TLCG that extends the Lambek calculus with a mode of implication that is dissociated from surface word order by building on the proposal outlined in Oehrle (1994, 1995) to model the prosodic component of linguistic signs via a lambda calculus. TLCG embodies a particularly satisfying framework from the point of view of explanatory capability in the following two respects. In the first place, as a true implicative logic of types, the system we explore and apply in this volume offers little or no room for the importation of special machinery or add-on devices: one has the lexicon and the rules of proof, and the claims and predictions of any given analysis are in very large part the forced consequences of these two components of the system. This kind of architecture amounts to a very strict accounting in reckoning up the pros and cons of specific analyses. Second, categorial grammar in general and TLCG in particular is known for an elegant and systematic interface between syntax and semantics—as van Benthem (1988a, 36) puts it, the calculus of syntactic types "wears its semantics upon its sleeves." This is an especially important property of the theory we propose in this book since the central target of our investigations is a set of complex (yet systematic) interactions between phenomena in natural language (specifically, scopal operators and noncanonical varieties of coordination and ellipsis) each of which itself exhibits considerable complexity in the mapping between form and meaning. These phenomena illustrate the power of logic-based theory in uncovering the systematicity underlying the surface observations, which initially tend to look just messy and complicated.

---

3. The term *Type-Logical Grammar* is more standard in the literature, but we stick to the terminology *Type-Logical Categorial Grammar* (TLCG) throughout this book in order to underscore the fact that Type-Logical Grammar is a version of categorial grammar.

The present volume consists of twelve chapters. The following diagram indicates the dependencies among the individual chapters:

(1)

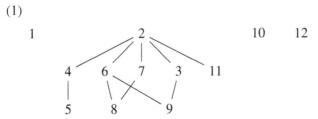

Chapter 1 lays out the general background of the ensuing discussion, tracing the history of contemporary syntactic theory, with special attention to what (on hindsight) seem to be largely accidental choices made at various points in the development of generative grammar that ultimately led to the central role that the notion of phrase structural constituency plays in practically all variants of contemporary generative grammar. As the discussion in this chapter provides the key motivation for the theory we present in this book, we recommend the reader at least skim through it. However, since this is not a technical chapter, the material in the following chapters does not directly depend on its content.

Chapter 2 presents the theory that is used (with only slight extensions in a couple of places) throughout the rest of the book for the analysis of various empirical phenomena. The theory we present, Hybrid Type-Logical Categorial Grammar (Hybrid TLCG), is a version of Type-Logical Categorial Grammar and builds on a large body of research in the literature of TLCG over the past thirty years. Though TLCG is a mathematically sophisticated formalism, we have tried to make the presentation in this chapter maximally accessible to ordinary linguists. We do not assume any background knowledge beyond solid understanding of the basics of formal semantics, especially the use of the lambda calculus (to write higher-order functions) as a "glue" language for meaning composition. Familiarity with standard propositional logic (especially the natural deduction system for it), versions of categorial grammar (such as CCG) and techniques in mathematical logic and computer science (such as type theory) would be useful but are not really required. The chapter is a self-contained introduction for the theory and prepares the reader for the technical analysis presented in the ensuing chapters.

The rest of the book up to chapter 9 deals with various empirical phenomena in English, mostly in the domains of coordination and ellipsis. Our empirical investigation starts with two types of "noncanonical" coordination phenomena, Gapping (chapter 3) and nonconstituent coordination (Right-Node Raising and Dependent Cluster Coordination; chapter 4). A central issue in these two chapters is the scopal interactions between coordination and scope-taking expressions such as generalized quantifiers and modal auxiliaries. As we discuss in detail in these chapters, the systematic link-ages among complex empirical patterns found in such interactions crucially distinguish the predictions of competing analyses of these phenomena. We show that two key properties of Hybrid TLCG—the flexible notion of constituency and the systematic mapping between syntax and semantics, both of which are direct consequences of the logic-based architecture of the theory in the sense outlined above—enable particularly simple analyses of these phenomena, which pose considerable difficulties for phrase structure–based theories of syntax (including both transformational and nontransformational variants). This discussion of the interactions between coordination and scopal expressions is followed by an in-depth analysis of more complex types of scope-taking expressions (symmetrical predicates such as *same* and *different*, so-called respective readings of conjoined and plural expressions, and summative predicates such as *a total of ten books*) in chapter 5. We show that the basic analysis of nonconstituent coordination from chapter 4 interacts with independently motivated analyses of these scopal phenomena to automatically make the right predictions for a wide range of complex phenomena involving these constructions.

In the latter half of the empirical investigations, we turn our attention to ellipsis phenomena, another major empirical domain which has been the target of extensive research in the contemporary syntactic literature. We start our investigations into ellipsis phenomena with an analysis of pseudogapping in chapter 6. Pseudogapping is a peculiar type of ellipsis phenomenon in English that is closely related to VP ellipsis. We formulate an analysis of this construction, which exploits the flexible notion of constituency that is at the heart of Hybrid TLCG. This is then followed by a brief chapter sketching the analysis of extraction in Hybrid TLCG (chapter 7), which provides the basis for a detailed analysis of the interactions between extraction and ellipsis in chapter 8. One of the central issues in the literature on ellipsis is whether covert structural representations are needed. Arguments for covert structural representations typically invoke interactions between ellipsis and extraction, where the latter is taken as a probe for covert structure, for example, by exhibiting sensitivity to island constraints. In chapter 8, we examine in detail the validity of this type of argument advocated by Kennedy (2003) by formulating an alternative analysis of the range of facts adduced by Kennedy which dispenses with covert structural representations.

The final chapter in the main part of the book (chapter 9) examines the syntax of auxiliary verbs in English (especially its interaction with scope of negation), a topic that is relevant for both coordination (in its relation to Gapping; chapter 3) and ellipsis (VP ellipsis; chapters 6 and 8). We show in this chapter that in Hybrid TLCG, we can formulate an analysis of English modal auxiliaries that offers a unifying perspective on the major types of analyses advocated in the literature of transformational and non-transformational variants of generative grammar respectively. Specifically, our analysis posits a higher-order entry for auxiliaries that mimics a movement-based analysis in the transformational literature, from which a sign corresponding to the "lexicalist" analyses of auxiliaries standardly adopted in the nontransformational theories can be derived as a theorem. This relationship between higher- and lower-order forms leads to an interesting synthesis of ideas from transformational and nontransformational variants of generative grammar. A broader implication that follows from this is that TLCG may be viewed as a common unifying framework for making explicit the hidden connections between analytic ideas explored in different strands of research in syntax and thereby clarifying the nature of the combinatoric system underlying human linguistic competence.

The remaining chapters (chapters 10–12) deal with some residual (but important) issues that have been left unaddressed in the main body of the book. Chapter 10 examines the issue of island constraints. Analyses of coordination and ellipsis phenomena in the transformational literature often invoke movement operations of various sorts, and such analyses are typically motivated by the (alleged) fact that they induce syntactic island effects. Though this type of argumentation has been standard practice in the syntactic literature over the last fifty years since Ross (1967) first discovered syntactic islands, recent reconsiderations of island effects call for fundamental rethinking of this research practice. In chapter 10, we first review the recent rethinking of island effects and alternative extragrammatical accounts of major types of syntactic islands. This part can be independently read as an up-to-date summary of the actively growing literature on this topic. This review of recent rethinking of island effects is followed by our own reassessment of various proposals about island sensitivity of the major types of coordination and ellipsis phenomena we have analyzed in the preceding chapters. The overall conclusion we reach is that the island-based arguments for the analyses of coordination and ellipsis phenomena in the transformational literature are uniformly untenable. In most cases, the reported data are neither robust nor representative enough to support the particular conclusions the authors draw based on such data.

Chapter 11 deals with another potential issue one may find with the type of theory advocated in this book. The key claim of the present book essentially amounts to the proposal to do away with the notion of constituency, or, to put it in a more nuanced way, to give it a much less central role than it happens to receive in most contemporary syntactic theories. But denying the relevance of syntactic constituency completely is also an extreme idea that is unlikely to be tenable. In this chapter, we sketch an extension of our theory, just to make it clear that we are in fact not advocating such an extreme position. The extended system is equipped with a mechanism for explicitly representing "grouping of words" and handling reordering of constituents in the morpho-phonological representation. (This type of architecture receives motivation mostly from languages other than English that display complex morpho-syntactic phenomena, which are beyond the scope of the present book.) We illustrate the workings of this system by formulating an analysis of a certain puzzling pattern in Right-Node Raising in English and other languages (here we take Japanese as an example) called Right-Node Wrapping.

Finally, in chapter 12, we provide a brief comparison between Hybrid TLCG and other variants of categorial grammar. The categorial grammar research community entertains a rather varied range of perspectives represented by a host of related yet distinct approaches (including our own), and it is sometimes difficult for outsiders to grasp the relationship between different variants and the different "philosophies" underlying coexisting alternative approaches. Putting our own approach in perspective helps clarify its primary goals and those respects in which it has made progress as well as respects in which it is underdeveloped relative to other related approaches. We hope to remind the reader through this comparison that categorial grammar research—just like any other scientific research in any other domain—is a collaborative endeavor in which related yet distinct approaches coexist and in which different perspectives mutually inform each other in a fruitful manner.

The present work itself has indeed benefited greatly from collaborations and interactions with our colleagues, and we would like to take this occasion to thank them. First and foremost, we'd like to thank our colleagues at Ohio State University, in particular, Carl Pollard. He was the first author's co-advisor (the second author being the other co-advisor) on the dissertation project (Kubota 2010) leading to the earliest version of the framework explored in the present book. Carl's critical feedback and constant engagement with the development of our approach has been invaluable in the refinement of our proposals, and our thinking in general. We are likewise indebted to current and former students at OSU, in particular, Noah Diewald, Scott Martin, Jordan Needle, Daniel Puthawala, Symon Stevens-Guille, Elena Vaiksnoraite, and Chris Worth.

Thanks are also due to the colleagues throughout the world with whom we have had ongoing discussions on several aspects of categorial grammar research over many years, including Chris Barker, Michael Moortgat, Richard Moot, and Glyn Morrill. Brendan Gillon gave us very useful feedback on parts of a near-final version of our manuscript. Input (in various forms at various occasions) from David Dowty, Polly Jacobson, Kyle Johnson, Mark Steedman, Mike White, Neal Whitman, Emmon Bach and Chung-chieh Shan has also been important. This is of course not to say that these people endorse the views advocated in the present volume. In fact, sometimes the feedback these scholars provided was valuable precisely because the alternative perspectives they offered helped articulate our own views. Likewise, we benefited greatly from input we have received from peer reviewers and audiences at conferences and summer schools (Formal Grammar, Logical Aspects of Computational Linguistics, Logic and Engineering of Natural Language Semantics, European Summer School in Logic, Language and Information and Linguistic Society of America Summer Institute). A special expression of gratitude is due our editors at three journals in which our work on Hybrid TLCG first appeared—Samuel Jay Keyser (*Linguistic Inquiry*), Louise McNally (*Natural Language and Linguistic Theory*), and Daniel Büring (*Linguistics and Philosophy*). In each case we were given the benefit of advice from an excellent selection of referees, along with invaluable input from the editors themselves.

We also profited from interactions with our colleagues in Japan, in particular, Daisuke Bekki and Koji Mineshima, who have commented on our work from the perspectives of logic and computer science research, and with whom we have recently started joint work extending our approach to syntax with the semantic theory (Dependent Type Semantics) they have been developing over the past several years. Much of the writing and revising for this volume was carried out while the second author was in residence at the University of Tsukuba on his sabbatical during 2018, whose faculty, staff, and students welcomed him with the utmost warmth and kindness to the intellectual life of the Linguistics Department there.

Our research was generously supported by the Japan Society for the Promotion of Science, which provided two postdoctoral fellowships (JSPS PD 10J02912 [2010–2013] and JSPS Postdoctoral Fellowship for Research Abroad [2013–2014]) for the first author. A subsequent research grant (JSPS KAKENHI JP15K16732) contributed significantly to the support of the second author during his research semester in Japan. The first author would also like to thank his previous and current employers, the University of Tsukuba and the National Institute for Japanese Language and Linguistics, for providing ideal research environments, in particular, the generous financial and administrational support for international collaboration. The research by the second author was supported by the College of Arts and Sciences at Ohio State University, through their Larger/Small Grant programs. We also wish to offer our thanks to the Department of Linguistics at OSU, which, during an extended period of budgetary constraint, nonetheless provided generous financial support for our research.

We emphatically thank our editors at MIT Press, Marc Lowenthal and Philip Laughlin, for their continuous guidance and expeditious treatment of the submission process. Thanks are also due to Arcadia Fund for its generous funding which made it possible to produce an open-access edition of this book. Theresa Carcaldi at Westchester Publishing Services deserves special thanks for guiding us smoothly through the production phase of the book. We would also like to thank Shinya Okano for his help at the copy-editing stage. And it goes without saying (but we will say it anyway) that the enthusiastic support of our families, to whom we dedicate our book, was essential to the completion of this project.

Finally, we take this opportunity to honor the memories of Joachim Lambek and Richard Oehrle, whose genius separately created the two respective formal systems that constitute the key components of the logical framework we employ in the present volume. We hope they would have been gratified at seeing how much analytic power and empirical reach follow from the combination of their brilliant contributions to the rigorously formal study of human language.

1 The Origins of Phrase Structure Constituency

In a remarkably prescient paper written for the 1989 Tilburg Conference on Discontinuous Constituency, David Dowty makes the following observations:

> No assumption is more fundamental in the theory (and practice) of syntax than that natural languages should always be described in terms of constituent structure, at least wherever possible. To be sure, certain kinds of cases are well-known where constituent structure of the familiar sort runs into problems . . . But even here, the strategy has usually been to accommodate these matters while modifying the received notion of constituent structure as little as possible.
>
> There are two things that worry me about the situation syntactic theory finds itself in. Since hierarchical syntactic structure is so often assumed, syntacticians don't usually ask questions—at least beyond the elementary syntax course—as to what the nature of evidence for a constituent structure in a particular sentence in a particular language is: we just take whatever structure our favorite syntactic theory would predict as the expected one for the string of words in questions—by the current X-bar theory, etc.—unless and until that assumption is contradicted by some particular fact.
>
> My second concern is closely related: I suspect syntacticians today have almost come to think of the primary empirical data of syntactic research as phrase structure trees, so firm are our convictions as to what the right S-structure tree for most any given sentence is. But speakers of natural languages do not speak trees, nor do they write trees on paper when they communicate. The primary data for syntax are of course only *strings* of words, and everything in syntactic description beyond that is part of a theory, invented by a linguist. (Dowty 1996b, 11–12)

Dowty's misgivings about the default status of phrase markers as the appropriate data structure for representation of the fundamental syntactic properties of sentences are, as we argue in this book, entirely justified, and in succeeding chapters we present a considerable body of additional phenomena, beyond those he cited in his paper, to support this negative view of configurational representations. But it is worth beginning this investigation by addressing the question of *why* we have this state of affairs in the first place. Where did the notion of phrase structure (PS) constituency come from, and why has it maintained such a grip on the analytic imagination of syntacticians—to an extent which makes it seem reasonable to posit all manner of complex, stipulative operations just to accommodate phenomena which stubbornly resist description in terms of hierarchical trees? As Dowty notes, various "fixes" have been proposed, essentially as add-ons to a phrase structure basis—indeed, in all but the most recent phase of transformational grammar, this was the essential architecture of the combinatoric component—but it still seems to be regarded as perverse, in some foundational way, to reject hierarchical phrase structure as the model of syntactic representation.

In this introductory chapter, we sketch what seems to us to be the main line of development in generative linguistics (and its precursor) which led to this state of affairs. Our view is that the notion of phrase structure hierarchy as a theoretical construct originates as a reification of analytic practice in the American Structuralist tradition originating with Bloomfield and his students. In the work of the Structuralists, this practice had no special theoretical status but rather represented a method of description which extended procedures applied and honed in the domain of morphology to the larger units beyond the word that the Structuralist found it necessary to recognize. And these morphologically based practices themselves originated, ultimately, in the linguistic relativism that Bloomfield's teacher, Franz Boas, introduced into the history of the field in the work he carried out and sponsored on the native languages of the New World. Our point in the following discussion is that phrase markers evolved out of a set of descriptive practices which reflect the analytic methods of Boas's intellectual descendants, rather than from some strongly motivated theoretical foundation. The long-established consensus that hierarchical constituency is the optimal data structure for syntactic representation is, in our view—and as per Dowty's caveat—a largely contingent development that calls for rethinking at a fundamental level.

1.1 The Boasian Era

Without any question, the dominant figure in American linguistics in the early twentieth century was the celebrated cultural anthropologist Franz Boas. When Boas first began working on native languages of North America, the dominant view of linguistic form was heavily Eurocentric, reflecting the views of the major nineteenth-century comparativists. On this view, the classical languages (Greek, Latin) and certain favored modern languages (e.g., German) embodied the "essence" of linguistic form, and all languages were to be described using, for example, Latin paradigms as models.

Boas took a radically different approach, concisely formulated in his remark in the introduction to the massive collection of descriptive grammars, *Handbook of American Indian Languages*:

> [T]he method of treatment has been throughout an analytical one. No attempt has been made to compare the forms of the Indian grammars with the grammars of English, Latin, or even among themselves; but in each case the psychological groupings which are given depend upon the inner form of each language. (Boas 1911, 68)

By "psychological groupings," Boas meant the grammatical categories revealed by morphological analysis, the point being that the authors of each of the grammatical descriptions in the *Handbook* understood the language so described to have its own formal organizing principles, with no language regarded as superior to, or entitled to serve as a model for, the analysis of any others.

The challenge in taking such an approach is of course to settle upon a method of analysis which does not make any reference whatever to some predetermined checklist of categories. From this point of view, one could view the movement which dominated American linguistics in the 1930s through the 1950s, *American Structuralism*, led by Leonard Bloomfield, one of Boas's two most important students, as in effect the operationalization of Boas's notion of "the inner form of each language." This fleshing out of Boas's conception could be summarized as the principle that any language was to be described in terms of classes of forms with parallel distributional properties. Thus, word parts, words, and strings of words could be assigned to equivalence classes based strictly on where they could appear in words (morphology) and sentences (syntax). The rules governing the arrangement of members of these equivalence classes (or "form classes") in any language constituted the grammatical rules of that particular language.

In structuralist analysis, morphological analysis—as expounded in detail in Nida's monumental 1949 text—was the model for syntactic analysis, a fact explicitly acknowledged in, for example, Zellig Harris's seminal "From Morpheme to Utterance" (Harris 1946) and Rulon Wells's more influential 1947 paper (Wells 1947) on the descriptive device he referred to as *Immediate Constituency* (IC). Harris (1946, 161) begins his paper with the following remarks:

> [T]his paper presents a formalized procedure for describing utterances directly in terms of sequences of morphemes rather than single morphemes . . . At present, morpheme classes are formed by placing in one class all morphemes substitutable for each other in utterances, as *man* replaces *child* in *The child disappeared.* The procedure outlined below consists, essentially in extending the technique of substitution from single morphemes (e.g. *man*) to sequences of morphemes (e.g. *intense young man*) . . . When applied to a particular language, the procedure yields a compact statement of what sequences of morphemes occur in the language, i.e., a formula for each utterance (sentence) structure in the language . . . The reason for a procedure of the type offered here is not far to seek. One of the chief objectives of syntactic analysis is a compact description of the structure of utterances in the given language.

Here and elsewhere in his paper, Harris is quite explicit that the "method of substitution" he alludes to as an extension of morphological analysis has as its objective a concise—that is, maximally general—statement of the distribution of words and word sequences in whatever language it is applied to. No theoretical content is claimed for the distributional statements arrived at in this fashion; Harris's goal, as he makes clear throughout the discussion, is the explicit codification of standard Structuralist analytic practice. As Harris (1946, 161) observes, "the proposed method does not involve new operations of analysis. It merely reduces to writing *the techniques of substitution which every linguist uses as he works over his material*" (emphasis added).

Essentially exactly the same method is presented in Wells (1947), more widely cited perhaps as a result of his possibly more intuitive use of bracket notation rather than the seemingly mathematical formulæ employed by Harris. So far as content is concerned, Wells's and Harris's respective papers share largely the same central premise: what Wells (1947, 82) identifies as "the simple but significant fact on which we base our whole theory of I[mmediate] C[onstituent]s . . .: that a sequence belonging to one sequence-class A is often substitutable for a sequence belonging to an entirely different sequence class B." By "sequence class," Wells is referring somewhat neutrally to sequences of morphemes, but in the context of the specific data and examples he provides, a sequence class is essentially a sequence of words with a parallel distribution with a sequence of words that has the same distribution as a single word taken to be an "expansion" of the sequence class to which that single word belongs. What Wells is in fact setting up is a definition of constituency in which constituents of a sentence are determined by parsing the sentences into strings whose distribution parallels that of single words in a range of contexts.

We can, however, be a bit more specific about the conceptual origins of constituency in Structuralists's standard practice. A substantial number of major Structuralists—including theoretical leaders such as Bloomfield and Hockett, and influential figures including Eugene Nida and Kenneth Pike—had continued the Boasian tradition of field linguistics with native languages of the western hemisphere, such as those of the Algonkian, Iroquoian, and Athapaskan families. In these languages, root morphemes were preceded and/or followed by sequences of affixes, many arranged in paradigmatic classes ("position classes"). Faced with such complexity, the standard methods of descriptive analysis pioneered by (post-)Boasian field linguists involved the elicitation of both inflectional and what might be called derivational paradigms, identifying recurrent pairings of phonetic form and grammatical function, where the analysis proceeds from the outside inwards peeling off layers of affixation until one arrives at the "roots" and "stems" referred to as such in, for example, Bloomfield (1933) and Nida (1949). Although the conclusion of this analytic practice was typically a statement of how morphological composition may proceed in the construction of lexical items, the practice itself orients the analyst to approach lexical items as a cluster of parts which are to be separated out in a series of steps, where at each step some of the material has been segmented off, a remainder which is then to undergo further analysis. This step-by-step method resolving words into sequences of morphemes is difficult to apply in any other way, for as a matter of practical necessity, the alternative would be to try to carry out segmentation medially, with unidentified phonological material on both sides of any given internal string of phonological segments, greatly increasing the uncertainty of the results.

The result of this kind of analytic practice ultimately had far-reaching implications for syntax. As Joos (1957, 185) notes, the Structuralists did not really start approaching syntactic description seriously until they had acquired considerable experience with morphology, where their distributional methods beyond the level of phonological segments had been honed—a fact which clearly predisposed them to use extensions of the familiar methods they had, in so many cases, brought to bear on morphologically very complex field languages and to view syntax from the perspective of those methods. Thus, Nida (1949, 86), for example, observes that "[t]he distribution of any morpheme must be given in terms of its environment, but some of its environment may be important and the rest unimportant. *This is true of both morphology and syntax.*"[1] In particular, the standard technique employed in descriptive linguistic practice when one has to analyze a word in a language different from one's own native language(s) has typically been to work from the outside in, observing what happens to word meanings when partials at the beginning or the end of a word are replaced while the rest is held constant, or, conversely, what constant contribution to meaning corresponds to a given stretch of phonological material at the edges of words across a number of data points. Once one has separated out the material on the periphery, the analytic procedure can be iterated, until the form is completely parsed.

This "decompositional" preference, arising from the practical methodology adopted by grammarians guided by distributional criteria, would have made it extremely natural for linguistic objects to be seen as assembled out of smaller parts, which in turn might themselves comprise subparts. Nida (1949, 101) in fact presents just such a treelike analysis for the Totonac word *kilila·pa·ški·qu·t* ('my necessity of loving them reciprocally'):

---

1. None of this is to say that Structuralist methodology was the sole contributor to the notion of hierarchy in human languages; thus, Percival (2018) identifies, as an important strand of Bloomfield's thinking, the influence of the psychologist and philosopher Wilhelm Wundt in his major work *Völkerpsychologie: Eine Untersuchung der Entwicklungsgesetze von Sprache, Mythus und Sitte* (Wundt 1900), arguing that Bloomfield's earlier major work on linguistics, published in 1914, was heavily indebted to Wundt's insistence that sentences have a primarily binary internal structure independent of the logical content the sentence expresses. In particular, as Percival notes, Wundt's own thinking was heavily influenced by the structure of formulæ in symbolic logic, whose connectives are primarily binary, and in which propositions are typically decomposed into a predicate and its argument. But it is unlikely that Wundt's logic-based binary view of the analysis of sentences and its influence on Bloomfield was the primary driver of the hierarchical analytic picture of sentence structure held by the leading Structuralist theorists. Percival himself acknowledges, in connection with the Structuralists's "preference for binary analysis" (clearly evident, for example, in Wells's formulation of IC analysis, to which we turn directly), that morphological practice played a major role in this attitude.

(2) kilila·pa·ški·qu·t

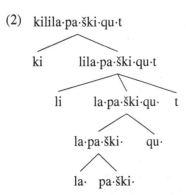

ki   lila·pa·ški·qu·t

li   la·pa·ški·qu·   t

la·pa·ški·   qu·

la· pa·ški·

From the analytic perspective given in the work by Harris and Nida, the graphic object in (2) is nothing more or less than a compact statement of the outer-to-inner segmentation of the complex Totonac word as motivated by the distribution of the substrings separated out in (2) on the basis of the recurrent semantic contributions of those subparts across the whole recorded Totonac lexicon: there is a "nucleus" comprising the immediate constituents *la·*, the reciprocal prefix and the verb stem *pa·ški·*, 'to love'; this sequence was in turn an immediate constituent, with the inflectional object suffix *qu·*, of the verb *la·pa·ški·qu·*, 'reciprocate love of someone'; and so on. These partials are identified via the distribution of form/meaning pairing, which was the major analytic tool in the Structuralists's arsenal, whereby a phonological sequence *ki-* has the constant meaning in all its occurrences of first-person possessive, *li-. . .-t* can be separated out from the rest of the word it appears in as a derivational circumfix denoting the necessity of the nominal it derives by combination with some verb, and so on. Essentially, the immediate constituent tree in (2) is nothing more or less than a graphic summary of this distribution of phonological/semantic covariation based on extensive elicitation and inspection of lexical and textual material.

Analyses of the sort summarized in (2) led to a certain view of word formation summarized in the following observation by Nida (1949, 98):

> [L]anguages with an extensive morphological structure frequently exhibit well-defined structural layers . . . The principle division is between derivational and inflectional formations. The derivational formations may in turn be divided between formations of the nuclei (these are compounds) and constructions consisting of nuclei and nonnuclei.

The history of the analyst's decomposition of the word into its distributionally determined subparts was thus seen as providing, in reverse order as it were, a guide to the morphological steps by which the word had been built up on the basis of its atomic root elements and affixes.

In view of the foregoing, it is hardly surprising that Structuralists's efforts to extend their methods to description and classification at the sentence level took the same form as their morphological descriptions. The basic thrust is evident from Wells's examples. Wells's central illustration of the method of immediate constituent analysis, for instance, starts with the sentence in (3):

(3) The King of England opened Parliament.

and breaks it down into immediate constituents based on substitution possibilities along the lines indicated. As Wells formulated his results, they took the explicit form of the following unlabeled bracketing (Wells 1947, 84):[2]

(4) [[the] [[king] [[of] [England]]]] [[opened] [Parliament]]

(4) simultaneously documents the *defensible* breakdown steps to arrive at the terminal yield of the analysis and displays the token existence of the strings derived in the breakdown at every level of the analysis. What is important in terms of the future development of linguistic theory in the post-Structuralist phase is that such objects essentially identify a relationship of "containment" among strings—simultaneously identifying, in particular, which strings any given word sequence is part of and what substrings it contains itself. These containment relations correspond at the syntactic level to exactly the information represented in the morphological analysis summarized in (2), and can be presented in the same graphical format:[3]

(5)   the King of England opened Parliament

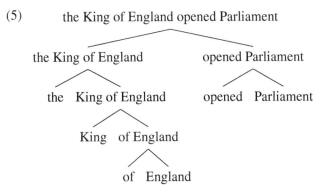

Such a labeled bracketing, by its very nature, depicts both the largest substring constituent parts of the sentence and the largest substring constituents of each of those parts, and so on. Because one is working top-down, so to speak, one first reveals the yield of the initial breakdown steps, then the breakdown of the latter into the largest strings they contain that meet Wells's substitutability criterion, repeating the procedure

2. Wells uses the vertical bar | instead of left and right brackets, but the information represented is the same.

3. Indeed, Nida (1949, 84) presents just this kind of tree in his representation of the structure of the sentence *Peasants throughout China work very hard.*

down to the individual words.[4] And because the critical relationship illustrated is containment, by far the most natural way to depict the totality of breakdown steps is by bracket annotation of the word sequence constituting the sentence.

IC analysis of the sort typified in (5) is clearly a major source of the dominant role that the notion of phrase structural constituency plays in modern linguistics, although during the Structuralist era it had, as already noted, no particularly rigorous methodological foundations. Wells's own characterization of the criteria by which alternative constituent analyses are arrived at is not particularly systematic and never gets around to explaining why such criteria are salient in the first place. At no point in his paper does Wells offer anything like a theoretical frame within which his classification criteria for determining the immediate constituents can be taken to yield a *better* result than some other set of criteria.[5] It is all the more interesting, then, that this exclusively methodological view of constituency was essentially enshrined as the canonical language of syntactic representation in the generative paradigm which succeeded Structuralism— a paradigm whose defining literature repeatedly emphasizes its theoretical content, in contrast to its taxonomic predecessor.[6]

1.2   Transformational Grammar: The Structuralist Legacy

It is by now fairly well accepted that many of the supposed innovations in transformational grammar were taken over, often with only cosmetic modification, from earlier

---

4. Wells does take the position that IC analysis can be construed as either a bottom-up or top-down process. But his examples uniformly reflect a top-down series of analyses, and when he says that "[t]his is the fundamental aim of IC-analysis: to analyze each utterance and each constituent into maximally independent sequences—sequences which, consistently preserving the same meaning, fit in the greatest number of environments" (Wells 1947, 88), it seems clear that the linguist is expected to identify a set of data and then apply the method illustrated in Wells's treatment of (3). Indeed, it is difficult to see how the particular methods Wells employs could be carried out in any *but* a top-down manner.

5. For example, the standard metric for evaluating scientific hypotheses—predictive success over the range of data to which the hypothesis applies—is not in play here, because there is no predictive content to Wells's proposal, nor, it is apparent, was there intended to be any. What Wells was outlining, as he makes clear throughout the paper, was a program for systematically applying the substitution criterion for defining constituents illustrated in some detail in Harris (1946). As such, it reflected the Structuralists's essentially exclusive concern with explicit procedures for classifying data.

6. Hyemes and Fought (1981, 125) make the rather odd claim that Wells was consciously engaged in linguistic theorizing because he uses the word *theory* in the first paragraph of his 1947 paper. It is instructive to recall what Wells actually says in that paragraph:

> We aim in this paper to replace by a unified, systematic theory the heterogeneous and incomplete *methods* hitherto offered for determining IMMEDIATE CONSTITUENTS . . . The unifying basis is furnished by the famous concept of patterning, applied repeatedly and in diverse special forms.   (Wells 1947, 81; emphasis added)

It is quite evident that by *theory* here, Wells intends nothing more than a systematic procedure, based on the parallel patterning of certain expressions and other much shorter ones, viz., that both can occur in a sufficiently large and diverse range of grammatical environments.

work in Structuralist linguistics on the one hand and mathematical logic on the other. Pullum (2011), for example, notes that Chomsky's watershed publication, *Syntactic Structures* (Chomsky 1957), offers a rule system which is, in the end, a more transparent version of formal generative technology than had been first devised in the mid-1940s by the logician Emil Post (see Post 1943, 1947). But what is particularly striking about the system which Chomsky presented in *Syntactic Structures* is the degree to which it took over what had been the methodological toolkit of Structuralist linguistics as the underlying component of syntactic theory. This is somewhat ironic, since generative grammar is standardly understood as having sharply broken with the Structuralists's practice of defining "discovery procedures" (of the sort described above) by emphasizing the primacy of "predictive success" as the criterion which, as in other nomological-deductive enterprises, grammatical analyses are to be evaluated against.

It is worth noting in this connection that early in generative grammar's career, after so-called generalized transformations were eliminated from the framework, the underlying context-free rule system (the so-called rules of the base) was *entirely* responsible for the infinite cardinality of the set of sentences each human language was taken to comprise. The open-endedness of the string sets that a language comprises is a by-product of the availability of chains of PS rule applications which expand some phrasal category X to yield, at some point in the series of rules applications, a string containing X. And collectively, these base rules were essentially a formalization of Harris's and Wells's immediate constituent analysis via a reader-friendly renotating of Post's generative technology (as per Pullum 2011).

In this context, it is useful to consider just what was involved in the transition from Wells's unlabeled bracketing representations to phrase markers with category-labeled nodes which became common at the end of the 1950s. The notion of constituent structure that Chomsky had inherited from the Structuralists reflected the containment relationship displayed in the hierarchically organized decomposition of sequences, as per (2) and (5). But the replacement of Wells's unlabeled bracketing capturing containment relationships among these constituents by labeled brackets made it possible to link such structures to the virtual automata which were increasingly coming into use as mathematical models of the generative systems enumerating those structures, where the categories labeling the brackets could be taken to correspond to the states of the automaton, and the PS rules to analogues of the transition functions defining such automata. Still more importantly, the category labels attached to bracketed strings, corresponding to the nodes in phrase markers, enable one to state generalizations over the behavior of all strings of words so labeled.

This point deserves some amplification, since it bears on the way in which a data structure made available in one analytic paradigm both fed into and helped shape the thinking of researchers working in succeeding paradigms. Phrase structure trees, widely adopted as a notation for syntactic representation soon after the appearance of *Syntactic Structures*, convey the same information content as labeled bracketings—but do so via a graphic organization of information which renders transparent the "genealogical relationship" among the category-labeled nodes in a way that bracketed objects do not. It is far easier to identify a string of words as descendants of a single category label when tree notation is used than with a flat string annotated with multiple subclusters of delimiters—and this, of course, matched perfectly with the appeal of transformational rules, originally proposed by Zellig Harris (1951), that Chomsky renotated and presented as the central innovation of his own framework. As structure-dependent mappings between hierarchical constituent representations, transformations depended, from their earliest formulations, on the possibility of identifying a string of words as the exhaustive descendants of a given category node.[7]

A key aspect of the role played by constituency in the transformationalist era is the way in which transformations, though nominally the major theoretical attraction in the new paradigm, frequently wound up playing the role of diagnostic probes for underlying phrase structure. Early textbooks, such as Jacobs and Rosenbaum (1968) and Akmajian and Heny (1975), argue for constituent structure at various points by pointing out various examples which appeal to movement in their derivations. The fact that transformations were taken to apply to major categories meant that the strings of words affected by such transformations were ipso facto analyzable as tokens of one or another of those categories. The role of the domination relation in identifying word sequences as analyzable with respect to some higher category node—and hence potentially part of the structural description of one or another transformational rule—ensured in turn that transformations could be used as diagnostic probes for phrase structure. But again, there was actually nothing fundamentally new in any of this. The Structuralists had, after all, insisted that shared distributional properties were the essential basis for taking (sequences of) grammatical formatives to belong to the same "form classes," and in Wells's analysis this diagnostic of parallel substitution possibilities is discussed at length. All that the use of transformations as probes for constituent structure represents is a systematization and extension of the range of substitution classes which were understood to be relevant for identifying the membership of some word sequence as an instance of a particular category. It is, again, an argument based on common distributional properties.

---

7. This essential reference to the history of a given substring is not immediately apparent in *Syntactic Structures*, where the statement of the structural analysis uses a flat, not hierarchical, representation; but the latter is inherent in the way the structural analysis identifies the target word strings for the application of each rule. Phrase markers, to which transformational rules make reference, thus allow substrings of the sentence to be identified as having a single ancestor that dominates them exhaustively, thereby defining the movable, replaceable, or deletable material in the "structural change" part of the transformation.

We thus have a somewhat curious situation. On the one hand, the transitivity of domination inherent in constituency created the "structural history" that was essential for the application of transformational rules, leading Chomsky to adopt the Structuralists's phrase marker notation (e.g., (2)) that permitted a transparent expression of those domination relations. The result was a data structure which made it possible to trace the sequence of domination relations holding for any terminal sequence arbitrarily far back into the rule expansion history licensing that sequence. On the other hand, transformational evidence was increasingly viewed as an essential part in validating specific phrase structure representation, based on the premise that if a string of words showed up in structural positions identified as solely the product of transformations (e.g., subjects of passive verbs), they were indeed necessarily to be regarded as syntactic constituents. The relationship between constituency and transformation thus verged on, and possibly into, circularity. The applicability of transformations, in itself, only defines objects to which the transformations are respectively applicable. Without some independent motivation for the increasingly intricate internal geometry attributed to the internal configurational structure of sentences via the rules of the base, the yield of these rules appeared to be doing little work, other than codifying the distribution of substrings labeled NP, AP, and so on. justified, in large part, on the basis of these same rules.

Perhaps not surprisingly, most of the explicit arguments on behalf of hierarchical constituent structures for syntactic representations are found in linguistic textbooks. One of the most extensive such defenses is given in Radford (1981), who provides the following distributional generalizations as the evidence that reference to such representations are necessary to account for the grammatical behavior of a word string:

1. recurrence of that string over a range of environments
2. coordinability
3. resistance to interposition of parenthetical material
4. proform replaceability
5. omissibility, for example, in ellipsis constructions

However, these criteria are plainly inadequate as either necessary or sufficient diagnostics for canonical phrase structure constituency. So far as sufficiency is concerned, we examine a wide range of cases in the following chapters in which both coordinability and omissibility fail as criteria for assigning the status of constituent to a word string.[8]

---

8. Parenthetical intrusion certainly fails as a criterion in English, as illustrated by the examples in (i) (where (ia) is a case of parenthetical intrusion into NP, and (ib), into PP):

(i) a. I can't find the, whatdya call it, SOCKET wrench that I need for this repair job.
     b. John contributed money to, if you can believe it, the Pythagorean Society!!

Nor, as Dalrymple (2001) notes, are all of Radford's criteria necessary to establish PS constituency. For example, we can hardly require that candidates for such constituent status be proform-replaceable, since there are many examples of accepted constituents which have no proforms (e.g., the canonical PPs *to John, of Mary*).[9] In the absence of much more sharply defined and precise versions of these criteria, they do nothing more than, at best, give the analyst some rules of thumb—in effect, hunches—for carrying out preliminary probes into novel data. But they can hardly be accorded the status of "just in case" criteria as Radford seeks to do. On the whole, then, most of Radford's criteria do not actually establish anything about constituency, because they do not yield the intended results.

The substitution test that Radford proposes is somewhat different, as are most of the diagnostics suggested by Dalrymple (2001).[10] This type of argument is highly effective as a defense of the claim that when word sequences combine with each other, the resulting longer word sequence is of a certain syntactic category, which can be referred to in stating the further combinatoric possibilities of that sequence; that is, one might argue on the basis of them that syntactic constituents corresponding to strings of words exist, with properties that are embodied in the category labels assigned to them, and with particular distributional properties.

This is actually a position that no major theoretical frameworks dispute. Strings of words may indeed instantiate some abstract syntactic type, such as NP or S, as opposed to being nothing more than lexical beads on a string, so to speak. But affirming the existence of such descriptions for strings of words in no way commits one to the position that when a pair of category-labeled strings A, B is combined by the composition rules of the syntax, the labels are retained in a hierarchically organized representation of a syntactic object that rules and constraints of the grammar can refer to. It is this latter, much stronger claim which is explicit in the representation of sentences as phrase markers, and so far as we can tell, none of Dalrymple's examples, or similar ones that have been offered as evidence for constituent structure, have any direct bearing on this

---

9. Conversely, the replacement test is not sufficient either: the $\overline{\text{N}}$ proform *one(s)* and the VP proform *do so* are known to pick out discontinuous strings as antecedents, to display significant mismatches with their supposed antecedents, to appear without any actual antecedent in discourse, and so on; see, for example, Miller (1991), Ward and Kehler (2005), Houser (2010), Miller and Pullum (2013). We return to the issue of identity conditions in ellipsis in chapter 6.

10. Dalrymple mentions a number of phenomena, such as the distribution of the English possessive clitic, the possible occurrences of extracted English *wh* phrases on the left periphery of clauses, and the linear position of verbal adjuncts in Icelandic, which can be captured only by making reference to the syntactic category types of the word sequences with which the linguistic expressions in question combine.

claim.[11] In other words, a defense of constituency does not in itself constitute a defense of phrase structure hierarchy, notwithstanding the fact that many defenses of the latter in the history of syntactic theory have amounted to little more than arguments on behalf of the former. What was (and is) missing from such arguments is a demonstration that one actually needs the extra information about the history of the branching from higher nodes in phrase marker representation. Facts about selectional possibilities, in and of themselves, do not supply such a demonstration.

For this reason, the inventory of restrictions on *wh* movement presented in Ross's (1967) MIT dissertation appeared to be a watershed in the development of the still-new framework.[12] What Ross's analysis appeared to establish was the fact that certain phrase structural configurations acted in effect as trip wires blocking the normal movement of *wh* phrases to their ordinary positions on the left periphery of root clauses. Consider, for example, the contrast in (6):

(6) a. Our research led us to believe that John was right to claim that matter could exist in ultra-condensed states.

    b. Which states did your research lead you to believe that John was right to claim that matter could occur in __?

    c. *Which states did your research lead you to believe John's claim that matter could occur in __?

    d. *Which states did your research lead you to the belief that John was right to claim that matter could occur in __?

At the time Ross's dissertation appeared, there was almost unanimous opinion in the field that the contrast between the judgments of well-formedness for (6b) on the one hand and (6c,d) on the other reflected facts about syntactic form. What Ross's account of such phenomena seemed to establish was that the syntactic failure responsible for the badness of the latter was a configurational condition, the Complex NP Constraint (CNPC), definable as a prohibition on the intervention of the configuration $[_{NP} \ldots [_S \ldots$, at any point on the extraction pathway between the *wh* extraction site and its surface position. In each of the ill-formed examples in question, there is a violation of the CNPC:

---

11. See the discussion of Generalized Phrase Structure Grammar (GPSG) in the next section in connection to this. Though GPSG took the notion of phrase structural constituency as part of its basic underlying architecture, due to its insistence of strict locality, the theory never made use of direct reference to hierarchical representations of sentence structures in stating the licensing conditions for well-formed sentences.

12. The rate of genuine progress in the early phase of transformational grammar was impressively rapid, and for those who went through the period it still seems a bit remarkable that Ross completed his thesis only a decade after the appearance of *Syntactic Structures*.

(7)   a. *Which states did your research lead you to believe [NP John's claim that [S matter could occur in __]]?

  b. *Which states did your research lead you to [NP the belief that [S John was right to claim that matter could occur in __]]?

In (7a), the critical boundaries occur closer to the extraction site than in (7b), but this doesn't matter: no matter where on the pathway this configuration occurs, moving the *wh* phrase past it results in the perception of major defectiveness. It follows that the CNPC, along with all of Ross's other conditions on extraction, jointly constituted support at the most fundamental level for the need to posit a hierarchy-based architecture for syntactic representations. In particular, without the hierarchical information recorded in phrase markers, there appeared to be no way to define the point in the application of movement transformations at which a fatal extraction occurred. During most of the history of transformational grammar, the existence of these constraints, reformulated though they were over the decades following Ross's original work, was taken as a "smoking gun" argument for a completely hierarchical representation of syntactic constituency that alternative approaches simply could not rebut.

During the past two decades, however, the picture of island effects as entirely (or even largely) syntactic in origin has undergone a very deep and extensive rethinking. Chapter 10 discusses a more recent, increasingly influential view of Ross's and similar restrictions on extraction which derives not solely from syntactic form but from the interaction of syntactic form with various functional factors (processing complexity, discourse coherence, and so on). A reassessment of the sources of islandhood along these lines seems very likely to drastically reduce the degree of confirmation island effects supply for the position which takes hierarchical configuration as the correct data structure for syntactic form. In this new picture, the compositional history of a sentence may still have a role to play in the conditions it must satisfy to ensure well-formedness, but the nature of this role need not constitute motivation for an architecture which incorporates a full representation of that history. We revisit this issue in greater detail in chapter 10.

1.3   Phrase Structure Grammar without Transformations

One of the most interesting (and perhaps perplexing) developments in the middle phase of syntactic theory post-*Syntactic Structures* was the fragmentation of generative grammar into a number of rival approaches, most of which rejected appeal to syntactic transformations. In the 1970s, the first work in Relational Grammar began to appear, followed by Generalized Phrase Structure Grammar (GPSG) and Lexical Functional Grammar (LFG), and subsequently the emergence of Head-Driven Phrase Structure Grammar (HPSG). The work of Michael Brame (see in particular Brame 1976, 1978), though it never led to the development of a distinct research community, was nonetheless highly influential as well (in particular, the critique of the transformational rule of Equi-NP deletion in Brame [1976]). What is striking, in retrospect, is the fact that apart from Relational Grammar, the major alternatives to transformational grammar continued to take for granted the use of phrase structure constituency.[13] This is particularly noteworthy in the case of GPSG, which merits detailed examination as an illustration of the persistence of the hierarchical phrase structure model in the nontransformationalist era—even where, as we argue directly, none of the transformationalist assumptions motivating that model held.[14]

The grip that the IC model (inherited from the Structuralists via its centrality in the language of syntactic representation enshrined in the dominant transformationalist paradigm) held on even non-derivational approaches is well illustrated in the case of GPSG. Of all the non-categorial models of grammar which emerged after the hegemony of transformational grammar began to break up in the early 1980s, GPSG, as we argue in detail in what follows, made the fewest assumptions that depended on hierarchical representations of syntactic form. The fact that such representations were assumed from the outset in GPSG thus testifies to the degree to which such representation had become an unquestioned default in linguistic theorizing.

Essentially, GPSG consists of a set of rules of immediate dominance, stating what the daughters of any given category may be, but not their linear order, and a set of constraints on the projection of two-generation phrase markers—"local trees," in the theory's parlance—from these rules. The major impact made by GPSG on a theoretical landscape in which Chomsky's Revised Extended Standard Theory constituted the default assumption of most syntacticians was as an existence proof that one could capture grammatical dependencies of both the local "relational" sort (e.g., passive and "raising" patterns) and unbounded dependencies (in particular filler-gap linkages) without transformations. In retrospect, however, one could argue that its most profound break with prior work was its adherence to the ethic of strict locality at its very foundations, in that it precluded at the threshold all global structural conditions constraining dependencies of the sorts just mentioned or other morpho-syntactic linkages such as agreement and case-marking. In particular, GPSG's architecture made it impossible to refer directly to aspects of the representation of a clausal structure beyond the syntactic properties of

---

13. The appearance of Ades and Steedman (1982), representing a renewal of a categorial grammar tradition largely dormant after Lambek (1958), was certainly important, but for some time after its appearance the sociological impact of this line of work was far less marked than was the case for GPSG and LFG.

14. Similar remarks apply to LFG, though for somewhat different reasons. In taking both configuration and grammatical relations to be primitive in its architecture, LFG appeared to be a kind of hybrid of phrase structure grammar and Relational Grammar.

a mother category and its daughters. In effect, a grammar can refer to no other aspect of a syntactic representation than what can be encoded in a single phrase structure rule.

GPSG's radical locality had obvious consequences for the kind of global restrictions that were routinely posited in transformational grammar following Ross (1967). Ross's CNPC as he stated it, for example, had no literal interpretation in the theory of GPSG in Gazdar et al. (1985); it had to be rephrased as a completely local constraint on the possible feature arrays attached to the nodes in which the dedicated gap-licensing feature SLASH appeared. This constraint, interacting with a network of similarly local restrictions, had the same effect as Ross's CNPC. The strict, absolute locality that was in a sense the central axiom of GPSG's architecture thus ensured that no reference to any configurational geometry beyond a mother node and its daughter nodes was either necessary or possible. Likewise, the theory of coordination and of feature sharing in Gazdar et al. (1985) ensured that a SLASH specification on a mother had to be shared with all its daughters, with lexical heads systematically excluded from this feature sharing, thereby capturing the Coordinate Structure Constraint. In retrospect, the lesson implicit in GPSG's account of islandhood is that the importance of syntactic hierarchy was much overrated.

One consequence of this strictly local formulation of island conditions is that, in an important sense, it undermines the role of islands in motivating hierarchical structure in syntactic representation. By treating unbounded dependencies via purely local feature percolation within two-generation trees, and stipulating that a nominal head daughter and a clause containing a nonempty SLASH specification could not compose, the system in Gazdar et al. (1985) made it unnecessary to assume the kind of global hierarchical structure that supposedly syntactic restrictions such as Ross's constraints seemed to vindicate. If the payoff of phrase structure hierarchy, via the dominance relation, was to make it possible to carry out operations on strings of words, then GPSG, which permitted no such operations, had no need for it, and this meant that the supposed rebuttal to such a view implicit in Ross (1967) no longer held.

From this point of view, one might read Gazdar et al. (1985) as an existence proof that reference to phrase markers was unnecessary in licensing natural language sentences. This situation is thus almost exactly the same as that of the steps in a standard logical proof, where earlier steps that led to the formulæ $\phi_1, \ldots, \phi_n$, which jointly allow one to infer ϕ_{n+1} play no role whatever in that inference step. In other words, the crucial aspect of phrase structure–based theories of syntax which distinguishes such theories from logical deductive calculi (including those in type logics, such as we introduce in chapter 2)—the freedom to incorporate conditions which apply over the entire history of a sentence's licensing—is completely proscribed in GPSG (recall the discussion of [alleged] evidence for phrase structural constituency in the previous subsection in this connection). It is thus rather easy to picture reformulating GPSG in a way very similar to that of a certain family of early categorial grammars (the so-called Ajdukiewicz/Bar-Hillel [AB]) calculus). Yet despite this fact, GPSG maintained a formal interpretation of its rules in which the latter license phrase markers rather than, for example, logical inferences. Thus, while the system presented in Gazdar et al. (1985) breaks profoundly with almost every aspect of the research tradition that emerged from Chomsky's work in the 1940s and 1950s, it preserves at its core Chomsky's reliance on the ultimately American Structuralist conception of phrase structure.[15] There would have been a very specific advantage in recasting GPSG as a logic of category types. The information content of the mother category in a local tree corresponds, broadly speaking, to the interaction between a head category and its nonhead sister, and indeed this was the point of the "type-driven translation" mapping from syntax to semantics developed in Klein and Sag (1985) and the semantics chapters in Gazdar et al. (1985), which, for the first time, linked a fully explicit theory of feature-based phrase structure to the fully explicit model-theoretic semantics of Montague (1973). This was a remarkable achievement, but the difficulty of implementing this mapping will be evident to anyone who studies these sources. The essential idea of type-driven translation, as presented in Klein and Sag (1985), was quite simple and appealing: in any local tree, the daughter constituents will correspond to semantical objects whose respective type assignments determine only one way in which they can participate in function/argument application, and the resulting denotation is the semantics of the mother category. The mother category will, however, be a daughter category in the "next tree up" and contribute its semantics to the yield of *that* tree, and so on.

But the extreme awkwardness of the syntax-semantics interface in the later GPSG literature is a sign that the phrase structure architecture in which the framework was cast was fundamentally ill-suited to the simple syntax-semantics translation that Gazdar et al. (1985) were rather heroically striving for. Despite their efforts to define a maximally natural semantic translation mechanism to link form and meaning, the dif-

---

15. The situation in HPSG, GPSG's immediate descendant, is somewhat different. In the "middle" phase of HPSG, represented by Pollard and Sag (1994), local domination relations are encoded in categories via the feature DAUGHTERS (DTRS), which appears in all phrasal constituents in a representation (apart from those dominating a gap site). It is thus possible to define a feature name/value pathway between a phrasal constituent, its daughters, its daughter's daughters, etc.—effectively making possible statements of global conditions (e.g., index identity) on what are, in effect, arbitrarily deep phrasal configurations. For example, Condition C of the HPSG binding theory is stated in terms of a relation, generalized o-command, which makes use of this possibility. Later versions of HPSG, however, modify the feature geometry to make this possibility in principle unavailable, making the formalism closer to that of GPSG.

Similarly, in LFG, use of the Kleene star operator in the specification of side conditions on phrase structure rules allows path identities to be stated over unboundedly large syntactic depths. Thus, one can, via the device of "functional uncertainty," identify an extracted *wh* element with the grammatical role assigned to some constituent in a deeply embedded clause, and this property of the architecture of LFG is also essential for the interpretation of generalized quantifiers (see, e.g., Dalrymple 2001, 139–143, 250 ff.).

ference between syntactic composition (via hierarchical constituency) and semantic composition (by functional applications)—a difference inherent in the nature of phrase structure syntax—created an irreducible divergence between the two lacking any analytically natural remedy. And this conceptual disconnection between the construction of form on the one hand and meaning on the other led directly to major analytic difficulties, perhaps most obviously the framework's failure to sponsor any well-defined characterization of what we might call nonconstituent coordination, discussed in detail in the present monograph. Thus, even though GPSG broke with the concept that phrase markers were the data structure of choice for syntactic representation, the persistent reliance on the characterization of constituency by reference to phrase structure rules led to a major impasse in its empirical coverage which was, so far as we are aware, never satisfactorily overcome.

1.4   Conclusions

It is tempting, then, to say that, in the break between GPSG (and LFG) and the mainstream transformational approach, one can see an ironic echo of the same continuity with the past that we have observed in connection with the development of transformational grammar as an outgrowth—and in some sense, the culmination—of American Structuralism. On the one hand, the radical locality of GPSG represents a notable break with a global conception of syntactic representation in transformational grammar, where transformational applicability, island constraints, and various kinds of command relations deemed essential for statements of anaphora possibilities and the like made reference to arbitrary syntactic depths essential. On the other hand, although phrase markers did no actual work in terms of the theory, GPSG still relied on a variant of context-free phrase structure rules as the combinatory machinery of the framework and the syntactic platform for the semantic interpretation of sentences. The notion of phrase structural constituency was carried over, essentially as an unquestioned given, to nontransformational approaches as the basis for syntactic representations (recall once again the quote from Dowty [1996b] that we started this chapter with), just as the notion of immediate constituency from the Structuralists's analytic practice was carried over into the theoretical foundations of transformational grammar. And here again, the supposedly fundamental break between derivational syntax and its monostratal offshoots concealed what, from a certain perspective, can reasonably be regarded as their deeper commonality.

But a still deeper break with the Structuralist analytic tradition had been available in the theoretical marketplace from the very beginnings of the transformational era. The approach to grammatical composition offered in Lambek (1958) made no use of phrase structure rules at all. Nor did it derive representations of clausal structure as the progressive construction of an increasingly complex branching structure which terminates in a string of words, substrings of which correspond to descendants of the root node and an arbitrarily large number of intermediate nodes. Instead, Lambek's system licensed sentences in precisely the way a logical proof licenses a conclusion based on one or more premises. In place of phrase structure rules, what has become known as the Lambek calculus provided an authentic logic—a set of connectives and rules of inference governing their use, which allowed one to deduce sentences as, quite literally, *theorems* of the lexicon under the proof theory provided by the calculus. It turns out that a principled extension of Lambek's proof theory leads directly to a drastic simplification in the syntax-semantics interface, whereby seemingly partial constituents in fact are derivable as full constituents, with a well-defined interpretation that enters into semantic composition in exactly the same way as phrase structure grammar's canonical phrasal types. In the following chapters we outline this extended proof theory and show how it accounts, in the most straightforward way, for a wide range of coordination and ellipsis phenomena that pose very difficult challenges for phrase structure–based approaches.

2 Hybrid Type-Logical Categorial Grammar

2.1 Introduction

In this chapter, we introduce *Hybrid Type-Logical Categorial Grammar* (Hybrid TLCG; Kubota 2010, 2014, 2015; Kubota and Levine 2012, 2013a,b, 2014a, 2016a). Hybrid TLCG is a variant of *categorial grammar* (CG; Ajdukiewicz 1935; Bar-Hillel 1953; Lambek 1958) that belongs to the tradition of Type-Logical Categorial Grammar (Morrill 1994; Moortgat 1997). We provide a gentle introduction of our framework for syntacticians and semanticists without prior familiarity with CG. Although familiarity with notions in (discrete) mathematics, logic, and computer science would be helpful, we hope to have made the ensuing exposition accessible to anybody with background in graduate introductory-level syntax and (formal) semantics.

As discussed in the previous chapter, the notion of phrase structural constituency is central to both transformational and nontransformational variants of generative grammar. For this reason, to make the ensuing exposition maximally transparent to our readers, we present our fragment in a step-by-step manner, starting with an equivalent of simple context-free grammar (known as the *AB Grammar* [Ajdukiewicz 1935, Bar-Hillel 1953]) and then working it up to a fragment that can (at an abstract level) be thought of as a formalization of the familiar movement-based model of syntax (in various incarnations of transformational grammar in the mainstream syntax literature). Up to this point, there is nothing that is fundamentally different from the mainstream approach as far as the basic architecture of the grammar is concerned, where the only major differences if any are notational and methodological (e.g., the explicit encoding of valence information in syntactic categories and an insistence on providing explicit compositional semantics that goes with the syntactic component). We illustrate the workings of this extended system with the basic analyses of quantification (for "covert movement") and topicalization (for "overt movement"). The analyses crucially exploit the notion of *hypothetical reasoning* that is characteristic of the *type-logical* variants of CG (as opposed to "rule-based" systems such as Combinatory Categorial Grammar [CCG; Steedman 1996, 2000]; see chapter 12 for a comparison with CCG).

The final part of the framework exposition embodies a radical departure from the familiar assumptions in standard approaches in generative grammar. Here, we show that a conceptually natural extension of the "AB Grammar + movement" fragment developed up to that point effectively amounts to abandoning the notion of phrase structural constituency as a primitive notion in the combinatoric system for natural language syntax. This is admittedly a radical move (though corresponding to the more dominant view within the CG literature), but we show that a number of important and interesting consequences directly follow from making this move. The present chapter illustrates some key cases involving nonconstituent coordination, and the ensuing chapters demonstrate the empirical payoff of this system with case studies with greater complexity.

The central property of Hybrid TLCG is that it employs the notion of hypothetical reasoning (a fundamental tool of logic-based systems of syntax) not just for the treatment of movement-like phenomena but for capturing the regularities in the local combinatorics too. This results in a "hybrid" implication system in which grammatical composition via local and nonlocal combinatorics are both governed by logical principles and in which the two types of grammatical composition smoothly interact with one another. The present chapter illustrates how this architecture offers a straightforward analysis of some of the basic phenomena we deal with more extensively in later chapters, namely, the patterns of nonconstituent coordination and the syntax-semantics interface of quantifier scope. Later chapters exploit this property of Hybrid TLCG more extensively, in the analyses of more complex linguistic phenomena, especially Gapping, the interaction of coordination and scope, and the so-called respective readings and related phenomena (including the semantics of *same* and *different*). Later chapters will also illustrate how the flexible notion of constituency is useful not only in the analyses of coordination (as is already well-known in the CG literature) but also in the characterization of elliptical linguistic expressions in Gapping, pseudogapping, and Stripping (the analysis of Stripping in Hybrid TLCG is due to Puthawala [2018]). The empirical phenomena we treat in this book have all posed recalcitrant problems for both transformational and nontransformational approaches in the previous syntactic literature. We show how the flexible and systematic syntax-semantics interface of Hybrid TLCG enables simple analyses of these phenomena that overcome the problems of previous proposals while at the same time integrating the key analytic insights from these previous proposals.

2.2   The AB Grammar

We start with a simple fragment of CG called the *AB Grammar*, and introduce some key concepts and notations along the way that are shared by many variants of CG. Following the standard practice in CG, linguistic expressions are written as triples of prosodic representation (i.e., "PF"—we gloss over fine details of this component, so this is just a string of words for all practical purposes except in chapter 11, in which we introduce a more sophisticated model of the prosodic component), semantic interpretation, and syntactic category, notated $\langle \pi; \sigma; \gamma \rangle$ (angle brackets will be omitted below). We assume that the set of syntactic categories is infinite and is recursively defined. This assumption reflects the view that natural language syntax is a kind of logic, a perspective that is particularly salient in the "type-logical" variants of CG (which Hybrid TLCG is an instance of). The underlying idea is that syntactic categories are like formulas in propositional logic. Just as the set of well-formed formulas in propositional logic is infinite in order to deal with unboundedly complex logical inferences, the set of syntactic categories is infinite in order to deal with (potentially) unboundedly complex combinatory properties of linguistic expressions.

We start with the following definition of *syntactic categories* (or *syntactic types*; following the convention in TLCG, we use the terms *syntactic type* and *syntactic category* interchangeably):[1]

(8) a. N, NP, and S are categories.

  b. If A and B are categories, then so are A/B and $B \backslash A$.

  c. Nothing else is a category.

The categories in (8a) are called *atomic categories* The ones involving slashes built from atomic categories via clause (8b) are called *complex categories*.

Note that this definition allows for an infinite set of syntactic categories. For example, by (8b) with $A = B = NP$, we have NP/NP as a category. Applying (8b) again, this time with $A = B = NP/NP$, yields $(NP/NP)/(NP/NP)$. Doing the same thing once again yields $((NP/NP)/(NP/NP))/((NP/NP)/(NP/NP))$. And so on. The definition of syntactic categories becomes slightly more complex once we introduce the vertical slash ($\upharpoonright$) below (see appendix A.1 for a complete definition), but for now, the simple definition in (8) (standard in the CG literature) suffices.

One important feature of CG is that it lexicalizes the valence (or subcategorization) properties of linguistic expressions via the use of complex syntactic categories. For example, lexical entries for intransitive and transitive verbs in English will look like the following (semantics is omitted here but will be supplied later):

(9) a. ran; NP\S

  b. read; (NP\S)/NP

---

1. We assume a small number of syntactic features for atomic categories, notated as subscripts as in NP_{nom} (for nominative NP) and NP_{acc} (for accusative NP). One way to formalize the notion of syntactic features in CG is by means of dependent types (Martin-Löf 1984; Ranta 1994), along the lines discussed in Morrill (1994) and Pogodalla and Pompigne (2012).

(9a) says that the verb *ran* combines with its argument NP *to its left* to become an S. Likewise, (9b) says that *read* first combines with an NP *to its right* and then another NP to its left to become an S. Thus, the slashes encode both the linear order in which the verb looks for its arguments and the number (and type) of arguments that it subcategorizes for. It is useful to introduce some terminology here: we say that complex categories (like the ones in (9)) designate *functors* that combine with *arguments* to return *results*.

As already noted, the distinction between the *forward slash* (/) and the *backward slash* (\) corresponds to the distinction in the directions (in the surface word order) in which functors look for arguments. That is, A/B is a functor looking for a *B to its right* (to become an *A*), whereas $B\backslash A$ is a functor looking for a *B to its left*. We adopt the so-called Lambek-style notation for syntactic categories, in which arguments are always written "under the slash." In the alternative notation adopted in CCG, the result category is always written on the left, with the consequence that the backward slash is written in the opposite way from the Lambek-style notation; that is, our $B\backslash A$ will be written $A\backslash B$ in the CCG notation. We omit outermost parentheses and parentheses for a sequence of the same type of slash, assuming that / and ↾ (introduced below) are left associative and \ is right associative. Thus, S/NP/NP, NP\NP\S, and S↾NP↾NP are abbreviations of ((S/NP)/NP), (NP\(NP\S)), and ((S↾NP)↾NP), respectively.

We first introduce the two basic rules in the grammar, namely, *Slash Elimination* rules for forward and backward slashes. In the so-called labeled deduction format of natural deduction (cf. Oehrle 1994; Morrill 1994), these rules are formulated as in (10).

(10) a. Forward Slash Elimination   b. Backward Slash Elimination

$$\frac{a;\,A/B \quad b;\,B}{a\circ b;\,A}\,/E \qquad\qquad \frac{b;\,B \quad a;\,B\backslash A}{b\circ a;\,A}\,\backslash E$$

The inputs to the rule are written above the horizontal line and the output is written below the line. In line with the analogy between language and logic underlying TLCG, we call the inputs of these rules *premises* and the outputs *conclusions*. The linear order between the two premises above the line has only mnemonic significance; as will become clear below, what *is* significant to word order is instead the order of *a* and *b* in the prosody of the expression obtained as the conclusion. The labeled deduction presentation is so called since, in addition to the syntactic categories of the premises and conclusions, the rules are also annotated (or labeled) with how the semantics and prosody of the conclusion are computed given the semantics and prosody of the premises.

The *proof* (or *derivation*; following the CG tradition, we use these two terms interchangeably, but it should be kept in mind that the notion of derivation in CG is quite different from that in standard derivational approaches) in (11) illustrates how larger linguistic expressions are built from smaller ones using the rules just introduced. Here, a transitive verb, of category $(NP\backslash S)/NP$, is combined with its two arguments on the right (object) and left (subject).

(11)
$$\cfrac{\text{john; } NP \qquad \cfrac{\text{mary; } NP \quad \text{loves; } (NP\backslash S)/NP}{\text{loves} \circ \text{mary; } NP\backslash S}/E}{\text{john} \circ \text{loves} \circ \text{mary; } S}\backslash E$$

Note that the object NP *Mary* is placed to the left of the verb in the proof tree, but this does not have any significance in the linear order of the string derived. Thus, unlike linguistic trees in ordinary syntactic theories (or in CCG), the left-to-right yield of the proof trees does not correspond to word order.

From a "logical" point of view, the two slashes should be thought of as directional variants of implication (that is, both A/B and $B\backslash A$ essentially mean '*if* there is a B, *then* there is an A'), and the two rules of Slash Elimination should be thought of as directional variants of *modus ponens* ($B \to A, B \vdash A$). Thus, (11) is literally a proof of the fact that a complete sentence exists if there is one NP to the right and one NP to the left of the verb *loves*.

We now turn to the syntax-semantics mapping. For expository ease, we assume a standard Montagovian model-theoretic semantics.[2] As is standard in CG, we assume a homomorphic mapping from syntactic categories to semantic types.[3] This means that, for each linguistic expression, given its syntactic category, one can determine uniquely and unambiguously its semantic type (e.g., individuals, sets of individuals, sets of sets of individuals, etc.). To work this out, we first assume that semantic types are recursively built from the basic types e (individuals) and t (truth values) in the standard fashion:[4]

(12) a. e and t are semantic types.

b. If α and β are semantic types, then so is $\alpha \to \beta$.

---

2. Since we do not deal with phenomena that crucially involve intensionality, we assume an extensional-ized fragment throughout. Also, our approach is in principle compatible with more sophisticated semantic theories such as dynamic semantics. See, for example, Martin (2013) and Martin and Pollard (2014) for a proposal for incorporating a compositional dynamic semantics to Linear Categorial Grammar (LCG), a version of CG closely related to Hybrid TLCG. See also Kubota et al. (2019) for a proposal for coupling Hybrid TLCG with Dependent Type Semantics (Bekki 2014; Bekki and Mineshima 2017), a recent proof-theoretic approach to compositional dynamic semantics.

3. Technically, this is ensured in TLCG by the homomorphism from the syntactic type logic to the semantic type logic (the latter of which is often implicit) and the so-called Curry-Howard correspondence (Howard 1969) between proofs and terms (van Benthem 1988b).

Linear Categorial Grammar (Mihalicek and Pollard 2012; Worth 2016) is different from other variants of CG in that it does not assume a functional mapping from syntactic types to semantic types. Instead, the mapping is relational (see in particular Worth [2014, section 1.1] for an explicit statement of this point).

4. We replace Montague's (1973) notation $\langle \beta, \alpha \rangle$ with $\beta \to \alpha$, so that the notation more transparently reflects the fact that the complex type is a functional type.

   c. Nothing else is a semantic type.

Then, we can define the function Sem that returns, for each syntactic category given as input, its semantic type:

(13) (Base Case)
     a. $\text{Sem}(NP) = e$
     b. $\text{Sem}(N) = e \rightarrow t$
     c. $\text{Sem}(S) = t$

(14) (Recursive Clause)
     For any complex syntactic category of the form A/B (or $B\backslash A$),
     $\text{Sem}(A/B) \; (= \text{Sem}(B\backslash A)) = \text{Sem}(B) \rightarrow \text{Sem}(A)$

(14) says that the semantic type of a complex syntactic category A/B (or $B\backslash A$) is that of a function that takes as its argument an expression that has the semantic type of its syntactic argument (i.e., $\text{Sem}(B)$) and returns an expression that has the semantic type of its result syntactic category (i.e., $\text{Sem}(A)$).

   We can now write full lexical entries that specify the semantics as well:

(15) a. ran; **ran**; $NP\backslash S$
     b. saw; **saw**; $(NP\backslash S)/NP$

Given the functional mapping from syntactic categories to semantic types in (14), we see that the intransitive verb *ran* is semantically of type $e \rightarrow t$ (set of individuals) and that the transitive verb *saw* is of type $e \rightarrow (e \rightarrow t)$ (a function from individuals to sets of individuals, i.e., a curried two-place relation).

   Syntactic rules with semantics can then be written as in (16) and a sample derivation with semantic annotation is given in (17).

(16) a. Forward Slash Elimination   b. Backward Slash Elimination

$$\frac{a; \mathcal{F}; A/B \quad b; \mathcal{G}; B}{a \circ b; \mathcal{F}(\mathcal{G}); A}\text{/E} \qquad\qquad \frac{b; \mathcal{G}; B \quad a; \mathcal{F}; B\backslash A}{b \circ a; \mathcal{F}(\mathcal{G}); A}\backslash\text{E}$$

(17)

$$\frac{john; \mathbf{j}; NP \quad \dfrac{loves; \mathbf{love}; (NP\backslash S)/NP \quad mary; \mathbf{m}; NP}{loves \circ mary; \mathbf{love(m)}; NP\backslash S}\text{/E}}{john \circ loves \circ mary; \mathbf{love(m)(j)}; S}\backslash\text{E}$$

Note that the semantic effect of Slash Elimination is *function application* in both of the two rules in (16).

   A system of CG with only the Slash Elimination rules such as the fragment above is called the *AB Grammar*, because it corresponds to the earliest form of CG formulated by Ajdukiewicz (1935) and Bar-Hillel (1953).

2.3 Adding the Vertical Slash to the AB Grammar

The AB Grammar introduced above is basically equivalent to phrase structure grammar (PSG) without elaborate additional mechanisms such as (overt or covert) movement, the SLASH feature inheritance mechanism in Generalized/Head-Driven Phrase Structure Grammar (G/HPSG), or quantifier storage due to Cooper (1983). In fact, the formal equivalence between the AB Grammar and context-free grammar (i.e., simple PSG) was proved as early as Bar-Hillel et al. (1960). This means that the AB Grammar is too impoverished for modeling complex empirical phenomena in natural language that have motivated the notion of "movement" in transformational grammar and various alternative mechanisms (like the SLASH feature and Cooper storage) in other frameworks.

In this section, we extend the AB Grammar by adding just one new mechanism—specifically, a new type of slash called the *vertical slash* ($\upharpoonright$), which, unlike the forward and backward slashes, does not encode linear order in syntactic categories (see Moortgat [1990] for a related earlier proposal involving the "q constructor" $\Uparrow$). This extended fragment can naturally model the notion of movement in derivational approaches. The mechanism of the vertical slash in Hybrid TLCG is moreover more general than that of movement in such approaches, and this difference becomes crucial in the analysis of Gapping we present in chapter 3. We will come back to this point in that chapter.

The problem with the AB Grammar can be illustrated by the failed derivation for the sentence *John met everyone yesterday* in (19), which attempts to mimic the Quantifier Raising (QR)-based analysis in a derivational framework in (18).

(18)

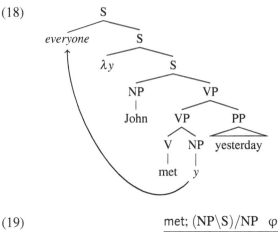

(19)

$$\frac{\dfrac{\text{met; } (NP\backslash S)/NP \quad \varphi; NP}{\text{met} \circ \varphi; NP\backslash S} \text{/E} \quad \begin{array}{c}\text{yesterday;}\\(NP\backslash S)\backslash(NP\backslash S)\end{array}}{\text{met} \circ \varphi \circ \text{yesterday; } NP\backslash S} \text{\textbackslash E}$$

$$\frac{\text{everyone; NP} \quad \dfrac{\text{john; NP} \quad \text{met} \circ \varphi \circ \text{yesterday; } NP\backslash S}{\text{john} \circ \text{met} \circ \varphi \circ \text{yesterday; } S} \text{\textbackslash E}}{\text{john} \circ \text{met} \circ \text{everyone} \circ \text{yesterday; } S} \text{????}$$

In (19), to model the covert movement of the quantifier, we start by positing a dummy expression, whose prosody is represented by the symbol φ. The derivation proceeds up to the point where a complete sentence is formed containing this "trace."

What we then need to do is combine the quantifier with this sentence so that it semantically scopes over the whole sentence but appears in the "trace" position in the prosodic form (since this is an instance of "covert movement").

However, things go wrong in all of the three components of the tripartite linguistic sign. First, syntactically, with the two Slash Elimination rules we have introduced above, we can only combine functors (i.e., expressions of the form A/B or $B\backslash A$, involving either the forward or the backward slash) with arguments, but neither S nor NP is a functor that takes the other as its argument. Prosodically, all we can do with the two rules we have introduced above is concatenate the two strings. But here, what we need to do is a more elaborate type of string manipulation whereby we replace the dummy string φ with the string of the quantifier *everyone* (i.e., an operation corresponding to Montague's (1973) syncategorematic rule of "quantifying-in"). Finally, semantically, the variable corresponding to the "trace" needs to be bound by the λ-operator and the property thus obtained given as an argument to the quantifier, but we currently do not have any rule in the grammar that allows for such a complex meaning assembly.

Are we then stuck? In a sense, yes, since the above illustration clearly shows that there is no natural way of modeling the notion of covert movement in the AB Grammar. Essentially the same point can be made with overt movement. But in fact, our attempt with the failed derivation in (19) was *almost* on the right track. Specifically, all that is missing is a mechanism that enables the last step to go through. And it turns out that such a mechanism is already available in CG, albeit outside of the AB Grammar and in a relatively recent line of development which has not yet gained due recognition in the linguistic literature.

Although approaches that distinguish word order by the forward and backward slashes (like the AB Grammar fragment formulated above) have been the mainstream in CG research, there is a relatively recent strand of research that relocates the word order information from the syntactic types to the prosodic component (Oehrle 1994; de Groote 2001; Muskens 2003; Mihalicek and Pollard 2012). Following Pollard (2013), we call this family of approaches *Linear Categorial Grammar* (LCG). LCG is characteristic for its use of the λ-calculus for modeling the prosody of linguistic expressions, and this plays a key role in encoding word order information in the prosodic representation directly.

Part of the motivation for LCG comes precisely from the recognition that variants of CG based on the distinction between forward and backward slashes are suboptimal for handling phenomena that are essentially insensitive to word order, such as quantification and extraction (see Muskens [2003] for a particularly lucid discussion on this point). We incorporate the key insight of LCG into our AB fragment and show that the extended fragment indeed gives us exactly the right tool to "fill in the gap" in the derivation in (19). The reason we make this move (of combining AB with LCG), rather than simply switching to LCG, will become clear later—it mainly has to do with the analysis of coordination. In a purely "nondirectional" calculus of LCG, the analysis of coordination quickly becomes extremely unwieldy, and, although there are some attempts at addressing this issue (Worth 2016; Kanazawa 2015; Pollard and Worth 2015), at this point it is still considerably unclear whether a completely general solution for this problem can be obtained in LCG. See chapter 12, section 12.3 for a more detailed discussion on this point.

The new mechanism we incorporate from LCG is an order-insensitive mode of implication $\upharpoonright$, called *vertical slash*. We introduce the *Introduction* and *Elimination* rules for this slash, which are formulated as follows (as with /, we write the argument to the right for $\upharpoonright$; the harpoon is there as a visual aide indicating that the right category is the argument):

(20) a. Vertical Slash Introduction

$$\frac{\vdots\quad[\varphi; x; A]^n\quad\vdots}{\vdots\qquad\vdots\qquad\vdots}$$
$$\frac{b; \mathcal{F}; B}{\lambda\varphi.b; \lambda x.\mathcal{F}; B\upharpoonright A}\upharpoonright I^n$$

b. Vertical Slash Elimination

$$\frac{a; \mathcal{F}; A\upharpoonright B \quad b; \mathcal{G}; B}{a(b); \mathcal{F}(\mathcal{G}); A}\upharpoonright E$$

The workings of these rules can be best illustrated with examples. We show in (21) the derivation for the sentence *John saw everyone yesterday*.

(21)

$$\cfrac{\lambda\sigma.\sigma(\text{everyone}); \mathbf{V_{person}}; S\upharpoonright(S\upharpoonright NP)}{}$$

$$\cfrac{ \begin{array}{c}\text{saw;}\\\mathbf{saw;}\\(NP\backslash S)/NP\end{array} \quad \begin{bmatrix}\varphi;\\x;\\NP\end{bmatrix}^1 }{\cfrac{\text{saw}\circ\varphi; \mathbf{saw}(x); NP\backslash S}{\cfrac{\text{saw}\circ\varphi\circ\text{yesterday}; \mathbf{yest(saw}(x)); NP\backslash S}{\cfrac{\text{john}\circ\text{saw}\circ\varphi\circ\text{yesterday}; \mathbf{yest(saw}(x))(\mathbf{j}); S}{\cfrac{\lambda\varphi.\text{john}\circ\text{saw}\circ\varphi\circ\text{yesterday}; \lambda x.\mathbf{yest(saw}(x))(\mathbf{j}); S\upharpoonright NP}{}\upharpoonright I^1}\backslash E}\backslash E}/E}$$

and the combined conclusion lines:

$$\mathbf{3}\to\cfrac{\lambda\sigma.[\sigma(\text{everyone})](\lambda\varphi.\text{john}\circ\text{saw}\circ\varphi\circ\text{yesterday}); \mathbf{V_{person}}(\lambda x.\mathbf{yest(saw}(x))(\mathbf{j})); S}{}\upharpoonright E$$

$$\cfrac{\lambda\varphi.[\text{john}\circ\text{saw}\circ\varphi\circ\text{yesterday}](\text{everyone}); \mathbf{V_{person}}(\lambda x.\mathbf{yest(saw}(x))(\mathbf{j})); S}{\text{john}\circ\text{saw}\circ\text{everyone}\circ\text{yesterday}; \mathbf{V_{person}}(\lambda x.\mathbf{yest(saw}(x))(\mathbf{j})); S}$$

with the labels ①→, ②→ marking intermediate lines: ①→ for the line *john* ∘ saw ∘ φ ∘ yesterday; **yest(saw**(x))(**j**); S and ②→ for the line λφ.john ∘ saw ∘ φ ∘ yesterday; λx.**yest(saw**(x))(**j**); S⌐NP.

The main new ingredient here is a type of inference called *hypothetical reasoning*. In ordinary kinds of logic, hypothetical reasoning is a type of proof in which one draws the conclusion $A \to B$ on the basis of a proof of B by first hypothetically assuming A.

As will become clear below (especially when we introduce hypothetical reasoning for the directional slashes in section 2.4), hypothetical reasoning is a very powerful (yet systematic) tool that is deeply rooted in the CG conception of natural language syntax as a kind of logic and which distinguishes CG from phrase structure–based theories of syntax (including both derivational and non-derivational approaches).

In (21), we first hypothesize an object NP with prosody φ and semantics x. In derivations, hypotheses are indicated by square brackets and are indexed. The indices are for keeping track of where the hypothesis is withdrawn in the whole proof—see below for more on this convention. The derivation proceeds in the same way as in (19) up to the point where the whole sentence is formed (①). At this point, we know that the string containing the prosodic variable φ is a full-fledged sentence. We then apply the *Vertical Slash Introduction* rule (20a) to withdraw this hypothesis (②). In this step, we are essentially concluding that the string *John saw __ yesterday* would be a well-formed sentence of English *if* there were an NP in the gap position notated by __. Note that this conclusion itself does not depend on the assumption that there is in fact an NP in the object position. It is in this sense that Vertical Slash Introduction *withdraws* the hypothesis posited at an earlier step in the proof. The hypothesis is there only for the sake of drawing this conclusion, and it doesn't play any other role in the grammar (and in this sense, it has a very different status from traces in derivational approaches, which are representational objects); rather, the hypothesis and its withdrawal are the type-logical analogue of the Implication Elimination rule in natural deduction formulations of intuitionistic propositional logic. The ↾I step is coindexed with the hypothesis that is withdrawn so as to keep track of which hypothesis is withdrawn at which step in the proof. The vertical dots around the hypothesis in the rule in (20a) abbreviate an arbitrarily complex proof structure. Thus, (20a) simply says that a hypothesis posited at some previous step can be withdrawn by ↾I at any step in the proof.

Let us now examine the effect of the Vertical Slash Introduction rule more closely. In the prosody of the derived expression, the gap position is explicitly represented by the prosodic variable φ bound by the λ-operator, resulting in a function from string to string (of type **st→st**, with **st** the type of strings). Correspondingly, the semantic action of ↾I is also variable binding—the variable x posited as the semantic placeholder for the "trace" is bound. Note that this creates the right property to be given as an argument to the quantifier. Finally, the syntactic category S↾NP, with the vertical slash ↾, indicates that the whole expression is a sentence missing an NP ('if there is an NP, then there is an S'), just like S/NP and NP\S. The difference from the directional slashes is that the vertical slash does not indicate where within the whole string the NP is missing, since that information is represented in the prosodic term itself via the use of λ-binding.

The quantifier then takes this **st→st** function as an argument and embeds its string component in the gap position (③). This step is licensed by the *Vertical Slash Elim-*

ination rule (20b). The dotted lines show reduction steps for the prosodic term (we often omit these in the derivations below) and should not be confused with the application of logical rules (of Slash Elimination and Introduction) designated by solid lines; unlike the latter, purely from a formal perspective, these reduction steps are redundant. Since the quantifier takes an **st→st** function as its argument, it has a higher-order prosody (of type (**st→st**)→**st**) itself. Semantically, the quantifier denotes a standard generalized quantifier (GQ) meaning of type $(e \rightarrow t) \rightarrow t$. **V**person abbreviates the term $\lambda P.\forall x[\mathbf{person}(x) \rightarrow P(x)]$ (similarly for the existential quantifier **∃person**). Since the $\upharpoonright$E rule does function application both in the semantic and prosodic components, the right string/meaning pair is assigned to the whole sentence by this derivation.

The analysis of scope ambiguity is then straightforward and is parallel to quantifying-in and QR. (22) shows the derivation for the inverse scope ($\forall > \exists$) reading of *Someone talked to everyone yesterday*:

(22)

$$
\begin{array}{l}
\text{talked} \circ \text{to;} \quad \left[\begin{array}{l}\varphi_1;\\ x_1;\\ \mathbf{NP}\end{array}\right]^1 \\
\mathbf{talked\text{-}to;} \\
\dfrac{(\mathbf{NP}\backslash \mathbf{S})/\mathbf{NP}}{} \\
\end{array}
$$

$$
\cfrac{
\cfrac{
\cfrac{
\cfrac{
\begin{array}{l}\text{talked} \circ \text{to;}\\ \mathbf{talked\text{-}to;}\\ (\mathbf{NP}\backslash\mathbf{S})/\mathbf{NP}\end{array}
\quad
\left[\begin{array}{l}\varphi_1;\\ x_1;\\ \mathbf{NP}\end{array}\right]^1
}{\begin{array}{l}\text{talked}\circ\text{to}\circ\varphi_1;\\ \mathbf{talked\text{-}to}(x_1);\mathbf{NP}\backslash\mathbf{S}\end{array}}{\scriptstyle /E}
}{\cfrac{
\left[\begin{array}{l}\varphi_2;\\ x_2;\\ \mathbf{NP}\end{array}\right]^2
\quad
\begin{array}{l}\varphi_2\circ\text{talked}\circ\text{to}\circ\varphi_1;\\ \mathbf{talked\text{-}to}(x_1)(x_2);\mathbf{S}\end{array}
}{}{\scriptstyle \backslash E}}
}{}
}{}
$$

The point here is that the scopal relation between multiple quantifiers depends on the order of application of the hypothetical reasoning steps involving $\upharpoonright$ to introduce quantifiers. We get the inverse scope reading in this derivation since the subject quantifier is introduced in the derivation first.

On the present approach, the difference between overt movement and covert movement comes down to a lexical difference in the "prosodic action" of the operator that triggers the "movement" operation in question. As shown above, covert movement is modeled by an operator which embeds some (non-empty) string in the gap position, whereas overt movement is modeled by an operator which embeds the empty string in the gap position. Thus, as shown by Muskens (2003), extraction can be analyzed quite elegantly in this type of CG with hypothetical reasoning for $\upharpoonright$, as in the derivation in (24) for the topicalization example (23).

(23) Bagels$_i$, Kim gave t_i to Chris.

(24)

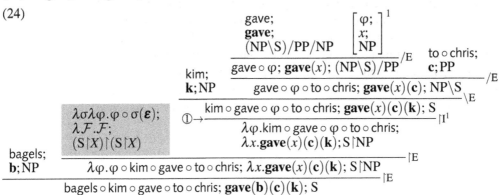

In (24), a gapped sentence is derived just in the same way as in the quantifier example above via hypothetical reasoning for $\upharpoonright$ (①). The difference from the quantifier example is that the topicalization operator, grayed in (24), embeds an empty string $\boldsymbol{\varepsilon}$ in the gap position, thereby closing off the gap, and then concatenates the string of the topicalized NP to the left of that string.

In short, what we have here can be thought of as a logical reconceptualization of transformational grammar; what we used to call "trace" in derivational approaches is just a hypothesis in a proof, and "movement" is just a metaphorical name for a particular type of hypothetical reasoning.[5] This key insight, which seems to stem from the early 1990s when the natural deduction formulations of various extensions of the Lambek calculus were introduced (see, e.g., Hepple 1990; Morrill 1994) and which is expressed particularly clearly in Oehrle (1994), not only is theoretically illuminating, capturing the tight correlation between the semantic and prosodic effects of quantification and extraction transparently, but also has a number of empirical advantages. Specifically, this approach enables an explicit and precise characterization of more complex types of scope-taking such as *parasitic scope* of symmetrical predicates (Barker 2007; Pollard and Smith 2012) and *split scope* of negative quantifiers (Kubota and Levine 2016a) and

---

5. But caution is in order here; this is just a rough and crude analogy. In fact, one important property of Slash Introduction rules (including the Vertical Slash Introduction rule above) is that, as inference rules in the logical deductive system, they *define* the properties of the slashes together with the Slash Elimination rules. For this reason, the grammar rules in (TL)CG have very different statuses conceptually from "corresponding" rules in other theories.

number determiners (Pollard 2014). Gapping is especially interesting in this connection in that it exhibits the properties of both "overt" and "covert" movement simultaneously, thus constituting a case that goes beyond the analytic possibilities available in the standard derivational architecture. We illustrate these points in later chapters.

2.4 Hypothetical Reasoning for All Slashes: Hybrid Type-Logical Categorial Grammar

At this point, we extend our fragment once more, this time by adding the Introduction rules for the forward and backward slashes. This gives us the full Hybrid TLCG, complete with both the Introduction and Elimination rules for all three slashes $/$, $\backslash$, and $\upharpoonright$. The main motivation for extending the system with the Introduction rules for the directional slashes comes from the analysis of coordination—including cases of nonconstituent coordination (Right-Node Raising [RNR] and Dependent Cluster Coordination [DCC]), as we illustrate below.

The Slash Introduction rules for $/$ and $\backslash$ are formulated as follows:

(25) a. Forward Slash Introduction

$$\frac{\dfrac{\vdots \quad [\varphi; x; A]^n \quad \vdots}{\vdots \quad \vdots \quad \vdots}}{\dfrac{b \circ \varphi; \mathcal{F}; B}{b; \lambda x.\mathcal{F}; B/A}/\mathrm{I}^n}$$

b. Backward Slash Introduction

$$\frac{\dfrac{\vdots \quad [\varphi; x; A]^n \quad \vdots}{\vdots \quad \vdots \quad \vdots}}{\dfrac{\varphi \circ b; \mathcal{F}; B}{b; \lambda x.\mathcal{F}; A\backslash B}\backslash\mathrm{I}^n}$$

The difference between the Introduction rule for the vertical slash and the Introduction rules for the directional slashes is that, unlike in $\upharpoonright$I, in $/$I and $\backslash$I, the prosodic variable φ for the hypothesis is simply thrown away in the conclusion on the condition of its presence at the (right or left) periphery of the prosody of the premise, instead of explicitly being bound by the λ-operator. The position of the missing expression is instead recorded in the forward versus backward slash distinction in the syntactic category.

As will become clear in a moment, with the Introduction rules for $/$ and $\backslash$, it becomes possible to reanalyze any substring of a sentence as a (derived) constituent. We first illustrate the workings of these rules with analyses of RNR and DCC and then come back to the relevant formal details. (27) shows how the string *John loves* in the RNR example in (26) is assigned the syntactic category S/NP via hypothetical reasoning involving $/$.

(26) John loves, and Bill hates, Mary.

(27)
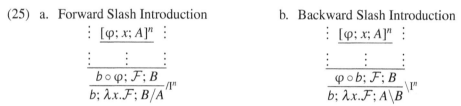

By hypothesizing a direct object NP, we first prove an S (①). At this point, since the prosody of the hypothesized NP φ appears on the right periphery, we can apply /I to withdraw the hypothesis (②). Intuitively, what is going on here can be paraphrased as follows: since we've proven that there is a complete S by assuming that there is an NP on the right periphery (①), we know that, without this hypothetical NP, what we have is something that becomes an S *if* there is an NP to its right (②). Thus, this is another instance of hypothetical reasoning. The difference from the case for ↾ is that, instead of explicitly keeping track of the position of the missing expression via λ-binding in the prosodic representation, the prosodic variable φ is simply thrown away, and the slash in the syntactic category records the fact that the NP is missing on the right periphery. Note also that the lambda abstraction on the corresponding variable in semantics assigns the right meaning (of type $e \to t$) to the derived S/NP.

In the CG analysis of RNR (see, e.g., Morrill 1994; the original analytic insight goes back to Steedman [1985]) such nonconstituents are directly coordinated as constituents and then combined with the RNR'ed expression as in (28):

(28)

$$
\begin{array}{c}
\begin{array}{cc}
\begin{array}{c}
\vdots \\
\text{john} \circ \text{loves;} \\
\lambda x.\textbf{love}(x)(\textbf{j}); \text{S/NP}
\end{array}
&
\dfrac{
\begin{array}{cc}
\begin{array}{c}
\text{and;} \\
\lambda\mathcal{W}\lambda\mathcal{V}.\mathcal{V}\sqcap\mathcal{W}; \\
(X\backslash X)/X
\end{array}
&
\begin{array}{c}
\vdots \\
\text{bill} \circ \text{hates;} \\
\lambda x.\textbf{hate}(x)(\textbf{b}); \text{S/NP}
\end{array}
\end{array}
}{
\begin{array}{c}
\text{and} \circ \text{bill} \circ \text{hates;} \\
\lambda\mathcal{V}.\mathcal{V}\sqcap\lambda x.\textbf{hate}(x)(\textbf{b}); (\text{S/NP})\backslash(\text{S/NP})
\end{array}
}\text{/E}
\end{array}
}{}
\end{array}
$$

$$
\dfrac{
\begin{array}{cc}
\dfrac{\text{john} \circ \text{loves} \circ \text{and} \circ \text{bill} \circ \text{hates;} \ \lambda x.\textbf{love}(x)(\textbf{j}) \sqcap \lambda x.\textbf{hate}(x)(\textbf{b}); \text{S/NP}}{}\backslash\text{E}
&
\begin{array}{c}
\text{mary;} \\
\textbf{m}; \text{NP}
\end{array}
\end{array}
}{\text{john} \circ \text{loves} \circ \text{and} \circ \text{bill} \circ \text{hates} \circ \text{mary;} \ \textbf{love}(\textbf{m})(\textbf{j}) \wedge \textbf{hate}(\textbf{m})(\textbf{b}); \text{S}}\text{/E}
$$

Note in particular that this analysis assigns the right meaning to the whole sentence compositionally. ⊓ designates *generalized conjunction* (Partee and Rooth 1983), defined as follows:[6]

(29) a. For p and q of type t, $p \sqcap q =_{def} p \wedge q$

  b. For $\mathcal{P}$ and $\mathcal{Q}$ of any conjoinable type other than t (where $\mathcal{P}$ and $\mathcal{Q}$ are of the same type), $\mathcal{P} \sqcap \mathcal{Q} =_{def} \lambda\mathcal{R}.\mathcal{P}(\mathcal{R}) \sqcap \mathcal{Q}(\mathcal{R})$

---

6. A conjoinable type is t and any functional type that "bottoms out" at t, such as $e \to t$, $t \to t$, $et \to t$, $et \to et$, etc. We illustrate generalized conjunction with some more examples in (i).

(i) a. $\textbf{bought}_{e \to et} \sqcap \textbf{ate}_{e \to et}$

$= \lambda x.\textbf{bought}(x)_{et} \sqcap \textbf{ate}(x)_{et}$	(by (29b))
$= \lambda x\lambda y.\textbf{bought}(x)(y)_t \sqcap \textbf{ate}(x)(y)_t$	(by (29b))
$= \lambda x\lambda y.\textbf{bought}(x)(y) \wedge \textbf{ate}(x)(y)$	(by (29a))

  b. $\textbf{yesterday}_{et \to et} \sqcap \textbf{today}_{et \to et}$

$= \lambda P.\textbf{yesterday}(P)_{et} \sqcap \textbf{today}(P)_{et}$	(by (29b))
$= \lambda P\lambda x.\textbf{yesterday}(P)(x)_t \sqcap \textbf{today}(P)(x)_t$	(by (29b))
$= \lambda P\lambda x.\textbf{yesterday}(P)(x) \wedge \textbf{today}(P)(x)$	(by (29a))

Thus, $\lambda u.\mathbf{love}(u)(\mathbf{j}) \sqcap \lambda x.\mathbf{hate}(x)(\mathbf{b}) = \lambda w.\mathbf{love}(w)(\mathbf{j}) \wedge \mathbf{hate}(w)(\mathbf{b})$.[7]

This analysis of RNR immediately extends to DCC. (30) shows the "reanalysis" of the string *Bill the book* as a derived constituent. This involves first hypothesizing a ditransitive verb and withdrawing that hypothesis after a whole verb phrase is formed (here, VP abbreviates NP\S):

(30)

$$\frac{\dfrac{[\varphi; f; \text{VP/NP/NP}]^1 \quad \text{bill}; \mathbf{b}; \text{NP}}{\varphi \circ \text{bill}; f(\mathbf{b}); \text{VP/NP}} /\text{E} \quad \text{the} \circ \text{book}; \iota(\mathbf{bk}); \text{NP}}{\dfrac{\varphi \circ \text{bill} \circ \text{the} \circ \text{book}; f(\mathbf{b})(\iota(\mathbf{bk})); \text{VP}}{\text{bill} \circ \text{the} \circ \text{book}; \lambda f.f(\mathbf{b})(\iota(\mathbf{bk})); (\text{VP/NP/NP})\backslash\text{VP}} \backslash\text{I}^1} /\text{E}$$

Then, after like-category coordination, the missing verb and the subject NP are supplied to yield a complete sentence (the last step is omitted):

(31)

$$\cfrac{\begin{array}{c}\text{gave};\\ \mathbf{gave};\\ \text{VP/NP/NP}\end{array} \quad \cfrac{\begin{array}{c}\vdots\\ \text{bill} \circ \text{the} \circ \text{book};\\ \lambda f.f(\mathbf{b})(\iota(\mathbf{bk}));\\ (\text{VP/NP/NP})\backslash\text{VP}\end{array} \quad \cfrac{\begin{array}{c}\text{and};\\ \lambda \mathcal{W}\lambda\mathcal{V}.\mathcal{V}\sqcap\mathcal{W};\\ (X\backslash X)/X\end{array} \quad \begin{array}{c}\vdots\\ \text{john} \circ \text{the} \circ \text{record};\\ \lambda f.f(\mathbf{j})(\iota(\mathbf{rc})); (\text{VP/NP/NP})\backslash\text{VP}\end{array}}{\begin{array}{c}\text{and} \circ \text{john} \circ \text{the} \circ \text{record};\\ \lambda\mathcal{V}.\mathcal{V}\sqcap\lambda f.f(\mathbf{j})(\iota(\mathbf{rc}));\\ ((\text{VP/NP/NP})\backslash\text{VP})\backslash((\text{VP/NP/NP})\backslash\text{VP})\end{array}}/\text{E}}{\begin{array}{c}\text{bill} \circ \text{the} \circ \text{book} \circ \text{and} \circ \text{john} \circ \text{the} \circ \text{record};\\ \lambda f.f(\mathbf{b})(\iota(\mathbf{bk})) \sqcap \lambda f.f(\mathbf{j})(\iota(\mathbf{rc})); (\text{VP/NP/NP})\backslash\text{VP}\end{array}}\backslash\text{E}}{\text{gave} \circ \text{bill} \circ \text{the} \circ \text{book} \circ \text{and} \circ \text{john} \circ \text{the} \circ \text{record}; \mathbf{gave}(\mathbf{b})(\iota(\mathbf{bk})) \sqcap \mathbf{gave}(\mathbf{j})(\iota(\mathbf{rc})); \text{VP}}\backslash\text{E}$$

We now turn to some formal details about the Introduction rules in (25). First, since $\circ$ is string concatenation, if we remove the rules for the vertical slash (i.e., $\upharpoonright$I and $\upharpoonright$E) from the present fragment, the system is identical to the product-free (associative) Lambek calculus **L** (Lambek 1958). This means that, with the /I and \I rules, a hypothesis can be withdrawn as long as its prosody appears on either the left or the right periphery of the prosody of the premise.[8] Note also that in this formulation, the prosodic term

---

7. A note is in order regarding the meaning of conjunction. Here, we have assumed that the word *and* denotes (generalized) boolean conjunction. In chapter 5, we examine various interactions between coordination and expressions denoting "structured" objects such as "respective" readings of plurals and symmetrical and summative predicates. We revise the meaning of *and* to a tuple-forming operator there ((181) in section 5.3.1), but keep the simpler generalized conjunction outside of that chapter since our discussion in the rest of the book does not hinge directly on the analysis of plurals and related phenomena in chapter 5.

8. One might worry about overgeneration in this regard. For example, note that the infamous Dekker's puzzle arises in our setup, just as in the Lambek calculus, overgenerating the following string as a sentence:

(i) *[Bill thinks]$_{\text{S/VP/NP}}$, and [the brother of]$_{\text{S/VP/NP}}$, John walks.

The standard response to this issue in contemporary CG is to control the availability of associativity in the prosodic calculus by the notion of *multi-modality* (Moortgat and Oehrle 1994; Dowty 1996b; Baldridge

labeling, rather than the left-to-right order of the premises in the proof tree, is relevant for the applicability conditions of the /I and \I rules (the latter presentation is more common in the literature of mathematical linguistics; so far as we are aware, Morrill (1994) was the first to recast the Lambek calculus in the former format). This point should be clear from the proof in (27), where we have deliberately placed the hypothetical object NP to the *left* of the verb in the proof tree. This also means that the order of the two premises in the Elimination rules does not play any role, as we have already noted above. In practice, we often write premises in an order reflecting the actual word order, but it should be kept in mind that this is only for the sake of maintaining the readability of derivations.

2.5   A Note on the Linearity of the Calculus

Since the treatment of quantification via prosodic λ-binding in the present framework is very powerful and flexible, one might worry about potential overgeneration of the following kind. Suppose we hypothesize the same variable in the two conjuncts of a conjoined sentence and bind them at once after the conjoined sentence is formed:

(32) $\lambda\varphi.\varphi \circ \text{is} \circ \text{male} \circ \text{or} \circ \varphi \circ \text{is} \circ \text{female}; \lambda x.\textbf{male}(x) \vee \textbf{female}(x); \text{S} \!\upharpoonright\! \text{NP}$

Then, by lowering the quantifier *everyone*, we seem to obtain the following:

(33) everyone $\circ$ is $\circ$ male $\circ$ or $\circ$ everyone $\circ$ is $\circ$ female;
       $\mathbf{V}_{\textbf{person}}(\lambda x.\textbf{male}(x) \vee \textbf{female}(x)); \text{S}$

In other words, we (apparently) incorrectly predict that *Everyone is male or everyone is female* has the reading 'everyone is either male or female.'

A sign such as (32) is not derivable in Hybrid TLCG. This follows from the fact that the vertical slash (as well as the forward and backward slashes) is a variant of *linear*

2002; Muskens 2007; Kubota 2010). This will, for example, prevent the inference $\text{S/S} \vdash \text{S/VP/NP}$ (valid in **L**) in the enriched calculus. Hybrid TLCG can be extended along these lines, as we discuss in chapter 11 (see also Kubota [2010, 2014] for a more detailed discussion of this general architecture of grammar enriching the morpho-phonological component).

   Another possibility is to seek explanation of the ill-formedness of (i) in processing terms. That is, in order to be able to interpret this sentence, speakers are required to process *John* simultaneously as the subject and *part* of the subject of a shared VP. This cognitive task is arguably something implausible for speakers to manage in the limited real-time window made available in working memory: the speaker, having encountered *Bill thinks, and*, is waiting for another expression of the same type S/S and a shared remnant, but what s/he finds instead is NP/NP followed by a complete S, very plausibly triggering backtracking/reparsing difficulties sufficient to make such examples unprocessable.

   This is an important issue, but a detailed investigation is beyond the scope of the present work. We leave it for future work to determine exactly how much overgeneration to rule out in the purely combinatoric component of grammar.

implication.[9] To put it differently, the three implication connectives $/$, $\backslash$, and $\upharpoonright$ can bind only one occurrence of a hypothesis at a time. The basic underlying linguistic intuition is that one token of a linguistic expression can fill in only one argument position of a subcategorizing predicate. The derivation above, in which one token of the quantifier *everyone* fills in the subject argument position of two distinct verbs simultaneously, is a textbook example of a violation of resource sensitivity and hence is ruled out in the present framework (as in any other variant of CG).[10]

This of course raises the question of how to treat ATB extraction and parasitic gaps:

(34) a. John met a man who Mary likes __ but Sue hates __.

b. Which paper did John file __ without reading __?

This is indeed a nontrivial problem. The analysis of *wh* extraction by Muskens (2003) via prosodic λ-binding, while capturing elegantly the basic patterns of overt movement, does not extend to multiple-gap phenomena straightforwardly. We will address the issue of multiple gaps in chapter 7.

2.6 Computational Issues

Although Hybrid TLCG is primarily meant to be a theory of competence grammar, and, moreover, we do not take practical applicability in parsing to be one of our primary goals (which sets it apart, we believe, from the research program of CCG), considerations of computational properties are an important issue for formally explicit frameworks of grammar. Moreover, the existence of an actually implemented parser—even one that does not compete realistically with efficient parsers designed to be applicable to practical purposes—would be useful for the purpose of grammar checking and can potentially provide a quite valuable tool for working linguists. In this section, we address these computational/implementation-related issues briefly. For an accessible

---

9. Note that, unlike (32), the following is a well-formed sign derivable in Hybrid TLCG:

(i) $\lambda\varphi_1\lambda\varphi_2.\varphi_1 \circ \text{is} \circ \text{male} \circ \text{or} \circ \varphi_2 \circ \text{is} \circ \text{female}; \lambda x\lambda y.\textbf{male}(x) \vee \textbf{female}(y); S \upharpoonright NP \upharpoonright NP$

Deriving (32) from (i) would be like deriving $A \rightarrow B$ from $A \rightarrow A \rightarrow B$ in classical propositional logic (where it is a theorem). In classical propositional logic, this is possible since using the same hypothesis A twice to cancel the two occurrences of A in the premise $A \rightarrow A \rightarrow B$ is allowed. The resource sensitivity of linear logic prohibits exactly this type of reuse of material.

10. This does not exclude a possibility in which a nonlinear semantic term is assigned as the translation for some linguistic expression (e.g., $\textbf{V}_{\textbf{man}}(\lambda x.\textbf{love}(x)(x))$ for *Every man loves himself*). This is possible in TLCG since nonlinear terms can be introduced as the translations of specific lexical items (such as reflexives). By the same token, nothing blocks the nonlinear term $\textbf{V}_{\textbf{person}}(\lambda x.\textbf{male}(x) \vee \textbf{female}(x))$ from being assigned as the translation for *Everyone is either male or female*. Here, the generalized conjunction meaning for *and* is the source of nonlinearity.

introduction to the logical and computational aspects of TLCG, see Moot and Retoré (2012).

It is known that a certain restricted form of Hybrid TLCG—specifically, one which does not contain empty operators or polymorphic specifications of lexical entries—is decidable and NP complete (Moot and Stevens-Guille 2019), just like related approaches in TLCG such as Displacement Calculus (Morrill et al. 2011) and NL_λ (Barker and Shan 2015). Decidability is an important property when considering the formal computational properties of a grammatical framework, since it ensures that the search space for the parser is finite in size for any given string.

As will become clear in the following chapters, we formulate analyses of linguistic phenomena making somewhat extensive use of empty operators and polymorphic specifications. Whether these empty operators and polymorphic specifications of lexical entries can be eliminated without sacrificing too much the generality of the linguistic analyses proposed below is a somewhat delicate question. There are a couple of points worth noting in connection to this issue. In certain cases (such as in the analysis of VP ellipsis and pseudogapping in chapter 6), the empty operator we introduce can be lexicalized, at the trivial cost of increasing lexical redundancy (but this is a bad consequence only on the linguistically unreasonable assumption that the lexicon is an unstructured list of words). But there are some instances of empty operators which do not seem to lend themselves to lexicalization as easily. An example of this is the type of empty operators that we extensively rely on in our analysis of "respective" readings and related phenomena in chapter 5. In general, there does seem to be a trade-off between computational concerns and elegance of linguistic analysis in the use of empty operators. For example, in the literature of plurality in theoretical linguistics in which computational issues are not the foremost concerns, empty operators are extensively employed for issues closely related to those we address in chapter 5. While we acknowledge this to be an important issue, addressing it properly is beyond the scope of the present work. We just note here that addressing this issue properly requires first and foremost making the assumptions about the relationship between the competence grammar and a theory of linguistic performance sufficiently explicit.

Hybrid TLCG has a parser, developed by Richard Moot as a component of the LinearOne system, which is a theorem prover for "first-order" linear logic. In particular, the module (contained in the LinearOne package, which is available at https://github.com/RichardMoot/LinearOne) that translates Hybrid TLCG into first-order linear logic is specific to Hybrid TLCG, and the rest of the parsing is done as proof search in first-order linear logic. Theoretical underpinnings of the translation from Hybrid TLCG to first-order linear logic is described in detail in Moot (2014), and the repository for the parser currently contains a toy grammar that can parse some sample sentences (mostly from the two articles on Gapping—Kubota and Levine [2012] and Kubota and Levine [2013b], which are earlier versions of chapter 3) with a brief documentation.

It is perhaps worth emphasizing here that the availability of a working parser is a significant advantage for theory development, since it gives us an indispensable tool for checking the consistency of handwritten theoretical analyses. In this respect, the similarity between Hybrid TLCG and the mainstream derivational architecture of grammar is especially noteworthy. Given the transparent correspondence between the two (in most cases), Hybrid TLCG + the LinearOne parser can, in addition to other purposes to which it can be put, be used as a practical tool for grammar checking for (the greater part of) mainstream syntax-semantics work.

3 Gapping

We start our case studies with a detailed analysis of Gapping in English. Gapping is a particularly odd instance of noncanonical coordination in which the (typically finite) main verb/auxiliary—or some larger string containing it—is missing from the noninitial conjunct(s):[1]

(35) Leslie bought a CD, and Robin ∅ a book.

What distinguishes Gapping from other kinds of noncanonical coordinations such as Dependent Cluster Coordination (DCC) and Right-Node Raising (RNR) is that the strings which appear to be coordinated in Gapping do not look very much like each other. In the case of DCC and RNR,

(36) a. I told the same joke to Robin on Friday and (to) Leslie on Sunday. (DCC)
      b. I gave Robin, and Leslie offered Terry, a pair of pliars. (RNR)

it is possible to identify two coordinated substrings which are parallel up to the point where they combine with the rest of the sentence; the problem is only that expressions such as *(to) Leslie on Sunday* (in (36a)) and *I gave Robin* (in (36b)) are not constituents of the traditional kind. We have seen in the previous chapter that hypothetical reasoning for the directional slashes can license such strings as constituents in TLCG, thereby enabling straightforward analyses of DCC and RNR. But in the case of Gapping, we seem to be coordinating a whole clause with a sequence of words which would be a clause if a copy of the verb in the first conjunct were introduced into the second

---

1. Instances of Gapping with nonfinite verbs can be found with "What—me worry?" sentences and infinitival optatives:

(i) a. What—Robin eat vegetables and Leslie whole-grain bread?? You're dreaming!
     b. Oh, for Robin to be convicted of fraud and her bootlicking minions fired!

We also find infinitival subject clauses parallel to (ib):

(ii) For Robin to be convicted of fraud and her bootlicking minions fired is all I would ask for in this life.

conjunct. As they stand, however, *Leslie bought a CD* in (35) has a completely different status from *Robin a book*.

The material overtly missing from, but seemingly present in the interpretation of, the second conjunct can be quite a bit more extensive than just the matrix verb of the first; in (37a), a larger string *gave me* properly containing a finite verb undergoes Gapping, and in (37b), the gapped material is an auxiliary + bare verb sequence:

(37) a. One gave me a book, and the other ∅ a CD.
      b. Terry can go with me, and Pat ∅ with you.

The examples in (38) are still more complex, where (38a) shows that a chain of infinitives plus the main verb can be gapped; (38b–d) show that the gapped material can even be a discontinuous substring of the sentence:

(38) a. John wants to try to begin to write a novel, and Mary ∅ a play.
      b. Robin put a dollar in the meter and Leslie ∅ three quarters ∅ .
      c. Some Republicans want Ford to run for the presidency, and others ∅ Reagan ∅ .
      d. Too many Irish setters are named Kelly, ∅ German shepherds ∅ Fritz, and ∅ huskies ∅ Nanook.

These examples illustrate the core syntactic properties of Gapping that must be accounted for in any adequate analysis.[2]

Gapping has continued to pose a difficult challenge in both derivational and nonderivational variants of generative grammar. The syntactic asymmetry noted above is already highly problematic, but things are actually worse. A further and even more vexing challenge for any analysis of Gapping comes from the scopal interactions with auxiliaries and quantifiers, exemplified by data such as the following (Siegel 1984, 1987; Oehrle 1987; McCawley 1993):[3]

---

2. In addition, it has often been observed that there are typically just two remnants in the gapped conjunct. (Remnants are expressions that remain in noninitial conjuncts.) Thus, examples like the following are marginal at best:

(i) a. ??Alan gave Sandy a book, and Peter Betsy a magazine.
     b. ??Alan told Harry that the sky was failing, and Sam Betsy that Chicken Little was right.

Sag (1976), however, notes that if the postverbal remnants contain PPs, the examples sound much better:

(ii) a. Peter talked to his boss on Tuesday, and Betsy to her supervisor on Wednesday.
      b. John talked to his supervisor about his thesis, and Erich to the dean about departmental politics.

We (like other authors) do not attempt to explain why (i) and (ii) differ in acceptability but assume that a processing basis is responsible for the difference.

3. Oehrle (1987) notes that this scope anomaly was discussed in Oehrle (1971).

(39) a. Mrs. J can't live in Boston and Mr. J ∅ in LA.

 b. Mrs. J can't live in Boston or Mr. J ∅ in LA.

 c. No dog eats Whiskas or ∅ cat ∅ Alpo.

Examples of this type are generally ambiguous between two readings. For example, on its most natural reading, (39a) means that it's not possible for Mrs. J and Mr. J to live in the two different respective cities at the same time ($\neg\Diamond(\varphi \wedge \psi)$), where the modal *can't* scopes over the conjunction. The sentence additionally has a reading denying *both* of the two possibilities ($\neg\Diamond\varphi \wedge \neg\Diamond\psi$), which is obtained by distributing the meaning of the modal to each conjunct. (39b) and (39c) are similarly ambiguous. Note here that the ambiguity is diminished or eliminated entirely by the typical prosody for these two distinct readings: in (39a), for example, the wide-scope modal interpretation emerges clearly when the two conjuncts are pronounced on a single prosodic monotone, suggesting a single intonational phrase, whereas for the distributive reading, the first syllable in *Boston* will receive conspicuous stress and the whole word will have sharply higher pitch, while in the second conjunct, both *Mr. J* and *LA* bear contrastive stress.[4]

The existence of the non-distributive, wide-scope reading of auxiliaries in Gapping, and particularly its default status in (39a) and similar examples, may appear rather surprising at first, since auxiliaries can't normally scope out of their local clauses to take scope in a higher clause (e.g., the modal *can't* can't scope over the matrix verb *thinks* in *Kevin thinks that Sandy can't rinse the sink*). Moreover, apart from Gapping, modals never outscope conjunction. Thus, *Mrs. J can't live in Boston and Mr. J lives in LA* does not have a reading analogous to (39a). The generalization here is that scopal operators, when they are gapped, can be interpreted *as if* they were not present in the first conjunct but instead were scoping over the whole coordinate structure (although not necessarily, since there is also the distributive reading). This "deep" symmetry between the two conjuncts is a big hint that the phenomenon itself conceals a hidden symmetry.

We wish to stress at the outset that in the discussion below, we assume (along with Kuno [1976] and many subsequent authors) that the actual set of interpretations available for a particular Gapping sentence results from an interaction between what the combinatoric system of grammar generates, lexical properties of the expressions chosen, and general pragmatic knowledge. The important point is that the combinatoric

---

4. If the distributive reading of negation "no dog eats Whiskas or no cat eats Alpo" seems difficult to get for (39c), consider the following, uttered in a "no matter which" type context:

(i) There's something wrong with public transportation—no bus is available from Düsseldorf to Cologne, or train from Cologne to Frankfurt—they never make it clear which one is the problem, but in either case, one thing is clear: there's no chance for us to get to Frankfurt in time.

component should make available both the distributive and non-distributive readings for both auxiliaries and quantifiers, leaving to other components of the grammar the relative accessibility of these respective interpretations (thus, one should not be misled by the fact that the distributive reading is difficult to get in some examples, especially without the right kind of contextual support).

The scope anomaly in Gapping, ignored in virtually all discussions of Gapping in the phrase structure theoretic literature (but see Park et al. [2019] for an exception; see below for a critique of phrase structure–based approaches to Gapping), has been addressed extensively in the recent Minimalist studies, starting from Johnson (2004) (originally written in 1996; cf. Johnson 2000, 2009; Lin 2000, 2002; Winkler 2005; Toosarvandani 2013). These proposals have in common the assumptions that, as per the subject-internal VP hypothesis, where subjects originate in the Spec position of VP, Gapping involves coordination at the low VP level (which is below the position where the modal auxiliary is base-generated) and that the subject of the first conjunct moves to some higher syntactic position while the subject of the second conjunct stays in its VP-internal position at surface structure. This approach thus attempts to derive the apparently anomalous scopal property of auxiliaries and quantifiers in examples like (39) from a posited syntactic asymmetry between the two conjuncts in Gapping, solving the two problems noted above (i.e., syntactic asymmetry and semantic scope anomaly) at once. Currently, this low VP coordination analysis is the only extant approach which links the two problems of Gapping and provides a uniform solution for them.[5]

The goal of this chapter is twofold. First, we present some new empirical arguments against the low VP coordination analysis of Gapping. Second, we propose an explicit alternative analysis of Gapping in Hybrid TLCG which does not suffer from the problems of the low VP coordination analysis, while entertaining at least comparable (or better) empirical coverage with respect to any previous account. The empirical arguments consist of both basic syntactic patterns of Gapping (involving largely neglected examples known since at least Sag [1976] as well as novel data reinforcing the point) and standard tests for constituency. These arguments rely on uncontroversial assumptions about syntax, and we believe that they convincingly show that the structural asymmetry that the low VP coordination analysis crucially rests on in deriving the scope anomaly is highly problematic.

The flexible syntax-semantics interface of Hybrid TLCG enables an analysis of Gapping as like-category coordination at the combinatoric structure, and the mismatch between this concealed structure and the visible string is mediated by hypothetical reasoning involving lambda binding in the prosodic component. It thus avoids the unde-

---

5. Except for Oehrle (1987) and Siegel (1987), whose analyses can, in a sense, be thought of as important precursors of this low VP coordination analysis as well as of our own analysis presented below.

sirable structural asymmetry that the low VP coordination analysis posits between the two conjuncts, which is essentially the source of its mispredictions. Our like-category coordination analysis of Gapping is, moreover, shown to interact properly with independently motivated analyses of scopal operators to immediately yield their apparently anomalous scopal properties in Gapping, offering, uniquely in the literature so far as we are aware, a conceptually simple and empirically adequate solution for both of the two challenges noted above that Gapping poses for previous accounts.

3.1 Gapping: The Research Background

As suggested above, Gapping presents two major challenges to grammatical theories:

- determination of the structural relationship between the two conjuncts
- identification of how this relationship yields the interpretation of the second conjunct based on the interpretation of the first conjunct

In this domain, phrase structure grammar has proven conspicuously inadequate. The difficulty that phrase structure–based approaches face can be illustrated succinctly by briefly reviewing the classical and still representative analysis of Gapping by Sag et al. (1985).

Sag et al. (1985) offer an account of the sentence *Terry likes Stacy, and Tracy Lee* along the following lines:

(40)

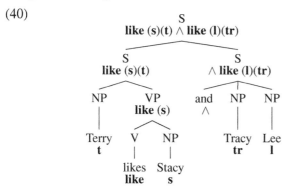

This analysis immediately raises the question of how the semantic interpretation of the whole sentence is obtained. Sag et al. (1985, 162) state that the interpretation for the second conjunct of this structure is given "by uniformly substituting its immediate constituents into some immediately preceding structure, and computing the interpretation of the results." Besides being stated in only very vague terms, such an analysis, requiring a global comparison of the two conjuncts, breaks sharply with the strictly local compositional interpretation mechanism assumed in GPSG (cf. chapter 1; see also Gazdar et al. 1985).

Still more important are the empirical consequences: the Sag et al. (1985) account mispredicts the modal scope ambiguity facts outlined above. For (39a), for example, there appears little basis for any other correlation between the two conjuncts than that in (41):

(41)   Mrs. J   can't   live   in   Boston
          ↕   ↕   ↕   ↕   ↕
        Mr. J   ∅   ∅   in   LA

But this gives us only the distributive reading as in the following:

(42)

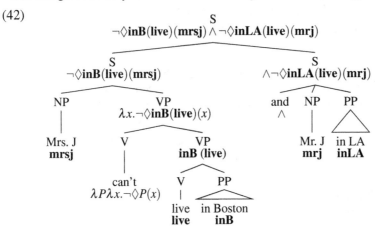

Park et al. (2019), the most recent analysis of Gapping in the HPSG literature, makes an important step of addressing the limitations of previous (H)PSG analyses of Gapping (Sag et al. 1985; Abeillé et al. 2014; Chaves 2005). In their analysis, couched in Lexical Resource Semantics (Richter and Sailer 2004), the lexical entries of the clause-level conjunction words *and* and *or* are underspecified as to the relative scope with respect to the propositional operator contributed by the modal auxiliary in the first conjunct. While this approach captures the anomalous scope patterns in Gapping, it does so by stipulation (in the lexical entries for the conjunction words) that does not seem to be motivated independently. Moreover, on Park et al.'s approach, extension to the determiner gapping case is left for future work.[6]

---

6. Park et al. (2019) note a potential overgeneration problem with our analysis of Gapping (Kubota and Levine 2016a; see section 3.2.1) in relation to cases of Gapping with (what they take to be) certain subordination markers such as *not to mention*:

Transformational approaches fare better with respect to the scope anomaly problem in Gapping. In fact, the family of low VP coordination approaches (for references, see above) are designed to solve precisely this problem. These proposals differ in some details, but they all have in common the assumption that Gapping sentences are derived from underlying sentences involving coordination at the lower VP level. In what follows, we review the adequacy of this assumption by taking Johnson (2000) as a representative case of such transformational analyses.[7]

3.1.1 Gapping as Low VP Coordination: Details and Motivation

The key innovation in Johnson's low VP coordination analysis is that, roughly speaking, what appears to be a coordination of a full clause with a partial clause missing its verb (and possibly other elements) is actually a coordination of two VPs—but where the second VP's subject is in situ in [Spec,VP] and the common verb of both is extracted via ATB movement to a position adjoining the T head whose complement is the conjoined VP. In addition to this more or less conventional movement, there is a second, non-ATB extraction which takes the subject of the first conjunct to the Spec position under the matrix AgrP, creating the illusion of a full clause on the left and a partial clause on the right. The actual structure is illustrated in (43).

(43)

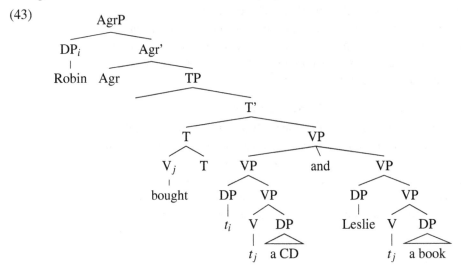

Cases of Gapping which include not just the verb but more complex structures in the righthand conjunct (e.g., (38a), where the nonconstituent string *wants to try to begin to write* goes missing) are presumably handled by multiple leftward raisings, along lines Johnson (2009) speculates on, though, to our knowledge, no detailed analysis has been offered to date.

Johnson's analysis contains a number of controversial features, such as the non-ATB movement of the first conjunct subject and the treatment of both conjuncts as VPs rather than clauses (with the second seemingly defective in some way) or a clause and a string of constituents (as in Sag et al. 1985, Culicover and Jackendoff 2005, and Abeillé et al. 2014). Our critique in section 3.1.2 essentially consists in questioning the plausibility of this structural asymmetry in the status of the subjects of the two conjuncts. But it is important to keep in mind that these moves are crucial to Johnson's account of the interaction of Gapping with scopal operators such as modal auxiliaries and negative determiners. Consider first the examples involving auxiliaries.

(44) a. Kim wouldn't play bingo or Sandy sit at home all evening.
      b. Kim wouldn't play bingo or Sandy chess.

While (44a) and (44b) differ in that only the auxiliary is gapped in (44a), the scopal facts are parallel. The key to an account of the auxiliary wide-scope reading for (44a) is to somehow separate the semantic action of the auxiliary from its apparent linear position—an outcome which follows directly from Johnson's proposal to take the two conjuncts in these examples to be VPs, creating a structure above which the auxiliary can appear. The remaining requirement, that of making the auxiliary appear to be embedded in the first conjunct, follows directly from the asymmetrical fronting of the first conjunct subject to [Spec,AgrP]. Thus, (44a) has the following structure:

(45)

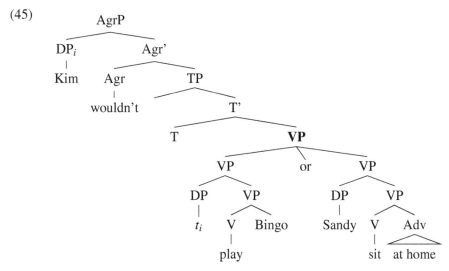

Examples like (44b) in which both the auxiliary and the verb are missing are licensed by moving the verb out of the two conjuncts in an ATB fashion (as in the basic Gapping example in (43)).

(46)

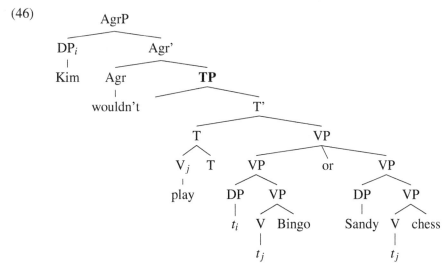

Finally, for cases involving negative determiners such as (47), Johnson adopts the split scope analysis (Jacobs 1980; Penka 2011) in which these determiners are decomposed into a higher sentential negation and a lower indefinite at LF, and he proposes an analysis along the lines of (48):

(47) No dog eats Whiskas or cat Alpo.

(48)

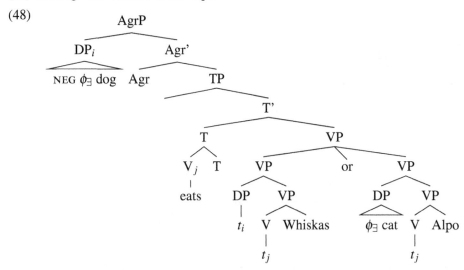

The ATB movement of the verb is licensed in the same way as (46). The only extra complication involved in this example is the split scope of the subject negative quantifier. The subjects in the two conjuncts both have a phonologically empty indefinite article $\phi_\exists$ as their determiners. This DP moves out of its VP-internal position in the first conjunct (just as in other examples) and attaches to a higher adverbial negation so that this negation and the indefinite $\phi_\exists$ fuse at PF to be spelled out as the morpheme *no*. $\phi_\exists$ and the head noun are reconstructed to their base positions at LF for the purpose of semantic interpretation. Thus, just as in the example above involving an auxiliary, the scopal relation between the quantifier and the coordinate structure is captured by assuming that the negation which is part of the negative quantifier originates syntactically *outside* the coordinate structure.

3.1.2 Low VP Coordination: Contraindications

As should be clear from the above, low VP coordination and the asymmetrical non-ATB movement of the subject of the first conjunct out of its VP-internal position is crucial in this approach for mediating the apparent mismatch between the surface positions of the scopal operators and their semantic scope. We now offer a host of empirical contraindications for this assumption. There are two lines of evidence against the low VP coordination analyses: on the one hand, the failure of constituency tests that VPs would be expected to satisfy, and on the other, a set of distributional patterns which strongly group Gapping conjuncts with clausal constituents as opposed to VPs. A complete argument against the transformational approach should also refute the islandhood-based arguments *for* it of the sort typically invoked in defense of movement-based analysis in the literature. We defer this task to a later chapter (chapter 10, section 10.2.1). Also, due to space limitations, the following discussion omits some arguments; for a more complete critique of the transformational analyses of Gapping, see Kubota and Levine (2016a). In particular, Johnson's analysis faces a major empirical difficulty in licensing the distributive readings of modals and negation quantifiers in the Siegel/Oehrle data, but we omit this discussion (see Kubota and Levine 2016a, section 2.2.1) in what follows.

3.1.2.1 Basic constituency tests The non-ATB movement of the first conjunct subject in the low VP coordination analysis creates a spurious surface VP (or TP)—the boldfaced constituents in (45) and (46)—asymmetrically containing the subject of the second conjunct. Thus, in (49) (which contains an auxiliary), the subject moves to a higher position, and the verb remains in either the T (in the case of auxiliary + verb gapping in (49a)) or the V (in the case of auxiliary alone gapping in (49b)) head, as in (50a) and (50b).

(49) No positron can occupy the INner shell and electron $\left\{ \begin{array}{l} \text{a. } \varnothing \\ \text{b. sit in} \end{array} \right\}$ the OUTer shell of the same atom.

(50) a. [$_{AgrP}$ No positron$_i$ [$_{Agr'}$ can [$_{TP}$ occupy$_j$ [$_{VP}$ [$_{VP}$ t_i t_j the INner shell] and [$_{VP}$ $\phi_\exists$ electron t_j the OUTer shell]]]]]]

b. [$_{AgrP}$ No positron$_i$ [$_{Agr'}$ can [$_{TP}$ [$_{VP}$ [$_{VP}$ t_i occupy the INner shell] and [$_{VP}$ $\phi_\exists$ electron sit in the OUTer shell]]]]]]

It is not necessarily clear in advance exactly which category is targeted by phenomena like VP fronting that are standardly taken to diagnose complements of auxiliaries (in theory neutral terms), but given the structures assigned to the two versions of (49) in (50), regardless of whether these tests apply to VP or to TP, one or the other of the two examples in (51)–(53) should be predicted to be grammatical. The robust unacceptability of all of these examples falsifies this prediction very clearly.

(51) a. No positron can [$_{TP_i}$ occupy the INner shell and electron the OUTer shell of the same atom]. #Not only that, no neutron can do so$_i$.   (*do so*)

b. No positron can [$_{VP_i}$ occupy the INner shell and electron sit in the OUTer shell of the same atom]. #Not only that, no neutron can do so$_i$.

(52) a. *[$_{TP_i}$ Occupy the INner shell and electron the OUTer shell of the same atom],
       no positron can t_i.   (*fronting*)

      b. *[$_{VP_i}$ Occupy the INner shell and electron sit in the OUTer shell of the same
       atom], no positron can t_i.

(53) a. *No positron can [$_{TP}$ occupy the INner shell and electron the OUTer shell of the
       same atom], or [$_{TP}$ occupy the inner shell of an atom with another positron].
                                                                                  (*coordination*)

      b. *No positron can [$_{VP}$ occupy the INner shell and electron sit in the OUTer shell
       of the same atom], or [$_{VP}$ occupy the inner shell of an atom with another
       positron].

It is true that failing a constituency test does not necessarily disprove the constituenthood of the string in question, since the failure may arise for nonstructural reasons.
Such accounts are of course always possible, and in certain cases seem quite likely as
the source of negative judgments. For example, in the case of (51), we might have used
VP ellipsis as our test, rather than *do so* replacement, and the anomalous result (#*Not
only that, no neutron can (either)*) might then have been taken to arise from the fact
that focused material cannot undergo ellipsis, assuming Gapping remnants are focused.
But so far as we can tell, there is no independent explanation—semantic, pragmatic,
psycholinguistic or prosodic—for the badness of the examples in (51)–(53). There is,
for example, no property of *do so* replacement analogous to that displayed by ellipsis
which would allow a parallel argument to be made for (51).[8] Thus, the examples in (51)
(at least one or the other) should be well-formed on the low VP coordination analysis,
and so should the others cited.[9] It thus seems safe to conclude that the misprediction

---

8. This of course does not mean that there are no semantic/pragmatic principles governing the use of *do
so* anaphora. In fact, there are: according to Ward and Kehler (2005), the acceptability difference in examples such as ?*The tallest teachers do so by example* vs. *The greatest teachers do so by example* (involving
deverbal nouns) depends on whether the nominalization makes the associated event (or property) salient
enough to support *do so* anaphora. The reason that *do so* has traditionally (but perhaps not totally unproblematically) been taken to be a syntactic constituency test is consistent with this view: if there is an overt
syntactic constituent that denotes the relevant property in the preceding discourse, that alone makes the
property salient enough. And since there would be nothing semantically or pragmatically incoherent in
the denotation of the alleged VP constituent in the case of (51), the prediction follows that, on the low VP
coordination analysis, the examples should be grammatical.

9. One might think that examples like (52) could be ruled out by assuming that reconstruction of the subject
of the first conjunct to a VP-internal position (which one might motivate either from the CSC (Lin 2001)
or perhaps just for the purpose of semantic interpretation) is blocked for fronted VPs. Such an assumption
might in turn be taken to receive independent support from the fact that the object quantifier cannot scope
over the subject quantifier in such an environment:

(i) See everyone, (I am sure) someone did.   ($\exists > \forall$, *$\forall > \exists$; Huang 1993)

But the argument that (i) motivates this assumption is decisively undermined by contrasts such as that
between (iia) and (iib).

noted is due to the fact that the low VP coordination approach analyzes Gapping via coordination at the VP level.

3.1.2.2 Gapped conjuncts: VP or S?

Moreover, just from the basic syntactic patterns of Gapping (not involving any interactions with other phenomena targeting "VP" constituents), we see evidence against the low VP coordination analysis. The relevant data come from Gapping sentences involving various fronted elements.

(54) a. At our house we play poker, and at Betsy's house, bridge.
     b. Yesterday we went to the movies, and last Thursday, to the circus.

(Sag 1976, 265)

(55) a. To Robin Chris gave the book __, and to Leslie, the magazine __.
     b. To Leslie I want to write a letter __, and to Robin, a short note __.
     c. To Leslie I (had) thought that we'd write a letter __, and to Robin, a short note __.
     d. Tweedledee, I intend to argue with __, and Tweedledum, to negotiate with __.
     e. Robin, I'm quite disappointed in __, and Leslie, very angry at __.

(56) Which abstract should we send to NELS and which manuscript to LI?

Some of these facts were already known since Sag (1976), and indeed, Repp (2009, 34) briefly notes that examples similar to (54) and (56) are problematic for the low VP coordination analysis of Gapping offered in Winkler (2005). On the low VP coordination analysis, by assumption, the second conjunct contains only an untensed lower VP projection, but then, there are no landing sites for the fronted elements, which are standardly taken to be somewhere above the T node.

Note crucially that, unlike subjects (for which there is at least a theory-internal motivation for a preverbal base position by adopting the VP-internal subject hypothesis), the fronted elements in (54)–(56) do not originate in the conjunct-initial positions in the second conjunct. Thus, the only way to accommodate these examples is to posit an ad hoc landing site just above the lower VP (Winkler [2005, 209] does indeed seem to be alluding to this possibility, without, however, noting its immediate consequence

---

(ii) a. Some student (or other) wants to hear stories about every physicist. $\quad$ ($\exists > \forall, \forall > \exists$)
     b. Stories about every physicist, some student (or other) wants to hear. $\quad$ ($\exists > \forall, {*}\forall > \exists$)

In (iib) there is no question of the existentially quantified subject reconstructing to a position within the fronted constituent, since it did not originate within that constituent to begin with. Yet just as in (i), we find that the wide scope available to the in situ universal is unavailable when the universal is part of a topicalized constituent. Hence the claim that subjects cannot reconstruct back into fronted VPs receives no support from the scopal facts about (i), and appealing to such a claim to explain the pattern in (52) must therefore be purely stipulative.

we discuss below). Positing such a landing site, however, is highly implausible, given the obvious impossibility of topicalizing to this position in non-Gapping contexts, as robustly exemplified in (57) and (58).

(57) a. *I intend$_i$ [$_{VP}$ Tweedledee$_k$ [$_{VP}$ t_i to negotiate with t_k]].   (cf. (55d))

     b. *I am Leslie$_i$ very angry at t_i .   (cf. (55e))

(58) a. *I want [to Robin]$_i$ to write a letter t_i .   (cf. (55b))

     b. *I thought [to Robin]$_i$ that we would write a letter t_i .   (cf. (55c))

     c. *I had [to Robin]$_i$ thought that we would write a letter t_i (cf. (55c))

Tweedledum is fronted in the second conjunct in (55d). The claim that the second conjunct is a VP thus entails that there is a position within a VP which can host a topicalized constituent. But then, this landing site should be available in non-Gapping clauses as well. However, this prediction fails, as attested by the ill-formedness of (57a). Similar arguments go with other examples. To rule out examples like (57) and (58), one would then need to invoke some constraint prohibiting the (future) fronted element to stay in the lower VP adjunction site if the subject moves out of its VP-internal position. But such a complex interdependency between movement operations not only is theoretically dubious but also lacks any independent empirical motivation.

The evidence just outlined from topicalization against the low VP coordination analysis uses a particular syntactic behavior characteristic of clauses but not of VPs as a diagnostic probe. A second argument of the same kind can be made based on a property characteristic of VPs as opposed to clauses: the distribution of the adverb *merely* is a case in point. As shown in (59), *merely* is strictly a VP adjunct; it cannot adjoin to S.

(59) a. Robin $\left\{ \begin{array}{l} \text{merely said} \\ \text{said merely} \end{array} \right\}$ that our footnotes were too long.

     b. *Merely, Robin said that our footnotes were too long.

On this basis, we predict that *merely* should be eligible to appear preceding the putative VP which the second conjunct consists of in Johnson's analysis. But this prediction is not borne out.

(60) Robin commented only that our margins were too small, and
$\left\{ \begin{array}{l} \text{a. Leslie merely} \\ \text{b. *merely Leslie} \end{array} \right\}$ that our footnotes were too long.

The badness of (60b) follows directly from the fact, exemplified in (59b), that *merely* is strictly a VP modifier, if we assume that the gapped conjunct is clausal. But it is completely unexpected if we take the gapped conjunct to be a VP.

We thus have two diagnostics which independently sort VPs from Ss converging on the identification of the gapped conjunct as an S, not a VP. Ordinary methodological considerations therefore suggest that, like the data in (51)–(53), these facts impose a very heavy burden of proof on the low VP coordination analysis.

Given the failure of the low VP coordination approach documented above, it seems fair to conclude that there is currently no successful analysis of the apparently anomalous scopal properties of auxiliaries and quantifiers in Gapping that is free from major empirical problems. On the whole, the low VP coordination analysis is the best story that has been produced in previous work on Gapping, but the empirical evidence we have discussed above seems to show conclusively that the particular way in which it links the two puzzles of Gapping is not on the right track.

3.2 An Analysis of Gapping in Hybrid Type-Logical Categorial Grammar

In this section, we propose an analysis of Gapping in Hybrid TLCG. The key property of Hybrid TLCG lies in its "hybrid" architecture involving both the standard directional slashes for regulating word order and the novel nondirectional slash stemming from Oehrle's (1994) work which is suitable for the modeling of movement-like phenomena. This enables simple analyses of various highly complex interactions between "order-sensitive" and "order-insensitive" phenomena in natural language that have proven problematic for previous syntactic theories, as we demonstrate further starting from this chapter. In particular, our analysis of Gapping in this chapter again crucially exploits the flexible (yet systematic) interactions between these two different modes of implication in capturing the apparently recalcitrant empirical properties that Gapping exhibits.

Our analysis of Gapping builds heavily on previous studies in the CG literature but extends their empirical coverage significantly. Implementational details aside, previous literature on Gapping in CG all agree on the fundamental hypothesis about the "underlying" syntactic structure of Gapping: Gapping instantiates like-category constituent coordination, despite the surface asymmetry between the initial and noninitial conjuncts. We take this hypothesis to be basically correct. However, previous analyses of Gapping in CG are all significantly limited in their empirical coverage. As we see it, the problem is that these previous analyses are couched in variants of CG that are suitable for handling only one or the other of the two problems that Gapping poses (i.e., describing the syntactic patterns and explaining the scope anomaly), thus leaving the analysis incomplete in the other respect (see Kubota and Levine [2012] for a more detailed critique of the major previous approaches to Gapping in the CG literature). For example, Steedman's (1990) analysis in CCG is the first analysis of Gapping as like category coordination, and it captures the basic syntactic patterns of Gapping quite successfully. However, it is not clear whether the complex interactions between Gapping and scope-taking expressions like quantifiers and auxiliaries observed above can be captured in a principled manner in CCG (which countenances a relatively constrained architecture of the syntax-semantics interface as compared to TLCG), even with the latest analysis of quantification proposed by Steedman (2012). By contrast, Oehrle (1987) and Siegel (1987) shed considerable light on this scope anomaly by casting their analyses in frameworks that are essentially the precursors of the contemporary "nondirectional" CGs. By relocating word order out of the combinatoric component, such frameworks are indeed suitable for capturing scope-related phenomena, but this comes with the cost that keeping track of linear order becomes notoriously difficult, resulting in an incomplete analysis of the basic syntactic patterns of Gapping. Our own analysis resembles most closely Morrill et al.'s (2011) (which is a refinement of Hendriks [1995b]) in treating Gapping essentially as coordination of sentences with medial gaps. However, neither Hendriks (1995b) nor Morrill et al. (2011) extend their analyses to the scope anomaly puzzle. (In an earlier version of this chapter, which has appeared as Kubota and Levine [2016a], we conjectured that our empirical analysis of Gapping would carry over straightforwardly to Morrill et al.'s [2011] setup. This point has in fact been demonstrated explicitly in Morrill and Valentín [2017].) We think that the main reason that the discovery of a TLCG solution for this problem did not become available until recently is that previous variants of TLCG employed very complex mechanisms for handling discontinuous constituency in Gapping and the syntax-semantics mismatch of scopal expressions, which obscured the underlying analytic insight considerably. Our setup improves these approaches in this respect, in treating (following Oehrle 1994) discontinuity simply by λ-binding in phonology, thereby making the underlying analytic intuition considerably more transparent.

Gapping presents an important case in relation to a comparison of (Hybrid) TLCG with the mainstream movement-based syntactic theory. At this point it may still appear as though Hybrid TLCG is just a nonstandard variant of movement-based theory which does away with the notion of phrase structural constituency. Gapping turns out to provide one answer to this question. Though the most basic use of the vertical slash connective is to model the notion of syntactic movement, inferences involving the vertical slash are much more general and powerful than the notion of syntactic movement, and this property of Hybrid TLCG turns out to be crucial in the analysis of Gapping.

3.2.1 Gapping as Hypothetical Reasoning

Our analysis of Gapping exploits the order-insensitive nature of the vertical slash $\upharpoonright$. As discussed in chapter 2, with the vertical slash, expressions containing medial gaps can be modeled straightforwardly via hypothetical reasoning. This enables us to analyze expressions like *Robin __ Bill* (a sentence missing the main verb) in Gapping as directly conjoinable constituents. Specifically, as illustrated in the following (partial) derivation, such expressions are derived as constituents of a syntactic category $S\upharpoonright((NP\backslash S)/NP)$ (i.e., an S missing a transitive verb $(NP\backslash S)/NP$ in the middle), with a functional phonology of type $\mathbf{st}{\rightarrow}\mathbf{st}$ (where the prosodic variable φ_1 of type $\mathbf{st}$ (string) bound by the lambda operator explicitly keeps track of the position of the gap in the string). The derivation is parallel to the topicalization derivation in (24) from the previous chapter, except that the missing category is $(NP\backslash S)/NP$ rather than NP.

(61)

$$\frac{\displaystyle \frac{[\varphi_1; P; (NP\backslash S)/NP]^1 \quad bill; \mathbf{b}; NP}{\text{robin}; \mathbf{r}; NP \quad \frac{\varphi_1 \circ bill; P(\mathbf{b}); NP\backslash S}{\text{robin} \circ \varphi_1 \circ bill; P(\mathbf{b})(\mathbf{r}); S}}{\lambda\varphi_1.\text{robin} \circ \varphi_1 \circ bill; \lambda P.P(\mathbf{b})(\mathbf{r}); S\upharpoonright((NP\backslash S)/NP)}}{\upharpoonright I^1} /E$$

Note that the matching index 1 on the hypothesis and the last inference step $\upharpoonright I^1$ indicate that the transitive verb hypothesis is withdrawn at this step. Because of this, the derived category is $S\upharpoonright((NP\backslash S)/NP)$, in accordance with what the rule dictates. Note also that the phonology and semantics of the derived expression is obtained by strictly following what is specified in the rule, that is, binding the variable corresponding to the hypothesis by a lambda operator.

The following Gapping-specific lexical entry for conjunction is responsible for coordinating such expressions with functional phonologies of type **st→st**:

(62) $\lambda\sigma_2\lambda\sigma_1\lambda\varphi.[\sigma_1(\varphi) \circ \text{and} \circ \sigma_2(\boldsymbol{\varepsilon})]; \lambda\mathcal{W}\lambda\mathcal{V}.\mathcal{V} \sqcap \mathcal{W}; (S\upharpoonright X)\upharpoonright(S\upharpoonright X)\upharpoonright(S\upharpoonright X)$

—where $\boldsymbol{\varepsilon}$ is the empty string and $X = \left\{ \begin{array}{c} Y_0\backslash S \\ S/Y_0 \end{array} \right\} /Y_1/\ldots/Y_n$ with $n \geq 1$

The side condition on X here is meant to capture the generalization that the gapped expression is of a verbal category (with at least two unsaturated arguments). In most cases, the last argument is an NP sought via $\backslash$, thus instantiating $Y_0\backslash S$ as $NP\backslash S$. (But see the topicalization interaction case in (65) for the need for the S/Y_0 case.) Syntactically, (62) coordinates two sentences missing the main verb (i.e., $S\upharpoonright((NP\backslash S)/NP)$ in the case at hand) to produce a larger expression of the same type, instantiating the general like-category coordination schema; correspondingly, the semantics is that of generalized conjunction, again conforming to the general treatment of coordination. The only slight complication is in the phonology. The output phonology is of the same type **st→st** as the input phonologies, but instead of binding the variables in each conjunct by the same λ-operator, the gap in the second conjunct is filled by an empty string $\boldsymbol{\varepsilon}$, capturing the idiosyncrasy of Gapping (where the verb is not pronounced in the second conjunct) via a lexical specification, without invoking any extra rule or prosodically empty operator.

A couple of comments are in order regarding the lexical entry in (62). First, the brace notation might give the misleading impression that the condition on the missing category is stated purely disjunctively. Recent work by Chris Worth (2016) suggests that it may be possible to model our directional mode of implication within a nondirectional CG via subtyping making use of higher-order logic. We envisage that in this more formally sophisticated implementation of our framework, it will be possible to treat the two directional slashes as subtypes of a single more general type, and that the disjunction in (62) can then be collapsed to a single more general condition, capturing the underlying analytic intuition more transparently. Second, to capture the generalization that the Gapping-specific entry of the form in (62) is available not just for *and* but for other conjunction markers as well, the entry should be thought of not as simply being listed in the lexicon but as being related to the ordinary string-conjoining entries of conjunction words via a lexical rule of the following form (with the same side condition on X as in (62)):

(63) $\varphi_0; \mathcal{F}; (Z \backslash Z)/Z \Rightarrow \lambda\sigma_2\lambda\sigma_1\lambda\varphi.[\sigma_1(\varphi) \circ \varphi_0 \circ \sigma_2(\boldsymbol{\varepsilon})]; \mathcal{F}; (S\upharpoonright X)\upharpoonright(S\upharpoonright X)\upharpoonright(S\upharpoonright X)$

This rule systematically relates a lexical entry for a conjunction word (which has the syntactic category $(Z \backslash Z)/Z$) to a lexical entry of the form in (62).[10] Gapping is associated with distinct properties both prosodically and pragmatically (cf. the Parallelism requirement [Kuno 1976; Levin and Prince 1986; Kehler 2002] for the latter).[11] The obligatory association with the special prosody and Parallel discourse relation can then be attributed to this lexical rule (or empty operator).[12]

With this conjunction lexical entry, a simple Gapping sentence can be derived as in (64) (in what follows, we abbreviate $(NP\backslash S)/NP$ and $NP\backslash S$ as TV and VP, respectively):

---

10. If desired, this lexical rule could be reformulated as an empty operator of the following form:

(i) $\lambda\varphi_0\lambda\sigma_2\lambda\sigma_1\lambda\varphi.[\sigma_1(\varphi) \circ \varphi_0 \circ \sigma_2(\boldsymbol{\varepsilon})]; \lambda\mathcal{F}.\mathcal{F}; (S\upharpoonright X)\upharpoonright(S\upharpoonright X)\upharpoonright(S\upharpoonright X)\upharpoonright((Z\backslash Z)/Z)$

11. This of course does not mean that such pragmatic and prosodic properties can be expressed/realized only in Gapping. It is possible to have a parallel discourse relation and a Gapping-like prosody at the same time in ordinary coordination as well in the right kind of context such as the following:

(i) A: Who ate what?
     B: John ate beans, and Bill ate rice.

The difference between Gapping and ordinary coordination is that while the association with this prosody/pragmatics pair is optional in the latter, it is obligatory in the former.

12. There is now increasing recognition in the literature that considerations of discourse coherence play a large role in judgments of well-formedness in such constructions. See, for example, Toosarvandani (2016) for one specific proposal to account for embedding asymmetries between the gapped and ungapped conjuncts in completely pragmatic terms.

(64)

$$\lambda\sigma_2\lambda\sigma_1\lambda\varphi.\sigma_1(\varphi)\circ$$
$$\text{and}\circ\sigma_2(\boldsymbol{\varepsilon});$$
$$\lambda\mathcal{W}\lambda\mathcal{V}.\mathcal{V}\sqcap\mathcal{W};$$
$$(S\vert X)\vert(S\vert X)\vert(S\vert X)$$

$$\vdots$$
$$\lambda\varphi_1.\text{robin}\circ\varphi_1\circ\text{bill};$$
$$\lambda P.P(\mathbf{b})(\mathbf{r});$$
$$S\vert TV$$

$$\vdots$$
$$\lambda\varphi_1.\text{leslie}\circ\varphi_1\circ\text{sandy};$$
$$\lambda Q.Q(\mathbf{s})(\mathbf{l});$$
$$S\vert TV$$

$$\cfrac{\lambda\sigma_1\lambda\varphi.\sigma_1(\varphi)\circ\text{and}\circ\text{robin}\circ\boldsymbol{\varepsilon}\circ\text{bill};}{\lambda\mathcal{V}.\mathcal{V}\sqcap\lambda P.P(\mathbf{b})(\mathbf{r});(S\vert TV)\vert(S\vert TV)}\ \lceil E$$

$$\cfrac{\lambda\varphi[\text{leslie}\circ\varphi\circ\text{sandy}\circ\text{and}\circ\text{robin}\circ\boldsymbol{\varepsilon}\circ\text{bill}];}{\lambda Q.Q(\mathbf{s})(\mathbf{l})\sqcap\lambda P.P(\mathbf{b})(\mathbf{r});S\vert TV}\ \lceil E$$

$$\vdots$$
$$\text{met};$$
$$\mathbf{met};$$
$$TV$$

$$\cfrac{\text{leslie}\circ\text{met}\circ\text{sandy}\circ\text{and}\circ\text{robin}\circ\boldsymbol{\varepsilon}\circ\text{bill};}{\mathbf{met}(\mathbf{s})(\mathbf{l})\wedge\mathbf{met}(\mathbf{b})(\mathbf{r});S}\ \lceil E$$

In this analysis, two gapped sentences are directly conjoined with each other first, and then the verb "lowers into" this conjoined gapped sentence phonologically. The right surface string is obtained for the whole sentence by giving the two type **st→st** functional phonologies of the conjuncts as arguments to the conjunction and then by applying the resultant **st→st** function to the string of the verb, via three successive applications of $\lceil E$. Note that the fact that the verb appears to the right of the coordinate structure in the derivation does not have any significance for the surface word order (thus, this should not be thought to reflect the status of the verb as being "extraposed" or "right-node raised"). The surface order is computed based on what is specified in the rules, in particular, here, the $\lceil E$ rule, according to which the phonology of the derived expression is the result of applying the phonology of the functor to that of its argument.

Note also that the right meaning for the sentence is obtained by letting the verb bind the gap positions in the two conjuncts after the coordinate structure is built via generalized conjunction instead of positing a phonetically empty copy of the verb in the gapped conjunct (if the reduction of the semantic translation at the last step isn't obvious, note that Partee and Rooth's [1983] definition of generalized conjunction entails that $[\phi\sqcap\psi](\alpha)=\phi(\alpha)\sqcap\psi(\alpha)$). This aspect of the semantics of coordination turns out to be crucial in assigning the right interpretations for the more complex cases involving scopal expressions like auxiliaries and quantifiers.

As should be clear at this point, the role of both directional and nondirectional implication is crucial in our analysis: the gapped sentence with syntactic type $S\vert TV$ explicitly keeps track of the position of the medial gap via λ-binding in phonology; on the other hand, directional slashes are crucially employed in the specification of the gapped material $(NP\backslash S)/NP$, which is reflected in the linear order in which its arguments appear in the string part of the gapped sentence. Thus, we exploit the hybrid implication architecture of Hybrid TLCG here; keeping track of the right word order becomes a very challenging problem in Linear Categorial Grammar (LCG; cf. chapter 12), which employs only the nondirectional mode of implication for syntactic composition.[13]

The analysis of Gapping presented above straightforwardly interacts with the analysis of topicalization from chapter 2 to yield an analysis of the topicalization/Gapping interaction example (55a). First, the gapped string *Chris gave* can be derived via hypothetical reasoning in the usual manner:

(65)
$$
\frac{
\dfrac{
\dfrac{
\dfrac{gave;\ \mathbf{gave};\ \mathrm{VP/PP/NP}\quad [\varphi_6;w;\mathrm{NP}]^1}{gave\circ\varphi_6;\ \mathbf{gave}(w);\ \mathrm{VP/PP}}\ _{/E}\quad [\varphi_7;u;\mathrm{PP}]^2}{gave\circ\varphi_6\circ\varphi_7;\ \mathbf{gave}(w)(u);\ \mathrm{VP}}\ _{/E}\quad chris;\ \mathbf{c};\ \mathrm{NP}}{chris\circ gave\circ\varphi_6\circ\varphi_7;\ \mathbf{gave}(w)(u)(\mathbf{c});\ \mathrm{S}}\ _{\backslash E}}{chris\circ gave\circ\varphi_6;\ \lambda u.\mathbf{gave}(w)(u)(\mathbf{c});\ \mathrm{S/PP}}\ _{/I^2}}
{chris\circ gave;\ \lambda w\lambda u.\mathbf{gave}(w)(u)(\mathbf{c});\ \mathrm{S/PP/NP}}\ _{/I^1}
$$

Then the two conjuncts to be coordinated are derived by binding a gap of type S/PP/NP in a topicalized sentence (note that two hypothetical reasonings are involved here, one for Gapping and the other for topicalization):

(66)

$$
\frac{
\left[\begin{matrix}\varphi_1;\\ x;\\ \mathrm{PP}\end{matrix}\right]^1\quad
\dfrac{
\dfrac{\left[\begin{matrix}\varphi_0;\\ P;\mathrm{S/PP/NP}\end{matrix}\right]^2\quad \dfrac{the\circ book;\ \mathbf{b};\mathrm{NP}}{}}{\varphi_0\circ the\circ book;\ P(\mathbf{b});\ \mathrm{S/PP}}\ _{/E}}{\varphi_0\circ the\circ book\circ\varphi_1;\ P(\mathbf{b})(x);\ \mathrm{S}}\ _{/E}
}{}
$$

$$
\frac{
\dfrac{\lambda\varphi_1.\varphi_0\circ the\circ book\circ\varphi_1;\ \lambda x.P(\mathbf{b})(x);\mathrm{S{\upharpoonright}PP}\qquad \dfrac{\lambda\sigma_1\lambda\varphi_3.\varphi_3\circ\sigma_1(\boldsymbol{\varepsilon});\ \lambda\mathcal{G}.\mathcal{G};(\mathrm{S{\upharpoonright}X}){\upharpoonright}(\mathrm{S{\upharpoonright}X})}{}}{\lambda\varphi_3.\varphi_3\circ\varphi_0\circ the\circ book;\ \lambda x.P(\mathbf{b})(x);\ \mathrm{S{\upharpoonright}PP}}\ _{{\upharpoonright}E}\qquad to\circ robin;\ \mathbf{r};\mathrm{PP}
}{
\dfrac{to\circ robin\circ\varphi_0\circ the\circ book;\ P(\mathbf{b})(\mathbf{r});\ \mathrm{S}}{\lambda\varphi_0.to\circ robin\circ\varphi_0\circ the\circ book;\ \lambda P.P(\mathbf{b})(\mathbf{r});\ \mathrm{S{\upharpoonright}(S/PP/NP)}}\ _{{\upharpoonright}I^2}
}\ _{{\upharpoonright}E}
$$

The derivation completes by conjoining two expressions of type S↾(S/PP/NP) and lowering the type S/PP/NP gapped expression to the first conjunct:

---

13. See chapter 12, section 12.3, and Moot (2014) for extensive discussions on this point. In particular, Moot (2014) discusses the particular difficulty that these approaches face in the context of Gapping (as well as other empirical phenomena such as [ordinary] coordination and adverb modification), where the interpretation "Leslie saw Sandy and Bill saw Robin" is predicted to be available for *Leslie saw Sandy, and Robin Bill* in a direct translation of the present analysis into LCG.

(67)

$$
\cfrac{
  \cfrac{
    \begin{array}{c}
    \lambda\sigma_2\lambda\sigma_1\lambda\varphi_5.\\
    \sigma_1(\varphi_5)\circ\\
    \text{and}\circ\sigma_2(\boldsymbol{\varepsilon});\\
    \lambda\mathcal{W}\lambda\mathcal{V}.\mathcal{V}\sqcap\mathcal{W};\\
    (S{\upharpoonright}X){\upharpoonright}(S{\upharpoonright}X){\upharpoonright}(S{\upharpoonright}X)
    \end{array}
    \qquad
    \begin{array}{c}
    \vdots\\
    \lambda\varphi_0.\text{to}\circ\text{leslie}\circ\\
    \varphi_0\circ\text{the}\circ\text{cd};\\
    \lambda P.P(\mathbf{cd})(\mathbf{l});\\
    S{\upharpoonright}(S/PP/NP)
    \end{array}
  }{
    \begin{array}{c}
    \lambda\sigma_1\lambda\varphi_5.\sigma_1(\varphi_5)\circ\\
    \text{and}\circ\text{to}\circ\text{leslie}\circ\boldsymbol{\varepsilon}\circ\text{the}\circ\text{cd};\\
    \lambda\mathcal{V}.\mathcal{V}\sqcap\lambda P.P(\mathbf{cd})(\mathbf{l});\\
    (S{\upharpoonright}(S/PP/NP)){\upharpoonright}(S{\upharpoonright}(S/PP/NP))
    \end{array}
  }{\upharpoonright}E
}{}
$$

$$
\begin{array}{c}
\vdots\\
\lambda\varphi_0.\text{to}\circ\text{robin}\circ\\
\varphi_0\circ\text{the}\circ\text{book};\\
\lambda P.P(\mathbf{b})(\mathbf{r});\\
S{\upharpoonright}(S/PP/NP)
\end{array}
$$

$$
\cfrac{
\lambda\varphi_5.\text{to}\circ\text{robin}\circ\varphi_5\circ\text{the}\circ\text{book}\circ\text{and}\circ\text{to}\circ\text{leslie}\circ\boldsymbol{\varepsilon}\circ\text{the}\circ\text{cd};}
{\lambda P.P(\mathbf{b})(\mathbf{r})\sqcap\lambda P.P(\mathbf{cd})(\mathbf{l});S{\upharpoonright}(S/PP/NP)}
$$

$$
\begin{array}{c}
\vdots\\
\text{chris}\circ\text{gave};\\
\lambda w\lambda u.\mathbf{gave}\\
(w)(u)(\mathbf{c});\\
S/PP/NP
\end{array}
$$

$$
\cfrac{}{
\begin{array}{c}
\text{to}\circ\text{robin}\circ\text{chris}\circ\text{gave}\circ\text{the}\circ\text{book}\circ\text{and}\circ\text{to}\circ\text{leslie}\circ\text{the}\circ\text{cd};\\
\mathbf{gave}(\mathbf{b})(\mathbf{r})(\mathbf{c})\wedge\mathbf{gave}(\mathbf{cd})(\mathbf{l})(\mathbf{c});S
\end{array}
}{\upharpoonright}E
$$

Before moving on to the more complex cases involving auxiliaries and determiners, we would like to clarify what our analysis above exactly amounts to. With the lexical entry (62) and the general availability of hypothetical reasoning, our analysis entails that *any* substring of the sentence that is a rightward looking (except for the last argument) functor rooted in S can undergo Gapping and that Gapping is restricted to noninitial conjuncts. As for the latter point, one might question our lexical treatment here since there are attempts to derive this property from basic word order, building on Ross's (1970) classical conjecture. However, the most successful such attempt by Steedman (1990) remains problematic due to the highly controversial status of the key combinatory rule ("Decompose") for deriving Gapping in English (see Kubota and Levine [2012] for some discussion), and for this reason we remain skeptical about such attempts. Moreover, in most other accounts of Gapping, including the low VP coordination analysis, this, or a related aspect, remains a stipulation. (On the latter, the question is why the subject of the second conjunct cannot undergo the non-ATB movement.)

The former question, namely, why Gapping is restricted to verbal categories, is currently a major open question for any theoretical account of Gapping.[14] We conjecture here that this may perhaps be understood as a grammaticalization of a functional constraint on the kinds of meanings typically expressed by Gapping sentences. As noted by many authors (see, e.g., Kuno [1976] for an early reference), Gapping invokes a

---

14. Yoshida et al. (2012) argue convincingly that the apparent Gapping in NPs like the following (noted by Jackendoff [1971]) had better be analyzed as an elliptical phenomenon licensed by an anaphoric mechanism:

(i) Bill's funny story about Sue and Max's ∅ about Kathy both amazed me.

contrast between parallel "pairs" of items. The relation holding between the elements of each pair is expressed by whatever material is contained in the initial conjunct that is missing in the noninitial conjunct(s). There is a sense in which the verb expresses the most central relation in the propositions expressed by each of the contrasted clauses. It then does not seem entirely implausible to speculate that, for this functionally motivated reason, there is a grammatical constraint that Gapping is restricted to verbs.[15] Cases of auxiliary-alone gapping such as (44a) may then be thought of as an extension of this pattern (where the missing relation is higher-order than in the case of plain verbs).

Finally, we would like to briefly comment on the relationship between the present proposal and the two types of major analyses of Gapping in the transformational literature. Our proposal shares one important property with Johnson's proposal involving ATB movement: in both approaches, Gapping is taken to be a sentence grammar phenomenon. We follow Johnson (2009) in taking this to be a correct feature of the analysis: as is well-known, Gapping is restricted to coordination environments (in the broader sense, including complex conjunction operators such as *not to mention*). In this respect, the present proposal contrasts with the proposals by Coppock (2001), Lin (2002), and Toosarvandani (2013), which crucially involve the anaphoric process of VP ellipsis for "removing" the verb from the second conjunct.[16] But despite the above similarity, the present proposal critically differs from Johnson's in that it does not take Gapping to involve VP coordination. In our analysis, coordination is at the S level, and this sets it free from all the problematic consequences entailed in Johnson's analysis. In a way, one might take Johnson's proposal to be an "approximation" of our S↾NP-coordination analysis within the movement-based setup. The various undermotivated transformational operations posited in Johnson's analysis seem to speak to the limitations of the transformational setup in mimicking the general mechanism of hypothetical reasoning that is fundamental to (Hybrid) TLCG, revealing the real difference between the transformational architecture of grammar and the logic-based architecture adopted here.

---

15. And to matrix verbs, not embedded verbs; thus, we take it that Johnson's (2009) "no embedding" constraint on Gapping follows from this.

16. In connection to this, one might wonder how cross-speaker Gapping like the following is to be handled:

(i) A: Delta will acquire Virgin America.
     B: *(And) Burger King, ∅ Wendy's.

Note that the conjunction marker is obligatory in B's utterance. We take this fact to indicate that this type of cross-speaker Gapping is felicitous only when the second speaker's utterance can in effect be interpreted as completing the utterance of the first speaker. As such, we take it that examples like (i) do not constitute counterevidence to our claim that Gapping is a strictly sentence grammar phenomenon licensed in conjunction environments only.

3.2.2 Scopal Interactions with Auxiliaries

The above analysis of the basic syntax of Gapping automatically interacts with independently motivated analyses of auxiliaries and quantifiers that take into account their scope-taking properties to predict their behaviors in Gapping examples.

The key assumption that enables a straightforward analysis of the scopal interactions between auxiliaries and Gapping is that auxiliaries are scope-taking expressions just like quantifiers. Specifically, we assume that morpho-phonologically auxiliaries have the distributional properties of a VP modifier of category VP/VP, but semantically, modals and negation are sentential operators μ, which take some proposition φ as an argument and return another proposition $\mu(\varphi)$. The idea in a nutshell is that auxiliaries are VP-type quantifiers in the same way that GQs are NP-type quantifiers. In the present approach, this syntax-semantics mismatch can be straightforwardly captured by assigning lexical entries of the following form to auxiliaries:

(68) $\lambda\sigma.\sigma(\mathsf{must})$; $\lambda\mathscr{F}.\Box\mathscr{F}(\mathsf{id}_{et})$; $\mathrm{S}{\restriction}(\mathrm{S}{\restriction}(\mathrm{VP/VP}))$

    ——where $\mathsf{id}_{et} =_{def} \lambda P_{et}.P$

This lexical entry says that the auxiliary verb *must* saturates a VP/VP (i.e., forward-looking VP modifier) gap in a sentence to return a fully saturated S. The VP modifier gap is vacuously bound by supplying an identity function id_{et} in its place, and the real semantic contribution of the auxiliary comes from the modal operator that takes as its scope the entire proposition obtained by binding this VP modifier gap of the gapped sentence.

The following derivation for the sentence *Someone must be present (at the meeting)* illustrates this scopal analysis of auxiliaries.[17] This derivation illustrates that the present analysis enables licensing the **must** $> \exists$ reading for the sentence without assuming that the modal subcategorizes for the subject in the GQ type.

---

17. As it is, the analysis of auxiliaries here overgenerates, since it does not capture the clause-boundedness of the scope of auxiliaries. See chapter 9, section 9.2.2, for how this constraint can be captured by an indexing mechanism we introduce in chapter 7 which keeps track of the depth of (clausal) embedding which is independently needed for other purposes.

(69)

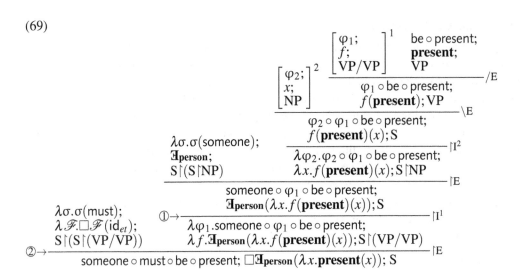

Just as in the quantifier example in (22), a hypothetical VP/VP expression is posited and this hypothesis is withdrawn once the whole sentence is built (①). This has the effect that the corresponding semantic and phonological variables are bound. The resultant type $S\!\restriction\!(VP/VP)$ expression is of the right type to be given as an argument to the auxiliary. The two are then combined by function application via $\restriction\!E$ (②), and the phonology of the auxiliary fills in the gap position of its argument. The semantic effect is somewhat more complex (and this might be thought of as a limiting case of "split scope" that we discuss below for negative quantifiers, where the lower meaning component is an identity function). An identity function is first filled in to the gap position of the sentence, which yields the proposition $\exists\mathbf{person}(\lambda x.\mathbf{present}(x))$. And then the modal operator $\square$ (which is the "real" semantic contribution of the auxiliary) scopes over this proposition to derive the translation of the whole sentence. As will become clear below, this higher-order treatment of auxiliaries turns out to be crucial in assigning the right meaning to the auxiliary gapping examples. Note also here that, since the quantifier is introduced in the derivation below the modal auxiliary, we obtain the $\mathbf{must} > \exists$ reading.

We are now ready to illustrate how the auxiliary wide-scope, non-distributive readings are obtained for Gapping sentences. We start with a variant in which only the auxiliary is gapped (70a) (the derivation for which is a bit simpler) and then move on to the case in which the whole auxiliary + verb sequence is gapped (70b).

(70) a. John can't eat steak and Mary eat pizza.
      b. John can't eat steak and Mary pizza.

The overall structure of the derivation for the auxiliary wide-scope reading is the same as in the simpler Gapping analysis in (64): we coordinate two expressions which are in effect clauses missing VP/VP functors, forming a larger expression of the same category:

(71)

$$
\begin{array}{c}
\cfrac{
\cfrac{
\cfrac{
\cfrac{
\begin{bmatrix} \varphi_1; \\ f; \mathrm{VP/VP} \end{bmatrix}^1 \quad
\begin{array}{c} \mathrm{eat} \circ \mathrm{steak}; \\ \mathbf{eat(s)}; \mathrm{VP} \end{array}
}{
\begin{array}{c} \varphi_1 \circ \mathrm{eat} \circ \mathrm{steak}; \\ f(\mathbf{eat(s)}); \mathrm{VP} \end{array}
}\ /\mathrm{E} \qquad \mathrm{john}; \ \mathbf{j}; \mathrm{NP}
}{
\begin{array}{c} \mathrm{john} \circ \varphi_1 \circ \mathrm{eat} \circ \mathrm{steak}; \\ f(\mathbf{eat(s)})(\mathbf{j}); \mathrm{S} \end{array}
}\ \backslash \mathrm{E}
}{
\begin{array}{c} \lambda \varphi_1 . \mathrm{john} \circ \varphi_1 \circ \mathrm{eat} \circ \mathrm{steak}; \\ \lambda f . f(\mathbf{eat(s)})(\mathbf{j}); \mathrm{S} \!\restriction\! (\mathrm{VP/VP}) \end{array}
}\ \restriction\! \mathrm{I}^1
}
\end{array}
$$

(the coordination structure with the right branch:)

$$
\cfrac{
\begin{array}{cc}
\begin{array}{c} \lambda \sigma_2 \lambda \sigma_1 \lambda \varphi . \sigma_1 (\varphi) \circ \\ \mathrm{and} \circ \sigma_2(\boldsymbol{\varepsilon}); \\ \lambda \mathcal{F}_2 \lambda \mathcal{F}_1 . \mathcal{F}_1 \sqcap \mathcal{F}_2; \\ (\mathrm{S}\!\restriction\! X)\!\restriction\! (\mathrm{S}\!\restriction\! X)\!\restriction\! (\mathrm{S}\!\restriction\! X) \end{array}
&
\begin{array}{c} \lambda \varphi_2 . \mathrm{mary} \circ \varphi_2 \circ \\ \mathrm{eat} \circ \mathrm{pizza}; \\ \lambda g . g(\mathbf{eat(p)})(\mathbf{m}); \\ \mathrm{S}\!\restriction\! (\mathrm{VP/VP}) \end{array}
\end{array}
}{
\begin{array}{c} \lambda \sigma_1 \lambda \varphi_0 . \sigma_1(\varphi_0) \circ \mathrm{and} \circ \\ \mathrm{mary} \circ \boldsymbol{\varepsilon} \circ \mathrm{eat} \circ \mathrm{pizza}; \\ \lambda \mathcal{F}_1 . \mathcal{F}_1 \sqcap \lambda g . g(\mathbf{eat(p)})(\mathbf{m}); \\ (\mathrm{S}\!\restriction\! (\mathrm{VP/VP}))\!\restriction\! (\mathrm{S}\!\restriction\! (\mathrm{VP/VP})) \end{array}
}\ \restriction\! \mathrm{E}
$$

$$
\cfrac{}{
\begin{array}{c} \lambda \varphi_0 . \mathrm{john} \circ \varphi_0 \circ \mathrm{eat} \circ \mathrm{steak} \circ \mathrm{and} \circ \mathrm{mary} \circ \boldsymbol{\varepsilon} \circ \mathrm{eat} \circ \mathrm{pizza}; \\ \lambda f . f(\mathbf{eat(s)})(\mathbf{j}) \sqcap \lambda g . g(\mathbf{eat(p)})(\mathbf{m}); \mathrm{S}\!\restriction\! (\mathrm{VP/VP}) \end{array}
}\ \restriction\! \mathrm{E}
$$

This coordinated "gapped" constituent is then given as an argument to the auxiliary to complete the derivation, in the same way as in the previous simpler example involving an auxiliary.

(72)

$$
\cfrac{
\begin{array}{cc}
\begin{array}{c} \lambda \sigma_0 . \sigma_0(\mathrm{can't}); \\ \lambda \mathcal{F} . \neg \Diamond \mathcal{F}(\mathrm{id}_{et}); \\ \mathrm{S}\!\restriction\! (\mathrm{S}\!\restriction\! (\mathrm{VP/VP})) \end{array}
&
\begin{array}{c} \lambda \varphi_0 . \mathrm{john} \circ \varphi_0 \circ \mathrm{eat} \circ \mathrm{steak} \circ \mathrm{and} \circ \mathrm{mary} \circ \boldsymbol{\varepsilon} \circ \mathrm{eat} \circ \mathrm{pizza}; \\ \lambda f . f(\mathbf{eat(s)})(\mathbf{j}) \sqcap \lambda g . g(\mathbf{eat(p)})(\mathbf{m}); \mathrm{S}\!\restriction\! (\mathrm{VP/VP}) \end{array}
\end{array}
}{
\mathrm{john} \circ \mathrm{can't} \circ \mathrm{eat} \circ \mathrm{steak} \circ \mathrm{and} \circ \mathrm{mary} \circ \boldsymbol{\varepsilon} \circ \mathrm{eat} \circ \mathrm{pizza}; \ \neg \Diamond [\mathbf{eat(s)(j)} \wedge \mathbf{eat(p)(m)}]; \ \mathrm{S}
}\ \restriction\! \mathrm{E}
$$

Note crucially that the auxiliary is a higher-order functor and what gets distributed to each conjunct is an identity function, not the modal meaning itself. More specifically, the reduction of the semantic term at the last step is unpacked in (73):

(73) $\lambda \mathcal{F}[\neg \Diamond \mathcal{F}(\mathrm{id}_{et})](\lambda f . f(\mathbf{eat(s)})(\mathbf{j}) \sqcap \lambda g . g(\mathbf{eat(p)})(\mathbf{m}))$
   $= \neg \Diamond [[\lambda f . f(\mathbf{eat(s)})(\mathbf{j}) \sqcap \lambda g . g(\mathbf{eat(p)})(\mathbf{m})](\mathrm{id}_{et})]$
   $= \neg \Diamond [[\lambda f . f(\mathbf{eat(s)})(\mathbf{j})](\mathrm{id}_{et}) \sqcap [\lambda g . g(\mathbf{eat(p)})(\mathbf{m})](\mathrm{id}_{et})]$
   $= \neg \Diamond [\mathbf{eat(s)(j)} \sqcap \mathbf{eat(p)(m)}]$
   $= \neg \Diamond [\mathbf{eat(s)(j)} \wedge \mathbf{eat(p)(m)}]$

Thus, we get an interpretation in which the modal scopes over the conjunction, as desired. Note also that the right surface string is obtained in which the auxiliary is pronounced only once in the first conjunct, as per the lexical specification of the Gapping-type conjunction.

The analysis of the full-gapping example like (70b) is somewhat more complex, but the way the wide-scope reading is predicted for the auxiliary is essentially the same. The technical complication lies in the fact that both the verb and the auxiliary strings need to be lowered to the first conjunct. We first lower a constituent of type TV (= VP/NP; consisting of the verb itself and an unbound variable representing the gap position for the auxiliary) to a gapped sentence of type $S \upharpoonright TV$. Then, by binding the VP/VP gap for the auxiliary with $\upharpoonright$, an $S \upharpoonright (VP/VP)$ expression is derived which can then be given as an argument to the auxiliary:

(74)

$$
\cfrac{\cfrac{\left[\begin{array}{l}\varphi_0; \\ f; \text{VP/VP}\end{array}\right]^0 \quad \cfrac{\text{eat;} \quad \left[\begin{array}{l}\varphi_1; \\ x; \text{NP}\end{array}\right]^1}{\text{eat} \circ \varphi_1; \textbf{eat}(x); \text{VP}}\text{/E}}{\cfrac{\varphi_0 \circ \text{eat} \circ \varphi_1; f(\textbf{eat}(x)); \text{VP}}{\varphi_0 \circ \text{eat}; \lambda x.f(\textbf{eat}(x)); \text{VP/NP}}\text{/I}^1}}{\cfrac{\begin{array}{l}\text{john} \circ \varphi_0 \circ \text{eat} \circ \text{steak} \circ \text{and} \circ \text{mary} \circ \boldsymbol{\varepsilon} \circ \text{pizza;} \quad f(\textbf{eat}(\textbf{s}))(\textbf{j}) \wedge f(\textbf{eat}(\textbf{p}))(\textbf{m}); S\end{array}}{\begin{array}{l}\lambda\varphi_0.\text{john} \circ \varphi_0 \circ \text{eat} \circ \text{steak} \circ \text{and} \circ \text{mary} \circ \boldsymbol{\varepsilon} \circ \text{pizza;} \\ \lambda f.[f(\textbf{eat}(\textbf{s}))(\textbf{j}) \wedge f(\textbf{eat}(\textbf{p}))(\textbf{m})]; S \upharpoonright (\text{VP/VP})\end{array}}\upharpoonright \text{I}^0} \quad \begin{array}{l}\vdots \\ \lambda\varphi_2.\text{john} \circ \varphi_2 \circ \text{steak} \circ \\ \text{and} \circ \text{mary} \circ \boldsymbol{\varepsilon} \circ \text{pizza;} \\ \lambda Q.[Q(\textbf{s})(\textbf{j})] \sqcap \lambda P.[P(\textbf{p})(\textbf{m})]; \\ S \upharpoonright (\text{VP/NP})\end{array}}\upharpoonright \text{E}
$$

Then, by giving the sign just derived as an argument to the auxiliary, the derivation completes and we obtain the same auxiliary wide-scope reading as in (71).

(75)

$$
\cfrac{\begin{array}{ll}\lambda\sigma_0.\sigma_0(\text{can't}); & \qquad \vdots \\ \lambda\mathscr{F}.\neg\Diamond\mathscr{F}(\text{id}_{et}); S \upharpoonright (S \upharpoonright (\text{VP/VP})) & \begin{array}{l}\lambda\varphi_0.\text{john} \circ \varphi_0 \circ \text{eat} \circ \text{steak} \circ \text{and} \circ \text{mary} \circ \boldsymbol{\varepsilon} \circ \text{pizza;} \\ \lambda f.[f(\textbf{eat}(\textbf{s}))(\textbf{j}) \wedge f(\textbf{eat}(\textbf{p}))(\textbf{m})]; S \upharpoonright (\text{VP/VP})\end{array}\end{array}}{\text{john} \circ \text{can't} \circ \text{eat} \circ \text{steak} \circ \text{and} \circ \text{mary} \circ \boldsymbol{\varepsilon} \circ \text{pizza;} \quad \neg\Diamond[\textbf{eat}(\textbf{s})(\textbf{j}) \wedge \textbf{eat}(\textbf{p})(\textbf{m})]; S}\upharpoonright\text{E}
$$

Essentially, in the present account, the wide-scope option for the auxiliary in examples like (70a) and (70b) trivially follows from the fact that the (combinatoric) syntax of Gapping involves *directly* coordinating sentences with missing elements and supplying the missing element at a later point in the derivation.

The present analysis predicts the availability of distributive readings for Gapping sentences with auxiliaries as well. Importantly (and interestingly), as shown in (76), in the present approach, a VP/VP entry for the auxiliary (identical to the familiar entry for auxiliaries in nontransformational approaches like G/HPSG and earlier versions of CG) that has a simple string phonology can be derived as a theorem from the more basic type assigned in the lexicon above in the category $S \upharpoonright (S \upharpoonright (\text{VP/VP}))$ (thus, the former does not need to be separately stipulated in the lexicon).

(76)

$$
\cfrac{
\cfrac{
\lambda\sigma.\sigma(\text{can't});\\
\lambda\mathscr{F}.\neg\Diamond\mathscr{F}(\text{id}_{et});\text{S}\!\upharpoonright\!(\text{S}\!\upharpoonright\!(\text{VP}/\text{VP}))
\qquad
\cfrac{
[\varphi_1;x;\text{NP}]^1
\qquad
\cfrac{
\cfrac{
\cfrac{\dfrac{[\varphi_2;g;\text{VP}/\text{VP}]^2 \quad [\varphi_3;f;\text{VP}]^3}{\varphi_2\circ\varphi_3;g(f);\text{VP}}/\text{E}}{}
}{\varphi_1\circ\varphi_2\circ\varphi_3;g(f)(x);\text{S}}\backslash\text{E}
}{\lambda\varphi_2.\varphi_1\circ\varphi_2\circ\varphi_3;\ \lambda g.g(f)(x);\text{S}\!\upharpoonright\!(\text{VP}/\text{VP})}\!\upharpoonright\!\text{I}^2
}{\varphi_1\circ\text{can't}\circ\varphi_3;\neg\Diamond f(x);\text{S}}\!\upharpoonright\!\text{E}
}{\cfrac{\text{can't}\circ\varphi_3;\lambda x.\neg\Diamond f(x);\text{VP}}{\text{can't};\lambda f\lambda x.\neg\Diamond f(x);\text{VP}/\text{VP}}/\text{I}^3}\backslash\text{I}^1
$$

Then, by giving this derived auxiliary as an argument to the same $\text{S}\!\upharpoonright\!(\text{VP}/\text{VP})$ constituent used in (75), we obtain the distributive reading for the auxiliary.

(77)

$$
\cfrac{
\begin{array}{cc}
\vdots & \vdots\\
\text{can't}; & \lambda\varphi.[\text{john}\circ\varphi\circ\text{eat}\circ\text{steak}\circ\text{and}\circ\text{mary}\circ\boldsymbol{\varepsilon}\circ\text{pizza}];\\
\lambda f\lambda x.\neg\Diamond f(x);\text{VP}/\text{VP} & \lambda h.[h(\textbf{eat}(\textbf{s}))(\textbf{j})\wedge h(\textbf{eat}(\textbf{p}))(\textbf{m})];\text{S}\!\upharpoonright\!(\text{VP}/\text{VP})
\end{array}
}{\text{john}\circ\text{can't}\circ\text{eat}\circ\text{steak}\circ\text{and}\circ\text{mary}\circ\boldsymbol{\varepsilon}\circ\text{pizza};\ \neg\Diamond\textbf{eat}(\textbf{s})(\textbf{j})\wedge\neg\Diamond\textbf{eat}(\textbf{p})(\textbf{m});\text{S}}\!\upharpoonright\!\text{E}
$$

The derivation of the VP/VP category from the lexically specified higer-order category $\text{S}\!\upharpoonright\!(\text{S}\!\upharpoonright\!(\text{VP}/\text{VP}))$ for the auxiliary in (76) is an instance of *slanting*, a family of theorems for deriving Lambek cateogry specifications from the more abstract vertically slashed category specifications for linguistic expressions in Hybrid TLCG. We discuss corresponding theorems for generalized quantifiers in chapter 4, section 4.5, and study in more detail the consequences of slanting for auxiliaries when we revisit the syntax-semantics interface of English auxiliaries in greater detail in chapter 9.

3.2.3 Scopal Interactions with Negative Quantifiers

We have seen above that the apparent scope anomaly in Gapping sentences with auxiliaries is in fact a *predicted* consequence of the most straightforward analysis of Gapping embodying the idea of like-category coordination in our approach. In short, the unexpected wide-scope interpretation for auxiliaries follows from the fact that the auxiliary is introduced in the derivation after the whole coordinate structure is built. This analysis extends directly to the case of determiner gapping, including cases involving negative quantifiers such as (39c). Here, too, the apparently anomalous scope relation between quantifiers and coordination immediately falls out from the fact that the quantificational determiner is gapped and appears only in the first conjunct on the surface string. Though conceptually the analysis is a straightforward extension, the technical details are somewhat demanding since quantifiers (and negative quantifiers in particular) are more complex types of scopal expressions than auxiliaries. For this reason, we choose to outline the key points of the analysis in broad terms in what follows. The full details of the analysis are found in appendix B of Kubota and Levine (2016a).

Following Johnson (2000), we take the split scope property of negative quantifiers to be the key driving force of their apparently anomalous scope in determiner gapping. Thus, we first need an analysis of "split scope," where negative quantifiers like *no*, *few*, and *hardly any* are decomposed into sentential negation and an existential quantifier (or an indefinite) that scopes below the negation (Jacobs 1980; Penka 2011). It turns out that a fully lexical analysis of split scope is available in the present framework.[18] Specifically, we assume that the quantificational determiners forming negative quantifiers are lexically type-raised higher-order determiners of type $S\upharpoonright(S\upharpoonright Det)$, where Det abbreviates the syntactic type of ordinary determiners $S\upharpoonright(S\upharpoonright NP)\upharpoonright N$. By assigning negative determiners in this type, it becomes possible to specify the scope of the higher negation and the lower existential separately in the lexical meaning of the negative determiner:[19]

(78) $[[no]] = \lambda \mathscr{P}_{(et\to et\to t)\to t}.\neg\mathscr{P}(\mathbf{\exists})$

That is, the lexically type-raised determiner feeds an ordinary positive quantifier meaning (of type $(et \to et \to t)$) to its argument, thus saturating its determiner-type variable position, and additionally contributes negation which scopes over the whole sentence.

The full lexical entry for the negative determiner is then formulated as follows:

(79) $\lambda\rho.\rho(\lambda\varphi\lambda\sigma.\sigma(no\circ\varphi)); \lambda\mathscr{P}.\neg\mathscr{P}(\mathbf{\exists}); S\upharpoonright(S\upharpoonright Det)$

——where Det abbreviates $S\upharpoonright(S\upharpoonright NP)\upharpoonright N$

Determiner gapping can then be treated as a case of multiple gapping involving both the verb and the determiner. The only complication here is that the "gap" corresponding to the determiner is of a higher-order type phonologically, so an identity element of this higher-order phonological type needs to be fed to the second conjunct. This is done by the following entry for the conjunction word, which generalizes the Gapping-type conjunction entry to the $S\upharpoonright Det\upharpoonright TV$ type (again, this is to be derived by a lexical rule):

(80) $\lambda\rho_2\lambda\rho_1\lambda\varphi\lambda\sigma.\rho_1(\varphi)(\sigma)\circ and\circ\rho_2(\boldsymbol{\varepsilon})(\varepsilon_d); \sqcap; \mathbf{GC}(S\upharpoonright Det\upharpoonright TV)$

——where $\mathbf{GC}(A) =_{def} A\upharpoonright A\upharpoonright A$ for any syntactic type A
and $\varepsilon_d =_{def} \lambda\varphi\lambda\sigma.\sigma(\boldsymbol{\varepsilon}\circ\varphi) = \lambda\varphi\lambda\sigma.\sigma(\varphi)$

Sentences containing both a verb gap and a determiner gap are obtained via hypothetical reasoning in the usual way:

---

18. For a recent alternative analysis of split scope, see Abels and Martí (2010). The key component of Abels and Martí's analysis consists in treating negative quantifiers (and related expressions) as quantifiers over choice functions (of type $((et \to e) \to t) \to t)$. We believe that this approach is also compatible with the syntax-semantics interface of determiner gapping in our analysis.

19. Steedman (2012) proposes an analysis of split scope in CCG that embodies a similar idea, though technically implemented in a somewhat different way.

(81) $\lambda\varphi_1\lambda\tau.\tau(\text{dog})(\lambda\varphi_2.\varphi_2 \circ \varphi_1 \circ \text{whiskas})$;

  $\lambda P \lambda \mathscr{F}.\mathscr{F}(\mathbf{dog})(\lambda x.P(\mathbf{w})(x))$; S↾Det↾TV

Then, conjunction of two such expressions via (80) yields the following sign:

(82) $\lambda\varphi_1\lambda\tau.\tau(\text{dog})(\lambda\varphi_2.\varphi_2 \circ \varphi_1 \circ \text{whiskas}) \circ \text{or} \circ \text{cat} \circ \text{alpo}$;

  $\lambda P \lambda \mathscr{F}.\mathscr{F}(\mathbf{dog})(\lambda x.P(\mathbf{w})(x)) \sqcup \lambda P \lambda \mathscr{F}.\mathscr{F}(\mathbf{cat})(\lambda x.P(\mathbf{a})(x))$; S↾Det↾TV

Note in particular that the right string is obtained for the second conjunct.

Finally, the missing verb and determiner are successively lowered to the first conjunct to yield the following sign:

(83) no $\circ$ dog $\circ$ eats $\circ$ whiskas $\circ$ or $\circ$ cat $\circ$ alpo;

  $\neg[\exists_{\mathbf{dog}}(\lambda x.\mathbf{eat}(\mathbf{w})(x)) \vee \exists_{\mathbf{cat}}(\lambda x.\mathbf{eat}(\mathbf{a})(x))]$; S

Crucially, just as in the analysis from the previous section, since the negative determiner scopes over the whole coordinated gapped sentence in the combinatoric structure, the right semantic scope between the two operators is predicted. Thus, here again, the apparently anomalous scope relation between the negative quantifier and disjunction is a predicted consequence of the "gapped" status of the former. The syntactic analysis of Gapping requires the determiner to syntactically scope over the whole coordinate structure, and the semantic scope between the two transparently reflects this underlying structural relationship.

Finally, just as a lower-order auxiliary entry of type VP/VP can be derived from the lexically specified higher-order entry of type S↾(S↾VP/VP), the higher-order entry for the negative determiner can be lowered to the ordinary determiner type Det (= S↾(S↾NP)↾N) via hypothetical reasoning in the present framework. The syntax and semantics of this derived entry is just the familiar GQ-type quantifier entry for the word *no*:[20]

(84) $\lambda\varphi\lambda\sigma.\sigma(\text{no} \circ \varphi)$; $\lambda P.\lambda Q.\neg\exists(P)(Q)$; S↾(S↾NP)↾N

With this derived entry for *no*, the distributive reading for the negative quantifier in examples like (39c) (or (i) in footnote 4 on p. 43) can be derived straightforwardly. The derivation will be identical in form to the one for the non-distributive reading for the negative quantifier up to the point where the verb is lowered into the first conjunct (which can be obtained by feeding a TV as an argument to (82)) and differs only in the last step, where we simply let the derived S↾Det take the lowered Det type determiner in (84) as an argument.[21]

---

20. Note that the derivability relation here is asymmetrical: (79) ⊢ (84) is a theorem but (84) ⊢ (79) isn't.

21. Note also that, in the present analysis, cases such as (38d) involving nonnegative quantifiers are equally straightforward. The only difference from the negative quantifier case outlined in the main text is that

Morrill and Valentín (2017) note an overgeneration problem for the analysis of determiner gapping we have presented above and argue that recasting essentially the same analysis in Displacement Calculus (Morrill et al. 2011) overcomes this problem while retaining all the essential features of the scopal interactions between Gapping and scopal operators. The problem essentially is that the lexical entry for the conjunction word for determiner gapping in (80) does not keep track of the relative order between the two gaps in the multiply-gapped sentences that it takes as its arguments. Thus, any sentence missing a determiner and a transitive verb somewhere inside can be licensed in the type S⌡Det⌡TV, overgenerating examples such as the following:

(85)   a. *Most cats like Alpo and John ~~likes most~~ dogs.

       b. *John likes most dogs and ~~most~~ cats ~~like~~ Alpo.

Since Morrill and Valentín's own proposal is technically quite complex and sophisticated, we do not review it here. The essential point is that in their approach, "gap" positions in the prosodic representations of linguistic expressions are explicitly indexed from left to right, and this enables them to keep track of the order of the determiner and verb gaps in examples like (39c). Morrill and Valentín additionally note that, unlike our analysis in Hybrid TLCG, the reformulation in Displacement Calculus enables them to collapse the lexical entries for the conjunction word for the continuous and discontinuous gapping into a single entry, thereby achieving a more uniform analysis of the two cases.

While Morrill and Valentín frame their discussion in terms of an overall comparison of Hybrid TLCG and Displacement Calculus as a theory of natural language syntax, we do not think that their argument conclusively eliminates the possibility that the overgeneration issue merely reflects inadequacies of the particular analysis of determiner gapping we have proposed in Kubota and Levine (2013b, 2016a) rather than showing fundamental inadequacy of the theory in which the analysis is formulated.

One possible response to the overgeneration issue would be to abandon the higher-order analysis of determiner gapping and stick to a simpler analysis in which all gapped constituents have simple string prosodies. This will still enable us to analyze determiner gapping since Hybrid TLCG allows for slanting of linguistic signs with higher-order prosodies. Specifically, since all (unequivocally) well-formed examples of determiner gapping have the determiner in the subject position, the following would be a reason-

---

non-negative quantifiers have only the ordinary GQ-type lexical entries, and thus, only the latter type of derivation is available for them. This yields the distributive reading for the quantifier. Since split scope is not an issue, so far as we can tell, this suffices to derive the correct truth conditions for sentences like (38d).

able entry for licensing determiner gapping, where *and* conjoins sentences missing a transitive verb and a subject position slanted GQ (where GQs = S/(NP\S)/N):[22]

(86) $\lambda\sigma_2\lambda\sigma_1\lambda\varphi_1\lambda\varphi_2.\sigma_1(\varphi_1)(\varphi_2) \circ \text{and} \circ \sigma_2(\boldsymbol{\varepsilon})(\boldsymbol{\varepsilon});$

      $\sqcap; (S\upharpoonright GQs\upharpoonright TV)\upharpoonright(S\upharpoonright GQs\upharpoonright TV)\upharpoonright(S\upharpoonright GQs\upharpoonright TV)$

A determiner in the object position slants down to the Lambek type $((S/NP)\backslash S)/N$. Since this type is distinct from the subject position determiner type $S/(NP\backslash S)/N$ (= GQs) in (86), this approach avoids the overgeneration problem noted by Morrill and Valentín. It is true that this approach still requires duplicate entries for continuous and discontinuous gapping. But the alternative, as embodied in Morrill and Valentín's analysis, requires an explicit indexing of gap positions involving a kind of counting mechanism implemented as part of the (extended) type logic. The comparison then seems to be one between lexical redundancy and an overall revision of the core architecture of the theory. While there may be other motivations (empirical or otherwise) to prefer Displacement Calculus, since the only known case documented in the literature is the one involving determiner gapping, we take the position that lexical redundancy is a more parsimonious choice.

---

22. The analysis of negative quantifiers needs to be modified slightly. One possible approach would be to replace the entry in (79) with the following one in which the negative determiner binds a type NP/N indefinite instead of an existential GQ (here ε_P is a term [of type e] corresponding to the "indefinite" satisfying the property P under the scope of negation introduced by the negative quantifier; we remain agnostic about the exact semantic analysis of indefinites—one could adopt the Skolem term analysis by Steedman [2012] or the proof theoretic analysis in Dependent Type Semantics [Bekki 2014; Bekki and Mineshima 2017] proposed by Kubota et al. [2019]):

(i) $\lambda\sigma.\sigma(\text{no}); \lambda\mathscr{P}.\neg\mathscr{P}(\lambda P.\varepsilon_P); S\upharpoonright(S\upharpoonright(NP/N))$

The derivation for the negation wide-scope reading then goes as follows:

(ii)

$$
\cfrac{
\lambda\sigma.\sigma(\text{no});\ \lambda\mathscr{P}.\neg\mathscr{P}(\lambda P.\varepsilon_P);\ S\upharpoonright(S\upharpoonright(NP/N))
\qquad
\cfrac{
\cfrac{
\cfrac{
\cfrac{
\left[\begin{array}{c}\varphi_3;\\ \mathscr{F};\\ NP/N\end{array}\right]^3
\quad
\left[\begin{array}{c}\varphi_4;\\ P;\\ N\end{array}\right]^4
}{\begin{array}{c}\varphi_3\circ\varphi_4;\\ \mathscr{F}(P);NP\end{array}}
\quad
\left[\begin{array}{c}\varphi_5;\\ Q;\\ NP\backslash S\end{array}\right]^5
}{\begin{array}{c}\varphi_3\circ\varphi_4\circ\varphi_5;\ \mathscr{F}(P)(Q);\ S\end{array}}
\ /\mathrm{I}^5
}{\varphi_3\circ\varphi_4;\ \lambda Q.\mathscr{F}(P)(Q);\ S/(NP\backslash S)}\ /\mathrm{I}^4
}{\varphi_3;\ \lambda P\lambda Q.\mathscr{F}(P)(Q);\ S/(NP\backslash S)/N}
\quad
\cfrac{
\cfrac{
\begin{array}{c}\lambda\varphi_2\lambda\varphi_1.\varphi_1\circ\text{dog}\circ\varphi_2\circ\\ \text{whiskas}\circ\text{or}\circ\text{cat}\circ\text{alpo};\\ \lambda R\lambda\mathscr{P}.\mathscr{P}(\textbf{dog})(R(\textbf{w}))\\ \vee\mathscr{P}(\textbf{cat})(R(\textbf{a}));\\ S\upharpoonright(GQs/N)\upharpoonright TV\end{array}
\quad
\begin{array}{c}\text{eats};\\ \textbf{eat};\\ TV\end{array}
}{\begin{array}{c}\lambda\varphi_1.\varphi_1\circ\text{dog}\circ\text{eats}\circ\\ \text{whiskas}\circ\text{or}\circ\text{cat}\circ\text{alpo};\\ \lambda\mathscr{P}.\mathscr{P}(\textbf{dog})(\textbf{eat}(\textbf{w}))\\ \vee\mathscr{P}(\textbf{cat})(\textbf{eat}(\textbf{a}));\\ S\upharpoonright(GQs/N)\end{array}}
}{\begin{array}{c}\varphi_3\circ\text{dog}\circ\text{eats}\circ\text{whiskas}\circ\text{or}\circ\text{cat}\circ\text{alpo};\\ \textbf{eat}(\textbf{w})(\mathscr{F}(\textbf{dog}))\vee\textbf{eat}(\textbf{a})(\mathscr{F}(\textbf{cat}));\ S\end{array}}\ \mathrm{I}^3
}{\begin{array}{c}\lambda\varphi_3.\varphi_3\circ\text{dog}\circ\text{eats}\circ\text{whiskas}\circ\text{or}\circ\text{cat}\circ\text{alpo};\\ \lambda\mathscr{F}.\textbf{eat}(\textbf{w})(\mathscr{F}(\textbf{dog}))\vee\textbf{eat}(\textbf{a})(\mathscr{F}(\textbf{cat}));\ S\upharpoonright(NP/N)\end{array}}
}{\begin{array}{c}\text{no}\circ\text{dog}\circ\text{eats}\circ\text{whiskas}\circ\text{or}\circ\text{cat}\circ\text{alpo};\\ \neg[\textbf{eat}(\textbf{w})(\varepsilon_{\textbf{dog}})\vee\textbf{eat}(\textbf{a})(\varepsilon_{\textbf{cat}})];\ S\end{array}}
$$

3.2.4 Is Gapping a Type of Movement?

At this point, we would like to step back from the specific analysis of Gapping and ponder a somewhat more general question of theory comparison. There are certain observations that seem to be relevant for clarifying the similarities and differences between hypothetical reasoning with ↾ and the notion of movement in derivational approaches. In the previous chapter, we noted that in our setup the difference between "overt" and "covert" movement boils down to what happens to the phonology of the "gap"-containing expression. "Covert" movement is modeled by an operator with a functional phonology whose string component is embedded in the "gap" position of its semantic argument. By contrast, for "overt" movement, we have an operator that fills in an empty string to the gap. But nothing in the formal setup says that these are the only two things that one can do with linguistic signs containing gap positions. This is perhaps a subtle, but, we think, crucial difference between our approach and the derivational architecture of grammar. In the latter, where movement is conceived of as inherently ordered structure-building/manipulation operations, these two options would indeed seem to exhaust the set of logical possibilities: if you move constituents before computing word order (i.e., before SpellOut), then what you have is an instance of overt movement, whereas if you move constituents after computing word order, then what you have is an instance of covert movement. But in our calculus, the two types of "movement" are not ordered with respect to one another. Rather, they are just two types of inference that are both simultaneously available at any step of the proof. (It is precisely for this reason that the analogies to "overt" and "covert" movements that we have informally introduced above should be taken only as rough and crude metaphors.)

This, then, opens up an interesting analytic possibility: in our system, it is possible to do "overt" movement and "covert" movement *at the same time*, as it were, or, to put it differently, do something that cannot be broken down into a successive application of separate overt and covert movements. An anonymous reviewer for an earlier version of this chapter (Kubota and Levine 2016a, published as an article in *Natural Language and Linguistic Theory*) made the following remark, which we think gets at the key difference between Hybrid TLCG and derivational frameworks:

> [In Hybrid TLCG, with the use of functional phonologies] it becomes possible to state a conjunction rule for gapping that combines likes. If I'm not mistaken, in a derivational framework like Minimalism, such signs cannot be created, since it does not countenance the idea of prosodic variables that can later be filled in. Traces of movement are semantic placeholders, but not phonological ones.

As this reviewer correctly notes, the analysis of Gapping we have presented above crucially exploits this property of the system: the coordination operator takes two pieces of phonology, both missing some material inside themselves. It fills in the gap of the second conjunct with an empty string (as in "overt" movement) and fills in the gap of the first conjunct with the phonology of the missing verb (as in "covert" movement). Crucially, there is no movement-based analog of a complex operation on functional phonologies like this, since there is no genuine analog of linguistic signs with functional phonologies in derivational approaches. We have already seen the robust empirical payoff of this analysis. The difference between this analysis and other competing analyses (such as one that posits an empty verb in the second conjunct) is not clear in simple cases in which what is missing is just the verb. However, in more complex cases where (part of) what is missing is a scopal operator, our analysis *predicts* the availability of both the wide-scope reading and the narrow-scope reading for the relevant operator, based on an independently motivated form/meaning mismatch encoded in the lexical entries of such operators.

3.3   A Note on Stripping

Interestingly, Gapping is not the only coordination construction which motivates the treatment of modal auxiliaries as higher-order operators. As noted by Puthawala (2018), Stripping displays the same pattern, as shown in (87):

(87) John didn't sleep, or Mary.

This example has both wide-scope ('neither John nor Mary slept') and narrow-scope ('John was the one who didn't sleep, or maybe that was Mary') interpretations for negation.

   Puthawala (2018) shows that the analysis of Gapping we have proposed in the present chapter straightforwardly extends to the Stripping cases as well. The key to this analysis is the lexical entry for the conjunction word in (88) which licenses Stripping. With this lexical entry, the complete derivation for (87) (for the wide-scope reading for negation) goes as in (89).

(88) $\lambda\varphi_1\lambda\varphi_2\lambda\sigma.\sigma(\varphi_2) \circ \text{or} \circ \varphi_1; \lambda z\lambda y\lambda Q.Q(y) \sqcup Q(z); S{\upharpoonright}(S{\upharpoonright}X){\upharpoonright}X{\upharpoonright}X$

(89)

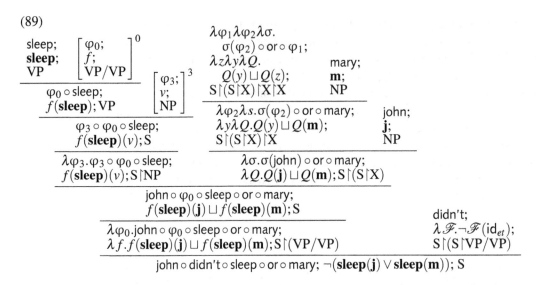

The narrow-scope reading for negation can be derived in a way parallel to the Gapping case. See Puthawala (2018) for further details.

4 Coordination and Scope

We have seen in the previous chapter that the interaction between the directional and nondirectional slashes in Hybrid TLCG is the key for the simple analysis of Gapping that captures the core properties of this construction, including the apparently anomalous scoping patterns of modal auxiliaries as they interact with Gapping. The advantage of the flexible yet systematic architecture of our framework is not limited to this particular type of noncanonical coordination construction. In fact, Hybrid TLCG allows for a systematic analysis of complex interactions between coordination (including both ordinary constituent coordination and the so-called nonconstituent coordination phenomena) and various types of scopal operators that have posed considerable difficulties for previous approaches to coordination in generative syntax (including both transformational and nontransformational approaches). The present chapter and the next chapter offer a detailed analysis of interactions between coordination and scopal operators, comparing the analysis in Hybrid TLCG with competing and/or related approaches in the current literature. We argue that the flexible syntax-semantics interface of Hybrid TLCG offers a general framework for formulating a simple analysis of apparently quite complex empirical patterns that the data in this domain exhibit.

4.1 The Coordination Problem in Modern Grammatical Theory

Coordination phenomena were one of the first syntactic patterns invoked to showcase the superiority of the generative transformational framework (see Chomsky 1957) but have emerged as one of the most problematic empirical domains in syntax, particularly in the interface with semantic interpretation. In the same year in which the grammar of coordination appeared to have finally received definitive treatment in Dougherty (1970) and Dougherty (1971) in the transformationalist paradigm, a short paper by Barbara Hall Partee (1970) appeared which made clear how problematic the relationship was between syntactic form and semantic interpretation involving coordination, scopal operators, and negation. Partee displayed data such as (90) to demonstrate that the standard approach to deriving the conjunction of non-clausal constituents by eliminating their apparently shared material via *Conjunction Reduction* was deeply misguided:

(90) a. Few rules are explicit and easy to read.

     b. Few rules are explicit and few rules are easy to read.

(90a) can be true even when (90b) is false, so that deriving the first from the structure giving rise to the second would, as Partee convincingly demonstrates, require distinctly ad hoc restrictions on the operations of the Conjunction Reduction transformation. Partee concluded her study with the observation that "[t]hose aspects of semantic interpretation which have been under consideration here appear to be explainable quite naturally on the basis of surface structure." In fact, however, data such as (90) proved to be only the easiest case of the problems posed by the interaction of scopal expressions under coordination.

In particular, in all of Partee's examples, the "surface" approach she argues for would simply combine a subject with a conjunction of VPs, with a transparent syntax-semantics mapping—an analysis which would combine two VP constituents into one, with the quantifier subject applying as an operator, with simple Montagovian semantics, to the intersection of properties corresponding to the conjunction. But consider what would be entailed by an analogous "surface" treatment in (91):

(91) John told a joke to Bill on Monday and Mary on Thursday.

A "surface" approach would be even less successful than an analysis based on Conjunction Reduction, since the operator denoted by *a joke* would have to scope over two nonconstituents—*Bill on Monday* and *Mary on Thursday*—which, under standard phrase structure assumptions, do not denote properties at all or indeed have any coherent semantic interpretations of their own. Thus, the fundamental question was not really that of "underlying structure" vs. "surface" interpretation, but rather the possibility of a syntax-semantics relationship based on the composition of material possibly lacking constituent status under phrase structure–based criteria.

Generalized Phrase Structure Grammar (GPSG) is an apt case in point. One of the earliest talking points in GPSG's rhetorical arsenal was the simplicity the framework made possible for analyses of coordination phenomena; indeed, coordination was in a sense the showpiece analysis in Gazdar's (1981) watershed paper, which, almost on its own, established the framework as a major competitor to the dominant tranformationalist consensus. The stipulativeness inherent in transformational rules such as Conjunction Reduction—purpose-built for syntactic conjunction and hence, in effect, simply an encoding of a specific construction—could be completely eliminated in favor of a few simple templates allowing various kinds of coordinations of like categories—and unlike categories as well—via GPSG's use of category underspecification. But things were quite different when the theorists working in GPSG attempted to confront data of the sort given in (92).

(92) a. John offered Mary, and Sue promised Bill, a lift home from the conference.
  b. John gave Mary a book and Bill a CD.
  c. John ate a pizza, and Mary, some tacos.

Each of these examples appears to display a coordination involving at least one non-constituent. (92a) conjoins two partial clauses, each of which is missing a final NP required by its valence specifications, whereas (92b) seems to have coordinated two sequences of NPs, where each NP sequence is combinable with the partial clause *John gave*. Strangest of all is (92c), an apparent coordination of a full sentence on the left with an NP sequence on the right. Nor are these the most extreme examples of such noncanonical coordinations, as (93) makes clear.

(93) a. John offered, and Mary presented, a book to Sue and a CD to Bill.
  b. John offered a book to Sue on Thursday and a CD to Bill on Saturday.

In (93a), illustrating *Right-Node Raising* (RNR), neither the partial clauses *John offered, Mary presented* nor the NP PP sequences *a book to Sue, a CD to Bill* have phrasal status within the theory. Similarly, in the Dependent Cluster Coordination (DCC) in (93b), *a book to Sue on Thursday* and *a CD to Bill on Saturday* do not count as constituents.

Moreover, these phenomena interact with one another in a fairly systematic manner:

(94) a. John offered a book, and Mary a CD, to Bill.   (Gapping + RNR)
  b. John offered a book to Sue on Thursday and a CD to Bill on Saturday, and Mary, a chess set to Ann on Wednesday and a decanter to Steve yesterday.
        (Gapping + DCC)
  c. John told Mary that Bill wanted, and Sue that Ann had bought, a red Lambourghini Centenario.   (DCC + RNR)

The theory of coordination given in Gazdar et al. (1985) does not come close to licensing any of these noncanonical coordinations, let alone provide an explicit compositional semantics for them. A more detailed treatment of coordination in GPSG appear in Sag et al. (1985), but the sketch of an account of Gapping in that work involved a completely ad hoc (and, compared to the rest of the framework, altogether inexplicit) mechanism that essentially jettisoned the otherwise strictly local nature of GPSG's syntax-semantics interface, as discussed in section 3.1.

As we argue below, at the heart of phrase structure–based frameworks' problems with noncanonical coordination—whether transformational or monostratal—is the unavailability of a simple treatment of seemingly partial and/or discontinuous constituents, allowing them full constituent status with a unitary semantic interpretation. But before we draw any theoretical conclusions, the empirical landscape needs to be clarified. For this purpose, we first make a systematic survey of the interactions between coordination and quantifier scope in section 4.2. We focus on (generalized) quantifiers in this chapter for the following two reasons. First, quantifiers are the most basic type of scope-taking expressions and for this reason illustrate the scopal interactions that coordination exhibits with other scopal expressions in the simplest form possible. Our discussion of the more complex types of scope-taking expressions in chapter 5 will be based on the analysis of the quantifier scope case in the present chapter. Second, the specific issue of how to account for coordination/scope interaction has been a central issue in the debate on the adequacy of a certain line of analysis developed in the HPSG literature we review in section 4.3.2 (see, e.g., Yatabe 2001; Beavers and Sag 2004; Chaves 2007; Levine 2011; Yatabe 2012; Yatabe 2013; Kubota and Levine 2015; Yatabe and Tam 2019). Moreover, the relevant issue has implications for other variants of phrase structure–based approaches (in the broader sense encompassing movement-based approaches as well), as should become clear in our critique of previous approaches in section 4.3. For this reason too, reviewing the empirical facts and their theoretical consequences in some detail is important. The empirical survey is followed by a critique of representative analyses of NCC in three major contemporary syntactic theories—the Minimalist framework, HPSG, and LFG in section 4.3. We then formulate our analyses of NCC in Hybrid TLCG in section 4.4 and compare it with these previous alternatives.

4.2 Coordination Scope Generalization

Though the implications of quantifier scope data for the analysis of coordination has often been noted in the literature (cf., e.g., the seminal work by Partee 1970, discussed above, Crysmann 2003, Beavers and Sag 2004, and Steedman 2012), a clear characterization of the empirical generalizations in this domain has remained rather elusive. Our first objective in this section is laying out what we take to be the full range of data bearing on this question and identifying the key descriptive generalization which emerges. Though our ultimate goal is to consider the theoretical implications of the relevant data, the empirical study itself should be of general interest, especially given the lack of a systematic investigation in this domain in the literature. We manipulate three parameters that potentially affect the available interpretations: downward entailing (DE) vs. non-DE quantifiers,[1] conjunction vs. disjunction, and constituent coordination vs. DCC vs. RNR. In sentences in which quantifiers appear outside of coordinate structure, there are in principle two scopal relations between the quantifier and the coordinate struc-

---

1. Here only the right argument of the quantificational determiner is relevant, since we are interested in the properties of quantificational NPs as a whole. Readers who are confused with our terminology should replace our *downward entailing* with *right downward entailing/monotone decreasing*.

ture: the quantifier either scopes over the whole coordinate structure (we call this the *non-distributive reading*) or its meaning is distributed to each conjunct (*distributive reading*).

As we show below, the generalization that emerges is simple and straightforward:

(95) Both the distributive and non-distributive readings are in principle available for both DE and non-DE quantifiers, regardless of the type of conjunction word (disjunction/conjunction) and regardless of the type of coordination (constituent coordination/DCC/RNR).

This generalization turns out to be crucial in the comparison of ellipsis-based and direct coordination analyses of NCC below.

There are, however, several (sometimes quite subtle) pragmatic factors that seem to affect the available interpretations in specific examples (in particular, the distributive reading turns out to be much harder to obtain than the non-distributive reading in many cases). We discuss these factors in what follows in an attempt to further clarify the interactions of grammatical and nongrammatical factors involved in inducing the patterns that are apparently found in the data. Readers who are comfortable in accepting the main generalization in (95) can skip this section by quickly glancing over the examples below (especially the ones illustrating the more difficult, distributive reading—(99), (101), and (103)) and checking whether the relevant readings are indeed available.

We start with non-DE quantifiers. The examples in (96) involve conjunction (with the (96a) examples instantiating constituent coordination and the (96b) examples NCC).

(96) a. $\left\{ \begin{array}{l} \text{Some minstrel} \\ \text{Every minstrel} \\ \text{Six minstrels} \\ \text{Most minstrels} \end{array} \right\}$ sang and danced.   (non-DE, CC, $\wedge$)

      b. I gave $\left\{ \begin{array}{l} \text{a minstrel} \\ \text{every minstrel} \\ \text{six minstrels} \\ \text{most minstrels} \end{array} \right\}$ presents on Thursday and food and wine on Saturday.   (non-DE, DCC, $\wedge$)

      c. Mary has already subscribed, and John plans to subscribe,
          to $\left\{ \begin{array}{l} \text{a journal} \\ \text{two journals} \end{array} \right\}$ of classical archaeology.   (non-DE, RNR, $\wedge$)

Parallel examples with disjunction can be readily constructed (by just replacing *and* with *or* in (96)), but with such examples, it is hard, or sometimes even impossible, to discern the relevant ambiguity, due to the logical equivalence or entailment relations that hold between the two readings ($\exists x P(x) \vee \exists y Q(y) \equiv \exists x[P(x) \vee Q(x)], \forall x P(x) \vee \forall y Q(y) \models \forall x[P(x) \vee Q(x)]$, and so on). Thus, we focus on conjunction here and assume that the same result carries over to disjunction. With conjunction, the two readings are clearly distinct. For example, the distributive reading for (96a) with *some* should be compatible with a situation in which different minstrels sang and danced, and with *six minstrels*, it should entail a total of maximally twelve (rather than six) minstrels to be involved. In examples like those above, the distributive reading might seem to be harder to obtain, but this is most likely a pragmatic blocking effect (that is, saying explicitly *Some minstrels sang and some minstrels danced* disambiguates the relevant reading). In fact, this pragmatic effect can be overridden quite readily with a judicious choice of lexical content:

(97) a. $\left\{ \begin{array}{c} \text{A mob boss was} \\ \text{Three mob bosses were} \end{array} \right\}$ assassinated in Boston earlier last month and executed for murder in New York this weekend.

   b. I gave $\left\{ \begin{array}{c} \text{an exam} \\ \text{three assignments} \end{array} \right\}$ to my advanced calculus seminar on Monday and my basket-weaving class on Thursday.

We thus take it that non-DE quantifiers induce scope ambiguity in coordination in general.

Turning to DE quantifiers such as *no*, *few*, and *hardly any*, we see an (apparently) quite different pattern. Ordinary constituent coordination with a DE quantifier in the subject position appears to strongly resist the distributive reading:

(98) a. $\left\{ \begin{array}{c} \text{No man} \\ \text{Few men} \\ \text{Hardly any man} \end{array} \right\}$ sang and danced.   (DE, CC, $\wedge$)

   b. $\left\{ \begin{array}{c} \text{No man} \\ \text{Few men} \\ \text{Hardly any man} \end{array} \right\}$ sang or danced.   (DE, CC, $\vee$)

However, there is reason to believe that the unavailability of the distributive reading here is not syntactic, for either conjunction or disjunction. We consider the disjunction case first, since the overall pattern is somewhat simpler with disjunction than with conjunction. Consider first the following example:

(99) Your family won't have any trouble getting past the border, as long as no one (either) is caught with a gun or has left their gun license at home.   (DE, CC, $\vee$)

Suppose (99) is uttered by a lawyer advising a family who are crossing the border into a country in which gun ownership is legal, but where guns are regarded as a family possession/responsibility. In this context, the native speakers whom we have consulted agree that (99) is unexceptional in the distributive reading, which essentially says that as long as either of the two conditions (no one getting caught; no one leaving their license at home) is satisfied, one is free to cross the border; in other words, if no one is caught with a gun, it doesn't matter if anyone has forgotten their gun license, and if no one has forgotten their license, it doesn't matter if anyone gets caught with a gun.[2]

Parallel patterns hold for DCC. Cases such as (100) are parallel to (98b) in seemingly resisting the distributive reading robustly:

(100) Terry gave $\left\{ \begin{array}{c} \text{no man} \\ \text{few men} \\ \text{hardly any men} \end{array} \right\}$ a book on Friday or a record on Saturday.

$$\text{(DE, DCC, } \vee\text{)}$$

But again, just a bit of pragmatic manipulation changes the situation dramatically. Suppose the speaker is planning to travel to Berlin, and the success of the trip is contingent on train transport being available *both* at Düsseldorf and Cologne. Then the following sentence easily allows for the distributive reading:[3]

(101) Deutche Bahn is routing no trains to (either) Düsseldorf on Thursday or to Cologne on Friday, but in either case, we won't be able to get to Berlin this week.

$$\text{(DE, DCC, } \vee\text{)}$$

The relevant reading (accepted by our informants) is one in which there are two possible states of affairs which have the consequence that our speaker's travel to Berlin will not be possible, and (at least) one of them holds, but the speaker doesn't know, or remember, which of the two it is. Thus, with careful preparation of the pragmatic context, the distributive reading of DE quantifiers is in fact available. The overwhelming preference for the non-distributive reading in "out of the blue" contexts, then, is presumably a consequence of some (in principle) overridable default interpretation strategy along the lines of the "strongest meaning principle" (Dalrymple et al. 1998).[4]

---

2. The distributive reading in addition involves a distinctive prosody, with a marked stress on *caught* and high intonation from that word to the end of the intonation phrase, followed by a slight but distinct pause, ending with moderately emphatic stress on *home*. This sort of specialized intonation is in itself hardly surprising; a distinct prosody is also typically required to enforce distributive readings arising from negated modals in Gapping sentences (see, e.g., Oehrle 1987; Kubota and Levine 2013a). The crucial factor that facilitates the distributive reading in this example seems to be the possibility of construing the conjuncts as instantiating what Kehler (2002) refers to as a *Resemblance* relation. When this relation holds between two clauses, the respective propositions they express are manifestations of some common and more general relation that is relevant in the larger discourse. In (99), what is common to the two conjuncts (under the distributive reading) is that they both alone count as sufficient conditions for passing the border without trouble, which is precisely the issue under discussion in the larger context.

3. Here, the two clauses have a parallel status to the larger discourse (instantiating a Resemblance relation) in that both count equally as a factor that results (*in either case*) in the eventual failure of the trip.

4. It may be that for some speakers, this default interpretive strategy is grammaticized to such an extent that the distributive reading is completely blocked.

RNR exhibits an opposite pattern. Examples such as the following seem to allow for only the distributive reading:[5]

(102) John said to Mary or Bill said to Ann nothing about the final report.

(DE, RNR, ∨)

Conjunction with DE quantifiers presents an apparently somewhat more complex pattern, since constituent coordination and NCC don't initially seem to behave in a completely parallel fashion. Let us examine constituent coordination first. Examples such as (98a) seem to rule out a distributive reading for negation. However, as noted by Szabolcsi and Haddican (2004), conjunction under negation in fact allows for the distributive reading much more readily than one might initially be led to believe (note, for example, their examples involving "stereotypical conjunction," such as *Mary didn't take math and physics* (cf. #*Mary didn't take math and hockey*)). The following example illustrates this point:[6]

(103) Nobody wants to help spammers and be taken advantage of by hackers, but the reality is, if you don't install the appropriate security software, you are vulnerable to both types of danger. (DE, CC, ∧)

Thus, the constituent coordination case for conjunction is very much like disjunction under negation in that contextual manipulation makes available an apparently unavailable distributive reading.

With RNR, the more readily available reading is similarly the quantifier wide-scope reading:

(104) John will bet five C-notes and Mary will bet double the kitty, on NONE of the poker hands this evening, I predict. (DE, RNR, ∧)

---

5. We are currently not sure why the quantifier wide-scope reading is unavailable in (102). It may have something to do with the fact that the right-peripheral position does not license most negative polarity items:

(i) a. I said nothing about the final report to anyone.
 b. I said to Terry NOTHING about the final report.
 c. *I said to anyone NOTHING about the final report.

6. Here again, what crucially supports the distributive reading seems to be the discourse relation. As Szabolcsi and Haddican (2004) note, one factor that facilitates the distributive reading for conjunction under negation is a "violation of expectation"–type discourse relation, supported by a parallel expectation for contrasted entities, which then ends up being denied by the negation of the two conjuncts (cf. their minimal pair in (43) and (44) [Szabolcsi and Haddican 2004, 235]). In (103), this common contextual expectation is to keep one's computer secure from external attack, and the sentence makes an assertion about two types of threat that have an equal status in counting as potential violations of this expectation. This parallel violation of expectation again establishes a Resemblance relation between the two conjuncts, supporting the distributive reading.

But the distributive reading seems available too, especially with comma intonation following *C-notes* and heavy emphatic stress on *none*.

We see a seemingly different (and initially somewhat surprising) pattern in the DCC case. In DCC examples like (105), it seems that the more easily available interpretation is actually the distributive reading:

(105) I intend to say nothing to Robin on Thursday and to Leslie on Friday.

(DE, DCC, ∧)

But in fact, the non-distributive reading is available too, if two nonstructural conditions are satisfied, as in the following example (106): on the prosodic side, a marked stress on both *no* and *and*, and on the semantic/pragmatic side, a referentially more specific nominal head, in contrast to the minimally informative *nothing* of (105).[7]

(106) I told NO joke to Robin on Thursday AND to Leslie on Friday.   (DE, DCC, ∧)

The intended reading here is that there is no one joke such that the speaker told it to Robin on Thursday and also to Leslie on Friday. As Szabolcsi and Haddican (2004, 226) note, a stress on *and* is actually required for the non-distributive reading in NP coordination cases as well:

(107) Mary didn't take hockey AND algebra.

Thus, the initial difficulty of obtaining the non-distributive reading for NCC like (105) is most likely due to the semantic/prosodic factors noted above (note that stressing *and* is not among the most natural prosodies for NCC sentences, unlike in NP coordination like (107)).

To summarize the findings in this section, both the distributive and non-distributive readings are in principle available for both DE and non-DE quantifiers, regardless of the type of the conjunction word (disjunction vs. conjunction) and regardless of the type of coordination (constituent coordination vs. DCC vs. RNR).

4.3   Current Approaches to Coordination and Scope in Major Syntactic Frameworks

In this section, we review representative analyses of NCC in three major contemporary syntactic theories—the Minimalist framework, HPSG, and LFG. We note at the outset that the purpose of the present subsection is *not* to give a comprehensive review of the literature on NCC in various grammatical theories. In particular, we will not attempt to

---

7. Pragmatic factors are likely to play a role here too. Not telling a single joke to two different people has a kind of real-world plausibility (for example, the two people in question might have completely incompatible senses of humor, so that at least one of them will probably hate the joke, regardless of what it is). But a general determination that, regardless of what one might say, one is not going to say it to *both* Robin and Leslie on different respective days seems quite odd and far more difficult to find a natural context for.

do justice to the literature on RNR, which is quite extensive (see Sabbagh [2014] and Chaves [2014] for some recent reviews). The common view across different theoretical frameworks seems to be that RNR is a label for a set of distinct grammatical phenomena (e.g., a surface-oriented ellipsis phenomenon and an extraposition-like phenomenon) which sometimes happen to yield the same surface string. The purpose of the present section is rather to highlight the similarities and differences between different analytic ideas entertained in phrase structure–based theories of syntax (in the broader sense) and thereby clarify the fundamental nature of the problem that the empirical patterns of coordination pose for such theories.

4.3.1 Transformational Approaches

While there are several approaches to RNR (e.g., the movement-based approach by Sabbagh [2007], the multidominance approach by Bachrach and Katzir [2008], and hybrid approaches like the ones proposed by Barros and Vicente [2011] and Belk and Neeleman [2018]; see Sabbagh [2014] for a recent overview), there is considerably less work on DCC in the transformational literature. Since the purpose of the present chapter is not to offer a comprehensive review of all kinds of previous approaches to NCC in major grammatical frameworks (which would be a worthwhile project on its own), we focus on the treatment of DCC in movement-based approaches in this section, which we believe highlights most clearly the kinds of challenges that the currently dominant transformational architecture of grammar faces in view of the empirical facts found in the domain of coordination.

The only concrete proposal for an analysis of DCC in the transformational literature we are aware of is that by Sailor and Thoms (2014). Their proposal is a version of the familiar movement + deletion type analysis for constructions involving apparent nonconstituents in the transformational literature. That is, an apparent nonconstituent is analyzed as a syntactic constituent by a series of movement operations of subconstituents out of some larger structure followed by the deletion of the entire extraction site, resulting in a surface structure consisting solely of the movement remnants.

This type of analysis is typically justified by the claim that the assumed movement operations obey the same syntactic constraints independently known to govern standard movement operations—most notably, island constraints (see chapters 6 and 8 for an extended critique of this type of approach in the domain of ellipsis phenomena). Indeed, Sailor and Thoms attempt to justify their proposal exactly along these lines, but the empirical argument they offer seems quite frail, as we discuss immediately.

The actual argument takes the following form. Sailor and Thoms start by noting the condition blocking fronting of clauses when a complementizer is left behind, as illustrated in (108):

(108) *He knows Icelandic, I'm $\left\{ \begin{array}{l} \text{sure that} \\ \text{not sure whether} \end{array} \right\}$.

They then offer (109) as evidence that movement must be involved in ellipsis, in particular DCC:

(109) The witness will testify to [whether John knew Icelandic] tomorrow and
       [*(whether) he knew Faroese] next week.

Since (108) shows that fronting of postcomplentizer clauses is prohibited, a movement-based account predicts that movement of such clauses out of the VP prior to deletion of the latter should be forbidden, as is indeed the case. Sailor and Thoms conclude from this observation that such data confirm the dependence of NCC on movement.

This line of argument, while widespread in the transformational literature, is in fact quite weak, or even worse: to the extent that a constraint against movement of a certain kind of syntactic material obliges a movement-based theory of NCC to predict that such material is barred from NCC constructions, the argument actually provides a powerful piece of evidence *against* a movement account of DCC.

To see this point, note that there are abundant cases of discrepancies of extractability and DCC licensing such as the following (note that emphatic contrast prosody does not materially improve (111b)):

(110) a. *What did you discuss John's __?
       b. I discussed John's BIRTHDAY with SUE and ANNIVERSARY with MARY.

(111) a. Which country is John the King of __?
       b. ??*I taught the King of NORWAY how to DANCE and SWEDEN how to SING.

(110) shows that stranding the possessive phrase inside an NP is prohibited for extraction while DCC formation is free from this constraint. (111) is an instance of the opposite pattern, where a movement operation acceptable for leftward extraction (out of the complement of the genitive *of*) produces an unacceptable string in the case of DCC. Since there is no obvious independent explanation for the ill-formedness of either (110a) or (111b), the above data contraindicate Sailor and Thoms's approach, which predicts that, other things being equal, the judgment patterns in extraction and DCC should strictly correlate with each other.[8]

---

8. A second line of argument for covert structure in NCC offered by Sailor and Thoms is based on the somewhat controversial claim that languages which block preposition (P-) stranding also block NCC. They offer Russian data to back up this claim and refer the reader to Frazier et al. (2012), in which the generalization is supposedly supported by a larger set of languages. The Frazier et al. paper actually does not offer any extensive cross-linguistic data, but merely lists the names of ten or so languages that are claimed to follow the generalization, including Japanese. Given the lack of actual empirical data, it is hard to accurately assess the validity of the generalization here. In particular, the fact that Japanese is included in the set of languages that exhibits P-stranding in NCC is puzzling, since it is well-known in the literature (see,

The noncorrelation between leftward extraction and DCC considerably weakens the movement-based analysis by Sailor and Thoms (2014), but the actual content of their analysis has other serious problems which the authors themselves do not address in any depth. Sailor and Thoms's approach is predicated on the assumption that "NCC always involves clausal ellipsis" (2014, 365) and is summarized in their depiction of the essential operations involved in deriving the sentence in (112), given in (113):

(112) I spoke to John on Thursday and Mary on Friday.

(113)

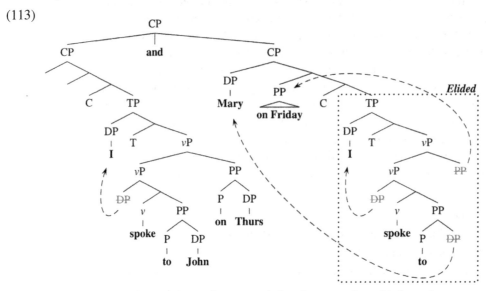

As shown in (113), Sailor and Thoms's approach involves a series of leftward movements and a deletion operation for which no independent motivation is given at any point. Movement of the *v*P specifier to the [Spec,TP] position has long been assumed as part of the derivation of basic English clause structure, but the topicalization operations that this scenario requires are certainly suspect—particularly in view of the fact that in the absence of ellipsis, the resulting structures are markedly ill-formed:

(114) *I spoke to John on Thursday and Mary₁ [on Friday]₂ [TP I spoke to t_1 t_2].

---

for example, Yatabe 2012) that the empirical pattern is the opposite of what Frazier et al. claim to be the case, if they have in mind the kinds of postposition-omission examples in Japanese such as the following (note that the first conjunct in (i) is unlikely to allow for the kind of silent copula analysis that Mukai [2003] suggests for caseless NCC examples):

(i) John-ga   Tookyoo, matawa Bill-ga   Kyooto-kara kuru-hazu-da.
    John-NOM Tokyo   or   Bill-NOM Kyoto-from come-must-COP

   'It must be that either John comes from Tokyo or Bill comes from Kyoto.'

More complex cases are still worse in the absence of ellipsis:

(115) *I spoke to John on Thursday about Bill at the office and Mary on Saturday about
        Sue in the park (*I spoke).

Whatever the source of the ill-formedness in such examples might be, it seems reasonable from a transformational point of view to regard them as arising from forbidden
movement operations. In the absence of a well-motivated basis for predicting that the
effects of this illicit movement will become acceptable through ellipsis—a line of argument that Thoms himself (Barros et al. 2014) has argued against—we have reason
to be skeptical of any account which depends on such movement. The Sailor-Thoms
analysis says nothing about this rather crucial issue.

  Furthermore, there is a specific problem arising from Sailor and Thoms's account of
the scopal interactions between quantifiers and DCC, exemplified by sentences such as
(116). Sailor and Thoms take the wide-scope interpretation for the quantifier to reflect
the position of the subject quantifier outside the vP conjunction via A-movement to TP:

(116) Few people went to the play on Thursday and the concert on Friday.

But what happens in a case such as (117), with the indicated compositional structure and wide-scoping indefinite, with a source (117a) giving rise to the ellipsed form
(117b):

(117) a. I [[bet John a certain amount of money on the ballgame] on Saturday] and
          [[bet John a certain amount of money on the horse race] on Wednesday].
       b. I [[bet John a certain amount of money on the ballgame] on Saturday] and
          [[on the horse race] on Wednesday].

Here, it is not the subject, on the left edge of the TP, which has to scope wide but a
secondary argument of the verb, buried in a Larsonian shell in both the left and right
conjuncts in the source, which has to scope over the conjunction, but with no plausible
landing site for this object. How then is this wide scoping over conjunction achieved?
Following Sailor and Thoms's analysis of the subject-quantifier example (116), we
seem to be led to the assumption that, just as in the case of (116), the direct object
NP *a certain amount of money* somehow moves out of the vP to a position sufficiently
high to scope over the entire conjunction. But this gives rise to a host of questions
whose answers are not at all clear (note in this connection that very similar questions
arise in connection with the transformational analyses of Gapping we have examined
in the preceding chapter): What is the landing site for such a movement, why is there
no evidence for this movement in the linear ordering of elements in the left conjunct

(which all appear to be exactly in situ in the positions they were Merged into), and why is the direct object moving in the first place?[9]

It should be clear from the above discussion that DCC poses a rather difficult empirical challenge to the standard transformational architecture of grammar. Sailor and Thoms's work—the only concrete proposal for DCC in the current literature—has several nontrivial issues in the basic analytic perspective, which, so far as we are aware, have never been addressed in the subsequent literature. We therefore conclude that DCC constitutes an empirical domain in which no satisfactory analysis currently exists in the mainstream transformational literature.

4.3.2 Linearization-Based Ellipsis in HPSG

4.3.2.1 Linearization-based ellipsis: An overview
Within phrase structure–based theories, by far the most formally well-developed approach to NCC is what we will call the *Linearization-Based Ellipsis* (LBE) approach to coordination, discussed and developed in Yatabe (2001), Crysmann (2003), Beavers and Sag (2004), Chaves (2007), and Yatabe and Tam (2019). The central claim of this approach is that apparently nonstandard coordinations such as those reviewed in section 4.1 all reduce to constituent coordination under prosodic ellipsis.[10] The analysis is technically implemented in a variant of HPSG that relaxes the mapping between the combinatoric structure and the surface string known as Linearization-Based HPSG (Reape 1996; Kathol 1995).[11]

The gist of the Linearization-Based framework involves associating a single combinatoric structure feeding into semantic interpretation with multiple possibilities of

---

9. Similar difficulties for Sailor and Thoms's proposal arise in connection with other scopal operators such as symmetrical predicates (see chapter 5 for an extensive discussion of the relevant data and the theoretical issues that such data raise):

(i) John introduced the same girl to Chris on Thursday and to Peter on Friday.

Assuming (as seems relatively uncontroversial in the transformational literature; cf., e.g., Sabbagh 2007) that the internal reading of *same* requires the NP containing *same* to outscope the conjunction at LF, essentially the same issue of the status of movement for the object NP *the same girl* arises in (i) as in the quantifier example (117b).

10. Maxwell and Manning (1996), Mouret (2006), and Abeillé et al. (2014) pursue a different type of approach where noncanonical coordinated strings are taken to reflect actual constituents directly licensed by the grammar. These approaches fail to provide satisfactory semantic analyses, as acknowledged in Mouret (2006). See section 4.3.3 for a critique of Maxwell and Manning (1996).

11. The general architecture of Linearization-Based HPSG has precedent in the "pheno/tectogrammar" distinction advocated in Curry (1961) and pursued in the context of CG in Dowty (1996b). The core of this proposal is a dramatic separation of prosodic representations, including word order, from syntactic combinatorics, so that, for example, words that are dependents of different subcategorizing heads may nonetheless be adjacent to each other in the surface string, while words that are dependents of the same head may be separated from each other by elements subcategorized by a different head. This broad idea has been adopted in the literatures of both HPSG and CG. See Mihalicek (2012) and Kubota (2010, 2014) for an application of this technique in the latter.

surface phonological realization. English exhibits flexibility of word order that this approach is designed to handle to a much more limited degree than languages like German and Japanese, but even in English, it considerably simplifies the analysis of phenomena such as adverb placement, where an adverb can appear in any of the four positions indicated in (118):

(118) Robin (*happily*) will (*happily*) give information (*happily*) to Leslie (*happily*).

In the linearization-based approach, variation in word order exhibited in (118) can be accounted for by allowing for a single combinatoric structure in (119) to be associated with the four different realizations of the surface string in (118).

(119)

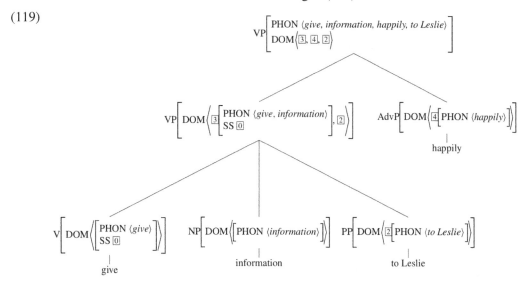

Unlike phrase structure trees, (119) does not represent word order as a left-to-right yield of the terminal nodes. The surface pronunciation is instead explicitly encoded in the PHON(OLOGY) feature on each node, and the list-valued DOM feature regulates the way in which the phonology of a mother node is determined based on the phonologies of its daughters. In (119), the verb and the direct object form one unit ③ (called "domain object") in the DOM specification of the VP, thus forming an inseparable unit in surface pronunciation. The PP *to Leslie*, on the other hand, forms a domain object by itself, and hence, the adverb *happily* can linearly intervene between the strings *give information* and *to Leslie*, giving rise to a mismatch between combinatoric structure and the surface string realization.

  This architecture potentially allows for a significant mismatch between underlying structure and surface pronunciation. The key idea of the LBE approach is to exploit the flexible mapping between surface form and combinatoric structure in the Linearization-

Based setup to implement a surface ellipsis-based analysis of noncanonical coordination along the lines of (120) (here and below, strikeout indicates the material that undergoes phonological ellipsis):

(120)   a.   [$_S$ I gave Robin a book on Thursday] and [$_S$ ~~(I) gave~~ Leslie a book on Friday].
        b.   [$_S$ I gave Robin ~~a pair of pliers~~] and [$_S$ Leslie offered Terry, a pair of pliers].
        c.   [$_S$ Leslie bought a CD], and [$_S$ Robin ~~bought~~ a book].

Since the mapping from the combinatoric structure to the surface string is not one-to-one, it is in principle possible to posit an expression in the underlying structure which does not correspond to an overt string. In the LBE approach, the condition of this surface deletion operation is stated in terms of identity in form to a "shared" string in the other conjunct. Essentially, this approach reconciles the mismatch between the overt forms of apparently anomalous coordination in (37) and the null hypothesis of "like category coordination" by faithfully embodying (in a contemporary guise) the key idea of the Conjunction Reduction analysis from the old transformational literature.

4.3.2.2   Problems with the LBE approach   An ellipsis-based analysis of noncanonical coordination along the lines of (120) encounters an immediate empirical challenge in the availability of the non-distributive reading in such noncanonical coordination constructions, as in, for example, (121) (= (100)):

(121)   Terry gave no man a book on Friday or a record on Saturday.

Assuming LBE automatically imposes, as the null hypothesis, the existence of an exclusive distributive interpretation.[12] This point emerges most clearly from Beavers

---

12. Yatabe (2001) and Yatabe and Tam (2019) (the latter of which contains a much more accessible exposition of essentially the same proposal as the former) propose a somewhat different analysis. Unlike Beavers and Sag, who assume that semantic composition is carried out on the basis of the meanings of *signs* on each node (which is the standard assumption about semantic composition in HPSG), Yatabe and Tam shift the locus of semantic composition to the list of domain objects, that is, the component that directly gets affected by the deletion operation that yields the surface string.

This crucially changes the default meaning predicted for examples such as (121). Specifically, in the Yatabe-Tam approach, the surface string for (121) is obtained by the "compaction" operation on word order domains that collapses two quantifiers originally contained in the two conjuncts into one. The semantics of the whole sentence is computed on the basis of this resultant word order domain representation, which contains only *one* instance of a domain object corresponding to the quantifier. The quantifier is then required to scope over the whole coordinate structure due to independently motivated principles of underspecification resolution. While this approach successfully yields the wide-scope reading for quantifiers, the distributive, narrow-scope reading for quantifiers (which is trivial for Beavers and Sag) now becomes a challenge. Yatabe and Tam simply stipulate a complex disjunctive constraint on semantic interpretation tied to the "compaction" operation that takes place in coordination so as to generate the two scopal readings—in effect, writing in a special exemption for an effect that contradicts their core proposal. Thus, though the specific details vary, the overall complexity of the proposal seems to be about the same in these two approaches in the LBE literature.

and Sag's (2004) proposal of *Optional Quantifier Merger* (OQM), a mechanism that is supposed to yield the non-distributive readings for quantifiers in NCC in the LBE approach. For ease of exposition, we keep the discussion in what follows at a somewhat informal level. For a more thorough critique, see Levine (2011).

Beavers and Sag sketch the content of OQM in the following terms:

(122) **Optional Quantifier Merger:** For any elided phrase denoting a generalized quantifier in the domain of either conjunct, the semantics of that phrase may optionally be identified with the semantics of its non-elided counterpart.

As should be evident, this is essentially an ad hoc fix for the marked discrepancy between the default predictions of the LBE analysis on the one hand and the empirical patterns observed in section 4.2 on the other. The point can be schematically summarized in (123):

(123)

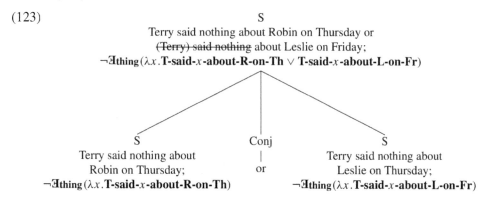

The quantifier $\neg\exists$thing, which on a strictly compositional account should be represented in the top-level clausal semantics by two separate tokens, instead is merged into one and takes scope over the whole disjunction.[13]

Though perspectives on compositionality vary among researchers, it is reasonable to assume, as Dowty (2007) emphasizes, that the null hypothesis for semantic interpretation incorporates a strictly local mapping from the denotations of subcomponents of a constituent to the denotation of that constituent (Dowty calls this "context-free semantics"). OQM clearly goes against this null hypothesis: it takes two conjuncts whose meanings have already been composed in a normal fashion, and on the basis of a purely prosodic (non-)realization in the second conjunct, removes an operator from

---

13. One might think that such an operation cannot be formulated, since it involves arbitrarily decomposing and rewriting the formulas that notate the translations of the two clauses. But note that (123) is a simplified notation for an expository purpose only. Beavers and Sag (2004) actually implement their analysis in the underspecified semantics framework of Minimal Recursion Semantics (Copestake et al. 2005), in which the effect represented in (123) can be encoded. See Levine (2011) for a detailed critique.

both conjuncts, replacing it with a new token of the same operator which scopes over the whole coordinate structure.[14]

We should hasten to add that a violation of compositionality by itself is not a problem. In fact, Beavers and Sag (2004) (along with much recent HPSG literature) assume that constructions themselves may supply extra components of meaning. The disconnection between input and output semantics embodied in OQM can therefore be attributed to the contribution of the coordination construction itself. However, note that invoking the notion of constructional meaning does not make the actual content of OQM any less ad hoc.

Moreover, this type of non-monotonic (or *subtractive*, as one might call it) constructional meaning is unheard of. Most constructional meanings proposed in the literature of Construction Grammar (Goldberg 1995) and Construction-based HPSG (Sag 1997, 2012) are *additive*, in the sense that, given the meanings of the daughter nodes f and g, the construction simply supplies some extra piece of meaning h when f and g are composed, producing, for example, $f(h(g))$ or $h(f(g))$ as the meaning of the mother node. (Sag's [1997] analysis of relativizer-less relative clauses is an instance of this; in effect, the headless relative clause construction contributes the meaning [roughly equivalent to the lambda term $\lambda P \lambda Q \lambda x [P(x) \wedge Q(x)]$] that takes the meaning of the single daughter (P) to form a proper meaning for a noun-modifying expression.) A somewhat more elaborate type of meaning composition has been proposed in the HPSG literature, where an adjunct scopes only over a subexpression of the head daughter that it locally combines with in the syntax (Cipollone 2001; Kubota 2007). But even such mechanisms—which one might characterize as *intrusive* meaning manipulation—are non-subtractive. In Cipollone's (2001) and Kubota's (2007) proposals, the adjunct meaning f is allowed to combine with the meaning representation of the head complex verb $g(h)$ to optionally return the output $g(f(h))$ or $f(g(h))$. Subtractive meaning manipulation embodied in OQM is crucially different from (and is arguably much more powerful than) both additive and intrusive meaning manipulation in that it *removes* a piece of meaning contributed by a subexpression (schematically: $f(g), f(h) \Rightarrow f(k(g)(h))$, where one token of f present in the input goes missing in the output). It is in this sense that we find the particular form of violation of compositionality incurred by OQM worrisome.

---

14. One point that Dowty (2007) emphasizes is that the best analysis is the one which balances criteria pertaining to the syntactic and semantic components respectively, as well as criteria pertaining to their interface (he moreover notes, correctly we think, that past research in syntax and semantics has tended to take the first two types of requirements to be predominant, overlooking the importance of the simplicity criteria for the interface component). Beavers and Sag's (2004) proposal can be thought of as an extreme example of prioritizing the simplicity of syntactic assumptions at the expense of excessive complications in the interface component.

Moreover, there is morpho-syntactic evidence against any ellipsis-based approach as well:

(124) I said nothing to Robin on Thursday nor (to) Leslie on Sunday.

For (124), simply recovering the "elided" material in the second conjunct results in a completely ungrammatical string, whereas deriving it from the grammatical source *I said nothing to Robin on Friday nor did I say anything to Leslie on Sunday* via neg-fronting would involve a host of ad hoc item-by-item replacements in the mapping to the surface form.[15]

Importantly, though OQM is a framework-specific mechanism, it is representative of the kind of solution one is forced to invoke in an ellipsis-based approach to NCC. By its very nature, ellipsis requires multiple tokens of the elided material in the underlying representation, and when these are (or contain) scopal elements, problems arise of exactly the sort that OQM was intended to solve. Given that OQM is a fairly straightforward implementation of a solution for this problem, it seems reasonable to take its failure to be symptomatic of some fundamental analytical difficulty that ellipsis-based approaches to NCC in general face (as noted in footnote 12, Yatabe and Tam [2019] propose a different approach to this problem within the larger LBE literature, but its failure to offer a more explanatory account than Beavers and Sag [2004] seems to reinforce the conclusion that the NCC paradigm poses a fundamental difficulty for the phrase structure–based architecture of grammar).

4.3.3 LFG

In comparison with HPSG, researchers in LFG have devoted little attention to non-canonical varieties of coordination. The most recent detailed treatment, which we consider in this section, is Maxwell and Manning (1996). Maxwell and Manning propose "an extension to LFG, which allows new forms of c-structure licensing" as a way to provide an analysis of nonconstituent coordination in LFG.[16] The extension they introduce is essentially a meta-notation added to phrase structure expansions of the form in (125).

(125) ZP → ZP-*x* [*x*-ZP-*y* Conj *x*-ZP-*y*] *y*-ZP

---

15. For some speakers, it appears that (*)*I said nothing to Robin on Thursday nor said nothing to Leslie on Sunday* is acceptable and could therefore be the underlying source for (124). However, in many speakers' variants of English (including the second author's), the neg-concord pattern in this example is robustly ill-formed, yet (124) is completely unexceptionable.

16. The topic receives a very brief discussion in Dalrymple (2001), which is largely a summary of Maxwell and Manning (1996), while the large-scale LFG textbook by Bresnan et al. (2016) explicitly excludes coordination of any kind from the scope of its coverage.

The intended effect of this rule is that, given a phrase structure rule (126), the tree in (127) is licensed, where x-VP is a "partial constituent" such that it would become a complete VP by being a right sister of VP-x. VP-x and x-VP are obtained by parsing the right-hand-side category "V PP PP" of the VP expansion rule (126).

(126) VP $\rightarrow$ V (NP) (NP) PP*

(127)

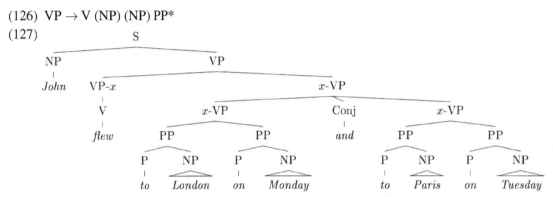

That is, (125) temporarily assigns a constituent status "on the fly," as it were, to a string of category symbols that is not licensed by the narrower grammar as the phrase structure rule (126) is expanded, and such phantom constituents are allowed to be conjoined as long as they correspond to the same sequence of category symbols.

The effect of this system is to allow the coordination of sequences of categories, each of which combines with some preceding (or following) part of a category C to yield a canonical realization of C. This is, of course, exactly what falls out of a variety of subvarieties of categorial grammar, as Maxwell and Manning themselves observe.[17]

There are both conceptual and empirical issues with this approach to NCC. The conceptual issue is the status of the coordination rule (125). The expansion of the x-VP category into a sequence of PP PP in (127) is based on the fact that this sequence can function as a "completion" of a VP node starting with the V category, which itself

---

17. Maxwell and Manning argue that the type-logical approach their rule system appears to simulate—specifically, the Lambek calculus—overgenerates to an extent that makes it undesirable as a framework for the analysis of coordination, based on data such as the following (on the reading where one person located was a friend of Mary and the other was the manufacturer of her handbag):

(i) *I found a friend of and the manufacturer of Mary's handbag.

They (correctly) note that the Lambek calculus overgenerates this example. This is in fact a version of Dekker's puzzle noted in chapter 2 (see footnote 8 on p. 35). As we noted in that discussion, however, remarks on inadequacies of associative systems as the underlying combinatoric system for English grammar of this sort critically overlook the considerable real-time processing difficulties that examples such as (i) present. Moreover, such criticisms only hold in versions of the Lambek system with completely unrestricted associativity. As we discuss in greater detail in chapter 11, the varieties of extensions of the Lambek calculus currently in play as frameworks for natural language grammars all have ways of controlling associativity, making the type of objection that Maxwell and Manning raise largely obsolete.

projects the VP-*x* category to indicate its status as a partial VP category corresponding to the left substring of the expansion. This effectively means that if one views (125) as a rule inside the narrow grammar, it is a device to introduce context sensitivity to the otherwise context-free c-structure component of LFG. It is unclear what consequences ensue by admitting such a mechanism in the overall architecture of LFG.

An alternative possibility (and this seems to be what is intended by Maxwell and Manning themselves) would be to view (125) as part of the human sentence parsing mechanism. That is, even though the competence grammar is not equipped with a mechanism to explicitly recognize NCC sentences as belonging to the set of well-formed sentences of English, native speakers can nevertheless parse such strings and make sense of them by somehow being guided by the processing strategy of parsing repeated occurrences of the same strings of categories as having an "equal" status (of being part of an expansion of some PS rule). While such a view may seem viable in view of the simplest instances of NCC, it is unclear whether it scales up properly to more complex examples involving interactions of DCC, RNR, and Gapping, of the sort exemplified by (94). At the very least, it is difficult to evaluate Maxwell and Manning's proposal in view of such data since they do not work out the relevant details of the parsing algorithm explicitly enough.

A related, empirical issue arises in connection to semantic interpretation. Whether one views the coordination rule (125) as part of the competence grammar or the processing mechanism, the fact that native speakers of English unambiguously understand the intended meanings of such strings needs to be accounted for. In particular, the coordination scope generalization from section 4.2 tells us that the coordinated nonconstituent strings behave just like coordinated ordinary constituents with respect to scopal interactions with generalized quantifiers (we will see in chapter 5 that this generalization extends to more complex types of scope-taking expressions such as symmetrical predicates and the so-called respective readings of plural and conjoined terms). It is rather unclear how (if at all) this type of complex interaction between coordination and scopal operators is to be accounted for in Maxwell and Manning's approach. The special status of the coordination rule entails that it somehow overrides the ordinary compositional semantics associated with the ordinary phrase structure rules, but the exact process by which complete interpretations of the sentences are built is nowhere stated explicitly in Maxwell and Manning's sketch of their proposal. Given these limitations and uncertainties, it seems reasonable to conclude that, at least as it stands, the Maxwell and Manning proposal does not count as an explicit analysis of NCC whose consequences can be meaningfully compared with other approaches (such as the LBE approaches in the HPSG literature) for which the relevant details are worked out in more detail.[18]

4.4   Coordination and Scope in Hybrid TLCG

Having reviewed the difficulties that NCC data pose for phrase structure–based approaches to syntax (both transformational and nontransformational), we are now ready to see how these same data are handled in Hybrid TLCG.

As illustrated in chapter 2, hypothetical reasoning with the directional slashes enables a simple and elegant analysis of coordination (including NCC). The real advantage of this approach, however, comes from a range of more complex examples involving interactions between coordination and scopal expressions. We briefly illustrate here the breadth of coverage inherent in our approach with examples involving generalized quantifiers. The issue will be discussed in greater detail with more complex types of scope-taking expressions (such as the "respective" readings of conjoined and plural expressions and the internal readings of symmetrical predicates such as *same* and *different*) in chapter 5.

The coordination scope generalization from section 4.2 says that when a scope-taking expression appears outside the coordinate structure in the surface string, both the *wide-scope reading* (in which the scopal operator scopes over the conjunction) and the *distributive reading* (in which the scope-taking expression scopes within each conjunct separately) are available. Which of the two readings is more prominent (or more readily available) in a particular sentence often depends heavily on pragmatic factors (in particular, the distributive reading tends to be more difficult in many examples), but there is reason to believe that the combinatoric component of grammar makes both $\Phi(\alpha \wedge \beta)$ and $\Phi(\alpha) \wedge \Phi(\beta)$ possible readings for all sentences of the form "Φ $[_A[_A\alpha]$ *and* $[_A\beta]]$," and likewise for disjunction.

For (128), the more prominent reading is the wide-scope reading for the quantifier, in which the negative quantifier scopes over the disjunction, yielding an entailment of negation of two propositions (i.e., $\neg(\varphi \vee \psi) \equiv \neg\varphi \wedge \neg\psi$).

(128) Terry said nothing to Robin on Thursday or to Leslie on Friday.

In Hybrid TLCG, the availability of both the wide-scope reading and the distributive reading is automatically predicted from the independently motivated analyses of coordination and quantification already introduced in chapter 2.

---

18. Dalrymple (2001) contains a summary of Maxwell and Manning (1996) but remains silent on how this approach may be combined with a modern approach to the syntax-semantics interface in LFG employing "glue semantics," a version of semantics that has an explicit account of quantifier scope.

We illustrate the analysis of the quantifier wide-scope reading first, since the derivation is somewhat simpler for this reading. The derivation is given in (129).

(129)

$$\frac{[\varphi_1; P; \text{VP/PP/NP}]^1 \quad [\varphi_2; x; \text{NP}]^2}{\varphi_1 \circ \varphi_2; P(x); \text{VP/PP}} /E \quad \frac{\text{to} \circ \text{robin};}{\mathbf{r}; \text{PP}}}{\frac{\varphi_1 \circ \varphi_2 \circ \text{to} \circ \text{robin}; P(x)(\mathbf{r}); \text{VP}}{\frac{\varphi_1 \circ \varphi_2 \circ \text{to} \circ \text{robin} \circ \text{on} \circ \text{thursday}; \mathbf{onTh}(P(x)(\mathbf{r})); \text{VP}}{\frac{\varphi_2 \circ \text{to} \circ \text{robin} \circ \text{on} \circ \text{thursday}; \lambda P.\mathbf{onTh}(P(x)(\mathbf{r})); (\text{VP/PP/NP})\backslash\text{VP}}{\text{to} \circ \text{robin} \circ \text{on} \circ \text{thursday}; \lambda x \lambda P.\mathbf{onTh}(P(x)(\mathbf{r})); \text{NP}\backslash(\text{VP/PP/NP})\backslash\text{VP}} \backslash I^2}} \backslash I^1}} /E}$$

$$\frac{\vdots \qquad\qquad \frac{\begin{array}{c}\text{or;}\\ \lambda\mathcal{V}\lambda\mathcal{W}.\mathcal{W}\sqcup\mathcal{V};\\ (X\backslash X)/X\end{array} \quad \begin{array}{c}\text{to} \circ \text{leslie} \circ \text{on} \circ \text{friday};\\ \lambda x\lambda P.\mathbf{onFr}(P(x)(\mathbf{l}));\\ \text{NP}\backslash(\text{VP/PP/NP})\backslash\text{VP}\end{array}}{\begin{array}{c}\text{or} \circ \text{to} \circ \text{leslie} \circ \text{on} \circ \text{friday};\\ \lambda\mathcal{W}.\mathcal{W}\sqcup[\lambda x\lambda P.\mathbf{onFr}(P(x)(\mathbf{l}))];\\ (\text{NP}\backslash(\text{VP/PP/NP})\backslash\text{VP})\backslash(\text{NP}\backslash(\text{VP/PP/NP})\backslash\text{VP})\end{array}} /E}{\begin{array}{c}\text{to} \circ \text{robin} \circ \text{on} \circ \text{thursday} \circ \text{or} \circ \text{to} \circ \text{leslie} \circ \text{on} \circ \text{friday};\\ \lambda x\lambda P\lambda z.\mathbf{onTh}(P(x)(\mathbf{r}))(z)\vee\mathbf{onFr}(P(x)(\mathbf{l}))(z); \text{NP}\backslash(\text{VP/PP/NP})\backslash\text{VP}\end{array}}} \backslash E$$

where the left premise is

$$\begin{array}{c}\vdots\\ \text{to} \circ \text{robin} \circ \text{on} \circ \text{thursday};\\ \lambda x\lambda P.\mathbf{onTh}(P(x)(\mathbf{r}));\\ \text{NP}\backslash(\text{VP/PP/NP})\backslash\text{VP}\end{array}$$

$$\frac{\begin{array}{c}\vdots\\ \frac{\left[\begin{array}{c}\varphi_3;\\ x;\\ \text{NP}\end{array}\right]^3 \quad \begin{array}{c}\text{to} \circ \text{robin} \circ \text{on} \circ \text{thursday} \circ \text{or} \circ\\ \text{to} \circ \text{leslie} \circ \text{on} \circ \text{friday};\\ \lambda x\lambda P\lambda z.\mathbf{onTh}(P(x)(\mathbf{r}))(z)\vee\\ \mathbf{onFr}(P(x)(\mathbf{l}))(z);\\ \text{NP}\backslash(\text{VP/PP/NP})\backslash\text{VP}\end{array}}{\begin{array}{c}\varphi_3 \circ \text{to} \circ \text{robin} \circ \text{on} \circ \text{thursday} \circ\\ \text{or} \circ \text{to} \circ \text{leslie} \circ \text{on} \circ \text{friday};\\ \lambda P\lambda z.\mathbf{onTh}(P(x)(\mathbf{r}))(z)\vee\\ \mathbf{onFr}(P(x)(\mathbf{l}))(z); (\text{VP/PP/NP})\backslash\text{VP}\end{array}} \backslash E\end{array}}{} $$

$$\begin{array}{c}\text{said;}\\ \mathbf{said};\\ \text{VP/NP/PP}\end{array}$$

$$\begin{array}{c}\text{terry;}\\ \mathbf{t}; \text{NP}\end{array}$$

$$\begin{array}{c}\text{said} \circ \varphi_3 \circ \text{to} \circ \text{robin} \circ \text{on} \circ \text{thursday} \circ\\ \text{or} \circ \text{to} \circ \text{leslie} \circ \text{on} \circ \text{friday};\\ \lambda z.\mathbf{onTh}(\mathbf{said}(x)(\mathbf{r}))(z)\vee\mathbf{onFr}(\mathbf{said}(x)(\mathbf{l}))(z); \text{VP}\end{array} \backslash E$$

$$\begin{array}{c}\text{terry} \circ \text{said} \circ \varphi_3 \circ \text{to} \circ \text{robin} \circ \text{on} \circ \text{thursday} \circ\\ \text{or} \circ \text{to} \circ \text{leslie} \circ \text{on} \circ \text{friday};\\ \mathbf{onTh}(\mathbf{said}(x)(\mathbf{r}))(\mathbf{t})\vee\mathbf{onFr}(\mathbf{said}(x)(\mathbf{l}))(\mathbf{t}); \text{S}\end{array} \backslash I^3$$

$$\begin{array}{c}\lambda\sigma.\sigma(\text{nothing});\\ \neg\exists\text{thing};\\ \text{S}\!\restriction\!(\text{S}\!\restriction\!\text{NP})\end{array}$$

$$\begin{array}{c}\lambda\varphi_3.\text{terry} \circ \text{said} \circ \varphi_3 \circ \text{to} \circ \text{robin} \circ \text{on} \circ \text{thursday} \circ\\ \text{or} \circ \text{to} \circ \text{leslie} \circ \text{on} \circ \text{friday};\\ \lambda x.\mathbf{onTh}(\mathbf{said}(x)(\mathbf{r}))(\mathbf{t})\vee\mathbf{onFr}(\mathbf{said}(x)(\mathbf{l}))(\mathbf{t}); \text{S}\!\restriction\!\text{NP}\end{array} \restriction E$$

$$\begin{array}{c}\text{terry} \circ \text{said} \circ \text{nothing} \circ \text{to} \circ \text{robin} \circ \text{on} \circ \text{thursday} \circ \text{or} \circ \text{to} \circ \text{leslie} \circ \text{on} \circ \text{friday};\\ \neg\exists\text{thing}(\lambda x.\mathbf{onTh}(\mathbf{said}(x)(\mathbf{r}))(\mathbf{t})\vee\mathbf{onFr}(\mathbf{said}(x)(\mathbf{l}))(\mathbf{t})); \text{S}\end{array}$$

The key point in this derivation is that, via hypothetical reasoning, the string *to Robin on Thursday or to Leslie on Friday* forms a syntactic constituent with a full-fledged meaning assigned to it in the usual way. The quantifier takes scope above this whole coordinate structure, yielding the non-distributive, quantifier wide-scope reading.

The derivation for the distributive reading is a bit more complex. We first illustrate the relevant steps with the constituent coordination example (130) and then show that the NCC case is treated in essentially the same way.

(130) During the past month, a mob boss was assassinated in Boston and executed in New York.

To see how the distributive reading is derived, note first that a quantifier entry of type $S{\upharpoonright}(S{\upharpoonright}NP)$ (with prosodic type $(\mathbf{st}{\to}\mathbf{st}){\to}\mathbf{st}$) can be converted to a sign with type $S/(NP\backslash S)$ (with a simple string prosody) as follows (see section 4.5 for a step-by-step "verbalization" of this proof):

(131)

$$\dfrac{\lambda\sigma.\sigma(\mathsf{a}\circ\mathsf{mob}\circ\mathsf{boss});\;\exists_{\mathbf{mb}};S{\upharpoonright}(S{\upharpoonright}NP)\qquad \dfrac{\dfrac{[\varphi_1;x;NP]^1\quad [\varphi_2;P;NP\backslash S]^2}{\varphi_1\circ\varphi_2;P(x);S}{\scriptstyle\backslash E}}{\lambda\varphi_1.\varphi_1\circ\varphi_2;\lambda x.P(x);S{\upharpoonright}NP}{\scriptstyle{\upharpoonright}I^1}}{\dfrac{\dfrac{\mathsf{a}\circ\mathsf{mob}\circ\mathsf{boss}\circ\varphi_2;\exists_{\mathbf{mb}}(\lambda x.P(x));S}{\mathsf{a}\circ\mathsf{mob}\circ\mathsf{boss};\lambda P.\exists_{\mathbf{mb}}(\lambda x.P(x));S/(NP\backslash S)}{\scriptstyle/I^2}}{}}{\scriptstyle{\upharpoonright}E}$$

This "lowered" quantifier sign, a theorem of our type logic applied to the higher-order lexical entry for the quantifier, is identical to the familiar type specification for quantifiers in variants of CG (such as CCG) with directional slashes only.

Once we have this derived entry, the distributive reading is straightforwardly obtained. The derivation involves first lifting the type of the VP to take GQ-type arguments in the subject position and then coordinating such higher-order VPs, to which the quantifier is then given as an argument:

(132)

We call the type of derivation shown in (131) *slanting*, in the sense that from an expression involving the vertical slash, a sign involving "slanted" (i.e., forward and backward) slashes is derivable by proof. As in (131), slanting exploits the "hybrid" architecture of the present framework, in which syntactic inferences involving the vertical slash freely interact with those involving the forward and backward slashes. See section 4.5 for more on slanting.

Note that the ambiguity for quantifiers in sentences involving coordination is due to the polymorphic specification for the conjunction word *and*. Without this lexical ambiguity for the conjunction word, slanting would just result in a detour in the proof that doesn't have any semantic consequence and which will be systematically eliminated in proof normalization.

Since slanting and type-lifting are generally available as theorems for any argument position of a verb, they can be applied to induce the distributive reading for quantifiers that occupy any argument position of a verb (extension to adjunct positions is also straightforward). In (133), the quantifier occupies the direct object position of a prepositional ditransitive verb.

(133) Terry gave a present to Robin on Thursday and to Leslie on Friday.

Thus, the distributive reading for this quantifier can be obtained by lifting the type of this argument position for the verb and slanting the quantifier accordingly. Note that the type of the argument clusters is a bit more complex than in the simpler cases above since they are specified to take the slanted quantifier as one of their arguments (so that the quantifier meaning is distributed to each conjunct). The derivation is given in (134). (Here, PTV abbreviates VP/PP; note that we are assuming an "already slanted" version of the quantifier in (134)—for the derivation of this $(\text{PTV}/\text{NP})\backslash\text{PTV}$ entry for the quantifier, see (137) in the next section.)

(134)

$$
\cfrac{
\cfrac{
\cfrac{
\left[\begin{matrix}\varphi_2;\\ P;\text{PTV}/\text{NP}\end{matrix}\right]^2 \quad \left[\begin{matrix}\varphi_1;\\ \mathscr{P};(\text{PTV}/\text{NP})\backslash\text{PTV}\end{matrix}\right]^1}{\varphi_2 \circ \varphi_1;\ \mathscr{P}(P);\ \text{PTV}}\ {}_{/\text{E}} \quad \begin{matrix}\text{to} \circ \text{robin};\\ \mathbf{r};\text{PP}\end{matrix}
}{
\cfrac{\varphi_2 \circ \varphi_1 \circ \text{to} \circ \text{robin};\ \mathscr{P}(P)(\mathbf{r});\ \text{VP}}{}\ {}_{/\text{E}} \quad \begin{matrix}\text{on} \circ \text{thursday};\\ \mathbf{onTh};\text{VP}\backslash\text{VP}\end{matrix}
}
}{
\cfrac{
\cfrac{\varphi_2 \circ \varphi_1 \circ \text{to} \circ \text{robin} \circ \text{on} \circ \text{thursday};\ \mathbf{onTh}(\mathscr{P}(P)(\mathbf{r}));\ \text{VP}}{\varphi_1 \circ \text{to} \circ \text{robin} \circ \text{on} \circ \text{thursday};\ \lambda P.\mathbf{onTh}(\mathscr{P}(P)(\mathbf{r}));\ (\text{PTV}/\text{NP})\backslash\text{VP}}\ {}_{\backslash\text{I}^2}
}{\text{to} \circ \text{robin} \circ \text{on} \circ \text{thursday};}
}\ {}_{\backslash\text{E}}
$$

$$
\lambda\mathscr{P}\lambda P.\mathbf{onTh}(\mathscr{P}(P)(\mathbf{r}));((\text{PTV}/\text{NP})\backslash\text{PTV})\backslash((\text{PTV}/\text{NP})\backslash\text{VP}) \quad {}_{\backslash\text{I}^1}
$$

$$\vdots$$

$$\text{to} \circ \text{robin} \circ \text{on} \circ \text{thursday} \circ$$
$$\text{and} \circ \text{to} \circ \text{leslie} \circ \text{on} \circ \text{friday};$$

$$\vdots$$

a $\circ$ present;

$$\lambda \mathscr{P} \lambda P.\mathbf{onTh}(\mathscr{P}(P)(\mathbf{r})) \sqcap$$

$$\lambda P \lambda y \lambda z.\mathbf{\exists pr}(\lambda x.P(x)(y)(z));$$

$$\lambda \mathscr{P} \lambda P.\mathbf{onFr}(\mathscr{P}(P)(\mathbf{l}));$$

$$(\text{PTV}/\text{NP}) \backslash \text{PTV}$$

$$((\text{PTV}/\text{NP}) \backslash \text{PTV}) \backslash ((\text{PTV}/\text{NP}) \backslash \text{VP})$$

$$\backslash \text{E}$$

gave;

a $\circ$ present $\circ$ to $\circ$ robin $\circ$ on $\circ$ thursday $\circ$

gave;

and $\circ$ to $\circ$ leslie $\circ$ on $\circ$ friday;

PTV/NP

$$\lambda P.\mathbf{onTh}(\lambda z.\mathbf{\exists pr}(\lambda x.P(x)(\mathbf{r})(z))) \sqcap \lambda P.\mathbf{onFr}(\lambda z.\mathbf{\exists pr}(\lambda x.P(x)(\mathbf{l})(z)));$$

$$(\text{PTV}/\text{NP}) \backslash \text{VP}$$

$$\backslash \text{E}$$

gave $\circ$ a $\circ$ present $\circ$ to $\circ$ robin $\circ$ on $\circ$ thursday $\circ$ and $\circ$ to $\circ$ leslie $\circ$ on $\circ$ friday;

$$\mathbf{onTh}(\lambda z.\mathbf{\exists pr}(\lambda x.\mathbf{gave}(x)(\mathbf{r})(z))) \sqcap \mathbf{onFr}(\lambda z.\mathbf{\exists pr}(\lambda x.\mathbf{gave}(x)(\mathbf{l})(z))); \text{VP}$$

Thus, the present approach licenses both the distributive and non-distributive readings for quantifiers when they interact with coordination, both in the constituent coordination and NCC cases. We take this to be an empirically correct result. As we discussed in section 4.2, the apparent difficulty for the distributive reading for downward entailing quantifiers disappears once appropriate contexts are established.[19]

4.5   A Note on Slanting

As discussed above, an operation (or a family of theorems) called *slanting* plays a crucial role in deriving entries of quantifiers that are used in licensing distributive readings

---

19. There does nonetheless seem to be an overwhelming preference for the non-distributive readings for downward entailing quantifiers in many cases, especially in "out of the blue" contexts. We believe that this is a reflection of a much larger generalization about the (preferred) scopal relation between negation (which is part of the meaning of downward entailing quantifiers) and other operators. Specifically, negation tends to resist inverse scope readings in relation to operators that it "c-commands":

(i)   a.   John didn't talk to every teacher. $(??\forall > \neg)$
      b.   No student/few students/hardly any student talked to every teacher. $(??\forall > \textit{no, few, hardly any})$

Note in particular that ordinary negation exhibits basically the same pattern as downward entailing quantifiers when it interacts with coordination:

(ii)   a.   Terry didn't say anything to Robin or Leslie. $(\neg > \lor, *\lor > \neg)$
       b.   Terry didn't say anything to Robin on Thursday or to Leslie on Friday. $(\neg > \lor, *\lor > \neg)$

At least in the disjunction cases like (ii), the dispreference for the distributive reading is clear in both constituent coordination and NCC. The relative inaccessibility of the distributive reading in such examples most likely results from a complex interaction of multiple factors, one of which is the absence (in ordinary contexts) of the relevant discourse relations supporting the distributive reading. As noted in section 4.2, the distributive "$\neg p \lor \neg q$" reading is inherently anomalous except in contexts where the speaker is known to be ignorant of which of two possibilities is true. In an "out of the blue" utterance especially, the discourse context fails completely to support this assumption of ignorance.

of quantifiers in coordination examples. We reproduce here the slanting derivation for the subject position quantifier (135) (= (131)), together with two more cases, one for the object position for transitive verbs (136) and the other for the direct object position of prepositional ditransitive verbs (137) (the latter is used in the derivation of the distributive reading for an NCC example in (134)).

Since slanting is a lemma (or, more precisely, a set of lemmas) applicable to a set of lexical entries rather than just to some specific words, we present it in a schematic form with quantifier entries with some string prosody p, where p is a metavariable ranging over the set of actual quantifier strings. We start with slanting for the subject position quantifier:

(135)

$$
\cfrac{\lambda\sigma.\sigma(p);\exists\mathbf{mb};S\!\upharpoonright\!(S\!\upharpoonright\!NP) \quad \cfrac{\cfrac{[\varphi_1;x;NP]^1 \quad [\varphi_2;P;NP\backslash S]^2}{\varphi_1\circ\varphi_2;P(x);S}\backslash E}{\lambda\varphi_1.\varphi_1\circ\varphi_2;\lambda x.P(x);S\!\upharpoonright\!NP}\!\upharpoonright\!I^1}{\cfrac{p\circ\varphi_2;\exists\mathbf{mb}(\lambda x.P(x));S}{p;\lambda P.\exists\mathbf{mb}(\lambda x.P(x));S/(NP\backslash S)}/I^2}\!\upharpoonright\!E
$$

The derivation in (135) can be understood as follows. We start by hypothesizing a VP (i.e., NP\S, indexed as 2) and an NP (indexed as 1). After a complete sentence is formed, the NP hypothesis is withdrawn so that the quantifier can take scope. The resulting expression is indeed of the right type (S↾NP) to be given as an argument to the quantifier, and the quantifier string is lowered to the subject position. This yields a string in which the prosody of the hypothesized VP φ_2 appears at the right periphery, satisfying the applicability condition of /I. By applying /I, the quantifier string p is paired with the original denotation of the quantifier (note that the final translation is equivalent to $\exists\mathbf{mb}$ via eta-equivalence) and the syntactic category $S/(NP\backslash S)$.

Similar steps of derivation yield alternative quantifier entries in other argument positions of the sentence, as follows:

(136)

$$
\cfrac{\lambda\sigma.\sigma(p);\exists\mathbf{mb};S\!\upharpoonright\!(S\!\upharpoonright\!NP) \quad \cfrac{\cfrac{[\varphi_2;P;S/NP]^2 \quad [\varphi_1;x;NP]^1}{\varphi_2\circ\varphi_1;P(x);S}\backslash E}{\lambda\varphi_1.\varphi_2\circ\varphi_1;\lambda x.P(x);S\!\upharpoonright\!NP}\!\upharpoonright\!I^1}{\cfrac{\varphi_2\circ p;\exists\mathbf{mb}(\lambda x.P(x));S}{p;\lambda P.\exists\mathbf{mb}(\lambda x.P(x));(S/NP)\backslash S}/I^2}\!\upharpoonright\!E
$$

(137)

$$
\dfrac{
\lambda\sigma.\sigma(p);\;\exists_{\mathbf{pr}};\;S{\upharpoonright}(S{\upharpoonright}NP)
\quad
\dfrac{
\left[\begin{matrix}\varphi_3;\\ z;NP\end{matrix}\right]^3
\quad
\dfrac{
\dfrac{
\dfrac{
\dfrac{[\varphi_0;P;VP/PP/NP]^0 \quad [\varphi_1;x;NP]^1}{\varphi_0\circ\varphi_1;P(x);VP/PP}/E
\quad
\left[\begin{matrix}\varphi_2;\\ y;PP\end{matrix}\right]^2
}{\varphi_0\circ\varphi_1\circ\varphi_2;P(x)(y);VP}/E
}{\varphi_3\circ\varphi_0\circ\varphi_1\circ\varphi_2;P(x)(y)(z);S}\backslash E
}{\lambda\varphi_1.\varphi_3\circ\varphi_0\circ\varphi_1\circ\varphi_2;\lambda x.P(x)(y)(z);S{\upharpoonright}NP}{\upharpoonright}I^1
}
{\varphi_3\circ\varphi_0\circ p\circ\varphi_2;\exists_{\mathbf{pr}}(\lambda x.P(x)(y)(z));S}{\upharpoonright}E
}
{\varphi_0\circ p\circ\varphi_2;\lambda z.\exists_{\mathbf{pr}}(\lambda x.P(x)(y)(z));VP}\backslash I^3
}
{\varphi_0\circ p;\lambda y\lambda z.\exists_{\mathbf{pr}}(\lambda x.P(x)(y)(z));PTV}/I^2
}
{p;\lambda P\lambda y\lambda z.\exists_{\mathbf{pr}}(\lambda x.P(x)(y)(z));(PTV/NP)\backslash PTV}\backslash I^0
$$

More generally, slanting is possible for any sentence-medial position. With S\$ abbreviating any arbitrary directional syntactic type ending in S (a notation we borrow from Steedman [2000], where two occurrences of S\$ with the same subscript instantiates the same category), slanting for quantifiers can be further schematized as follows:

(138) $\lambda\sigma.\sigma(p);\mathscr{P};S{\upharpoonright}(S{\upharpoonright}NP)\vdash$
$\quad p;\lambda P\lambda x_1\ldots x_n.\mathscr{P}(\lambda x.P(x)(x_1)\ldots(x_n));S\$_1/(NP\backslash S\$_1)$

(139) $\lambda\sigma.\sigma(p);\mathscr{P};S{\upharpoonright}(S{\upharpoonright}NP)\vdash$
$\quad p;\lambda P\lambda x_1\ldots x_n.\mathscr{P}(\lambda x.P(x)(x_1)\ldots(x_n));(S\$_2/NP)\backslash S\$_2$

It is important to note that, although Slanting is a very flexible operation, it never yields entries of quantifiers that disrupt word order. For example, it is impossible to derive an entry for the quantifier of type $(NP\backslash S)\backslash S$ from the lexically specified type $S{\upharpoonright}(S{\upharpoonright}NP)$. (If such a derivation were possible, it would overgenerate the string *Loves a sailor every boy* with the reading 'Every boy loves a sailor,' clearly a wrong result.)

The following failed derivation for $S{\upharpoonright}(S{\upharpoonright}NP)\vdash(NP\backslash S)\backslash S$ illustrates the point succinctly:

(140)

$$
\dfrac{
\lambda\sigma.\sigma(p);\exists_{\mathbf{mb}};S{\upharpoonright}(S{\upharpoonright}NP)
\quad
\dfrac{
\dfrac{[\varphi_1;x;NP]^1 \quad [\varphi_2;P;NP\backslash S]^2}{\varphi_1\circ\varphi_2;P(x);S}\backslash E
}{\lambda\varphi_1.\varphi_1\circ\varphi_2;\lambda x.P(x);S{\upharpoonright}NP}{\upharpoonright}I^1
}{
\dfrac{p\circ\varphi_2;\exists_{\mathbf{mb}}(\lambda x.P(x));S}{\text{FAIL}}{}^{**}\backslash I^{2**}
}{\upharpoonright}E
$$

The proof starts by hypothesizing $NP\backslash S$, since this is the category that needs to be withdrawn at the last step via $\backslash I$ to obtain the category $(NP\backslash S)\backslash S$. Then the proof proceeds in the same way as (135) until the very final step, at which point it fails. At this final step, in order to obtain the $(NP\backslash S)\backslash S$ category instead of the $S/(NP\backslash S)$ category as in (135), we need to apply $\backslash I$. However, this is impossible since the applicability condition of the \I rule requires the prosody of the hypothesis to be withdrawn to appear on the left periphery of the input string—a condition that is not satisfied in (140). Thus, this derivation is correctly blocked.

Interestingly—and in contrast to quantifiers—verb lexical entries can be slanted and *un*slanted back and forth. The following derivations for a transitive verb illustrate this point:

(141)
$$\cfrac{[\varphi_2;y;\mathrm{NP}]^2 \quad \cfrac{\cfrac{p;R;(\mathrm{NP}\backslash\mathrm{S})/\mathrm{NP} \quad [\varphi_1;x;\mathrm{NP}]^1}{p\circ\varphi_1;R(x);\mathrm{NP}\backslash\mathrm{S}}/\mathrm{E}}{\cfrac{\varphi_2\circ p\circ\varphi_1;R(x)(y);\mathrm{S}}{\cfrac{\lambda\varphi_2.\varphi_2\circ p\circ\varphi_1;\lambda y.R(x)(y);\mathrm{S}\!\upharpoonright\!\mathrm{NP}}{\lambda\varphi_1\lambda\varphi_2.\varphi_2\circ p\circ\varphi_1;\lambda x\lambda y.R(x)(y);(\mathrm{S}\!\upharpoonright\!\mathrm{NP})\!\upharpoonright\!\mathrm{NP}}\upharpoonright\!\mathrm{I}^1}\upharpoonright\!\mathrm{I}^2}}{}\backslash\mathrm{E}$$

(142)
$$\cfrac{[\varphi_2;y;\mathrm{NP}]^2 \quad \cfrac{\cfrac{\lambda\varphi_3\lambda\varphi_4.\varphi_4\circ p\circ\varphi_3;R;(\mathrm{S}\!\upharpoonright\!\mathrm{NP})\!\upharpoonright\!\mathrm{NP} \quad [\varphi_1;x;\mathrm{NP}]^1}{\lambda\varphi_4.\varphi_4\circ p\circ\varphi_1;R(x);\mathrm{S}\!\upharpoonright\!\mathrm{NP}}\upharpoonright\!\mathrm{E}}{\cfrac{\varphi_2\circ p\circ\varphi_1;R(x)(y);\mathrm{S}}{\cfrac{p\circ\varphi_1;\lambda y.R(x)(y);\mathrm{NP}\backslash\mathrm{S}}{p;\lambda x\lambda y.R(x)(y);(\mathrm{NP}\backslash\mathrm{S})/\mathrm{NP}}/\mathrm{I}^1}\backslash\mathrm{I}^2}}{}\upharpoonright\!\mathrm{E}$$

Slanting and unslanting that disrupt word order are underivable in Hybrid TLCG since the prosodic labeling keeps track of the string positions of both hypothesized and real expressions. That is, inferences that go against the linear order properties encoded via / and \ in the syntactic categories of the relevant expressions will be automatically ruled out in the calculus. This was illustrated for the failed quantifier slanting in (140). Similarly, the unslanted category $\mathrm{S}\!\upharpoonright\!\mathrm{NP}\!\upharpoonright\!\mathrm{NP}$ for the transitive verb obtained in the derivation in (141) does not give rise to any additional word order possibilities, since the word order information originally encoded in the / vs. \ distinction in the syntactic category is "transferred" to the explicit encoding of word order in the (functional) prosodic specification of the derived expression. In this sense, proofs in the present calculus are strictly order-preserving.

4.6   A Note on Summative Agreement

As we have shown above, the "constituent coordination" analysis of NCC in CG straightforwardly captures the scopal interactions between NCC and quantifiers. We argue in the next chapter that further support for this approach comes from similar scope interactions involving more complex types of scope-taking expressions. While we believe that the CG analysis represents the most successful analysis of coordination that is currently available, there are opposing views in the literature. In this subsection, we address one specific issue involving an empirical phenomenon called "summative agreement," which in our view is possibly the strongest piece of evidence that has so far been identified in the literature as a potential problem for the direct coordination analysis of NCC in CG.

4.6.1 Summative Agreement

Summative agreement is exemplified in the following example from Postal (1998):

(143) The pilot claimed that the first nurse, and the sailor proved that the second nurse, were spies.

This agreement pattern appears problematic under the assumption that the "raised" VP in such data is a single token of VP linked to two separate gap sites, with its form regulated by the morpho-syntactic condition in each of the corresponding gaps' sites:

(144) The pilot claimed that the first nurse $\left\{ \begin{array}{l} \text{was a spy} \\ \text{*were spies} \end{array} \right\}$ and the sailor proved that

the second nurse $\left\{ \begin{array}{l} \text{was a spy} \\ \text{*were spies} \end{array} \right\}$.

Postal (1998, 172) argues that (143) could conceivably be explained by "the possibility of seeing *were spies* . . . as some sort of realization of an *n*-ad of ATB extracted singulars," a suggestion that is difficult to assess since nothing beyond this speculation is offered that would make formal sense of the notion of a filler as an "*n*-ad" of singulars. Below, however, we offer a reinterpretation of Postal's idea in terms of semantic conditions involving the speaker's perspective.

Yatabe and Tam (2019) claim that the pattern exhibited in (143) poses a "potential empirical problem" for the analysis of RNR—and with the treatment of coordination more generally—in Hybrid TLCG. The crux of their argument is the contrast between the respective patterns in (143) and in (145):

(145) a. ??The pilot claimed that the first nurse, or the sailor proved that the second nurse, were spies.

   b. ?*The pilot claimed that the nurse from the United States, and the sailor also claimed that the nurse from the United States, were spies.

   c. ?*The pilot claimed that the nurse from the United States, and the sailor claimed that no one, were spies.

The conjoined expressions are uniformly of type S/VP_{sing} in both (143) and (145), and this syntactic category does not directly encode the information about the semantics of the subject NPs in each conjunct. Yatabe and Tam (2019) conclude from this that there is no way of capturing the acceptability contrast between (143) and (145) in the CG analysis of RNR. At first sight, this argument appears quite compelling.

Summative agreement is a peculiar phenomenon. Intuitively (and informally speaking), this agreement pattern is induced by the fact that the speaker has reason to believe that the RNR'ed VP is predicated of a plural individual. This is the key intuition common to all previous accounts of summative agreement (including Beavers and Sag [2004] and Chaves [2014]), and our own account, which we articulate below, also builds on this idea.

But before examining the relevant details of the syntax and semantics of RNR that induce summative agreement, it is worth noting, in support of the general approach just alluded to, that we have prima facie evidence for this "speaker's perspective" interpretation available to—and perhaps preferred for—RNR. Note the following examples exhibiting the effect of this interpretation on the form of the pronominal determiners in the RNR'ed expression:

(146) a. Mr. J_1 sent a Christmas card, and Mrs. J_2 sent a party invitation, to their$_{1+2}$ next-door neighbors.
   b. *Mr. J_1 sent a Christmas card to their next-door neighbors$_{1+2}$, and Mrs. J_2 sent a party invitation to their$_{1+2}$ next-door neighbors.

(147) a. John$_1$ sent a Christmas card, and Mary$_2$ sent a party invitation, to each other's$_{1+2}$ bosses.
   b. *John$_1$ sent a Christmas card to each other's$_{1+2}$ bosses, and Mary$_2$ sent a party invitation to each other's$_{1+2}$ bosses.

It is evident that in such cases, the RNR'ed expression contains a determiner which does not reflect anaphoric reference to the relevant NP in either of the conjoined clauses, but rather receives an interpretation reflecting the speaker's retrieval of these NPs and their referents, to form a set which the anaphoric expression refers to. This retrieval is possible in contexts embedded under propositional attitude predicates:

(148) John suspected that Mary, and Bill thought that Ann, were $\left\{ \begin{array}{l} \text{each} \\ \text{both} \end{array} \right\}$ involved in the robbery.

Getting back to the examples in (145), (145c) is particularly interesting. Note that the same singular agreement pattern appears in (149):

(149) The pilot claimed that the nurse from the United States, and the sailor claimed that every nurse from Scotland, $\left\{ \begin{array}{l} \text{?*were spies} \\ \text{was a spy} \end{array} \right\}$.

The pattern in (145c) and (149) is in fact characteristic of a much broader class of coordination phenomena involving singular determiners corresponding to universal quantification. Even with a background assumption that the set of nurses from Scotland is non-empty, a singular VP agreement pattern is mandated for (149). To provide a complete answer to the apparent problem posed by (145c) and (149), therefore, we need to determine just what underlies the singular agreement pattern associated with singular universals and how it impacts the agreement patterns associated with coordination.

The most basic morpho-syntactic fact about universal singular determiners is that they require a singular-marked VP:

(150) $\left\{ \begin{array}{l} \text{Every} \\ \text{Each} \end{array} \right\}$ submission was/*were sent to the referees.

The morphological marking on the determiner's nominal argument suggests that *every/each* do not permit interpretation of the subject as a plural/aggregate/collective object that can enter into collective predication relations, in contrast to the plural determiner *all*, a suggestion strongly supported by other data. Consider the difference between the cases displayed in (151):[20]

(151) a. All (the) participants met in the park.

b. $\left\{ \begin{array}{l} \text{John and Mary} \\ \text{An author and an editor} \\ \text{The author and the editor} \end{array} \right\}$ met in the park.

c. #Every/each man and every/each woman met in the park.

These examples show that a coordination of atomic individuals can be construed, in effect, as a collective object. For notational convenience, we introduce two subtypes for the type e: e_t for atomic individuals and e_σ for sums. What (151c) shows is that coordination of "quantified NPs" cannot undergo this collective interpretation when the determiner is a singular universal GQ. The predicate **meet** (i.e., the denotation of *meet*) can only hold of entities with aggregate structure, and evidently the coordination of *each/every* subjects does not yield a functor which can apply to **meet**. This conclusion is made more or less explicit by the parallel contrast in the agreement facts:

(152) a. All (the) participants are getting an award.

b. $\left\{ \begin{array}{l} \text{John and Mary} \\ \text{An author and an editor} \\ \text{The author and the editor} \end{array} \right\}$ are getting an award.

c. Every/each mathematician and every/each physicist $\left\{ \begin{array}{l} \text{*are} \\ \text{is} \end{array} \right\}$ getting an award.

Thus, the morphological number marking displayed in the VP corresponds to the properties of the subject along the following lines:[21]

---

20. The issues on collective interpretation raised in the following discussion have a long history in the formal semantics literature; see, e.g., Bennett (1974); Scha (1981); Dowty (1987).

21. See the discussion of the distributivity of *each/every* in Beghelli and Stowell (1997) and Winter (2001) in this connection. We propose an analysis of distributive quantifiers *every* and *each* as denoting sums (or,

- The subjects of plural-marked VPs are also possible subjects of VPs which can combine to give a semantically well-formed result only with collectivities, e.g., *meet*, *gather*, *assemble*, and *interact*.
- The subjects of singular-marked VPs (including quantifiers with *each/every*, which invariably contain a singular nominal, even when two or more such quantified phrases are conjoined) cannot, as a rule, combine with VPs which denote properties of collectivities.

4.6.2   Semantic Agreement and Summative Agreement

With the semantics for morphological number marking introduced above, the summative agreement facts in question fall readily into place.

Suppose that RNR is licensed by the grammar by a special entry for *and* with the syntactic type $((S/VP_{sg})\backslash(S/VP_{pl}))/(S/VP_{sg})$, which comes with the additional pragmatic condition for its felicitous use: the summative agreement *and* is possible only when the speaker can entertain a perspective (which she or he does not necessarily endorse) which guarantees the existence of some plural entity (of type e_σ) of which the RNR'ed VP predicate can be appropriately predicated. We have seen clear independent evidence for the sensitivity of the RNR'ed expression to the speaker's perspective in, for example, (148): in this type of example, the RNR'ed expression contains an anaphoric element reflecting the speaker's assessment of the relevant state of affairs, which the attitude holders in the respective two clauses do not necessarily have direct access to.

Summative agreement can then be taken to be a grammaticalized extension, as it were, of this anaphoric possibility sensitive to the speaker's perspective.[22] When the

---

more precisely, tuples) in chapter 5, in order to capture their behavior in relation to symmetrical predicates such as *same* and *different*. Our assumption in the current chapter is consistent with such an analysis of *every* and *each*. The sum/tuple-based analysis of universals requires a covert distributive/respective operator to be present to ensure distributive readings for *every* and *each*. Thus, in this alternative analysis, even though *every/each N* and *all Ns* both denote sum/tuple-type objects, the crucial difference between them—that only the latter can combine with collective predicates—is ensured by the obligatory presence of the distributive/respective operator when *every/each* enters into a predication relation with some $e \rightarrow t$ property.

22. See Chaves (2014) for a similar view on summative agreement as a constructional property of RNR. Note that the speaker's "role" here is merely that of summarizing the reported speeches, from which it does not necessarily follow that the speaker endorses the truth of the reported statements, as can be clearly seen from the fact that examples like the following are possible:

(i) The pilot claimed that the first nurse, and the sailor insisted that the second nurse, were spies, and then everybody got terrified, but it later turned out that both reports were unfounded rumors.

Though our approach is inspired by an earlier proposal by Beavers and Sag (2004), it (as well as Chaves's [2014] account) crucially differs from the latter in that it takes summative agreement to be a phenomenon licensed by the grammar (under certain pragmatic conditions), rather than characterizing it as a case of tolerated performance error.

subjects of the two clauses corresponding to the reported propositions are denoted by, for example, definite descriptions, the speaker can *construe* the "referents" of the embedded subjects in the two clauses (i.e., *the first nurse* and *the second nurse*) as forming the sum **nurse1** $\oplus$ **nurse2**, which is appropriate as an argument of plural predicates, for example, *were spies*, since this semantic object is of the right type to serve as an argument to a sum-seeking plural VP. The same holds for other singular existentials, for example, names and *a/the* terms, and for certain plural universals as well. But when these subjects are represented by singular universals, no appropriate plural individual (i.e., sum) can be constructed within the speaker's perspective to support agreement with a plural VP, paralleling the judgment patterns of the simpler non-RNR examples of conjoined singular quantifiers in (150).

Thus, all we need assume in order to account for summative agreement in RNR is the existence of the syntactic type $((S/VP_{sg})\backslash(S/VP_{pl}))/(S/VP_{sg})$ for *and* and the following three independently motivated assumptions:[23]

- Names, definites, indefinites, and plurals of the form *all (the) Ns* denote individuals, all of which can be conjoined to form an individual of type e_σ.
- Singular quantifiers of the form *each N*, *every N*, and *no N* all denote generalized quantifiers of type $(e_\iota \to t) \to t$.
- The RNR'ed expression can reflect a speaker's perspective in which the separate arguments of the single VP predicate are in effect retrieved by the speaker from their separate S/VP_{sg} clauses and thrown together by the speaker's construal of them as forming a single plural entity to which the RNR'ed VP applies, just in case it can take such arguments.

The three principles itemized—each of which, as noted earlier, is separately supported—interact to yield (143) as a straightforward consequence. Definite descriptions such as *the first nurse* and *the second nurse* can form plural objects under implicit summative conjunction and hence are legitimate antecedents for plural anaphoric expressions such as personal pronouns, reflexives, and reciprocals—and, in the case of verbal morphology, the plural number marking that reflects summative agreement. This combination of pragmatic assumptions (needed in order to understand data such as (146)) and the behavior of coordinate subjects of explicitly plurality-seeking VPs suffice to account for the summative agreement facts. The syntactic type $((S/VP_{sg})\backslash(S/VP_{pl}))/(S/VP_{sg})$ may well have the status of an emergent category, ac-

---

23. In the revised version of the analysis of *every* and *each* introduced in chapter 5, the distributive/respective operator that forces the obligatorily distributive interpretations of these quantifiers converts the sum/tuple-type denotations to "singular" quantifiers of type $(e_\iota \to t) \to t$ that are only compatible with "singular" predicates.

cessible for certain speakers under certain pragmatic conditions, but does not represent an "established," canonical type available to all English speakers.[24]

To conclude, despite what may initially appear, summative agreement facts are amenable to a relatively simple treatment in the CG analysis of RNR.

---

24. In this connection, it is worth recalling the point made in Beavers and Sag (2004) that "Yatabe's work with native speaker informants reveals that such sentences [as (143)] are of intermediate acceptability (only 7 of the 23 subjects he studied found this sentence to be perfectly acceptable)." This fact suggests that the type $((S/VP_{sg})\backslash(S/VP_{pl}))/(S/VP_{sg})$ is still missing from the lexicon of the majority of English speakers. It is of course possible, though, that such a type has been fully grammaticized in the syntax-semantics interface of other languages, corresponding to Yatabe and Tam's (2019) claim that summative agreement is standard in RNR in a number of languages.

5 The Semantics of "Respective," Symmetrical, and Summative Predicates

The analyses of Gapping and NCC in the previous two chapters have demonstrated that the flexible but systematic interaction between the vertical slash and the directional slashes in Hybrid TLCG can be profitably exploited in making sense of the complex empirical patterns exhibited by the Gapping construction in English. In this chapter, we present an analysis of yet another complex interaction between syntactic and semantic phenomena, namely the so-called "respective" predication and related phenomena (such as symmetrical predicates), and argue that Hybrid TLCG again enables a successful analysis of the seemingly quite complex set of empirical phenomena exhibited by these expressions. The analysis we propose not only accounts for the basic properties of "respective" predicates and related phenomena but also extends straightforwardly to interactions between these phenomena and noncanonical coordination (RNR and DCC), as well as interactions among these phenomena themselves.

The so-called "respective" readings of plural and conjoined expressions and the internal readings of symmetrical predicates such as *same* and *different* in (153a,b) have posed difficult challenges to theories of the syntax-semantics interface. Summative predicates such as *a total of X* in (153c) present a similar problem.

(153) a. John and Bill sang and danced, respectively.
             (= 'John sang and Bill danced')
       b. {The same performer/Different performers} sang and danced.
             (≈ 'The performer who sang and the performer who danced are the same/different')
       c. John and Bill spent a total of $10,000 last year.
             (= 'The amount that John spent last year and the amount that Bill spent last year add up to $10,000')

These phenomena interact with coordination, including nonconstituent coordination (NCC; both Right-Node Raising and Dependent Cluster Coordination):

(154) a. John read, and Bill reviewed, *Barriers* and *LGB* (respectively).

b. John introduced the same girl to Chris on Thursday and (to) Peter on Friday.

c. John spent, and Bill lost, a total of $10,000 last year.
   (= 'The amount that John spent last year and the amount that Bill lost last year add up to $10,000')

Moreover, these expressions can themselves be iterated and interact with one another to induce multiple dependencies:

(155) a. John and Bill introduced Mary and Sue to Chris and Pat (respectively).

b. John and Bill gave the same book to the same man.

c. John and Mary showed the same book to his brother and her sister (respectively).

d. John and Mary collected a total of $10,000 for charity from his family and her clients, respectively.

e. John and Mary gave a total of $10,000 to the same man.

Any adequate analysis of these phenomena needs to account for these empirical facts. In particular, the parallel between the phenomena in the multiple dependency cases in (155), especially the interdependency between "respective," symmetrical, and summative predicates in (155c–e), raises the possibility that the same (or a similar) mechanism is at the core of the semantics of these three phenomena.

Our goal in this chapter is precisely such a unified analysis of the three phenomena. While the "respective" readings and symmetrical predicates have been extensively studied in the previous literature, there does not currently exist an analysis, at any level of formal explicitness, which offers a systematic explanation for their parallel behaviors observed above. By building on several analyses of these phenomena from the previous literature, we develop an analysis that posits a common mechanism of pairwise predication involving multiple list-like data structures and show that this analysis straightforwardly captures their parallel behaviors.

5.1 The Meanings of "Respective," Symmetrical, and Summative Predicates

"Respective" readings of plural and conjoined expressions (cf., e.g., Kay 1989; McCawley 1998; Gawron and Kehler 2004; Winter 1995; Bekki 2006; Chaves 2012) and the semantics of symmetrical predicates such as *same* and *different* (cf., e.g., Carlson 1987; Moltmann 1992; Beck 2000; Barker 2007; Brasoveanu 2011) have been known to pose significant challenges to theories of compositional semantics. Each of these two constructions alone presents a set of quite complex problems, and previous authors have thus mostly focused on studying the properties of one or the other. However, as we discuss below, the problems that the two phenomena exhibit are remarkably similar. A less frequently discussed type of sentence but one which raises essentially the same problem for compositionality comes from the interpretation of expressions such as *a total of X* and *X in total*. We call these expressions "summative" predicates. Summative predicates have been discussed in the literature mostly in the context of Right-Node Raising (RNR) (Abbott 1976; Jackendoff 1977). Some representative examples of each construction were given in (153)–(155).

The difficulty that these phenomena pose can be illustrated by the following examples involving "respective" readings:[1]

(156) a. John and Bill bought the book and the CD, respectively. (NP coordination)
    b. John and Bill ran and danced, respectively.   (VP coordination)
    c. John read, and Bill listened to, the book and the CD, respectively.   (RNR)
    d. John gave the book and the CD to Sue on Wednesday and to Mary on Thursday, respectively.   (Dependent-Cluster Coordination [DCC])

These examples exhibit readings that can be paraphrased by the sentences in (157).[2]

---

1. It has been noted by Postal (1998), Kehler (2002), and Chaves (2012) that "respective" readings interact with extraction, as exemplified by the following data (called "interwoven dependency" by Postal (1998)):

(i) a. Which pilot$_i$ and which sailor$_j$ will Joan invite __$_i$ and Greta entertain __$_j$ respectively?
    b. What book$_i$ and what magazine$_j$ did John buy __$_i$ and Bill read __$_j$ respectively?

It is possible to construct parallel examples involving summative readings (symmetrical predicates seem to be uncomfortable in fronted *wh* or topicalized positions, and we weren't able to construct relevant examples):

(ii) How many frogs in total did Greg capture __ and Lucille train __?

The semantic analysis of "respective" predication we propose in section 5.3.1 is in principle compatible with these data. However, since there is a technical problem in the syntactic analysis of ATB extraction (which constitutes an exception to the linearity of the calculus underlying TLCG), we will not attempt to formulate an explicit analysis.

2. One might be inclined to think that the adjective *respective* in examples like the following should be given a parallel treatment:

(i) John and Bill talked to their respective supervisors.

However, as convincingly argued by Okada (1999) and Gawron and Kehler (2002), the properties of the adjective *respective* are significantly different from those of the *respectively* sentences in (156). In particular, contrasts such as the following suggest that the adjective *respective* takes scope strictly within the NP in which it occurs:

(ii) a. Intel and Microsoft combined their respective assets.
    b. #Intel and Microsoft combined their assets respectively.

We thus set aside the adjective *respective* in the rest of this chapter. See Gawron and Kehler (2002) for an analysis of *respective* that captures its strictly local scope correctly.

Other expressions whose interpretations are similarly sensitive to the order of mention include *successively*, *progressively*, and *increasingly*:

(iii) Robin, Terry, and Leslie got successively higher grades on the SAT.

(157) a. John bought the book and Bill bought the CD.
       b. John ran and Bill danced.
       c. John read the book and Bill listened to the CD.
       d. John gave the book to Sue on Wednesday and gave the CD to Mary on Thursday.

The difficulty that these examples pose essentially lies in the fact that they seem to require having access to the denotations of parts of a phrase (for example, the meaning **ran** is not retrievable from the boolean conjunction $\lambda x.\mathbf{ran}(x) \wedge \mathbf{danced}(x)$ that is standardly taken to be the meaning of *ran and danced*). This violates the principle of compositionality at least in its strictest formulation, which dictates that, once the meaning of a phrase is constructed, the grammar should no longer have direct access to the meanings of its parts. Things are especially tricky in examples like (156c) and (156d), where neither the whole nor the part of the coordinate structure is even a constituent in the standard sense. So far as we are aware, there is no explicit analysis of these *respectively*/NCC interactions in the literature. In particular, it is worth noting that the proposals by Gawron and Kehler (2004) and Chaves (2012) that we review below both fail to extend to these NCC cases since they assume phrase structure–based syntax for formulating their analyses (but to be fair, it should be noted that, at least in the case of Gawron and Kehler [2004], the semantic analysis they propose does not depend in any crucial way on the syntactic assumptions they make).

One might object to the characterization we have just given (see, e.g., Chaves [2012] and Schwarzschild [1996]—but see also Gawron and Kehler [2002] for a critique of Schwarzschild [1996]; we address Chaves's [2012] approach in detail in section 5.4.1.3): at least cases like (156a) can be dealt with by an independently needed mechanism for yielding the so-called cumulative readings of plurals (Scha 1981):

(158) Seven hundred Dutch companies have used ten thousand American computers.

In the cumulative reading of (158), a set of seven hundred Dutch companies is related to a set of ten thousand American computers in the "*x*-used-*y*" relation. The sentence does not specify which particular company used which particular computer, but it only says that the total number of companies involved is seven hundred and the total number of computers involved is ten thousand.

The "respective" reading in (156a) could then be thought of as a special case of this cumulative reading. Unlike the more general cumulative reading, the "respective" reading is sensitive to an established order among elements in each of the conjoined or plural terms (that is, (156a) is false in a situation in which John bought the CD and Bill bought the book), but one could maintain that the core compositional mechanism is the same.

However, an attempt to reduce the "respective" reading to the cumulative reading fails, at least if we adhere to the conventional assumption about the latter that it is

induced by a lexical operator that directly applies to the meanings of verbs. As should
be clear from the examples in (156b–d), it is not just co-arguments of a single verb that
can enter into the "respective" relation. Thus, a lexical operator–based approach is not
general enough.[3]

But we think there is a grain of truth in this attempt to relate cumulative and "respective" readings. The "violation" of compositionality under discussion exhibited
by "respective," symmetrical, and summative readings arises only in connection with
coordinated or plural expressions. (Examples involving symmetrical and summative
predicates are introduced below.) Thus, instead of claiming that these constructions
pose serious challenges to the tenet of compositionality (as some authors indeed have;
cf. Kay 1989), it seems more plausible to find ways to relax compositionality just in
the context of coordination and plural expressions, in such a way that these apparent
violations of compositionality (but nothing more) are allowed.

Building on related ideas explored by previous authors, in particular, Gawron and
Kehler (2004) and Barker (2007), we argue precisely for such an approach in this chapter. In fact, in the case of conjoined NPs, which are standardly taken to denote sums
(or, more correctly, joins in a semilattice, but for convenience of presentation we will
continue to use the informal locution of plurals "denoting" sums), the issue of compositionality is already moot since the denotation itself ($\mathbf{j} \oplus \mathbf{b}$) retains the internal structure
of the conjunction that can be accessed by other operators such as the distributivity
operator commonly assumed in the semantics literature (compare this situation to the
generalized conjunction of the lifted versions of the individual terms $\lambda P.P(\mathbf{j}) \wedge P(\mathbf{b})$,
for which the individual parts are no longer directly accessible). As shown in detail
for "respective" readings by Gawron and Kehler (2004), by generalizing this approach
to non-NP-type meanings, the complex semantics that "respective" readings and related phenomena exhibit can be uniformly handled by modeling the meanings of expressions involving plurals or conjunction by a structured object—either (generalized)
sums (Gawron and Kehler 2004) or tuples (Winter 1995; Bekki 2006).

The idea, in a nutshell, is to keep track of the meanings of components (e.g., the
meanings of each verb **ran** and **danced** for the conjoined VP *ran and danced*) as distinct tuple (or sum) elements so that they can be separately retrievable from the meaning
of the whole conjoined expression. The grammar conforms to the standard notion of
compositionality in all other respects, and in this sense, this approach involves only a
limited degree of noncompositionality, as it were. The present chapter extends this approach to the other two empirical phenomena (symmetrical and summative predicates),

---

3. An event-based analysis (along the lines, e.g., of Lasersohn [1992]) is conceivable for examples like
(156b) (and possibly for (156c) and (156d) as well, though working out the details would be nontrivial).
See the discussion about (225) in section 5.4.1 for why we do not pursue this approach.

as well as embedding the analysis in Hybrid TLCG, which offers a flexible and explicit syntax-semantics interface. As will become clear below, our choice of tuples over sums for the underlying data structure—departing, in this respect, from Gawron and Kehler's (2004) original proposal—is primarily motivated by the need to generalize the analysis to the other two phenomena (see section 5.4 for discussion). Our analysis of the class of predicates under consideration has the advantage that the interactions with NCC exhibited by data such as (156c) and (156d) (and their counterparts involving symmetrical and summative predicates introduced below) become straightforward. This is especially important since interactions between NCC and each of these phenomena have been known to pose significant problems for analyses of coordination in the literature (see, e.g., Abbott 1976, Jackendoff 1977, and Beavers and Sag 2004 for some discussion), and a fully general solution is still missing in previous proposals.

We now turn to the specifics of each of the three phenomena. For the "respective" reading, note first that if we remove the adverb *respectively*, the sentences still have the "respective" interpretation as one of their possible senses.

(159) John and Bill bought the book and the CD.

But in this case, the sentence is multiply ambiguous. For example, in (159), both the subject and object NPs could be construed collectively: the two people bought the two things together. The sentence also allows for readings in which only the subject or the object NP exhibits a distributive reading (e.g., 'John bought the book and the CD and Bill also bought the book and the CD'). The presence of the adverb *respectively* disambiguates the interpretation to the "respective" reading.

In the "respective" readings with overt conjunction (as in the examples in (156)), the *n*-th conjunct in one term is matched up with the *n*-th conjunct in the other term. As noted by many (cf. McCawley 1998, Kay 1989, among others), if the order of elements is clear from the (nonlinguistic) context, then not just conjoined NPs but plural NPs can also enter into "respective" predication, as in the following examples:

(160) a. [Caption under a picture showing five men standing next to each other:] These five men are Polish, Irish, Armenian, Italian, and Chinese, respectively.
       b. The three best students received the three best scores, respectively.

McCawley (1998) also notes that, when there are more than two plural or conjoined terms in the sentence, multiple "respective" relations can be established among them. Disambiguation with *respectively* works in the same way as in the simpler examples, with the consequence that (161b) with a single *respectively* is ambiguous whereas (161a) with two occurrences of *respectively* is unambiguous:

(161) a. George and Martha sent a bomb and a nasty letter respectively to the president and the governor respectively.
       b. George and Martha sent a bomb and a nasty letter to the president and the governor respectively.

As we discuss below, the availability of this multiple "respective" reading turns out to be particularly important in formulating a compositional semantic analysis of "respective" interpretations. Moreover, a parallel multiple dependency is observed with symmetrical predicates, and this poses a severe problem for the compositional analysis of *same* and *different* by Barker (2007, 2012) (see section 5.4.1.2). So far as we are aware, Gawron and Kehler (2004) was the first to propose a formally explicit solution for this problem in the analysis of "respective" readings, and our own analysis generalizes the solution to all of the three phenomena we consider in this chapter.

Turning now to symmetrical predicates, note first that symmetrical predicates such as *same*, *different*, *similar*, and *identical* exhibit an ambiguity between the so-called internal and external readings (Carlson 1987).

(162) a. The same waiter served Robin and poured the wine for Leslie.
       b. Different waiters served Robin and poured the wine for Leslie.

When uttered in a context in which some waiter is already salient (for example, when (162a) is preceded by *I had a very entertaining waiter when I went to that restaurant last week, and yesterday evening . . .), the same waiter* in (162a) anaphorically refers to that individual already introduced in the discourse. This is called the *external reading*, corresponding to an anaphoric expression such as *that very waiter*. But this sentence can be uttered in an "out of the blue" context too, and in this case, it simply asserts that the individual who acted as Robin's server and the one who poured Leslie's wine were identical and that that individual, whoever s/he was, was indeed a waiter—the so-called *internal reading*. The external reading is just an anaphoric use of these expressions and does not pose a particularly challenging problem for compositional semantics. For this reason, we set it aside and focus on the internal reading in the rest of this chapter (but see section 5.3.2, where we briefly discuss a possibility in which the internal and external readings may be related in our setup).

The distribution of the internal reading of symmetrical predicates is remarkably similar to that of "respective" readings. First, like "respective" readings, the internal reading is available in all types of coordination:

(163) a. John and Bill read {the same book/different books}.   (NP coordination)
       b. {The same waiter/Different waiters} served Robin and poured the wine for Leslie.   (VP coordination)
       c. John read, and Bill reviewed {the same book/different books}.   (RNR)

d. I gave {the same book/different books} to John on Wednesday and to Bill on Thursday.   (DCC)

Examples like (163c) and (163d) are especially problematic since they show that deletion-based analyses of NCC (which derive, for example, the RNR example (163c) from an underlying source *John read the same book and Bill reviewed the same book*) do not work (Abbott 1976; Jackendoff 1977; Carlson 1987).

Second, both plural and conjoined expressions induce the internal reading. Thus, by replacing *John and Bill* in (163a) by *the men*, both the external and internal readings are available:

(164) The men read {the same book/different books}.

Third, just like multiple "respective" readings, multiple internal readings are possible:

(165) a. John and Bill bought the same book at the same store.
       b. John and Bill bought the same book at different stores.
       c. John and Bill bought the same book at the same store on the same day for the same price.

Note moreover that the "respective" reading and the internal reading interact with one another:

(166) a. John and Mary showed the same book to his brother and her sister respectively.
       b. The White House proposed, and the Justice Department formally recommended, different codes of conduct to the Boy Scouts and the CIA Operations Section respectively on the same day.

These similarities, especially the fact that the two phenomena interact with one another systematically as in (166), strongly suggest that one and the same mechanism is at the core of the compositional semantics of these constructions.

The parallel distributional pattern in fact extends to the interpretations of summative predicates such as *a total of N* and *N in total* as well. The problem that summative predicates pose for the syntax-semantics interface is best known in the context of RNR, in examples such as the following (Abbott 1976):

(167) John spent, and Bill lost, a total of $10,000 last year.

Just like the internal reading for symmetrical predicates (cf. (163c)), (167) has a reading that is not equivalent to its "paraphrase" with clausal coordination:

(168) John spent a total of $10,000 last year and Bill lost a total of $10,000 last year.

But the summative reading exhibited by (167) (where $10,000 corresponds to the sum of amounts that respectively satisfy the two predications) is not limited to RNR. The same reading is found in the full range of coordination constructions:

(169) a. The two men spent a total of $10,000.   (NP coordination)

      b. A total of $10,000 was spent and lost.   (VP coordination)

      c. John donated a total of $10,000 to the Red Cross on Thursday and to the Salvation Army on Friday.   (DCC)

Note that here too, both plural NPs (as in (169a)) and conjoined expressions (as in (169b,c)) can enter into summative predication.

Moreover, just as with "respective" readings and internal readings, iterated summative readings are also possible, and these phenomena interact with one another:

(170) a. A total of three boys bought a total of ten books.

      b. John collected, and Mary got pledges for, a total of $10,000 for charity from his family and her clients, respectively.

      c. John gave, and Bill lent, a total of $10,000 to $\left\{ \begin{array}{l} \text{the same student} \\ \text{different students} \end{array} \right\}$.

We are not aware of any explicit previous analysis that accounts for the interactions of these phenomena with each other as exemplified by (170b,c) and (166) above. We take it that these examples provide a particularly strong argument for a unified analysis of these phenomena.

In the next section, we propose just such an analysis of "respective," symmetrical, and summative predicates, accounting for the parallels and interactions among these phenomena straightforwardly. The key idea that we exploit is that all these expressions denote tuples—that is, ordered lists of items—and the same "respective" predication operator mediates the complex (yet systematic) interactions they exhibit that pose apparent challenges to compositionality. While the semantics of each of these phenomena have been studied extensively in the previous literature by several authors, to our knowledge, a unitary and fully detailed compositional analysis—especially one that extends straightforwardly to cases involving interactions with NCC—has not yet been achieved. (But see Chaves [2012] for a recent attempt, some of whose key ideas we inherit in our own analysis; see section 5.4.1.3 for a comparison.) We believe that the unified analysis we offer below clarifies the compositional mechanism underlying these phenomena—in particular, illuminating the way it interacts with the general syntax and semantics of coordination, including both standard constituent coordination and NCC.

5.2   Some Residual Issues Regarding the Empirical Properties of "Respective," Symmetrical, and Summative Predicates

Before moving on to the analysis, we would like to address residual issues, some of which might initially appear to threaten the unified treatment of "respective," symmetrical and summative predicates presented in the next section.

5.2.1   Apparent Nonparallels between "Respective," Symmetrical, and Summative Predicates

As we have discussed above, the analysis presented below builds on the idea that a single common mechanism is at the core of the semantics of the three phenomena reviewed above. One might object to this assumption by noting cases where these phenomena apparently do not behave in a completely parallel fashion. We believe that in each such case, the superficial difference can be attributed to independent factors orthogonal to the core semantic mechanism common to these phenomena.

5.2.1.1   Interactions with universal quantifiers   The first alleged discrepancy among the three phenomena comes from examples involving the universal quantifiers *every* and *each*. Note first that *every* and *each* license internal readings of symmetrical predicates quite readily:

(171)   a.   Every student read {the same book/a different book}.

        b.   Each student read {the same book/a different book}.

Given the parallel between symmetrical predicates on the one hand and "respective" and summative predicates on the other, as noted above, one might then expect the latter two to induce the relevant readings with universal quantifiers similarly. This expectation seems initially falsified by data such as the following:

(172)   a.   {Each/Every} student read a total of twenty books.

        b. #{Each/Every} student read *War and Peace*, *Anna Karenina*, and *The Idiot*, respectively.

These sentences lack the relevant "respective"/summative readings. (172a) can be interpreted only on the strictly distributive reading of *each/every* (where each of the students read a total of twenty books separately) and (172b) is simply infelicitous since the adverb *respectively* is incompatible with the distributive reading of *each* and *every*.

However, it has been noted in the literature that the relevant readings are available at least in certain examples:

(173)   a.   Three copy-editors (between them) caught every mistake in the manuscript.

                                                         (Kratzer 2007)

b. (. . .) it is essential that an agreement be reached as to the costs that each party will respectively bear.   (Chaves 2012)

There seem to be several factors involved in the contrast between the examples in (173) and those in (172). One relevant factor is arguably pragmatic. Both the "respective" reading and the summative reading seem to require that the totality of the set identified by the quantified NP containing *every* or *each* be identifiable, so that a proper correspondence between each member of that set and the corresponding subparts of the other plurality can be established. For the "respective" reading, there also needs to be at least an implicit linking between specific members of one set to the members of the other. Typically, this is established by a linguistically or contextually invoked ordering (as already discussed), but an implicit dependency between the members of the two sets (as facilitated by the expression *costs*, which readily invokes such dependency) seems to play the role of establishing the relevant linking in examples like (173b).

Another relevant factor seems to be real-time sentence processing. Note that, in both of the examples in (173), where the "respective"/summative readings are licensed with *each/every*, the NP containing *each/every* linearly follows the plural that it relates to.[4] While a complete account of why linear order would matter in inducing "respective" predication is beyond the scope of our proposal, we believe that something along the following lines is at work. The "respective" and summative readings are, in a sense, more complex than distributive readings and internal readings of symmetrical predicates in that they involve codependency of interpretation between the sets identified by *every/each N* and the other plural. Distributive and internal readings, by contrast, involve only quantification over the set of objects identified by *each/every* (the internal reading is somewhat more complex than the distributive reading, but the extra complexity boils down to the (non-)distinctness of the property predicated of each object that the quantifier ranges over). When the plural precedes the quantifier, the codependency relation can be established more easily since by the time the processor encounters the quantifier, the plural NP that it associates with is already identified. By contrast, in examples like (172), the NP containing *each/every* appears sentence-initially, and this sets a strong bias for a distributive quantification interpretation (in the broader sense encompassing the internal readings of symmetrical predicates) in which the quantifier meaning is processed without taking into account its codependency to another expression.

---

4. Kratzer (2007) attributes the contrast between (173a) and *Every copy editor caught five hundred mistakes in the manuscript* (which does not induce the relevant summative reading) to differences in grammatical relations. However, see Champollion (2010) for a discussion that grammatical relation is not the relevant factor.

Thus, while there apparently is an asymmetry between "respective" and summative predicates on the one hand and symmetrical predicates on the other as to how readily the relevant reading is available, we believe that the contrast observed in (171)–(173) receives independent explanation and that it is not problematic for the unified analysis we propose below.

5.2.1.2 The incompatibility of overt *respectively* with symmetrical and summative predicates Unlike "respective" readings, symmetrical and summative predicates are incompatible with the adverb *respectively*:

(174) a. #John and Bill read {the same book/different books}, respectively.

      b. #John and Bill spent a total of $10,000, respectively.

This does not pose any problem for our unified analysis of "respective," symmetrical, and summative predicates. As noted by Chaves (2012), the function of the adverb *respectively* is to ensure that the bijection established is in accordance with the contextually provided ordering (where the relevant ordering is either given by the linguistic context [i.e., order of mention] or the pragmatic context). Although the technical analysis we propose below makes use of the same mechanism for establishing a bijective mapping in the three phenomena, the nature of the ordering is crucially different in the case of *respectively* sentences on the one hand and symmetrical and summative predicates on the other. In the latter two cases, the relevant ordering is introduced purely for the sake of ensuring that a proper bijective mapping is established. Thus, since there is no contextually salient ordering involved, these expressions are incompatible with the meaning of the adverb *respectively*.

5.2.1.3 "Respective" readings with disjunction As noted by Eggert (2000) and Yatabe and Tam (2019), there are examples in which the "respective" reading is induced by disjunction rather than conjunction, such as the following:

(175) a. If the cup is too small or too large, then you should go up or down, respectively, in cup size.

      b. The n and N commands repeat the previous search command in the same or opposite direction, respectively.

One might think that this type of example would pose a challenge to the analysis of the "respective" reading that we propose in the next section, since our analysis takes a generalized version of the distributivity operator to be responsible for inducing the "respective" reading.

We suspect that all such examples involve the alternative-invoking meaning of *or* in English (cf., e.g., Alonso-Ovalle 2006), rather than boolean disjunction. Once this possibility is recognized, it seems to us to be premature to draw the conclusion that these data pose a problem for our approach, since alternative semantic values in alternative semantics (Rooth 1985) are model-theoretic objects that can enter into more complex compositional operations, just like elements of a sum in sum-based semantics for plurality. This being said, we leave a detailed examination of these disjunctive "respective" reading examples to another occasion.

5.2.2   Non-coordinate RNR and Dependent Clusters

It is well-known that RNR is not restricted to coordination (Hudson 1976; Phillips 1996):

(176) a. Stone also suggests that Nixon knew of, though he did not attempt to partic-
           ipate in, US attempts to assassinate Fidel Castro.

                                                    (*Boston Globe* Sunday movie section)

       b. The people who liked, easily outnumbered the people who disliked, the
           movie we saw yesterday.

Interestingly, some instances of "non-coordinate" RNR can induce the "respective" reading and the internal reading of symmetrical predicates:[5]

(177) a. John defeated, {whereas/although} Mary lost to, the exact same opponent.

       b. John defeated, whereas Mary lost to, Sam and Kim, respectively.

Note further that, as pointed out by Beavers and Sag (2004), the disjunction *or* is seriously degraded in the internal reading, and other types of non-coordinate RNR whose (truth-conditional) meanings do not correspond to conjunction similarly fail to induce the relevant readings:

(178) a. #John hummed, or Mary sang, the same tune.   (Beavers and Sag 2004)

       b. #The people who liked, easily outnumbered the people who disliked, the
           same movie.

We think that the relevant generalization is whether the construction in question has the meaning of conjunction. *Whereas* and *although* are truth-conditionally equivalent to conjunction, with an extra pragmatic function of indicating a particular discourse relation (some kind of contrast) between the two clauses. Since the analysis we present below is predicated of the conjunctive meaning of *and* rather than its syntactic coordinatehood, the examples in (177), rather than undermining our analysis, in fact provide further corroboration for it.

---

5. The following example, however, does not induce the summative reading:

(i) John spent, whereas Mary lost, a total of $10,000.

This seems to be due to the fact that the "contrast" discourse relation lexically invoked by *whereas* is inherently incompatible with the pragmatics of summative interpretation (in which the two clauses need to be construed to pertain to some common point rather than being in contrast with one another).

More challenging to our approach are cases like the following, in which dependent cluster formation interacts with comparatives. As noted by Moltmann (1992) and Hendriks (1995a), comparatives license the internal reading of *same* (but this does not seem to be possible with other symmetrical predicates such as *different* and *similar*), and this works in examples involving nonconstituents in the comparative clause also:

(179) a. I gave the same girl more books on Saturday than CDs on Sunday.

  b. ??I gave {different/similar} girls more books on Saturday than CDs on Sunday.

We do not know of any compositional analysis of internal readings of symmetrical predicates that can account for the interaction of *same* and comparatives in examples like (179a). It is tempting to speculate that the internal reading here is supported by some core meaning (something like "parallel predications" involving multiple clauses) common to conjunction and comparatives and that, once this core meaning is identified, the existing analyses of internal readings would straightforwardly carry over to cases like (179a). However, given the lack of a concrete proposal, we simply leave this as an open issue for future study.

5.3 The Compositional Semantics of "Respective" Predication

In this section, we present a unified analysis of "respective," symmetrical, and summative predicates in Hybrid TLCG. Key to our proposal is the idea that the same underlying mechanism of pairwise predication between terms that denote tuples is involved in the semantics of these phenomena. This analytic idea itself is theory-neutral, but we show that formulating the analysis in Hybrid TLCG enables us to capture the complex yet systematic properties of this class of phenomena particularly transparently. More specifically, the order-insensitive mode of implication involving the "vertical slash" ($\restriction$), the key novel feature of Hybrid TLCG, enables a unified analysis of the two essential properties of these phenomena identified in section 5.1: (i) interactions with NCC; and (ii) multiple dependency that these predicates exhibit, including the interactions of the three phenomena with one another.

5.3.1 Hypothetical Reasoning and "Respective" Predication

We start with the analysis of "respective" readings since our analysis of the other two phenomena builds on the core semantic operator that we introduce for this construction. The underlying intuition of most formal analyses of "respective" readings (cf. Gawron and Kehler 2004; Winter 1995; Bekki 2006) (which we also adopt) is that sentences like (180) involve pairwise predication between two (or more) sets of entities where the "corresponding" elements of the two sets are related by some predicate in the sentence.

(180) Mary and Sue married John and Bill (respectively).

In the case of (180), this "predicate" is simply the lexical meaning of the verb, but in certain cases that we discuss below, the predicate that relates the elements of the two sets (as well as the elements in the two sets themselves) can be of a more complex type.

Among the previous approaches, Gawron and Kehler (2004) (G&K) work out the relevant compositional mechanism in most detail (see section 5.4.1.1 for more on their approach). G&K model the meanings of expressions to be related in a "respective" manner in terms of the notion of sums. While this works well with cases of "respective" readings, G&K's approach faces a technical difficulty if one attempts to extend it directly to the case of symmetrical predicates (see section 5.4.1.1). Since our goal is to provide a unified analysis of the three phenomena, we adopt a different approach. Specifically, following Winter (1995) and Bekki (2006), we first recast the relevant aspects of G&K's analysis in terms of the notion of tuple, which is essentially a list that comes with an ordering of elements. Our reasons for taking the ordering of elements to be part of the denotation of plural and conjoined expressions are given in section 5.4.2. As we discuss there, this choice is purely for expository convenience; a multiset-based reformulation of the analysis (which relocates the ordering information to pragmatics) is conceivable, but then the relevant compositional mechanism becomes much more complex.

Tuples can be formally defined in several different ways.[6] Here, we adopt a functional definition, where an n-tuple $\langle a_1, a_2, \ldots, a_n \rangle$ is a function whose domain is a set of integers $\{1, \ldots, n\}$ such that

$$\langle a_1, a_2, \ldots, a_n \rangle =_{def} \begin{bmatrix} 1 \longmapsto a_1 \\ 2 \longmapsto a_2 \\ \vdots \\ n \longmapsto a_n \end{bmatrix}$$

---

6. A standard definition in mathematics is in terms of ordered pairs:

(i)   a.   For any a and b, the ordered pair $\langle a, b \rangle$ is a two-tuple and is written as (a, b).
      b.   If $A (= (a_1, a_2, \ldots, a_n))$ is an n-tuple, then for any b, the ordered pair $\langle A, b \rangle$ is an $(n+1)$-tuple and is written as $(a_1, a_2, \ldots, a_n, b)$.

However, this formulation has the problem that an n-tuple and an $(n-1)$-tuple whose first component is itself a tuple are formally indistinguishable (e.g., the triple $\langle a, b, c \rangle$ and the double $\langle \langle a, b \rangle, c \rangle$ are identical under this definition). This is problematic for our purposes since an n-tuple does not behave like an $(n-1)$-tuple in the "respective" readings:

(ii) #Alice, Betty, and Cathy met Dan and Eric, respectively.
      intended: 'Alice and Betty met Dan and Cathy met Eric.'

Importantly, unlike sums (or sets), tuples are inherently ordered. Thus, $a \oplus b \oplus c = a \oplus c \oplus b$, but $\langle a,b,c \rangle \neq \langle a,c,b \rangle$.

We assume that the conjunction word *and* denotes the following tuple-forming operator (this needs to be generalized to cases involving more than two conjuncts, but we omit this detail since it is not directly relevant for the ensuing discussion):[7]

(181) and; $\lambda \mathcal{W} \lambda \mathcal{V}.\langle \mathcal{V}, \mathcal{W} \rangle$; $(X \backslash X)/X$

This enables us to assign tuples of individuals like $\langle \mathbf{mary}, \mathbf{sue} \rangle$ and $\langle \mathbf{mary}, \mathbf{sue}, \mathbf{ann} \rangle$ as the meanings of expressions like *Mary and Sue* and *Mary, Sue, and Ann*.[8] Then, to assign the right meaning to (180), the two tuples $\langle \mathbf{mary}, \mathbf{sue} \rangle$ and $\langle \mathbf{john}, \mathbf{bill} \rangle$, each denoted by the subject and object NPs, need to be related to each other in a "respective" manner via the relation **married**: Mary married John and Sue married Bill. Establishing this "respective" relation is mediated by the **resp** operator in (182), which is a prosodically empty operator that takes a relation and two tuple-denoting terms as arguments and returns a tuple consisting of propositions obtained by relating each member of the two tuples in a pairwise manner with respect to the relation in question (see below for the denotation for the adverb *respectively*; the role of *respectively* is essentially to ensure that the bijective mapping obtained by this covert **resp** operator conforms to the contextually established ordering):

(182) $\mathbf{resp} = \lambda \mathcal{R} \lambda \mathcal{T}_{\times_n} \lambda \mathcal{U}_{\times_n} . \prod_i^n \mathcal{R}(\pi_i(\mathcal{T}_{\times_n}))(\pi_i(\mathcal{U}_{\times_n}))$

$\mathcal{T}_{\times_n}$ and $\mathcal{U}_{\times_n}$ range over n-tuples. We omit the subscript n if its value is contextually obvious. Thus, in (182), the cardinality of the input tuples needs to match. π_i is the projection function which returns the i-th member of the tuple. $\prod_i^n$ is a tuple constructor defined as follows:

(183) $\prod_i^n a_i = \langle a_1, a_2, \ldots, a_n \rangle$

From this, it should be clear that the cardinality of the input and output tuples matches.

---

7. At this point, one might wonder whether the tuple meaning in (181) is the only meaning of conjunction that we need, or if we need to assume the boolean conjunction meaning in addition. As discussed in Kubota and Levine (2014b), the two rules in (252) in section 5.5 become derivable in our setup. Sentences like (ia) and the distributive readings of sentences like (ib) can then be obtained with these rules.

(i) a. John walked and talked.
     b. John and Bill walked.

Alternatively, boolean conjunction meanings (for any given type) can be derived as a theorem from the tuple-type meaning for *and* in (181) via hypothetical reasoning with the **resp** operator in (182) and the tuple constructor in (183). Thus, boolean conjunction does not need to be separately posited. See Krifka (1990) for some discussion about the relationship between boolean and non-boolean *and*.

8. We assume, as per our discussion in the preceding chapter, that plural NPs denote sums lexically and that they are converted to tuples via an empty operator when some contextually salient ordering is available.

By giving the relation denoted by the verb and the two tuples denoted by the object and subject NPs as arguments to the **resp** operator, we obtain the following result:

(184) $\mathbf{resp}(\mathbf{married})(\langle \mathbf{j}, \mathbf{b}\rangle)(\langle \mathbf{m}, \mathbf{s}\rangle) = \prod_i \mathbf{married}(\pi_i(\langle \mathbf{j}, \mathbf{b}\rangle))(\pi_i(\langle \mathbf{m}, \mathbf{s}\rangle))$
$\qquad = \langle \mathbf{married}(\mathbf{j})(\mathbf{m}), \mathbf{married}(\mathbf{b})(\mathbf{s})\rangle$

This tuple of two propositions is then mapped to a boolean conjunction via a phonologically empty operator with the following meaning:

(185) $\lambda p_\times . \bigwedge_i \pi_i(p_\times)$

By applying (185) to (184), we obtain the proposition $\mathbf{married}(\mathbf{j})(\mathbf{m}) \wedge \mathbf{married}(\mathbf{b})(\mathbf{s})$. As will become clear below, keeping the two components separate in the form of a tuple after the application of the **resp** operator is crucial for dealing with multiple "respective" (or symmetrical/summative) readings in examples like those in (161), (165), and (170).

The next question is how to get this semantic analysis to mesh with a compositional analysis of the sentence. Things may seem simple and straightforward in examples like (180), where the two terms to be related to each other in a pairwise manner are co-arguments of the same predicate. However, as noted already, this is not always the case. For treating more complex cases, G&K propose to treat "respective" predication in terms of a combination of recursive applications of both the "respective" operator and the distributive operator, but their approach quickly becomes unwieldy. Since we need to deal with complex examples involving interactions with nonconstituent coordination, we simply note here that the compositional mechanism assumed by G&K is not fully general and turn to an alternative approach (see section 5.4.1.1 for a more complete critique of their approach; see also section 5.5 for some more general remarks about the relationship between the present proposal and G&K's approach).

It turns out that a more general (and simpler) approach which serves our purpose here is straightforwardly available in Hybrid TLCG by (two instances of) hypothetical reasoning with the vertical slash, as we show momentarily. Crucially, the interdependence between the two product-type terms is mediated by double abstraction via ↾ in the syntax, whose output (together with the two product-type terms themselves) is immediately given to the **resp** operator, which then relates them in a pairwise manner with respect to some relation $\mathcal{R}$. This is essentially an implementation of Barker's (2007) "parasitic scope" strategy. (For a comparison between the present proposal and Barker's analysis of *same*, see section 5.4.1.2.)

In Hybrid TLCG, we can abstract over any arbitrary positions in a sentence to create a relation that obtains between objects belonging to the semantic types of the variables that are abstracted over. This is illustrated in the following partial derivation for (180). By abstracting over the subject and object positions of the sentence, we obtain an expression of type S↾NP↾NP, where the "gaps" in the subject and object positions are kept track of via explicit λ-binding in the phonology, just in the same way as in the analysis of quantifier scope in chapter 2.

(186)

$$
\cfrac{
  [\varphi_2; y; \mathrm{NP}]^2 \quad
  \cfrac{
    \cfrac{
      \text{married}; \textbf{married}; \mathrm{VP/NP} \quad [\varphi_1; x; \mathrm{NP}]^1
    }{
      \text{married} \circ \varphi_1; \textbf{married}(x); \mathrm{VP}
    } /E
  }{
    \cfrac{
      \cfrac{
        \varphi_2 \circ \text{married} \circ \varphi_1; \textbf{married}(x)(y); \mathrm{S}
      }{
        \lambda\varphi_2.\varphi_2 \circ \text{married} \circ \varphi_1; \lambda y.\textbf{married}(x)(y); \mathrm{S}{\upharpoonright}\mathrm{NP}
      }{\upharpoonright}\mathrm{I}^2
    }{
      \lambda\varphi_1\lambda\varphi_2.\varphi_2 \circ \text{married} \circ \varphi_1; \lambda x\lambda y.\textbf{married}(x)(y); \mathrm{S}{\upharpoonright}\mathrm{NP}{\upharpoonright}\mathrm{NP}
    }{\upharpoonright}\mathrm{I}^1
  }
}{} /E
$$

The "respective" operator, defined as in (187), then takes such a doubly abstracted proposition as an argument to produce another type $\mathrm{S}{\upharpoonright}\mathrm{NP}{\upharpoonright}\mathrm{NP}$ expression. Phonologically, it is just an identity function, and its semantic contribution is precisely the **resp** operator defined above.

(187) $\lambda\sigma\lambda\varphi_1\lambda\varphi_2.\sigma(\varphi_1)(\varphi_2)$; **resp**; $(Z{\upharpoonright}X{\upharpoonright}Y){\upharpoonright}(Z{\upharpoonright}X{\upharpoonright}Y)$

The derivation completes by giving the two product-type arguments denoted by *John and Bill* and *Mary and Sue* to this "respectivized" type $\mathrm{S}{\upharpoonright}\mathrm{NP}{\upharpoonright}\mathrm{NP}$ predicate and converting the pair of propositions to a boolean conjunction by the boolean reduction operator in (185). (As per our standard practice, dotted lines in derivations correspond to reductions of semantic translations to enhance readability and should not be confused with the application of logical rules designated by solid lines. Unlike the latter, purely from a formal perspective, these reduction steps are redundant.)

(188)

$$
\cfrac{
  \lambda\varphi.\varphi; \lambda p_\times. \bigwedge_i \pi_i(p_\times); \mathrm{S}{\upharpoonright}\mathrm{S}
  \quad
  \cfrac{
    \cfrac{
      \begin{array}{l} \text{mary} \circ \\ \text{and} \circ \\ \text{sue}; \\ \langle\textbf{m},\textbf{s}\rangle; \mathrm{NP} \end{array}
      \quad
      \cfrac{
        \begin{array}{l} \text{john} \circ \\ \text{and} \circ \\ \text{bill}; \\ \langle\textbf{j},\textbf{b}\rangle; \mathrm{NP} \end{array}
        \quad
        \cfrac{
          \begin{array}{l} \lambda\sigma\lambda\varphi_1\lambda\varphi_2. \\ \sigma(\varphi_1)(\varphi_2); \\ \textbf{resp}; \\ (Z{\upharpoonright}X{\upharpoonright}Y){\upharpoonright}(Z{\upharpoonright}X{\upharpoonright}Y) \end{array}
          \quad
          \begin{array}{l} \lambda\varphi_3\lambda\varphi_4. \\ \varphi_4 \circ \text{married} \circ \varphi_3; \\ \textbf{married}; \mathrm{S}{\upharpoonright}\mathrm{NP}{\upharpoonright}\mathrm{NP} \end{array}
        }{
          \begin{array}{c} \lambda\varphi_1\lambda\varphi_2.\varphi_2 \circ \text{married} \circ \varphi_1; \\ \textbf{resp}(\textbf{married}); \mathrm{S}{\upharpoonright}\mathrm{NP}{\upharpoonright}\mathrm{NP} \end{array}
        }{\upharpoonright}E
      }{
        \begin{array}{c} \lambda\varphi_2.\varphi_2 \circ \text{married} \circ \text{john} \circ \text{and} \circ \text{bill}; \\ \textbf{resp}(\textbf{married})(\langle\textbf{j},\textbf{b}\rangle); \mathrm{S}{\upharpoonright}\mathrm{NP} \end{array}
      }{\upharpoonright}E
    }{
      \begin{array}{c} \text{mary} \circ \text{and} \circ \text{sue} \circ \text{married} \circ \text{john} \circ \text{and} \circ \text{bill}; \\ \textbf{resp}(\textbf{married})(\langle\textbf{j},\textbf{b}\rangle)(\langle\textbf{m},\textbf{s}\rangle); \mathrm{S} \\ \cdots\cdots\cdots\cdots\cdots\cdots\cdots\cdots\cdots \\ \text{mary} \circ \text{and} \circ \text{sue} \circ \text{married} \circ \text{john} \circ \text{and} \circ \text{bill}; \\ \langle\textbf{married}(\textbf{j})(\textbf{m}), \textbf{married}(\textbf{b})(\textbf{s})\rangle; \mathrm{S} \end{array}
    }{\upharpoonright}E
  }
}{
  \begin{array}{c} \text{mary} \circ \text{and} \circ \text{sue} \circ \text{married} \circ \text{john} \circ \text{and} \circ \text{bill}; \\ \textbf{married}(\textbf{j})(\textbf{m}) \wedge \textbf{married}(\textbf{b})(\textbf{s}); \mathrm{S} \end{array}
} {\upharpoonright}E
$$

Note in particular that prosodic λ-binding with ${\upharpoonright}$ enables "lowering" the phonologies of the two product-type terms in their respective positions in the sentence, thus mediating the syntax-semantics mismatch between their surface positions and semantic scope (of the **resp** operator that they are arguments of) in essentially the same way as with quantifiers.

We now turn to the treatment of the adverb *respectively*. We assume that the function of *respectively* is to ensure that the order of elements in the tuples that the covert **resp** operator takes as arguments conforms to some contextually established ordering. This can be encoded as a condition on the arguments via the predicate **order**$_C$ (with contextual parameter C), where **order**$_C(X_\times)$ is true of a tuple $X_\times$ if and only if the ordering of elements encoded in $X_\times$ conforms to the contextual ordering of its elements in C. The lexical entry for *respectively* can then be written as follows:

(189) $\lambda\sigma\lambda\varphi_1\lambda\varphi_2.\sigma(\varphi_1)(\varphi_2) \circ$ respectively;

$\lambda\mathcal{R}\lambda\mathcal{T}_{\times:\mathbf{order}_C(\mathcal{T}_\times)} \lambda\mathcal{U}_{\times:\mathbf{order}_C(\mathcal{U}_\times)}.\mathcal{R}(\mathcal{T}_\times)(\mathcal{U}_\times); (Z{\upharpoonright}X{\upharpoonright}Y){\upharpoonright}(Z{\upharpoonright}X{\upharpoonright}Y)$

By applying this operator to the "respectivized" relation **resp**(**marry**), we obtain

(190) $\lambda\mathcal{T}_{\times:\mathbf{order}_C(\mathcal{T}_\times)} \lambda\mathcal{U}_{\times:\mathbf{order}_C(\mathcal{U}_\times)}.\mathbf{resp}(\mathbf{marry})(\mathcal{T}_\times)(\mathcal{U}_\times)$

It might appear that the function of *respectively* is completely redundant in examples like (180), since the tuples already record the correct ordering reflecting the order of mention. However, this is an artificial consequence of adopting a tuple-based formulation of the analysis. In a multiset-based reformulation (which we discuss briefly in section 5.4.2), *respectively* does make a substantial contribution to the meaning of the sentence by filtering out ordering possibilities that do not conform to the contextual ordering (e.g., #*The front and the back of the ship are called the bow and the stern, respectively, but which is which?*).

Another point which needs to be noted about *respectively* is that it is an adverb, and just like other adverbs, its surface word order is relatively flexible.

(191) a. John and Mary will meet Peter and Sue, respectively.
      b. John and Mary respectively will meet Peter and Sue.
      c. John and Mary will respectively meet Peter and Sue.

With the lexical entry in (189), our analysis attaches *respectively* at the end of the whole string. We assume that surface reordering principles (of the sort that can be implemented in our system by enriching the prosodic component along the lines discussed in chapter 11) are responsible for generating the other orders such as (191b,c).

It should be clear that the analysis extends straightforwardly to cases where one of the product-type terms appears in a sentence-internal position, such as the following:

(192) John and Bill sent the bomb and the letter to the president yesterday, respectively.

For this sentence, we first obtain the following doubly abstracted proposition in the same way as in the simpler example above:

(193) $\lambda\varphi_1\lambda\varphi_2.\varphi_1 \circ \text{sent} \circ \varphi_2 \circ \text{to} \circ \text{the} \circ \text{president} \circ \text{yesterday};$

$\lambda x\lambda y.\textbf{yest}(\textbf{sent}(y)(\textbf{the-pres}))(x); \text{S}\!\restriction\!\text{NP}\!\restriction\!\text{NP}$

The **resp** operator then takes this and the two product-type terms as arguments to produce a sign with the surface string in (192) paired with the following semantic interpretation (after the application of boolean reduction):

(194) $\textbf{yest}(\textbf{sent}(\textbf{the-bomb})(\textbf{the-pres}))(\textbf{j}) \wedge \textbf{yest}(\textbf{sent}(\textbf{the-letter})(\textbf{the-pres}))(\textbf{b})$

We now turn to an interaction with NCC, taking the following example as an illustration:

(195) John and Bill met Robin on Thursday and Chris on Friday, respectively.

The analysis is in fact straightforward. As discussed in chapter 2, Dependent Cluster Coordination is analyzed by treating the apparent nonconstituents that are coordinated in examples like (195) to be (higher-order) derived constituents via hypothetical reasoning (with the directional slashes / and \).

Specifically, via hypothetical reasoning, the string *Robin on Thursday* can be analyzed as a constituent of type $(\text{VP}/\text{NP})\backslash\text{VP}$, an expression that combines with a transitive verb and an NP (in that order) to its left to become an S (see (253) in section 5.6 for a complete proof):

(196) $\text{robin} \circ \text{on} \circ \text{thursday}; \lambda R.\textbf{onTh}(R(\textbf{r})); (\text{VP}/\text{NP})\backslash\text{VP}$

We then derive a sentence containing gap positions corresponding to this derived constituent and the subject NP (see (254) in section 5.6):

(197) $\lambda\varphi_1\lambda\varphi_2.\varphi_1 \circ \text{met} \circ \varphi_2; \lambda x\lambda\mathscr{P}.\mathscr{P}(\textbf{met})(x); \text{S}\!\restriction\!((\text{VP}/\text{NP})\backslash\text{VP})\!\restriction\!\text{NP}$

The rest of the derivation involves giving this relation and the two product-type arguments of types NP and $(\text{VP}/\text{NP})\backslash\text{VP}$ as arguments to the **resp** operator, which yields the following translation for the whole sentence:

(198) $\textbf{onTh}(\textbf{met}(\textbf{r}))(\textbf{j}) \wedge \textbf{onFr}(\textbf{met}(\textbf{c}))(\textbf{b})$

Finally, multiple "respective" readings, exemplified by (199), are straightforward.

(199) Tolstoy and Dostoevsky sent *Anna Karenina* and *The Idiot* to Dickens and Thackeray (respectively).

As in G&K's analysis, the right meaning can be compositionally assigned to the sentence via recursive application of the **resp** operator, without any additional mechanism. The key point of the derivation is that we first derive a three-place predicate of type $\text{S}\!\restriction\!\text{NP}\!\restriction\!\text{NP}\!\restriction\!\text{NP}$, instead of a two-place predicate of type $\text{S}\!\restriction\!\text{NP}\!\restriction\!\text{NP}$ (as in the simpler case in (188)), to be given as an argument to the first **resp** operator:

(200) $\lambda\varphi_1\lambda\varphi_2\lambda\varphi_3.\varphi_3 \circ \text{sent} \circ \varphi_1 \circ \text{to} \circ \varphi_2; \textbf{sent}; \text{S}\!\restriction\!\text{NP}\!\restriction\!\text{NP}\!\restriction\!\text{NP}$

After two of the tuple-denoting terms are related to each other with respect to the predicate denoted by the verb, the resultant $S{\upharpoonright}NP$ expression denotes a tuple of two properties (see (255) in section 5.6 for a complete proof):

(201) $\lambda\varphi_3.\varphi_3 \circ \text{sent} \circ \text{AK} \circ \text{and} \circ \text{Id} \circ \text{to} \circ \text{Di} \circ \text{and} \circ \text{Th};$ $\langle \mathbf{sent(ak)(di)}, \mathbf{sent(id)(th)} \rangle;$ $S{\upharpoonright}NP$

And the remaining conjoined term $\langle \mathbf{to}, \mathbf{do} \rangle$ is related to this product-type property by a derived two-place "respective" operator in the following way:

(202)

$$
\cfrac{
\begin{array}{cc}
\vdots & \vdots \\
\begin{array}{l}
\lambda\sigma\lambda\varphi.\sigma(\varphi); \\
\lambda P_\times\lambda X_\times. \prod_i \pi_i(P_\times)(\pi_i(X_\times)); \\
(S{\upharpoonright}NP){\upharpoonright}(S{\upharpoonright}NP)
\end{array}
&
\begin{array}{l}
\lambda\varphi_3.\varphi_3 \circ \text{sent} \circ \text{AK} \circ \text{and} \circ \text{Id} \circ \\
\text{to} \circ \text{Di} \circ \text{and} \circ \text{Th}; \\
\langle \mathbf{sent(ak)(di)}, \mathbf{sent(id)(th)} \rangle; S{\upharpoonright}NP
\end{array}
\end{array}
}{}
$$

$$
\cfrac{
\begin{array}{l}
\text{To} \circ \text{and} \circ \text{Do}; \\
\langle \mathbf{to}, \mathbf{do} \rangle; NP
\end{array}
\quad
\cfrac{
\begin{array}{l}
\lambda\varphi.\varphi \circ \text{sent} \circ \text{AK} \circ \text{and} \circ \text{Id} \circ \text{to} \circ \text{Di} \circ \text{and} \circ \text{Th}; \\
\lambda X_\times. \prod_i \pi_i(\langle \mathbf{sent(ak)(di)}, \mathbf{sent(id)(th)} \rangle)(\pi_i(X_\times)); S{\upharpoonright}NP
\end{array}
}{}{\upharpoonright}E
}{
\begin{array}{l}
\text{To} \circ \text{and} \circ \text{Do} \circ \text{sent} \circ \text{AK} \circ \text{and} \circ \text{Id} \circ \text{to} \circ \text{Di} \circ \text{and} \circ \text{Th}; \\
\prod_i \pi_i(\langle \mathbf{sent(ak)(di)}, \mathbf{sent(i)(th)} \rangle)(\pi_i(\langle \mathbf{to}, \mathbf{do} \rangle)); S
\end{array}
}{\upharpoonright}E
$$

$$
\begin{array}{l}
\text{To} \circ \text{and} \circ \text{Do} \circ \text{sent} \circ \text{AK} \circ \text{and} \circ \text{Id} \circ \text{to} \circ \text{Di} \circ \text{and} \circ \text{Th}; \\
\langle \mathbf{sent(ak)(di)(to)}, \mathbf{sent(id)(th)(do)} \rangle; S
\end{array}
$$

The two-place **resp** operator, which directly relates the product-type property (of type $S{\upharpoonright}NP$) with the product-type NP occupying the subject position via pairwise function application of the corresponding elements, can be derived from the lexically specified three-place **resp** operator via hypothetical reasoning. The proof is given in (256) in section 5.6.

5.3.2 Extending the Analysis to Symmetrical and Summative Predicates

We exploit the **resp** operator introduced above in the analysis of symmetrical and summative predicates as well. The intuition behind this approach is that NPs containing *same*, *different*, and the like (we call such NPs symmetrical terms below) in examples like (203) denote tuples (linked to the other tuple denoted by the plural *John and Bill* in the same way as in the "respective" readings above) but impose special conditions on each member of the tuple.

(203) John and Bill read the same book.

In (203), John and Bill need to be each paired with an identical book, and in the case of *different*, they need to be paired with distinct books. To capture this additional constraint on the tuples denoted by symmetrical terms, we assign to them GQ-type meanings of type $S{\upharpoonright}(S{\upharpoonright}NP)$, where the abstracted NP in their arguments are product-type expressions semantically. More specifically, we posit the following lexical entries for *the same* and *different*:[9]

(204) a. $\lambda\varphi\lambda\sigma.\sigma(\text{the}\circ\text{same}\circ\varphi)$;

$\lambda P\lambda Q.\exists X_\times \forall i\, P(\pi_i(X_\times)) \wedge \forall i \forall j [\pi_i(X_\times) = \pi_j(X_\times)] \wedge Q(X_\times)$;

$S\!\upharpoonright\!(S\!\upharpoonright\!NP)\!\upharpoonright\!N$

b. $\lambda\varphi\lambda\sigma.\sigma(\text{different}\circ\varphi)$;

$\lambda P\lambda Q.\exists X_\times \forall i\, P(\pi_i(X_\times)) \wedge \forall i \forall j [i \neq j \rightarrow \pi_i(X_\times) \neq \pi_j(X_\times)] \wedge Q(X_\times)$;

$S\!\upharpoonright\!(S\!\upharpoonright\!NP)\!\upharpoonright\!N$

In both cases, the relevant tuple (which enters into the "respective" relation with another tuple via the **resp** operator) consists of objects that satisfy the description provided by the noun. The difference is that in the case of *same*, the elements of the tuple are all constrained to be identical, whereas in the case of *different*, they are constrained to differ from one another.

We now outline the analysis for (203) (the full derivation is given in (257) in section 5.6). The key point is that we first posit a variable that semantically denotes a tuple and relate it to the other tuple-denoting expression (*John and Bill* in this case) via the **resp** operator. This part of the analysis follows proof steps completely parallel to the analysis of "respective" readings shown in the previous section. Specifically, by hypothetically assuming an NP with phonology φ and semantics $X_\times$, we can derive the expression in (205).

(205) john $\circ$ and $\circ$ bill $\circ$ read $\circ$ φ; $\bigwedge_i \pi_i(\textbf{resp}(\textbf{read})(X_\times)(\langle \mathbf{j}, \mathbf{b}\rangle))$; S

At this point (where boolean reduction has already taken place), we withdraw the hypothesis to obtain an expression of type $S\!\upharpoonright\!NP$. This is then given as an argument to the symmetrical term *the same book*, which, as noted above, has the GQ-type category $S\!\upharpoonright\!(S\!\upharpoonright\!NP)$. The symmetrical term lowers its phonology to the gap and semantically imposes the identity condition on the members of the relevant tuple. These last steps are illustrated in (206).

---

9. There is a close connection between the lexical entries for the internal readings posited in (204) and those for the external readings. The lexical entries in (204) essentially establish (non-)identity among each element of a tuple, and in this sense, they can be thought of as involving a reflexive anaphoric reference. By replacing this reflexive anaphoric reference with an anaphoric reference to some external object and stating the (non-)identity conditions to pertain to the object identified by the symmetrical term and the anaphorically invoked external object, we obtain a suitable lexical meaning for the external readings for *same* and *different*. Thus, while it may not be possible to unify the lexical entries for the two readings completely, we believe that our approach provides a basis for understanding the close relationship between the two readings. In fact, whether a unified analysis of internal and external readings is desirable seems still controversial. See Brasoveanu (2011) and Bumford and Barker (2013) for discussion.

(206)

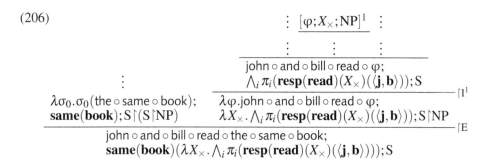

The reason that boolean reduction precedes the abstraction over the product-type NP in (206)/(257) is that the meaning of the symmetrical term is a GQ over product-type NPs. That is, the type S$\upharpoonright$NP property given to it as an argument is a property of product-type NPs that returns a truth value, rather than a tuple, by taking its product-type NP argument. One way to see what's going on in this derivation is that the hypothetical reasoning with the tuple-denoting variable $X_\times$ and "respective" predication involving it is needed since a symmetrical term denotes a quantifier over tuple-denoting expressions and hence cannot directly fill in an argument slot of a lexical verb (which is looking for non-tuple-denoting expressions as its arguments).

The final translation is unpacked in (207):

(207) $\mathbf{same}(\mathbf{book})(\lambda X_\times . \bigwedge_i \pi_i(\mathbf{resp}(\mathbf{read})(X_\times)(\langle \mathbf{j}, \mathbf{b} \rangle)))$

$= \exists X_\times \forall i \, \mathbf{book}(\pi_i(X_\times)) \wedge \forall i \forall j [\pi_i(X_\times) = \pi_j(X_\times)] \wedge \bigwedge_i \pi_i(\mathbf{resp}(\mathbf{read})(X_\times)(\langle \mathbf{j}, \mathbf{b} \rangle))$

$= \exists X_\times \forall i \, \mathbf{book}(\pi_i(X_\times)) \wedge \forall i \forall j [\pi_i(X_\times) = \pi_j(X_\times)] \wedge$

$\qquad \mathbf{read}(\pi_1(X_\times))(\mathbf{j}) \wedge \mathbf{read}(\pi_2(X_\times))(\mathbf{b})$

Since $\pi_1(X_\times) = \pi_2(X_\times)$, this correctly ensures that the book that John read and the one that Bill read are identical.

Before moving on to more complex cases, a comment is in order on the semantic analysis of *same* and *different* in (204). So far as we can tell, the lexical meanings given in (204) capture the truth conditions for the internal readings of *same* and *different* correctly. One might think that (204a) is too weak as the meaning of *same* since according to this definition, (203) can be true in a situation in which the sets of books that John and Bill read are different, as long as one can identify some common book read by both individuals. Thus, one might think that some kind of maximality condition should be imposed on the set of books identified by *same*. We do not agree with this judgment. We believe that (203) is true and felicitous as long as one can identify (at least) one book commonly read by John and Bill. They may have read other books in addition, but that doesn't make (203) false or infelicitous. Such an implication, if felt to be present, is presumably a conversational implicature since it is clearly cancelable:

(208) John and Bill read the same book, although they both read several different books in addition.

Similarly, (204b), as it stands, does not exclude a possibility in which there is some set of books commonly read by John and Bill. We again take this to be the correct result. The following example shows that the implication excluding the existence of common books read by the two (which indeed seems to be present) is not part of the entailment of the sentence:[10]

(209) John and Bill read different books, although they read the same books too.

We now move on to multiple dependency cases. In fact, the present analysis already assigns the right meanings to these sentences. Specifically, since the same **resp** operator is at the core of the analysis as in the case of "respective" readings, we immediately predict that symmetrical predicates can enter into multiple dependencies both among themselves and with respect to "respective" predication, as exemplified by examples like the following:

(210) a. John and Bill gave the same book to Mary and Sue (respectively).
       b. John and Bill gave the same book to the same man.

Since the relevant derivations can be reconstructed by taking the derivation for multiple "respective" readings presented in the previous section as a model, we omit the details and reproduce here only the derived meanings for (210a) and (210b) in (211) and (212), respectively (see (258) in section 5.6 for a complete derivation for (210b)).

(211) $\mathbf{same}(\mathbf{book})(\lambda X_\times.\mathbf{gave}(\mathbf{m})(\pi_1(X_\times))(\mathbf{j}) \wedge \mathbf{gave}(\mathbf{s})(\pi_2(X_\times))(\mathbf{b}))$

$= \exists X_\times \forall i\, \mathbf{book}(\pi_i(X_\times)) \wedge \forall i \forall j[\pi_i(X_\times) = \pi_j(X_\times)] \wedge$
$\quad \mathbf{gave}(\mathbf{m})(\pi_1(X_\times))(\mathbf{j}) \wedge \mathbf{gave}(\mathbf{s})(\pi_2(X_\times))(\mathbf{b})$

(212) $\mathbf{same}(\mathbf{book})(\lambda X_\times.\mathbf{same}(\mathbf{man})(\lambda Y_\times.\mathbf{gave}(\pi_1(Y_\times))(\pi_1(X_\times))(\mathbf{j}) \wedge$
$\quad \mathbf{gave}(\pi_2(Y_\times))(\pi_2(X_\times))(\mathbf{b})))$

$= \exists X_\times \forall i\, \mathbf{book}(\pi_i(X_\times)) \wedge \forall i \forall j[\pi_i(X_\times) = \pi_j(X_\times)] \wedge \exists Y_\times \forall i\, \mathbf{man}(\pi_i(Y_\times)) \wedge$
$\quad \forall i \forall j[\pi_i(Y_\times) = \pi_j(Y_\times)] \wedge \mathbf{gave}(\pi_1(Y_\times))(\pi_1(X_\times))(\mathbf{j}) \wedge$
$\quad \mathbf{gave}(\pi_2(Y_\times))(\pi_2(X_\times))(\mathbf{b})$

The derivation for the multiple *same* sentence (210b) involves first positing two product-type variables $X_\times$ and $Y_\times$, which are linked to the plural term *John and Bill* via the recursive application of the **resp** operator and then bound by the two GQs over product-type terms *the same man* and *the same book*.

---

10. There is a certain awkwardness to (209). But again, we believe that this arises from a Gricean implicature. Had the speaker known that (209) were the case, s/he could have less confusingly and more cooperatively said *John and Bill read some of the same books, but some different ones too*, or something equivalent. Thus, we take (209) to be only awkward, but crucially, not contradictory.

In the present analysis, the interaction between multiple "respective" predication with NCC, exemplified by sentences like the following, is similarly straightforward:

(213) Terry gave the same gift to Bill and Sue as a Christmas present on Thursday and as a New Year's gift on Saturday (respectively).

The full derivation, which combines the proof steps for the NCC/"respective" interaction and multiple "respective" readings already outlined, is given in (259) in section 5.6. We reproduce here the final translation and unpack it:

(214) $\mathbf{same}(\mathbf{gift})(\lambda X_\times . \mathbf{onTh}(\mathbf{asChP}(\mathbf{gave}(\pi_1(X_\times)(\mathbf{b})))) (\mathbf{t})$
$\qquad \wedge \mathbf{onS}(\mathbf{asNYG}(\mathbf{gave}(\pi_2(X_\times)(\mathbf{s}))))(\mathbf{t}))$
$\quad = \exists X_\times . \forall i\, \mathbf{gift}(\pi_i(X_\times)) \wedge \forall i \forall j [\pi_i(X_\times) = \pi_j(X_\times)] \wedge$
$\qquad \mathbf{onTh}(\mathbf{asChP}(\mathbf{gave}(\pi_1(X_\times))(\mathbf{b})))(\mathbf{t}) \wedge \mathbf{onS}(\mathbf{asNYG}(\mathbf{gave}(\pi_2(X_\times))(\mathbf{s})))(\mathbf{t})$

The present analysis also assigns intuitively correct truth conditions for sentences such as the following, where two symmetrical terms exhibit interdependency with each other without being mediated by a separate plural term (unlike (210b)):

(215) a. Different students bought different books.
　　　 b. The same student bought different books.

The derivation proceeds by abstracting over the subject and object positions, "respectivizing" the relation thus obtained, and then "quantifying-in" the symmetrical terms in the subject and object positions one by one. This yields the following translation for (215a):

(216) $\exists X_\times . \forall i\, \mathbf{student}(\pi_i(X_\times)) \wedge \forall i j [i \neq j \rightarrow \pi_i(X_\times) \neq \pi_j(X_\times)] \wedge$
$\quad \exists Y_\times . \forall i\, \mathbf{book}(\pi_i(Y_\times)) \wedge \forall i j [i \neq j \rightarrow \pi_i(Y_\times) \neq \pi_j(Y_\times)] \wedge \mathbf{resp}(\mathbf{bought})(X_\times)(Y_\times)$

This asserts the existence of a set of students and a set of books such that the buying relation is a bijection between these two sets. Thus, no two students bought the same book and no two books were bought by the same students. This corresponds to one of the intuitively available readings of the sentence. In section 5.4.2, we discuss a more complex type of reading for the same sentence according to which the sets of books that each student bought are different from one another, where, for any given pair of students s_1 and s_2, there could be a partial (but not total) overlap between the sets of books that s_1 and s_2 respectively bought.

Examples like (217), in which the universal quantifiers *every* and *each* interact with symmetrical predicates, can be analyzed by treating NPs containing universal quantifiers like *every/each N* as maximal pluralities satisfying the description N that are obligatorily associated with a distributive or "respective" operator (see also Barker [2007] for a similar idea, but one that is technically implemented in a somewhat different way).[11]

(217) {Every/Each} student read {the same book/a different book}.

The assumption that universal quantifiers in English (effectively) denote "sums" (or pluralities) is advocated by several authors, including Szabolcsi (1997), Landman (2000), Matthewson (2001) and Champollion (2010).[12] This assumption also accounts for the interactions between universal quantifiers and "respective" and summative predicates as exemplified by (173) from section 5.2.1.1. In the present setup, the obligatory "distributive" nature of *every* and *each* can be captured by specifying in their lexical entries that they take as arguments sentences missing product-type NPs. This can be done by syntactically encoding the semantic distinction between product-type and non-product-type NPs via some feature.[13]

The present analysis straightforwardly extends to scope interactions between symmetrical predicates and negation and quantifiers in examples like the following:

(218)   a.   John and Bill didn't read the same book.
        b.   John and Bill didn't read different books.
        c.   Every boy gave every girl a different poem.

(218a) has a reading (perhaps the most prominent one) which seems to intuitively mean the same thing as 'John and Bill read different books.' Similarly, (218b), again on its perhaps most prominent reading, seems to mean the same thing as 'John and Bill read the same book.' By having the negation scope over the symmetrical predicate (which is straightforward by adopting the analysis of auxiliaries that we proposed in chapter 3), we obtain the following translations for (218a) and (218b):

---

11. We take distributive readings to be derived by the **resp** operator we posit in our system (see footnote 7), following a proposal by Bekki (2006). Our assumption here is in the same spirit as G&K's suggestion of unifying the distributive and "respective" operators in their system.

12. Dotlacil (2010) objects to this idea by noting the infelicity of the following (the judgments are his):

(i)   a.   *Each boy each read a book.
      b.   *Each boy read a book each.
      c.   *Each boy talked to each other.

But the awkwardness of these examples seems to be due to the redundant marking of distributivity by the same word (albeit perhaps in distinct uses of it; compare, for example, the sentences in (i) with ??*All boys all went swimming*, which is degraded for precisely the same reason of redundancy). Thus, we do not take these data to provide a convincing counterevidence to the family of "universal as sum" type approaches.

13. One issue that remains is why the NP containing *different* is singular if the licensor is a distributive quantifier rather than a plural NP. In order to get our compositional mechanism to yield the right result, we need to assume that *a different book* in (217) denotes a tuple just like *different books*. We suspect that the singular marking here is a matter of morphological agreement with the licensor, but leave a detailed investigation of this matter for a future study.

(219) a. $\neg[\exists X_\times \forall i\, \textbf{book}(\pi_i(X_\times)) \wedge \forall i \forall j[\pi_i(X_\times) = \pi_j(X_\times)] \wedge$
$\textbf{read}(\pi_1(X_\times))(\textbf{j}) \wedge \textbf{read}(\pi_2(X_\times))(\textbf{b})]$

   b. $\neg[\exists X_\times \forall i\, \textbf{book}(\pi_i(X_\times)) \wedge \forall i \forall j[i \neq j \rightarrow \pi_i(X_\times) = \pi_j(X_\times)] \wedge$
$\textbf{read}(\pi_1(X_\times))(\textbf{j}) \wedge \textbf{read}(\pi_2(X_\times))(\textbf{b})]$

It may appear that these truth conditions do not quite match the intuitive meanings of the sentences. But note that both (218a) and (218b) seem to implicate that both John and Bill read at least one book (we do not attempt here to characterize the nature of this implication, but given that it is available in the nonnegative counterparts of (218a) and (218b), and moreover seems to survive other presupposition holes [such as conditionals], this implication is most likely a presupposition of *same/different*). By taking these implications into account, the intuitively observed meanings of (218a) and (218b) do in fact follow from (219a) and (219b).

As noted by Bumford and Barker (2013), (218c) is ambiguous between two readings: if the subject quantifier scopes over the object quantifier, it means that no boy gave the same poem to multiple girls, whereas if the object quantifier scopes over the subject quantifier, the sentence means that no girl received the same poem from multiple boys. Since our approach has a fully general mechanism for scope-taking for quantifiers and symmetrical predicates (via hypothetical reasoning involving $\upharpoonright$), this scope ambiguity is straightforwardly predicted.

We now turn to an analysis of summative predicates such as *a total of $10,000*. The approach to symmetrical predicates above uses the **resp** operator to create pairings between corresponding elements of two tuples and then imposes a further condition on one of the two tuples involved. The (in)equality relation incorporated in this analysis is only one possible condition that could be so imposed, however; theoretically there are an unlimited number of other possible conditions, and we could expect a certain variety in the way natural language grammars exploit such possibilities. It turns out that we indeed see evidence of exactly this type of variety (for example, *an average of X* is yet another such expression, as discussed by Kennedy and Stanley [2008]). In particular, in examples like (220) involving summative predicates, the tuple elements are required to (together) satisfy a quantity condition: taking $n^\$$ and $m^\$$ to be the tuple elements denoting amounts of money, then, roughly speaking, (220) asserts that $\textbf{spent}(\textbf{r}, n^\$)$ and $\textbf{lose}(\textbf{l}, m^\$)$ and that $n^\$ + m^\$ = \$10,000$.

(220) Robin spent and Leslie lost a total of $10,000.

In other words, the condition "adds up to $10,000" is imposed on the members of the tuple, instead of the (in)equality or similarity relations.

To capture this idea, we once again treat the relevant expressions as GQs over product-type terms of type $S \upharpoonright (S \upharpoonright NP)$, assigning to *a total of* the following meaning:

(221) $\lambda\varphi\lambda\sigma.\sigma(a \circ \text{total} \circ \text{of} \circ \varphi); \lambda S\lambda P.\exists X_{\times_n} \sum_{1 \leq i \leq n} \pi_i(X_{\times_n}) = S \wedge P(X_{\times_n}); S\!\restriction\!(S\!\restriction\!NP)$

This operator takes a sum S and a predicate P (over product-type terms) as arguments and asserts the existence of some tuple $X_{\times_n}$ where the sum of all of the elements of $X_{\times_n}$ equals S and $X_{\times_n}$ itself satisfies the predicate P. Since P is a predicate of product-type terms, this effectively means that $X_{\times_n}$ enters into a "respective" relation with some other product-type term in the sentence. The tuple $X_{\times_n}$ can be thought of as a possible partitioning of the sum S into subportions that can respectively be related to the other tuple(s), which, in the case of (220), is contributed by the plural NP.

(220) is then analyzed in a way parallel to the symmetrical predicate example above. We first derive a sentence in which a hypothetically assumed tuple-denoting expression (φ_1; $X_\times$; NP) enters into a "respective" predication with an overt conjoined term (which, in this case, is a "nonconstituent" *John spent and Bill lost*; for details, see the full derivation in (260)):

(222) $\text{john} \circ \text{spent} \circ \text{and} \circ \text{bill} \circ \text{lost} \circ \varphi_1; \mathbf{spent}(\mathbf{j}, \pi_1(X_\times)) \wedge \mathbf{lost}(\mathbf{b}, \pi_2(X_\times)); S$

By abstracting over $X_\times$, we obtain an expression of type $S\!\restriction\!NP$. This is then given as an argument to the GQ-type $S\!\restriction\!(S\!\restriction\!NP)$ expression denoted by *a total of \$10,000*, and we obtain the final translation in (223), which captures the intuitively correct meaning of the sentence:

(223) $\mathbf{total}(\$10k)(\lambda X_\times.\mathbf{spent}(\mathbf{j}, \pi_1(X_\times)) \wedge \mathbf{lost}(\mathbf{b}, \pi_2(X_\times)))$
$= \exists X_{\times_2}.\pi_1(X_{\times_2}) \oplus \pi_2(X_{\times_2}) = \$10k \wedge \mathbf{spent}(\mathbf{j}, \pi_1(X_{\times_2})) \wedge \mathbf{lost}(\mathbf{b}, \pi_2(X_{\times_2}))$

5.4 Comparisons and Larger Issues

5.4.1 Comparisons with Related Approaches

In the previous section, we have proposed a unified analysis of "respective," symmetrical, and summative predicates. The key components of our analysis are the treatment of expressions involving conjunction as denoting tuples and the flexible syntax-semantics interface of Hybrid TLCG. As demonstrated above, in our analysis, hypothetical reasoning for relating the relevant tuples in the "respective" manner that underlies the semantics of these expressions interacts fully systematically with hypothetical reasoning for forming syntactic constituents that enter into that "respective" predication. While our proposal builds on several key insights from previous proposals on these phenomena, we are unaware of any other proposal, at any level of formal explicitness, which accounts for the same range of data for which we have provided an explicit account. In this section, we present three previous approaches, namely, Gawron and Kehler (2004), Barker (2007, 2012) and Chaves (2012), that are closely related to our own and discuss their key insights as well as limitations.

We focus on these three approaches here since, as we discuss below, we build on and combine key ideas that are most explicitly embodied in these proposals. But before moving on, we would like to briefly comment on other previous proposals. As for symmetrical predicates in particular, there are various accounts that contain important insights but which are not explicitly formalized, such as Dowty (1985), Carlson (1987) and Oehrle (1996). See Barker (2007) for a useful summary of these previous proposals. Barker's proposal and our own refinement of it can be thought of as an attempt to explicitly formalize the analytic intuitions embodied in these earlier works.

A more formally developed analysis of symmetrical predicates has been offered by Brasoveanu (2011). Though technically implemented in a different way, Brasoveanu's (2011) analysis of *different* embodies essentially the same analytic intuition as ours (see also Dotlacil 2010; Bumford and Barker 2013). Brasoveanu accounts for the pairwise matching between the sets of objects designated by the NP containing *different* and the correlate NP (i.e., a quantifier or a plural) via a device in an extended DRT called "plural information states," which are formally sets of assignment functions and which can be thought of as stack-like objects. There is an obvious relation between tuples and stacks in that they are both formal constructs that keep track of the internal structures of complex objects with some ordering imposed on their elements.[14]

Moltmann (1992) perhaps deserves a special comment as well. In this work, Moltmann develops an approach to coordination which is essentially a version of multidominance analysis. This allows her to analyze interactions between RNR and symmetrical predicates such as the following via the notion of "implicit coordination," where *John* and *Mary*, "parallel" elements within conjuncts in RNR, are effectively treated as if they were coordinated for the purpose of interpretation of the shared element *the same book*.

(224) John read, and Mary reviewed, the same book.

This approach raises many questions about compositionality and the architecture of the syntax-semantics interface (in particular, it is unclear what exactly is the status of the "implicitly coordinated" *John and Mary* within the overall interpretation of the sentence). Moreover, since Moltmann's (1992) approach and ours start from totally different sets of assumptions, comparing the two directly does not seem to be very useful. However, there are two points which seem to be worth noting. First, although the key underlying intuitions are similar, Moltmann takes the *syntactic* coordinate structure to provide the basis for "respective" readings (and related phenomena). Following authors

---

14. Since Brasoveanu's approach and our own primarily focus on different sets of issues pertaining to the semantics of symmetrical predicates, a direct comparison does not seem to be very meaningful, but we would nevertheless like to note that it is unclear whether Brasoveanu's DRT-based system extends in any straightforward way to the interactions of symmetrical predicates (and related phenomena) and NCC.

such as G&K, we take this assumption to be implausible, since this account does not extend in any straightforward way to "respective" readings of non-conjoined plural NPs. The other point which seems worth noting is that, unlike RNR, DCC seems less straightforward to analyze in a multidominance-type approach. The difficulty essentially lies in the fact that, unlike RNR, the shared string in DCC involves two separate constituents. It is unclear how the semantics of the sentence can be properly assigned in such a complex multidominance structure (especially in cases involving interactions with "respective," symmetrical, and summative predicates). Moltmann does not discuss how her approach may be extended to DCC, and, so far as we are aware, this issue has not been addressed in any of the more recent variants of multidominance analyses of coordination such as Bachrach and Katzir (2007, 2008).

Finally, we would like to briefly comment on event-based approaches, along the lines, for example, of Lasersohn (1992). One might think that, in an event-based approach, by introducing the notion of "event sums," many of the examples discussed above can be treated without tweaking the notion of compositionality and representing the meanings of conjoined predicates directly as a tuple (or sum) of atomic predicates. We do not think that this type of approach is general enough for the problem at hand. Note in particular that "respective" readings (and related phenomena) are possible with non-eventive predicates such as the following:[15]

(225) The numbers nine and six are odd and even, respectively.

In order to extend an event sum–based account to examples like this, one would need to assume an abstract conceptualization of the notion of event devoid of any independent empirical justification.[16] Moreover, in examples like (225), the issue of event individuation, an inherent problem of event-based semantics in general, seems to become particularly unwieldy. Given the murkiness of these issues, we find an event-based approach less than ideal for the class of phenomena considered in this chapter.

5.4.1.1 Gawron and Kehler (2004)

As noted in the previous section, our own analysis builds directly on Gawron and Kehler's (2004) (G&K's) proposal in the core semantic analysis of "respective" readings. The key difference between our proposal and G&K's is that G&K take the ordering of elements in the denotations of plural or conjoined expressions to be given by an external contextual parameter of sequencing

---

15. Note also that the adverb *alternately*, on which Lasersohn (1992) focuses in his event sum–based approach, similarly allows the relevant reading with non-eventive predicates:

(i) The coefficients in this expansion of the function are alternately positive and negative integers.

16. See also Barker (2007, 418) for essentially the same point in connection to a similar example with *same*.

functions, whereas in our analysis, this information is directly encoded in the denotation of the expressions themselves in the form of tuples. With the ordering information removed from the denotations of the expressions themselves, G&K can model the meanings of plural and conjoined expressions in terms of sums, in line with one established tradition in the literature on plurality (cf., e.g., Link 1983, Lasersohn 1988, and Schwarzschild 1996, but see also Landman 1989). As we discuss below, this tuple/sum difference in the two approaches has some important implications when extending the analysis to symmetrical predicates. Another, perhaps less essential (but nonetheless important) difference between the two approaches is that G&K's proposal is formulated in a strictly phrase structure–based syntax-semantics interface. For this reason, their analysis, at least in its original form, does not extend straightforwardly to interactions with NCC.[17]

G&K's approach presupposes that the argument of the sequencing function is a sum and not an atom. This assumption is necessary in their analysis for ensuring that the right matching of elements is established between the two sums in the case of "respective" readings, but it causes a problem for at least a subset of symmetrical predicates. Recall from the previous section that the symmetrical predicate *the same* imposes an equality relation among each member of the tuple. If we recast this analysis in a sum-based analysis à la G&K, then the n-tuple denoted by *the same N* that is to be related to another n-tuple in a pairwise manner collapses to a single object, since a sum of multiple "tokens" of the same object collapses to that object itself (i.e., $a \oplus a = a$ by definition). But then, it would be predicted that *John and Bill read the same book* is infelicitous since in G&K's analysis, the sequencing function is defined only for sums that have proper subparts (lifting this condition would incorrectly admit into their analysis examples like #*Sue and Bob like Fred, respectively*).[18]

---

17. There is an additional technical problem in G&K's proposal. Their analysis, in which "respective" readings are analyzed via a series of successive applications of the distributive and "respective" operators, turns out to be rather unwieldy in cases such as the following ((ib) is the same example as (192)):

(i) a. John and Bill read and reviewed the book, respectively.
     b. John and Bill sent the bomb and the letter to the president yesterday, respectively.

The problem essentially is that the distributive operator that G&K posit (which is identical in all relevant respects to the distributive operator standardly assumed in the formal semantics literature) can only distribute a functor over the components of a sum of argument objects, not vice versa. But the analysis of (ia) requires distributing the object argument to the conjoined functor *read and reviewed*. See Kubota and Levine (2014b) for a more detailed discussion of this problem and possible solutions for it (the most straightforward of which is to extend the phrase structure–based setup of G&K to an architecture like our own, which recognizes hypothetical reasoning fully generally).

18. Gawron and Kehler (2004, 174) claim that this assumption explains the ill-formedness of the following:

(i) ??Sue and Bob like Fred and Fred, respectively.

But note that (i) is just a clumsy way of saying the same thing as the following:

An essentially analogous problem arises with *similar*. The similarity condition that *similar* imposes on its tuple elements does not exclude a possibility that the elements are completely identical. Suppose, for example, Alice suggests to her collaborator Betty:

(226) Ok, Betty, let's work on these problems separately first, and then if we run into similar problems, let's get together and discuss.

They later confer by email and discover that they are stuck on exactly the same problem. Alice refuses to get together and discuss and insists that they keep working separately, since they've run into exactly the same problem, not similar problems. We think that Alice would be a perverse person in such a situation. Thus, the implication of 'similar but not the same' is arguably a Gricean implicature. But then, this means that if the tuple elements happen to be identical, a G&K-based analysis predicts sentences containing *similar* to be infelicitous. In other words, (the *if* clause of) (226) is predicted to be infelicitous just in case Alice and Betty run into exactly the same problem. This does not seem to be a correct prediction.

It then seems fair to conclude that G&K's sum-based approach does not extend straightforwardly to the analysis of symmetrical predicates. As we have discussed in section 5.1, we take the parallel between "respective" readings on the one hand and symmetrical and summative predicates on the other to be robust. Thus, in the absence of an explicit and fully general analysis of symmetrical predicates in a sum-based approach (in this connection, see also the discussion of the empirical problems of Barker's [2007, 2012] approach in the next section), we take our tuple-based analysis to be an improvement over G&K's original sum-based analysis of "respective" readings.

5.4.1.2 Barker (2007, 2012)   Barker (2007) proposes an analysis of symmetrical predicates via the notion of "parasitic scope," which captures the syntax-semantics interface underlying the compositional semantics of these predicates quite elegantly. In his analysis, *same* receives the following translation:

(227) $\lambda \mathscr{F} \lambda X \exists \mathfrak{f} \forall x <_a X . \mathscr{F}(\mathfrak{f})(x)$

Here, $\mathscr{F}$ is of type $(et \rightarrow et) \rightarrow et$. That is, $\mathscr{F}$ denotes a relation between adjectives (i.e., modifiers of common nouns) on the one hand and individuals on the other, with X a variable over sums of individuals and $\mathfrak{f}$ a variable over *choice functions* (a choice function is a function that takes a set as argument and returns as output a singleton set containing a member of that set). Roughly speaking, *same* converts a relation between functors on some property on the one hand and an individual on the other into a re-

---

(ii) Sue and Bob like Fred.

Thus, we see no reason for excluding (i) in the combinatoric component of grammar.

lation between inhabitants of that property on the one hand and sums of individuals on the other, guaranteeing a unique inhabitant of that property to which each individual in the sum is mapped. Thus, for example, in the case of (228), an abstraction first on a variable over individual types and then over adjective types yields the relation $\lambda \xi \lambda y.\mathbf{read}(\iota(\xi(\mathbf{book}))(y))$.

(228) John and Bill read the same book.

The *same* operator in (227) then maps this relation to a relation between the sum of individuals $\mathbf{j} \oplus \mathbf{b}$ on the one hand and a single element of the set **book** such that each member of the sum is in the **read** relation to that element.

It should be clear from the above that our own analysis takes Barker's work as its basis. In particular, we take Barker's double abstraction treatment of *same* as the core of our own compositional analysis, though the specific semantic analyses differ in important ways. We aim at a unitary analysis of symmetrical, "respective," and summative predicates; hence, the key semantic commonality we have identified in these three cases—the mapping relationship between elements of two (or more) different composite data structures—correspond to a single source, the **resp** operator, which crosscuts the specific semantic (and pragmatic) properties of the three. By contrast, in Barker's analysis, the operation corresponding to our **resp** is directly encoded in the lexical meaning of symmetrical predicates, effectively ruling out a unified analysis of the larger class of predicates discussed above.

But quite apart from this issue, the lack of a recursive mechanism that keeps track of the structure of a sum/tuple-type object entails severe empirical difficulties when multiple instances of symmetrical predicates are present. We illustrate this problem with (229), for which Barker's analysis yields a particularly strange semantics.[19]

(229) John and Bill gave different things to different people.

Barker (2007) gives the semantics of *different* as in (230),

(230) $\lambda \mathscr{F} \lambda X \forall \mathfrak{g} \forall z, v <_a X.\ [\mathscr{F}(\mathfrak{g})(z) \wedge \mathscr{F}(\mathfrak{g})(v)] \rightarrow [z = v]$

with which the translation in (231b) is assigned to (231a) (ε here is the meaning of the indefinite article *a*; since the choice function returns a singleton set, the choice of the article [between *the* for *same* and *a* for *different*] is immaterial in Barker's analysis).

(231) a. John and Bill read a different book.

---

19. Barker (2012) partially addresses the multiple symmetrical predicate issue by revising the translation for *same* in Barker (2007) slightly, removing the distributive operator from the meaning of *same* (and instead assuming that it is implicit in the lexical meaning of the verb). However, this approach does not seem to work for the case of *different* (within the set of assumptions that Barker [2007, 2012] makes), and Barker (2012) remains silent about cases like (229).

    b. $\forall \mathfrak{f} \forall z, v <_a \mathbf{j} \oplus \mathbf{b}[\mathbf{read}(\varepsilon(\mathfrak{f}(\mathbf{book})))(z) \wedge \mathbf{read}(\varepsilon(\mathfrak{f}(\mathbf{book})))(v)] \rightarrow [z = v]$

To paraphrase, (231b) says that whatever choice function one chooses, the only way in which two (potentially distinct) people out of the set $\{\mathbf{j}, \mathbf{b}\}$ read the book that the choice function returns is when the two people are the same ones. In other words, there is no single common book that John and Bill both read.

    Assuming Barker's semantics for *different*, and following the procedure for multiple *same* discussed in Barker (2012), we wind up with the translation for the VP for (229) in (232).

(232) $\lambda U \forall w, y <_a U \forall \mathfrak{f} \forall \mathfrak{g}$
$$\lambda W[\forall z, v <_a W[\mathbf{gave}(\varepsilon(\mathfrak{f}(\mathbf{thing})))(\varepsilon(\mathfrak{g}(\mathbf{person})))(z) \wedge$$
$$\mathbf{gave}(\varepsilon(\mathfrak{f}(\mathbf{thing})))(\varepsilon(\mathfrak{g}(\mathbf{person})))(v)] \rightarrow [z = v]](w) \wedge$$
$$\lambda W[\forall z, v <_a W[\mathbf{gave}(\varepsilon(\mathfrak{f}(\mathbf{thing})))(\varepsilon(\mathfrak{g}(\mathbf{person})))(z) \wedge$$
$$\mathbf{gave}(\varepsilon(\mathfrak{f}(\mathbf{thing})))(\varepsilon(\mathfrak{g}(\mathbf{person})))(v)] \rightarrow [z = v]](y) \rightarrow [y = w]$$

We see here a subtyping mismatch problem whose resolution leads to a severe mischaracterization of the truth conditions of the sentence. The problem in a nutshell is that each token of *different* introduces an abstraction on a sum type, each of whose atoms are to be related to a member of some set of entities which is identical to no other member of that set. But only the wider-scoping token of *different* will get an actual sum (in this case, $\mathbf{john} \oplus \mathbf{bill}$) supplied as its argument; the narrower-scoping token will be able to apply only to the universally bound atomic elements introduced by the wider-scoping instance of *different*. The only way we can see to resolve this apparent incoherence in the semantics of such examples is to treat the "part-whole" relation $<_a$ as simple equality in the case where the second relatum is an atom, as indeed intimated in Barker (2012) in his treatment of the *same/same* examples. But the assumption that $x <_a u$ entails $u = x$ has, as a corollary, the consequence that $x, y <_a u$ entails $u = x = y$. The result is that (232) reduces to (233):

(233) $\lambda U \forall w, y <_a U \forall \mathfrak{f} \forall \mathfrak{g} \, [[\mathbf{gave}(\varepsilon(\mathfrak{f}(\mathbf{thing})))(\varepsilon(\mathfrak{g}(\mathbf{person})))(w)] \rightarrow [w = w] \wedge$
      $[\mathbf{gave}(\varepsilon(\mathfrak{f}(\mathbf{thing})))(\varepsilon(\mathfrak{g}(\mathbf{person})))(y)] \rightarrow [y = y]] \rightarrow [y = w]$

But this result makes no sense. What we have in (233) is an implication, whose antecedent is a tautology (itself composed of a conjunction of tautologies of the same general form $\psi \rightarrow (\alpha = \alpha)$), which means that the whole conditional statement is equivalent to its consequent $y = w$. The variables w and y range over the atoms of the sum that (233) takes as its argument. Thus, it is predicted that (229) means that John and Bill are the same person.[20]

---

20. Similar difficulties arise in an only slightly less striking fashion in *John and Bill put the same object in different boxes*, where Barker's analysis predicts that on the inverse scoping of the two symmetrical

In summary, Barker's analysis of symmetrical predicates loses generality in two directions, and these problems, we believe, essentially derive from the same limitation in his analysis. On the one hand, unlike G&K's and our proposal, Barker's analysis lacks a mechanism for making the internal structure of a sum simultaneously visible to multiple tokens of *same/different*. For this reason, it does not extend to multiple *same/different* sentences fully generally. On the other hand, the fundamentally parallel semantic action of "respective" interpretations and summative predicates cannot be captured in Barker's implementation because the crucial sum-to-individual mapping is directly encoded in the lexical meaning of the symmetrical predicate operators in his proposal. To remove these obstacles, a different strategy seems to be needed, in which a mapping between composite objects is mediated by a separate general operator that allows for recursive application, as in G&K's and our own proposal.[21]

5.4.1.3 Chaves (2012)   Chaves's (2012) account has the virtue of identifying "respective," symmetrical, and summative interpretations as unitary phenomena (see especially pp. 319–321)—a view we inherit in our own analysis. The mechanism Chaves proposes for the compositional analysis of these predicates is, however, fundamentally different from our approach; Chaves takes "respective" readings in cases such as *Bill and Tom invited Sue and Anne to the party (respectively)* to be nothing more than particular instances of the so-called cumulative reading (Scha 1981), along the lines discussed in section 5.1.

But as noted by Gawron and Kehler (2004) in their critique of Schwarzschild's (1996) analysis of "respective" readings, such an approach does not extend to examples like (234) (= (153)), in which one of the sums related in the "respective" manner is a sum of predicates rather than a sum of entities:

(234) John and Bill sang and danced, respectively.   (= 'John sang and Bill danced')

Chaves therefore proposes the translation in (235) for the coordination marker *and*, which, according to him, has the effect of providing two possible interpretations for (234) and similar examples (we have modified Chaves's [2012] original translation

---

predicates it is impossible for John to have put *any* object in a box that Bill put some other, distinct object in. While the surface scope (*same > different*) does yield the correct interpretation for this example, the picture changes when the subject is singular rather than plural: in the case of *John put the same object in different boxes*, the surface scoping yields a tautology predicting that the sentence is true in all conceivable circumstances.

21. Given the parallel semantic action of symmetrical predicates on the one hand and "respective" readings on the other, it is worth observing that Kubota's (2015) extension of Barker's (2007) analysis of *same* to "respective" readings fails to generalize to multiple "respective" readings. The problem in these cases is the same dilemma with type mismatch blocking recursive application of operators: after the first application of the "respective" operator, the result is a boolean conjunction whose parts are no longer accessible as sum components, making further application of the same operator in principle impossible.

slightly to accommodate it with the description of the *and* operator he gives in the text—note that the event variable *e* isn't existentially bound in our reformulation; nothing crucially hinges on this modification).

(235) $\lambda P \lambda Q \lambda z_0 \ldots \lambda z_n \lambda e. [e = (e_1 \oplus e_2) \wedge Q(x_0) \ldots (x_n)(e_1) \wedge P(y_0) \ldots (y_n)(e_2) \wedge z_0 = (x_0 \oplus y_0) \wedge \ldots \wedge z_n = (x_n \oplus y_n)]$

This operator conjoins two relations, and either identifies (i.e., if $x_n = y_n$) or distributes (i.e., if $x_n \neq y_n$) their conjoined shared dependents. With (235), (234) receives the following interpretation (after the event variable *e* is existentially closed):

(236) $\exists e''. e'' = (e_1 \oplus e_2) \wedge \mathbf{sang}(x_0)(e_1) \wedge \mathbf{danced}(y_0)(e_2) \wedge (\mathbf{j} \oplus \mathbf{b}) = (x_0 \oplus y_0)$

The idea is that if $x_n = y_n$, then both John and Bill sang and both danced, whereas if $x_n \neq y_n$, then either John danced and Bill sang or Bill danced and John sang. The adverb *respectively* imposes a further constraint on the interpretation obtained above, to force the pairings $\mathbf{j} = x_0, \mathbf{b} = y_0$ (which effectively restricts the interpretation to the $x_n \neq y_n$ case).

Note that, in this analysis, except for complicating the meaning of *and*, no special mechanism is needed in the grammar to license "respective" readings (and related phenomena), giving us an overall very simple analysis of a complex class of phenomena. But the success of this approach is only apparent; once we extend the data pool beyond the most simple class of examples (such as (234)), Chaves's analysis quickly becomes problematic. NCC/"respectively" interaction examples such as (237) illustrate the point persuasively:

(237) I bet $50 and $100 with John on the football game and (with) Mary on the basketball game (respectively).

Since (237), by virtue of its nonconstituent conjuncts, cannot be directly interpreted, the syntactic source of this sentence must be presumed to arise under the prosodic ellipsis analysis Chaves explicitly assumes (as per Beavers and Sag 2004; Chaves 2008; and Hofmeister 2010; see section 4.3.2), with (238) the necessary input to the semantic interpretation:[22]

---

22. Chaves (2012) extensively relies on the ellipsis strategy, even in cases like the following that do not involve nonconstituent coordination:

(i) Different newspapers are running conflicting reports. The *Guardian* and the *Telegraph* reported that Michael Phelps won the silver medal and the gold medal respectively.   (Chaves 2012, 316)

According to Chaves (2012), the "respective" reading of (i) is obtained from the underlying structure in (ii):

(ii) The *Guardian* and the *Telegraph* reported [that Michael Phelps won the silver medal] and [~~that Michael Phelps won~~ the gold medal] respectively.

(238) I bet $50 and $100 with John on the football game and ~~(I) bet $50 and $100~~ (with) Mary on the basketball game (respectively).

No cumulative interpretations are available for the conjoined clauses or verb phrases in (238). Thus, the source of the "respective" reading in (237) must arise from the action of the *and* operator in (235). But the necessary conditions on *and* are not satisfied in (238). In order for Chaves's setup to work as required, it is crucial that the arguments corresponding to x_k, y_k be actual conjuncts, but this critical condition is not fulfilled in (238), where the terms that need to enter into the "respective" relation belong to completely different clauses/VPs, appearing (on the surface string) to be parts of con-joined expressions only via the strictly prosodic deletion operation which yields the surface string (237). The operator in (235) therefore provides no account of how the "respective" readings arise in examples of this type.

In a sense, Chaves's proposal can be thought of as an attempt to lexicalize (in the meanings of conjoined predicates) the effects of the "respective" operator of the sort posited in G&K's and our approach. While a strictly lexical approach may be attractive if it can handle all the relevant data uniformly, the discussion above suggests that such an approach is not general enough.

5.4.2 A Note on the Treatment of Plurality

One might wonder how the tuple-based analysis of "respective" readings and related phenomena presented above extends (or does not extend) to other interpretations of plural and conjoined expressions, such as collective and cumulative readings. These phenomena are themselves quite complex, and each of them deserves a treatment on its own. Thus, addressing them fully is clearly beyond the scope of our coverage in this chapter. But given that the phenomena treated above are clearly related to the more general empirical domain of plurality, some comments seem to be necessary, and we will try to explicate our position here.

In a comparison of our tuple-based approach with a sum-based alternative (which is more standard, at least for the treatment of plurality), it is useful to distinguish three properties of different types of formal objects that are (or can be) used for modeling entities having complex internal structures, so as to avoid confusion about points of (non-)controversy. Tuples have more complex structures than sums or sets in that (i) they have ordering, (ii) they allow for identical elements to appear twice (iterability), and (iii) they can be nested (nestability). A comparison of different data structures with respect to these properties is as follows:

(239)

	Ordering	Iterability	Nestability
Tuple	Yes	Yes	Yes
Multiset	No	Yes	Yes
Set	No	No	Yes
Sum	No	No	No

To state the conclusion first, the only property we crucially need for our unified analysis of the three phenomena is iterability. We have chosen tuples over multisets purely for the sake of simplifying the technical exposition, and there is no fundamental conceptual or empirical reason for us to favor a tuple-based formulation over a multiset-based formulation. As we discuss below, many apparently problematic aspects of our analysis can be eliminated by adopting a multiset-based reformulation.

Nestability also complicates the analysis of plurals in a nontrivial manner. Here, we have to say that this is an unfortunate consequence. As we have already discussed in relation to G&K's proposal, we have adopted tuples/multisets instead of sums since iterability is crucially needed for extending the analysis to symmetrical predicates. Ideally, we would want some formal object with iterability but not nestability. But as the table in (239) makes clear, there is no known formal object that has the right property, at least none that we are aware of.[23] Thus, it seems that we have to live with the artificial complication introduced by the nestability property of tuples/multisets, that is, the so-called overrepresentation problem in the plurality literature (discussed below). However, we do not find this to be a serious problem, since overrepresentation, by its very nature, does not constitute any empirical problem. It only means that the theoretical distinctions that one makes are *unnecessary*, and eliminating these distinctions can always be done uniquely and unambiguously.

Regarding the overrepresentation issue, we find Schwarzschild's (1996) argument against groups convincing. The argument runs roughly as follows. An example like (240) apparently unambiguously means that the separation was done by kind. But things are not so clear-cut once we take into consideration more complex examples like (241).

(240) The cows and the pigs were separated.

(241) a. The cows and the pigs were separated by age.

---

23. We could, of course, add constraints on multisets or tuples so that no nesting is allowed. This can be done by explicitly imposing typing restrictions on membership. But again, we have not chosen to implement this explicitly here since this option does not seem to be very different from choosing tuples or multisets as the underlying mathematical structure but not making use of their nestability property.

b. The animals were separated by age. That is, the cows and the pigs were separated.

In a world in which there are only cows and pigs, the second sentence of (241b) means the same thing as (241a). Schwarzschild (1996) concludes from this that the subgrouping of a sum in sentences like (240) is provided by a contextual parameter (which he calls "covers") rather than explicitly represented at the level of semantics. It indeed seems that, if one limits one's attention to the treatment of plurality (in the nominal domain), the overrepresentation problem of the group-based approach (which our tuple/multiset-based approach inherits) speaks in favor of Schwarzschild's neo-Linkean sum-based approach.

There are, however, other points of consideration that come into play once we extend our empirical domain to a wider range of linguistic phenomena. First, as noted by G&K, though Schwarzschild (1996) sketches an extension of his cover-based analysis to the NP-NP cases of "respective" readings (e.g., (242a)), his analysis does not generalize fully to other types of "respective" readings (e.g., (242b); see the discussion of Chaves's [2012] proposal above).

(242) a. John and Bill married Mary and Sue, respectively.
      b. John and Bill walked and talked, respectively.

It is unclear whether an extension of Schwarzschild's (1996) cover-based analysis is motivated for examples like (242b) and, more generally, for a still larger (and more complex) data set encompassing examples involving interactions with NCC such as (156c,d).

Another, perhaps more important, point is that, as we have discussed in section 5.4.1.1, a tuple-based analysis enables a straightforward extension to the analysis of symmetrical predicates, whereas a sum-based analysis doesn't. To be fair, Schwarzschild's (1996) proposal was not intended to cover symmetrical predicates, but to the extent that one finds the parallel between "respective" readings and symmetrical predicates (of the sort noted in the previous section) to be intriguing, a unified analysis seems more preferable.

For these reasons, we tentatively conclude that overrepresentation in the domain of nominal plurality is a price that has to be paid in view of the overall generality of the analysis in a wider empirical domain. We recognize that this is a potentially controversial claim but believe that the burden of proof is on those who would subscribe to the neo-Linkean sum-based treatment of plurality to develop an explicit account that has the same empirical coverage as ours (or else show that the empirical generalization that we have drawn across the three phenomena is in fact a false generalization).

Coming back to the "ordering" issue, note first that, as noted by Lasersohn (1988, 87–88), representing the meanings of conjoined NPs in the form of tuples complicates the semantics of collective readings in examples like the following:

(243) Lennon and McCartney wrote "Across the Universe" and "Sexy Sadie."
       (= 'They both coauthored')

The ordering of elements doesn't make any truth-conditional difference for collective readings, and to capture this fact on a tuple-based approach, one would either need to write a bunch of meaning postulates for the lexical meanings of verbs that induce collective readings or posit an empty operator that eliminates the ordering information by converting tuples to sums. This indeed seems to be a purely artificial complication introduced in the theory.

Even more problematic for the tuple-based approach are examples like (244), where an order-insensitive bijective relation is established between two conjoined expressions:

(244) a. The front and the back of the ship are called the bow and the stern, but which is which?
       b. We know houses four and five are the Swede and the German, but which is which?   (Chaves 2012)

To account for these examples, a tuple-based analysis would have to assume an operator that reorders the elements of a tuple and underspecifies the ordering.

In view of the above observations, we think that reformulating our analysis by replacing tuples with multisets and relocating the ordering information to a contextual parameter along the lines of G&K's proposal is ultimately more plausible (at least for the treatment of nominal plurality). Multisets are different from tuples in that they do not encode ordering (but the two are similar in not collapsing two occurrences of an identical element to a single object; thus, this reformulation retains the extendability to symmetrical predicates), and, for this reason, examples like those in (243) and (244) become unproblematic. However, we have refrained from reformulating the analysis presented above since relocating the ordering information to a contextual parameter makes the formulation of the recursive compositional mechanism of "respective" predication nontrivially more complex. It should, however, be kept in mind that this decision is purely for expository ease.

Finally, we would like to discuss briefly how one might go about extending the present tuple- (or multiset-)based analysis of "respective" readings to cumulative predication. With a slight extension, the tuple-based analysis of "respective" predication that we have proposed offers a simple way of characterizing cumulative readings. Specifically, all we need to do is to assume that tuples corresponding to plural terms can contain elements that are themselves sums of individuals rather than just atomic individuals. We sketch here a basic analysis of (245) and then discuss some implications.

(245) A total of four students read a total of five books.

Assuming that we have four students $s1, s2, s3, s4$ and five books $b1, b2, b3, b4, b5$ and that the reading relation that holds between the two sets is given by the following,

(246) $\{ \langle s1, b1 \rangle, \langle s1, b2 \rangle, \langle s2, b1 \rangle, \langle s2, b2 \rangle, \langle s2, b3 \rangle, \langle s3, b2 \rangle, \langle s3, b4 \rangle, \langle s4, b5 \rangle \}$

then the situation can be modeled by a "respective" predication between two tuples $X_\times = \langle s1, s2, s3, s4 \rangle$ and $Y_\times = \langle b1 \oplus b2, b1 \oplus b2 \oplus b3, b2 \oplus b4, b5 \rangle$. Thus, the following translation that is assigned to the sentence compositionally by the present analysis suffices to capture the cumulative reading of (245):

(247) $\exists S. |S| = 4 \wedge \mathbf{student}(S) \wedge \exists X_\times \sum_i^n \pi_i(X_\times) = S \wedge \exists S'. |S'| = 5 \wedge \mathbf{book}(S') \wedge$
$\exists Y_\times. \sum_i^n \pi_i(Y_\times) = S' \wedge \mathbf{resp}(X_\times)(Y_\times)(\mathbf{read})$

This extension offers a promising approach to characterizing the more complex reading for sentences involving two occurrences of *different*, such as the following (cf. section 5.3.2).

(248) Different students read different books.

The relevant reading links students to sets of books that they read and asserts that for no two students, the sets of books that they respectively read are completely identical. Thus, (248) is true on this reading in a situation (call it situation 1) described in (246) but false in a situation where $s1$ read $b3$ in addition (call it situation 2), since in situation 2, the sets of books that $s1$ and $s2$ read are exactly identical. By assuming that the tuple of students consists of atomic students but that the tuple of books can consist of sums of books, we can model this reading with our **resp** operator and the semantics for *different* already introduced above. The sentence comes out true in situation 1 but false in situation 2, since, according to the semantics of *different*, each element of the book tuple needs to be distinct from each other, a condition satisfied in situation 1 but not in situation 2.

The analysis of cumulativity sketched above, although preliminary, is promising in that it already extends straightforwardly to quite complex examples such as the following, a type of sentence originally discussed by Schein (1993), where cumulativity and distributivity interact:

(249) A total of three ATMs gave a total of one thousand customers two new passwords.

There is a reading of this sentence in which *three ATMs* is related to *one thousand customers* in the cumulative manner, and *two new passwords* distributes over each ATM-customer pair (thus involving two thousand distinct passwords issued).

To derive this reading, all we need to assume is that the plural term *two new passwords* denotes an ordinary cardinal quantifier that scopes below the "respective" operator that establishes the cumulative relation between the other two plural terms (by alternating scope, we can account for other scope readings for the sentence too). The full derivation is given in (261) in section 5.6. The translation obtained is as follows:

(250) $\textbf{total}(\textbf{3-atms})(\lambda X_\times.\textbf{total}(\textbf{1k-cus})$
$(\lambda W_\times.\textbf{bool}(\textbf{resp}(\lambda x.\textbf{dist}(\lambda y.\textbf{two-pw}(\lambda z.\textbf{gave}(y)(z)(x))))(X_\times)(W_\times))))$

Assuming that the sum of ATMs consists of three ATMs $\textbf{atm1}$, $\textbf{atm2}$, and $\textbf{atm3}$ and that the tuple corresponding to this sum consists of atomic ATMs as its members in this order, that is, $X_\times = \langle\textbf{atm1},\textbf{atm2},\textbf{atm3}\rangle$, the final translation reduces to the following:

(251) $\exists W_{\times_3}. \sum\limits_{1\leq i\leq 3} \pi_i(W_{\times_3}) = \textbf{1k-cus} \land$
$\quad\textbf{dist}(\lambda y.\textbf{two-pw}(\lambda z.\textbf{gave}(y)(z)(x)))(\textbf{atm1})(\pi_1(W_{\times_3})) \land$
$\quad\textbf{dist}(\lambda y.\textbf{two-pw}(\lambda z.\textbf{gave}(y)(z)(x)))(\textbf{atm2})(\pi_2(W_{\times_3})) \land$
$\quad\textbf{dist}(\lambda y.\textbf{two-pw}(\lambda z.\textbf{gave}(y)(z)(x)))(\textbf{atm3})(\pi_3(W_{\times_3}))$

This means that the total of one thousand customers can be partitioned into three groups such that for each of these groups, one of the three ATMs gave two distinct passwords to each individual in that group. This corresponds to the relevant reading of the sentence.

5.5   Conclusion

Our analysis of "respective" readings and related phenomena incorporates ideas from both G&K's analysis of "respective" readings and Barker's analysis of symmetrical predicates. While the strictly local approach in G&K's original formulation and the nonlocal approach by Barker via "parasitic scope" may initially look quite different, the effects of the two types of operations (or series of operations) that they respectively invoke are rather similar: they both establish some correspondence between the internal structures of two terms that do not necessarily appear adjacent to each other in the surface form of the sentence. The main difference is *how* this correspondence is established: G&K opt for a series of local composition operations (somewhat reminiscent of the way long-distance dependencies are handled in lexicalist frameworks such as CCG and G/HPSG), whereas Barker does it by a single step of nonlocal mechanism (in a way analogous to a movement-based analysis of long-distance dependencies).

A question that arises at this point is whether we gain any deeper understanding of the relationship between the respective solutions proposed by these authors, by recasting them within the general syntax-semantics interface of Hybrid TLCG. We do think that we have. Note first that, by recasting these proposals in our setup, we have a clearer picture of the core mechanism underlying these phenomena. This in turn has enabled us to overcome the major empirical limitations of both G&K's analysis (with respect to NCC) and Barker's analysis (with respect to iterated symmetrical predicates).

But we can go even further. As discussed in detail in Kubota and Levine (2014b), building on some key ideas originally proposed by Bekki (2006), the local and nonlocal modeling of "respective" predication from the two previous works can be shown to have a very close relationship formally, since in Hybrid TLCG, the local composition rules for "percolating up" the tuple structure from coordination that are crucially involved in G&K's setup can be derived as theorems in a grammar that essentially implements Barker's approach of nonlocal "respective" predication via hypothetical reasoning. More specifically, by introducing some auxiliary assumptions, the following two rules (where Rule 1 corresponds to G&K's **Dist** operator and Rule 2 corresponds to the **Dist**$'$ operator needed but apparently missing from G&K's setup) are both derivable as theorems in the system we presented in section 5.3.1 (for proofs, see Kubota and Levine [2014b]):

(252) a. Rule 1

$$\frac{a; \mathcal{F}; A/B \qquad b; \langle a_1, \ldots, a_l \rangle; B}{a \circ b; \langle \mathcal{F}(a_1), \ldots, \mathcal{F}(a_l) \rangle; A}$$

b. Rule 2

$$\frac{a; \langle \mathcal{F}_1, \ldots, \mathcal{F}_n \rangle; A/B \qquad b; a; B}{a \circ b; \langle \mathcal{F}_1(a), \ldots, \mathcal{F}_n(a) \rangle; A}$$

It can moreover be formally proven that the local and nonlocal modelings of "respective" predication make exactly the same predictions as to the range of available "respective" readings and internal readings for symmetrical predicates: in both approaches, it is possible to relate two (or more) terms embedded arbitrarily deeply in different parts of the sentence in the "respective" manner. This is an interesting result, since one might a priori be inclined to think that the local modeling would be inherently less powerful than the nonlocal modeling. It is of course conceivable to entertain a constrained version of local modeling in which percolation of a tuple structure is blocked in certain syntactic environments (such as islands and complements of certain types of predicates). But similar effects can probably be achieved in the nonlocal modeling as well, by constraining the steps of hypothetical reasoning involved in "respective" predication in some way or other (in relation to this, see Pogodalla and Pompigne [2012] for an implementation of scope islands in Abstract Categorial Grammar, a framework of CG closely related to Hybrid TLCG).

Choosing between these two alternative approaches on empirical grounds seems to be a complex matter. But whatever conclusion one draws on this issue, we believe that the kind of general setup we have offered in this chapter should be useful for comparing different hypotheses about them, as it enables one to formulate both the local and nonlocal modeling of "respective" predication within a single platform. At the very least, we believe that the unifying perspective we have offered on these two approaches is interesting in that it relativizes the debate between "derivational" and "non-derivational" theories (where the difference between the two architectures may at times have been overemphasized by proponents of each): so far as the semantics of "respective" predicates is concerned, our analysis shows that the extra machinery one needs to introduce in the grammar in each setup is largely equivalent, and that the difference in the two types of strategies representative in the two theories is more superficial than real.

5.6 Ancillary Derivations

(253)

$$
\cfrac{
\cfrac{[\varphi_3; R; \mathrm{VP/NP}]^3 \quad \mathrm{robin}; \mathbf{r}; \mathrm{NP}}{\varphi_3 \circ \mathrm{robin}; R(\mathbf{r}); \mathrm{VP}}{}_{/E} \quad
\begin{array}{c}\mathrm{on} \circ \mathrm{thursday}; \\ \mathbf{onTh}; \mathrm{VP}\backslash\mathrm{VP}\end{array}
}{
\cfrac{\varphi_3 \circ \mathrm{robin} \circ \mathrm{on} \circ \mathrm{thursday}; \mathbf{onTh}(R(\mathbf{r})); \mathrm{VP}}{\mathrm{robin} \circ \mathrm{on} \circ \mathrm{thursday}; \lambda R.\mathbf{onTh}(R(\mathbf{r})); (\mathrm{VP/NP})\backslash\mathrm{VP}}{}_{\backslash I^3}
}{}_{\backslash E}
$$

(254)

$$
\cfrac{
[\varphi_1; x; \mathrm{NP}]^1 \quad
\cfrac{\mathrm{met}; \mathbf{met}; \mathrm{VP/NP} \quad [\varphi_2; \mathscr{P}; (\mathrm{VP/NP})\backslash\mathrm{VP}]^2}{\mathrm{met} \circ \varphi_2; \mathscr{P}(\mathbf{met}); \mathrm{VP}}{}_{\backslash E}
}{
\cfrac{\cfrac{\varphi_1 \circ \mathrm{met} \circ \varphi_2; \mathscr{P}(\mathbf{met})(x); \mathrm{S}}{\lambda\varphi_2.\varphi_1 \circ \mathrm{met} \circ \varphi_2; \lambda\mathscr{P}.\mathscr{P}(\mathbf{met})(x); \mathrm{S}\!\restriction\!((\mathrm{VP/NP})\backslash\mathrm{VP})}{}_{\restriction I^2}}{\lambda\varphi_1\lambda\varphi_2.\varphi_1 \circ \mathrm{met} \circ \varphi_2; \lambda x \lambda\mathscr{P}.\mathscr{P}(\mathbf{met})(x); \mathrm{S}\!\restriction\!((\mathrm{VP/NP})\backslash\mathrm{VP})\!\restriction\!\mathrm{NP}}{}_{\restriction I^1}
}{}_{\backslash E}
$$

(255)

$$
\vdots
$$

$$
\cfrac{
\mathrm{Di} \circ \mathrm{and} \circ \mathrm{Th}; \langle\mathbf{di},\mathbf{th}\rangle; \mathrm{NP} \quad
\cfrac{
\mathrm{AK} \circ \mathrm{and} \circ \mathrm{Id}; \langle\mathbf{ak},\mathbf{id}\rangle; \mathrm{NP} \quad
\cfrac{
\begin{array}{c}\lambda\sigma_0\lambda\varphi_1\lambda\varphi_2.\sigma_0(\varphi_1)(\varphi_2); \\ \mathbf{resp}; \\ (Z\!\restriction\!X\!\restriction\!Y)\!\restriction\!(Z\!\restriction\!X\!\restriction\!Y)\end{array} \quad
\begin{array}{c}\lambda\varphi_1\lambda\varphi_2\lambda\varphi_3. \\ \varphi_3 \circ \mathrm{sent} \circ \\ \varphi_1 \circ \mathrm{to} \circ \varphi_2; \\ \mathbf{sent}; \\ \mathrm{S}\!\restriction\!\mathrm{NP}\!\restriction\!\mathrm{NP}\!\restriction\!\mathrm{NP}\end{array}
}{\begin{array}{c}\lambda\varphi_1\lambda\varphi_2\lambda\varphi_3.\varphi_3 \circ \mathrm{sent} \circ \varphi_1 \circ \mathrm{to} \circ \varphi_2; \\ \mathbf{resp}(\mathbf{sent}); \mathrm{S}\!\restriction\!\mathrm{NP}\!\restriction\!\mathrm{NP}\!\restriction\!\mathrm{NP}\end{array}}{}_{\restriction E}
}{\begin{array}{c}\lambda\varphi_2\lambda\varphi_3.\varphi_3 \circ \mathrm{sent} \circ \mathrm{AK} \circ \mathrm{and} \circ \mathrm{Id} \circ \mathrm{to} \circ \varphi_2; \\ \mathbf{resp}(\mathbf{sent})(\langle\mathbf{ak},\mathbf{id}\rangle); \mathrm{S}\!\restriction\!\mathrm{NP}\!\restriction\!\mathrm{NP}\end{array}}{}_{\restriction E}
}{\begin{array}{c}\lambda\varphi_3.\varphi_3 \circ \mathrm{sent} \circ \mathrm{AK} \circ \mathrm{and} \circ \mathrm{Id} \circ \mathrm{to} \circ \mathrm{Di} \circ \mathrm{and} \circ \mathrm{Th}; \\ \mathbf{resp}(\mathbf{sent})(\langle\mathbf{ak},\mathbf{id}\rangle)(\langle\mathbf{di},\mathbf{th}\rangle); \mathrm{S}\!\restriction\!\mathrm{NP}\end{array}}{}_{\restriction E}
$$

$$
\cdots\cdots\cdots\cdots\cdots\cdots\cdots\cdots\cdots\cdots
$$

$$
\begin{array}{c}\lambda\varphi_3.\varphi_3 \circ \mathrm{sent} \circ \mathrm{AK} \circ \mathrm{and} \circ \mathrm{Id} \circ \mathrm{to} \circ \mathrm{Di} \circ \mathrm{and} \circ \mathrm{Th}; \\ \langle\mathbf{sent}(\mathbf{ak})(\mathbf{di}), \mathbf{sent}(\mathbf{id})(\mathbf{th})\rangle; \mathrm{S}\!\restriction\!\mathrm{NP}\end{array}
$$

(256)

$$
\cfrac{
\begin{array}{c}\lambda\rho\lambda\sigma\lambda\varphi.\rho(\sigma)(\varphi); \\ \lambda\mathcal{R}\lambda\mathcal{T}_\times\lambda\mathcal{U}_\times.\prod_i\mathcal{R}(\pi_i(\mathcal{T}_\times))(\pi_i(\mathcal{U}_\times)); \\ (Z\!\restriction\!X\!\restriction\!Y)\!\restriction\!(Z\!\restriction\!X\!\restriction\!Y)\end{array} \quad
\cfrac{
\cfrac{
\cfrac{[\sigma; f; \mathrm{S}\!\restriction\!\mathrm{NP}]^1 \quad [\varphi; x; \mathrm{NP}]^2}{\sigma(\varphi); f(x); \mathrm{S}}{}_{\restriction E}
}{\lambda\varphi.\sigma(\varphi); \lambda x.f(x); \mathrm{S}\!\restriction\!\mathrm{NP}}{}_{\restriction I^2}
}{\lambda\sigma\lambda\varphi.\sigma(\varphi); \lambda f\lambda x.f(x); (\mathrm{S}\!\restriction\!\mathrm{NP})\!\restriction\!(\mathrm{S}\!\restriction\!\mathrm{NP})}{}_{\restriction I^1}
}{\lambda\sigma_1\lambda\varphi_1.\sigma_1(\varphi_1); \lambda P_\times\lambda X_\times.\prod_i\pi_i(P_\times)(\pi_i(X_\times)); (\mathrm{S}\!\restriction\!\mathrm{NP})\!\restriction\!(\mathrm{S}\!\restriction\!\mathrm{NP})}{}_{\restriction E}
$$

(257)

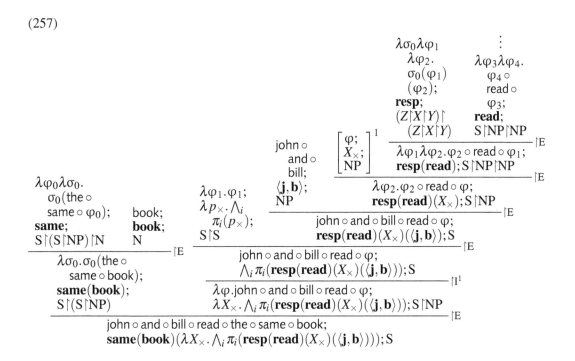

(258)

$$
\vdots
$$

$$
\begin{array}{c}
\dfrac{
\begin{array}{cc}
\begin{array}{l}
\lambda\varphi_1\lambda\varphi_2\lambda\varphi_3.\\
\quad \varphi_2\circ\mathsf{gave}\circ\\
\quad \varphi_1\circ\mathsf{to}\circ\varphi_3;\\
\lambda x\lambda y\lambda w.\\
\quad \mathbf{gave}(x)\\
\quad (w)(y);\\
\mathrm{S}{\restriction}\mathrm{NP}{\restriction}\mathrm{NP}{\restriction}\mathrm{NP}
\end{array}
&
\begin{array}{l}
\lambda\sigma_0\lambda\varphi_4\lambda\varphi_5\\
\quad \sigma_0(\varphi_4)(\varphi_5);\\
\lambda\mathcal{R}\lambda\mathcal{T}_{\times_n}\lambda\mathcal{U}_{\times_n}.\\
\quad \prod_i^n\mathcal{R}(\pi_i(\mathcal{T}_{\times_n}))\\
\quad (\pi_i(\mathcal{U}_{\times_n}));\\
(\mathrm{Z}{\restriction}\mathbf{X}{\restriction}\mathbf{Y}){\restriction}(\mathrm{Z}{\restriction}\mathbf{X}{\restriction}\mathbf{Y})
\end{array}
\end{array}
}{}{\restriction}\mathrm{E}
\end{array}
$$

$$
\dfrac{\lambda\varphi_4\lambda\varphi_5\lambda\varphi_3.\varphi_5\circ\mathsf{gave}\circ\varphi_4\circ\mathsf{to}\circ\varphi_3;\;
\lambda\mathcal{T}_\times\lambda\mathcal{U}_\times\prod_i^n\lambda w.\mathbf{gave}(\pi_i(\mathcal{T}_\times))(w)(\pi_i(\mathcal{U}_\times));\;
\mathrm{S}{\restriction}\mathrm{NP}{\restriction}\mathrm{NP}{\restriction}\mathrm{NP}}{}
$$

$$
\begin{bmatrix}\varphi_6;\\X_\times;\\\mathrm{NP}\end{bmatrix}^6
$$

$$
\begin{array}{c}
\text{john}\circ\\
\text{and}\circ\\
\text{bill};\\
\langle\mathbf{j},\mathbf{b}\rangle;\\
\mathrm{NP}
\end{array}
\qquad
\begin{array}{l}
\lambda\sigma_2\lambda\varphi_7.\\
\quad \sigma_2(\varphi_7);\\
\lambda P_\times\lambda W_\times.\\
\quad \prod_i\pi_i(P_\times)\\
\quad (\pi_i(W_\times));\\
(\mathrm{S}{\restriction}\mathrm{NP}){\restriction}\\
(\mathrm{S}{\restriction}\mathrm{NP})
\end{array}
$$

$$
\dfrac{\lambda\varphi_5\lambda\varphi_3.\varphi_5\circ\mathsf{gave}\circ\varphi_6\circ\varphi_3;\;
\lambda\mathcal{U}_\times\prod_i^n\lambda w.\mathbf{gave}(\pi_i(X_\times))(w)(\pi_i(\mathcal{U}_\times));\mathrm{S}{\restriction}\mathrm{NP}{\restriction}\mathrm{NP}}{}{\restriction}\mathrm{E}
$$

$$
\begin{bmatrix}\varphi_8;\\Y_\times;\\\mathrm{NP}\end{bmatrix}^8
$$

$$
\dfrac{\lambda\varphi_3.\text{john}\circ\text{and}\circ\text{bill}\circ\mathsf{gave}\circ\varphi_6\circ\mathsf{to}\circ\varphi_3;\;
\langle\lambda w.\mathbf{gave}(\pi_1(X_\times))(w)(\mathbf{j}),\lambda w.\mathbf{gave}(\pi_2(X_\times))(w)(\mathbf{b})\rangle;\mathrm{S}{\restriction}\mathrm{NP}}{}{\restriction}\mathrm{E}
$$

$$
\begin{array}{l}
\lambda\varphi.\varphi;\\
\lambda p_\times.\bigwedge_i\\
\pi_i(p_\times);\\
\mathrm{X}{\restriction}\mathrm{X}
\end{array}
$$

$$
\dfrac{\lambda\varphi_3.\text{john}\circ\text{and}\circ\text{bill}\circ\mathsf{gave}\circ\varphi_6\circ\mathsf{to}\circ\varphi_3;\;
\lambda W_\times.\langle\mathbf{gave}(\pi_1(X_\times))(\pi_1(W_\times))(\mathbf{j}),\mathbf{gave}(\pi_2(X_\times))(\pi_2(W_\times))(\mathbf{b})\rangle;\mathrm{S}{\restriction}\mathrm{NP}}{}{\restriction}\mathrm{E}
$$

$$
\dfrac{\text{john}\circ\text{and}\circ\text{bill}\circ\mathsf{gave}\circ\varphi_6\circ\mathsf{to}\circ\varphi_8;\;
\langle\mathbf{gave}(\pi_1(X_\times))(\pi_1(Y_\times))(\mathbf{j}),\mathbf{gave}(\pi_2(X_\times))(\pi_2(Y_\times))(\mathbf{b})\rangle;\mathrm{S}}{}{\restriction}\mathrm{E}
$$

$$
\text{john}\circ\text{and}\circ\text{bill}\circ\mathsf{gave}\circ\varphi_6\circ\mathsf{to}\circ\varphi_8;\;
\mathbf{gave}(\pi_1(X_\times))(\pi_1(Y_\times))(\mathbf{j})\wedge\mathbf{gave}(\pi_2(X_\times))(\pi_2(Y_\times))(\mathbf{b});\mathrm{S}
$$

$$
\vdots
$$

$$
\begin{array}{l}
\text{john}\circ\text{and}\circ\text{bill}\circ\mathsf{gave}\circ\varphi_6\circ\mathsf{to}\circ\varphi_8;\\
\mathbf{gave}(\pi_1(X_\times))(\pi_1(Y_\times))(\mathbf{j})\wedge\\
\mathbf{gave}(\pi_2(X_\times))(\pi_2(Y_\times))(\mathbf{b});\mathrm{S}
\end{array}
$$

$$
\vdots
$$

$$
\begin{array}{l}
\lambda\sigma_3.\sigma_3(\text{the}\circ\\
\quad \text{same}\circ\text{man});\\
\mathbf{same}(\mathbf{man});\\
\mathrm{S}{\upharpoonright}(\mathrm{S}{\restriction}\mathrm{NP})
\end{array}
$$

$$
\dfrac{}{\lambda\varphi_8.\text{john}\circ\text{and}\circ\text{bill}\circ\mathsf{gave}\circ\varphi_6\circ\mathsf{to}\circ\varphi_8;\;
\lambda Y_\times.\mathbf{gave}(\pi_1(X_\times))(\pi_1(Y_\times))(\mathbf{j})\wedge
\mathbf{gave}(\pi_2(X_\times))(\pi_2(Y_\times))(\mathbf{b});\mathrm{S}{\restriction}\mathrm{NP}}{\restriction}\mathrm{I}^8
$$

$$
\begin{array}{l}
\lambda\sigma_4.\sigma_4(\text{the}\circ\\
\quad \text{same}\circ\text{book});\\
\mathbf{same}(\mathbf{book});\\
\mathrm{S}{\upharpoonright}(\mathrm{S}{\restriction}\mathrm{NP})
\end{array}
$$

$$
\dfrac{\text{john}\circ\text{and}\circ\text{bill}\circ\mathsf{gave}\circ\varphi_6\circ\mathsf{to}\circ\text{the}\circ\text{same}\circ\text{man};\;
\mathbf{same}(\mathbf{man})(\lambda Y_\times.\mathbf{gave}(\pi_1(X_\times))(\pi_1(Y_\times))(\mathbf{j})\wedge\mathbf{gave}(\pi_2(X_\times))(\pi_2(Y_\times))(\mathbf{b}));\mathrm{S}}{}{\restriction}\mathrm{I}^6
$$

$$
\dfrac{}{\begin{array}{l}\lambda\varphi_6.\text{john}\circ\text{and}\circ\text{bill}\circ\mathsf{gave}\circ\varphi_6\circ\mathsf{to}\circ\text{the}\circ\text{same}\circ\text{man};\\
\lambda X_\times.\mathbf{same}(\mathbf{man})(\lambda Y_\times.\mathbf{gave}(\pi_1(X_\times))(\pi_1(Y_\times))(\mathbf{j})\wedge\mathbf{gave}(\pi_2(X_\times))(\pi_2(Y_\times))(\mathbf{b}));\\
\mathrm{S}{\restriction}\mathrm{NP}\end{array}}{\restriction}\mathrm{E}
$$

$$
\begin{array}{l}
\text{john}\circ\text{and}\circ\text{bill}\circ\mathsf{gave}\circ\text{the}\circ\text{same}\circ\text{book}\circ\mathsf{to}\circ\text{the}\circ\text{same}\circ\text{man};\\
\mathbf{same}(\mathbf{book})(\lambda X_\times.\mathbf{same}(\mathbf{man})(\lambda Y_\times.\mathbf{gave}(\pi_1(X_\times))(\pi_1(Y_\times))(\mathbf{j})\wedge\mathbf{gave}(\pi_2(X_\times))(\pi_2(Y_\times))(\mathbf{b})));\mathrm{S}
\end{array}
$$

(259)

$$
\cfrac{
\cfrac{
\cfrac{
\cfrac{
\cfrac{
\cfrac{
\cfrac{
\cfrac{
\begin{array}{l} \text{gave;} \\ \textbf{gave;} \\ \text{VP} \\ \text{/PP} \\ \text{/NP} \end{array}
\quad
\left[\begin{array}{l} \varphi_1; \\ x; \\ \text{NP} \end{array}\right]^1
}{
\begin{array}{l} \text{gave} \circ \varphi_1; \\ \textbf{gave}(x); \text{VP/PP} \end{array}
}\,{}^{/\text{E}}
\quad
\left[\begin{array}{l} \varphi_2; \\ y; \\ \text{PP} \end{array}\right]^2
}{
\begin{array}{l} \text{gave} \circ \varphi_1 \circ \varphi_2; \\ \textbf{gave}(x)(y); \text{VP} \end{array}
}\,{}^{/\text{E}}
\quad
\left[\begin{array}{l} \varphi_3; \\ \mathscr{F}; \\ \text{VP}\backslash\text{VP} \end{array}\right]^3
}{
\begin{array}{l} \text{gave} \circ \varphi_1 \circ \varphi_2 \circ \varphi_3;\ \mathscr{F}(\textbf{gave}(x)(y)); \text{VP} \end{array}
}\,{}^{\backslash\text{E}}
}{
\begin{array}{l} \text{terry} \circ \text{gave} \circ \varphi_1 \circ \varphi_2 \circ \varphi_3;\ \mathscr{F}(\textbf{gave}(x)(y))(\textbf{t}); \text{S} \end{array}
}
}{
\begin{array}{l} \lambda\varphi_3.\text{terry} \circ \text{gave} \circ \varphi_1 \circ \varphi_2 \circ \varphi_3; \\ \lambda\mathscr{F}.\mathscr{F}(\textbf{gave}(x)(y))(\textbf{t}); \text{S}{\upharpoonright}(\text{VP}\backslash\text{VP}) \end{array}
}\,{}^{{\upharpoonright}\text{I}^3}
}{
\begin{array}{l} \lambda\varphi_2\lambda\varphi_3.\text{terry} \circ \text{gave} \circ \varphi_1 \circ \varphi_2 \circ \varphi_3; \\ \lambda y\lambda\mathscr{F}.\mathscr{F}(\textbf{gave}(x)(y))(\textbf{t}); \text{S}{\upharpoonright}(\text{VP}\backslash\text{VP}){\upharpoonright}\text{PP} \end{array}
}\,{}^{{\upharpoonright}\text{I}^2}
}{
\begin{array}{l} \lambda\varphi_1\lambda\varphi_2\lambda\varphi_3.\text{terry} \circ \text{gave} \circ \varphi_1 \circ \varphi_2 \circ \varphi_3; \\ \lambda x\lambda y\lambda\mathscr{F}.\mathscr{F}(\textbf{gave}(x)(y))(\textbf{t}); \text{S}{\upharpoonright}(\text{VP}\backslash\text{VP}){\upharpoonright}\text{PP}{\upharpoonright}\text{NP} \end{array}
}
$$

Left margin labels and terminals (as placed in the tree):

$$
\begin{array}{l} \text{terry;} \\ \textbf{t}; \text{NP} \end{array}
$$

$$
\begin{array}{l} \lambda\sigma_0\lambda\varphi_1 \\ \lambda\varphi_2. \\ \sigma_0(\varphi_1) \\ (\varphi_2); \\ \textbf{resp}; \\ (Z{\upharpoonright}X{\upharpoonright}Y){\upharpoonright} \\ (Z{\upharpoonright}X{\upharpoonright}Y) \end{array}
$$

$$
\cfrac{
\cfrac{
\cfrac{
\begin{array}{l} \lambda\varphi_1\lambda\varphi_2\lambda\varphi_3.\text{terry} \circ \text{gave} \circ \varphi_1 \circ \varphi_2 \circ \varphi_3; \\ \textbf{resp}(\lambda x\lambda y\lambda\mathscr{F}.\mathscr{F}(\textbf{gave}(x)(y))(\textbf{t})); \text{S}{\upharpoonright}(\text{VP}\backslash\text{VP}){\upharpoonright}\text{PP}{\upharpoonright}\text{NP} \end{array}
\quad
\left[\begin{array}{l} \varphi_4; \\ X_\times; \\ \text{NP} \end{array}\right]^4
}{
\begin{array}{l} \lambda\varphi_2\lambda\varphi_3.\text{terry} \circ \text{gave} \circ \varphi_4 \circ \varphi_2 \circ \varphi_3; \\ \textbf{resp}(\lambda x\lambda y\lambda\mathscr{F}.\mathscr{F}(\textbf{gave}(x)(y))(\textbf{t}))(X_\times); \text{S}{\upharpoonright}(\text{VP}\backslash\text{VP}){\upharpoonright}\text{PP} \end{array}
}\,{}^{{\upharpoonright}\text{E}}
\quad
\begin{array}{l} \text{to} \circ \\ \text{bill} \circ \\ \text{and} \circ \\ \text{sue;} \\ \langle\textbf{b},\textbf{s}\rangle; \\ \text{PP} \end{array}
}{
\begin{array}{l} \lambda\varphi_3.\text{terry} \circ \text{gave} \circ \varphi_4 \circ \text{to} \circ \text{bill} \circ \text{and} \circ \text{sue} \circ \varphi_3; \\ \textbf{resp}(\lambda x\lambda y\lambda\mathscr{F}.\mathscr{F}(\textbf{gave}(x)(y))(\textbf{t}))(X_\times)(\langle\textbf{b},\textbf{s}\rangle); \text{S}{\upharpoonright}(\text{VP}\backslash\text{VP}) \end{array}
}\,{}^{{\upharpoonright}\text{E}}
$$

$$
\cdots\cdots\cdots\cdots\cdots\cdots\cdots\cdots\cdots\cdots\cdots\cdots
$$

$$
\begin{array}{l} \lambda\varphi_3.\text{terry} \circ \text{gave} \circ \varphi_4 \circ \text{to} \circ \text{bill} \circ \text{and} \circ \text{sue} \circ \varphi_3; \\ \langle\lambda\mathscr{F}.\mathscr{F}(\textbf{gave}(\pi_1(X_\times))(\textbf{b}))(\textbf{t}), \lambda\mathscr{F}.\mathscr{F}(\textbf{gave}(\pi_2(X_\times))(\textbf{s}))(\textbf{t})\rangle; \text{S}{\upharpoonright}(\text{VP}\backslash\text{VP}) \end{array}
$$

$\vdots$

$$\lambda\varphi_3.\text{terry} \circ \text{gave} \circ$$
$$\varphi_4 \circ \text{to} \circ \text{bill} \circ$$
$$\text{and} \circ \text{sue} \circ \varphi_3;$$

$\vdots$

$\lambda\sigma_1\lambda\varphi_1.$ $\langle\lambda\mathscr{F}.\mathscr{F}$
$\sigma_1(\varphi_1);$ $(\textbf{gave}(\pi_1(X_\times))$
$\lambda Y_\times\lambda P_\times.$ $(\textbf{b}))(\textbf{t}), \lambda\mathscr{F}.$
$\prod_i \pi_i(P_\times)$ $\mathscr{F}(\textbf{gave}(\pi_2(X_\times))$
$(\pi_i(Y_\times));$ $(\textbf{s}))(\textbf{t})\rangle;$
$(X{\upharpoonright}Y){\upharpoonright}(X{\upharpoonright}Y)$ $S{\upharpoonright}(VP\backslash VP)$
————————————— ${\upharpoonright}E$

as $\circ$ a $\circ$ christmas $\circ$ $\lambda\varphi_3.\text{terry} \circ \text{gave} \circ$
present $\circ$ on $\circ$ $\varphi_4 \circ \text{to} \circ \text{bill} \circ \text{and} \circ \text{sue} \circ \varphi_3;$
thursday $\circ$ and $\circ$ as $\circ$ $\lambda Y_\times.\prod_i \pi_i(\langle\lambda\mathscr{F}.$
a $\circ$ new $\circ$ year's $\circ$ gift $\circ$ $\mathscr{F}(\textbf{gave}(\pi_1(X_\times))(\textbf{b}))(\textbf{t}),$
on $\circ$ saturday; $\lambda\mathscr{F}.\mathscr{F}(\textbf{gave}(\pi_2(X_\times))(\textbf{s}))$
$\langle\lambda P.\textbf{onTh}(\textbf{asChP}(P)),$ $(\textbf{t})\rangle)(\pi_i(Y_\times));$
$\lambda P.\textbf{onS}(\textbf{asNYG}(P))\rangle;$ $S{\upharpoonright}(VP\backslash VP)$
$VP\backslash VP$
——————————————————— ${\upharpoonright}E$

terry $\circ$ gave $\circ$ φ_4 $\circ$ to $\circ$ bill $\circ$ and $\circ$ sue $\circ$ as $\circ$
$\lambda\varphi_1.\varphi_1;$ a $\circ$ christmas $\circ$ present $\circ$ on $\circ$ thursday $\circ$ and $\circ$
$\lambda p_\times.\bigwedge_i$ as $\circ$ a $\circ$ new $\circ$ year's $\circ$ gift $\circ$ on $\circ$ saturday;
$\pi_i(p_\times);$ $\langle\textbf{onTh}(\textbf{asChP}(\textbf{gave}(\pi_1(X_\times))(\textbf{b})))(\textbf{t}),$
$S{\upharpoonright}S$ $\textbf{onS}(\textbf{asNYG}(\textbf{gave}(\pi_2(X_\times))(\textbf{s})))(\textbf{t})\rangle; S$
——————————————————— ${\upharpoonright}E$

terry $\circ$ gave $\circ$ φ_4 $\circ$ to $\circ$ bill $\circ$ and $\circ$ sue $\circ$ as $\circ$ a $\circ$ christmas $\circ$ present $\circ$
on $\circ$ thursday $\circ$ and $\circ$ as $\circ$ a $\circ$ new $\circ$ year's $\circ$ gift $\circ$ on $\circ$ saturday;
$\textbf{onTh}(\textbf{asChP}(\textbf{gave}(\pi_1(X_\times))(\textbf{b})))(\textbf{t})\wedge$
the $\circ$ $\textbf{onS}(\textbf{asNYG}(\textbf{gave}(\pi_2(X_\times))(\textbf{s})))(\textbf{t}); S$
same $\circ$ ——————————————————— ${\upharpoonright}I^4$
gift; $\lambda\varphi_4.\text{terry} \circ \text{gave} \circ \varphi_4 \circ \text{to} \circ \text{bill} \circ \text{and} \circ \text{sue} \circ \text{as} \circ \text{a} \circ \text{christmas} \circ \text{present} \circ$
$\textbf{same}(\textbf{gift});$ on $\circ$ thursday $\circ$ and $\circ$ as $\circ$ a $\circ$ new $\circ$ year's $\circ$ gift $\circ$ on $\circ$ saturday;
$S{\upharpoonright}(S{\upharpoonright}NP)$ $\lambda X_\times.\textbf{onTh}(\textbf{asChP}(\textbf{gave}(\pi_1(X_\times))(\textbf{b})))(\textbf{t})\wedge$
   $\textbf{onS}(\textbf{asNYG}(\textbf{gave}(\pi_2(X_\times))(\textbf{s})))(\textbf{t}); S{\upharpoonright}NP$
——————————————————— ${\upharpoonright}E$

terry $\circ$ gave $\circ$ the $\circ$ same $\circ$ gift $\circ$ to $\circ$ bill $\circ$ and $\circ$ sue $\circ$ as $\circ$ a $\circ$ christmas $\circ$ present $\circ$
on $\circ$ thursday $\circ$ and $\circ$ as $\circ$ a $\circ$ new $\circ$ year's $\circ$ gift $\circ$ on $\circ$ saturday;
$\textbf{same}(\textbf{gift})(\lambda X_\times.\textbf{onTh}(\textbf{asChP}(\textbf{gave}(\pi_1(X_\times))(\textbf{b})))(\textbf{t})\wedge$
$\textbf{onS}(\textbf{asNYG}(\textbf{gave}(\pi_2(X_\times))(\textbf{s})))(\textbf{t})); S$

(260)

$$\dfrac{[\varphi_1; f; S/NP]^1 \quad [\varphi_2; x; NP]^2}{\dfrac{\dfrac{\varphi_1 \circ \varphi_2; f(x); S}{\lambda\varphi_2.\varphi_1 \circ \varphi_2; \lambda x.f(x); S{\upharpoonright}NP} {\upharpoonright}I^2}{\lambda\varphi_1\lambda\varphi_2.\varphi_1 \circ \varphi_2; \lambda f\lambda x.f(x); S{\upharpoonright}NP{\upharpoonright}(S/NP)} {\upharpoonright}I^1} {\upharpoonright}E$$

$\lambda\sigma\lambda\varphi_1\lambda\varphi_2.\sigma(\varphi_1)(\varphi_2);$
$\textbf{resp};$
$(Z{\upharpoonright}X{\upharpoonright}Y){\upharpoonright}(Z{\upharpoonright}X{\upharpoonright}Y)$

—————————————————————————————— ${\upharpoonright}E$

$\lambda\varphi_1\lambda\varphi_2.\varphi_1 \circ \varphi_2; \lambda P_\times\lambda X_\times.\prod_i \pi_i(P_\times)(\pi_i(X_\times)); S{\upharpoonright}NP{\upharpoonright}(S/NP)$

$$
\begin{array}{c}
\vdots \qquad\qquad \vdots \\
\lambda\varphi_1\lambda\varphi_2.\varphi_1\circ\varphi_2; \qquad \text{john}\circ\text{spent}\circ \\
\lambda P_\times\lambda X_\times.\prod_i \qquad \text{and}\circ\text{bill}\circ\text{lost}; \\
\pi_i(P_\times)(\pi_i(X_\times)); \qquad \langle\lambda x.\mathbf{spent}(\mathbf{j},x), \\
\text{S}\!\upharpoonright\!\text{NP}\!\upharpoonright\!(\text{S/NP}) \qquad \lambda x.\mathbf{lost}(\mathbf{b},x)\rangle; \\
\text{S/NP}
\end{array}
$$

(261)

$$
\lambda\varphi_1\lambda\varphi_2.\varphi_1\circ\text{gave}\circ\varphi_2\circ\text{two}\circ\text{passwords}; \ \lambda x.\mathbf{dist}(\lambda y.\mathbf{two\text{-}pw}(\lambda z.\mathbf{gave}(y)(z)(x))); \ \text{S}\!\upharpoonright\!\text{NP}\!\upharpoonright\!\text{NP}
$$

$$\vdots$$

$$
\begin{array}{cc}
\begin{array}{c}\lambda\sigma_0\lambda\varphi_1\\ \lambda\varphi_2.\\ \sigma_0(\varphi_1)\\ (\varphi_2);\\ \mathbf{resp};\\ (Z{\uparrow}X{\uparrow}Y){\uparrow}\\ (Z{\uparrow}X{\uparrow}Y)\end{array}
&
\begin{array}{c}\lambda\varphi_1\lambda\varphi_2.\varphi_1\circ\\ \mathrm{gave}\circ\\ \varphi_2\circ\mathrm{two}\circ\\ \mathrm{passwords};\\ \lambda x.\mathbf{dist}(\lambda y.\\ \mathbf{two\text{-}pw}\\ (\lambda z.\mathbf{gave}\\ (y)(z)(x)));\\ S{\uparrow}NP{\uparrow}NP\end{array}
\end{array}
$$

$$\rule{6cm}{0.4pt}\; {\uparrow}E$$

$$
\begin{array}{cc}
\left[\begin{array}{c}\varphi_1;\\ X_\times;\\ NP\end{array}\right]^4
&
\begin{array}{c}\lambda\varphi_1\lambda\varphi_2.\varphi_1\circ\mathrm{gave}\circ\\ \varphi_2\circ\mathrm{two}\circ\mathrm{passwords};\\ \mathbf{resp}(\lambda x.\mathbf{dist}(\lambda y.\mathbf{two\text{-}pw}\\ (\lambda z.\mathbf{gave}(y)(z)(x))));\\ S{\uparrow}NP{\uparrow}NP\end{array}
\end{array}
$$

$$\rule{6cm}{0.4pt}\; {\uparrow}E$$

$$
\begin{array}{cc}
\left[\begin{array}{c}\varphi_2;\\ W_\times;\\ NP\end{array}\right]^5
&
\begin{array}{c}\lambda\varphi_2.\varphi_1\circ\mathrm{gave}\circ\varphi_2\circ\mathrm{two}\circ\mathrm{passwords};\\ \mathbf{resp}(\lambda x.\mathbf{dist}(\lambda y.\\ \mathbf{two\text{-}pw}(\lambda z.\mathbf{gave}(y)(z)(x))))(X_\times);\\ S{\uparrow}NP\end{array}
\end{array}
$$

$$\rule{6cm}{0.4pt}\; {\uparrow}E$$

$$
\begin{array}{cc}
\begin{array}{c}\lambda\varphi.\\ \varphi;\\ \mathbf{bool};\\ S{\uparrow}S\end{array}
&
\begin{array}{c}\varphi_1\circ\mathrm{gave}\circ\varphi_2\circ\mathrm{two}\circ\mathrm{passwords};\\ \mathbf{resp}(\lambda x.\mathbf{dist}(\lambda y.\\ \mathbf{two\text{-}pw}(\lambda z.\mathbf{gave}(y)(z)(x))))(X_\times)(W_\times);S\end{array}
\end{array}
$$

$$\rule{6cm}{0.4pt}\; {\uparrow}E$$

$$
\begin{array}{cc}
\begin{array}{c}\lambda\sigma.\sigma(a\circ\\ \mathrm{total}\circ\mathrm{of}\circ\\ 1000\circ\\ \mathrm{customers});\\ \mathbf{total}\\ (\mathbf{1k\text{-}cus});\\ S{\uparrow}(S{\uparrow}NP)\end{array}
&
\begin{array}{c}\varphi_1\circ\mathrm{gave}\circ\varphi_2\circ\mathrm{two}\circ\mathrm{passwords};\\ \mathbf{bool}(\mathbf{resp}(\lambda x.\mathbf{dist}(\lambda y.\\ \mathbf{two\text{-}pw}(\lambda z.\mathbf{gave}(y)(z)(x))))(X_\times)(W_\times));S\\ \hline \begin{array}{c}\lambda\varphi_2.\varphi_1\circ\mathrm{gave}\circ\varphi_2\circ\mathrm{two}\circ\mathrm{passwords};\\ \lambda W_\times.\mathbf{bool}(\mathbf{resp}(\lambda x.\mathbf{dist}(\lambda y.\\ \mathbf{two\text{-}pw}(\lambda z.\mathbf{gave}(y)(z)(x))))(X_\times)(W_\times));\\ S{\uparrow}NP\end{array}\end{array}
\end{array}\;{\uparrow}I^5
$$

$$\rule{6cm}{0.4pt}\; {\uparrow}E$$

$$
\begin{array}{cc}
\begin{array}{c}\lambda\sigma.\sigma(a\circ\\ \mathrm{total}\circ\mathrm{of}\circ\\ 3\circ\mathrm{atms});\\ \mathbf{total}\\ (\mathbf{3\text{-}atms});\\ S{\uparrow}(S{\uparrow}NP)\end{array}
&
\begin{array}{c}\varphi_1\circ\mathrm{gave}\circ a\circ\mathrm{total}\circ\mathrm{of}\circ1000\circ\mathrm{customers}\circ\mathrm{two}\circ\mathrm{passwords};\\ \mathbf{total}(\mathbf{1k\text{-}cus})(\lambda W_\times.\mathbf{bool}(\mathbf{resp}(\lambda x.\mathbf{dist}(\lambda y.\\ \mathbf{two\text{-}pw}(\lambda z.\mathbf{gave}(y)(z)(x))))(X_\times)(W_\times));S\\ \hline \begin{array}{c}\lambda\varphi_1.\varphi_1\circ\mathrm{gave}\circ a\circ\mathrm{total}\circ\mathrm{of}\circ1000\circ\mathrm{customers}\circ\mathrm{two}\circ\mathrm{passwords};\\ \lambda X_\times.\mathbf{total}(\mathbf{1k\text{-}cus})(\lambda W_\times.\mathbf{bool}(\mathbf{resp}(\lambda x.\mathbf{dist}(\lambda y.\\ \mathbf{two\text{-}pw}(\lambda z.\mathbf{gave}(y)(z)(x))))(X_\times)(W_\times)));S{\uparrow}NP\end{array}\end{array}
\end{array}\;{\uparrow}I^4
$$

$$\rule{6cm}{0.4pt}\; {\uparrow}E$$

$$
\begin{array}{c}
a\circ\mathrm{total}\circ\mathrm{of}\circ3\circ\mathrm{atms}\circ\mathrm{gave}\circ a\circ\mathrm{total}\circ\mathrm{of}\circ1000\circ\mathrm{customers}\circ\mathrm{two}\circ\mathrm{passwords};\\
\mathbf{total}(\mathbf{3\text{-}atms})(\lambda X_\times.\mathbf{total}(\mathbf{1k\text{-}cus})(\lambda W_\times.\mathbf{bool}(\mathbf{resp}(\lambda x.\mathbf{dist}(\lambda y.\\
\mathbf{two\text{-}pw}(\lambda z.\mathbf{gave}(y)(z)(x))))(X_\times)(W_\times))));S
\end{array}
$$

6 Pseudogapping

We have, in previous chapters, presented evidence of the advantages of TLCG's flexible constituency vis-à-vis the syntax-semantics interface problems posed by coordination. It is true, however, that coordination has been the empirical "set piece" of CG for several decades, and it is legitimate to ask at this point whether, apart from this one (admittedly vast) domain of phenomena, the flexibility of CG is needed in empirical studies of natural language grammars. We argue in this chapter that ellipsis phenomena provide an emphatically positive answer to this question. Like coordination, ellipsis frequently involves apparently missing material which does not correspond to a phrase structural constituent, and which, just as in the case of coordination, has typically been treated in derivational approaches via complex movement operations, with a separate series of deletion steps. In this chapter, we take up one specific type of ellipsis phenomenon in English, namely, *pseudogapping*, and argue that neither movement nor deletion is required or motivated for its analysis; on the contrary, not only are neither necessary, but the specific analyses which have appealed to them are dubious on both conceptual and empirical grounds. The failure of the movement + deletion type approach is perhaps most dramatic in the case of pseudogapping, but we believe that our argument can be extended to other major ellipsis constructions which have attracted much attention in recent theorizing. Hybrid TLCG offers a particularly natural way of reformulating the syntactic and semantic licensing conditions for ellipsis and has the potential of overcoming the major problems of both the transformational and nontransformational accounts of ellipsis in the previous literature. We return to this issue in chapter 8, where we examine more complex types of ellipsis phenomena in which ellipsis interacts with another major grammatical phenomenon, namely, extraction.

Pseudogapping is a somewhat odd instance of ellipsis in which a lexical verb under an auxiliary is deleted, leaving behind its own complement(s). There are clear family resemblances between pseudogapping on the one hand and Gapping and VP ellipsis on the other.

(262) Mary hasn't **dated** Bill, but she has ∅ Harry.   (*pseudogapping*)

(263) Smoke **bothers** Fred, and loud music, ∅ Fred's parents.   (*Gapping*)

(264) Smoke might have **bothered Fred**, but it didn't ∅ .   (*VP ellipsis*)

In both pseudogapping and Gapping, the lexical verb is missing, leaving behind some (or all) of its complements as remnants, but in pseudogapping, an auxiliary in the elided clause must be present (just as in VP ellipsis), whereas in gapping no auxiliary is found. Gapping also differs from the other two in that it is restricted to coordination environments (e.g., *I'll contact John if you will (Mary)* vs. **I'll contact John if you Mary*).

The proper analysis of pseudogapping has long been a problem in the literature (e.g., Kuno 1981; Jayaseelan 1990; Miller 1990; Lasnik 1999; Baltin 2000; Takahashi 2004; Hoeksema 2006; Gengel 2013; Miller 2014). The shared-auxiliary requirement and distributional parallelisms of pseudogapping and VP ellipsis (where, unlike the pattern with Gapping, these elliptical constructions are not restricted to coordination environments) suggest a unitary analysis in which the latter is nothing but a limiting case of the former with all the verb's complements elided. In transformational approaches (e.g., Jayaseelan 1990), this unification has been implemented by treating pseudogapping as VP ellipsis in which a remnant (*Harry* in (262)) has been moved out of a subsequently deleted VP, thereby escaping ellipsis. The disagreements among previous proposals pertain to differences in (i) the kinds of movements proposed (A- vs. $\overline{\text{A}}$-movement) and (ii) the direction of movement (leftward vs. rightward). However, as we will show, regardless of which choices are made, the various movement operations employed for this purpose by different authors are not only undermotivated but empirically problematic. The nontransformational literature, by contrast, has given relatively little attention to pseudogapping, with Miller (1990, 2014) being virtually the only exception. Building on Schachter's (1978) analysis of VP ellipsis (see also Hardt 1993), Miller (1990) proposes that the meaning of the missing verb (such as *dated* in (262)) in pseudogapping is simply recovered by an anaphoric mechanism. This approach is quite successful in providing a relatively simple mechanism for correlating form and meaning, and we have adopted its core ideas into our own proposals. But it has one major drawback: the complete dissociation between the syntactic and semantic licensing conditions for pseudogapping underlying Miller's analysis (which is common to many nontransformational analyses of ellipsis phenomena) overgenerates in a way never expected in a transformational approach.

We argue in this chapter that a synthesis of the transformational and nontransformational approaches to pseudogapping becomes possible in Hybrid TLCG. As we have demonstrated in the previous chapters, the flexible interactions between the directional and nondirectional modes of implication are at the heart of our approach. We show that the "hybrid" architecture of Hybrid TLCG once again yields an elegant analysis of a highly problematic empirical phenomenon, namely, pseudogapping. Our analysis characterizes the syntactic properties of the "antecedent" of the pseudogapped verb in the preceding clause via the flexible notion of constituency with directional slashes and captures the anaphoric relation between the antecedent and the ellipsis clauses via order-insensitive inference with the nondirectional slash. This essentially amounts to augmenting the interpretive analysis of Miller (1990) with the insight from transformational approaches that syntactic information is also relevant in the licensing of pseudogapping, resulting in a synthesis of the seemingly antithetical transformational and nontransformational analytic strategies.

6.1   Syntactic and Semantic Constraints on Pseudogapping

6.1.1   Basic Patterns and Sensitivity to Discourse-Oriented Factors

Pseudogapping is most typical with transitive verbs (with NP or PP complements).

(265)   a.   Mary hasn't dated Bill, but she has ∅ Harry.

         b.   Mary dates Bill more frequently than she does ∅ Harry.

(266)   a.   You can't count on a stranger, but you can ∅ on a friend.

         b.   John speaks to Mary more civilly than he does ∅ Anne.

Though both the comparative and the non-comparative variants are clearly acceptable in such simple examples, pseudogapping is a somewhat marginal phenomenon at best, and judgments are often unstable. For this reason, it is important to first clarify the factors that affect the felicity of pseudogapping and to control for them as much as possible.[1]

The most fundamental property of pseudogapping, which is particularly important to bear in mind, is that, as noted by Hoeksema (2006), this construction must satisfy the Contrast relation in Kehler's (2002) classification of discourse relations.[2] Thus, note that the highly marginal (267a) improves with the use of contrastive *but* in (267b) and becomes virtually unexceptionable with the use of the comparative structure in (267c).

---

1. Since judgments on pseudogapping examples are often subtle and complex, we adopt a somewhat elaborate system for marking the acceptability of examples in this chapter. We use * for marking examples that, in our view, cannot be ameliorated by pragmatic manipulation (lexical choice, discourse context, world knowledge, and so on). In this section, we mark examples with intermediate levels of acceptability with %. Since we take all such examples to be grammatical (but degraded for pragmatic reasons), we generally eliminate this marking in later sections of this chapter to avoid overload of notation. When a (gradient) acceptability difference is at issue, we indicate different degrees of acceptability with the number of % symbols (where %% is worse than %). Outside of the particular set of contrasted examples, this should not be taken to have any significance. For examples from the literature, we have (except where noted) replaced the original judgments with our own.

2. The Contrast relation is typically expressed by *but*, as in *Mary went to the movies, but Bill went to a rock concert*, and is often manifested (as in this example) by the juxtaposition of two clauses having overall parallel structures but with at least one "slot" that is different; the material in this slot is in some sense opposed to the material in the corresponding slot in the other clause.

(267) a. %%John will write essays and he will ∅ novels.

     b. %John won't write essays but he will ∅ novels.

     c. John will write essays much more successfully than he will ∅ novels.

Note moreover that in all these cases, contrastive emphasis on *essays* and *novels* increases acceptability of the sentence as uttered (other sources of increased acceptability include the use of the demonstratives *this/that* [see section 6.3.5], which corroborates the same point).

Indeed, Hoeksema (2006) notes a strong statistical association between pseudogapping and comparative constructions, where 87 percent of his attested examples involve comparatives or constructions for comparison (with expressions such as *like* and *the way/manner*). This makes sense given the tight correlation between pseudogapping and the Contrast relation.

Also, as noted by Levin (1979), Hoeksema (2006), and Miller (2014), keeping the subject of the antecedent and the pseudogapping clause identical greatly increases the acceptability of pseudogapping (in fact, Miller notes that 85 percent of the pseudogapping examples in his corpus sample contain a pronoun as the subject of the ellipsis clause). Thus, compared with (267a,b), (268a,b) are somewhat degraded.

(268) a. %%%John will write essays and Mary will ∅ novels.

     b. %%John will write essays but Mary will ∅ novels.

The effect of the Contrast requirement and the "same subject" preference is that the least acceptable example in this paradigm is (268a), with no contrastive stress on the remnants (and no discourse context suggesting that essays and novels are contrasted), and the best is (267c), with strong contrastive stress on the remnants. Thus, we do not regard (268a) as ungrammatical; it just fails to satisfy all the relevant discourse conditions affecting the felicity of pseudogapping.[3] When presenting our examples below, we will control for these factors so that the examples will not violate these interfering discourse conditions. This is especially important for examples with more complex structures, in which such effects (unsurprisingly) tend to be aggravated. For example, even with single remnants, when the syntactic and semantic types are not the simple NP individual-denoting type as in (265) and (266), acceptability noticeably drops, as in the following (but note that the comparative structure is consistently better than the non-comparative structure).

---

3. It is well-known in the literature on island effects that cumulative effects of such extragrammatical factors can lead to unacceptability practically indistinguishable from ungrammaticality. See chapter 10 for more discussion on this point.

(269) a. %%John will bet an entire fortune that the METS will win the pennant, but he won't ∅ that the BRAVES will win.

(Culicover and Jackendoff 2005, 294)

   b. %John would bet an entire fortune that the METS will win the pennant more readily than he would ∅ that the BRAVES will win.

6.1.2 Complex Pseudogapping Patterns

Beyond the "base cases" involving direct objects of transitive verbs as remnants, there are a variety of more complex pseudogapping examples that are well within the range of acceptable patterns. We take all these examples to be generated in the syntax since doing so will make the overall analysis simpler. Wherever relevant, we offer some observations on the extragrammatical factors possibly affecting their perceived acceptability.

6.1.2.1 Multiple remnants   Pseudogapping is possible with multiple remnants in the ellipsis clause (we show the antecedent of the "elided verb" in boldface and the remnant(s) in italics).

(270) a. %Although I wouldn't **introduce** THOSE people to Tom and SALLY, I WOULD ∅ THESE *people to each* OTHER.   (Gengel 2013, 58)

   b. I would **introduce** THOSE people to Tom and SALLY with more hesitation than I would ∅ THESE *people to each* OTHER.

The moderately degraded status of (270a) essentially disappears when the sentence is reframed as a comparative as in (270b), suggesting that the degree of contrast in (270a) is not quite sufficient to completely satisfy the Contrast relation.

We believe that the number of remnants is not limited to two. Though (271) is admittedly somewhat awkward, we take its decreased acceptability to be due to processing difficulty.[4]

(271) %I'd **bet** a FRIEND more DOLLARS that something UNLIKELY was true than I would ∅ *an* ENEMY EUROS *that the* SUN *will rise tomorrow*.

6.1.2.2 Nonconstituent ellipsis targets   The elided material is not necessarily a standard constituent.

(272) a. %You can't **take the lining out of** that coat. You can ∅ *this one*.

(Levin 1979, 77)

---

4. As noted in chapter 3 (footnote 2), multiple remnants are difficult in Gapping as well, presumably for a similar reason.

b. You can **take the lining out of** that coat more easily than you can ∅ *this one*.

c. You can't **pay more attention to** John than you do ∅ *Mary*!

These examples are particularly important since they seem to militate against analyses that depend on rightward movements to evacuate the remnants out of the deleted VP. Our analysis allows the elided material in these examples to constitute combinatorial units with proper semantic interpretations, enabling us to subsume these cases under the normal licensing mechanism of pseudogapping.

6.1.2.3 Discontinuous ellipsis There are also data displaying apparently discontinuous ellipsis.

(273) a. She **found** her coworker **attractive** but she didn't ∅ *her husband* ∅.

b. I didn't **expect** your mother **to like the picture**, but I did ∅ *you* ∅.

These examples seem particularly problematic to some of the movement-based approaches (again, ones involving rightward movement). They also have some interesting implications for our own analysis, and they raise an important (open) question: Namely, how much flexibility should be allowed in the syntax proper in capturing the possible patterns of pseudogapping adequately? We return to this issue in section 6.3.3.

6.1.3 Analytically Problematic Patterns

As noted at the beginning of this chapter, two major approaches have been taken to pseudogapping: (i) transformational analyses with movement + VP ellipsis and (ii) nontransformational analyses that rely on purely anaphoric mechanisms to retrieve the meaning of the missing verb. We now turn to data that prove to be especially difficult (or even intractable) for one or the other of these approaches.

6.1.3.1 Problems for covert structure Movement-based approaches find support in essentially two types of evidence: (i) syntactic identity conditions between the antecedent and the elided VPs and (ii) manifestations of island constraints governing the movement operations involved. Here we focus on the former. Islandhood-based evidence is discussed in chapter 10, together with similar evidence for other constructions analyzed in other chapters.

Evidence for identity conditions is taken to come from data such as (274), which according to Merchant (2008a) is ungrammatical because of voice mismatch.

(274) %%Klimt is admired by Abby more than anyone does Klee.

(Merchant 2008a, 170).

However, as noted by Tanaka (2011, 476) and Miller (2014, 87), there are well-formed instances of voice-mismatch pseudogapping such as the following, casting serious doubt on an argument for hidden syntactic structure based on data such as (274):[5]

(275) a. %MY problem will be investigated by Tom, but he won't YOURS.
       b. These savory waffles are ideal for brunch, served with a salad as you would a quiche.

A subtler type of tolerated mismatch is noted in Miller 2014, where the pseudogapped verb has a different valence from the token that appears in the antecedent clause.

(276) Ask Doll, who spoke as much about his schoolboy career ending as he did of the season in general.   (Miller 2014, 83)

(275) and (276) are clearly problematic for "deletion under structural identity" type approaches.

There is further evidence against syntactic identity in pseudogapping. Miller (2014, 85) notes examples such as the following, in which there is no overt syntactic constituent in the antecedent clause corresponding to the elided material in the pseudogapping clause:

(277) a. They all called him Pa Tommy, just as they would any village elder in Sierra Leone.
           = '. . . just as they would *call* any village elder in S. L. *by his first name*'
       b. Type in your PIN, just hit those buttons like you would a phone.
           = '. . . like you would *use* a phone'
       c. EPA urged the Corps "to work directly with the affected communities as well as seek professional assistance in this matter as they would any other environmental issue."
           = '. . . as they would *act with respect to* any other environmental issue'

Here, the ellipsis clauses are interpreted along the lines of the paraphrases given, but there are no corresponding syntactic constituents in the preceding clauses that would match these paraphrases (or any other paraphrase that would work for these examples).

Note also that pseudogapping allows for split antecedents, which are similarly problematic for syntactic approaches.

---

5. Nakamura (2013), building on Kertz (2010, 2013), argues convincingly that the asymmetry between cases such as (274) and (275) reflects the manner in which the Contrast relation is satisfied. Specifically, when the (intended) contrast is between the subject in the antecedent clause and the corresponding demoted argument in the pseudogapped clause, voice mismatch is barred, whereas if the contrast is established between the auxiliaries in different polarities in the two clauses, voice mismatch does not lead to unacceptability. See also Miller (2014, 87) for some discussion on the role of discourse constraints in acceptable examples of voice mismatch in pseudogapping.

(278) a. %John saw Mary and Peter heard Ann, but neither did me.

(Miller 1990, 296)

b. John saw Mary and Peter heard Ann more clearly than either of them did me.

Data such as (277) and (278) obviously present severe challenges to arguments for covert structure based on the premise that straightforward syntactic identity conditions hold between the elided material and its antecedent.

6.1.3.2 Problems for purely interpretive approaches Purely interpretive approaches can handle the kinds of data given above without trouble. But such approaches, too, face empirical contraindications from a certain type of data, namely, those displaying syntactic connectivity between the antecedent and the ellipsis site (Miller [1990] marks (279a) with ?? and takes it to be semantically, rather than syntactically, ill-formed; see section 6.2.2).

(279) a. *John spoke to Mary more often than he did for Anne.

b. *John will accuse Bill of perjury more readily than he would Mary with forgery.

For example, (279a) is ungrammatical since the preposition in the remnant (*for*) does not match the one in the antecedent clause (*to*). It should be clear that these patterns do not fall out in any straightforward way in an approach relying solely on a semantic process of anaphora retrieval.[6]

6.2 Previous Proposals

We now review representative analyses of pseudogapping in the literature. As we discuss in more detail below, both the (majority of) transformational analyses and Miller's (1990) nontransformational alternative take pseudogapping and VP ellipsis to be derived by essentially the same mechanism. Our own analysis in section 6.3 follows these proposals in this respect. Though this assumption has been challenged by some

6. Regarding connectivity, some authors have discussed the interactions between pseudogapping and binding conditions (such as Principle A [Baltin 2000] and Principle C [Sauerland 1998; Takahashi 2004]) and have drawn various theoretical conclusions. Unfortunately, exploring this issue is beyond the scope of the present work. For one thing, at least for some of these conditions (most notably, Principle C), their exact status—in particular, whether they are syntactic in nature—has been controversial (see Büring [2005] for a lucid review). Another reason for postponing this issue for future work is that (syntactic) binding is an area that is relatively underdeveloped in CG research (but see Szabolcsi 1992; Steedman 1996; Jacobson 2007). That being said, the interaction between binding and ellipsis is an important area for future research since typical accounts of both phenomena in CG eschew reference to syntactic structures, yet the relevant empirical observations in this domain have usually been taken to present evidence for structure-based accounts.

authors (most notably, Hoeksema [2006]), we believe that Miller (2014, section 5) shows convincingly that the various distributional differences between pseudogapping and VP ellipsis identified in the literature can be explained by means of independent non-syntactic (i.e., discourse- and/or processing-oriented) differences between the two constructions and thus do not constitute convincing enough evidence to posit a syntactic difference between them.

6.2.1 Pseudogapping as VP Ellipsis: Movement-Based Approaches

There are two aspects to movement-based approaches that need to be kept separate. One is the characterization of pseudogapping (and ellipsis more generally) as an operation that makes reference to purely syntactic information. The second is the specific implementation of this syntactic dependency via structure-changing operations.

The essential insight of movement-based approaches seems to lie largely in the first of these aspects. Movement-based approaches immediately explain the category-matching connectivity effect in pseudogapping, which can be accommodated only by an ad hoc stipulation in the interpretive approaches. At the same time, as we discuss in detail below, previous transformational analyses are unsatisfactory on both empirical and conceptual grounds: the various movement operations utilized either lack independent motivation or (when an independently motivated movement is retooled) do not match the actual distributional properties of pseudogapping. Moreover, movement-based approaches do not by themselves illuminate the question of why we might expect something like pseudogapping to be a possible type of ellipsis in English.

The transformational literature has essentially followed Kuno (1981), who took pseudogapping to be a case of VP ellipsis in which various constituents are moved out of the VP via adjunction operations, thus "surviving" VP ellipsis. Adopting this general idea, Jayaseelan (1990) analyzes (280) (= (262)) as in (281), via Heavy NP Shift (HNPS).

(280) Mary hasn't dated Bill, but she has ∅ Harry.

(281)

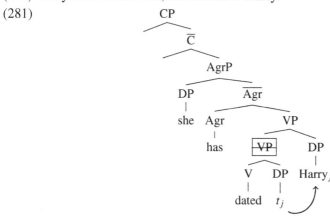

Various empirical challenges have been identified in the literature for this analysis of pseudogapping. See, for example, Lasnik (1999) and Kubota and Levine (2017) for some extensive critiques. The most striking problem is perhaps the fact that it predicts that pronouns are not good remnants of pseudogapping since they are not right-shiftable in HNPS. Miller (2014), however, shows that pronouns are in fact one of the most typical types of remnants in many naturally occurring instances of pseudogapping, such as the following:

(282) It hurt me as much as it did *her*.

Subsequent transformational literature has seen several alternatives to Jayaseelan's (1990) proposal, but in a sense these are minor variants of the original idea embodied in his analysis. The only differences consist in whether the movement is taken to be A or $\overline{\text{A}}$ movement and rightward or leftward movement. Among these various suggestions, Takahashi's (2004) "eclectic" analysis is empirically the most successful. For this reason, we focus on his analysis in what follows.

The background for Takahashi's (2004) solution is that neither an exclusively rightward movement analysis (such as Jayaseelan's [1990]) nor an exclusively leftward movement analysis (such as Lasnik's [1999]) can cover the whole range of data that pseudogapping displays. The gist of Takahashi's (2004) own proposal, then, is to admit both leftward and rightward movement as sources of pseudogapping and to capture data that are problematic for either one of the two approaches by the other movement mechanism. In a sense, this "eclectic" approach can be seen as the limiting case of the movement strategy: given that neither the leftward nor the rightward analysis covers all cases, the next (and the last) analytic alternative is to combine all approaches that have worked in particular cases. Unfortunately, however, a wider set of data reveals problems similar to those that undermine the previous accounts.

In the following (283), for example, there are three remnants.

(283) %I'd bet a FRIEND more DOLLARS that something UNLIKELY was true than I would an ENEMY EUROS that the sun will RISE tomorrow.

Takahashi's analysis would take the leftmost complement *an enemy* to undergo Object-shift to the left, followed by either two rightward movements targeting each of the remaining complements or a second movement to the left, applying to *Euros*, and a movement of the clausal complement to the right. But both of these possibilities are ruled out by Takahashi's own respective arguments against Jayaseelan's analysis on the one hand and Lasnik's on the other. In the former case, leaving aside the legality of multiple HNPS, the first of the rightward movements must move the indirect object *Euros* over the clausal complement. However, this is not a legal type of HNPS (see Kubota and Levine [2017, section 3.1] for a detailed discussion). In the latter case, the first movement must displace the indirect object over the direct object—again, an option precluded for Takahashi's approach, since admitting such movement would incorrectly license the passivization of an indirect object.[7]

Aside from the specific empirical problems noted above, there is one fundamental issue for all movement-based analyses of pseudogapping (and of VP ellipsis more generally). As noted in the previous section, under the right conditions, pseudogapping is possible without any overt syntactic antecedent (cf. the antecedentless and split-antecedent pseudogapping examples (277) and (278) noted in section 6.1). These examples suggest that, despite the initial appeal of the movement + deletion strategy, descriptively speaking, the type of ellipsis involved in pseudogapping is anaphoric rather than being licensed syntactically. But then the fact that pseudogapping leaves a remnant (displaying connectivity effects) is particularly troublesome, since extraction "out of" unequivocally anaphoric expressions is generally prohibited. Note, for example, the following contrast between antecedent-contained ellipsis and its counterpart involving *do so* anaphora:

(284) John talked to everyone who Peter did (*so).   (Haïk 1987, 513)

Previous syntactic accounts of pseudogapping remain silent about this tension between (apparent) evidence for a structural account and evidence against it.

6.2.2 The Anaphoric-Interpretive Strategy

During the past three decades, an alternative approach to ellipsis has emerged, whose central claim is that ellipsis never involves covert structure (e.g., Schachter 1978; Sag et al. 1985; Miller 1990; Dalrymple et al. 1991; Hardt 1993; Culicover and Jackendoff 2005). Versions of this approach typically invoke some kind of anaphoric process based on the semantics of the antecedent clause. We illustrate this strategy by reference to Miller (1990), which offers the most explicit proposal of this sort to date for pseudogapping (see Culicover and Jackendoff [2005] for a similar idea, worked out in less detail).

The key idea of Miller's (1990) non-derivational analysis of pseudogapping, couched in Generalized Phrase Structure Grammar, is that auxiliaries can appear as the head verb in the same set of phrase structure rules that license projections of lexical verbs. For example, in (262), reproduced here as (285), the auxiliary *has* is effectively treated as a transitive verb and directly combines with the remnant *Harry*.

---

7. Takahashi (2004, 579) suggests the possibility of multiple leftward movements for the two objects in multiple remnant pseudogapping with ditransitives. But this directly contradicts Takahashi's (2004, 575) own argument against Lasnik (1999) just a few pages earlier. Since Takahashi suggests an alternative leftward + rightward movement analysis for ditransitives immediately after this puzzling mention of the multiple leftward movement possibility, we take the latter to be his real proposal (which is by far more in line with the spirit of his "eclectic" approach).

(285) Mary hasn't dated Bill, but she has ∅ Harry.

Miller implements this strategy by assuming that auxiliaries can appear not only in subcategorization frames taking nonfinite VP complements but also in frames instantiating any subcategorization frame of a lexical verb in English. This means that the auxiliary *has* is specified in the lexicon to be compatible with the [SUBCAT 2] specification, which is associated with the following phrase structure rule licensing lexically transitive verbs such as *drink*:

(286) VP → H[SUBCAT 2], NP

This rule licenses (285), and the meaning of the "missing" verb is then supplied by anaphoric reference to some "corresponding" verb in the preceding clause.

Elegant though it is, this analysis has one serious source of overgeneration. The problem, in a nutshell, is that Miller's anaphora resolution procedure makes no reference to any syntactic information of the antecedent clause—in particular, to the syntactic selectional properties of the head verb, which must be matched by the auxiliary in the pseudogapped clause, as discussed above. This indeterminacy entails that if some complement in the pseudogapping clause has a denotation that corresponds to the denotation of a syntactically different complement in the antecedent clause, then it is in principle possible to obtain a coherent interpretation in Miller's analysis even though the verb in the antecedent clause cannot actually combine with the pseudogapping clause complement. Thus, this account as it stands does not predict the anomaly of (279a), repeated here as (287).

(287) *John spoke to Mary more often than he did for Anne.

Here, the individual denotation **anne** is a possible interpretation for *for Anne* (cf. *John waited for Anne*, where the preposition *for* is standardly taken to be meaningless). But then, the meaning of the auxiliary *did* can be anaphorically resolved as the meaning of the verb *spoke* in the antecedent clause (note that *to* in *spoke to Mary* is similarly meaningless), leading to the misprediction that (287) should be well-formed with the same interpretation as *John spoke to Mary more often than he did to Anne*.

Miller takes (287) to be ruled out by a semantic selectional restriction analogous to the gender restriction on pronouns. This selectional restriction applies to the anaphoric auxiliary and imposes the constraint that it is felicitous just in case the verb meaning that is anaphorically retrieved is compatible with the overt preposition that heads the PP that the auxiliary syntactically combines with. Thus, for example, (287) is predicted to be semantically anomalous since "NP1 *speak to* NP2" and "NP1 *speak for* NP2" mean different things (NP2 is a participant in the act of speaking in the former but not in the latter). Thus, when appearing with *for* (as in the pseudogapping clause), the meaning of *speak* in the antecedent clause would not be the "appropriate" one, and anaphora resolution therefore fails. Though this approach seems in principle implementable in an interpretive approach, it is unclear to us what the motivation could be for anaphoric auxiliaries (which are all identical in form in the relevant respect) to carry *semantic* restrictions based on the intended antecedent target, which according to Miller is no different from the gender restriction on pronouns (the latter of which has a clear morphological reflex on the overt form of the pronouns).[8] In the next section, we offer an alternative formulation of the syntactic connectivity restrictions that keeps the core insight of Miller's proposal but implements the relevant constraint in a way we believe is much more straightforward.

6.3 Pseudogapping as Pseudo-VP Ellipsis

In this section, we propose an analysis of pseudogapping in Hybrid TLCG. Our analysis aims to synthesize the key insights from both transformational and nontransformational approaches. Specifically, we follow Miller (1990) in taking pseudogapping to be licensed by an anaphoric mechanism, thereby avoiding the various problems associated with previous transformational analyses. However, unlike Miller's purely interpretive approach, the specific way in which we unify the syntactic licensing mechanism of pseudogapping and VP ellipsis naturally predicts that pseudogapping is sensitive to certain syntactic information (specifically, the syntactic selectional restrictions that the antecedent verb imposes on its complements). This way, the analysis naturally incorporates the connectivity requirement on pseudogapping from transformational approaches as well.

The key analytic idea of our proposal is largely theory-independent and can be formulated in any syntactic theory that has an explicit syntax-semantics interface and countenances a relatively flexible notion of syntactic constituency. We believe that one of the reasons that pseudogapping has turned out to be so problematic in both the transformational and the nontransformational literature is that previous syntactic theories do not have these properties in a fully general manner. Hybrid TLCG is uniquely distinct from previous transformational and nontransformational syntactic theories in that

---

8. Since this condition cannot be hooked to the morphological form of the anaphoric auxiliary, the formulation of the relevant condition (Miller's [1990] (41)) is rather complicated.

(i) The functor from the antecedent of *do* which applies to the denotation of the complement (respectively complements) of *do* (that functor is either the denotation of a verb or of a preposition) must be an appropriate denotation for that verb or preposition when it is used with a subcategorization frame comprising a complement (respectively complements) of the same syntactic category as that of the complement (respectively complements) of *do*. (This presupposes that such a subcategorization frame exists.)

Moreover, this alleged "semantic" selectional restriction is very different from the gender restriction on pronouns (which has the simple function of restricting the domain for the referent) in that it refers to the subcategorization frame (which is syntactic, rather than semantic, information) of the target antecedent verb.

it satisfies both of these two requirements adequately. In particular, the flexible notion of syntactic constituency that it shares with many other variants of CG enables a straightforward characterization of the meaning-category pair of the "elided" material, and a novel mechanism of prosodic λ-binding (originally due to Oehrle [1994]) that enables a generalization of the notion of "movement" from the transformational literature offers a simple characterization of the relevant anaphoric process.

6.3.1 VP Ellipsis in Hybrid TLCG

Since we take pseudogapping to be a special case of VP ellipsis, we start with an analysis of VP ellipsis. In chapter 3, we posited a higher-order entry for the auxiliary verb and showed that the following VP/VP-type entry (where VP is an abbreviation for NP\S), familiar in the nontransformational syntax literature, is derivable from that higher-order entry.

(288) can; $\lambda Q \lambda x. \Diamond Q(x)$; VP/VP

Since the lower-order entry suffices for the purpose of the analysis of ellipsis phenomena for the most part, in this chapter and in chapter 8, we make the simplifying assumption that auxiliaries have entries of the form in (288) with the syntactic type VP/VP. But such entries should not be taken to be separately posited in the lexicon, but should be thought of as "theorems" derived from the more basic higher-order entries, as per (76). In chapter 9, we analyze modal auxiliaries in English in greater detail. We discuss cases of VP ellipsis and pseudogapping that require the higher-order versions of the auxiliary entry in that chapter (section 9.3.3).

We take VP ellipsis to be licensed by an alternative sign for the auxiliary verb, which unlike the VP/VP entry in (288), does not subcategorize for a VP but instead anaphorically retrieves the relevant VP meaning in reference to the preceding discourse. For this purpose, we posit an empty operator that applies to the lexical sign of auxiliaries and saturates the VP argument slot of the latter. This "VP ellipsis" operator is defined as in (289).

(289) **VP ellipsis operator, version 1**
       $\lambda \varphi. \varphi$; $\lambda \mathscr{F}. \mathscr{F}(P)$; VP$\upharpoonright$(VP/VP)
       ——where P is a free variable whose value is identified with the meaning of some linguistic sign in the preceding discourse with category VP

By applying (289) to (288), we obtain a derived auxiliary entry of category VP as in (290).

(290)
$$\frac{\begin{array}{cc} \lambda\varphi.\varphi; & \text{can;} \\ \lambda\mathscr{F}.\mathscr{F}(P); \text{VP}\upharpoonright(\text{VP}/\text{VP}) & \lambda Q\lambda x.\Diamond Q(x); \text{VP}/\text{VP} \end{array}}{\text{can; } \lambda x.\Diamond P(x); \text{VP}} \upharpoonright \text{E}$$

A simple VP ellipsis example such as (291) can then be derived as in (292) (here and below, the syntactic category of the expression that serves as an antecedent of VP ellipsis is shaded).

(291) John can sing. Bill can't.

(292)

$$
\frac{\displaystyle \text{john;} \quad \frac{\begin{array}{c}\text{can;}\\ \lambda P\lambda x.\Diamond P(x);\\ \text{VP/VP}\end{array} \quad \frac{\begin{array}{c}\text{sing;}\\ \mathbf{sing;}\\ \boxed{\text{VP}}\end{array}}{}}{\text{can} \circ \text{sing;}\ \lambda x.\Diamond \mathbf{sing}(x);\ \text{VP}}/E}{\text{john} \circ \text{can} \circ \text{sing;}\ \Diamond \mathbf{sing}(\mathbf{j});\ S} \backslash E
$$

$$
\frac{\displaystyle \text{bill;} \quad \frac{\begin{array}{c}\lambda\varphi.\varphi;\\ \lambda\mathscr{F}.\mathscr{F}(\mathbf{sing});\\ \text{VP}{\upharpoonright}(\text{VP/VP})\end{array} \quad \frac{\begin{array}{c}\text{can't;}\\ \lambda P\lambda x.\neg\Diamond P(x);\\ \text{VP/VP}\end{array}}{}}{\text{can't;}\ \lambda x.\neg\Diamond \mathbf{sing}(x);\ \text{VP}}{\upharpoonright}E}{\text{bill} \circ \text{can't;}\ \neg\Diamond \mathbf{sing}(\mathbf{b});\ S} \backslash E
$$

Note that, since the operator directly applies to the auxiliary to modify its subcategorization property, no phonologically empty verb is involved.

At this point, some comments are in order about our choice of an analysis involving an empty syntactic operator. There are at least three alternatives to this approach: (i) a binding-based analysis in which a hypothetical VP is bound by an antecedent VP via a syntactic mechanism of variable binding (Morrill et al. 2011; Barker 2013), (ii) an analysis that posits an empty VP (this would correspond most closely to a deletion-based analysis in derivational approaches), and (iii) an analysis that posits an alternative auxiliary entry (identical to the output of our syntactic empty operator) in the lexicon (Jäger 2005).

We think that our empty operator–based approach has certain advantages over these three alternatives, although admittedly the third alternative in particular is very close (both in spirit and in content) to our own approach. The binding approach does not easily extend to intersentential anaphora; especially problematic are cases where VP ellipsis (and pseudogapping) takes place across speakers. The present approach is superior to an empty VP approach in that it can straightforwardly capture the generalization that auxiliaries (including the "infinitive marker" *to*) are the triggers of VP ellipsis.[9] The main difference between our own approach and a lexical approach along the lines of the third alternative is that the former straightforwardly extends to the pseudogapping case (see below), with a uniform ellipsis operator (schematically) of the form $A{\upharpoonright}(A/A)$.

---

9. (289) involves a simplification in this respect, since, as it stands, the VP ellipsis operator can combine with any VP/VP. In a more complete account, auxiliaries need to be distinguished from VP adverbs. A well-established approach in lexicalist theories (such as HPSG and CCG) is to introduce syntactic features to classify different types of VPs (for example, the auxiliary *have* will be specified as $\text{VP}_{bse}/\text{VP}_{pst}$, a verb taking a past participle and returning a base form VP). Once this modification is made, we can refine the syntactic category of the VP ellipsis operator so that it takes as an argument $\text{VP}_\alpha/\text{VP}_\beta$, where $\alpha \neq \beta$ (which suffices to distinguish auxiliaries from adverbs).

It should, however, be noted that lexicalizing the effect of the ellipsis operator in the Jäger-type approach is definitely possible.

Interactions between VP ellipsis and other phenomena such as quantifier scope and the strict/sloppy ambiguity of pronouns can be handled in essentially the same way as in previous analyses of VP ellipsis in TLCG (Morrill and Merenciano 1996; Jäger 2005).

(293) a. John thinks he is a genius. Bill does, too.

     b. John read every book before Bill did.

(294) shows the sloppy reading of (293a).

(294)

$$
\cfrac{
\cfrac{
\begin{array}{c}
\lambda\sigma.\sigma(\text{he}); \\
\lambda R\lambda x.R(x)(x); \\
\text{VP}\!\upharpoonright\!(\text{VP}\!\upharpoonright\!\text{NP})
\end{array}
\quad
\cfrac{
\text{thinks}; \; \textbf{think}; \text{VP/S}
\quad
\cfrac{
[\varphi_1; x; \text{NP}]^1 \quad \text{is} \circ \text{a} \circ \text{genius}; \textbf{is-a-gens}; \text{VP}
}{
\varphi_1 \circ \text{is} \circ \text{a} \circ \text{genius}; \textbf{is-a-gens}(x); \text{S}
}\scriptstyle\backslash\text{E}
}{
\cfrac{
\text{thinks} \circ \varphi_1 \circ \text{is} \circ \text{a} \circ \text{genius}; \textbf{think}(\textbf{is-a-gens}(x)); \text{VP}
}{
\begin{array}{c}
\lambda\varphi_1.\text{thinks} \circ \varphi_1 \circ \text{is} \circ \text{a} \circ \text{genius}; \\
\lambda x.\textbf{think}(\textbf{is-a-gens}(x)); \text{VP}\!\upharpoonright\!\text{NP}
\end{array}
}\scriptstyle\upharpoonright\text{I}^1
}{}
}{
\text{thinks} \circ \text{he} \circ \text{is} \circ \text{a} \circ \text{genius}; \lambda x.\textbf{think}(\textbf{is-a-gens}(x))(x); \boxed{\text{VP}}
}\scriptstyle\upharpoonright\text{E}
}{}
}{}
$$

(Proof tree for (294): john; **j**; NP combined with the VP derivation to yield: john ∘ thinks ∘ he ∘ is ∘ a ∘ genius; **think(is-a-gens(j))(j)**; S)

$$
\cfrac{
\text{bill}; \textbf{b}; \text{NP}
\quad
\cfrac{
\lambda\varphi.\varphi; \; \lambda\mathscr{F}.\mathscr{F}(\lambda x.\textbf{think}(\textbf{is-a-gens}(x))(x)); \text{VP}\!\upharpoonright\!(\text{VP/VP})
\quad
\text{does}; \lambda P.P; \text{VP/VP}
}{
\text{does}; \lambda x.\textbf{think}(\textbf{is-a-gens}(x))(x); \text{VP}
}\scriptstyle\upharpoonright\text{E}
}{
\text{bill} \circ \text{does}; \textbf{think}(\textbf{is-a-gens}(\textbf{b}))(\textbf{b}); \text{S}
}\scriptstyle\backslash\text{E}
$$

We assume the so-called "binding at VP" analysis of pronouns in (294) (see Bach and Partee 1980, 1984). In this analysis, after the binding of the pronoun to the subject NP, the right meaning (self-ascription of the property of being a genius) is assigned to the VP, which the VP ellipsis operator can then take as the antecedent. The strict reading, on the other hand, is obtained by letting the pronoun *he* in the antecedent clause pick up *John* as its own antecedent, not by binding but by a general mechanism for anaphora resolution for free pronouns (notated in the following proof by α). This, then, creates the property $\lambda y.\textbf{think}(\textbf{is-a-gens}(\textbf{j}))(y)$ that serves as an appropriate antecedent for the elided VP in the ellipsis clause as in (295).

(295)

$$\frac{\text{is} \circ \text{a} \circ \text{genius}; \textbf{genius}; \text{VP} \quad \text{he}; \alpha; \text{NP}}{\text{he} \circ \text{is} \circ \text{a} \circ \text{genius}; \textbf{genius}(\alpha); \text{S}} \quad \frac{\text{thinks};}{\textbf{think}; \text{VP/S}}$$

$$\frac{\text{thinks} \circ \text{he} \circ \text{is} \circ \text{a} \circ \text{genius}; \textbf{think}(\textbf{genius}(\alpha)); \text{VP}}{\text{thinks} \circ \text{he} \circ \text{is} \circ \text{a} \circ \text{genius}; \textbf{think}(\textbf{genius}(\textbf{j})); \boxed{\text{VP}} \quad \text{john}; \textbf{j}; \text{NP}}$$

$$\text{john} \circ \text{thinks} \circ \text{he} \circ \text{is} \circ \text{a} \circ \text{genius}; \textbf{think}(\textbf{genius}(\textbf{j}))(\textbf{j}); \text{S}$$

$$\frac{\text{does} \circ \text{too}; \textbf{think}(\textbf{genius}(\textbf{j})); \text{VP} \quad \text{bill}; \textbf{b}; \text{NP}}{\text{bill} \circ \text{does} \circ \text{too}; \textbf{think}(\textbf{genius}(\textbf{j}))(\textbf{b}); \text{S}}$$

The interactions between quantifier scope and VP ellipsis are also straightforward in our approach. (296) shows the *every* > *before* reading of (293b).

(296)

In (296), the VP ellipsis operator takes the VP in the antecedent clause containing a free variable x (to be later bound by the universal quantifier) as the antecedent. The quantifier scopes over the whole sentence after this anaphora resolution takes place and binds the variable x in both the antecedent clause and the ellipsis clause. The narrow-scope reading for the quantifier (*before* > *every*) is obtained by first forming a sentence with a hypothetical subject over which the quantifier takes scope and then abstracting over the subject position to obtain the property $\lambda x.\textbf{V}_{\textbf{book}}(\lambda y.\textbf{read}(y)(x))$ within the antecedent clause (which then gets picked up as the meaning of the missing VP in the ellipsis clause).

6.3.2 Pseudogapping

We analyze pseudogapping in (297) via transitive verb (TV = (NP\S)/NP) ellipsis (Jacobson [2019] independently arrives at the same conclusion).

(297) John should eat the banana. Bill should ~~eat~~ the apple.

In the present setup, this involves making only a minimal extra assumption: all that is necessary is to make the VP ellipsis operator in (289) polymorphic. Polymorphism is a standard technique for generalizing the lexical definitions of semantic operators independently needed in the grammar in the analysis of coordination and certain adverbial operators (cf. the "cross-categorial" analysis of focus particles in Rooth [1985]).

Moreover, there is independent evidence that English allows for TV ellipsis. Jacobson (1992, 2008) argues that antecedent-contained deletion (ACD) is to be analyzed in terms of TV ellipsis rather than VP ellipsis. The idea is that in (298), what is missing after *had* is just the transitive verb *showed* instead of a full VP.[10]

(298) John showed Bill every place that Harry already had.

We refer the reader to Jacobson's work for a detailed empirical justification and technical execution of this analysis of ACD (see also Jäger [2005] for a TLCG implementation of Jacobson's analysis), but one big advantage should be immediately obvious: in this

---

10. Pseudogapping and ACD are sometimes thought to display different distributions. First, Jacobson (1998, 80) reports the following contrast (her (17), judgment hers):

(i) a. John thought that Mary read everything that Bill (also) did (= think that Mary read).
     b. *John thought that Mary read *Crime and Punishment* and Bill did *The Brothers Karamazov* (= think that Mary read).

But note that the structure in (ib) improves considerably in an example like the following:

(ii) John would claim Bill is a SPY more confidently than I would a SABOTEUR.

We therefore take it that the unacceptability of (ib) is not due to a combinatoric constraint but rather derives from the requirement that the elided material correspond to some "coherent semantic unit" so as to support the Contrast relation between the two clauses. ACD is not so constrained, presumably because the object is shared in the two clauses and hence the construction is not associated with the Contrast discourse relation. See section 6.3.5 for some relevant discussion. We leave it for future work to clarify exactly what is going on in data such as (i) and (ii). The notion of "coherent semantic unit" here is admittedly vague, but such a notion does seem to play a role in accounting for certain linguistic phenomena that resist a purely syntactic characterization—see, for example, Kubota and Lee's (2015) analysis of CSC patterns in Japanese and Korean for another such case. Second, Lasnik (1999, 169) reports contrasts like (iii), arguing that pseudogapping is limited to direct objects but ACD is not.

(iii) a. John stood near everyone Bill did.
      b. *John stood near Bill and Mary should Susan.

Again, the alleged restriction on pseudogapping is dubious at best. Miller (2014, 81) reports attested examples analogous in structure to (iiib). Finally, one might wonder how "Kennedy's puzzle" (Kennedy 1994/2008) would be treated in this approach. See Jacobson (2009) for a non-representational account of this phenomenon.

analysis, the notorious problem of "infinite regress" simply does not arise, since a VP containing a trace is not reconstructed in the ellipsis site to begin with.

Since pseudogapping is not restricted to transitive verbs but can involve ditransitive verbs and so on, we make the VP ellipsis operator polymorphic, employing Steedman's (2000) $ notation for polymorphic lexical entries.

(299) **VP ellipsis/pseudogapping operator, version 2**
$\lambda\varphi.\varphi; \lambda\mathscr{F}.\mathscr{F}(P); (\text{VP}/\$)\upharpoonright((\text{VP}/\$)/(\text{VP}/\$))$

——where P is a free variable whose value is identified with the meaning of some linguistic sign in the preceding discourse with category VP/\$

VP/\$ is a metavariable notation for a set of categories where any number of arguments (of any category) are sought via / (VP, VP/NP, VP/NP/PP, and so on). The three occurrences of VP/\$ are to be instantiated in the same way. The key idea behind this extension is that the ellipsis operator is generalized to apply to any syntactic category that the auxiliary itself can be derived in (as will become clear momentarily).

The TV/TV (= (VP/VP)/(VP/VP)) entry of the auxiliary that this operator applies to in the analysis of (297) can be derived from the lexically assigned VP/VP entry and does not need to be posited separately. This is an instance of the Geach rule, which is a theorem in the Lambek calculus and TLCG (as long as the calculus is associative).

(300)
$$\dfrac{\text{should}; \lambda P\lambda y.\Box P(y); \text{VP/VP} \quad \dfrac{[\varphi_2; f; \text{TV}]^2 \quad [\varphi_3; x; \text{NP}]^3}{\varphi_2 \circ \varphi_3; f(x); \text{VP}}/\text{E}}{\dfrac{\dfrac{\text{should} \circ \varphi_2 \circ \varphi_3; \lambda y.\Box f(x)(y); \text{VP}}{\text{should} \circ \varphi_2; \lambda x\lambda y.\Box f(x)(y); \text{TV}}/\text{I}^3}{\text{should}; \lambda f\lambda x\lambda y.\Box f(x)(y); \text{TV/TV}}/\text{I}^2}/\text{E}$$

The analysis of a basic pseudogapping example like (297) is then straightforward.

(301)

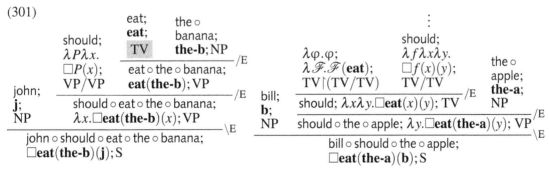

Here, the auxiliary is in the derived TV/TV category. The VP ellipsis/pseudogapping operator in (299) takes this auxiliary category as an argument and saturates its TV argument by anaphorically referring to the transitive verb *eat* in the antecedent clause.

As discussed in section 6.1, the "deleted" material in pseudogapping does not necessarily correspond to a syntactic constituent in the traditional sense. The present approach straightforwardly handles such cases of "nonconstituent" pseudogapping (like those in (272)) by treating the "nonconstituent" strings in the preceding clause as syntactic constituents that can serve as antecedents in pseudogapping. We illustrate in (303) the derivation for (the antecedent clause of) (302) (= (272a)).

(302) You can't **take the lining out of** that coat. You can ∅ this one.

(303)

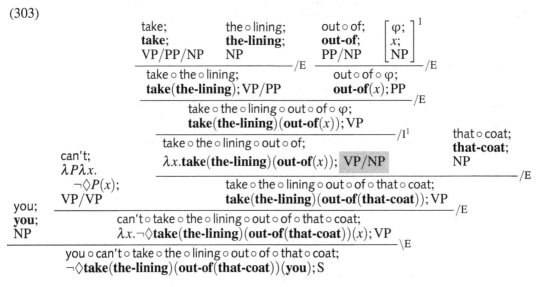

Via hypothetical reasoning involving directional slashes, the string *take the lining out of* is derived as a syntactic constituent of category VP/NP. The denotation of this sign can then be identified as the antecedent of the relevant anaphoric process in the target clause. Examples like those in (272) are especially important in that they show the significance of the flexible notion of constituency available in CG in an empirical domain other than coordination. Note that these nonconstituent pseudogapping examples pose significant problems for many previous transformational accounts, since deriving these examples via movement + ellipsis entails positing various otherwise unmotivated movement operations.

As discussed in section 6.2.1, pseudogapping with multiple remnants like the following are also highly problematic for movement-based approaches:

(304) a. I won't introduce THOSE GIRLS to my SISTER, but I WOULD these boys to my BROTHER.

    b. I bet more money with JOHN that the game would go into OVERTIME than I did with MARY that the final score would be a TIE.

Multiple-remnant pseudogapping is straightforward in our approach. The key point is that the following PDTV/PDTV (where PDTV = VP/PP/NP) version of the auxiliary can be derived from the lexically specified VP/VP entry via the Geach rule:

(305) *would*; $\lambda f \lambda x \lambda y \lambda z. f(x)(y)(z)$; PDTV/PDTV

Since the derivation is parallel to the one for the TV/TV entry above (hypothesizing a PDTV, NP, and PP to the right of the auxiliary and withdrawing these hypotheses one by one after combining them with the auxiliary), we omit it here.

Since the VP ellipsis/pseudogapping operator is polymorphic, it can take this derived auxiliary verb as an argument and anaphorically saturate the missing PDTV argument position in the same way as in the simpler examples above. Here, we show only the derivation for the target clause of pseudogapping. The VP ellipsis/pseudogapping operator makes reference to the ditransitive verb in the antecedent clause with category PDTV and semantics **introduce** (here we ignore the modal meaning of the auxiliary *would*).

(306)

$$
\begin{array}{l}
\lambda\varphi.\varphi; \\
\lambda\mathcal{F}.\mathcal{F}(\lambda x\lambda y\lambda z. \\
\quad \mathbf{intro}(y)(x)(z)); \\
\text{PDTV} \upharpoonright (\text{PDTV}/\text{PDTV})
\end{array}
\qquad
\begin{array}{l}
\text{would}; \\
\lambda f\lambda x\lambda y\lambda z. \\
\quad f(x)(y)(z); \\
\text{PDTV}/\text{PDTV}
\end{array}
$$

i; i; NP

would; $\lambda x\lambda y\lambda z.\mathbf{intro}(y)(x)(z)$; PDTV   these ∘ boys; **these-boys**; NP   to ∘ my ∘ brother; **my-bro**; PP

would ∘ these ∘ boys; $\lambda y\lambda z.\mathbf{intro}(y)(\mathbf{these\text{-}boys})(z)$; VP/PP

would ∘ these ∘ boys ∘ to ∘ my ∘ brother; $\lambda z.\mathbf{intro}(\mathbf{my\text{-}bro})(\mathbf{these\text{-}boys})(z)$; VP

i ∘ would ∘ these ∘ boys ∘ to ∘ my ∘ brother; $\mathbf{intro}(\mathbf{my\text{-}bro})(\mathbf{these\text{-}boys})(\mathbf{i})$; S

The present analysis also correctly predicts the interactions between pseudogapping and strict/sloppy readings and quantifier scope in examples like the following:

(307) a. John forwarded HIS address to Ann before BILL did to SUE.

    b. John read every book to MARY before Bill did to SUE.

We omit the derivations, which are parallel to the VP ellipsis cases in (294) and (296).

Since in CG the combinatorial properties of linguistic expressions (including those corresponding to nontraditional constituents) are represented explicitly in their syntactic categories, our approach overcomes the major problem for previous nontransformational approaches as well. Recall from section 6.2.2 that Miller's (1990) interpretive approach requires a rather cumbersome "add-on" in order to explain the ungrammaticality of preposition mismatch examples like (308).

(308) *John spoke to Mary more often than he did for Anne.

Our approach rules out this type of example straightforwardly. In the antecedent clause, we have an instance of the verb *speak* that subcategorizes for a *to*-PP (of syntactic category VP/PP_{to}). But in the target clause, we need to recover the meaning of *speak* associated with a different subcategorization frame VP/PP_{for}. Because of the syntactic category mismatch, the relevant anaphoric mechanism fails and hence (308) is correctly blocked.

Interestingly, the present proposal can also correctly capture cases of tolerated category mismatch, exemplified by data such as (309) (= (276)).

(309) Ask Doll, who spoke as much about his schoolboy career ending as he did of the season in general.

Miller (2014) makes the important observation that (309) is licensed despite the preposition mismatch because of the closeness of the lexical meaning of the verb in the different subcategorization frames. This condition is not satisfied in the minimally different (308), resulting in the degraded status of the latter.

To see how the contrast between (308) and (309) can be accounted for in the present approach, note first that exactly the same contrast is found in unlike-category coordination (UCC).

(310) a. Robin spoke about the war and of similar events.

        b. *John didn't speak to Mary or for Susan at the meeting.

This contrast motivates assigning the category $VP/PP_{of} \wedge VP/PP_{about}$ involving the meet connective $\wedge$ to the verb *speak*, following the general analysis of UCC by Morrill (1994) and Bayer (1996) (see also Kubota and Levine 2013a). We assume that / and \ associate more strongly than $\wedge$; thus, $VP/PP_{of} \wedge VP/PP_{about}$ is an abbreviation for $(VP/PP_{of}) \wedge (VP/PP_{about})$. In (311), the two (related yet distinct) meanings of *speak* associated with different subcategorization frames are represented separately in the form of a tuple.[11]

(311) speak; $\langle$**speak-about**, **speak-of**$\rangle$; $VP/PP_{about} \wedge VP/PP_{of}$

---

11. This corresponds to "semantically potent" meet in Bayer 1996. Bayer rejects this type of lexical entry by claiming that admitting such entries would incorrectly overgenerate violations of Zaenen and Karttunen's (1984) Anti-Pun Ordinance (*I can tuna and get a job*). We don't find this argument convincing. By assuming that lexical entries involving meet are restricted to ones in which the two meanings listed together in a single entry are related (as in (311) and (317)), and by ensuring that meet cannot be syntactically introduced, the Anti-Pun Ordinance can be maintained while still admitting semantically potent meet.

With this lexical assignment and the *Meet Elimination* rules in (643) (where π_1 and π_2 are the standard projection functions such that $\pi_1(\langle \alpha, \beta \rangle) = \alpha$ and $\pi_2(\langle \alpha, \beta \rangle) = \beta$), the analysis for (310a) is straightforward, as in (313). Recall that the index 1 at the last step of the first chunk of the derivation in (313) is for indicating the hypothesis that is withdrawn at that step. For this reason, the PP *about the war* is derived in a functor category that seeks as its argument a conjunctively specified verb.

(312) a. Left Meet Elimination

$$\dfrac{a;\, \mathcal{F};\, A \wedge B}{a;\, \pi_1(\mathcal{F});\, A}\wedge\!E_l$$

b. Right Meet Elimination

$$\dfrac{a;\, \mathcal{F};\, A \wedge B}{a;\, \pi_2(\mathcal{F});\, B}\wedge\!E_r$$

(313)

$$\dfrac{\dfrac{[\varphi; F; \mathrm{VP/PP}_{about} \wedge \mathrm{VP/PP}_{of}]^1}{\varphi;\, \pi_1(F);\, \mathrm{VP/PP}_{about}}\wedge\!E_l \quad \text{about} \circ \text{the} \circ \text{war};\, \mathbf{w};\, \mathrm{PP}_{about}}{\dfrac{\varphi \circ \text{about} \circ \text{the} \circ \text{war};\, \pi_1(F)(\mathbf{w});\, \mathrm{VP}}{\text{about} \circ \text{the} \circ \text{war};\, \lambda F.\pi_1(F)(\mathbf{w});\, (\mathrm{VP/PP}_{about} \wedge \mathrm{VP/PP}_{of})\backslash \mathrm{VP}}\backslash\!I^1}/E$$

$$\vdots$$

$$\dfrac{\begin{matrix}\text{robin};\\ \mathbf{r};\mathrm{NP}\end{matrix} \quad \dfrac{\begin{matrix}\text{spoke};\\ \langle\mathbf{spoke\text{-}about},\mathbf{spoke\text{-}of}\rangle;\\ \mathrm{VP/PP}_{about} \wedge \mathrm{VP/PP}_{of}\end{matrix} \quad \begin{matrix}\text{about} \circ \text{the} \circ \text{war} \circ \text{and} \circ \text{of} \circ \text{similar} \circ \text{events};\\ \lambda F.\pi_1(F)(\mathbf{w}) \sqcap \lambda F.\pi_2(F)(\mathbf{s\text{-}ev});\\ (\mathrm{VP/PP}_{about} \wedge \mathrm{VP/PP}_{of})\backslash \mathrm{VP}\end{matrix}}{\begin{matrix}\text{spoke} \circ \text{about} \circ \text{the} \circ \text{war} \circ \text{and} \circ \text{of} \circ \text{similar} \circ \text{events};\\ \mathbf{spoke\text{-}about}(\mathbf{w}) \sqcap \mathbf{spoke\text{-}of}(\mathbf{s\text{-}ev});\mathrm{VP}\end{matrix}}\backslash E}{\begin{matrix}\text{robin} \circ \text{spoke} \circ \text{about} \circ \text{the} \circ \text{war} \circ \text{and} \circ \text{of} \circ \text{similar} \circ \text{events};\\ \mathbf{spoke\text{-}about}(\mathbf{w})(\mathbf{r}) \wedge \mathbf{spoke\text{-}of}(\mathbf{s\text{-}ev})(\mathbf{r});\mathrm{S}\end{matrix}}\backslash E$$

The contrast in (310) then follows from the assumption that *speak* with a *for*-PP complement is simply listed as a separate entry in the lexicon. We take it that the "closeness" of meaning that Miller (2014) alludes to governs which subcategorization frames can be "packaged" into a single lexical entry involving the meet connective for any given verb.

The parallel contrast between (308) and (309) in the pseudogapping case follows from the same assumption. The preposition-mismatch pseudogapping apparently violating connectivity is licensed in the present analysis without any extra machinery, except that the anaphoric retrieval mechanism is a bit more involved in this case. We assume that the VP ellipsis/pseudogapping operator can access either of the two category-meaning pairs stored in a linguistic sign involving the meet connective such as (311). With this assumption, examples such as (309) can be accounted for straightforwardly. We provide an analysis of (314), a slight variant of (309), in (315).

(314) Robin has spoken about the war, and Leslie has of similar events.

(315)

$$
\begin{array}{c}
\text{spoken;} \\
\langle\mathbf{speak\text{-}about},\mathbf{speak\text{-}of}\rangle; \\
\dfrac{\text{VP}/\text{PP}_{about}\wedge\text{VP}/\text{PP}_{of}}{\text{spoken;}\ \mathbf{speak\text{-}about};\ \text{VP}/\text{PP}_{about}}\ {\scriptstyle\wedge E_l} \quad \dfrac{\text{about}\circ\text{the}\circ\text{war;}}{\mathbf{w};\text{PP}_{about}}
\end{array}
$$

Derivation (315):

- robin; **r**; NP
- has; $\lambda P.P$; VP/VP
- spoken; $\langle$**speak-about**, **speak-of**$\rangle$; VP/PP$_{about}$ $\wedge$ VP/PP$_{of}$ $\dfrac{}{}$ $\wedge E_l$ → spoken; **speak-about**; VP/PP$_{about}$
- about ∘ the ∘ war; **w**; PP$_{about}$
- spoken ∘ about ∘ the ∘ war; **speak-about(w)**; VP   /E
- has ∘ spoken ∘ about ∘ the ∘ war; **speak-about(w)**; VP   /E
- robin ∘ has ∘ spoken ∘ about ∘ the ∘ war; **speak-about(w)(r)**; S   \E

$\vdots$

Derivation (second):

- leslie; **l**; NP
- $\lambda\varphi.\varphi$; $\lambda\mathcal{F}.\mathcal{F}(\mathbf{speak\text{-}of})$; $(\text{VP}/\text{PP}_{of})\!\upharpoonright\!((\text{VP}/\text{PP}_{of})/(\text{VP}/\text{PP}_{of}))$
- has; $\lambda f\lambda x\lambda y.f(x)(y)$; $(\text{VP}/\text{PP}_{of})/(\text{VP}/\text{PP}_{of})$ ↿E → has; $\lambda x\lambda y.\mathbf{speak\text{-}of}(x)(y)$; VP/PP$_{of}$
- of ∘ similar ∘ events; **s-ev**; PP$_{of}$
- has ∘ of ∘ similar ∘ events; $\lambda y.\mathbf{speak\text{-}of}(\mathbf{s\text{-}ev})(y)$; VP   /E
- leslie ∘ has ∘ of ∘ similar ∘ events; **speak-of(s-ev)(y)(l)**; S   \E

The ungrammaticality of (308) still follows, since the meaning of *speak* associated with the different lexical entry with syntactic category VP/PP$_{for}$ cannot be anaphorically retrieved from an occurrence of the VP/PP$_{of}$ $\wedge$ VP/PP$_{about}$ entry in the antecedent.

Furthermore, the following related example noted by Miller (1990, 300), in which a ditransitive verb instantiates different subcategorization frames (V NP NP vs. V NP PP) in the antecedent and the pseudogapping clauses, can be analyzed in essentially the same way (see Kubota and Levine 2014a for a complete derivation):

(316) John gave Mary more books than he did ∅ records to Ann.

The key assumption is the following entry for the ditransitive verb *give* involving the meet connective (which again is motivated by the pattern in UCC (Kubota and Levine 2013a)):

(317) give;
$\langle\lambda x\lambda y\lambda z.\mathbf{give}(x)(y)(z),\lambda y\lambda x\lambda z.\mathbf{give}(x)(y)(z)\rangle;$
$(\text{VP}/\text{PP}/\text{NP})\wedge(\text{VP}/\text{NP}/\text{NP})$

We take voice-mismatch examples such as (318) from Tanaka (2011) (= (275a)) to be licensed in a similar way.

(318) $^{\%}$MY problem will be investigated by Tom, but he won't YOURS.

Though the active/passive alternation is different from the argument structure alternation involving ditransitive verbs in that a morphological marking is involved (thus, the meet connective would be of no use here), there is an obvious similarity between examples like (316) and voice-mismatch examples involving the active form in the antecedent clause licensing a passive pseudogapped verb or vice versa. The key in both cases is lexical relatedness and the mutual entailment of the two related meanings.[12] Following the standard assumption in the nontransformational literature (cf. Bresnan 1982; Pollard and Sag 1994), we take passivization to be a lexical relationship. Since the argument structure and the morphological form are different, the passive form of a verb is listed in the lexicon as a distinct entry separate from the active form. However, they are related to each other via some explicit lexical operation (one standard way of formalizing this is in terms of lexical rules), and the active and the passive forms have identical meanings in terms of their truth-conditional entailments. It is then not unreasonable to assume that the pseudogapping operator can have access to the lexical entry of the passive form from the occurrence of the active form in the preceding clause and vice versa, because of this close relation between the lexical entries for the active and passive forms in the lexicon. Thus, voice-mismatch examples like (318) do not pose problems for the present approach.

6.3.3   Discontinuous Pseudogapping

As discussed in the previous section, our approach extends smoothly to quite complex types of data such as multiple-remnant pseudogapping (304), "nonconstituent" pseudogapping (302), and "unlike-category" pseudogapping (309) and (316), all of which are highly problematic for many previous approaches. However, as it stands, the present analysis does not yet cover cases of discontinuous pseudogapping exemplified by the following data:

(319) a. Although I didn't **give** Bill **the book**, I did $\varnothing$ Susan $\varnothing$.
       b. She **found** her coworker **attractive** but she didn't $\varnothing$ her husband $\varnothing$.

There are at least two possible approaches to this problem, and deciding between them is a delicate matter, given the somewhat marginal status of the pseudogapping construction itself and especially its discontinuous variant. Here, we simply lay out the two options and leave it for future work to determine which is the better alternative.

One possible approach would be to deal with discontinuity via the prosodic λ-binding mechanism already available in the grammar. Since this alternative does not involve adding any new machinery to the grammar, we will be relatively brief in sketching the main idea. See Kubota and Levine 2014a for a more detailed demonstration of this approach with example derivations. Essentially, the idea of this vertical slash–based approach is that in order to license (319a), for example, we can derive the following

---

12. Mutual entailment is a crucial factor. For example, the conative alternation is treated (under certain theories) via a lexical rule, but *He kicked Bill more than he did at John* does not seem to be as acceptable as (318).

expression of type VP↾NP and identify it as the antecedent for the VP ellipsis/pseudo-gapping operator (whose syntactic category also needs to be changed slightly) in the target clause:

(320) $\lambda\varphi.\text{give} \circ \varphi \circ \text{the} \circ \text{book}; \lambda x.\textbf{give}(x)(\textbf{the-book}); \text{VP}{\upharpoonright}\text{NP}$

This would suffice to license (319a) ((319b) could be derived analogously).

One concern about this type of approach is its overgeneration. One concrete case that the vertical slash–based approach would overgenerate is (321).

(321) *John **laughed when** BILL **arrived**, but he didn't ∅ SUE ∅.
       intended: '. . . he didn't laugh when Sue arrived.'

Here, the same VP↾NP category as in (320) could be assigned to the string *laughed when __ arrived*. It is not immediately clear whether this example could be ruled out by any of the known pragmatic properties associated with pseudogapping.[13]

While pushing the "syntax overgenerates, pragmatics constrains" approach to its limits is certainly an attractive option (especially if doing so avoids the need to introduce new theoretical machinery), we would like to offer another possibility, if only as a point of comparison for future investigations. The guiding intuition behind this alternative is the observation (which itself needs to be scrutinized, but which seems to match the overall empirical patterns we have been able to identify) that there is an intriguing overlap between the cases of discontinuous pseudogapping and patterns of (apparent) discontinuity traditionally analyzed by the "wrapping" operation in the CG literature.[14] Wrapping is a mechanism originally proposed by Bach (1979) and Dowty (1982) in the

---

13. One might think that (i) (from Miller 2014, 83) would have the same structure as (321):

(i) . . . they would **examine what** I **wore** as intensely as anything else—as they would ∅ any woman who met with them ∅

If the elided material were to correspond to the boldfaced material in the antecedent clause, this example indeed would not seem to lend itself to any well-motivated wrapping analysis (discussed below). However, (i) seems to allow for an alternative parse in which the elided material is just the verb *examine* (note from above that, as in (277), pseudogapping is sometimes possible without any matching syntactic antecedent), and it is hard to clearly establish that this example is consistent only with the former interpretation. For this reason, we do not take (i) to provide a conclusive enough argument for the vertical slash–based analysis of discontinuous pseudogapping.

14. Levin (1979) provides several examples of (apparent) discontinuous pseudogapping. So far as we can tell, all of her examples belong to one of the following three classes: (i) antecedentless pseudogapping (similar to the cases discussed in section 6.3.4), (ii) pseudogapping combined with an independent nominal ellipsis or adjunct ellipsis, (iii) wrapping-type pseudogapping. For example, her (36) on p. 77 *Does it [writing a check at a grocery store] usually take this long? – No, it never did me before* can be analyzed as an instance of (i), where what is missing after *did* is simply the verb (plus preposition) *happen to*. See section 6.3.4 for antecedentless pseudogapping. We take an example such as Levin's (1) on p. 75 *We'll share it–like we do ∅ the pink [blouse]* as an instance of (ii), where the ellipsis of *blouse* after *pink* is nominal ellipsis independent of pseudogapping.

early Montague Grammar literature for treating discontinuous strings (such as *make __ up*, *pull __ out* in verb-particle constructions) as combinatoric units. For example, in a wrapping-based analysis, the verb-adjective pair *found __ attractive* in (319b) is analyzed as an "underlying" constituent, and it "wraps" around the object NP *her coworker* in the surface form of the sentence.

We now give a somewhat detailed sketch of this alternative, which treats discontinuous pseudogapping like that in (319) via an interaction between pseudogapping and wrapping. In contemporary TLCG, wrapping is modeled by enriching the prosodic component of the theory (roughly corresponding to PF) via the notion of "multimodality" (Moortgat and Oehrle 1994; Dowty 1996a,b; Muskens 2007; Kubota 2010, 2014; Mihalicek 2012). We discuss this type of extension of Hybrid TLCG in chapter 11 in greater detail. Here we provide a brief sketch of the main idea as it pertains to the analysis of discontinuous pseudogapping. The notion of "modality" here pertains to different "modes" of composition in the prosodic component governing various reordering and restructuring operations related to surface morpho-phonological constituency; it has nothing to do with the notion of modality in the semantics literature. Following Kubota (2010, 2014), we call this surface morpho-phonological component of grammar the "prosodic algebra."

For our purposes, it suffices to distinguish between two modes of composition in the prosodic algebra: the ordinary concatenation mode ($\circ$) and the infixation mode (which we notate as $\circ_\bullet$). Prosodic terms are ordered in the prosodic algebra by the *deducibility* relations between terms (where $\varphi_1 \leq \varphi_2$ is to be read 'φ_2 is deducible from φ_1'). Specifically, to model wrapping, we posit the following rule:

(322) $(A \circ_\bullet B) \circ C \leq (A \circ C) \circ B$

The intuition behind this is that when A and B are combined in the infixation mode, an expression C that combines with that unit at a later point in the derivation can be infixed in the middle by a surface morpho-phonological reordering operation. To refer to the deducibility relation in the prosodic algebra from the combinatoric component during the course of a derivation, we posit the following P(rosodic)-Interface rule:

(323) P-Interface Rule
$$\frac{\varphi_1; \mathcal{F}; A}{\varphi_2; \mathcal{F}; A}\text{PI}$$
——where $\varphi_1 \leq \varphi_2$ holds in the prosodic algebra

The syntactic rules are also revised to take into account the sensitivity to modes of composition (for space reasons, we only reproduce the rules for $/$, but the rules for $\backslash$ are similarly revised; the rules for $\upharpoonright$ remain the same as above).

(324)   a. Forward Slash Introduction   b. Forward Slash Elimination

$$\dfrac{a;\, \mathcal{F};\, A/_iB \quad b;\, \mathcal{G};\, B}{a \circ_i b;\, \mathcal{F}(\mathcal{G});\, A}\, /_iE$$

$$\vdots \quad [\varphi;\, x;\, A]^n \quad \vdots$$

$$\dfrac{\vdots \qquad \vdots \qquad \vdots}{\dfrac{b \circ_i \varphi;\, \mathcal{F};\, B}{b;\, \lambda x.\mathcal{F};\, B/_iA}}\, /_iI^n$$

In these revised rules, the modes encoded in the slashes match those that are used to combine the phonologies of the functor expressions with those of their arguments.

   With this small extension, a simple wrapping example such as (325) can be analyzed as in (326).

(325) Mary found Chris attractive.

(326)

$$\dfrac{\dfrac{\text{found};\, \textbf{find};\, \text{VP}/\text{NP}/.\,\text{Adj} \quad \text{attractive};\, \textbf{attractive};\, \text{Adj}}{\text{found} \circ.\, \text{attractive};\, \textbf{find}(\textbf{attractive});\, \boxed{\text{VP}/\text{NP}} \quad \text{chris};\, \textbf{c};\, \text{NP}}\, /.E}{}$$

mary; **m**; NP

(found ∘. attractive) ∘ chris; **find**(**attractive**)(**c**); VP /E

mary ∘ ((found ∘. attractive) ∘ chris); **find**(**attractive**)(**c**)(**m**); S \E

mary ∘ found ∘ chris ∘ attractive; **find**(**attractive**)(**c**)(**m**); S PI

The point here is that the (surface) discontinuous string *found __ attractive* behaves as a unit in the combinatoric component (motivation for this assumption comes from patterns of argument structure–sensitive phenomena such as passivization and binding; see, for example, Dowty 1982, 1996a). The pseudogapping operator can then directly refer to the syntactic category and the semantics of this "underlying constituent" to supply the relevant subcategorization frame and meaning of the missing TV to the auxiliary, in exactly the same way as in the simpler examples above. Thus, (319b) is licensed as follows:

(327)

$$\lambda\varphi.\varphi;$$
$$\lambda\mathscr{F}.\mathscr{F}(\textbf{find}(\textbf{attractive}));$$
$$\text{TV}\!\restriction\!(\text{TV}/\text{TV})$$

didn't;
$$\lambda f\lambda x\lambda y.\neg f(x)(y);\text{TV}/\text{TV}$$

$$\dfrac{\text{didn't};\, \lambda x\lambda y.\neg\textbf{find}(\textbf{attractive})(x)(y);\, \text{TV} \quad \text{her} \circ \text{husband};\, \textbf{her-h};\, \text{NP}}{\text{didn't} \circ \text{her} \circ \text{husband};\, \lambda y.\neg\textbf{find}(\textbf{attractive})(\textbf{her-h})(y);\, \text{VP}}\, /E$$

The wrapping-based alternative just sketched does not admit discontinuous constituents involving the vertical slash $\restriction$ (such as VP$\restriction$NP), since VP/\$ ranges over categories involving directional slashes only. With this restriction, it is predicted that discontinuous pseudogapping is possible only when the deleted discontinuous string corresponds to an "underlying" constituent in the combinatoric component involving wrapping. The data reported in the literature seem to conform to this prediction, but it remains an open question whether this analysis is adequate or whether true counterexamples can be found that would suggest that the other approach involving the vertical slash would be better.

6.3.4   The Nature of the Syntactic Identity Condition

The analysis of VP ellipsis and pseudogapping given above is actually a bit too simplistic in assuming that there is always a syntactic antecedent that the ellipsis operator anaphorically refers to (see the side condition in (299)). This requirement is clearly too strong for VP ellipsis and arguably also for pseudogapping. As noted by Miller and Pullum (2013), if appropriate discourse conditions are satisfied, purely exophoric VP ellipsis is possible.

(328)   a.   Once in my room, I took the pills out. "Should I?" I asked myself.
                                     [Corpus of Contemporary American English]
         b.   [Entering a construction site, somebody hands a hard hat to the speaker:]
               Do I have to?

  While it seems considerably more difficult to construct analogous purely exophoric cases of pseudogapping (presumably because of the requirement specific to pseudogapping that the remnant needs to be contrasted with some "corresponding" item),[15] as we have already noted, there are cases of pseudogapping in which there are no appropriate syntactic antecedents in the preceding clauses (Miller 2014) and also instances of split-antecedent pseudogapping, which essentially establish the same point.

(329)   a.   Type in your PIN, just hit those buttons like you would $\varnothing$ a phone.
         b.   John saw Mary and Peter heard Ann, but neither of them did $\varnothing$ me.

While these examples clearly show that the condition encoded in (299) (which requires the existence of a syntactic antecedent) is too strong, purely interpretive approaches such as Miller's (1990) would overgenerate radically, as Miller (2014) himself acknowledges.

---

15. To our knowledge, the literature does not report any case of purely exophoric pseudogapping, but the following example may count as one (which to the ears of the native-speaker author sounds acceptable):

(i)   [You stop in at a (German) friend's house, and he holds out to you a huge one-liter mug of beer. You look at it quickly, smile and shake your head, and say:]
      No, but I COULD a small glass of wine.

We think the right empirical pattern can be captured by relaxing the condition on the VP ellipsis/pseudogapping operator (reproduced in (330)) slightly, along the lines of (331).

(330) **VP ellipsis/pseudogapping operator, final version**

$\lambda \varphi. \varphi; \lambda \mathscr{F}. \mathscr{F}(P); (VP/\$) \restriction ((VP/\$)/(VP/\$))$

——where P is a free variable whose value is resolved anaphorically

(331) Anaphora resolution condition on the VP ellipsis/pseudogapping operator:

   a. If there is a syntactic constituent with category VP/$ in the antecedent clause matching the syntactic category of the missing verb in the target clause, then the value of P is identified with the denotation of that constituent.

   b. If there is no such syntactic constituent, then the value of P is anaphorically identified with some salient property in the discourse that is not inconsistent with the syntactic category VP/$.

With these conditions, the preposition mismatch case in (287), repeated here as (332), is still correctly ruled out.

(332) *John spoke to Mary more often than he did for Anne.

The remnant PP_{for} forces the syntactic category of the derived auxiliary to be VP/PP_{for}, but then, there is no matching syntactic antecedent in the preceding clause. Crucially, recovering the "speak to" meaning of *speak* from the preceding clause via a purely anaphoric process (clause (ii)) is not an option either, since that meaning is associated with a distinct subcategorization frame VP/PP_{to} and thus is inconsistent with the VP/PP_{for} frame.[16]

The revised condition in (331) is clearly in the same spirit as Miller's (1990) selectional restriction–based treatment (see section 6.2.2) in embodying the intuition that, essentially, (332) is ill-formed because the verb has distinct meanings depending on which of the two subcategorization frames it appears in. But it achieves the same effect by simply making the anaphora resolution process be sensitive to both the syntactic and the semantic information of the antecedent simultaneously, rather than by making

---

16. Though the formulation in (330) and (331) predicts morphological identity between the remnant and its correlate in the antecedent clause, it does not require the morphological forms of the elided verb and the antecedent verb to be identical. This is because the VP in the result category of (330) and the VP in the anaphora resolution condition (331) do not need to match in terms of their morpho-syntactic features. Thus, well-known form mismatches in VP ellipsis and pseudogapping (e.g., in *I talked to John, though I didn't want to ∅* with VP_{fin} vs. VP_{bse}) are not problematic. The anaphora condition in (331) essentially says that it doesn't care about either the number or the category of the elided material, as long as they match in the antecedent clause and the ellipsis site. This seems to correspond to the relevant generalization on connectivity in ellipsis cross-linguistically (cf. Merchant 2004).

the *semantic* restriction on the denotation of the anaphoric verb directly access the sub-categorization frame of the antecedent.[17]

The antecedentless and split-antecedent examples in (329) are no longer problematic for the revised formulation of the anaphora resolution condition in (331). In these cases, there are no syntactic antecedents matching in category with the "missing verbs." However, unlike the case of (332), the relevant relations appropriate as antecedents (such as "use" for (329a) and "saw or heard" for (329b)) are salient in the preceding discourse; moreover, there is no interference from a lexically associated conflicting subcategorization frame. Thus, anaphora is resolved by a purely semantic/pragmatic mechanism in these cases.

6.3.5   A Note on Overgeneration

We believe that the above discussion has made it clear that our analysis of pseudo-gapping achieves better empirical coverage than any of the transformational analyses. At the same time, the flexible CG-based syntax-semantics interface enables us to formulate the restrictions pertaining to syntactic connectivity much more simply than in purely anaphoric approaches. Nonetheless, the present proposal leaves open one major issue, which we should note explicitly: overgeneration owing to the flexible architecture of CG. For example, on our account, nothing in the syntax predicts (333a) to be unacceptable. We take this to be the correct result, since the structurally parallel (333b), an attested example from Levin (1979, 77), is an acceptable example of pseudogapping.

(333)   a.   %%%I took a book out of the box. But I didn't ∅ the bookcase.

      b.   %You can't take the lining out of that coat. You can ∅ this one.

But then, how can we account for the unacceptability of (333a)? Here, too, we feel sympathetic to the general perspective advocated by Miller (2014), in which the syntax overgenerates somewhat wildly and additional processing-oriented and pragmatic factors constrain the acceptability of specific examples further. It is beyond the scope of the present work to fully articulate these extragrammatical conditions, but we would like to note some potentially relevant factors, in the hope that our discussion will at

---

17. We believe that this is a subtle but important difference between the present proposal and related proposals in the anaphoric approaches. For example, Ginzburg and Sag's (2000) SAL-UTT feature (invoked in their analysis of sluicing and fragment answers and also employed in other recent work such as Chaves [2014]) does roughly the same work; however, a criticism one might raise, that it builds strictly morpho-syntactic specifications of linguistic expressions into supposedly purely discourse-based information (under CONTEXT) to capture morpho-syntactic connectivity by fiat, does not apply to our approach.

Note also that formulating a syntax-semantics interface condition along the lines of (331) seems less straightforward in phrase structure–based frameworks such as HPSG, since such frameworks do not have a fully general "built-in device" for representing the notion of flexible incomplete constituents with some valent(s) unsaturated. In our CG-based approach, hypothetical reasoning is the device that gives us this flexibility.

least provide a starting point for further investigating this quite complex issue in more detail.

The acceptability of complex instances of pseudogapping (such as those in (333)) seems to be particularly sensitive to pragmatic factors such as prototypicality and plausibility of the event described by the sentence in view of general world knowledge.[18] For example, the intended interpretation of (333b) is presumably supported by the fact that linings are components of coats that are detachable for some types of coats, but not all. In (333a), by contrast, there is no such inherent part-whole relation between books and boxes.

Note further that the contrast in (333) becomes less clear if we manipulate certain lexical choices. (334b) is less natural than (333b) since skirts and dresses don't normally have linings. By contrast, (334a) is more natural than (333a) since the use of the demonstratives *this* and *that* naturally invokes a contrast between the two remnants.

(334) a. %%I took a book out of this box. But I didn't ∅ that one.
       b. %%I took the lining out of the skirt. But I didn't ∅ the dress.

Given the diversity of the possibly relevant factors, predicting the acceptability of specific examples in some precisely measurable manner is a potentially limitless open question, and we do not attempt to answer it here. But the overall conclusion from the above discussion should be clear: in general, one should be extra careful in assessing the acceptability of pseudogapping examples; in particular, when some example seems to sound bad, one should not immediately attribute its unacceptability to grammatical factors. Such a conclusion is justified only if the unacceptability cannot be ameliorated by carefully controlling for all possible confounding factors.

6.4 Toward an Account of "Partial" Syntactic Sensitivity

Pseudogapping has remained problematic for both transformational and nontransformational approaches because of what has recently been identified in a different domain of ellipsis as "partial syntactic sensitivity" (Chung 2013; Barker 2013; Yoshida et al. 2015): with respect to subcategorization-related properties, the elided verb and the remnant exhibit morpho-syntactic matching, apparently motivating an analysis in terms of syntactic movement; in other respects, however, the movement operations required in syntactic deletion–based analyses do not exhibit the expected distributional properties (such as island sensitivity), and the movements required are themselves typically dubious, as detailed in Kubota and Levine (2017). These considerations cast consider-

---

18. The greater role of extragrammatical factors in regulating acceptability here is reminiscent of the similarly nontrivial role that such factors play in the so-called gapless relative clauses in Japanese and Korean (Kuno 1973; Yoon 1993; Matsumoto 1997).

able doubt on movement-based analyses. Interpretive approaches can account for the island insensitivity straightforwardly (and avoid various other problems for movement-based analyses), but on this type of approach, connectivity effects in subcategorization-related properties remain puzzling. In fact, Miller (1990)—who provides the only extant proposal that explicitly attempts to capture syntactic connectivity in pseudogapping in an interpretive approach—invokes for this purpose a quite complex and abstract type of semantic selectional restriction that does not resemble any other well-known types of selectional restrictions. Importantly, neither the transformational nor the non-transformational approach explains *why* pseudogapping exhibits only partial syntactic sensitivity and why it is that, among the various pieces of syntactic information encoded in the "elided" material, what matters are the selectional requirements that the elided verb imposes on the remnant.

It is then interesting to see that, from the CG perspective, this partial syntactic sensitivity is exactly what is expected in an analysis that embodies the null hypothesis about pseudogapping. Pseudogapping involves anaphorically retrieving the meaning of the missing verb. In CG, there is a tight connection between the syntactic category of any linguistic expression and its semantic denotation (even in cases in which the linguistic expression in question does not correspond to a traditional constituent). Thus, it is naturally expected that the relevant anaphoric process is sensitive not just to the meaning of the antecedent but also to its syntactic category, which encodes the relevant subcategorization information. But this anaphora resolution process does not involve any movement operation, and, for this reason, the account is free from the problems facing movement-based approaches. As we have argued here, this CG perspective enables us to naturally synthesize the insights of both transformational and nontransformational approaches, paving the way toward a truly explanatory account of the phenomenon.[19]

Evidence of a possible line of convergence between the approach we take here and the standard transformational "move and delete" scenario for analyzing ellipsis is to be found in the recent work on problems posed by the differential sensitivity of various kinds of ellipsis to island effects. A number of different approaches to this problem have been proposed, which try to reconcile the immunity of certain versions of ellipsis, such as sluicing, to island violations with the supposed vulnerability of VP ellipsis and pseudogapping to such effects. In some proposals, for example, Merchant (2008b), various complex representations and conditions are posited to explain this difference in behavior; Barros et al. (2014) convincingly refutes such an account, arguing instead for an "evasion" explanation in which the covert structure from which movement occurs in the case of sluicing differs in form from the overt, problematic configuration in the

---

19. In this connection, see also Barker (2013), who arrives at a conclusion very similar to ours in the analysis of another major and controversial type of ellipsis, namely, sluicing.

antecedent, although the remnant in the ellipsis clause corresponds semantically to the material within the island in the antecedent. The difference in syntactic form is hypothesized to be such that movement of the remnant out of the ellipsed material does not cross any island boundaries. But this approach has been shown to have its own major flaws, in work both outside the transformational approach (e.g., Jacobson 2016) and within, as in Abels (2018), the most recent and comprehensive overview of the issues raised by the interaction of ellipsis and extraction phenomena. As Abels (2018, 424) soberly observes of his own findings,

> It was shown that the most immediate empirical consequence of the two canonical theories of ellipsis, that is of theories that posit no (variable) syntactic structure at the ellipsis site and theories that demand syntactic identity between antecedent and ellipsis site, radically different though they are, is Ross's conjecture. Ross's conjecture says that, ceteris paribus, all cases of ellipsis give rise to island amelioration. On the surface, the conjecture is false. As a result, the various conclusions based on canonical theories of ellipsis are weakened. The most promising competing approach, the approach based on island evasion, cannot be considered a successful theory until a principled account of case connectivity is presented and the too-many-paraphrases problem is solved.

Our own assessment of such efforts to motivate covert syntactic structure in ellipsis is given in chapter 8, where we extend the present analysis of ellipsis to somewhat more complex cases involving interactions between ellipsis and extraction phenomena. In the literature, such complex interactions between major grammatical phenomena have been taken to provide strong evidence for the hypothesis that ellipsis requires positing invisible syntactic structures (see in particular Kennedy 2003 and Kennedy and Merchant 2000). We argue in chapter 8 that an alternative analysis of the relevant empirical patterns is not only available in Hybrid TLCG but is actually both empirically and conceptually superior to the traditional structural accounts offered in the previous literature. Specifically, our approach offers a principled explanation for *why* ellipsis exhibits only *partial* syntactic sensitivity with respect to these more complex data involving ellipsis/extraction interactions as well, thereby offering one possible answer to the question that Abels (2018) identifies as the major remaining issue. This conclusion suggests once again that the synthesis of transformational and nontransformational perspectives on grammar that Hybrid TLCG offers is not just a matter of theoretical elegance but has substantial empirical and conceptual consequences directly relevant for grammatical theory development.

7 Filler-Gap Dependency

In this chapter, we extend the analysis of long-distance dependencies sketched briefly in chapter 2. The main purpose of this extension is twofold. First, there are certain empirical phenomena discussed extensively in the literature of phrase structure–based syntactic theories under the rubric of "syntactic binding domain phenomena" or "extraction pathway marking" (e.g., Zaenen 1983; Levine and Hukari 2006, 119; Chaves 2009, 48), which initially seem to pose significant difficulties to the type of analysis of extraction in terms of hypothetical reasoning from chapter 2, whose key analytic idea goes back to Muskens (2003). Though a complete analysis of this rather intricate empirical domain (which involves several languages with well-attested patterns of this sort) is beyond the scope of the present monograph, we find it important to skech the core idea of a possible elaboration of the Muskens-style analysis of extraction in TLCG. The account we formulate here should not be understood as a full-fledged analysis but rather as a proof of concept that the logical deductive system underlying our approach can be augmented with devices (which have empirical motivation in other domains) to deal with the locality effects exhibited by the extraction pathway marking data.

   The second reason for extending the fragment of long-distance dependencies here is that the central focus of the next chapter is an interaction between ellipsis and extraction, and for this reason, we need to broaden the coverage of the simple analysis of extraction in chapter 2 so that it can deal with a wider range of data. In particular, an explicit analysis of parasitic gap licensing is needed in order to deal with the parasitic gap licensing by elided VPs discussed by Postal (1993), Shimada (1999), and Kennedy (2003). Since multiple-gap phenomena (including parasitic gaps) pose a potentially deep foundational issue for TLCG, we do not mean to offer here a definitive answer to the question of how best to deal with multiple gaps in TLCG. Our goal here is more modest. We sketch an outline of one possible approach that does not involve a radical reworking of the foundations of the architecture of the syntax-semantics interface. We then show, in the next chapter, that this analysis interacts in a simple and direct fashion with the analysis of VP ellipsis from chapter 6 to straightforwardly predict the ellipsis/extraction interaction data that Kennedy (2003) adduces for his deletion-based analysis of VP ellipsis in English.

It may ultimately turn out that the specific analyses of extraction pathway marking and multiple-gap phenomena we introduce in this chapter need to be replaced by more elaborate/sophisticated analyses, possibly together with some major reformulations of (at least part of) the logical deductive system itself, for example, along the lines of a recent proposal by Morrill (2017) for the analysis of multiple gaps. If this turns out to be the case, the specific analysis we formulate below should be viewed as a touchstone that any analysis that supersedes it should be able to account for, with comparable or (ideally) less extra machinery involved. In any event, the treatment of long-distance dependencies is a relatively underdeveloped domain of inquiry in TLCG research, and for this reason, our own investigations in this chapter have a more exploratory nature than the material presented in previous chapters. Where there are open issues and alternative analytic perspectives, we note them as such in the ensuing discussions.

7.1   Extraction Pathway Marking

7.1.1   The Reality of Extraction Pathway Marking

There is a basis for viewing extraction as a series of locally constructed linkages: the existence of languages which distinctively mark in some way the syntactic domains intervening between fillers and their associated gaps. This pattern, first identified as a cross-linguistic pattern in Zaenen (1983), immediately confronts accounts such as Muskens's (2003) with a descriptive difficulty which, unlike island effects, is unlikely to originate in non-syntactic factors. The problem is that, on Muskens's account, the morpho-syntactic/prosodic "registration" of a filler-gap pathway will not be possible. In Muskens's analysis of extraction, the linkage between the gap and filler is established via a single step of hypothetical reasoning via the vertical slash, and given the nature of hypothetical reasoning, whether or not a particular linguistic expression "contains a gap" is impossible to tell since a hypothesis does not necessarily correspond to a gap within the overall architecture of grammar.

Consider, for concreteness, the facts first reported by James McCloskey (1979) for Irish:

(335) Shíl   mé **goN**   mbeadh sé ann.
       thought I   COMP would-be he there
       'I thought that he would be there.'

(336) Dúirt mé **gurL**   shíl   me **goN** mbeadh   sé ann.
       said I   **goN**+PAST thought I   **goN** would-be he there
       'I said that I thought that he would be there.'

In (335)–(336), we see multiple instances of *g-* complementizers, as is appropriate to a series of clauses in which all valence requirements are locally satisfied by overt constituents. In (337), however, while the lower clause contains no gap "sites" and is appropriately marked with a *g-* complementizer, the upper clause, which is missing its subject (as indicated by the gap marker __), is identified via an *a-* form.[1]

(337) an fear **aL** shíl __ **goN** mbeadh sé ann
      the man COMP thought __ COMP would-be he there
      'the man that thought he would be there'

Finally, the examples in (338)–(339) display the characteristic local registration in Irish of the linkage between the filler and the gap over an arbitrary number of structural levels.

(338) an fear **aL** shíl mé **aL** bheadh __ ann
      the man COMP thought I COMP would-be __ there
      'the man that I thought would be there'

(339) an fear **aL** dúirt mé **aL** shíl mé **aL** bheadh __ ann
      the man COMP said I COMP thought I COMP would-be __ there
      'The man that I said I thought would be there'

Moreover, regardless of the depth of the extraction, as soon as the gap site is identified, all lower clauses which themselves are not associated with an extraction will be marked by *g-* class complementizers, a point illustrated in (337) and at still greater structural depth in (340).

(340) an fear **aL** dúirt sé **aL** shíl __ **goN** mbeadh sé ann
      the man COMP said he COMP thought __ COMP would-be he there
      'the man that he said thought he would be there'

Apart from its inherent interest as a convincing demonstration of the local nature of information sharing in extraction dependencies, the grammatical marking of extraction pathways in Irish provides further corroboration of the convergence between valent and adjunct extraction.

Note first that Irish supports the argument that extraction of adjuncts (corresponding to functors in our framework) is mediated by exactly the same mechanisms as are required for the extraction of arguments:

(341) an lá **aL** bhí muid nDoire __
      [the day]$_j$ COMP were we in Derry e$_j$

---

1. The locution "gap site" is used here as an informal abbreviation for "string position in which a phono-logically overt substring would normally appear in the saturation of some functor type."

'the day we were in Derry'

(342) Cén   uair   **aL**   tháinig siad na bhaile __
      [which time]$_j$ COMP came   they home   e$_j$
      'What time did they come home?'

Neither the copula in Irish nor *tháinig* selects a constituent corresponding to a temporal description, but in both of these cases we find a fronting of these modificatory phrases associated with one or more *a-* series complementizers. Similarly, *béarfaí* in (343) does not select a constituent indicating location, but when an adjunct is extracted from a multiply-embedded position, all the clause boundaries between the extraction site and the filler are marked by the *a-* complementizer.

(343) I mBetlehem **aL**   dúirt na targaireachtaí **aL**   béarfaí   an
      in Bethlehem COMP said the prophecies   COMP would-be-born the
      Slánaitheoir __
      Savior   __
      'It was in Bethlehem that the prophecies said the Savior would be born.'

The data in (341)–(343) establish conclusively that the displacement of adjuncts is mediated by the same mechanism as the displacement of material selected by a head.

But this family of morpho-syntactic patterns presents a major challenge to the Muskens treatment of filler-gap dependencies. Since the history of proof does not correspond to a representational object expressing the description of natural language sentences, there is no obvious locus for the identification of the notion "connectivity pathway" that would be a direct analogue for the appearance of traces in a chain of functional projections at clause boundaries in P&P formulations of these pathways or the appearance of nonempty SLASH specifications in various avatars of phrase structure grammar, starting with Gazdar et al. (1985) and maintained and applied to the marking of extraction locality in, e.g., Bouma et al. (2001). Since the order of proof steps corresponding to the embedding of material via functor saturations has no comparable standing in the representation language of TLCG, we seem to be at a loss for resources applicable to capturing patterns such as the *goN/aL* alternations in (335)–(342).

7.1.2 Marking Extracted Arguments with a Syntactic Feature

We first elaborate the analysis of extraction from chapter 2 by adding a syntactic feature for distinguishing extracted and overt phrases. The extraction operator is thus revised to specifically require the missing NP to carry the +*wh* feature:

(344) $\lambda\sigma.$what $\circ$ $\sigma(\boldsymbol{\varepsilon})$; **wh**(**obj**); Q$\upharpoonright$(S$\upharpoonright$NP$_{+wh}$)

This modest elaboration has an apparently significant technical consequence (which, however, turns out to be a nonissue). Consider a very simple sentence such as (345):

(345) I wonder what John ate.

In order to supply a variable whose abstraction can feed the extraction operator (344), we need to saturate *ate* with an NP_{+wh} variable. But *eat* can combine with other NPs in non-extraction constructions as well, making the default statement of this verb's syntactic type $VP/(NP_{+wh} \vee NP_{-wh})$.[2]

Disjunctive categories have their own inference rules—duals, in a specific sense, of the rules for the conjunctive type constructor $\wedge$ discussed in section 6.3—which are independently motivated empirically in the analysis of feature neutralization effects, as discussed in detail in Bayer (1996). We reproduce here the $\vee$ Introduction rules from Bayer (1996):[3]

(346) a. Left Join Introduction

$$\frac{a;\, \mathcal{F};\, B}{a;\, \mathcal{F};\, A \vee B}\vee I_l$$

  b. Right Join Introduction

$$\frac{a;\, \mathcal{F};\, A}{a;\, \mathcal{F};\, A \vee B}\vee I_r$$

Using these rules, we can directly prove the lemma (or theorem) $VP/(NP_{+wh} \vee NP_{-wh})$ $\vdash VP/NP_{+wh}$. The proof is straightforward, completely cognate to that for the elementary theorem in classical propositional logic $(\phi \vee \psi) \supset \rho \vdash \phi \supset \rho$:

---

2. We use the notation $NP_{\#wh}$ as an abbreviation for $NP_{+wh} \vee NP_{-wh}$ throughout the rest of this chapter and chapter 8. Since NP itself is an abbreviation for a fully specified syntactic category in which all feature values are fully specified (cf. A.4 in the appendix), we need to be more precise about what we actually mean by saying that $NP_{\#wh}$ abbreviates $NP_{+wh} \vee NP_{-wh}$. What we mean here is that the symbol "NP" in the abbreviatory notation $NP_{\#wh}$ for the disjunctively specified category is to be understood as a *fully specified* NP category (modulo the *wh* feature), such as $NP_{+p,sg}$ (assuming that, aside from *wh*, *p* and *sg/pl* are the only syntactic features appropriate for NP). Given this assumption, the abbreviatory notation for the transitive verb $(NP_{\#wh}\backslash S)/NP_{\#wh}$ can, for example, be instantiated either as (ia) or (ib), but *not* as (ic) or (id):

(i) a. $((NP_{+p,sg,+wh} \vee NP_{+p,sg,-wh})\backslash S)/(NP_{+p,pl,+wh} \vee NP_{+p,pl,-wh})$
   b. $((NP_{-p,sg,+wh} \vee NP_{-p,sg,-wh})\backslash S)/(NP_{+p,pl,+wh} \vee NP_{+p,pl,-wh})$
   c. $((NP_{+p,pl,+wh} \vee NP_{+p,sg,-wh})\backslash S)/(NP_{+p,pl,+wh} \vee NP_{+p,pl,-wh})$
   d. $((NP_{+p,sg,+wh} \vee NP_{+p,sg,-wh})\backslash S)/(NP_{+p,pl,+wh} \vee NP_{-p,pl,-wh})$

In (ic), the subject NP has conflicting number specifications, and in (id), the value for the *p* (pronominal) feature for the object NP doesn't match.

3. Bayer assumes that terms inhabiting conjoined and disjoined types cannot differ in their semantics, regardless of which subtype they belong to. Such signs, in his terminology, reflect a semantically "nonpotent" interpretation of the meet and join connectives, in contrast to Morrill's (1994) treatment, in which $X \vee Y$ can combine different semantics for X, Y to yield ordered-pair interpretations. We follow Bayer's analysis for join, taking the semantics of disjoined types to be nonpotent—but, per our analysis of examples such as (316) (from chapter 6), we assume the meet connective to be associated with a semantically potent denotation, whose component meanings are obtained along the lines outlined in Carpenter (1997) for the treatment of "sum" types.

(347)

$$\cfrac{k; \text{VP}/(\text{NP}_{+wh} \vee \text{NP}_{-wh}) \quad \cfrac{\cfrac{[\varphi_0; \text{NP}_{+wh}]^1}{\varphi_0; \text{NP}_{+wh} \vee \text{NP}_{-wh}} \vee \text{I}}{k \circ \varphi_0; \text{VP}} /\text{E}}{\cfrac{k; \text{VP}/\text{NP}_{+wh}}{} /\text{I}^1}$$

This proof can be trivially generalized schematically in the form of $X\|Y \vdash X\|Z$ (where $Z \vdash Y$), with X, Y, Z variables over syntactic types and $\|$ a variable over implicational connectives (i.e., $/$, $\backslash$, and $\upharpoonright$). In writing proofs, we suppress the steps explicitly shown in (347) and pretend as if NPs with the *wh* feature specified (either as $+$ or $-$) can directly saturate $\text{NP}_{\#wh}$ arguments of verbs, as in the following derivation:

(348)

$$\cfrac{\cfrac{\cfrac{\cfrac{\text{ate}; \textbf{eat}; \text{VP}/\text{NP}_{\#wh} \quad [\varphi_0; x; \text{NP}_{+wh}]^1}{\text{ate} \circ \varphi_0; \textbf{eat}(x); \text{VP}} \quad \cfrac{\text{john};}{\textbf{j}; \text{NP}_{-wh}}}{\text{john} \circ \text{ate} \circ \varphi_0; \textbf{eat}(x)(\textbf{j}); \text{S}}}{\lambda\varphi_0.\text{john} \circ \text{ate} \circ \varphi_0; \lambda x.\textbf{eat}(x)(\textbf{j}); \text{S}\upharpoonright\text{NP}_{+wh}} \upharpoonright\text{I}^1 \quad \cfrac{\lambda\sigma.\text{what} \circ \sigma(\boldsymbol{\varepsilon}); \textbf{wh}(\textbf{obj}); \text{Q}\upharpoonright(\text{S}\upharpoonright\text{NP}_{+wh})}{}}{\text{what} \circ \text{john} \circ \text{ate} \circ \boldsymbol{\varepsilon}; \textbf{wh}(\textbf{obj})(\lambda x.\textbf{eat}(x)(\textbf{j})); \text{Q}}$$

7.1.3   Modeling Extraction Pathway Marking

We now assume a systematic encoding of "level of clausal embedding" by means of a numerical index attached to syntactic categories to keep track of the "extraction pathway" of expressions extracted out of embedded positions. For this purpose, we follow the approach of Pogodalla and Pompigne (2012), who employ this type of feature encoding (formally implemented in terms of subtypes in their formulation) for the purpose of syntactically encoding scope islands.[4] We thus assume the following lexicon for Irish:

(349)   a. an; $\lambda P.\iota(P)$; $\text{NP}^n_{-wh}/\text{N}^n$

   b. dól; $\lambda x \lambda y.\textbf{drink}(y)(x)$; $(\text{S}^n/\text{NP}^n_{\#wh})/\text{NP}^n_{\#wh}$

   c. ghiseach; **girl**; N^n

   d. tuische; **water**; N^n

   e. $\lambda\sigma_1\lambda\varphi_1.\text{aL} \circ \sigma_1(\varphi_1)$; $\lambda P.P$; $(\text{S}'^{n+1}\upharpoonright\text{NP}^{n+1}_{+wh})\upharpoonright(\text{S}^n\upharpoonright\text{NP}^n_{+wh})$

---

4. We do not, however, follow Pogodalla and Pompigne (2012) in encoding island constraints as syntactic constraints. See chapter 10 for our view on island constraints, where, following many authors in the recent literature, we take (most of) island constraints to follow from extragrammatical factors such as processing difficulty or prosodic/pragmatic incongruence. However, even assuming island constraints to be essentially extragrammatical, syntactic factors that are relevant for the formulations of such extragrammatical principles need to be captured by some kind of interface conditions making reference to essentially syntactic properties such as levels of clausal embedding. Thus, although we do not literally adopt Pogodalla and Pompigne's (2012) syntactic encoding of (a subtype of) island constraints, the formal machinery that they propose will very likely turn out to be essential in formulating explicitly the relevant interface conditions mediating syntax and other components of grammar (including the online processing component).

f. goN; $\lambda p.p$; S'^{n+1}/S^n

g. $\lambda\sigma_2\lambda\varphi_2.\varphi_2\circ\sigma_2(\boldsymbol{\varepsilon})$; $\lambda P\lambda Q\lambda y.Q(y)\wedge P(y)$; $(N^n\backslash N^n)\!\upharpoonright\!(S'^n\!\upharpoonright\!NP^n_{+wh})$

(349g) is the null relativizer that combines the modifying property sign with the nominal predicates (349c) and (349d). With this lexicon, we obtain the following derivation for (350).

(350) An ghirseach aL dól an t-uisce
       'the girl that drank the water'

(351)

$$
\begin{array}{c}
\text{dól;} \\
\lambda x\lambda y.\mathbf{drink}(y)(x); \\
(S^1/NP^1_{\#wh})/ \\
NP^1_{\#wh}
\end{array}
\qquad
\begin{bmatrix}\varphi_0; \\ z; \\ NP^1_{+wh}\end{bmatrix}^0
\qquad
\begin{array}{c}
\text{an}\circ \\
\text{tuische;} \\
\iota(\mathbf{water}); \\
NP^1_{-wh}
\end{array}
$$

$$
\dfrac{\text{dól}\circ\varphi_0;\ \lambda y.\mathbf{drink}(y)(z); S^1/NP^1_{\#wh}\qquad NP^1_{-wh}}{}
$$

$$
\begin{array}{c}
\lambda\sigma_2\lambda\varphi_2. \\
\varphi_2\circ\sigma_2(\boldsymbol{\varepsilon}); \\
\lambda P\lambda Q\lambda y. \\
Q(y)\wedge P(y); \\
(N^2\backslash N^2)\!\upharpoonright \\
(S'^2\!\upharpoonright\!NP^2_{\#wh})
\end{array}
\qquad
\begin{array}{c}
\text{dól}\circ\varphi_0\circ\text{an}\circ\text{tuische;} \\
\mathbf{drink}(\iota(\mathbf{water}))(z); S^1 \\
\hline
\lambda\varphi_0.\text{dól}\circ\varphi_0\circ\text{an}\circ\text{tuische;} \\
\lambda z.\mathbf{drink}(\iota(\mathbf{water}))(z); S^1\!\upharpoonright\!NP^1_{+wh} \\
\hline
\lambda\varphi_1.\text{aL}\circ\text{dól}\circ\varphi_1\circ\text{an}\circ\text{tuische;} \\
\lambda z.\mathbf{drink}(\iota(\mathbf{water}))(z); S'^2\!\upharpoonright\!NP^2_{+wh}
\end{array}
\qquad
\begin{array}{c}
\lambda\sigma_1\lambda\varphi_1. \\
\text{aL}\circ\sigma_1(\varphi_1); \\
\lambda P.P; \\
(S'^{n+1}\!\upharpoonright\!NP^{n+1}_{+wh})\!\upharpoonright \\
(S^n\!\upharpoonright\!NP^n_{+wh})
\end{array}
$$

$$
\begin{array}{c}
\lambda\varphi_2.\varphi_2\circ\text{aL}\circ\text{dól}\circ\boldsymbol{\varepsilon}\circ\text{an}\circ\text{tuische;} \\
\lambda Q\lambda y.Q(y)\wedge\mathbf{drink}(\iota(\mathbf{water}))(y); N^2\backslash N^2
\end{array}
\qquad
\begin{array}{c}
\text{ghiseach;} \\
\mathbf{girl}; N^2
\end{array}
$$

$$
\begin{array}{c}
\text{an;} \\
\lambda P.\iota(P); \\
NP^2_{-wh}/N^2
\end{array}
\qquad
\dfrac{\text{ghiseach}\circ\text{aL}\circ\text{dól}\circ\boldsymbol{\varepsilon}\circ\text{an}\circ\text{tuische;}}{\lambda y.\mathbf{girl}(y)\wedge\mathbf{drink}(\iota(\mathbf{water}))(y); N^2}
$$

$$
\dfrac{\text{an}\circ\text{ghiseach}\circ\text{aL}\circ\text{dól}\circ\boldsymbol{\varepsilon}\circ\text{an}\circ\text{tuische;}}{\iota(\mathbf{girl}(y)\wedge\mathbf{drink}(\iota(\mathbf{water}))(y)); NP^2_{-wh}}
$$

The key point to note here is that the empty relativizer requires both the body of the relative clause and the gap NP to carry the same clause-level index as the modified noun. This requirement can be satisfied by using *aL*, which explicitly passes the gap NP from the lower clause to the higher clause by incrementing the clause-level index of the gap NP by one.

Note in particular that using *goN* instead of *aL* here results in a failed derivation:

(352)

$$\frac{\genfrac{}{}{0pt}{}{\vdots}{\text{dól} \circ \varphi_0 \circ \text{an} \circ \text{tuische}; \, \textbf{drink}(\iota(\textbf{water}))(z); \, \text{S}^1} \qquad \genfrac{}{}{0pt}{}{\text{goN};}{\lambda p.p; \, \text{S}'^{n+1}/\text{S}^n}}{}$$

$$\frac{\genfrac{}{}{0pt}{}{\text{goN} \circ \text{dól} \circ \varphi_0 \circ \text{an} \circ \text{tuische}; \, \textbf{drink}(\iota(\textbf{water}))(z); \, \text{S}'^2}{\begin{array}{l} \lambda\varphi_0.\text{goN} \circ \text{dól} \circ \varphi_0 \circ \text{an} \circ \text{tuische}; \\ \lambda z.\textbf{drink}(\iota(\textbf{water}))(z); \text{S}'^2 \!\upharpoonright\! \text{NP}^1_{+wh} \end{array}} \Pi^0 \qquad \frac{\begin{array}{l} \lambda\sigma_2\lambda\varphi_2.\varphi_2 \circ \sigma_2(\boldsymbol{\varepsilon}); \\ \lambda P\lambda Q\lambda y.Q(y) \wedge P(y); \\ (\text{N}^n\backslash\text{N}^n) \!\upharpoonright\! (\text{S}'^n \!\upharpoonright\! \text{NP}^n_{\#wh}) \end{array}}{}}{}$$

FAIL

goN increments the index of the S it selects, but it does not increment the index of the gap NP. The consequence of this is that when the NP_{+wh} hypothesis is withdrawn, the resultant expression has a syntactic type that is not compatible with the index requirement imposed by the relativizer.

This analysis entails the multiple appearances of *aL*, and only *aL*, along an extended filler-gap linkage exactly where we find them. Consider the following example from McCloskey (1979):

(353) an fear **aL** dúirt me **aL** shil me **aL** bheadh __ ann
     'The man that I said I thought would be there.'

Assuming the following lexical entries for verbs that take clausal complements in (354), the derivation for (350) now proceeds as in (355)–(358).

(354) a. dúirt; $\lambda x\lambda p.\textbf{said}(p)(x); \text{S}^n/\text{S}'^n/\text{NP}^n_{\#wh}$
      b. shíl; $\lambda x\lambda p.\textbf{think}(p)(x); \text{S}^n/\text{S}'^n/\text{NP}^n_{\#wh}$

In the first stage of the derivation shown in (355), we obtain the innermost appearance of *aL*, corresponding in phrase structure–based approaches to the smallest clause actually "housing" the extraction site:

(355)

$$\frac{\genfrac{}{}{0pt}{}{\begin{array}{l}\text{bheadh};\\ \lambda x\lambda y.\textbf{exist}(y)(x);\\ \text{S}^n/\text{PP}^n/\text{NP}^n_{\#wh}\end{array} \quad \begin{bmatrix}\varphi_0;\\ w;\\ \text{NP}^1_{+wh}\end{bmatrix}^0}{\text{bheadh} \circ \varphi_0; \, \lambda y.\textbf{exist}(y)(w); \, \text{S}^1/\text{PP}^1} \qquad \genfrac{}{}{0pt}{}{\text{ann};}{\textbf{there};}{\text{PP}^1}}{}$$

$$\frac{\genfrac{}{}{0pt}{}{\text{bheadh} \circ \varphi_0 \circ \text{ann}; \, \textbf{exist}(\textbf{there})(w); \, \text{S}^1}{\begin{array}{l}\lambda\varphi_0.\text{bheadh} \circ \varphi_0 \circ \text{ann};\\ \lambda w.\textbf{exist}(\textbf{there})(w); \text{S}^1 \!\upharpoonright\! \text{NP}^1_{+wh}\end{array}} \Pi^0 \qquad \begin{array}{l}\lambda\sigma_1\lambda\varphi_1.\text{aL} \circ \sigma_1(\varphi_1);\\ \lambda P.P;\\ (\text{S}'^{n+1} \!\upharpoonright\! \text{NP}^{n+1}_{+wh}) \!\upharpoonright\! (\text{S}^n \!\upharpoonright\! \text{NP}^n_{+wh})\end{array} \quad \begin{bmatrix}\varphi_2;\\ v;\\ \text{NP}^2_{+wh}\end{bmatrix}^2}{}$$

$$\frac{\lambda\varphi_1.\text{aL} \circ \text{bheadh} \circ \varphi_1 \circ \text{ann}; \, \lambda w.\textbf{exist}(\textbf{there})(w); \, \text{S}'^2 \!\upharpoonright\! \text{NP}^2_{+wh}}{\text{aL} \circ \text{bheadh} \circ \varphi_1 \circ \text{ann}; \, \textbf{exist}(\textbf{there})(v); \, \text{S}'^2}$$

At this point, at the penultimate proof step, *aL* has been composed into the clause representing the initial extraction domain. To complete this part of the derivation, we then saturate the resulting $S \!\!\restriction\!\! NP$ sign to make it eligible for selection by *shíl*.

(356)

$$\begin{array}{c}
\dfrac{\begin{array}{cc}
\begin{array}{c}
\text{shíl;} \\
\lambda x \lambda p.\mathbf{think}(p)(x); \\
S^n/S'^n/NP^n_{\#wh}
\end{array} &
\begin{array}{c}
\text{me;} \\
\mathbf{1st;} \\
NP^2_{-wh}
\end{array} &
\begin{array}{c}
\vdots \\
\text{aL} \circ \text{bheadh} \circ \\
\varphi_2 \circ \text{ann;} \\
\mathbf{exist}(\mathbf{there})(v); \\
S'^2
\end{array}
\end{array}}
{\begin{array}{c}
\text{shíl} \circ \text{me;} \\
\lambda p.\mathbf{think}(p)(\mathbf{1st}); S^2/S'^2
\end{array}}
\end{array}$$

$$\dfrac{\dfrac{\begin{array}{c}\text{shíl} \circ \text{me} \circ \text{aL} \circ \text{bheadh} \circ \varphi_2 \circ \text{ann;} \\ \mathbf{think}(\mathbf{exist}(\mathbf{there})(v))(\mathbf{1st}); S^2\end{array}}{\begin{array}{c}\lambda\varphi_2.\text{shíl} \circ \text{me} \circ \text{aL} \circ \text{bheadh} \circ \varphi_2 \circ \text{ann;} \\ \lambda v.\mathbf{think}(\mathbf{exist}(\mathbf{there})(v))(\mathbf{1st}); S^2\!\!\restriction\!\!NP^2_{+wh}\end{array}} \; \restriction\! I^2 \quad \begin{array}{c}\lambda\sigma_2\lambda\varphi_3.\text{aL} \circ \sigma_2(\varphi_3); \\ \lambda P.P; \\ (S'^{n+1}\!\!\restriction\!\!NP^{n+1}_{+wh})\!\!\restriction\!\!(S^n\!\!\restriction\!\!NP^n_{+wh})\end{array} \quad \left[\begin{array}{c}\varphi_4; \\ z; \\ NP^3_{+wh}\end{array}\right]^4}
{\begin{array}{c}\lambda\varphi_3.\text{aL} \circ \text{shíl} \circ \text{me} \circ \text{aL} \circ \text{bheadh} \circ \varphi_3 \circ \text{ann;} \\ \lambda v.\mathbf{think}(\mathbf{exist}(\mathbf{there})(v))(\mathbf{1st}); S^3\!\!\restriction\!\!NP^3_{+wh}\end{array}}$$

$$\text{aL} \circ \text{shíl} \circ \text{me} \circ \text{aL} \circ \text{bheadh} \circ \varphi_4 \circ \text{ann;} \; \mathbf{think}(\mathbf{exist}(\mathbf{there})(z))(\mathbf{1st}); S'^3$$

That is, once *shíl* has composed into the derivation, we bind the new φ_2 variable—thus in effect renewing the abstraction corresponding to the original gap in the first step of the proof. A final iteration of the same proof sequence—in abstract terms, λ-bind a variable, saturate the associated functor, compose the result with a new selector, and then rebind the variable—will yield the final form of the relative clause:

(357)

$$\dfrac{\begin{array}{cc}
\dfrac{\begin{array}{cc}\begin{array}{c}\text{dúirt;} \\ \lambda x \lambda p.\mathbf{said}(p)(x); \\ S^n/S'^n/NP^n_{\#wh}\end{array} & \begin{array}{c}\text{me;} \\ \mathbf{1st;} NP^3_{-wh}\end{array}\end{array}}{\text{dúirt} \circ \text{me;} \; \lambda p.\mathbf{said}(p)(\mathbf{1st}); S^n/S'^n} &
\begin{array}{c}\vdots \\ \text{aL} \circ \text{shíl} \circ \text{me} \circ \text{aL} \circ \text{bheadh} \circ \varphi_4 \circ \text{ann;} \\ \mathbf{think}(\mathbf{exist}(\mathbf{there})(z))(\mathbf{1st}); S'^3\end{array}
\end{array}}
{\begin{array}{c}\text{dúirt} \circ \text{me} \circ \text{aL} \circ \text{shíl} \circ \text{me} \circ \text{aL} \circ \text{bheadh} \circ \varphi_4 \circ \text{ann;} \\ \mathbf{said}(\mathbf{think}(\mathbf{exist}(\mathbf{there})(z))(\mathbf{1st}))(\mathbf{1st}); S^3\end{array}}$$

$$\dfrac{}{\begin{array}{c}\lambda\varphi_4.\text{dúirt} \circ \text{me} \circ \text{aL} \circ \text{shíl} \circ \text{me} \circ \text{aL} \circ \text{bheadh} \circ \varphi_4 \circ \text{ann;} \\ \lambda z.\mathbf{said}(\mathbf{think}(\mathbf{exist}(\mathbf{there})(z))(\mathbf{1st}))(\mathbf{1st}); S^3\!\!\restriction\!\!NP^3_{+wh}\end{array}} \; \restriction\! I^4$$

The proof concludes with the linkage among the relative clause, the null relativizer, and the "head" noun of the NP:

(358)

$$\vdots$$

$$\lambda\varphi_2\lambda\varphi_5.$$
$$\varphi_5 \circ \sigma_2(\boldsymbol{\varepsilon});$$
$$\lambda P\lambda Q\lambda y.$$
$$Q(y) \wedge P(y);$$
$$(N^n\backslash N^n)\!\upharpoonright$$
$$(S'^n\!\upharpoonright\!NP^n_{+wh})$$

$$\lambda\varphi_4.\text{dúirt} \circ \text{me} \circ \text{aL} \circ \text{shíl} \circ \text{me} \circ$$
$$\text{aL} \circ \text{bheadh} \circ \varphi_4 \circ \text{ann};$$
$$\lambda z.\textbf{said}(\textbf{think}$$
$$(\textbf{exist}(\textbf{there})(z))(\textbf{1st}))(\textbf{1st});$$
$$S^3\!\upharpoonright\!NP^3_{+wh}$$

$$\lambda\sigma_1\lambda\varphi_1.$$
$$\text{aL} \circ \sigma_1(\varphi_1);$$
$$\lambda P.P;$$
$$(S'^{n+1}\!\upharpoonright\!NP^{n+1}_{+wh})\!\upharpoonright$$
$$(S^n\!\upharpoonright\!NP^n_{+wh})$$

fear;
man;
$$N^4$$

$$\lambda\varphi_4.\text{aL} \circ \text{dúirt} \circ \text{me} \circ$$
$$\text{aL} \circ \text{shíl} \circ \text{me} \circ \text{aL} \circ \text{bheadh} \circ \varphi_4 \circ \text{ann};$$
$$\lambda z.\textbf{said}(\textbf{think}(\textbf{exist}(\textbf{there})(z))(\textbf{1st}))(\textbf{1st}); S^4\!\upharpoonright\!NP^4_{+wh}$$

$$\lambda\varphi_5.\varphi_5 \circ \text{aL} \circ \text{dúirt} \circ \text{me} \circ \text{aL} \circ \text{shíl} \circ \text{me} \circ \text{aL} \circ \text{bheadh} \circ \boldsymbol{\varepsilon} \circ \text{ann};$$
$$\lambda Q\lambda y.Q(y) \wedge \textbf{said}(\textbf{think}(\textbf{exist}(\textbf{there})(y))(\textbf{1st}))(\textbf{1st}); N^4\backslash N^4$$

an;
$$\lambda P.\iota(P);$$
$$NP^4_{-wh}/N^4$$

$$\text{fear} \circ \text{aL} \circ \text{dúirt} \circ \text{me} \circ \text{aL} \circ \text{shíl} \circ \text{me} \circ \text{aL} \circ \text{bheadh} \circ \boldsymbol{\varepsilon} \circ \text{ann};$$
$$\lambda y.\textbf{man}(y) \wedge \textbf{said}(\textbf{think}(\textbf{exist}(\textbf{there})(y))(\textbf{1st}))(\textbf{1st}); N^4\backslash N^4$$

$$\text{an} \circ \text{fear} \circ \text{aL} \circ \text{dúirt} \circ \text{me} \circ \text{aL} \circ \text{shíl} \circ \text{me} \circ \text{aL} \circ \text{bheadh} \circ \boldsymbol{\varepsilon} \circ \text{ann};$$
$$\iota(\lambda y.\textbf{man}(y) \wedge \textbf{said}(\textbf{think}(\textbf{exist}(\textbf{there})(y))(\textbf{1st}))(\textbf{1st})); NP^4_{-wh}$$

Note further that examples such as those in (359) are correctly predicted to be impossible on this analysis:

(359) a. *an fear **aL** duiirt me **aL** shil me **goN** bheadh __ ann
      'The man that I said I thought would be there.'

   b. *an fear **goN** duiirt me **aL** shil me **aL** bheadh __ ann
      'The man that I said I thought would be there.'

In the case of (359a), *goN* will combine with a clause containing a hypothesized NP^1_{+wh}, shifting the index of that clause to 2, and the *shíl* clause will maintain this index on the resulting S', as will *dúirt*. In order to combine with *aL*, however, the original NP^1_{+wh} hypothesis at the "bottom" will have to be withdrawn from the *dúirt* clause, yielding an argument of the form $S^2\!\upharpoonright\!NP^1_{+wh}$—an unacceptable argument type for *aL*, which requires the same index on both argument and yield. More generally, anytime *goN* appears between a filler and a gap, it will have been necessary to saturate the functor corresponding to the gap with an NP (or other filler type) at the same index level as its selector, since *goN* requires a complete S to combine with. But any *aL* higher up requires an $S\!\upharpoonright\!NP$ category where the argument and the result share the same index value. This will be impossible, since once the hypothesized NP that saturated the *goN* clause is withdrawn, the result—due to the index effect of *goN*—will be a constituent of the form $S^n\!\upharpoonright\!NP^m$ with $n > m$. If the hypothesis is withdrawn at the very top of the dependency, as in (359b), then the result will fail for essentially the same reason, since not just *aL* but the relativizer and all *wh* terms require arguments of the form $S^n\!\upharpoonright\!NP^n$.

Thus *goN* is blocked from any appearance between a filler and a "gap," and it is also obvious that *aL* will be blocked in any context where there is no extraction dependency (note that the "missing" NP in the lexical specification for *aL* is specifically marked as +*wh*). The complementarity between *goN* and *aL*, and the mandatory appearance of *aL* at every point along a filler gap pathway, thus follows directly. For if *aL* is missing at some point, then the string in question will be typed $S^n \!\uparrow\! NP^n$, rather than the $S'^n \!\uparrow\! NP^n$ required of arguments to Irish predicates seeking clausal complements. Hence *aL* is obligatory in each clausal sign along the extraction pathway, just as *goN* is obligatory for clauses in nonextraction constructions.[5]

7.2 Linearity of the Underlying Logic and the Treatment of Parasitic Gaps

Multiple-gap phenomena (of which parasitic gaps are an instance) perhaps pose a somewhat more serious issue for the treatment of extraction in terms of the linear implication connective $\uparrow$ as the key device for mediating the linkage between the filler and the gap. While extraction pathway marking can be modeled by encoding the level of clause embedding via a syntactic feature (a mechanism which can potentially be retooled for other purposes along lines briefly discussed above), the fact that at least in some languages (including English) a single filler can correspond to multiple gaps simultaneously, as in the following parasitic gap examples in English, seems to be directly at odds with the assumption that the underlying logic for the combinatoric component of natural language grammar is resource-sensitive linear logic.

(360) a. This is the article that John filed __ without reading __.
        b. Peter is a guy who even the best friends of __ tend to avoid hanging around with __.

Unlike the possibilities available in classical logic, in which $A, A \to (A \to B) \vdash B$ is a valid theorem (by using the minor premise A twice in Modus Ponens), in linear logic, the corresponding inference $A, A \multimap (A \multimap B) \vdash B$ is *not* a theorem since reuse of a resource is not an option. But if we model the extraction phenomena via hypothetical reasoning, along the lines of Muskens (2003), the derivation for multiple-gap sentences would seem to necessarily correspond to the unavailable theorem in linear logic.

Does this mean, after all, that the implication connective mediating long-distance dependencies in English (and other languages that allow for multiple-gap constructions)

---

5. Readers familiar with the syntax-semantics interface presented in Gazdar et al. (1985) will find our analysis of "extraction pathway marking" as the clause-by-clause saturation and rebinding of the variable associated with the prosodic gap site rather familiar: it is simply the TLCG version of the way Gazdar et al. treated filler-gap interpretation as the semantic correspondent of the SLASH feature's locally mediated distribution through all clause levels separating fillers from their matching gap sites.

is *not* linear? Some authors have indeed drawn this conclusion and have proposed analyses which explicitly reject linearity, at least in contexts in which multiple gaps are licensed in extraction constructions. The most recent and the most detailed proposal embodying this idea can be found in Morrill (2017). Here, we opt for a less radical departure from the assumption of linearity, not because we find the extensive revision of the underlying logic undertaken by Morrill (2017) implausible, but merely because we wish to remain agnostic about this potentially quite deep and fundamental question that has direct ramifications to the architecture of the syntax-semantics interface. For this reason, we sketch below a lexical operator–based analysis of parasitic gaps in English which retains the linearity of the underlying logic and introduces resource duplication via an empty operator that is associated with a nonlinear term as its semantic translation. We then formulate our account of the Kennedy ellipsis/extraction paradigm in the next chapter on the basis of this analysis of parasitic gaps.[6]

We can overcome the technical difficulty noted above by positing a lexical operator that introduces multiple tokens of a variable which are "pre-bound," along the lines of (361):[7]

(361) $\lambda\sigma_1\lambda\sigma_2\lambda\varphi.\sigma_2(\varphi)\circ\sigma_1(\varphi);$

   $\lambda R\lambda g\lambda x.R(x)(g(x)); (S\upharpoonright NP_{+wh})\upharpoonright(NP_{-wh}\upharpoonright NP_{+wh})\upharpoonright((NP_{-wh}\backslash S)\upharpoonright NP_{+wh})$

---

6. As will become clear in the next chapter, the only crucial assumption for our analysis of the Kennedy paradigm is that the "existence" of a gap within an "elided" VP is marked in the syntactic category of the latter. In order to see whether our analysis carries over to other TLCG approaches, detailed assumptions about how exactly the analyses of ellipsis and extraction interact with one another in each approach needs to be spelled out. This is of course not a trivial task, but we believe that a translation of our analysis to other TLCG approaches (including Morrill [2017]) should be mostly straightforward, since the encoding of extracted elements in the category of linguistic signs is a property that is for the most part orthogonal to the question of whether the implicational connective employed is linear or not. In any event, regardless of what conclusion one draws on the linearity issue, we take the Kennedy paradigm to be one of the empirical criteria for judging the adequacy of an analysis of extraction phenomena (in particular, the licensing of multiple gaps) in English.

7. This operator, on its own, licenses parasitic gaps in the subject position only. In order to license parasitic gaps in adjunct clauses, a second, separate operator is needed. One might object to this type of analysis on the ground that it fails to capture parasitic gaps in the two environments via a uniform mechanism. However, it is questionable whether a uniform analysis is desirable to begin with. Culicover (1999, 179–181) notes that "there appear to be many languages that have *without*-parasitic gaps and parasitic gaps in adjuncts, but lack parasitic gaps in subjects," giving Spanish and German as two such languages. We therefore take the need for separate operators for adjunct and subject parasitic gaps to be well supported empirically. Questions, however, remain regarding the much larger issue of how to deal with a wider range of multiple-gap phenomena in Hybrid TLCG. We can find in English a variety of other multiple-gap/single-filler constructions, including "parasitic" gaps in adjuncts, ATB extraction in coordination, the "symbiotic" gaps pointed out in Levine and Sag (2003), and cases such as (i), where both gaps are in extractable positions within a single VP:

(i) Which people$_i$ did you show pictures of ___$_i$ to ___$_i$?

We leave it for future work to extend our analysis to such cases.

This operator takes a VP missing an NP and an NP missing an NP and in effect fuses the missing NP argument variables, and likewise for the prosodic variables. The result, supplied as an argument to the *wh* operator, yields a sign with the empty string in two separate positions, corresponding to two tokens of a single variable in the semantic component of the sign, bound by a single abstraction operator.[8] The action of the gap-multiplying operator (361) is illustrated in (362):

(362)

$$\lambda\sigma_1\lambda\sigma_2\lambda\varphi.$$
$$\sigma_2(\varphi)\circ\sigma_1(\varphi);$$
$$\lambda R\lambda g\lambda x.R(x)(g(x));$$
$$(S\!\upharpoonright\!NP_{+wh})\!\upharpoonright$$
$$(NP_{-wh}\!\upharpoonright\!NP_{+wh})\!\upharpoonright$$
$$((NP_{-wh}\backslash S)\!\upharpoonright\!NP_{+wh})$$

$$\lambda\varphi.\text{admire}\circ\varphi;$$
$$\textbf{admire};$$
$$(NP_{-wh}\backslash S)\!\upharpoonright\!NP_{+wh}$$

$$\lambda\varphi.\text{the}\circ\text{close}\circ$$
$$\text{friends}\circ\text{of}\circ\varphi;$$
$$\lambda x.\iota(\lambda y.\textbf{close-fr}$$
$$(x)(y));$$
$$NP_{-wh}\!\upharpoonright\!NP_{+wh}$$

$$\lambda\sigma_2\lambda\varphi.\sigma_2(\varphi)\circ\text{admire}\circ\varphi;$$
$$\lambda g\lambda x.\textbf{admire}(x)(g(x));$$
$$(S\!\upharpoonright\!NP_{+wh})\!\upharpoonright(NP_{-wh}\!\upharpoonright\!NP_{+wh})$$

$$\lambda\sigma.\text{who}\circ\sigma(\boldsymbol{\varepsilon});$$
$$\lambda P\lambda Q\lambda x.$$
$$Q(x)\wedge P(x);$$
$$(N\backslash N)\!\upharpoonright(S\!\upharpoonright\!NP_{+wh})$$

$$\lambda\varphi.\text{the}\circ\text{close}\circ\text{friends}\circ\text{of}\circ\varphi\circ\text{admire}\circ\varphi;$$
$$\lambda x.\textbf{admire}(x)(\iota(\lambda y.\textbf{close-fr}(x)(y)));S\!\upharpoonright\!NP_{+wh}$$

$$\text{who}\circ\text{the}\circ\text{close}\circ\text{friends}\circ\text{of}\circ\text{admire};$$
$$\lambda Q\lambda x.Q(x)\wedge\textbf{admire}(x)(\iota(\lambda y.\textbf{close-fr}(x)(y)));N\backslash N$$

8. A similar strategy for dealing with nonlinearity in natural language is pursued in the cross-categorial analysis of coordination via "generalized conjunction" by Partee and Rooth (1983) and analyses which build the distribution of reflexive pronouns into the semantics of such pronouns along the lines of Bach and Partee (1980).

8 Extraction/Ellipsis Interactions

Building on the analysis of ellipsis in chapter 6 and the analysis of extraction in chapter 7, this chapter addresses what we take to be the central question posed by ellipsis phenomena: Do the latter receive an adequate explanation only if we posit covert syntactic structure at the ellipsis site? The great bulk of the literature on ellipsis has always assumed a positive answer to this question, if only implicitly, and the authors of much of the more recent work have taken pains to offer arguments defending that view (e.g., Kennedy and Merchant 2000; Johnson 2001; Kennedy 2003; Merchant 2015; and Thoms 2016).

Kennedy (2003) in particular offers a clear, concise summary of five of the seemingly strongest such arguments focusing on VP ellipsis:

1. The distribution of ellipsis remnants reflects sensitivity to island conditions on configurations which are not visible in the surface string at the ellipsis site.
2. The interpretations available in ellipsis data exhibit Strong Crossover effects that imply the existence of syntactic gaps within the ellipsis site.
3. The anaphora possibilities available in the interpretations of VP ellipsis reflect Binding Condition B effects, implying the existence of pronouns within the ellipsis site.
4. Parasitic gap licensing behavior requires the presence of a syntactic gap within the ellipsed material in order to license a visible gap in an island context within the remnant material.
5. The "attributive comparative" construction permits certain possibilities which appear to violate the "Left Branch Constraint" just in case ellipsis is also involved, a pattern that can be accounted for as an instance of repair, via deletion, of an offending covert structure.

We evaluate these five arguments, concluding that each of them is either empirically deficient or predicated on an undermotivated treatment of the relevant data. In the latter case, there are alternative analyses which are at least as successful in accounting for the facts and require no reference at all to configurational properties of the ellipsed material. Our conclusion is that the various data sets offered in Kennedy (2003) in support of covert structural analyses for ellipsis phenomena do not in fact motivate such analyses.

8.1 Kennedy's Arguments for Covert Structure in Ellipsis

Each of Kennedy's five arguments is based on a syntactic pattern which is either commonly held, or explicitly argued, to require appeal to a specific syntactic configuration for a satisfactory explanation. In all but the last case, the ellipsed clause displays parallel behavior to its unellipsed counterpart, and since that behavior is supposedly motivated by specific structural facts, it would follow that the observed parallelism is eo ipso a sufficient basis to posit covert structure. We begin by outlining the storyline of each of Kennedy's arguments, returning in section 8.3 for a reassessment of them.

8.1.1 Island Effects

Probably the most frequently encountered argument for covert structure in ellipsis is the claim that ellipsis possibilities mirror the (un)acceptability of their unellipsed counterparts with respect to island effects.[1] Kennedy (2003) offers an instance of this argument for VP ellipsis in English based on the paradigm in (363) and (364):

(363) a. Sterling criticized every decision that Lou $\left\{ \begin{array}{l} \text{did} \\ \text{criticized } t \end{array} \right\}$.

   b. *Sterling criticized every decision that Doug was upset because Lou $\left\{ \begin{array}{l} \text{did} \\ \text{criticized } t \end{array} \right\}$.

(364) Max refused to buy the shirt that I picked out even though it was less expensive than the one that (*the salesperson complimented him after) he $\left\{ \begin{array}{l} \text{did} \\ \text{picked out } t \end{array} \right\}$.

Extraction in the "full" version of (363a) is impeccable, and so is the ellipsed version. When the material destined for ellipsis appears in an adjunct island, however, the extraction is bad, as is the ellipsed variant, as in (363b). Since the basis for islandhood in Kennedy's framework is assumed to be structural, the parallel behavior of full and ellipsed clauses with respect to islandhood is taken as a strong argument that ellipsis

---

1. Such arguments, however, typically offer little detailed consideration of the well-formedness of certain species of ellipsis in which island violations do not appear to incur any penalty. This problem for the islandhood argument was in fact already noted in Ross's (1969) watershed paper on sluicing, in which Ross explicitly acknowledges that he has no account to offer for it. One relatively recent strategy for dealing with this problem, pursued, for example, in considerable detail in Barros et al. (2014), is to deny that the covert syntax of the ellipsed material involves any islandhood in the first place. Jacobson (2016), however, offers a persuasive rebuttal to this line of solution. At present it seems fair to say that there is no consensus among researchers advocating covert structure in ellipsis about these difficulties.

must apply to a structural object which either complies with island conditions and is acceptable or fails to comply and is judged ill-formed. Likewise, we see that in (364), both the full and VP ellipsis versions are fine when the gap is within an extraction-accessible complement but are bad when the ellipsed VP hosting the gap is within an island.

8.1.2 Strong Crossover

The second major argument for covert structure in Kennedy (2003) hinges on the Strong Crossover (SCO) Condition discussed at length in Postal (1971, 2004). SCO blocks the appearance of a pronoun on a filler-gap pathway which is coreferential with, and in some sense structurally superior to, the gap. Thus, (365) does not allow the interpretation 'for which male person is it the case that that person is always criticizing himself?':

(365) *Who_i is he_i always criticizing t_i ?

Unlike islandhood, the kind of gradient effects noted in recent processing-oriented approaches such as Kluender (1998), Hofmeister et al. (2013), and Chaves (2013) have never been reported in connection with SCO judgments. This absolute character seems to give appeal to SCO considerable weight as evidence for covert structure in data such as (366):

(366) Who_i will Mary vote for t_i if $he_{j/*i}$ does ~~vote for t_i~~?

It is not possible to construe the referent of *he* as the candidate in question.[2] But when the pronoun is clearly not to be construed as coreferential with the gap following *for* (i.e., $j \neq i$), the sentence is acceptable. This pattern follows more or less immediately by assuming that there is covert syntactic structure featuring a movement trace within the ellipsis site. By contrast, (according to Kennedy) it is difficult to see how a purely interpretive approach could account for the fact that the sentence is either acceptable or unacceptable depending on the interpretation of the pronoun *he*. The point is that purely interpretive approaches do not posit any sort of trace or gap in the ellipsis site. But without such a gap somewhere in the representation, there is no straightforward way to induce the SCO effect in (366).

---

2. If we were to replace the trace in (366) with a pronoun, the result in (i) will still be bad due to Condition B effects (see section 8.1.3):

(i) Who_i will Mary vote for if $he_{j/*i}$ does ~~vote for him_i~~?

Thus, the only alternative is for the object of *for* to be a real gap, which leads to the ill-formedness of (366), on the assumption that a trace is present at the gap site.

8.1.3 Ellipsis and Binding Condition B

Kennedy's argument from Binding Condition B hinges on data such as (367):

(367) John$_k$ takes care of him$_i$ because he$_{j/*i}$ won't $\left\{ \begin{array}{l} \text{a. take care of him}_i \\ \text{b. } \text{take care of him}_i \end{array} \right\}$.

Condition B, first stated in Chomsky (1981), blocks coreference between an NP and a pronoun within a certain locality domain. The generalization itself is taken to be relevant in the more recent literature, though there does not seem to be a clear, broadly accepted formulation of this condition in the Minimalist framework. Condition B effects are evident in the unellipsed form, (367a): when the subject of the adjunct clause is interpreted as coreferential with the direct object, the example is bad. On the assumption that (367b) is derived by deleting a VP that has the same syntactic form as its unellipsed counterpart, we predict that the status of the example depends entirely on the adjunct subject pronoun's index. In contrast, on a purely semantic treatment of ellipsis, there is supposedly no reason why a predicate of the form $\lambda y.\textbf{take-care-of}(y)(\textbf{k})$ cannot take $\textbf{k}$ as an argument (with $\textbf{k}$ the denotation of the pronoun *he*); after all, the semantics of *He takes care of himself* requires exactly this type of interpretation. Hence, the argument goes, to capture the ill-formedness of (367b) on the coreferential interpretation, there must be an actual pronoun in the representation for the sentence at the level at which Condition B applies.[3]

8.1.4 Ellipsis and Parasitic Gaps

Parasitic gap licensing is standardly taken to be a matter of syntax. (368) illustrates the basis for the common claim that subjects cannot host gaps unless at least one gap also appears in the main VP.

(368) a. *Who$_i$ did close friends of __$_i$ become famous?
      b. Who$_i$ do close friends of __$_i$ always defend __$_i$?

The examples in (369) exhibit a slightly more complex pattern. Standard islandhood tests seem to confirm that the gap in the adjunct in (369) is derived by *wh* extraction. As (369a) shows, when no gap appears in the adjunct's own VP, the gap in its clausal subject yields an ill-formed result, as would be expected on the basis of (368).

(369) a. *Otis is a person who$_i$ I admire __$_i$ because close friends of __$_i$ became famous.

---

3. Kennedy's reasoning here depends on an implicit assumption which is open to question, viz., that the relevant locality condition accounting for Condition B effects is to be formulated in terms of syntactic configurations. Jacobson (2007) has in fact thoroughly argued that this assumption is deeply problematic, showing that such approaches require quite elaborate and indirect mechanisms to overcome a number of serious empirical mispredictions.

b. Otis is a person who$_i$ I admire because close friends of ___$_i$ admire ___$_i$/*him$_i$.

In contrast, in (369b), a gap in the adjunct subject position is licensed since it is legally parasitized on the VP internal gap. Here there are two separate extraction chains, with a presumed empty operator binding both the licensing gap following *admire* and the parasitic subject-internal gap. But this derivation is only legal on condition that the gap within the adjunct VP is indeed a trace. If, instead, a null pronoun were the object of *admire*, the results would be unacceptable—something we know because, if the pronoun is overt, as per (369b), the result is bad. Since, however, (369b) (in its gap version) is good, we can be sure that what is missing in this example is a true gap, licensing the parasitic gap in the subject position. From this conclusion, Kennedy infers that in the example (370), a true gap must somehow be located within the ellipsis site:

(370) Otis is a person who$_i$ I admire ___$_i$ because close friends of ___$_i$ seem to $\varnothing$.

(Engdahl 1985; Kennedy 2003)

That is, $\varnothing$ must be [~~$_{VP}$ admire ___$_i$~~] entailing a covert structure analysis for such examples.

8.1.5 The Argument from Comparatives

There is one more argument that Kennedy (2003) adduces on behalf of covert structure—in effect, a very compressed synopsis of the argument based on properties of comparative (sub)deletion phenomena presented in Kennedy and Merchant (2000). The argument runs as follows: ordinary comparatives, of the sort illustrated in (371a), are arguably best analyzed as instances of *wh* movement involving a null operator, along the lines of (371b):

(371) a. Pico's novel was much more interesting than Brio thought it would be ___.
       b. Pico's novel was much more interesting than [O$_{deg_i}$ Brio thought it would be t_i]

The movement account of comparative "deletion" is supported by the fact that it predicts the ill-formedness of examples such as (372a), presumably with the structure (372b):

(372) a. *John buys more expensive wine than he buys beer.
       b. John buys more expensive wine than [O$_{deg_i}$ he buys [$_{NP}$ t_i beer]]

In (372), the gap is in the "left branch" position (Ross 1967), which is known to disallow extraction:

(373) *Whose did you borrow [$_{NP}$ ___ book]?

But this seemingly straightforward account of (372a) is at odds with the fact, apparently not noticed prior to Kennedy and Merchant (2000), that pseudogapped analogues of (372a) are impeccable:

(374) John buys more expensive wine than he does beer.

Without argument, Kennedy and Merchant take the discrepancy between (372a) and (374) to be syntactic in nature. They offer a complex account which in its essence derives the ill-formedness of (372a) from a lexical condition on the highest functional head position (FocP, in their account) in the constituent from which the null degree operator in left-branch position is extracted. This condition makes lexical insertion of an actual head unavailable, with the result that the Spec of this focal projection bears a certain unchecked feature which cannot be interpreted at LF, leading the derivation to crash. If, however, the constituent [$_{DetP}$ t_i beer] escapes by rightward movement to surface as a pseudogapping remnant, the uninterpretable feature is "trapped" within FocP and deleted along with the rest of the VP, as shown in (375):

(375) . . . than he does [$_{VP}$ ~~[$_{VP}$ buy [$_{FocP}$ O_i t_j]]~~ [$_{DetP_j}$ t_i beer]]

Thus, on Kennedy and Merchant's account, the contrast between (372a) and (374) is the direct result of the structural deletion operation responsible for ellipsis—a powerful argument, in their view, for treating ellipsis as a reduction of syntactic structures.

Furthermore, a prediction follows directly from their analysis which they argue is confirmed cross-linguistically, namely, that in languages in which left-branch extraction is permitted—and in which, therefore, the lexical condition Kennedy and Merchant posit for English does not hold—we should expect to find attributive comparatives not only in ellipsed forms of the construction but in their unellipsed counterpart as well. They cite Polish and Czech, in which left-branch extraction is legal, in support of this prediction: in both languages, examples comparable to (372a) are altogether unproblematic. In Greek and Bulgarian, on the other hand, which mirror the prohibition in English against left-branch extraction, the judgment patterns in the attributive comparative data parallel the patterns found in English, as indeed predicted on their account.

8.1.6 Summary

The preceding arguments appear to implicate unavoidably the presence of structure at the ellipsis site in VP ellipsis—but, as we argue below, the logic of Kennedy's (and Merchant's) argument hinges crucially on two key assumptions. First, it takes as a given the structural basis of the various diagnostics that are invoked to probe for concealed configuration at VP ellipsis. Second, it assumes that the extracted material in cases such as (376) is linked to a position *within* the missing material following the auxiliary rather than to a complement position directly associated with the auxiliary itself:

(376) I know what John ate for lunch, but I don't know what Bill did.

In the discussion below, we argue that there is no compelling basis for either of these assumptions. We argue further that there is an alternative, processing-based explanation for the attributive adjective comparative pattern in which the data, including the cross-linguistic facts, have a markedly simpler explanation without reference at all to particular structural conditions.

8.2   Extraction/Ellipsis Interaction in Hybrid TLCG

In this section, we extend the analysis of ellipsis in chapter 6 to the basic cases of ellipsis/extraction interaction and ellipsis in comparatives.

8.2.1   "Extraction from Elided VP" Revisited

Examples like the following seem to have been taken as prima facie evidence for the presence of covert structure, even without consideration of specific structure-dependent effects along the lines Kennedy pursues.

(376) I know what John ate for lunch, but I don't know what Bill did.

For example, referring to data such as (376), Johnson (2001) remarks, "In these cases too the ellipsis site seems to have internal parts." (Elbourne 2008, 216) echoes this assessment, referring the reader to Johnson's article

> for a summary of the controversy about whether theories without normal syntactic structures in the ellipsis sites can deal with examples like these. The upshot is not encouraging, and things seem especially difficult for [the version in Hardt (1999)], according to which there is nothing whatsoever in ellipsis sites.

As we show below, however, our own proposal, which posits no syntactic material at all in the supposed ellipsis site, is vulnerable to none of the objections Johnson and Elbourne raise.[4] Our own analysis is immune to this criticism since it analyzes apparent extraction from an ellipsis site as a genuine syntactic extraction—but not extraction

---

4. A certain caution is necessary in evaluating these objections, however. Elbourne apparently regards the problem with Hardt's analysis, vis-à-vis the extraction data, as the fact that since the latter hinges on a purely semantic recovery process, it ipso facto cannot include syntactic information, such as the presence of a syntactic gap site. But this criticism assumes that Hardt's approach still incorporates a movement-based source for *wh* fillers (or some analogous mechanism for syntactically registering the connectivity relationship). But nothing in Hardt's paper requires such a source; for example, if *wh*-fillers are licensed in place, and the linkage to their gap sites is treated as a matter of interpretation, then data such as (376) do not present a problem for a direct interpretation approach.

The real difficulty that Hardt's approach faces is precisely the kind of structure-dependent patterns which Kennedy adduces in his paper. A purely interpretive account of apparent extraction from VP ellipsis contexts runs into trouble not, *pace* Johnson and Elbourne, because of the extraction itself (which might indeed be only apparent as per the scenario just sketched); rather, the serious challenges arise when the extraction clause displays behavior which in its unellipsed counterparts appears to be strictly syntactic. It is precisely facts such as the parallelism between ellipsed and unellipsed clauses with respect to, for example, Condition

from an ellipsed position. Rather, we propose that apparent extraction from an ellipsed VP is in fact extraction from one or another argument of the "transitive" auxiliary which is associated with the general ellipsis operator introduced in chapter 6. That is, examples such as (376) involve not just a semantic object, as in Hardt's analysis, but an actual syntactic extraction from an ordinary overt VP, as we show below. Hence, these constructions are predicted to conform to whatever conditions hold on extraction in general without any concomitant assumption of covert structure corresponding to an "ellipsed" VP.

To flesh out the analysis outlined above, consider first a VP from which material is missing in some unknown, possibly non-peripheral position. Such a VP—which is just what is captured by the description $VP{\upharpoonright}XP$—corresponds to a VP in a filler-gap relationship with an XP filler. Thus, in *I wonder what John said to Mary*, the subconstituent *said __ to Mary* constitutes a VP with a medial NP gap, meeting the description $VP{\upharpoonright}NP$. It follows, then, that in principle, a sentence such as (376) can be licensed by mapping the auxiliary, not to VP but to a VP looking for an NP missing from *somewhere* "inside" it. Such a predicate is in the simplest case a transitive verb which can take an object argument (cf. the analysis of pseudogapping in chapter 6) but could in fact represent any VP from which an NP is missing, as in (377).

(377) John was someone whom I had $[_{VP{\upharpoonright}NP}$ heard [stories about __] for a long time].

Our generalized ellipsis operator in (299) from chapter 6 won't quite be sufficient here, because it is stated in terms of categories of the form $VP/\$$, which targets categories seeking arguments only to the right and thus excludes VPs with medial gaps. To correct this omission, we amend the definition of the ellipsis operator to give it still greater generality.

We start by demonstrating that a Geach-style proof is available for auxiliaries which will map them to types of the form $(VP{\upharpoonright}XP){\upharpoonright}(VP{\upharpoonright}XP)$:

(378)

$$\cfrac{k;\,\mathcal{O};\,VP/VP \quad \cfrac{[\sigma_1;f;VP{\upharpoonright}NP_{\#wh}]^1 \quad [\varphi_2;x;NP_{\#wh}]^2}{\sigma_1(\varphi_2);\,f(x);\,VP}}{\cfrac{\cfrac{k\circ\sigma_1(\varphi_2);\,\mathcal{O}(f(x));\,VP}{\lambda\varphi_2.k\circ\sigma_1(\varphi_2);\,\lambda x.\mathcal{O}(f(x));\,VP{\upharpoonright}NP_{\#wh}}{\upharpoonright}I^2}{\lambda\sigma_1\lambda\varphi_2.k\circ\sigma_1(\varphi_2);\,\lambda f\lambda x.\mathcal{O}(f(x));\,(VP{\upharpoonright}NP_{\#wh}){\upharpoonright}(VP{\upharpoonright}NP_{\#wh})}{\upharpoonright}I^1}$$

B, which Hardt's analysis cannot handle easily because, given the existence of reflexives, a purely semantic approach such as his cannot rule out interpretations in which a subject and object are coreferential.

The generalized ellipsis operator then takes such "Geached" auxiliaries and maps them to type VP↾XP, anaphorically supplying the meaning of the gapped VP:[5]

(379) $\lambda \rho \lambda \varphi_1 . \rho(\lambda \varphi_0 . \varphi_0)(\varphi_1)$; $\lambda \mathscr{F} . \mathscr{F}(R)$; $(VP \upharpoonright NP_{\#wh}) \upharpoonright ((VP \upharpoonright NP_{\#wh}) \upharpoonright (VP \upharpoonright NP_{\#wh}))$

——where R is the semantic term of a sign retrieved from the context whose type is $VP \upharpoonright NP_{\#wh}$

The analysis of (the antecedent clause of) (380) then goes as in (381).

(380) I know what John ate for lunch, but I don't know what$_i$ Bill did ~~eat~~ ___$_i$ ~~for lunch~~.

(381)

$$[\varphi_1; x; NP_{\#wh}]^1$$

$$\vdots$$

①→ $\dfrac{\dfrac{\text{ate} \circ \varphi_1 \circ \text{for} \circ \text{lunch}; \ \mathbf{ate}(x)(\mathbf{lunch}); VP}{\lambda \varphi_1 . \text{ate} \circ \varphi_1 \circ \text{for} \circ \text{lunch}; \ \boxed{\lambda x . \mathbf{ate}(x)(\mathbf{lunch})}; VP \upharpoonright NP_{\#wh}} \upharpoonright I^1 \quad \begin{bmatrix} \varphi_2; \\ u; \\ NP_{+wh} \end{bmatrix}^2}{}$$

John $\dfrac{\begin{matrix} \text{ate} \circ \varphi_2 \circ \text{for} \circ \text{lunch}; \ \mathbf{ate}(u)(\mathbf{lunch}); VP \end{matrix}}{}$ $\begin{matrix} \text{john}; \\ \mathbf{j}; \\ NP_{-wh} \end{matrix}$

$\dfrac{\text{john} \circ \text{ate} \circ \varphi_2 \circ \text{for} \circ \text{lunch}; \ \mathbf{ate}(u)(\mathbf{lunch})(\mathbf{j}); S}{\lambda \varphi_2 . \text{john} \circ \text{ate} \circ \varphi_2 \circ \text{for} \circ \text{lunch}; \ \lambda u . \mathbf{ate}(u)(\mathbf{lunch})(\mathbf{j}); S \upharpoonright NP_{+wh}} \upharpoonright I^2$ $\begin{matrix} \lambda \sigma . \text{what} \circ \sigma(\boldsymbol{\varepsilon}); \\ \lambda P . \mathbf{what}(P); \\ Q \upharpoonright (S \upharpoonright NP_{+wh}) \end{matrix}$

$$\text{what} \circ \text{john} \circ \text{ate} \circ \boldsymbol{\varepsilon} \circ \text{for} \circ \text{lunch}; \ \mathbf{what}(\lambda u . \mathbf{ate}(u)(\mathbf{lunch})(\mathbf{j})); Q$$

The derivation of the ellipsis clause involves free instantiation of the VP↾NP variable introduced in the generalized ellipsis operator defined above. We take R to be the grayed-in semantic term obtained in the proof line ①. The first part of the proof for *what Bill did* then takes the following form:

(382)

$$\vdots$$

$\begin{matrix} \lambda \sigma \lambda \varphi . \text{did} \circ \sigma(\varphi); \\ \lambda f \lambda x \lambda y . f(x)(y); \\ (VP \upharpoonright NP_{\#wh}) \upharpoonright (VP \upharpoonright NP_{\#wh}) \end{matrix}$ $\begin{matrix} \lambda \rho \lambda \varphi . \rho(\lambda \varphi_0 . \varphi_0)(\varphi); \\ \lambda \mathscr{F} . \mathscr{F}(\lambda x . \mathbf{ate}(x)(\mathbf{lunch})); \\ (VP \upharpoonright NP_{\#wh}) \upharpoonright \\ ((VP \upharpoonright NP_{\#wh}) \upharpoonright (VP \upharpoonright NP_{\#wh})) \end{matrix}$

$\dfrac{}{\lambda \varphi . \text{did} \circ \varphi; \ \lambda x \lambda y . \mathbf{ate}(x)(\mathbf{lunch})(y); VP \upharpoonright NP_{\#wh}}$ $\begin{bmatrix} \varphi_3; \\ v; \\ NP_{+wh} \end{bmatrix}^3$ $\begin{matrix} \text{bill}; \\ \mathbf{b}; \\ NP_{-wh} \end{matrix}$

$\dfrac{\text{did} \circ \varphi_3; \ \lambda y . \mathbf{ate}(v)(\mathbf{lunch})(y); VP}{}$

$\dfrac{\text{bill} \circ \text{did} \circ \varphi_3; \ \mathbf{ate}(v)(\mathbf{lunch})(\mathbf{b}); S}{\lambda \varphi_3 . \text{bill} \circ \text{did} \circ \varphi_3; \ \lambda v . \mathbf{ate}(v)(\mathbf{lunch})(\mathbf{b}); S \upharpoonright NP_{+wh}} \upharpoonright I^3$

---

5. One might wonder whether this operator needs to be further generalized via a vertical-slash version of $. We will not address this question here.

The term obtained at the last step of this proof, supplied as an argument to the extraction operator, yields an interpretation identical to the unellipsed embedded question *what bill ate for lunch.*

The above (re)analysis of "extraction out of an elided VP" as extraction of a pseudogapping remnant gives us, in effect, a proof-of-concept argument for rejecting the assumption that covert structures in VP ellipsis necessarily exist in order that a "site of origin" exist for filler-gap linkages that appear to implicate material missing from deleted VPs. While various versions of this approach have been challenged in previous work, we show in section 8.4 that the empirical basis for these objections is quite fragile and problematic when a larger range of relevant data is taken into account.

8.2.2 Ellipsis and Comparatives

The other technical piece that is needed is an analysis of comparatives. For this purpose, we outline here our assumptions about the syntax and semantics of comparatives, implementing in Hybrid TLCG the basic semantic characterization of comparative constructions in standard accounts (see, e.g., Kamp 1975; Cresswell 1976; Hellan 1981; von Stechow 1984; Hendriks 1995a; Kennedy 2005). As we show below, hypothetical reasoning with the vertical slash tied to prosodic λ-abstraction enables a flexible and simple treatment of the complex syntax-semantics interface of the comparative construction, which straightforwardly interacts with an independently motivated analysis of VP ellipsis to yield the right results in cases in which these two phenomena interact. This interaction between comparatives and ellipsis also plays a crucial role in the non-deletion analysis of the "attributive comparative" data we formulate in the next section.

8.2.2.1 The basic syntax-semantics interface of comparatives   The semantics of comparatives reflects an (in)equality in the degree of some property or predicate. Thus, in the following examples, what is asserted is a proposition of the form $d_1 > d_2$, where d_1 and d_2 are, in the case of (383a), for example, the degrees to which Mary and Ann are tall respectively.

(383) a. Mary is taller than Ann is.

 b. Mary runs faster than John runs.

Other forms of the comparative equate two degrees (e.g., *John runs as fast as Mary runs*) or quantify the difference (e.g., *Mary runs twice as fast as John runs*).

One way to compositionally derive the comparative meaning from the surface form of the sentence in examples like those in (383) is to assume that both the main clause and the *than* clause denote predicates of degree of type $d \rightarrow t$. For example, (383a) is derived (either via ellipsis of the adjective *tall* in the *than* clause or by some other means that derives the same semantic effect) from the following source,[6]

(384) (?)Mary is taller than Ann is tall.

with an "LF" that looks like the following:

(385) er-than $[\lambda d.$ Mary is d-tall$]$ $[\lambda d.$ Ann is d-tall$]$

That is, at the level relevant for semantic interpretation, the comparative operator *er-than* takes two degree descriptions of type $d \to t$ and compares the maximum degrees that satisfy each of these degree descriptions. Here, we assume (following many previous authors) that gradable adjectives take a degree argument (which is often implicit). In Hybrid TLCG, this can be modeled by assuming that adjectives are of type $d \to e \to t$ semantically and Adj$\restriction$Deg syntactically.

Putting aside the exact morpho-syntax of comparative forms, the degree operator can be defined as follows:

(386) $\quad \lambda\sigma_1\lambda\sigma_2.\sigma_1(\text{er}) \circ \text{than} \circ \sigma_2(\boldsymbol{\varepsilon});$

$\quad\quad \lambda P \lambda Q.\mathbf{max}(P) > \mathbf{max}(Q); S\restriction(S\restriction\text{Deg})\restriction(S\restriction\text{Deg})$

$\quad\quad$ where $\mathbf{max} =_{def} \lambda P.\iota d.P(d) \wedge \neg\exists d'[P(d') \wedge d' > d]$

The derivation for (385) then goes as follows:

(387)

$$
\begin{array}{c}
\begin{array}{ccc}
 & & \begin{array}{c} \lambda\varphi.\text{tall} \circ \varphi; \\ \mathbf{tall}; \\ \text{Adj}\restriction\text{Deg} \end{array} \; \left[\begin{array}{c}\varphi; \\ d; \\ \text{Deg}\end{array}\right]^1 \\
 & \begin{array}{c}\text{is;} \\ \lambda P.P; \\ \text{VP/Adj}\end{array} & \overline{\text{tall} \circ \varphi; \mathbf{tall}(d); \text{Adj}} \\
\begin{array}{c}\text{mary;} \\ \mathbf{m}; \\ \text{NP}\end{array} & \multicolumn{1}{c}{\overline{\text{is} \circ \text{tall} \circ \varphi; \mathbf{tall}(d); \text{VP}}}
\end{array} \\
\end{array}
$$

(derivation figure — see image)

Whether (383a) is derived from (384) via VP ellipsis or the missing adjective meaning is instead supplied by the comparative operator is debatable, but since the latter option is needed in the analysis of "attributive comparative deletion" examples, we illustrate this latter option here. This option also makes it possible to encode the comparative

---

6. (384) may sound less natural than (383a), but this is arguable due to the redundancy of repeating the adjective *tall* in the *than* clause.

morphology via a functional prosodic term, which is convenient for the treatment of suppletive forms. Specifically we assume that the **st→st** function ER takes the string prosody of the base form of an adjective and returns the comparative form of the adjective.

On this assumption, there is a slightly more complicated variant of the comparative operator defined as in (388):

(388) $\lambda\sigma_0\lambda\sigma_1\lambda\sigma_2.\sigma_1(\text{ER}(\sigma_0(\boldsymbol{\varepsilon}))) \circ \text{than} \circ \sigma_2(\boldsymbol{\varepsilon});\quad \lambda f\lambda P\lambda Q.\textbf{max}(\lambda d.P(f(d))) >$
$\quad\textbf{max}(\lambda d.Q(f(d)));\, S\upharpoonright(S\upharpoonright\text{Adj})\upharpoonright(S\upharpoonright\text{Adj})\upharpoonright(\text{Adj}\upharpoonright\text{Deg})$

The difference between (386) and (388) is that in (388), the two clauses are missing the entire adjective rather than just the degree argument. Correspondingly, in (388), the comparative operator lowers the comparative form of the adjective in the first clause in the prosodic component. Obtaining the right degree descriptions for the two clauses is straightforward given the semantics of the comparative operator in (388).

With the definition in (388), the derivation for (383a) goes as in (389):

(389)

$\lambda\sigma_0\lambda\sigma_1\lambda\sigma_2.\sigma_1(\text{ER}(\sigma_0(\boldsymbol{\varepsilon}))) \circ$
$\quad\text{than} \circ \sigma_2(\boldsymbol{\varepsilon});$
$\lambda f\lambda P\lambda Q.\textbf{max}(\lambda d.P(f(d))) >$ 　$\lambda\varphi.\text{tall} \circ \varphi;$
$\quad\textbf{max}(\lambda d.Q(f(d)));$ 　　　**tall**;
$S\upharpoonright(S\upharpoonright\text{Adj})\upharpoonright(S\upharpoonright\text{Adj})\upharpoonright(\text{Adj}\upharpoonright\text{Deg})$ 　$\text{Adj}\upharpoonright\text{Deg}$

$\dfrac{}{}$

$\lambda\sigma_1\lambda\sigma_2.\sigma_1(\text{ER}(\text{tall})) \circ \text{than} \circ \sigma_2(\boldsymbol{\varepsilon});$
$\lambda P\lambda Q.\textbf{max}(\lambda d.P(\textbf{tall}(d))) >$
$\quad\textbf{max}(\lambda d.Q(\textbf{tall}(d)));$
$S\upharpoonright(S\upharpoonright\text{Adj})\upharpoonright(S\upharpoonright\text{Adj})$

is;
$\lambda P.P;$
VP/Adj
mary;
m;
NP

$\begin{bmatrix}\varphi;\\P;\\\text{Adj}\end{bmatrix}^1$

$\dfrac{}{\text{is} \circ \varphi;\, P;\, \text{VP}}$

mary $\circ$ is $\circ \varphi$; $P(\textbf{m})$; S

$\lambda\varphi.\text{mary} \circ \text{is} \circ \varphi;$
$\lambda P.P(\textbf{m}); S\upharpoonright\text{Adj}$

$\lambda\varphi.\text{ann}\circ$
is $\circ \varphi;$
$\lambda P.P(\textbf{a});$
$S\upharpoonright\text{Adj}$

$\lambda\sigma_2.\text{mary} \circ \text{is} \circ \text{tall} \circ \text{er} \circ \text{than} \circ \sigma_2(\boldsymbol{\varepsilon});$
$\lambda Q.\textbf{max}(\lambda d.\textbf{tall}(d)(\textbf{m})) > \textbf{max}(\lambda d.Q(\textbf{tall}(d)));\, S\upharpoonright(S\upharpoonright\text{Adj})$

$\dfrac{}{\text{mary} \circ \text{is} \circ \text{tall} \circ \text{er} \circ \text{than} \circ \text{ann} \circ \text{is};\ \textbf{max}(\lambda d.\textbf{tall}(d)(\textbf{m})) > \textbf{max}(\lambda d.\textbf{tall}(d)(\textbf{a}));\, S}$

8.2.2.2 VP ellipsis in comparatives The analysis of comparatives sketched above interacts straightforwardly with the analysis of VP ellipsis from chapter 6 to yield the right meanings for examples like the following:

(390) John ran faster than Mary did.

Here again, there can be two possible analyses of the missing status of *fast* in the *than* clause. We assume without argument here that the adverb is part of the "elided material." An analysis in which the comparative operator is responsible for the recovery of the adverb meaning (corresponding to the derivation in (389)) is also straightforward in our approach.

We assume that, like adjectives, adverbs that have a gradable component in meaning take an additional degree argument (syntactically of type Deg and semantically of type d).

(391) $\lambda\varphi.\text{fast} \circ \varphi$; **fast**; $(\text{VP}\backslash\text{VP})\upharpoonright\text{Deg}$

With this lexical entry for the adverb *fast*, the derivation for (390) goes as follows (here, we abbreviate Deg as D):

(392)

$$
\cfrac{
\cfrac{
\lambda\sigma_2.\text{john} \circ \text{ran} \circ \text{fast} \circ \text{er} \circ \text{than} \circ \sigma_2(\boldsymbol{\varepsilon});\ \lambda Q.\mathbf{max}(\lambda d.\mathbf{fast}(d)(\mathbf{ran})(\mathbf{j})) > \mathbf{max}(Q); S\upharpoonright(S\upharpoonright\text{D})
}{}
}{}
$$

$$
\cfrac{
\lambda\sigma_1\lambda\sigma_2.\sigma_1(\text{er}) \circ \text{than} \circ \sigma_2(\boldsymbol{\varepsilon});\ \lambda P\lambda Q.\mathbf{max}(P) > \mathbf{max}(Q); S\upharpoonright(S\upharpoonright\text{D})\upharpoonright(S\upharpoonright\text{D})
\qquad
\cfrac{
\begin{array}{c}
\text{john;}\\ \mathbf{j;}\\ \text{NP}
\end{array}
\quad
\cfrac{
\left[\begin{array}{c}\varphi;\\ d;\\ \text{D}\end{array}\right]^2
\quad
\cfrac{
\cfrac{
\begin{array}{c}\text{ran;}\\ \mathbf{ran;}\\ \text{VP}\end{array}
\quad
\cfrac{\lambda\varphi.\text{fast} \circ \varphi;\ \mathbf{fast};(\text{VP}\backslash\text{VP})\upharpoonright\text{D} \quad \left[\begin{array}{c}\varphi;\\ d;\text{D}\end{array}\right]^3}{\text{fast} \circ \varphi;\ \mathbf{fast}(d);(\text{VP}\backslash\text{VP})}
}{
\cfrac{\text{ran} \circ \text{fast} \circ \varphi;\ \mathbf{fast}(d)(\mathbf{ran}); \text{VP}}{\lambda\varphi.\text{ran} \circ \text{fast} \circ \varphi;\ \lambda d.\mathbf{fast}(d)(\mathbf{ran}); \boxed{\text{VP}\upharpoonright\text{Deg}}}\ \upharpoonright I^3
}
}{\text{ran} \circ \text{fast} \circ \varphi;\ \mathbf{fast}(d)(\mathbf{ran}); \text{VP}}
}{
\cfrac{\text{john} \circ \text{ran} \circ \text{fast} \circ \varphi;\ \mathbf{fast}(d)(\mathbf{ran})(\mathbf{j}); S}{\lambda\varphi.\text{john} \circ \text{ran} \circ \text{fast} \circ \varphi;\ \lambda d.\mathbf{fast}(d)(\mathbf{ran})(\mathbf{j}); S\upharpoonright\text{D}}\ \upharpoonright I^2
}
}{}
}{\lambda\sigma_2.\text{john} \circ \text{ran} \circ \text{fast} \circ \text{er} \circ \text{than} \circ \sigma_2(\boldsymbol{\varepsilon});\ \lambda Q.\mathbf{max}(\lambda d.\mathbf{fast}(d)(\mathbf{ran})(\mathbf{j})) > \mathbf{max}(Q); S\upharpoonright(S\upharpoonright\text{D})}
$$

$$
\cfrac{
\begin{array}{c}
\vdots\\
\lambda\sigma_2.\text{john} \circ \text{ran} \circ \text{fast} \circ \text{er} \circ \text{than} \circ \sigma_2(\boldsymbol{\varepsilon});\\ \lambda Q.\mathbf{max}(\lambda d.\mathbf{fast}(d)(\mathbf{ran})(\mathbf{j})) > \mathbf{max}(Q);\\ S\upharpoonright(S\upharpoonright\text{D})
\end{array}
\quad
\cfrac{
\begin{array}{c}\text{mary;}\\ \mathbf{m;}\\ \text{NP}\end{array}
\quad
\cfrac{
\left[\begin{array}{c}\varphi;\\ d;\\ \text{D}\end{array}\right]^1
\quad
\cfrac{
\begin{array}{c}\lambda\rho\lambda\varphi.\rho(\lambda\varphi.\varphi)(\varphi);\\ \lambda\mathcal{G}.\mathcal{G}(\lambda d.\mathbf{fast}(d)(\mathbf{ran}));\\ (\text{VP}\upharpoonright\text{D})\upharpoonright((\text{VP}\upharpoonright\text{D})\upharpoonright(\text{VP}\upharpoonright\text{D}))\end{array}
\quad
\begin{array}{c}\lambda\sigma\lambda\varphi.\text{did} \circ \sigma(\varphi);\\ \lambda\mathcal{F}.\mathcal{F};\\ (\text{VP}\upharpoonright\text{D})\upharpoonright(\text{VP}\upharpoonright\text{D})\end{array}
}{\lambda\varphi.\text{did} \circ \varphi;\ \lambda d.\mathbf{fast}(d)(\mathbf{ran}); \text{VP}\upharpoonright\text{D}}
}{\text{did} \circ \varphi;\ \mathbf{fast}(d)(\mathbf{ran}); \text{VP}}
}{
\cfrac{\text{mary} \circ \text{did} \circ \varphi;\ \mathbf{fast}(d)(\mathbf{ran})(\mathbf{m}); S}{\lambda\varphi.\text{mary} \circ \text{did} \circ \varphi;\ \lambda d.\mathbf{fast}(d)(\mathbf{ran})(\mathbf{m}); S\upharpoonright\text{D}}\ \upharpoonright I^1
}
}{\text{john} \circ \text{ran} \circ \text{fast} \circ \text{er} \circ \text{than} \circ \text{mary} \circ \text{did};\ \mathbf{max}(\lambda d.\mathbf{fast}(d)(\mathbf{ran})(\mathbf{j})) > \mathbf{max}(\lambda d.\mathbf{fast}(d)(\mathbf{ran})(\mathbf{m})); S}
$$

In somewhat informal terms, on this analysis what is "elided" in the *than* clause in (390) is a VP containing a "gap" position for the degree argument: "ran __ fast." In Hybrid TLCG terms, this will correspond to an expression of type VP⌐Deg, with the denotation $\lambda d.\mathbf{fast}(d)(\mathbf{ran})$. Thus, the derivation is parallel to the extraction/ellipsis interaction case in (382) from section 8.2.1, with the only difference being that the missing expression here is of type Deg rather than type NP.

8.3 Kennedy's Arguments: A Second Look

We now revisit Kennedy's arguments as summarized in section 8.1, in light of the alternative analysis of extraction/ellipsis interaction just sketched, apart from his island arguments (which we take up in chapter 10). In the following discussion we demonstrate that, in every case, the data that Kennedy takes to establish the inevitability of a covert structure analysis for ellipsis phenomena can be accounted for far more straightforwardly on a "direct interpretation" approach. In some cases, Kennedy's assumptions about the structural basis of the diagnostic probes he employs are undermotivated, while in others, the fact that on our approach examples such as (376) do involve an actual extraction renders his argument moot.

8.3.1 Ellipsis and Islandhood

As noted above, we discuss Kennedy's arguments involving islandhood in chapter 10 (section 10.2.4), together with similar arguments for structural analyses of other phenomena. To preview the conclusion, the judgment patterns that Kennedy gives to support his deletion analyses either receive alternative explanations or simply are not robust enough to support the existence of islandhood as a syntactic condition.

8.3.2 Ellipsis and SCO

Kennedy's argument based on SCO, as outlined in section 8.1.2, hinges on the assumption that data such as (366) indeed reflect extraction from an elided VP.

(366) Who$_i$ will Mary vote for t_i if he$_{j/*i}$ does ~~vote for t_i~~?

However, on the alternative analysis presented in section 8.2.1, an analogue of the following representation of the relevant coindexing relations in (366) is licensed:

(393) *wh$_i$ ... he$_i$ [$_{VP}$ [$_{VP/NP}$ does] t_i]

The point is that what is extracted in (393) could correspond, on this analysis, to an argument of the auxiliary itself. Thus, any account of SCO which motivates ordinary cases such as (365) will predict SCO in pseudogapping + extraction cases of the sort exhibited in (366) on exactly the same basis, with no covert structure.[7]

In other words, it follows that on the extended valence analysis of auxiliaries, the SCO facts that Kennedy takes as prima facie support for covert structure in VP ellipsis

---

7. Although it is true that, in principle, nothing excludes a transformational counterpart to our pseudogapping-based analysis and that any such analysis undercuts Kennedy's use of SCO effects to defend covert structure, whether or not such a transformational treatment is possible is a complex question. The remnants in pseudogapping examples represent the survivors of a movement + deletion process in transformational approaches. The eligibility of such an expression for further movement depends on a possibly intricate network of further assumptions about iterated movement which in practice appear to vary from author to author.

are just another expected consequence of auxiliary behavior, fully compatible with a nonstructural treatment of those facts.

We do not formulate an account of SCO in our approach, and acknowledge that the phenomenon originally described in Postal (1971) is difficult to analyze—with the caveat that this holds for all current theories, including the Principles and Parameters approach.

8.3.3 Ellipsis and Condition B

For the analysis of the so-called Binding Condition B, we adopt Jacobson's approach, representing part of a long tradition of non-configurational approaches to anaphoric relations amongst nominal terms. In this work, Jacobson offers a thorough critique of the standard configuration-based approach to "Condition B" effects, concluding that it faces "problems which seem insurmountable" (2007, 218).[8] The key idea in Jacobson's alternative, non-configurational account of Condition B effects is that NPs are divided by a binary-valued feature $\pm p$, with pronouns marked NP_{+p} and all other NPs NP_{-p}. In all lexical entries of the form in (394), all NP (and PP) arguments in any realization of $/\$$ are specified as $-p$.[9]

(394) k; P; $VP/\$$

The effect of this restriction is to rule out pronouns from argument positions of verbs with ordinary semantic denotations. On this approach, the only way a lexically specified functional category can take $+p$ arguments is via the application of the following irreflexive operator:[10]

---

8. The pioneering study of anaphora in Bach and Partee (1980) offered a purely compositional semantic treatment of reflexives which hinges on treating anaphors in a fashion parallel to generalized quantifiers as scope-taking elements. In HPSG, on the other hand, anaphoric possibilities are determined by neither phrase structure configuration nor semantic composition but by the combinatory argument structure specified for heads (Pollard and Sag 1983, 1992, 1994), an approach subsequently adopted by LFG (Bresnan et al. 2016). Even within the general Principles and Parameters framework, there are both older and more recent treatments which do not derive the anaphora possibilities from configurational representations (see, e.g., Reinhart and Reuland 1993; Safir 2004). It is worth noting that efforts to extend the Bach-Partee approach to cover Condition B were not particularly successful until Jacobson's (2007) work; see Jäger (2005, chap. 2) and Morrill (2010, 124–125) for discussion.

9. We take VP to abbreviate NP\S, where NP is underspecified for the value of the feature p. Unlike pronouns in the object position, no special conditions or restrictions apply to subject pronouns, hence the choice of $\pm$ value for such pronouns need not be specified.

10. For expository purposes, we state the operator in (395) in its most restricted form, dealing with only the case where there is a single syntactic argument apart from the subject. A much broader coverage is of course necessary in order to handle cases like the following:

(i) a. *John$_i$ warned Mary about him$_i$.
     b. *John talked to Mary$_i$ about her$_i$.
     c. *John explained himself$_i$ to him$_i$.

(395) $\lambda\varphi.\varphi;\ \lambda f\lambda u\lambda v.f(u)(v),\ \boxed{u\neq v}\ ;\ (VP/NP_{+p})\upharpoonright(VP/NP_{-p})$

The grayed-in part $u\neq v$ separated from the truth conditional meaning by a comma is a presupposition introduced by the pronoun-seeking variant of the predicate. It says that the subject and object arguments are forced to pick out different objects in the model. For the semantics of pronouns themselves, we continue to assume from chapter 6 that free (i.e., unbound) pronouns are simply translated as arbitrary variables (cf. Cooper 1979).

Crucially, the operator in (395) is restricted in its domain of application to the set of signs which are specified in the lexicon. We notate this restriction by using the dashed line notion in what follows. Then *John praises him* will be derived as in (396):

(396)

$\lambda\varphi.\varphi;$
$\lambda f\lambda u\lambda v.f(u)(v),u\neq v;$ praises;
$(VP/NP_{+p})\upharpoonright(VP/NP_{-p})$ **praise**; VP/NP_{-p}

----

praises; $\lambda u\lambda v.\mathbf{praise}(u)(v),u\neq v;$ VP/NP_{+p} him; z; NP_{+p}

praises $\circ$ him; $\lambda v.\mathbf{praise}(z)(v),z\neq v;$ VP   john; **j**; NP_{-p}

john $\circ$ praises $\circ$ him; $\mathbf{praise}(z)(\mathbf{j}),z\neq\mathbf{j};$ S

The presupposition $z\neq\mathbf{j}$ ensures that the referent of the pronoun is different from John.

This approach extends straightforwardly to bound variable readings of pronouns. We first illustrate how a well-formed example of bound variable anaphora such as (397) can be analyzed in this setup, and then explain the Condition B effects for bound pronouns.

(397) Every editor$_i$ believes that John admires him$_i$.

For the bound variable reading of pronouns, we assume the following lexical entry, which encodes nonlinearity enforced by binding in the lexical specification (note that,

---

What we need in effect is a schematic type specification that applies to a pronoun in any or all argument positions, i.e., stated on an input of the form $VP/\$/XP_{-p}/\$$ to yield an output of the form $VP/\$/XP_{+p}/\$$. To ensure the correct implementation of this extension, some version of the "wrapping" analysis needs to be assumed (cf. Jacobson 2007), so that the order of the arguments in verbs' lexical entries is isomorphic to the obliqueness hierarchy (of the sort discussed by Pollard and Sag [1992]).

Cases such as the following also call for an extension (also a relatively straightforward one):

(ii) *John$_i$ is proud of him$_i$.

By assuming (following Jacobson 2007) that the $\pm p$ feature percolates from NPs to PPs and by generalizing the irreflexive operator still further so that it applies not just to VP/XP_{-p} but also to AP/XP_{-p}, the ungrammaticality of (ii) follows straightforwardly.

in the semantic term, two tokens of the same variable w are bound by the same lambda operator):[11]

(398) $\lambda\sigma.\sigma(\text{him}); \lambda\mathscr{F}\lambda w.\mathscr{F}(w)(w); \text{VP}\!\uparrow\!(\text{VP}\!\uparrow\!\text{NP}_{+p})$

With this lexical sign for *him*, we obtain the correct interpretation of (397) as follows (here, $\mathbf{V}_{\textbf{editor}}$ is an abbreviation for the term $\lambda Q.\forall x[\mathbf{editor}(x) \rightarrow Q(x)]$):

(399)

$\vdots$

admires;
$\lambda u \lambda v.$
  $\mathbf{admire}$
  $(u)(v),$
  $u \neq v;$ $\begin{bmatrix} \varphi_0; \\ z; \\ \text{NP}_{+p} \end{bmatrix}^0$
  VP/NP_{+p}

───────────────────────────────
admires $\circ \varphi_0;$ john;
$\lambda v.\mathbf{admire}(z), z \neq v;$ $\mathbf{j};$
VP NP_{-p} thinks;
─── $\mathbf{think};$
  john $\circ$ admires $\circ \varphi_0;$ VP/S
  $\mathbf{admire}(z)(\mathbf{j}), z \neq \mathbf{j}; \text{S}$ $\lambda\sigma_0.$
─── $\sigma_0(\text{him});$
  thinks $\circ$ john $\circ$ admires $\circ \varphi_0;$ $\lambda\mathscr{F}\lambda w.$
  $\mathbf{think}(\mathbf{admire}(z)(\mathbf{j})), z \neq \mathbf{j}; \text{VP}$ $\mathscr{F}(w)(w);$
──────────────────────────────────── $\!\!\upharpoonright^0$ $\text{VP}\!\uparrow$
  $\lambda\varphi_0.\text{thinks} \circ \text{john} \circ \text{admires} \circ \varphi_0;$ $(\text{VP}\!\uparrow\!\text{NP}_{+p})$ $\begin{bmatrix} \varphi_1; \\ y; \\ \text{NP} \end{bmatrix}^1$
  $\lambda z.\mathbf{think}(\mathbf{admire}(z)(\mathbf{j})), z \neq \mathbf{j};$
  $\text{VP}\!\uparrow\!\text{NP}_{+p}$
───
  thinks $\circ$ john $\circ$ admires $\circ$ him; $\lambda\sigma_1.\sigma_1$
  $\lambda w.\mathbf{think}(\mathbf{admire}(w)(\mathbf{j}))(w), w \neq \mathbf{j}; \text{VP}$ (every $\circ$
───   editor);
  $\varphi_1 \circ$ thinks $\circ$ john $\circ$ admires $\circ$ him; $\mathbf{V}_{\textbf{editor}};$
  $\mathbf{think}(\mathbf{admire}(y)(\mathbf{j}))(y), y \neq \mathbf{j}; \text{S}$ $\text{S}\!\uparrow\!(\text{S}\!\uparrow\!\text{NP}_{-p})$
──────────────────────────────────── $\!\!\upharpoonright^1$
  $\lambda\varphi_1.\varphi_1 \circ$ thinks $\circ$ john $\circ$ admires $\circ$ him;
  $\lambda y.\mathbf{think}(\mathbf{admire}(y)(\mathbf{j}))(y), y \neq \mathbf{j}; \text{S}\!\uparrow\!\text{NP}$
───
  every $\circ$ editor $\circ$ thinks $\circ$ john $\circ$ admires $\circ$ him;
  $\mathbf{V}_{\textbf{editor}}(\lambda y.\mathbf{think}(\mathbf{admire}(y)(\mathbf{j}))(y), y \neq \mathbf{j}); \text{S}$

─────────────────────────────

11. One might worry about the duplication of lexical entries for pronouns for the free and bound uses. It is in fact straightforward to unify the two by deriving the bound form from the free form by the following operator (which, like the irreflexive operator, is a lexical operator), with α a variable over case values:

(i) $\lambda\varphi\lambda\sigma.\sigma(\varphi); \lambda v\lambda\mathscr{G}\lambda w.\mathscr{G}(w)(w); (\text{VP}\!\uparrow\!(\text{VP}\!\uparrow\!\text{NP}_{+p,\alpha}))\!\uparrow\!\text{NP}_{+p,\alpha}$

By applying (i) to the free pronoun (ii), we obtain the bound pronoun entry identical to (398).

(ii) *him*; u; $\text{NP}_{+p,acc}$

The bound variable reading for the following example is blocked for essentially the same reason that the coreferential reading is blocked in simpler examples like (396).

(400) *Every editor$_i$ congratulated him$_i$.

The forced application of the irreflexive operator to the verb lexical entry dictated by the pronoun has the effect that the verb's subject and object have disjoint reference. However, this directly contradicts the subject quantifier's binding the object pronoun, thus rendering the sentence uninterpretable on the intended reading. The derivation is shown in (401):

(401) $\vdots$

$$
\frac{
\begin{array}{ll}
\text{congratulated;} \\
\lambda u \lambda v.\textbf{congratulated}(u)(v), & \left[\begin{array}{l} \varphi_0; \\ w; \\ NP_{+p} \end{array}\right]^0 \\
\quad u \neq v; \\
VP/NP_{+p}
\end{array}
}{
\begin{array}{l}
\text{congratulated} \circ \varphi_0; \\
\lambda v.\textbf{congratulated}(w)(v), w \neq v; VP
\end{array}
} \upharpoonright I^0
$$

$$
\frac{
\begin{array}{ll}
\lambda\varphi_0.\text{congratulated} \circ \varphi_0; & \text{him;} \\
\lambda w \lambda v.\textbf{congratulated}(w)(v), w \neq v; & \lambda\mathscr{G}\lambda y.\mathscr{G}(y)(y); \\
VP\upharpoonright NP_{+p} & VP\upharpoonright(VP\upharpoonright NP_{+p})
\end{array}
}{
\begin{array}{l}
\text{congratulated} \circ \text{him;} \\
\lambda y.\textbf{congratulated}(y)(y), y \neq y; VP
\end{array}
\quad \left[\begin{array}{l} \varphi_1; \\ x; \\ NP \end{array}\right]^1
}
$$

$$
\frac{
\begin{array}{l}
\varphi_1 \circ \text{congratulated} \circ \text{him;} \\
\textbf{congratulated}(x)(x), x \neq x; S
\end{array}
}{
\begin{array}{l}
\lambda\varphi_1.\varphi_1 \circ \text{congratulated} \circ \text{him;} \\
\lambda x.\textbf{congratulated}(x)(x), x \neq x; S\upharpoonright NP
\end{array}
} \upharpoonright I^1
\qquad
\begin{array}{l}
\lambda\sigma_1.\sigma_1(\text{every} \circ \\
\quad \text{editor}); \\
\textbf{V}_{\textbf{editor}}; \\
S\upharpoonright(S\upharpoonright NP_{-p})
\end{array}
$$

$$
\begin{array}{l}
\text{every} \circ \text{editor} \circ \text{congratulated} \circ \text{him;} \\
\textbf{V}_{\textbf{editor}}(\lambda x.\textbf{congratulated}(x)(x), x \neq x); S
\end{array}
$$

With this strictly semantic approach to "Condition B" effects in hand, let us return to Kennedy's argument based on such effects. Recall that Kennedy's argument rested on the assumption that in examples such as (402) (= (367) from section 8.1.3) the obligatorily disjoint interpretation of the two pronouns requires a specific covert structure as the supposed basis for this enforced interpretation.

(402) John$_k$ takes care of him$_i$ because he$_{j/*i}$ won't.

But the interaction of our lexically based semantic treatment of "Condition B" effects with the analysis of ellipsis from section 8.2 automatically accounts for the pattern in

(402). The derivation is given in (403) (here, we ignore the tense and modal meaning of the future tense auxiliary *won't*; **irr** abbreviates the term $\lambda f \lambda u \lambda v. f(u)(v), u \neq v$).[12]

(403)

$$\frac{\begin{array}{cc} \text{takes} \circ \text{care} \circ \text{of;} \\ \textbf{irr}(\textbf{take-care}); \text{VP}/\text{NP}_{+p} \quad \text{him}; w; \text{NP}_{+p} \end{array}}{\begin{array}{cc} \text{takes} \circ \text{care} \circ \text{of} \circ \text{him;} \ \textbf{irr}(\textbf{take-care})(w); \text{VP} \quad \text{john; } \textbf{j}; \text{NP}_{-p} \\ \hline \text{john} \circ \text{takes} \circ \text{care} \circ \text{of} \circ \text{him;} \ \textbf{irr}(\textbf{take-care})(w)(\textbf{j}); \text{S} \end{array}}$$

$$\frac{\text{won't;} \ \neg\textbf{irr}(\textbf{take-care})(w); \text{VP} \quad \text{he; } y; \text{NP}_{+p}}{\text{he} \circ \text{won't;} \ \neg\textbf{irr}(\textbf{take-care})(w)(y); \text{S}}$$

Since $\textbf{irr}(\textbf{take-care})(w)(y) \equiv \textbf{take-care}(w)(y), w \neq y$, it is guaranteed that the subject pronoun is disjoint in reference from the object (note that the term $w \neq y$, when evaluated at a given model and a value assignment g, entails that the individuals assigned to w and y by g are distinct).

Examples like (402), therefore, offer no support to the claim that covert syntactic structure must be present in VP ellipsis. The disjoint reference requirement follows equally straightforwardly in a nonstructural analysis of VP ellipsis combined with a nonstructural analysis of "Condition B" effects. It is important to keep in mind that, though these perspectives on ellipsis and binding depart from the standard view, they both receive ample empirical support, since their advantages over the standard view have independently been established in the literature.

8.3.4 Ellipsis and Parasitic Gaps

We now extend our approach to Kennedy's parasitic gap data, demonstrating that, again, appeal to hidden configuration is unnecessary. Consider again (404) and (405) ((369) and (370) from section 8.1.4):

(404) a. *Otis is a person who$_i$ I admire __$_i$ because close friends of __$_i$ became famous.

   b. ?Otis is a person who I admire because close friends of __$_i$ admire __$_i$/*him$_i$.

(405) Otis is a person who$_i$ I admire __$_i$ because close friends of __$_i$ seem to $\varnothing$.

---

12. We take the idiom *takes care of* to be a complex transitive verb, as per (i):

(i) take $\circ$ care $\circ$ of; **take-care-of**; VP/NP

The treatment reflected in (i) is strongly supported by the passivization and extraction pattern in (ii).

(ii) a. Our problem seems to have been taken care of.
   b. *Care was taken of that problem.
   c. ??*Of which problem have you taken care?

Here we annotate Kennedy's original datum in (404b) with our own judgment, which, while taking this example to be grammatical, assigns it a rather more diminished status than does Kennedy.

The central issue about parasitic gaps comes down to the following question: Why is (404b) (in the gap version) reasonably acceptable but (404a) bad? It has been widely assumed in the literature that the contrast between (404a) and (404b) is a grammatical one, that is, that the "parasitic" gap in the subject position cannot be licensed except for the presence of a supporting "real gap" in the main VP. But in recent years, this position has begun to give way to an alternative perspective, in which processing-based factors bear the primary responsibility for the contrast between (404a) and (404b), as we discuss in greater detail below (see also section 10.1.3.1).

Note first that, just as in the case of extractions from other putative island positions, subject gap sites are more or less permissible in principle. Thus we find examples such as the following (where the $[_\pi \ldots]$ notation identifies the bracketed material as a prosodic phrase):

(406) a. There are certain topics which $[_\pi$ jokes about ___ $]$ $[_\pi$ are completely unacceptable.$]$ (Levine and Sag 2003).

      b. $[_\pi$ Of which cars$]$ $[_\pi$ were only the hoods ___ $]$ $[_\pi$ damaged by the explosion?$]$
                                                            (Ross 1967, 252, cited in Chaves 2013)

      c. They have eight children $[_\pi$ of whom$]$ $[_\pi$ five ___ are still living at home.$]$
                                                (Huddleston et al. 2002, 1093, cited in Chaves 2013)

      d. $[_\pi$ That is the lock$]$ $[_\pi$ to which$]$ $[_\pi$ the key ___ has been lost.$]$
                                                                        (Levine and Hukari 2006)

      e. $[_\pi$ Which disease$]$ $[_\pi$ will the cure for ___ $]$ $[_\pi$ never be discovered$]$?
                                                                              (Chaves 2013, 17)

Chaves (2013) and Chaves and Dery (2019) contain many such examples, which point to the conclusion that subjects are not, in themselves, island contexts. On this view, examples such as (407) are grammatical, but unacceptable for reasons explored in Kluender (2004), Chaves (2013), and Chaves and Dery (2019).

(407) ??*Which people did friends of ___ become famous?

But there appears to be an important exception to this pattern. When otherwise reasonably acceptable examples of subject-internal gaps appear as adjunct clauses in parasitic gap constructions (i.e., when the relevant gap is an adjunct parasitic gap) rather than as main clauses, there is a dramatic drop in speakers' assessments of their status.

(408) a. ??*Which disease$_i$ do people rightly fear ___$_i$ because the cure for ___$_i$ will never be discovered?

    b. ??*There are certain topics which$_i$ comedians ignore __$_i$ because jokes about __$_i$ are completely unacceptable.

These examples essentially have the same syntactic structure as (404a).

Thus, we have four classes of data to account for (the contrast between 3 and 4 is what crucially supports Kennedy's argument from parasitic gap–licensing patterns):

1. unsupported *wh* extraction from subjects (sometimes good (407); sometimes bad (406))
2. supported *wh* extraction from subjects (typically fine)
3. embedded unsupported *wh* extraction from subjects ((408); markedly worse than 1)
4. embedded supported *wh* extraction from subjects ((404b); markedly better than 3)

The key explanatory mechanism for 1–2 is offered in Chaves (2013), based on the premise that parsing efficiency considerations have led to a strategy in which, once a filler has been encountered and stored, the processor expects to find no corresponding gap within the subject, but strongly anticipates a gap in the immediately following VP. This is discussed in greater detail in chapter 10. Cases such as (407), on this view, are unacceptable precisely because they violate both of these presumptions. As Chaves notes, prosodic or pragmatic cues can ameliorate these violations and allow the processor to successfully link the filler to gap sites even where neither of the parser's wired-in "first pass" expectations is satisfied (as attested in (406)), but such cues have to be quite prominent to offset the effect of those expectations failing. On the other hand, simple subject parasitic gap cases as in 2 violate only one of the parser's expectations and are thus predicted to be significantly better than 1.

The final issue corresponds to cases in which we have an unsupported and supported parasitic gap in an adjunct clause subject (3 and 4). Here too, we have an answer ready. Pattern 3 is significantly worse than pattern 1 since it violates a parser's expectations in *three* ways. Specifically, the gap is inside an adjunct clause, it is in the subject position, and there is no supporting gap in the following VP. With three independent violations of the processor's parsing strategy, it is not surprising that such examples are severely ill-formed.[13] By contrast, 4 is markedly better than 3 because it violates only two of the three conditions. Thus, with no further development or modification, Chaves's model

---

13. As noted in Kluender (1998), each successive clausal boundary (or its real-time parsing analogue) represents an additional processing bottleneck which adds significant costs to the parser's efforts to link stored fillers with identifiable gap sites. Subsequent work reported in Kluender (2004) suggests that subject-internal gaps are intrinsically harder to process than gaps in other parts of the sentence, but are not ruled out in the grammar. Kluender (2004) offers well-formed examples (including some first noted in Ross [1967]) in support of this claim but does not offer an explanation for why subsequent gaps within the VP ameliorate the processing difficulties involved.

already accounts for what we have identified as the key problems posed by subject-internal gaps.

We summarize the situation in the following table. The check mark indicates that the pattern violates the condition in question.

(409)

	Gap in subject position	No gap in the following VP	Embedding in adjunct clause
1	✓	✓	
2	✓		
3	✓	✓	✓
4	✓		✓

Against the background of this account of parasitic gap licensing, the well-formedness and interpretation of (405), which adds ellipsis in the adjunct clause to the mix, now follows automatically, with no further conditions, restrictions, or machinery. Recall that in the case of the simpler "extraction out of an elided VP" example (380), we identified the extraction "site" as the direct object of the transitive auxiliary *did*. Exactly the same analysis is available in the case of (405). Using the gap-multiplying operator introduced at the end of the preceding chapter, we have proofs such as the following:

(410)
$$\vdots$$

$$\frac{\begin{array}{c}\lambda\varphi.\text{to}\circ\varphi;\\ \lambda x\lambda y.\\ \mathbf{admire}(x)(y);\\ \text{VP}{\restriction}\text{NP}_{\#wh}\end{array}\quad\left[\begin{array}{c}\varphi_1;\\ u;\\ \text{NP}_{+wh}\end{array}\right]^1}{\begin{array}{c}\text{to}\circ\varphi_1;\\ \lambda y.\mathbf{admire}(u)(y);\text{VP}\end{array}}\quad\begin{array}{c}\text{seem};\\ \mathbf{seem};\\ \text{VP/VP}\end{array}$$

$$\frac{\begin{array}{c}\text{seem}\circ\text{to}\circ\varphi_1;\\ \lambda w.\mathbf{seem}(\mathbf{admire}(u)(w));\text{VP}\end{array}}{\begin{array}{c}\lambda\varphi_1.\text{seem}\circ\text{to}\circ\varphi_1;\\ \lambda u\lambda w.\mathbf{seem}(\mathbf{admire}(u)(w));\text{VP}{\restriction}\text{NP}_{+wh}\end{array}}{\restriction}I^1$$

$$\vdots$$

$$\frac{\begin{array}{c}\lambda\varphi_1.\text{seem}\circ\text{to}\circ\varphi_1;\\ \lambda u\lambda w.\mathbf{seem}(\mathbf{admire}(u)(w));\\ (\text{NP}_{-wh}\backslash\text{S}){\restriction}\text{NP}_{+wh}\end{array}\quad\begin{array}{c}\lambda\sigma_1\lambda\sigma_2\lambda\varphi.\\ \sigma_2(\varphi)\circ\sigma_1(\varphi);\\ \lambda R\lambda g\lambda x.R(x)(g(x));\\ (\text{S}{\restriction}\text{NP}_{+wh}){\restriction}\\ (\text{NP}_{-wh}{\restriction}\text{NP}_{+wh}){\restriction}\\ ((\text{NP}_{-wh}\backslash\text{S}){\restriction}\text{NP}_{+wh})\end{array}}{\begin{array}{c}\lambda\sigma_2\lambda\varphi.\sigma_2(\varphi)\circ\text{seem}\circ\text{to}\circ\varphi;\\ \lambda g\lambda x.\mathbf{seem}(\mathbf{admire}(x)(g(x)));(\text{S}{\restriction}\text{NP}_{+wh}){\restriction}(\text{NP}_{-wh}{\restriction}\text{NP}_{+wh})\end{array}}\quad\begin{array}{c}\lambda\varphi_3.\text{the}\circ\text{close}\circ\\ \text{friends}\circ\text{of}\circ\varphi_3;\\ \lambda v.\iota(\lambda z.\\ \mathbf{close\text{-}fr}(v)(z));\\ \text{NP}_{-wh}{\restriction}\text{NP}_{+wh}\end{array}$$

$$\begin{array}{c}\lambda\varphi.\text{the}\circ\text{close}\circ\text{friends}\circ\text{of}\circ\varphi\circ\text{seem}\circ\text{to}\circ\varphi;\\ \lambda x.\mathbf{seem}(\mathbf{admire}(x)(\iota(\lambda z.\mathbf{close\text{-}fr}(x)(z))));\text{S}{\restriction}\text{NP}_{+wh}\end{array}$$

On our analysis, cases such as (405), licensed by the derivation in (410), should have exactly the same status as their overt counterpart; like the latter, (405) displays a gap in subject position and a corresponding gap in the VP, the critical requirement for full acceptability in English when a subject gap is involved. The gap corresponds to an argument of a transitive auxiliary, but this fact in itself does not make any difference to the status of the example. What is crucial is that there be an actual syntactic "gap" involved and that this gap need not be a configurational object (this latter assumption is shared widely among so-called lexicalist theories of syntax such as G/HPSG and most versions of categorial grammar).[14]

Thus, Kennedy's argument for covert structure based on the distribution of parasitic gaps proves unfounded as well. Combining the independently required operator treatments of simple extraction and parasitic gaps with a generalization of the analysis of pseudogapping in chapter 6 automatically yields the parallelism between the "real" and "deleted" host VPs for subject position parasitic gaps attested in (404b) and (405), without recourse to any actual configurational object that undergoes syntactic deletion. At the same time, the combinatorics of our system (without augmentation of syntactic mechanisms blocking islands along the lines proposed, for example, in Morrill [2017]) license subject island violation examples such as (368a) and (404a), whose deviant status follows on independent grounds from the interactions of the factors discussed in detail in Kluender (2004), Chaves (2013), and Chaves and Dery (2019). On this view, the "parasitism" of subject-internal gaps is not a strictly syntactic phenomenon but an emergent effect of real-time parsing strategy.[15]

---

14. In fact, the processing-based account of parasitic gap acceptability essentially leads us to this conclusion directly. The arguments in Chaves (2013), which present a strong case for this processing basis, can be adopted directly on our account on the assumption that the processing of filler-gap linkages is not dependent on the gap being a configurational object. Pickering and Barry (1991, 250) defend just this possibility (see also Pickering 1993), namely,

> that a categorial grammar can recover information that is specified in phrase structural accounts by the use of empty categories, and . . . that a categorial processing model is capable of making the associations that we have argued to be appropriate to the processing of unbounded dependencies.

The rules in the version of categorial grammar they assume (which is based on CCG) are theorems of the proof theory of Hybrid TLCG and other versions of TLCG, and the analysis of extraction in the two (broad) versions of categorial grammar are the same in the relevant respects. Most important, the specific processing mechanism Pickering and Barry hypothesize—a direct association between the filler and a functional category which is specified for an argument of the same type as the filler—can be carried over directly to our analysis of extraction via hypothetical reasoning. Thus, their arguments and conclusion about the direct linkage of fillers with the predicates that select them directly carry over to our approach.

15. However, while we believe that Chaves's processing account of parasitic gap patterns is very much on the right track, this issue is in a sense orthogonal to the question of whether or not such patterns support the existence of covert structure. On our analysis, an ordinary elided VP and an elided VP supposedly containing a gap site have different syntactic types: the former is VP while the latter is VP↾XP. Correspondingly, their semantic types are different. Thus, as long as there is some way (either processing-based, as we have

8.3.5 Ellipsis and Attributive Comparatives

Kennedy's (and Merchant's) argument for covert syntactic structure in VP ellipsis in the attributive comparative construction rests on the premise that the contrast between the elided and non-elided counterparts of attributive comparatives such as the following reflects a difference in *syntactic* well-formedness:

(411)   a. *John buys more expensive wine than he buys beer.

   b. John buys more expensive wine than he does beer.

We disagree with Kennedy and Merchant on the assessment of the relevant data. Specifically, we take both (411a) and (411b) to be licensed by the grammar and assume that the unacceptability of the former is explained by a processing-based factor (which is essentially a form of garden path effect). We address this issue in detail in section 10.2.4.2.

In this section, we formulate an explicit compositional analysis that derives both (411a) and (411b) as syntactically well-formed sentences of English, with the same meaning (after the VP ellipsis in the latter is resolved appropriately). As we show below, the basic analysis of the syntax-semantics interface of comparatives and its interactions with VP ellipsis introduced in section 8.2.1 extends straightforwardly to these somewhat more complex attributive comparative data.

There is one technical complication that needs to be addressed when formulating a compositional analysis of attributive comparatives: in examples like those in (411), the comparative form is in the attributive modifier position of an existentially quantified (or indefinite) NP, and we need to make sure that the **max** operator introduced by the comparative operator scopes lower than this existential quantifier. For this purpose, the definition of the comparative operator needs to be made slightly more complex. We first illustrate the new definition of the comparative operator with the simple example (412) (= (383a) from section 8.2.2), showing that the new definition yields exactly the same truth conditions for this sentence as the older definition.

(412) Mary is taller than Ann is.

We then show that with this new definition of the comparative operator, the attributive comparative examples in (411) can be analyzed in a way fully parallel to the analysis of (412), with the only difference being that the adjective is in the prenominal attributive position rather than in the predicative position.

---

assumed here, or syntactic, as is more traditionally entertained) of accounting for the acceptability contrast between "supported" and "unsupported" subject parasitic gaps, then that account straightforwardly carries over to the VP ellipsis cases. In categorial grammar, if one wanted to encode the parasitic gap licensing patterns in the syntax, the category distinction between VP|XP and VP already present would provide just enough information to implement such a syntactic condition.

The new comparative operator has the same syntactic type and prosodic form as the second version of the comparative operator from section 8.2.2 in (388):

(413) $\lambda \sigma_0 \lambda \sigma_1 \lambda \sigma_2 . \sigma_1 (ER(\sigma_0(\boldsymbol{\varepsilon}))) \circ \text{than} \circ \sigma_2(\boldsymbol{\varepsilon});$

$\quad \lambda f \lambda \mathscr{P} \lambda \mathscr{Q} \exists d_1, d_2 . \mathscr{P}(\lambda x . \mathbf{max}(\lambda d . f(d)(x)) = d_1) \wedge$

$\qquad \mathscr{Q}(\lambda x . \mathbf{max}(\lambda d . f(d)(x)) = d_2) \wedge d_1 > d_2;$

$\quad S \upharpoonright (S \upharpoonright Adj) \upharpoonright (S \upharpoonright Adj) \upharpoonright (Adj \upharpoonright Deg)$

The difference lies in the semantic component. Instead of directly forming degree predicates with the two clauses whose degree argument positions are abstracted over, the new operator first identifies the maximal degrees that satisfy the relevant degree descriptions and then compares the two degrees thus obtained. The crucial difference from the older definition in (388) is that the new definition forces the relevant degree descriptions (and hence the **max** operator that scopes immediately over these degree descriptions) to be included in the scope of other scopal expressions (if there are any) in the sentence.

Since the syntactic type of the comparative operator remains the same, the structure of the derivation for (412) is identical to (389) from section 8.2.2. The following translation is obtained by replacing the comparative operator in (389) with the new one in (413):

(414) $\exists d_1, d_2 . \mathbf{max}(\lambda d . \mathbf{tall}(d)(\mathbf{m})) = d_1 \wedge \mathbf{max}(\lambda d . \mathbf{tall}(d)(\mathbf{a})) = d_2 \wedge d_1 > d_2$

This is semantically equivalent to the older translation except that there is (in this case) redundant existential quantification over the two degrees d_1 and d_2.

As noted above, the only (substantial) difference between the simpler example in (412) and the attributive comparative example in (411a) is that the gradable adjective is in the predicative position in the former, whereas it is in the prenominal attributive modifier position in the latter. We assume that prenominal adjectives are of type N/N (semantically, $et \to et$). The (polymorphic) definition of the comparative operator needs to be slightly adjusted to accommodate this type difference. The version of the comparative operator for the prenominal adjective is as follows:

(415) $\lambda \sigma_0 \lambda \sigma_1 \lambda \sigma_2 . \sigma_1 (ER(\sigma_0(\boldsymbol{\varepsilon}))) \circ \text{than} \circ \sigma_2(\boldsymbol{\varepsilon});$

$\quad \lambda f \lambda \mathscr{P} \lambda \mathscr{Q} \exists d_1, d_2 . \mathscr{P}(\lambda P \lambda x . \mathbf{max}(\lambda d . f(d)(P)(x)) = d_1) \wedge$

$\qquad \mathscr{Q}(\lambda P \lambda x . \mathbf{max}(\lambda d . f(d)(P)(x)) = d_2) \wedge d_1 > d_2;$

$\quad S \upharpoonright (S \upharpoonright (N/N)) \upharpoonright (S \upharpoonright (N/N)) \upharpoonright ((N/N) \upharpoonright Deg)$

With this definition, the derivation for (411a) is straightforward. Just as in the simpler example in (412), the derivation proceeds by abstracting over the position of the adjective in the main clause and the *than* clause to form two clauses that have adjectival gaps (of type $S \upharpoonright (N/N)$). Two such gapped clauses are then given as arguments to the comparative operator. The full derivation is given in (417) (here, $\mathbf{int} = \lambda d \lambda P \lambda x.P(x) \wedge \mathbf{interesting}_{d \to t \to t}(d)(x)$). The final translation obtained in (417) can be unpacked as in (416).

(416) $\exists d_1, d_2.\mathbf{\exists}_{(\lambda x.\mathbf{max}(\lambda d.\mathbf{int}(d)(\mathbf{novel})(x))=d_1)}(\lambda x.\mathbf{wrote}(x)(\mathbf{j})) \wedge$
$\qquad \mathbf{\exists}_{(\lambda x.\mathbf{max}(\lambda d.\mathbf{int}(d)(\mathbf{play})(x))=d_2)}(\lambda x.\mathbf{wrote}(x)(\mathbf{m})) \wedge d_1 > d_2$
$\qquad = \exists d_1, d_2.\exists x.[\mathbf{max}(\lambda d.\mathbf{novel}(x) \wedge \mathbf{interesting}(d)(x)) = d_1 \wedge \mathbf{wrote}(x)(\mathbf{j})]$
$\qquad \wedge \exists y.[\mathbf{max}(\lambda d.\mathbf{play}(y) \wedge \mathbf{interesting}(d)(y)) = d_1 \wedge \mathbf{wrote}(y)(\mathbf{m})]$
$\qquad \wedge d_1 > d_2$

This says that there is a novel that John wrote and there is a play that Mary wrote and that the former is more interesting than the latter. This corresponds to the intuitive meaning of the sentence.

(417)

$$\lambda\sigma_0\lambda\sigma_1\lambda\sigma_2.\sigma_1(\mathsf{ER}(\sigma_0(\boldsymbol{\varepsilon}))) \circ \mathsf{than} \circ \sigma_2(\boldsymbol{\varepsilon});$$
$$\lambda f \lambda \mathscr{P} \lambda \mathscr{Q} \exists d_1, d_2.$$
$$\mathscr{P}(\lambda P \lambda x.\mathbf{max}(\lambda d.f(d)(P)(x)) = d_1) \wedge \qquad \lambda \varphi.\mathbf{interesting} \circ \qquad \lambda\varphi.\mathsf{john} \circ$$
$$\mathscr{Q}(\lambda P \lambda x.\mathbf{max}(\lambda d.f(d)(P)(x)) = d_2) \wedge \qquad \varphi; \qquad\qquad \mathsf{wrote} \circ$$
$$d_1 > d_2; \qquad\qquad\qquad\qquad\qquad\qquad\qquad \mathbf{int}; \qquad\qquad\qquad \mathsf{a} \circ \varphi \circ$$
$$\mathsf{S}{\upharpoonright}(\mathsf{S}{\upharpoonright}(\mathsf{N/N})){\upharpoonright}(\mathsf{S}{\upharpoonright}(\mathsf{N/N})){\upharpoonright}((\mathsf{N/N}){\upharpoonright}\mathsf{Deg}) \qquad (\mathsf{N/N}){\upharpoonright}\mathsf{Deg} \qquad \mathsf{novel};$$

$$\lambda\sigma_1\lambda\sigma_2.\sigma_1(\mathsf{ER}(\mathbf{interesting})) \circ \mathsf{than} \circ \sigma_2(\boldsymbol{\varepsilon}); \qquad\qquad\qquad \lambda f.\mathbf{\exists}_{f(\mathbf{novel})}$$
$$\lambda \mathscr{P} \lambda \mathscr{Q} \exists d_1, d_2.\mathscr{P}(\lambda P \lambda x.\mathbf{max}(\lambda d.\mathbf{int}(d)(P)(x)) = d_1) \wedge \qquad (\lambda x.\mathbf{wrote}$$
$$\mathscr{Q}(\lambda P \lambda x.\mathbf{max}(\lambda d.\mathbf{int}(d)(P)(x)) = d_2) \wedge d_1 > d_2; \qquad (x)(\mathbf{j}));$$
$$\mathsf{S}{\upharpoonright}(\mathsf{S}{\upharpoonright}(\mathsf{N/N})){\upharpoonright}(\mathsf{S}{\upharpoonright}(\mathsf{N/N})) \qquad\qquad\qquad\qquad\qquad \mathsf{S}{\upharpoonright}(\mathsf{N/N})$$

$$\lambda\sigma_2.\mathsf{john} \circ \mathsf{wrote} \circ \mathsf{a} \circ \mathsf{ER}(\mathbf{interesting}) \circ \mathsf{novel} \circ \mathsf{than} \circ \sigma_2(\boldsymbol{\varepsilon}); \qquad \lambda f.\mathbf{\exists}_{f(\mathbf{play})}$$
$$\lambda \mathscr{Q} \exists d_1, d_2.\mathbf{\exists}_{(\lambda x.\mathbf{max}(\lambda d.\mathbf{int}(d)(\mathbf{novel})(x))=d_1)}(\lambda x.\mathbf{wrote}(x)(\mathbf{j})) \wedge \qquad (\lambda x.\mathbf{wrote}$$
$$\mathscr{Q}(\lambda P \lambda x.\mathbf{max}(\lambda d.\mathbf{int}(d)(P)(x)) = d_2); \wedge d_1 > d_2; \qquad (x)(\mathbf{m}));$$
$$\mathsf{S}{\upharpoonright}(\mathsf{S}{\upharpoonright}(\mathsf{N/N})) \qquad\qquad\qquad\qquad\qquad\qquad\qquad\qquad \mathsf{S}{\upharpoonright}(\mathsf{N/N})$$

$$\mathsf{john} \circ \mathsf{wrote} \circ \mathsf{a} \circ \mathsf{ER}(\mathbf{interesting}) \circ \mathsf{novel} \circ \mathsf{than} \circ \mathsf{mary} \circ \mathsf{wrote} \circ \mathsf{a} \circ \mathsf{play};$$
$$\exists d_1, d_2.\mathbf{\exists}_{(\lambda x.\mathbf{max}(\lambda d.\mathbf{int}(d)(\mathbf{novel})(x))=d_1)}(\lambda x.\mathbf{wrote}(x)(\mathbf{j})) \wedge$$
$$\mathbf{\exists}_{(\lambda x.\mathbf{max}(\lambda d.\mathbf{int}(d)(\mathbf{play})(x))=d_2)}(\lambda x.\mathbf{wrote}(x)(\mathbf{m})) \wedge d_1 > d_2; \mathsf{S}$$

At this point, it should be obvious that (411b) is merely a pseudogapping counterpart of (411a), where the auxiliary *did* in the *than* clause stands in for the main verb *wrote*, with the syntactic type and semantic translation identical to the latter:

(418) did; **wrote**; VP/NP

The sign in (418) can be obtained straightforwardly in the analysis of pseudogapping from chapter 6. The derivation for (411b) can thus be obtained by replacing the lexical verb *wrote* in the *than* clause in (417) with the "pseudogapped" anaphoric auxiliary *did* in (418).

Thus, fully compositional analyses for the sentences in (411) can be obtained without recourse to deletion of abstract syntactic representations. Note in particular that our analysis consists solely of independently motivated assumptions about the relevant phenomena (the general syntax-semantics interface of comparatives and VP ellipsis/pseudogapping in the case of the "attributive comparative" construction analyzed in this section).

8.4 Apparent Challenge to the "Remnant-Extraction" Analysis

One issue needs to be addressed before concluding this chapter, in relation to our analysis of "extraction out of elided VPs" essentially as extraction *of* pseudogapping remnants. This type of analytic possibility has been considered previously in the literature. In particular, Johnson (2001) gives an informal sketch of a version of this analysis and rejects it by citing several examples which supposedly display non-parallelism between pseudogapping and extraction from VP ellipsis sites. We show here that the nonparallel behavior displayed by these examples is, contra Johnson, not a consequence of a systematic syntactic difference between the two constructions but rather a direct result of the nonparallelism in the way the specific examples have been constructed. Once these examples are corrected to eliminate the confounding factor that has led to the misinterpretation of the data, the differences between the extraction and pseudogapping cases that Johnson's claims rest on essentially disappear.

8.4.1 Johnson's Argument

The principal argument in Johnson (2001) is that pseudogapping obeys constraints on the ellipsis remnants not found in the apparent VP ellipsis + extraction cases; thus Johnson argues that pseudogapping "cannot elide part of a prepositional phrase . . . nor . . . remove part of a noun phrase," offering the examples in (419)–(420) to support this claim:

(419)   a.   *Sally will stand near Mag, but he won't Holly.

       b.   *While Holly didn't discuss a report about every boy, she did every girl.

(420)   I know which woman HOLLY will discuss a report about, but I don't know which woman YOU will.

Since pseudogapping, as in (419), apparently cannot "reach into" PPs to access their NP objects, whereas extraction from elided VP can, as in (420), Johnson argues that such extraction cannot be reduced to pseudogapping plus movement of the remnant.

However, Johnson's argument is problematic since the alleged generalization that pseudogapping is limited to the direct object position of the verb is factually wrong: there is ample evidence from the literature that counterexemplifies this claim.[16]

8.4.2   Counterexamples from the Literature

There is ample data already attested in the literature displaying the possibility of pseudogapping remnants corresponding to NP-internal positions in the antecedent clause; see Miller (2014) and chapter 6 for many such examples. In particular, examples such as (421), first documented in Levin (1979), were already known long before Johnson (2001):

(421) You can take the lining out of that coat more easily than you can this one.

Examples such as those in (422) seem unproblematic as well.

(422) a. You'll find more illustrated books on golf than you will on ping-pong.
       b. I've collected more somewhat embarrassing stories about John than I have about Bill.
       c. As a fruitpacker, I can tell you that the key to high production is fruit size. For example, in one hour I can pack many more boxes of GRAPEFRUIT, especially those enormous Rio Reds, than I can ORANGES.

It is somewhat difficult to pin down exactly the conditions governing the felicity of these examples involving pseudogapping from "embedded" positions, but it seems uncontroversial that the relevant factor is pragmatic rather than syntactic. See section 6.3.5, where we have briefly speculated on the possibility of explaining the difference in acceptability among individual examples analogous to what is found in (421) and (422) versus (419) in terms of a complex set of conditions including factors such as prototypicality and inherent relatedness between the remnant and the elided head noun.

---

16. Johnson's argument has other serious empirical problems. In particular, he assumes the claims in Haïk (1987), who implicitly invokes a second kind of supposed contrast:

(i) *Mary talked about everyone that Peter did ∅ about __.

The point of (i), so far as Johnson's argument is concerned, is that, since this example supposedly shows that extraction from within a pseudogapping remnant is prohibited, it is difficult to justify a treatment of the elided VP extraction data which takes them to reflect extraction *of* such a remnant itself. But this argument too fails on factual grounds, for it is not difficult to find far better cases of extraction from pseudogapping "remnants":

(ii) a. I can predict/say who John will vote FOR __ more confidently than who he will AGAINST __.
      b. (?)I can say who John will vote FOR __ more easily than I can who he will AGAINST __.

(iia) in particular seems quite acceptable.

Note in this connection that examples that are syntactically identical in form to (419b) in relevant respects improve significantly by making the elided predicate semantically more natural. For example, *write a report about* is arguably a much more natural predicate than *discuss a report about*. As expected, (423), while not totally impeccable for all speakers, seems to be distinctly better than (419b):

(423) Given his background and experiences, I'd expect that John could write a report about EUROPE much more easily than he could CHINA.

Further corroboration for the current view comes from the fact that when *near* is replaced by *next to* in (419a), the example improves, particularly if the example also takes into account the strong preference for the very marked contrast in comparatives:

(424) I suspect Mary would sit next to John more readily than she would Bill.

This effect is particularly noticeable if, as suggested in (424), the discourse context is one in which people are making a conscious choice, in response to a request, of who they will sit in immediate proximity to. This fact suggests that pragmatic factors of the sort alluded to above indeed crucially affect the felicity of pseudogapping examples.[17]

8.5   A Note on the P-Stranding Generalization

We have focused on the interactions between extraction and VP ellipsis in our discussion, mostly responding to a particular set of claims made by Kennedy (2003) (and Kennedy and Merchant [2000]). The literature on ellipsis and extraction contains another type of argument, originally due to Merchant (2001), that has become quite influential. The argument (in its original form) involves the sluicing construction and is called the "P-stranding (preposition-stranding) generalization." The P-stranding generalization is often invoked as a strong piece of argument in favor of covert structural representations in ellipsis, though there are recent discussions casting considerable doubt on the validity of this empirical generalization.[18] In what follows, we demonstrate that

---

17. One might still wonder why a contrast exists in Johnson's original examples: while the same predicate *discuss a report about* is used in both (419b) and (420), the former is unacceptable while the latter is acceptable. We speculate that the improved status of (420) has to do with the fact that extraction is involved in this example. In particular, note that in (420), due to the extraction of the complement NP of the preposition *about*, the material that needs to be recovered in the ellipsis clause (i.e., *discuss a report about __*) is a surface syntactic constituent. This arguably would help greatly in the pragmatic ellipsis resolution process as compared to the case (such as (419b)) in which such a condition does not hold.

18. For example, Sag and Nykiel (2011) argue that Polish counterexemplifies this generalization; Merchant (2019) himself refers to the literature on several such cases and suggests the possibility that in these cases "the P-less 'sluices' in fact derive from a copular or reduced cleft-like source," a possibility which he refers to as pseudosluicing. Recent work, however, challenges this alternative derivation of apparent exception: Nykiel (2013) offers a suite of experimental psycholinguistic tests whose results suggest that in general the

even if the P-stranding generalization were a cross-linguistically valid generalization, there is a relatively straightforward way of capturing it in the type of approach to ellipsis phenomena we have advocated in this book that is arguably no more stipulative than the popular configurational analysis in the mainstream syntactic literature. Taken together with the recent reconsideration of the empirical status of the generalization itself, the "existence proof" we offer below for a nonstructural account of the P-stranding generalization removes the force of the argument for covert structure that the P-stranding generalization is typically associated with.

8.5.1 The P-Stranding Generalization

Merchant (2001, 92) contains an argument for covert structure in sluicing based on what has come to be known as the P-stranding generalization:

(425) A language *L* will allow preposition stranding under sluicing iff *L* allows preposition stranding under regular *wh*-movement.

The pattern noted in (425) can be illustrated by the contrast between English and Spanish:

(426) a. John was talking to someone, but I don't know who __.
       b. *Juan ha hablado con una chica rubia, pero no sé qué chica más.
           'John has talked with a blond girl, but I don't know which other girl (John
           has talked with).'   (Rodrigues et al. 2009)

English permits preposition stranding; Spanish does not. This pattern appears to persist in sluicing constructions where the ellipsed material, corresponding to the portion of the antecedent presumably left behind by *wh* movement, contains a preposition stranded by such movement. The empirical basis for the generality of Merchant's claim is a set of data from eighteen languages: six Germanic languages which support P-stranding (both in the regular *wh* movement context and in sluicing) and twelve from a wide variety of languages (including a variety of Indo-Iranian and Semitic languages, as well as Basque) which do not. On the basis of these facts and the descriptive generalization in (425), Merchant (2001, 107) argues that

> the usual mechanisms for case-assignment and determination of targets of *wh*-movement that operate in a given language to regulate the shapes of *wh*-phrases in non-elliptical questions operate in identical ways under sluicing as well. All of these facts strongly suggest that *wh*-movement of the usual sort has taken place, displacing an IP-internal *wh*-phrase to SpecCP. . . . Similar considerations suggest a movement approach to a variety of parallel . . . form-identity effects in stripping, comparatives, fragment answers, [and] the remnants of gapping, which often show case and P-stranding dependencies like their sluicing cousins.

---

acceptability of sluicing with a lone preposition remnant is unrelated to the acceptability of *wh* extraction of NPs from PPs.

By the same reasoning, the putative generalization should be observable in examples like the following, where (427a) is standardly analyzed as extraction out of elided VPs and (427b) is a case of pseudogapping:

(427) a. I know whom John argued with, but I don't know whom Mary did.
     b. I can deal with Mary more easily than I can Sue.

In (427a) the *wh* filler has moved to the left, leaving behind a VP with a trace in it (*argued with __*), which is subsequently deleted on Merchant's analysis. In a language that allows extraction out of VP ellipsis sites but which has a ban on P-stranding, data such as (427a) should never exist, and likewise for analogues of (427b).[19]

8.5.2 English*

For the purpose of illustration we now consider a language English* (instead of a real language such as German), which is exactly like English except that preposition stranding is forbidden. We demonstrate how our general approach to ellipsis, with no additions or modifications, yields the P-stranding generalization for the so-called extraction out of elided VP cases like (427a) (for which we have defended an analysis [essentially] in terms of extraction of pseudogapping remnants). Assume that in English* we have only (428) as the lexical entry for the preposition *to*.

(428) *to*; $\lambda x.x$; PP_{to}/NP_{-wh}

This specification differs crucially from the lexical description of *to* in English in that the syntactic type of the latter will be $PP_{to}/NP_{\#wh}$ (see below), with both NP_{+wh} and NP_{-wh} as possible instantiations for $NP_{\#wh}$.

    Given the lexical specifications for prepositions in English*, indirect questions such as *I wonder who John spoke to* cannot be formed. Since only an NP_{-wh} variable can be supplied to the object of *to*, a sentence missing an NP object of a preposition such as *John spoke to __* can only be derived in type $S \restriction NP_{-wh}$. But such a description fails to satisfy the fronted *wh* word's argument description $S \restriction NP_{+wh}$ (cf. (344)). And precisely the same will hold in the attempt to derive the corresponding elided VP. Consider (429):

(429) JOHN talked to BILL, but I don't know whom MARY did.

This example is acceptable in English (as long as the proper intonational and contextual cues are given) but would be ill-formed in English*. The antecedent upon which the ellipsis clause depends will have the following derivation:

---

19. Matters may be a bit more complex in the case of pseudogapping, though. On some analyses, remnant movement in pseudogapping is to the right, leaving open the possibility that in a language with a P-stranding prohibition on leftward movement only, something like (427b) could be legal.

(430)

$$\begin{bmatrix} \varphi_0; \\ u; \\ NP_{-wh} \end{bmatrix}^1 \quad \begin{array}{l} \text{to;} \\ \lambda\varphi.\varphi; \\ PP_{to}/NP_{-wh} \end{array} \quad \begin{array}{l} \text{talked;} \\ \mathbf{talk;} \\ VP/PP_{to} \end{array}$$

$$\cfrac{\cfrac{\cfrac{\cfrac{\cfrac{\cfrac{\text{to} \circ \varphi_0; u; PP_{to}}{\text{talked} \circ \text{to} \circ \varphi_0; \mathbf{talk}(u); VP}}{\boxed{\lambda\varphi_0.\text{talked} \circ \text{to} \circ \varphi_0; \lambda u.\mathbf{talk}(u); VP{\restriction}NP_{-wh}} \quad \lceil I^1 \quad \begin{bmatrix} \varphi_1; \\ w; \\ NP_{-wh} \end{bmatrix}^2}{\text{talked} \circ \text{to} \circ \varphi_1; \mathbf{talk}(w); VP} \quad \begin{array}{l} \text{john;} \\ \mathbf{j;} \\ NP_{-wh} \end{array}}{\text{john} \circ \text{talked} \circ \text{to} \circ \varphi_1; \mathbf{talk}(w)(\mathbf{j}); S}}{\lambda\varphi_1.\text{john} \circ \text{talked} \circ \text{to} \circ \varphi_1; \lambda w.\mathbf{talk}(w)(\mathbf{j}); S{\restriction}NP_{-wh}} \quad \lceil I^2 \quad \begin{array}{l} \text{bill;} \\ \mathbf{b;} \\ NP_{-wh} \end{array}}{\text{john} \circ \text{talked} \circ \text{to} \circ \text{bill}; \mathbf{talk}(\mathbf{b})(\mathbf{j}); S} \quad \lceil E$$

And for the VP ellipsis auxiliary, we obtain:

(431)

$$\begin{array}{l} \lambda\rho\lambda\varphi.\rho(\lambda\varphi_0.\varphi_0)(\varphi); \\ \lambda\mathscr{F}.\mathscr{F}(P); \\ (VP{\restriction}NP_{-wh}){\restriction} \\ ((VP{\restriction}NP_{-wh}){\restriction}(VP{\restriction}NP_{-wh})) \end{array}$$

$$\textcircled{1} \rightarrow \cdots\cdots\cdots\cdots\cdots\cdots\cdots\cdots\cdots\cdots\cdots$$

$$\cfrac{\cfrac{\cfrac{\begin{array}{l} \lambda\sigma\lambda\varphi.\text{did} \circ \sigma(\varphi); \\ \lambda f\lambda x\lambda y.f(x)(y); \\ (VP{\restriction}NP_{-wh}){\restriction} \\ (VP{\restriction}NP_{-wh}) \end{array} \quad \begin{array}{l} \lambda\rho\lambda\varphi.\rho(\lambda\varphi_0.\varphi_0)(\varphi); \\ \lambda\mathscr{F}.\mathscr{F}(\lambda u.\text{talked}(u)); \\ (VP{\restriction}NP_{-wh}){\restriction} \\ ((VP{\restriction}NP_{-wh}){\restriction}(VP{\restriction}NP_{-wh})) \end{array}}{\lambda\varphi.\text{did} \circ \varphi; \lambda x\lambda y.\mathbf{talk}(x)(y); VP{\restriction}NP_{-wh} \quad \begin{bmatrix} \varphi_3; \\ v; \\ NP_{-wh} \end{bmatrix}^3}{\text{did} \circ \varphi_3; \lambda y.\text{talked}(v)(y); VP} \quad \begin{array}{l} \text{mary;} \\ \mathbf{m;} \\ NP_{-wh} \end{array}}{\cfrac{\text{mary} \circ \text{did} \circ \varphi_3; \mathbf{talk}(v)(\mathbf{m}); S}{\lambda\varphi_3.\text{mary} \circ \text{did} \circ \varphi_3; \lambda v.\mathbf{talk}(v)(\mathbf{m}); S{\restriction}NP_{-wh}} \quad \lceil I^3}$$

The ellipsis operator has a syntactic type schematically of the form $X{\restriction}(X{\restriction}X)$, and the anaphora resolution condition requires that X match the category of the relevant antecedent whose meaning is recovered in ellipsis resolution (see chapter 6 for details). In the case at hand, the appropriate antecedent is the grayed-in expression in (430), with semantics $\lambda u.\mathbf{talked}(u)$. The free variable P in the ellipsis operator thus gets resolved as this term at the step (which, strictly speaking, is outside of the syntactic derivation) marked as ①. But then, any attempt to compose the sign derived in (431) with the extraction operator will fail:

(432)

$$\cfrac{\lambda\varphi_3.\text{mary} \circ \text{did} \circ \varphi_3; \lambda v.\mathbf{talk}(v)(\mathbf{m}); S{\restriction}NP_{-wh} \qquad \begin{array}{l} \lambda\sigma.\text{whom} \circ \sigma(\boldsymbol{\varepsilon}); \\ \mathbf{wh}(\mathbf{person}); Q{\restriction}(S{\restriction}NP_{+wh}) \end{array}}{\mathbf{FAIL}}$$

In a nutshell, the extraction operator can only compose with a sentence missing an NP_{+wh}, but the conditions imposed on prepositions in English* allow *to* to combine only with NP_{-wh}, leading to a continuation typed $S{\upharpoonright}NP_{-wh}$, an invalid argument for the extraction operator. Such extractions therefore cannot give rise to well-formed VP ellipsis strandings. No special mechanisms are required, and nothing has to be stipulated other than the lexical condition illustrated in (428), which simply expresses the ban on preposition stranding in such languages. In particular, no covert syntactic structure is required as long as the required syntactic information about category type is made available to the anaphoric process.

In English, in contrast, sentences such as (429) are licensable because in place of (428), the lexical entry for *to* is (433):

(433) *to*; $\lambda x.X$; $PP_{to}/NP_{\#wh}$

Since *to* can combine with an NP of either polarity for the *wh* feature, we will have a derivation along the following lines:

(434)

$$
\begin{array}{l}
\begin{bmatrix} \varphi_0; \\ u; \\ NP_{\#wh} \end{bmatrix}^1 \quad
\begin{array}{l} to; \\ \lambda\varphi.\varphi; \\ PP_{to}/NP_{\#wh} \end{array} \quad
\begin{array}{l} \text{talked}; \\ \textbf{talk}; \\ VP/PP_{to} \end{array} \\[1em]
\hline
\quad\quad \text{to} \circ \varphi_0; u; PP_{to} \quad\quad\quad VP/PP_{to} \\[0.5em]
\hline
\quad\quad\quad \text{talked} \circ \text{to} \circ \varphi_0; \textbf{talk}(u); VP
\end{array}
$$

$$
\begin{array}{l}
\boxed{\begin{array}{l} \lambda\varphi_0.\text{talked} \circ \text{to} \circ \varphi_0; \\ \lambda u.\textbf{talk}(u); VP{\upharpoonright}NP_{\#wh} \end{array}}{\upharpoonright}I^1 \quad
\begin{bmatrix} \varphi_1; \\ w; \\ NP_{\#wh} \end{bmatrix}^2 \quad
\begin{array}{l} \text{john}; \\ \textbf{j}; \\ NP_{-wh} \end{array}
\end{array}
$$

$$
\begin{array}{l}
\hline
\quad \text{talked} \circ \text{to} \circ \varphi_1; \textbf{talk}(w); VP \\[0.5em]
\hline
\quad \text{john} \circ \text{talked} \circ \text{to} \circ \varphi_1; \textbf{talk}(w)(\textbf{j}); S \\[0.5em]
\hline
\lambda\varphi_1.\text{john} \circ \text{talked} \circ \text{to} \circ \varphi_1; \lambda w.\textbf{talk}(w)(\textbf{j}); S{\upharpoonright}NP_{\#wh} \quad {\upharpoonright}I^2 \quad
\begin{array}{l} \text{bill}; \\ \textbf{b}; \\ NP_{-wh} \end{array} \\[0.5em]
\hline
\quad \text{john} \circ \text{talked} \circ \text{to} \circ \text{bill}; \textbf{talk}(\textbf{b})(\textbf{j}); S
\end{array}
$$

The grayed-in line is the critical proof step for anaphoric retrieval. The argument of this expression is $NP_{\#wh}$. So, we can derive an auxiliary in the entry $VP{\upharpoonright}NP_{\#wh}$ by anaphorically retrieving its meaning from this antecedent as follows:

(435)

$$\lambda\rho\lambda\varphi.\rho(\lambda\varphi_0.\varphi_0)(\varphi);$$
$$\lambda\mathscr{F}.\mathscr{F}(P);$$
$$(VP{\upharpoonright}NP_{\#wh}){\upharpoonright}$$
$$((VP{\upharpoonright}NP_{\#wh}){\upharpoonright}(VP{\upharpoonright}NP_{\#wh}))$$

$$\vdots \qquad\qquad ①\rightarrow \cdots\cdots\cdots\cdots\cdots\cdots\cdots\cdots\cdots\cdots\cdots\cdots\cdots\cdots\cdots$$

$$\lambda\sigma\lambda\varphi.\text{did}\circ\sigma(\varphi); \qquad \lambda\rho\lambda\varphi.\rho(\lambda\varphi_0.\varphi_0)(\varphi);$$
$$\lambda f\lambda x\lambda y.f(x)(y); \qquad \lambda\mathscr{F}.\mathscr{F}(\lambda u.\textbf{talked}(u));$$
$$(VP{\upharpoonright}NP_{\#wh}){\upharpoonright} \qquad (VP{\upharpoonright}NP_{\#wh}){\upharpoonright}$$
$$(VP{\upharpoonright}NP_{\#wh}) \qquad ((VP{\upharpoonright}NP_{\#wh}){\upharpoonright}(VP{\upharpoonright}NP_{\#wh})) \qquad \begin{bmatrix}\varphi_2; \\ w; \\ NP_{\#wh}\end{bmatrix}^2 \qquad \begin{matrix}\text{mary}; \\ \textbf{m}; \\ NP_{-wh}\end{matrix}$$

$$\overline{\lambda\varphi.\text{did}\circ\varphi;\ \lambda x\lambda y.\textbf{talk}(x)(y);\ VP{\upharpoonright}NP_{\#wh}}$$

$$\overline{\text{did}\circ\varphi_2;\ \textbf{talk}(w);\ VP}$$

$$\overline{\text{mary}\circ\text{did}\circ\varphi_2;\ \textbf{talk}(w)(\textbf{m});\ S}$$

$$\overline{\lambda\varphi_2.\text{mary}\circ\text{did}\circ\varphi_2;\ \lambda w.\textbf{talk}(w)(\textbf{m});\ S{\upharpoonright}NP_{\#wh}}\ {\upharpoonright}I^2$$

$$\vdots$$

$$\overline{\lambda\varphi_2.\text{mary}\circ\text{did}\circ\varphi_2;\ \lambda w.\textbf{talk}(w)(\textbf{m});\ S{\upharpoonright}NP_{+wh}}$$

The difference between the failed derivation in English* and the unproblematic derivation in English is a direct reflection of the different valence possibilities for prepositions in the two languages, with no reference to any structure ever coming into the picture. As the proof for English* makes clear, the enforced selection of NP_{-wh} by prepositions translates, through the chain of hypothetical reasoning displayed above, into a sign typed $S{\upharpoonright}NP_{-wh}$, which is unable to compose with the extraction operator to complete the derivation. Since the $\pm wh$ distinction is an independently motivated distinction that needs to be encoded in the syntactic type of NPs, the valence information is all that is needed to institute the P-stranding generalization for the "extraction out of VP ellipsis" pattern. We now demonstrate that exactly the same purely valence-based account is sufficient for the P-stranding generalization in the case of sluicing as well.

8.5.3 Sluicing

Following the overall strategy in Barker (2013), we posit the following operator for the analysis of sluicing:

(436) $\lambda\rho.\rho(\lambda\varphi.\varphi);\ \lambda\mathscr{W}.\mathscr{W}(P);\ Q{\upharpoonright}(Q{\upharpoonright}(S{\upharpoonright}NP_{+wh}))$

——where P is a property matching a contextually salient sign compatible with the type description $S{\upharpoonright}NP_{+wh}$ in the preceding discourse

In simple cases of sluicing, we obtain derivations such as that given in (438) for (437):

(437) John criticized someone, but Mary doesn't know who(m).

(438)

$$\frac{\text{criticized};\ \textbf{criticize};\ \text{VP}/\text{NP}_{\#wh}\quad [\varphi_0; x; \text{NP}_{\#wh}]^1}{\text{criticized} \circ \varphi_0;\ \textbf{criticize}(x);\ \text{VP}}\quad\frac{\text{john};}{\textbf{j};\text{NP}_{-wh}}$$

$$\frac{\text{john} \circ \text{criticized} \circ \varphi_0;\ \textbf{criticize}(x)(\textbf{j});\ S}{\boxed{\lambda\varphi_0.\text{john} \circ \text{criticized} \circ \varphi_0;\ \lambda x.\textbf{criticize}(x)(\textbf{j});\ S\!\restriction\!\text{NP}_{\#wh}}}\restriction\!\text{I}^1$$

$$\vdots$$

$$\frac{\lambda\varphi_0.\text{john} \circ \text{criticized} \circ \varphi_0;\ \lambda x.\textbf{criticize}(x)(\textbf{j});\ S\!\restriction\!\text{NP}_{-wh}\qquad\begin{array}{c}\lambda\sigma_0.\sigma_0(\text{someone});\\\textbf{∃person};\\S\!\restriction\!(S\!\restriction\!\text{NP}_{-wh})\end{array}}{\text{john} \circ \text{criticized} \circ \text{someone};\ \textbf{∃person}(\lambda x.\textbf{criticize}(x)(\textbf{j}));\ S}$$

$$\frac{\begin{array}{c}\lambda\rho.\rho(\lambda\varphi.\varphi);\\\lambda\mathscr{W}.\mathscr{W}(P);Q\!\restriction\!(Q\!\restriction\!(S\!\restriction\!\text{NP}_{+wh}))\\\cdots\cdots\cdots\cdots\cdots\\\lambda\rho.\rho(\lambda\varphi.\varphi);\\\lambda\mathscr{W}.\mathscr{W}(\lambda x.\textbf{criticize}(x)(\textbf{j}));\\Q\!\restriction\!(Q\!\restriction\!(S\!\restriction\!\text{NP}_{+wh}))\end{array}\quad\begin{array}{c}\lambda\sigma_1.\\\text{whom} \circ \sigma_1(\boldsymbol{\varepsilon});\\\textbf{wh}(\textbf{person});\\Q\!\restriction\!(S\!\restriction\!\text{NP}_{+wh})\end{array}}{\begin{array}{c}\text{whom};\\\textbf{wh}(\textbf{person})(\lambda x.\textbf{criticize}(x)(\textbf{j}));\ Q\end{array}}$$

$$\frac{\frac{\begin{array}{c}\text{whom};\\\textbf{wh}(\textbf{person})(\lambda x.\textbf{criticize}(x)(\textbf{j}));\ Q\end{array}\quad\begin{array}{c}\text{know};\\\textbf{know};\\\text{VP}/Q\end{array}}{\begin{array}{c}\text{know} \circ \text{whom};\\\textbf{know}(\textbf{wh}(\textbf{person})(\lambda x.\textbf{criticize}(x)(\textbf{j})));\ \text{VP}\end{array}\quad\begin{array}{c}\text{doesn't};\\\lambda Q\lambda y.\\\neg Q.Q(y);\\\text{VP}/\text{VP}\end{array}}{\begin{array}{c}\text{doesn't} \circ \text{know} \circ \text{whom};\\\lambda y.\neg\textbf{know}(\textbf{wh}(\textbf{person})(\lambda x.\textbf{criticize}(x)(\textbf{j})))(y);\ \text{VP}\end{array}\quad\begin{array}{c}\text{mary};\\\textbf{m};\\\text{NP}_{-wh}\end{array}}{\begin{array}{c}\text{mary} \circ \text{doesn't} \circ \text{know} \circ \text{whom};\\\neg\textbf{know}(\textbf{wh}(\textbf{person})(\lambda x.\textbf{criticize}(x)(\textbf{j})))(\textbf{m});\ S\end{array}}$$

The lexical entry for the *wh* word *whom* and the sluicing operator (436) are taken to be common to English* and English and, more generally, to all languages with *wh* extraction and sluicing regardless of whether they allow stranded prepositions. Again, the sole difference is in the specification of the class of NPs with which prepositions can combine.

Given the entry for *to* in (428), preposition stranding is already automatically blocked in English* sluicing, just as it is for VP ellipsis extraction. For example, consider the following example:

(439) John talked to someone, but I don't know who(m).

In order to create the appropriate expression to serve as the antecedent in the first clause, *to* needs to combines with a variable, but in view of (428), this variable will necessarily be $-wh$. When the hypothesis corresponding to this variable is withdrawn, the result, $S\!\restriction\!\text{NP}_{-wh}$, will be unable to serve as an antecedent for the sluicing operator, which explicitly requires the antecedent to be compatible with type $S\!\restriction\!\text{NP}_{+wh}$.

(440)

$$\frac{\dfrac{\text{talked;}}{\textbf{talk;}}\quad \dfrac{\text{to;}\ \lambda\varphi.\varphi;\text{PP}_{to}/\text{NP}_{-wh}\quad \left[\begin{matrix}\varphi_1;\\v;\text{NP}_{-wh}\end{matrix}\right]^1}{\text{to}\circ\varphi_1;\ v;\ \text{PP}}}{\text{talked}\circ\text{to}\circ\varphi_1;\ \textbf{talk}(v);\ \text{VP}}$$

$$\frac{\text{talked}\circ\text{to}\circ\varphi_1;\ \textbf{talk}(v);\ \text{VP}\qquad \dfrac{\text{john;}}{\textbf{j};\text{NP}}}{\dfrac{\text{john}\circ\text{talked}\circ\text{to}\circ\varphi_1;\ \textbf{talk}(v)(\textbf{j});\ \text{S}}{\ }\upharpoonright\text{I}^1}$$

$$\frac{\dfrac{\lambda\sigma_1.\sigma_1(\text{someone});}{\exists\textbf{person};\text{S}\upharpoonright(\text{S}\upharpoonright\text{NP}_{-wh})}\qquad \boxed{\begin{matrix}\lambda\varphi_1.\text{john}\circ\text{talked}\circ\text{to}\circ\varphi_1;\\ \lambda v.\textbf{talk}(v)(\textbf{j});\text{S}\upharpoonright\text{NP}_{-wh}\end{matrix}}}{\text{john}\circ\text{talked}\circ\text{to}\circ\text{someone};\ \exists\textbf{person}(\lambda v.\textbf{talk}(v)(\textbf{j}));\ \text{S}}$$

$$\frac{\lambda\rho.\rho(\lambda\varphi.\varphi);\ \lambda\mathscr{W}.\mathscr{W}(P);\ Q\upharpoonright(Q\upharpoonright(\text{S}\upharpoonright\text{NP}_{+wh}))}{\cdots\cdots\cdots\cdots\cdots\cdots\cdots\cdots\cdots\cdots\text{FAIL}}\quad \dfrac{\lambda\sigma.\text{who}\circ\sigma(\boldsymbol{\varepsilon});}{\textbf{wh}(\textbf{person});}$$
$$\boxed{\lambda\rho.\rho(\lambda\varphi.\varphi);\ \lambda\mathscr{W}.\mathscr{W}(\lambda v.\textbf{talk}(v)(\textbf{j}));\ Q\upharpoonright(Q\upharpoonright(\text{S}\upharpoonright\text{NP}_{+wh}))}\qquad Q\upharpoonright(\text{S}\upharpoonright\text{NP}_{+wh})$$

$$\overline{\text{who};\ \textbf{wh}(\textbf{person})(\lambda v.\textbf{talk}(v)(\textbf{j}));\ Q}$$

By contrast, in English, since the argument of *to* is underspecified for the *wh* feature, the following derivation is available:

(441)

$$\frac{\dfrac{\text{talked;}}{\textbf{talk;}}\quad \dfrac{\text{to;}\ \lambda\varphi.\varphi;\ \text{PP}_{to}/\text{NP}_{\#wh}\quad \left[\varphi_1;v;\text{NP}_{\#wh}\right]^1}{\text{to}\circ\varphi_1;\ v;\ \text{PP}}}{\text{talked}\circ\text{to}\circ\varphi_1;\ \textbf{talk}(v);\ \text{VP}}$$

$$\frac{\text{talked}\circ\text{to}\circ\varphi_1;\ \textbf{talk}(v);\ \text{VP}\qquad \dfrac{\text{john;}}{\textbf{j};}}{\dfrac{\text{john}\circ\text{talked}\circ\text{to}\circ\varphi_1;\ \textbf{talk}(v)(\textbf{j});\ \text{S}}{\boxed{\lambda\varphi_1.\text{john}\circ\text{talked}\circ\text{to}\circ\varphi_1;\ \lambda v.\textbf{talk}(v)(\textbf{j});\ \text{S}\upharpoonright\text{NP}_{\#wh}}}\upharpoonright\text{I}^1}$$

$$\frac{\dfrac{\lambda\sigma_1.\sigma_1(\text{someone});}{\exists\textbf{person};\text{S}\upharpoonright(\text{S}\upharpoonright\text{NP}_{-wh})}\qquad \dfrac{\vdots}{\lambda\varphi_1.\text{john}\circ\text{talked}\circ\text{to}\circ\varphi_1;\ \lambda v.\textbf{talk}(v)(\textbf{j});\ \text{S}\upharpoonright\text{NP}_{-wh}}}{\text{john}\circ\text{talked}\circ\text{to}\circ\text{someone};\ \exists\textbf{person}(\lambda v.\textbf{talk}(v)(\textbf{j}));\ \text{S}}$$

$$\frac{\begin{matrix}\lambda\rho.\rho(\lambda\varphi.\varphi);\\ \lambda\mathscr{W}.\mathscr{W}(P);Q\upharpoonright(Q\upharpoonright(\text{S}\upharpoonright\text{NP}_{+wh}))\end{matrix}}{\cdots\cdots\cdots\cdots\cdots\cdots\cdots\cdots\cdots}\quad \dfrac{\lambda\sigma.\text{whom}\circ\sigma(\boldsymbol{\varepsilon});}{\textbf{wh}(\textbf{person});}$$
$$\boxed{\begin{matrix}\lambda\rho.\rho(\lambda\varphi.\varphi);\\ \lambda\mathscr{W}.\mathscr{W}(\lambda v.\textbf{talk}(v)(\textbf{j}));Q\upharpoonright(Q\upharpoonright(\text{S}\upharpoonright\text{NP}_{+wh}))\end{matrix}}\qquad Q\upharpoonright(\text{S}\upharpoonright\text{NP}_{+wh})$$

$$\overline{\text{whom};\ \textbf{wh}(\textbf{person})(\lambda v.\textbf{talk}(v)(\textbf{j}));\ Q}$$

Here, the free variable P in the sluicing operator can be instantiated as a contextually appropriate predicate $\lambda v.\textbf{talk}(v)(\textbf{j})$ denoted by the grayed-in expression of type $\text{S}\upharpoonright\text{NP}$ in the antecedent clause, since $\text{S}\upharpoonright\text{NP}_{\#wh}$, which entails $\text{S}\upharpoonright\text{NP}_{+wh}$ (that is, $\text{S}\upharpoonright\text{NP}_{\#wh}\vdash$

$S \upharpoonright NP_{+wh}$ is a theorem), is clearly compatible with the description $S \upharpoonright NP_{+wh}$. It then follows that in English, preposition stranding is possible in sluicing.

Hence the P-stranding generalization in the case of sluicing falls out directly from the simple lexical treatment in (428) and (436), with no need to posit covert configurations.

The technical details of the proofs given above are necessary so that readers can verify for themselves that our proposal does exactly what we claim it does: guarantee that the P-stranding generalization does indeed fall out of our type-logical framework with no appeal whatever to configurational representations characterizing the "missing" material in any ellipsis construction. We hope, however, that the fundamental simplicity of our solution will not become lost in these technical details. The central point is that in order to capture the P-stranding generalization, nothing more need be assumed than the independently needed lexical prohibition on NP_{+wh} arguments to prepositions in non-stranding languages and the independently motivated assumption that the anaphora recovery process in ellipsis is sensitive to the syntactic category of the antecedent expression (cf. chapter 6).

Importantly, access to syntactic category information that our anaphora-based approach crucially exploits is not something that is "added on" to the theory but is a direct consequence of the fundamental architecture of (most versions of) categorial grammar: at each stage of syntactic derivation, the prosody, semantics, and syntactic type of the linguistic expression are fully explicit. The correlation between a particular semantics and specific syntactic type is thus built into the fundamental architecture of the theory. This architecture, however, does not allow access to the "history of derivation" (i.e., the structure of the proof) up to the point that the expression in question is obtained, and it is in this respect that categorial grammar departs most crucially from derivational variants of syntax that in principle allow (unless additional theory-internal assumptions are made) full access to the internal syntactic structure of a linguistic expression.

Both Hybrid TLCG and the P&P analyses of ellipsis essentially rely on specifications of lexical valence to rule out overgeneration that would arise in purely interpretive accounts, and in this respect, at the descriptive level, both are getting at more or less the same insight. However, covert structure analyses add a further component of hierarchical representations projected from these lexically specified argument structure possibilities—representations which, given the foregoing discussion, are not necessary to capture the P-stranding generalization. Basic considerations of parsimony (i.e., Occam's razor) thus seem to rule in favor of the Hybrid TLCG account (unless it can be shown that this approach incurs some hidden or overlooked additional complexity that is not present in the derivational approach) and the view that syntactic information as reflected in the syntactic categories of linguistic expressions is sufficient in the licensing of elliptical constructions, without the need for hidden configurational structure.

8.6   Conclusions: Covert Structure and the Burden of Proof

The overall architecture of the transformational framework, despite its successive re-casting in at least seemingly quite different versions over the past seven decades, in-corporates a syntax-semantics interface which most naturally handles form/meaning discrepancies in terms of hidden structures which contribute crucial components of the required semantic interpretations but which are subsequently suppressed by deletion operations of one or another sort. The invisibility of this deleted material inherently puts a burden of proof on any covert structural analysis: in any theory, the presence of a syntactic configuration inevitably entails certain empirical predictions as the null hypothesis, and the burden of proof is satisfied by demonstrating that, all other things being equal, constructions derived by movement and deletion conform to these predic-tions. The clear intent of Kennedy (2003) is to make an overwhelming demonstration along these lines.

But there are two deep, interlocking problems with all such attempts. In the first place, such arguments are only effective cross-theoretically if there is broad consensus that the constraints themselves cannot be explained satisfactorily except by appeal to syntactic structure, and for none of the probes for structure invoked by Kennedy, as we have discussed in detail earlier, does such a consensus exist: islands are increasingly widely assumed to represent functional obstacles not native to the combinatorics them-selves; Condition B effects are cogently argued by Jacobson (2007) to correspond to semantic irreflexivity; Strong Crossover effects do not appear to have a clear explana-tion at all. Even more problematic, a number of the key factual claims in Kennedy and Merchant (2000), Kennedy (2003), and some of the important prior literature on which these claims implicitly rest are robustly counterexemplified in our informants' data, in corpora, or in earlier work on pseudogapping and ellipsis generally. It seems fair to conclude, therefore, that none of the arguments in Kennedy (2003) privilege a covert structure treatment of ellipsis over the kind of direct interpretation approach we have argued for in this book.

9 English Modal Auxiliaries

By this point, the reader should have noticed one property that distinguishes our approach from earlier or competing proposals in other lexicalist theories of syntax such as HPSG. As compared to theories such as HPSG, Hybrid TLCG (and TLCG in general) assumes a more abstract interface between surface syntax and semantic interpretation. The (seemingly) abstract and complex lexical entries for scopal operators involving prosodic lambda abstraction that we have introduced in the analyses of various phenomena in the preceding chapters all embody this (from a certain perspective) somewhat untransparent perspective on the architecture of the syntax-semantics interface. We have shown above that this approach can successfully handle a number of complex empirical phenomena that have proven refractory for previous lexicalist/phrase structure–based theories, but one question naturally arises at this point: To what extent is our approach compatible with previous analyses of major syntactic phenomena in the lexicalist tradition?

Addressing this issue properly would call for another monograph-length discussion, one clearly beyond the scope of the present work. Instead, in this chapter we attempt to achieve a more modest goal of clarifying a hidden connection between our approach and previous lexicalist approaches by focusing on a specific empirical domain, namely, the analysis of English modal auxiliaries (in particular, as they interact with the scope of negation). The point we would like to make in this case study is that the somewhat abstract analyses of (semantic) operators and scope we have proposed in the present work is not so distant from the lexicalist analyses familiar in the literature as it may initially appear since the two are indeed closely related to one another from a certain perspective.

The grammar of English modal auxiliaries is a particularly suitable topic for this purpose for the following reasons. First, the treatment of English auxiliary verbs has been one of the central topics in the literature of lexicalist syntactic theories from the early days of GPSG (e.g., Gazdar et al. 1982) up to the most recent version of HPSG (see Sag et al. 2020). Second, in our analysis of the scope anomaly in Gapping in chapter 3, we assumed an analysis of modal auxiliaries as higher-order scopal operators that departed from the traditional VP/VP analysis in lexicalist theories of syntax. While this assumption is crucial for giving a systematic account of the scoping patterns of auxiliaries in Gapping sentences, one may naturally wonder whether an analysis along these lines can capture the properties of modal auxiliaries that the traditional VP/VP analysis is designed to account for. In any event, while we have shown that the more traditional VP/VP analysis is derivable as an entailment in our type logic from the somewhat novel higher-order operator treatment proposed in chapter 3, the relationship between the two is not yet entirely clear, and a more systematic comparison is called for at this point. The discussion in the present chapter aims to shed light on this question by formulating an explicit analysis of the scopal interactions between modal auxiliaries and negation, an empirical domain which, so far as we are aware, has not received attention in the previous literature on TLCG.

9.1   Modals and Negation: The Empirical Landscape

A review of the basic data illustrating scopal relationship between modals and negation reveals little in the way of systematic semantic conditions which allow one to predict this relationship for any given modal, despite certain semantic aspects of modal operators which appear to be relevant. No single semantic dimension seems to be sufficient to account for the differences in behavior of the modals with respect to negation, let alone explain why the operators introduced by some modals must outscope negation, others must scope under negation, and still others scope freely. The modals differ from each other in terms of quantificational force—in effect, the sets of worlds they quantify over—and modal base, that is, whether they have deontic, epistemic, or bouletic interpretations. But no combination of these semantic properties accounts for the particular scope relation which any given modal auxiliary has with respect to negation. Thus in (442), *should/must* and *need* denote (respectively different flavors of) universal quantification over the relevant possible worlds but have opposite scoping vis-à-vis negation. And this scoping holds regardless of the type of modal base:

(442) a. John should/must not criticize Mary. $\Box\neg\mathbf{criticize}(\mathbf{m})(\mathbf{j})$, deontic

b. Mary must not have arrived yet. $\Box\neg\mathbf{yet}(\mathbf{arrive}(\mathbf{m}))$, epistemic

c. That rook should not leave the sixth rank.

$\Box\neg\mathbf{leave}(\mathbf{6th})(\iota(\mathbf{rook}))$, bouletic

(443) a. John need not criticize Mary. $\neg\Box\mathbf{criticize}(\mathbf{m})(\mathbf{j})$, deontic

b. Mary need not have arrived yet. $\neg\Box\mathbf{yet}(\mathbf{arrive}(\mathbf{m}))$, epistemic

c. That rook need not leave the sixth rank. $\neg\Box\mathbf{leave}(\mathbf{6th})(\iota(\mathbf{rook}))$, bouletic

Must invariably scopes over negation, regardless of which of three possible interpretations it conveys, whereas exactly the opposite holds for *need*. Thus, despite their shared quantificational force, all that they have in common is that each permits only one scopal ordering of $\Box$ and $\neg$.

This in itself might be taken to support at least a semantically based distinction between the (universal) modals displaying a fixed order with respect to negation and the (existential) modals which, as shown by *can*, *could*, and *may*, can scope either above or below negation, across all available interpretations:

(444) John may/can/could not criticize Mary.

$$\Diamond\neg\textbf{criticize}(\textbf{m})(\textbf{j}), \neg\Diamond\textbf{criticize}(\textbf{m})(\textbf{j}) \text{ (epistemic/deontic)}$$

But this generalization does not extend to *might*, whose quantificational force is also existential but which only has a single scopal ordering with respect to negation:

(445) You might not criticize Mary quite so much.

$$\Diamond\neg\textbf{criticize}(\textbf{m})(\textbf{j}), \#\neg\Diamond\textbf{criticize}(\textbf{m})(\textbf{j}) \text{ (epistemic/deontic)}$$

Might, it is true, does not always display a prominent deontic interpretation. But in (445), there is arguably an interpretation of *might* which suggests that the speaker is advocating for the hearer's forbearance in the latter's interactions with Mary, rather than merely noting the possibility of such forbearance in one or another set of circumstances. Yet even with its existential status and dual deontic/existential versions, *might* can only scope wider than negation, never narrower.

These considerations reflect the difficulty in identifying a consistent set of semantic factors which jointly covary with—let alone determine—the relative order of modal scope with respect to negation in the case of any given auxiliary. The following table lists the relevant patterns for the major familiar modal auxiliaries:

(446)

Modal	Scopal pattern
will	$\textbf{F} > \neg$
would	$\mathfrak{W} > \neg$
shall	$\textbf{F} > \neg$
should	$\Box > \neg$
ought	$\Box > \neg$
might	$\Diamond > \neg$
must	$\Box > \neg$
may	$\Diamond < > \neg$
can	$\Diamond < > \neg$
could	$\Diamond < > \neg$
need	$\neg > \Box$

Iatridou and Zeijlstra (2013) argue that a principled account of the patterns in (446) can be given directly in terms of the sensitivity displayed by the individual modals to the scope of negation. *Need* is a known negative polarity item (NPI; see Levine [2013] for discussion of the somewhat unusual behavior of this NPI), and hence, when it appears with a local negator such as *not* or *never*, it always scopes under negation. Iatridou and Zeijlstra propose that the invariably wide scope of *must, should, ought,* and so on, with respect to local negation reflects their status as *positive* polarity items (PPIs). On their account, the different scopal relations between different types of modals and negation is a consequence of the "reconstruction" possibilities of modals depending on their polarity statuses—NPI, PPI, or neutral modals—as summarized in the following table:[1]

(447)

	PPI modals	Neutral modals	NPI modals
Universal	*must, should, ought to, to be to*	*have to, need to*	*need*
Existential	—	*can, may*	—

On Iatridou and Zeijlstra's account, the auxiliaries are raised to the head of TP, and hence above negP. In the case of a sentence such as *John need not worry, need* cannot be licensed unless it is reconstructed back under negP, due to its NPI status. By contrast, PPI modals such as *must, should,* and *ought* are prohibited from reconstruction, again due to their lexical property as PPIs. Neutral modals such as *can* and *may* optionally reconstruct to their original sites, giving rise to scope ambiguity with negation.

---

1. One might wonder about the classification of *must* and *should* as PPIs, given that they can appear unproblematically in the scope of negation in sentences such as *I don't think that John should be even one little bit nice to anyone in that room,* where the NPIs *even, anyone,* and *one little bit* appear with no hint of ill-formedness. But here it is crucial to bear in mind that polarity items as a broad class are known to be sensitive to not only semantic scope effects but syntactic contexts as well; see Richter and Soehn (2006) for a survey of syntactic conditions on a range of NPIs in German. Iatridou and Zeijlstra (2013) argue that the same syntactic sensitivity holds for PPIs and note that

> PPIs . . . are fine in the scope of negation or any other context that is known to ban PPIs if this context is clause-external (Szabolcsi 2004, 24–27), as illustrated in (i)–(iv):

> (i) I don't think that John called someone.   not > $[_{CP/IP}$ some
>
> (ii) No one thinks/says that John called someone.   no one > $[_{CP/IP}$ some
>
> (iii) I regret that John called someone.   regret > $[_{CP/IP}$ some
>
> (iv) Every boy who called someone got help.   every $[_{CP/IP}$ some

What seems to hold for the PPI modals, then, is that they cannot be in the scope of negation that originates in syntactically *local* operators.

Thus, Iatridou and Zeijlstra's approach accounts for the scopal relations between modals and negation in terms of the structural relationships between them at LF, induced by the polarity properties of different types of modals. The TLCG account we propose below follows Iatridou and Zeijlstra in taking this correlation between polarity and relative scope of semantic operators to be the key property underlying the superficially observed scope relations between modals and negation. But the specific assumptions about the syntax-semantics interface is different, mainly due to the different assumptions about the status of covert structural representations underlying semantic interpretation.

9.2 Capturing the Modal/Negation Scope Interaction

9.2.1 NPI and PPI Modals

In order to capture the polarity sensitivity of different types of modal auxiliaries in English, we posit a syntactic feature *pol* for category S that takes one of the three values $+$, $-$, and $\varnothing$. The treatment of polarity here follows the general approach to polarity marking in the CG literature by Dowty (1994), Bernardi (2002), and Steedman (2012) but differs from them in some specific details. Intuitively, S_{pol+} and S_{pol-} are positively and negatively marked clauses respectively, and $S_{pol\varnothing}$ is a "smaller" clause that isn't yet assigned polarity marking. To avoid cluttering the notation, we suppress the feature name *pol* in what follows and write S_{pol+}, S_{pol-}, and $S_{pol\varnothing}$ simply as S_+, S_-, and $S_\varnothing$, respectively. Positive-polarity modals are then lexically specified to obligatorily take scope at the level of S_+. Negative-polarity modals, on the other hand, are lexically specified to take scope at the level of $S_\varnothing$, before negation turns an "unmarked" clause to a negatively marked clause. We assume further that complete sentences in English are marked either *pol+* or *pol−*; thus, inhabitants of the type $S_\varnothing$ do not appear as stand-alone sentences.

The analysis of PPI and NPI modals outlined above can be technically implemented by positing the following lexical entries for the modals and the negation morpheme (where $\alpha, \beta \in \{\varnothing, -\}$ and $\gamma \in \{b(se), f(in)\}$):

(448)   a. $\lambda\sigma.\sigma(\text{should}); \lambda\mathscr{G}.\Box\mathscr{G}(\text{id}_{et}); S_{f,+}\!\restriction\!(S_{f,\beta}\!\restriction\!(VP_{f,\alpha}/VP_{b,\alpha}))$

       b. $\lambda\sigma.\sigma(\text{need}); \lambda\mathscr{G}.\Box\mathscr{G}(\text{id}_{et}); S_{f,\varnothing}\!\restriction\!(S_{f,\varnothing}\!\restriction\!(VP_{f,\varnothing}/VP_{b,\varnothing}))$

       c. $\lambda\sigma.\sigma(\text{not}); \lambda\mathscr{G}.\neg\mathscr{G}(\text{id}_{et}); S_{\gamma,-}\!\restriction\!(S_{\gamma,\varnothing}\!\restriction\!(VP_{b,\varnothing}/VP_{b,\varnothing}))$

We assume that different modals are assigned the following syntactic categories, depending on their polarity sensitivity:

(449)

PPI	NPI
$S_{f,+} \upharpoonright (S_{f,\beta} \upharpoonright (VP_{f,\alpha}/VP_{b,\alpha}))$	$S_{f,\varnothing} \upharpoonright (S_{f,\varnothing} \upharpoonright (VP_{f,\varnothing}/VP_{b,\varnothing}))$
should	*need*
must	*dare*
ought	
might	
can	*can*
could	*could*
may	*may*
will	*will*
would	*would*

We now illustrate the working of this fragment with the analyses for (450a) (which involves a PPI modal) and (450b) (which involves an NPI modal).

(450)   a. John should not come.

  b. John need not come.

The derivation for (450a) goes as follows:

(451)

$$\text{john; } \mathbf{j}; NP \quad \frac{\left[\begin{array}{c}\varphi_4; \\ h; VP_{f,\varnothing}/VP_{b,\varnothing}\end{array}\right]^4 \quad \frac{[\varphi_1; f; VP_{b,\varnothing}/VP_{b,\varnothing}]^1 \quad \text{come; } \mathbf{come}; VP_{b,\varnothing}}{\varphi_1 \circ \text{come}; f(\mathbf{come}); VP_{b,\varnothing}}}{\varphi_4 \circ \varphi_1 \circ \text{come}; h(f(\mathbf{come})); VP_{f,\varnothing}}$$

$$\text{john} \circ \varphi_4 \circ \varphi_1 \circ \text{come}; h(f(\mathbf{come}))(\mathbf{j}); S_{f,\varnothing}$$

$$\vdots$$

$$\lambda \sigma.\sigma(\text{should}); \\ \lambda \mathcal{G}.\Box\mathcal{G}(\text{id}_{et}); \\ S_{f,+} \upharpoonright (S_{f,\beta} \upharpoonright (VP_{f,\alpha}/VP_{b,\alpha}))$$

$$\frac{\begin{array}{c}\lambda \sigma.\sigma(\text{not}); \\ \lambda \mathcal{G}.\neg\mathcal{G}(\text{id}_{et}); \\ S_{\gamma,-} \upharpoonright (S_{\gamma,\varnothing} \upharpoonright (VP_{b,\varnothing}/VP_{b,\varnothing}))\end{array} \quad \frac{\begin{array}{c}\text{john} \circ \varphi_4 \circ \varphi_1 \circ \text{come}; \\ h(f(\mathbf{come}))(\mathbf{j}); S_{f,\varnothing}\end{array}}{\begin{array}{c}\lambda\varphi_1.\text{john} \circ \varphi_4 \circ \varphi_1 \circ \text{come}; \\ \lambda f.h(f(\mathbf{come}))(\mathbf{j}); \\ S_{f,\varnothing} \upharpoonright (VP_{b,\varnothing}/VP_{b,\varnothing})\end{array}} \upharpoonright I^1}{\begin{array}{c}\text{john} \circ \varphi_4 \circ \text{not} \circ \text{come}; \neg h(\mathbf{come})(\mathbf{j}); S_{f,-}\end{array}} \upharpoonright I^4$$

$$\frac{\lambda\varphi_4.\text{john} \circ \varphi_4 \circ \text{not} \circ \text{come}; \\ \lambda h.\neg h(\mathbf{come})(\mathbf{j}); S_{f,-} \upharpoonright (VP_{f,\varnothing}/VP_{b,\varnothing})}{\text{john} \circ \text{should} \circ \text{not} \circ \text{come}; \Box\neg\mathbf{come}(\mathbf{j}); S_{f,+}}$$

The key point here is that although both *should* and *not* are lexically specified to take scope at the clausal level, their scopal relation is fixed. Specifically, once *should* takes scope, the resultant clause is S_+, which is incompatible with the specification on the argument category for *not*. This means that negation is forced to take scope before the PPI modal does.

Exactly the opposite relation holds between the NPI modal *need* and negation. Here, after negation takes scope, we have S_-, but this specification is incompatible with the argument category for the NPI modal, which requires the clause it scopes over to be $S_\varnothing$. Thus, as in (452), the only possibility is to have *need* take scope before the negation does, which gives us the $\neg > \square$ scopal relation.

(452)

$$\dfrac{\dfrac{\text{john;}}{\mathbf{j};\text{NP}} \quad \dfrac{\begin{bmatrix} \varphi_4; \\ h; \text{VP}_{f,\varnothing}/\text{VP}_{b,\varnothing} \end{bmatrix}^4 \quad \dfrac{[\varphi_1; f; \text{VP}_{b,\varnothing}/\text{VP}_{b,\varnothing}]^1 \quad \text{come}; \mathbf{come}; \text{VP}_{b,\varnothing}}{\varphi_1 \circ \text{come}; f(\mathbf{come}); \text{VP}_{b,\varnothing}}}{\varphi_4 \circ \varphi_1 \circ \text{come}; h(f(\mathbf{come})); \text{VP}_{f,\varnothing}}}{\text{john} \circ \varphi_4 \circ \varphi_1 \circ \text{come}; h(f(\mathbf{come}))(\mathbf{j}); S_{f,\varnothing}}$$

$$\vdots$$

$$\dfrac{\dfrac{\lambda\sigma.\sigma(\text{not});}{\lambda\mathcal{G}.\neg\mathcal{G}(\text{id}_{et}); \\ S_{\gamma,-} \upharpoonright (S_{\gamma,\varnothing} \upharpoonright (\text{VP}_{b,\varnothing}/\text{VP}_{b,\varnothing}))} \quad \dfrac{\dfrac{\lambda\sigma.\sigma(\text{need});}{\lambda\mathcal{G}.\square\mathcal{G}(\text{id}_{et}); \\ S_{f,\varnothing} \upharpoonright (S_{f,\varnothing} \upharpoonright (\text{VP}_{f,\varnothing}/\text{VP}_{b,\varnothing}))} \quad \dfrac{\dfrac{\text{john} \circ \varphi_4 \circ \varphi_1 \circ \text{come};}{h(f(\mathbf{come}))(\mathbf{j}); S_{f,\varnothing}}}{\dfrac{\lambda\varphi_4.\text{john} \circ \varphi_4 \circ \varphi_1 \circ \text{come};}{\lambda h.h(f(\mathbf{come}))(\mathbf{j}); \\ S_{f,\varnothing} \upharpoonright (\text{VP}_{f,\varnothing}/\text{VP}_{b,\varnothing})}} \upharpoonright I^4}{\dfrac{\text{john} \circ \text{need} \circ \varphi_1 \circ \text{come}; \square f(\mathbf{come})(\mathbf{j}); S_{f,\varnothing}}{\dfrac{\lambda\varphi_1.\text{john} \circ \text{need} \circ \varphi_1 \circ \text{come};}{\lambda f.\square f(\mathbf{come})(\mathbf{j}); S_{f,\varnothing} \upharpoonright (\text{VP}_{b,\varnothing}/\text{VP}_{b,\varnothing})}} \upharpoonright I^1}}{\text{john} \circ \text{need} \circ \text{not} \circ \text{come}; \neg\square\mathbf{come}(\mathbf{j}); S_{f,-}}$$

We assume that modals that give rise to scope ambiguity with negation are simply ambiguous between PPI and NPI variants, as in (449). This accounts for the scope ambiguity of examples such as (444).[2]

Contracted negation presents no special problems, except for one small idiosyncrasy with "neutral" modals that needs to be taken into account. Contracted forms of (un-ambiguously) PPI and NPI modals such as *shouldn't* and *needn't* simply preserve the

---

2. Though we have chosen to posit two distinct lexical entries for the "neutral" modals (*can*, *could*, and *may*) for high and low scoping possibilities with respect to negation, corresponding respectively to the scoping properties of the unambiguous modals, it is easy to collapse these two entries for these modals by making the polarity features for the two Ss and two VPs in the complex higher-order category for the modal totally underspecified and unconstrained (except for one constraint $\langle\alpha,\beta\rangle \neq \langle\varnothing,-\rangle$, to exclude the possibility of double negation marking *can not not*), along the following lines:

(i) $\lambda\sigma.\sigma(\text{can}); \lambda\mathcal{G}.\diamond\mathcal{G}(\text{id}_{et}); S_{f,\alpha} \upharpoonright (S_{f,\beta} \upharpoonright (\text{VP}_{f,\delta}/\text{VP}_{b,\zeta}))$

By (partially) resolving underspecification, we can derive both the "PPI" and "NPI" variants of the modal lexical entry in (449) from (i), thus capturing scope ambiguity via a single lexical entry. (i) allows for other instantiations of feature specification, but these are either redundant (yielding either high or low scope that is already derivable with the PPI and NPI instantiations in (449)) or useless (i.e., cannot be used in any well-formed syntactic derivation) and hence harmless. Thus, if desired, the lexical ambiguity we have tentatively assumed in the main text can be eliminated by adopting the more general lexical entry along the lines of (i) without the danger of overgeneration.

scope relation between the modal meanings and negation identical to the uncontracted forms (i.e., *should not*, *need not*, and so on.). However, for the "neutral" modals such as *can*, which induce ambiguity in the uncontracted forms, the contracted variants (e.g., *can't*) only have the negation wide-scope meanings ($\neg > \Diamond$). Whatever the source of this idiosyncrasy, assuming that the contracted forms are all stored in the lexicon, the proper scope relation between the modal and negation can be readily captured in the present approach.[3]

9.2.2 Imposing the Clause-Bounded Scope Restriction on Modals and Negation

One issue that needs to be addressed in the higher-order operator analysis of modal auxiliaries and negation we have proposed above is potential overgeneration regarding the syntactic scope of the modal and negation operators. For example, in the following, neither the negation nor the modal auxiliary in the embedded clause can scope over the matrix clause:

(453) John may think Ann should not buy the car.

This clause-boundedness restriction on the scope of modal and negation operators can be captured via the clause-level indexing mechanism we employed in the analysis of extraction pathway marking in chapter 7. To avoid notational clutter, we have not made explicit the relevant assumptions in presenting the lexical entries for the modal and negation operators above, but this can be implemented easily by revising those lexical entries along the following lines:

(454) a. $\lambda \sigma. \sigma(\text{should}); \lambda \mathcal{G}.\Box \mathcal{G}(\text{id}_{et}); S^n_{f,+} \upharpoonright (S^n_{f,\beta} \upharpoonright (VP^n_{f,\alpha} / VP^n_{b,\alpha}))$
       b. $\lambda \sigma. \sigma(\text{need}); \lambda \mathcal{G}.\Box \mathcal{G}(\text{id}_{et}); S^n_{f,\varnothing} \upharpoonright (S^n_{f,\varnothing} \upharpoonright (VP^n_{f,\varnothing} / VP^n_{b,\varnothing}))$
       c. $\lambda \sigma. \sigma(\text{not}); \lambda \mathcal{G}.\neg \mathcal{G}(\text{id}_{et}); S^n_{\gamma,-} \upharpoonright (S^n_{\gamma,\varnothing} \upharpoonright (VP^n_{b,\varnothing} / VP^n_{b,\varnothing}))$

The explicit indexing on the S and VP/VP categories in these lexical entries ensures that the modal and negation operators take scope directly over the clauses that are "projections" of the VP/VP gaps that they bind. This ensures the clause-boundedness of the scope of these operators.

We illustrate in (455) a failed derivation for (453) in which the embedded negation tries to take scope at the matrix level. The derivation fails due to the mismatch in the index between the VP/VP gap and the outer S for the sign that is given as an argument to the negation operator in (454c) (to make the derivation easier to read, we have used

---

3. An alternative would be to assume a syntactic derivation for auxiliary contraction. On this approach, the inability of the PPI variant of *can* to morphologically merge with contracted negation needs to be stipulated in some way or other.

the "slanted" variants of the modals *should* and *may* here (cf. section 9.3.1); this choice is immaterial for the (failed) status of the derivation in (455)).[4]

(455)

$$\frac{\frac{\text{buy} \circ \text{the} \circ \text{car};}{\textbf{buy}(\iota(\textbf{car})); \text{VP}_{b,\varnothing}^1} \quad \left[\begin{matrix} \varphi_1; \\ f; \text{VP}_{b,\varnothing}^1/\text{VP}_{b,\varnothing}^1 \end{matrix}\right]^1}{\dfrac{\varphi_1 \circ \text{buy} \circ \text{the} \circ \text{car};}{f(\textbf{buy}(\iota(\textbf{car}))); \text{VP}_{b,\varnothing}^1}} \quad \frac{\vdots}{\dfrac{\text{should};}{\lambda P \lambda y.\Box P(y);}}{\text{VP}_{f,+}^1/\text{VP}_{b,\varnothing}^1}}$$

$$\frac{\dfrac{\text{should} \circ \varphi_1 \circ \text{buy} \circ \text{the} \circ \text{car};}{\lambda y.\Box f(\textbf{buy}(\iota(\textbf{car}))); \text{VP}_{f,+}^1} \qquad \dfrac{\text{ann};}{\dfrac{\textbf{a};}{\text{NP}}}}{\text{ann} \circ \text{should} \circ \varphi_1 \circ \text{buy} \circ \text{the} \circ \text{car}; \Box f(\textbf{buy}(\iota(\textbf{car})))(\textbf{a}); \text{S}_{f,+}^1}$$

$$\frac{\dfrac{\begin{matrix} \text{ann} \circ \text{should} \circ \varphi_1 \circ \\ \text{buy} \circ \text{the} \circ \text{car}; \\ \Box f(\textbf{buy}(\iota(\textbf{car})))(\textbf{a}); \\ \text{S}_{f,+}^1 \end{matrix} \quad \dfrac{\begin{matrix}\text{think};\\ \textbf{think};\end{matrix}}{\text{VP}_{b,\varnothing}^{n+1}/\text{S}_{f,+}^n}}{\begin{matrix} \text{think} \circ \text{ann} \circ \text{should} \circ \varphi_1 \circ \\ \text{buy} \circ \text{the} \circ \text{car}; \\ \textbf{think}(\Box f(\textbf{buy}(\iota(\textbf{car})))(\textbf{a})); \text{VP}_{b,\varnothing}^2 \end{matrix}} \quad \dfrac{\vdots}{\dfrac{\begin{matrix}\text{may};\\ \lambda Q \lambda z.\\ \Diamond Q(z);\end{matrix}}{\text{VP}_{f,+}^2/\text{VP}_{b,\varnothing}^2}}}{\dfrac{\text{may} \circ \text{think} \circ \text{ann} \circ \text{should} \circ \varphi_1 \circ \text{buy} \circ \text{the} \circ \text{car};}{\lambda z.\Diamond \textbf{think}(\Box f(\textbf{buy}(\iota(\textbf{car})))(\textbf{a}))(z); \text{VP}_{f,+}^2} \quad \dfrac{\text{john};}{\dfrac{\textbf{j};}{\text{NP}}}}$$

$$\frac{\dfrac{\text{john} \circ \text{may} \circ \text{think} \circ \text{ann} \circ \text{should} \circ \varphi_1 \circ \text{buy} \circ \text{the} \circ \text{car};}{\Diamond \textbf{think}(\Box f(\textbf{buy}(\iota(\textbf{car})))(\textbf{a}))(\textbf{j}); \text{S}_{f,+}^2}}{\dfrac{\lambda \varphi_1.\text{john} \circ \text{may} \circ \text{think} \circ \text{ann} \circ \text{should} \circ \varphi_1 \circ \text{buy} \circ \text{the} \circ \text{car};}{\lambda f.\Diamond \textbf{think}(\Box f(\textbf{buy}(\iota(\textbf{car})))(\textbf{a}))(\textbf{j}); \text{S}_{f,+}^2\!\upharpoonright\!(\text{VP}_{b,\varnothing}^1/\text{VP}_{b,\varnothing}^1)}}{\text{FAIL}} \!\upharpoonright\!{}^{I^1} \quad \dfrac{\begin{matrix}\lambda \sigma.\sigma(\text{not});\\ \lambda \mathscr{G}.\neg \mathscr{G};\\ \text{S}_{\gamma,-}^n\!\upharpoonright\\ (\text{S}_{\gamma,\varnothing}^n\!\upharpoonright\!(\text{VP}_{b,\varnothing}^n/\text{VP}_{b,\varnothing}^n))\end{matrix}}{}$$

To avoid notational clutter, we omit the clause-level indexing feature altogether in the rest of this chapter (and throughout the whole monograph), but it should be assumed that it is implemented along the lines explained above for the purpose of controlling overgeneration.

---

4. The same failure of wide scoping over embedded propositional content is observed in connection with negation inside complement VPs in cases such as (i) involving a control verb, cited in Sag et al. (2020, 41) as supporting the interpretation of narrow-scoping negation operators as adjuncts:

(i) Pat considered not doing the homework assignments.

Such cases are straightforward in our account, on the assumption that the lexical entry for *considered*, like other nonauxiliary verbs which embed propositional arguments, will have the syntactic type $\text{VP}_{f,\alpha}^{n+1}/\text{VP}_{ger,\alpha}^n$, which, combining with its gerundive argument, increments the clause level by one.

9.3   Consequences of the Higher-Order Analysis of Modals and Negation

In this section, we discuss some consequences of the higher-order analysis of modals and negation we have presented above. As will be discussed below, the present analysis extends straightforwardly to more complex examples involving these modal and negation operators in ways that may not be fully obvious initially.

9.3.1   Slanting and the VP/VP Analysis of Auxiliaries

The analysis of modal scope presented above can, in a sense, be thought of as a logical reconceptualization of the configurational account proposed by Iatridou and Zeijlstra (2013). Instead of relying on reconstruction and movement, our analysis simply regulates the relative scope relations between the auxiliary and negation via the three-way distinction of the polarity-marking feature *pol*, but aside from this technical difference, the essential analytic idea is the same: the semantic scope of the modal and negation operators transparently reflects the form of the abstract combinatoric structure that is not directly visible from surface constituency, be it a level of syntactic representation (i.e., LF, as in Iatridou and Zeijlstra's account) or the structure of the proof that yields the pairing of surface string and semantic translation (as in our approach, and more generally, in CG-based theories of natural language syntax-semantics).

One might then wonder whether the two analyses are mere notational variants or if there is any advantage gained by recasting the LF-based analysis in a type-logical setup. We do think that our approach has the advantage of being fully explicit, without relying on the notions of reconstruction and movement, whose exact details remain somewhat elusive. However, rather than dwelling on this point, we would like to point out an interesting consequence that immediately follows from our account and which illuminates the relationship between the "transformational" analysis of auxiliaries (of the sort embodied in our analysis of modal auxiliaries as "VP-modifier quantifiers") and the lexicalist alternatives in the tradition of nontransformational syntax (such as G/HPSG and CG).

To see the relevant point, note first that PPI modals such as *should* can be derived in the lower-order category $\mathrm{VP}_{f,+}/\mathrm{VP}_{b,\delta}$ as follows (where $\alpha, \beta, \delta \in \{\varnothing, -\}$):

(456)

$$
\cfrac{\cfrac{\begin{bmatrix}\varphi_3;\\x;\mathrm{NP}\end{bmatrix}^3 \quad \cfrac{\begin{bmatrix}\varphi_1;\\f;\mathrm{VP}_{f,\delta}/\mathrm{VP}_{b,\delta}\end{bmatrix}^1 \quad \begin{bmatrix}\varphi_2;\\g;\mathrm{VP}_{b,\delta}\end{bmatrix}^2}{\varphi_1\circ\varphi_2; f(g); \mathrm{VP}_{f,\delta}}}{\cfrac{\varphi_3\circ\varphi_1\circ\varphi_2; f(g)(x); S_{f,\delta}}{\lambda\varphi_1.\varphi_3\circ\varphi_1\circ\varphi_2; \lambda f.f(g)(x); S_{f,\delta}\!\restriction\!(\mathrm{VP}_{f,\delta}/\mathrm{VP}_{b,\delta})}\;\!\restriction\!\mathrm{I}^1}}{\cfrac{\cfrac{\varphi_3\circ\mathsf{should}\circ\varphi_2; \Box g(x); S_{f,+}}{\mathsf{should}\circ\varphi_2; \lambda x.\Box g(x); \mathrm{VP}_{f,+}}\backslash\mathrm{I}^3}{\mathsf{should}; \lambda g\lambda x.\Box g(x); \mathrm{VP}_{f,+}/\mathrm{VP}_{b,\delta}}/\mathrm{I}^2}
$$

Left premise (456):
$$\lambda\sigma.\sigma(\mathsf{should});\ \lambda\mathcal{G}.\Box\mathcal{G}(\mathrm{id}_{et});\ S_{f,+}\!\restriction\!(S_{f,\beta}\!\restriction\!(\mathrm{VP}_{f,\alpha}/\mathrm{VP}_{b,\alpha}))$$

Similarly, the negation morpheme *not* can be slanted to the $\mathrm{VP}_{b,-}/\mathrm{VP}_{b,\varnothing}$ category:

(457)

$$
\cfrac{\cfrac{\begin{bmatrix}\varphi_3;\\x;\mathrm{NP}\end{bmatrix}^3 \quad \cfrac{\begin{bmatrix}\varphi_1;\\f;\mathrm{VP}_{b,\varnothing}/\mathrm{VP}_{b,\varnothing}\end{bmatrix}^1 \quad \begin{bmatrix}\varphi_2;\\g;\mathrm{VP}_{b,\varnothing}\end{bmatrix}^2}{\varphi_1\circ\varphi_2; f(g); \mathrm{VP}_{b,\varnothing}}}{\cfrac{\varphi_3\circ\varphi_1\circ\varphi_2; f(g)(x); S_{b,\varnothing}}{\lambda\varphi_1.\varphi_3\circ\varphi_1\circ\varphi_2; \lambda f.f(g)(x); S_{b,\varnothing}\!\restriction\!(\mathrm{VP}_{b,\varnothing}/\mathrm{VP}_{b,\varnothing})}\;\!\restriction\!\mathrm{I}^1}}{\cfrac{\cfrac{\varphi_3\circ\mathsf{not}\circ\varphi_2; \neg g(x); S_{b,-}}{\mathsf{not}\circ\varphi_2; \lambda x.\neg g(x); \mathrm{VP}_{b,-}}\backslash\mathrm{I}^3}{\mathsf{not}; \lambda g\lambda x.\neg g(x); \mathrm{VP}_{b,-}/\mathrm{VP}_{b,\varnothing}}/\mathrm{I}^2}
$$

Left premise (457):
$$\lambda\sigma.\sigma(\mathsf{not});\ \lambda\mathcal{G}.\neg\mathcal{G}(\mathrm{id}_{et});\ S_{\gamma,-}\!\restriction\!(S_{\gamma,\varnothing}\!\restriction\!(\mathrm{VP}_{b,\varnothing}/\mathrm{VP}_{b,\varnothing}))$$

These two lowered categories can be combined to produce the following sign:

(458)

$$
\cfrac{\mathsf{should}; \lambda g\lambda x.\Box g(x); \mathrm{VP}_{f,+}/\mathrm{VP}_{b,\delta} \quad \cfrac{\mathsf{not}; \lambda g\lambda x.\neg g(x); \mathrm{VP}_{b,-}/\mathrm{VP}_{b,\varnothing} \quad [\varphi_1; g; \mathrm{VP}_{b,\varnothing}]^1}{\mathsf{not}\circ\varphi_1; \lambda x.\neg g(x); \mathrm{VP}_{b,-}}}{\cfrac{\mathsf{should}\circ\mathsf{not}\circ\varphi_1; \lambda x.\Box\neg g(x); \mathrm{VP}_{f,+}}{\mathsf{should}\circ\mathsf{not}; \lambda g\lambda x.\Box\neg g(x); \mathrm{VP}_{f,+}/\mathrm{VP}_{b,\varnothing}}/\mathrm{I}^1}
$$

Slanting the NPI modal *need*, on the other hand, yields the following result:

(459)

$$
\cfrac{\cfrac{\begin{bmatrix}\varphi_3;\\x;\mathrm{NP}\end{bmatrix}^3 \quad \cfrac{\begin{bmatrix}\varphi_1;\\f;\mathrm{VP}_{f,\varnothing}/\mathrm{VP}_{b,\varnothing}\end{bmatrix}^1 \quad \begin{bmatrix}\varphi_2;\\g;\mathrm{VP}_{b,\varnothing}\end{bmatrix}^2}{\varphi_1\circ\varphi_2; f(g); \mathrm{VP}_{f,\varnothing}}}{\cfrac{\varphi_3\circ\varphi_1\circ\varphi_2; f(g)(x); S_{f,\varnothing}}{\lambda\varphi_1.\varphi_3\circ\varphi_1\circ\varphi_2; \lambda f.f(g)(x); S_{f,\varnothing}\!\restriction\!(\mathrm{VP}_{f,\varnothing}/\mathrm{VP}_{b,\varnothing})}\;\!\restriction\!\mathrm{I}^1}}{\cfrac{\cfrac{\varphi_3\circ\mathsf{need}\circ\varphi_2; \Box g(x); S_{f,\varnothing}}{\mathsf{need}\circ\varphi_2; \lambda x.\Box g(x); \mathrm{VP}_{f,\varnothing}}\backslash\mathrm{I}^3}{\mathsf{need}; \lambda g\lambda x.\Box g(x); \mathrm{VP}_{f,\varnothing}/\mathrm{VP}_{b,\varnothing}}/\mathrm{I}^2}
$$

Left premise (459):
$$\lambda\sigma.\sigma(\mathsf{need});\ \lambda\mathcal{G}.\Box\mathcal{G}(\mathrm{id}_{et});\ S_{f,\varnothing}\!\restriction\!(S_{f,\varnothing}\!\restriction\!(\mathrm{VP}_{f,\varnothing}/\mathrm{VP}_{b,\varnothing}))$$

Note that this resultant category cannot be combined with the lowered negation category in (457) due to feature mismatch (*need* requires its argument to be $\text{VP}_{b,\varnothing}$, but *not* marks the VP as $\text{VP}_{b,-}$). Thus, the lowered *need* is correctly prevented from outscoping negation.

It is, however, possible to derive *need not* as a complex auxiliary with the correct negation-outscoping semantics:

(460)

$$
\cfrac{
\begin{bmatrix} \varphi_3; \\ x; \text{NP} \end{bmatrix}^3 \quad
\cfrac{
\begin{bmatrix} \varphi_4; \\ h; \text{VP}_{f,\varnothing}/\text{VP}_{b,\varnothing} \end{bmatrix}^4 \quad
\cfrac{
\begin{bmatrix} \varphi_1; \\ f; \text{VP}_{b,\varnothing}/\text{VP}_{b,\varnothing} \end{bmatrix}^1 \quad
\begin{bmatrix} \varphi_2; \\ g; \text{VP}_{b,\varnothing} \end{bmatrix}^2
}{\varphi_1 \circ \varphi_2; \, f(g); \, \text{VP}_{b,\varnothing}}
}{\varphi_4 \circ \varphi_1 \circ \varphi_2; \, h(f(g)); \, \text{VP}_{f,\varnothing}}
}{\varphi_3 \circ \varphi_4 \circ \varphi_1 \circ \varphi_2; \, h(f(g))(x); \, \text{S}_{f,\varnothing}}
$$

$$\vdots$$

$$
\cfrac{
\begin{array}{c}
\lambda\sigma.\sigma(\text{not}); \\
\lambda\mathcal{G}.\neg\mathcal{G}(\text{id}_{et}); \\
\text{S}_{\gamma,-}\!\upharpoonright(\text{S}_{\gamma,\varnothing}\!\upharpoonright(\text{VP}_{b,\varnothing}/\text{VP}_{b,\varnothing}))
\end{array}
\quad
\cfrac{
\cfrac{
\begin{array}{c}
\lambda\sigma.\sigma(\text{need}); \\
\lambda\mathcal{G}.\Box\mathcal{G}(\text{id}_{et}); \\
\text{S}_{f,\varnothing}\!\upharpoonright(\text{S}_{f,\varnothing}\!\upharpoonright(\text{VP}_{f,\varnothing}/\text{VP}_{b,\varnothing}))
\end{array}
\quad
\cfrac{
\begin{array}{c}
\varphi_3 \circ \varphi_4 \circ \varphi_1 \circ \varphi_2; \\
h(f(g))(x); \text{S}_{f,\varnothing}
\end{array}
}{
\begin{array}{c}
\lambda\varphi_4.\varphi_3 \circ \varphi_4 \circ \varphi_1 \circ \varphi_2; \\
\lambda h.h(f(g))(x); \\
\text{S}_{f,\varnothing}\!\upharpoonright(\text{VP}_{f,\varnothing}/\text{VP}_{b,\varnothing})
\end{array}
}\Pi^4
}{
\cfrac{\varphi_3 \circ \text{need} \circ \varphi_1 \circ \varphi_2; \, \Box f(g)(x); \, \text{S}_{f,\varnothing}}{
\begin{array}{c}
\lambda\varphi_1.\varphi_3 \circ \text{need} \circ \varphi_1 \circ \varphi_2; \\
\lambda f.\Box f(g)(x); \text{S}_{f,\varnothing}\!\upharpoonright(\text{VP}_{b,\varnothing}/\text{VP}_{b,\varnothing})
\end{array}
}\Pi^1
}
}{
\cfrac{
\cfrac{\varphi_3 \circ \text{need} \circ \text{not} \circ \varphi_2; \, \neg\Box g(x); \, \text{S}_{f,-}}{\text{need} \circ \text{not} \circ \varphi_2; \, \lambda x.\neg\Box g(x); \, \text{VP}_{f,-}}\backslash\text{I}^3
}{\text{need} \circ \text{not}; \, \lambda g \lambda x.\neg\Box g(x); \, \text{VP}_{f,-}/\text{VP}_{b,\varnothing}}/\text{I}^2
}
$$

In short, in our type-logical setup, alternative lexical signs that correspond to the lexical entries for the relevant expressions that are directly specified in the lexicon in lexicalist theories of syntax are all derivable as theorems from the more abstract, higher-order entries we have posited above. This is essentially the consequence of the slanting lemma in the revised system augmented with polarity markings. Significantly, the polarity markings ensure that slanting of the higher-order modals and negation preserves the correct scope relations between these operators.

The formal derivability of the lower-order entry from the higher-order entry is an interesting result, as it potentially illuminates the deeper relationship between the "transformational" and "lexicalist" analyses of auxiliaries in the different traditions of the generative grammar literature. The two approaches have tended to be seen as reflecting fundamentally incompatible assumptions about the basic architecture of grammar, but if a formal connection can be established between the two at an abstract level by making certain (not totally implausible) assumptions, then the two may not be as different from each other as they have appeared to be throughout the whole history of the controversy between the transformational and nontransformational approaches to syntax. In any event, we take our result above to indicate that the logic-based setup of TLCG can be fruitfully employed for the purpose of meta-comparison of different approaches to grammatical phenomena in the syntactic literature.[5]

9.3.2 Some Further Consequences of Slanting

We believe that the above discussion of the derivability relation between the higher-order entries of modals and negation and their lower-order counterparts corresponding to the more familiar VP/VP entries in lexicalist theories of syntax has clarified the relationship between our proposal and previous approaches in the lexicalist tradition considerably. At a suitably abstract level, one can see the former as a proper generalization of the latter, rather than seeing the two as embodying mutually incomparable analytic ideas.

But the role of the slanting lemma in our theory is not merely to relate the more abstract analysis to a more surface-oriented familiar analysis in the lexicalist tradition. In fact, slanting plays a crucial role in analyzing certain types of examples that are otherwise difficult to analyze without duplicating the lexicon. Here, we illustrate two such cases, one involving coordination of the modals themselves (this section) and the other involving VP ellipsis with the higher-order modal interpretation (section 9.3.3).

Consider first the conjunction of modals in (461).

(461) Every physicist can and should learn how to teach quantum mechanics to the undergraduate literature majors.

There is a reading for this sentence in which the two modals outscope the subject universal quantifier in each conjunct ('it is possible that every physicist learns . . . and it is deontically necessary that every physicist learn . . .').

Assuming that *and* is of type $(X \backslash X)/X$, combining only expressions whose prosodies are strings, it may appear impossible to derive (461) on the relevant reading, since the modals in (461) must be higher-order to outscope the subject quantifier and therefore must have functional prosodies. In fact, however, a straightforward derivation is avail-

---

5. Familiar examples such as (i) provide motivation for higher-order versions of raising verbs such as *seem*, *tend*, *happen*, and so on:

(i) A unicorn seems to be approaching.

It is straightforward to show that the higher-order lexical entries for such verbs yield, by exactly the same proof narratives as for modals, the lower-order VP/VP signs that correspond to the argument structure taken as standard in a variety of nontransformational frameworks. On the basis of such higher-order $S\!\upharpoonright\!(S\!\upharpoonright\!(VP/VP))$ types, we would expect to find cases of raising predicates scoping wide over conjunctions and disjunctions, but the semantics of these verbs makes it difficult to come up with clear cases that would enable us to test this prediction.

able with no additional assumptions or machinery. Note first that the modal auxiliary can be derived in the $((S/VP)\backslash S)/VP$ type:

(462)

$$\cfrac{[\varphi_3; \mathscr{P}; S_{f,\alpha}/VP_{f,\alpha}]^3 \quad \cfrac{\cfrac{[\varphi_2; f; VP_{f,\alpha}/VP_{b,\alpha}]^2 \quad [\varphi_1; P; VP_{b,\alpha}]^1}{\varphi_2 \circ \varphi_1; f(P); VP_{f,\alpha}}}{\cfrac{\varphi_3 \circ \varphi_2 \circ \varphi_1; \mathscr{P}(f(P)); S_{f,\alpha}}{\lambda\varphi_2.\varphi_3 \circ \varphi_2 \circ \varphi_1; \lambda f.\mathscr{P}(P); S_{f,\alpha}\upharpoonright(VP_{f,\alpha}/VP_{b,\alpha})} \upharpoonright I^2} \quad \cfrac{\lambda\sigma.\sigma(can);}{\lambda\mathscr{F}.\Diamond\mathscr{F}(id_{et});} }{\cfrac{\cfrac{\varphi_3 \circ can \circ \varphi_1; \Diamond\mathscr{P}(P); S_{f,+}}{can \circ \varphi_1; \lambda\mathscr{P}.\Diamond\mathscr{P}(P); (S_{f,\alpha}/VP_{f,\alpha})\backslash S_{f,+}} \backslash I^3}{can; \lambda P\lambda\mathscr{P}.\Diamond\mathscr{P}(P); ((S_{f,\alpha}/VP_{f,\alpha})\backslash S_{f,+})/VP_{b,\alpha}} /I^1}$$

By conjoining two such modals via generalized conjunction, we obtain

(463) can $\circ$ and $\circ$ should; $\lambda R\lambda\mathscr{R}.\Diamond\mathscr{R}(R) \wedge \Box\mathscr{R}(R); ((S_{f,\alpha}/VP_{f,\alpha})\backslash S_{f,+})/VP_{b,\alpha}$

We apply this functor first to the sign with VP type derived for *learn how to teach quantum mechanics to the undergraduate literature majors* and then to the slanted version of the quantified subject *every physicist*, derivable as in (464):

(464)

$$\cfrac{\cfrac{\cfrac{[\varphi_1; y; NP]^1 \quad [\varphi_2; P; VP_{f,\alpha}]^2}{\varphi_1 \circ \varphi_2; P(y); S_{f,\alpha}}}{\lambda\varphi_1.\varphi_1 \circ \varphi_2; \lambda y.P(y); S_{f,\alpha}\upharpoonright NP} \upharpoonright I^1 \quad \cfrac{\lambda\sigma_1.\sigma_1(every \circ physicist);}{\mathbf{V_{phys}}; S_{f,\alpha}\upharpoonright(S_{f,\alpha}\upharpoonright NP)}}{\cfrac{every \circ physicist \circ \varphi_2; \mathbf{V_{phys}}(\lambda y.P(y)); S_{f,\alpha}}{every \circ physicist; \lambda P.\mathbf{V_{phys}}(\lambda y.P(y)); S_{f,\alpha}/VP_{f,\alpha}} /I^2}$$

This yields the following result, with the correct semantic translation for (461):

(465)

$$\cfrac{\cfrac{\vdots}{\cfrac{\substack{every \circ physicist;\\ \mathbf{V_{phys}}; S_{f,\alpha}/VP_{f,\alpha}}} \quad \cfrac{\substack{can \circ and \circ should;\\ \lambda R\lambda\mathscr{R}.\Diamond\mathscr{R}(R) \wedge \Box\mathscr{R}(R); ((S_{f,\alpha}/VP_{f,\alpha})\backslash S_{f,+})/VP_{b,\alpha}} \quad \substack{\vdots\\ learn...;\\ \mathbf{LHT}; VP_{b,\alpha}}}{\substack{can \circ and \circ should \circ learn...;\\ \lambda\mathscr{R}.\Diamond\mathscr{R}(\mathbf{LHT}) \wedge \Box\mathscr{R}(\mathbf{LHT}); (S_{f,\alpha}/VP_{f,\alpha})\backslash S_{f,+}}}}{\substack{every \circ physicist \circ can \circ and \circ should \circ learn...;\\ \Diamond\mathbf{V_{phys}}(\mathbf{LHT}) \wedge \Box\mathbf{V_{phys}}(\mathbf{LHT}); S_{f,+}}}$$

9.3.3 Higher-Order Modals and Ellipsis

A natural question that arises at this point is whether our analysis of VP ellipsis and pseudogapping will extend to cases in which the higher-order entry for the modal is involved in the ellipsis site, due to scopal interaction with other elements in the sentence (typically, the subject quantifier scoping lower than the auxiliary).

There are indeed examples of exactly this pattern, such as the following:

(466) a. A mathematician will solve this physics problem, someday, but no physicist
           ever will.
       b. Maybe John and Bill don't solve math problems, but surely every physicist
           should physics problems.

For example, (466b) has two possible readings. On one reading (*every* > *should*),
the sentence asserts the obligation held by actual physicists of solving physics problems. On the other reading (*should* > *every*), the sentence says something about what
has to be the case about whoever happen to be physicists in the relevant (deontically
necessary) possible worlds, so, on this reading it can be (non-vacuously) true even in
situations in which there are no physicists in the actual world. These two readings are
thus truth-conditionally distinct. A similar, modal wide-scope reading is available in
the VP ellipsis example (466a) as well. To obtain this second type of reading, we need
the higher-order *will* rather than the lower-order VP/VP entry to host VP ellipsis. Perhaps surprisingly, the analysis of VP ellipsis and pseudogapping from chapter 6 can
license the relevant readings for (466) without introducing any additional machinery.
We illustrate this point in what follows.

We start with the proof that an $S{\upharpoonright}(S{\upharpoonright}(TV/TV))$ expression for the higher-order modal
is an entailment of the $S{\upharpoonright}(S{\upharpoonright}(VP/VP))$ entry posited in the lexicon:

(467)

$$
\cfrac{
\left[\begin{array}{l}\sigma_1;\\ \mathscr{C};\\ S_{f,\beta}{\upharpoonright}(TV_{f,\alpha}/TV_{b,\alpha})\end{array}\right]^4
\quad
\cfrac{
\cfrac{
\cfrac{
\cfrac{
\cfrac{
\left[\begin{array}{l}\varphi_1;\\ f;\\ VP_{f,\alpha}/VP_{b,\alpha}\end{array}\right]^1
\quad
\cfrac{
\left[\begin{array}{l}\varphi_2;\\ R;\\ TV_{b,\alpha}\end{array}\right]^2
\quad
\left[\begin{array}{l}\varphi_3;\\ x;\\ NP\end{array}\right]^3
}{\varphi_2 \circ \varphi_3;\ R(x);\ VP_{b,\alpha}}
}{\varphi_1 \circ \varphi_2 \circ \varphi_3;\ f(R(x));\ VP_{f,\alpha}}/I^3
}{\varphi_1 \circ \varphi_2;\ \lambda x.f(R(x));\ TV_{f,\alpha}}/I^2
}{\varphi_1;\ \lambda R\lambda x.f(R(x));\ TV_{f,\alpha}/TV_{b,\alpha}}
}{\sigma_1(\varphi_1);\ \mathscr{C}(\lambda R\lambda x.f(R(x)));\ S_{f,\beta}}
}{\lambda\varphi_1.\sigma_1(\varphi_1);\ \lambda f.\mathscr{C}(\lambda R\lambda x.f(R(x)));\ S_{f,\beta}{\upharpoonright}(VP_{f,\alpha}/VP_{b,\alpha})}{\upharpoonright}I^1
\quad
\begin{array}{l}\lambda\sigma_0.\sigma_0(\text{should});\\ \lambda\mathscr{F}.\Box\mathscr{F}(\text{id}_{et});\\ S_{f,+}{\upharpoonright}(S_{f,\beta}{\upharpoonright}(VP_{f,\alpha}/VP_{b,\alpha}))\end{array}
}{\sigma_1(\text{should});\ \Box\mathscr{C}(\lambda R\lambda x.R(x));\ S_{f,+}}
}{\lambda\sigma_1.\sigma_1(\text{should});\ \lambda\mathscr{C}.\Box\mathscr{C}(\text{id}_{et});\ S_{f,+}{\upharpoonright}(S_{f,\beta}{\upharpoonright}(TV_{f,\alpha}/TV_{b,\alpha}))}{\upharpoonright}I^4
$$

With this derived entry for the auxiliary, the derivation for the ellipsis clause of (466b)
is straightforward. The derivation is shown in (468).

(468)

$$\dfrac{\lambda\sigma_1.\sigma_1(\text{every}\circ\text{physicist});\ \mathbf{V_{phys}};\ \mathrm{S}_{f,\varnothing}\upharpoonright(\mathrm{S}_{f,\varnothing}\upharpoonright\mathrm{NP})}{}$$

$$\cfrac{\cfrac{\begin{bmatrix}\varphi_1;\\x;\\\mathrm{NP}\end{bmatrix}^1\quad\cfrac{\cfrac{\lambda\varphi_0.\varphi_0;\ \lambda\mathscr{F}.\mathscr{F}(\mathbf{solve});\ \mathrm{TV}_{f,\varnothing}\upharpoonright(\mathrm{TV}_{f,\varnothing}/\mathrm{TV}_{b,\varnothing})\quad\begin{bmatrix}\varphi;\\\mathscr{G};\\\mathrm{TV}_{f,\varnothing}/\mathrm{TV}_{b,\varnothing}\end{bmatrix}^0}{\varphi;\ \mathscr{G}(\mathbf{solve});\ \mathrm{TV}_{f,\varnothing}}\ {\scriptstyle/\mathrm{E}}\quad\begin{matrix}\text{physics}\circ\\\text{problems};\\\mathbf{physp};\mathrm{NP}\end{matrix}}{\varphi\circ\text{physics}\circ\text{problems};\ \mathscr{G}(\mathbf{solve})(\mathbf{physp});\ \mathrm{VP}_{f,\varnothing}}}{\cfrac{\varphi_1\circ\varphi\circ\text{physics}\circ\text{problems};\ \mathscr{G}(\mathbf{solve})(\mathbf{physp})(x);\ \mathrm{S}_{f,\varnothing}}{\lambda\varphi_1.\varphi_1\circ\varphi\circ\text{physics}\circ\text{problems};\ \lambda x.\mathscr{G}(\mathbf{solve})(\mathbf{physp})(x);\ \mathrm{S}_{f,\varnothing}\upharpoonright\mathrm{NP}}\ {\scriptstyle\upharpoonright\mathrm{I}^1}}\ {\scriptstyle\upharpoonright\mathrm{I}^1}}{\text{every}\circ\text{physicist}\circ\varphi\circ\text{physics}\circ\text{problems};\ \mathbf{V_{phys}}(\lambda x.\mathscr{G}(\mathbf{solve})(\mathbf{physp})(x));\ \mathrm{S}_{f,\varnothing}}$$

$$\dfrac{}{\lambda\varphi.\text{every}\circ\text{physicist}\circ\varphi\circ\text{physics}\circ\text{problems};\ \lambda\mathscr{G}.\mathbf{V_{phys}}(\lambda x.\mathscr{G}(\mathbf{solve})(\mathbf{physp})(x));\ \mathrm{S}_{f,\varnothing}\upharpoonright(\mathrm{TV}_{f,\varnothing}/\mathrm{TV}_{b,\varnothing})}\ {\scriptstyle\upharpoonright\mathrm{I}^0}$$

$$\vdots \qquad\qquad\qquad\qquad\qquad\qquad\vdots$$

$$\dfrac{\begin{matrix}\lambda\sigma_1.\sigma_1(\text{should});\\\lambda\mathscr{C}.\square\mathscr{C}(\mathrm{id}_{et});\\\mathrm{S}_{f,+}\upharpoonright(\mathrm{S}_{f,\beta}\upharpoonright(\mathrm{TV}_{f,\alpha}/\mathrm{TV}_{b,\alpha}))\end{matrix}\qquad\begin{matrix}\lambda\varphi.\text{every}\circ\text{physicist}\circ\varphi\circ\text{physics}\circ\text{problems};\\\lambda\mathscr{G}.\mathbf{V_{phys}}(\lambda x.\mathscr{G}(\mathbf{solve})(\mathbf{physp})(x));\ \mathrm{S}_{f,\varnothing}\upharpoonright(\mathrm{TV}_{f,\varnothing}/\mathrm{TV}_{b,\varnothing})\end{matrix}}{\begin{matrix}\text{every}\circ\text{physicist}\circ\text{should}\circ\text{physics}\circ\text{problems};\\\square\mathbf{V_{phys}}(\lambda x.\mathbf{solve}(\mathbf{physp})(x));\ \mathrm{S}_{f,+}\end{matrix}}$$

The key point of the derivation here is that a hypothetical TV/TV (which later gets bound by the "Geachified" higher-order modal derived in (467)) feeds the ordinary pseudogapping operator (of type TV$\upharpoonright$(TV/TV)) that supplies the meaning of the missing verb. Since the Geachified higher-order modal enters the derivation after the subject quantifier takes scope, we obtain the desired $\square > \forall$ reading for the sentence. Note in particular that via the systematic interaction of hypothetical reasoning, no special entry for the ellipsis operator (e.g., one that directly takes the higher-order modal as an argument) needs to be posited to derive the relevant modal wide-scope reading for the sentence.

9.3.4 VP Fronting

Work in phrase structure–theoretic approaches to the syntax-semantics interface has tended to follow the treatment of negation in Kim and Sag (2002), which distinguishes *not* (and possibly *never*) as a complement of auxiliaries from *not* as an adjunct to the auxiliaries' VP complements (see section 9.4 for more on this). This approach is supposedly motivated by the ambiguity of sentences with *could not/never* sequences, where both $\neg > \Diamond$ and $\Diamond > \neg$ readings are available.

There is, in fact, only a very sparse empirical base in English for this phrase structure–based analysis of modal/negation scoping relations, a fact that Kim and Sag (2002) themselves tacitly acknowledge. One of the few lines of argument that they appeal to is the fact that fronted VPs containing *not* adjuncts are always interpreted with narrowly scoping negation, as illustrated in (469):

(469) ... and NOT vote, you certainly can __, if the nominees are all second-rate.

Data of this sort are intended to provide empirical support for the putative correlation of phrase structural position with the scope of negation (see section 9.4 for further discussion).

But we can readily capture the pattern in (469) in our approach by requiring that clauses hosting topicalization be subject to polarity conditions which induce the effect of entailing narrow scope for the negation within the fronted VP. We start by presenting the topicalization operator in (470a) (with the polymorphic syntactic type X), illustrating its ordinary operation to produce (470b) (where the semantics is simply an identity function, since we ignore the pragmatic effects of topicalization):

(470)   a. $\lambda\varphi\lambda\sigma.\varphi \circ \sigma(\boldsymbol{\varepsilon}); \lambda\mathcal{F}\lambda\mathcal{G}.\mathcal{G}(\mathcal{F}); (S_{f,\beta} \upharpoonright (S_{f,\beta} \upharpoonright X)) \upharpoonright X$ where $\beta \in \{+, -\}$

     b. ... and vote, John can __.

     c. #... and not vote, John can __. $(\neg > \Diamond)$

The derivation for (470b) is given in (471).

(471)

$$\cfrac{\cfrac{\cfrac{\text{can;} \quad \lambda P\lambda y.\Diamond P(y); \text{VP}_{f,+}/\text{VP}_{b,\alpha} \qquad \begin{bmatrix} \varphi_1; \\ Q; \text{VP}_{b,\alpha} \end{bmatrix}^1}{\text{can} \circ \varphi_1; \lambda y.\Diamond Q(y); \text{VP}_{f,+}} \qquad \begin{matrix} \text{john;} \\ \mathbf{j}; \text{NP} \end{matrix}}{\cfrac{\text{john} \circ \text{can} \circ \varphi_1; \Diamond Q(\mathbf{j}); S_{f,+}}{\lambda\varphi_1.\text{john} \circ \text{can} \circ \varphi_1; \lambda Q.\Diamond Q(\mathbf{j}); S_{f,+} \upharpoonright \text{VP}_{b,\alpha}} \uparrow 1^1 \qquad \cfrac{\begin{matrix} \lambda\varphi\lambda\sigma.\varphi \circ \sigma(\boldsymbol{\varepsilon}); & \text{vote;} \\ \lambda P\lambda\mathcal{C}.\mathcal{C}(P); & \textbf{vote;} \\ (S_{f,\beta} \upharpoonright (S_{f,\beta} \upharpoonright X)) \upharpoonright X & \text{VP}_{b,\alpha} \end{matrix}}{\begin{matrix} \lambda\sigma.\text{vote} \circ \sigma(\boldsymbol{\varepsilon}); \\ \lambda\mathcal{C}.\mathcal{C}(\textbf{vote}); \\ S_{f,\beta} \upharpoonright (S_{f,\beta} \upharpoonright \text{VP}_{b,\alpha}) \end{matrix}}}{\text{vote} \circ \text{john} \circ \text{can} \circ \boldsymbol{\varepsilon}; \Diamond\textbf{vote}(\mathbf{j}); S_{f,+}}$$

The requirement on the topicalization operator in (470a) effectively means that $S_\varnothing$ is "too small" to host a topicalized phrase. That is, in order to license topicalization, the clause needs to have already "fixed" the polarity value to either $+$ or $-$. This condition turns out to have the immediate effect of enforcing narrow scope on negation in fronted VPs.

To see how this condition works, let's suppose it did not hold; that is, suppose that β could take any of the three polarity values. Then the following would be one way in which *not* inside a topicalized phrase would outscope the modal.

$$(472) \quad \frac{[\varphi_4; Q; \mathrm{VP}_{b,\varnothing}]^1 \quad [\varphi_5; g; \mathrm{VP}_{b,\varnothing}/\mathrm{VP}_{b,\varnothing}]^2}{\varphi_5 \circ \varphi_4; g(Q); \mathrm{VP}_{b,\varnothing}} \quad \begin{array}{l} \text{john;} \\ \mathbf{j}; \mathrm{NP} \end{array}$$

$$\frac{\mathrm{john} \circ \varphi_5 \circ \varphi_4; g(Q)(\mathbf{j}); S_{b,\varnothing}}{\lambda\varphi_5.\mathrm{john} \circ \varphi_5 \circ \varphi_4; \lambda g.g(Q)(\mathbf{j}); S_{b,\varnothing} \restriction (\mathrm{VP}_{b,\varnothing}/\mathrm{VP}_{b,\varnothing})} \upharpoonright^2 \quad \begin{array}{l} \lambda\sigma_0.\sigma_0(\mathrm{can}); \\ \lambda\mathscr{F}.\Diamond\mathscr{F}(\mathrm{id}_{et}); \\ S_{f,\varnothing} \restriction (S_{b,\varnothing} \restriction (\mathrm{VP}_{b,\varnothing}/\mathrm{VP}_{b,\varnothing})) \end{array}$$

$$\frac{\mathrm{john} \circ \mathrm{can} \circ \varphi_4; \Diamond Q(\mathbf{j}); S_{f,\varnothing}}{\lambda\varphi_4.\mathrm{john} \circ \mathrm{can} \circ \varphi_4; \Diamond Q(\mathbf{j}); S_{f,\varnothing} \restriction \mathrm{VP}_{b,\varnothing}} \upharpoonright^1$$

$$\begin{array}{cc} \begin{array}{c} \vdots \\ \lambda\varphi_4.\mathrm{john} \circ \\ \mathrm{can} \circ \varphi_4; \\ \Diamond Q(\mathbf{j}); \\ S_{f,\varnothing} \restriction \mathrm{VP}_{b,\varnothing} \end{array} & \begin{array}{c} \begin{array}{cc} \begin{array}{c} \text{vote;} \\ \mathbf{vote;} \\ \mathrm{VP}_{b,\varnothing} \end{array} & \left[\begin{array}{c} \varphi_1; \\ f; \\ \mathrm{VP}_{b,\varnothing}/\mathrm{VP}_{b,\varnothing} \end{array}\right]^3 \end{array} & \begin{array}{c} \lambda\varphi_2\lambda\sigma_1. \\ \varphi_2 \circ \sigma_1(\boldsymbol{\varepsilon}); \\ \lambda\mathcal{F}\lambda\mathcal{G}.\mathcal{G}(\mathcal{F}); \\ (S_{f,\beta} \restriction (S_{f,\beta} \restriction X)) \restriction X \end{array} \\ \hline \begin{array}{c} \varphi_1 \circ \mathrm{vote}; f(\mathbf{vote}); \mathrm{VP}_{b,\varnothing} \end{array} \\ \hline \begin{array}{c} \lambda\sigma_1.\varphi_1 \circ \mathrm{vote} \circ \sigma_1(\boldsymbol{\varepsilon}); \\ \lambda\mathscr{C}.\mathscr{C}(f(\mathbf{vote})); S_{f,\varnothing} \restriction (S_{f,\varnothing} \restriction \mathrm{VP}_{b,\varnothing}) \end{array} \end{array} \end{array}$$

$$\frac{\varphi_1 \circ \mathrm{vote} \circ \mathrm{john} \circ \mathrm{can} \circ \boldsymbol{\varepsilon}; \Diamond f(\mathbf{vote})(\mathbf{j}); S_{f,\varnothing}}{\begin{array}{c} \lambda\varphi_1.\varphi_1 \circ \mathrm{vote} \circ \mathrm{john} \circ \mathrm{can} \circ \boldsymbol{\varepsilon}; \\ \lambda f.\Diamond f(\mathbf{vote})(\mathbf{j}); S_{f,\varnothing} \restriction (\mathrm{VP}_{b,\varnothing}/\mathrm{VP}_{b,\varnothing}) \end{array}} \upharpoonright^3 \quad \begin{array}{l} \lambda\sigma.\sigma(\mathrm{not}); \\ \lambda\mathcal{G}.\neg\mathcal{G}(\mathrm{id}_{et}); \\ S_{f,-} \restriction (S_{f,\varnothing} \restriction (\mathrm{VP}_{b,\varnothing}/\mathrm{VP}_{b,\varnothing})) \end{array}$$

$$\mathrm{not} \circ \mathrm{vote} \circ \mathrm{john} \circ \mathrm{can}; \neg\Diamond\mathbf{vote}(\mathbf{j}); S_{f,-}$$

Here, the derivation uses the NPI version of *can* in order to license the negation wide-scope reading. Since the negation is inside the topicalized phrase rather than the main clause, topicalization needs to be hosted by a clause to which negation hasn't yet combined. But this is precisely the possibility that the restriction $\beta \in \{+, -\}$ excludes. That is, the derivation in (472) actually fails to be licensed in our fragment since β in the topicalization operator cannot be instantiated as $\varnothing$ (as in the grayed-in part of the derivation in (472)).

Using the other version of *can* produces the other scopal relation ($\Diamond > \neg$) for (470c), as in the following derivation:

$$(473) \qquad\qquad\qquad \vdots$$

$$\frac{\begin{array}{cc} \begin{array}{c} \text{vote;} \\ \mathbf{vote}; \mathrm{VP}_{b,\varnothing} \end{array} & \begin{array}{c} \text{not;} \\ \lambda Q\lambda y.\neg Q(y); \mathrm{VP}_{b,-}/\mathrm{VP}_{b,\varnothing} \end{array} \end{array}}{\mathrm{not} \circ \mathrm{vote}; \lambda y.\neg\mathbf{vote}(y); \mathrm{VP}_{b,-}} \quad \begin{array}{l} \lambda\varphi_2\lambda\sigma_1.\varphi_2 \circ \sigma_1(\boldsymbol{\varepsilon}); \\ \lambda\mathcal{F}\lambda\mathcal{G}.\mathcal{G}(\mathcal{F}); (S_{f,\beta} \restriction (S_{f,\beta} \restriction X)) \restriction X \end{array}$$

$$\lambda\sigma_1.\mathrm{not} \circ \mathrm{vote} \circ \sigma_1(\boldsymbol{\varepsilon}); \lambda\mathscr{C}.\mathscr{C}(\lambda y.\neg\mathbf{vote}(y)); S_{f,\beta} \restriction (S_{f,\beta} \restriction \mathrm{VP}_{b,-})$$

$$
\cfrac{
\cfrac{
\begin{bmatrix}\varphi_1;\\ P;\\ VP_{b,-}\end{bmatrix}^1 \quad
\cfrac{
\cfrac{
\begin{bmatrix}\varphi_3;\\ f;\\ VP_{b,-}/VP_{b,-}\end{bmatrix}^3 \quad \begin{array}{c}\text{john};\\ \mathbf{j};\\ NP\end{array}
}{\varphi_3\circ\varphi_1;\ f(P);\ VP_{b,-}}
}{
\begin{array}{c}\lambda\varphi_3.\text{john}\circ\varphi_3\circ\varphi_1;\\ \lambda P.f(P)(\mathbf{j});\ S_{f,+}\end{array}
}
}{
\begin{array}{c}\lambda\varphi_3.\text{john}\circ\varphi_3\circ\varphi_1;\\ \lambda P.f(P)(\mathbf{j});\ S_{f,+}\!\upharpoonright\!(VP_{b,-}/VP_{b,-})\end{array}
}\ {\upharpoonright}\mathrm{I}^3
}{
}
$$

$$
\lambda\sigma_0.\sigma_0(\text{can});\ \lambda\mathscr{F}.\Diamond\mathscr{F}(\mathrm{id}_{et});\ S_{f,+}\!\upharpoonright\!(S_{b,-}\!\upharpoonright\!(VP_{b,\alpha}/VP_{b,\alpha}))
$$

$$
\vdots
$$

$$
\lambda\sigma_1.\text{not}\circ\text{vote}\circ\sigma_1(\boldsymbol{\varepsilon});\ \lambda\mathscr{C}.\mathscr{C}(\lambda y.\neg\mathbf{vote}(y));\ S_{f,\beta}\!\upharpoonright\!(S_{f,\beta}\!\upharpoonright\!VP_{b,-})
$$

$$
\cfrac{\text{john}\circ\text{can}\circ\varphi_1;\ \Diamond P(\mathbf{j});\ S_{f,+}}{\lambda\varphi_1.\text{john}\circ\text{can}\circ\varphi_1;\ \lambda P.\Diamond P(\mathbf{j});\ S_{f,+}\!\upharpoonright\!VP_{b,-}}\ {\upharpoonright}\mathrm{I}^1
$$

$$
\text{not}\circ\text{vote}\circ\text{john}\circ\text{can}\circ\boldsymbol{\varepsilon};\ \Diamond\neg\mathbf{vote}(\mathbf{j});\ S_{f,+}
$$

The slanted version of *not* combines freely with its VP argument to yield a topicalized VP_, but the type of the mother—in particular, its polarity specification—is determined by the highest scoping operator, *can*, which yields a positive polarity clause.

Cases of VP fronting involving quantified subjects are also straightforward in the present approach. For example, (474) involves VP fronting, but the scopal relation between the subject quantifier and the negated modal is the same as in examples that don't involve VP fronting. Thus, on one reading, it has the $\neg > \Diamond > \forall$ scopal relation (consider, for example, a [typical] situation of a physics department at which some of the professional physicists are employed as technical staff who don't have rights to vote at the department chair election).

(474) But vote, EVERY physicist could not __.

We illustrate below how this reading is derived in the present approach.

Given what has been said so far, it will be clear that if the negative operator scopes highest in deriving the continuation clause, that clause will be S_, in compliance with the conditions on the topicalization operator. A proof along these lines will thus take the following form:

(475)

$$
\cfrac{
\cfrac{
[\varphi_2;f;VP_{b,\varnothing}/VP_{b,\varnothing}]^2 \quad [\varphi_1;P;VP_{b,\varnothing}]^1
}{\varphi_2\circ\varphi_1;\ f(P);\ VP_{b,\varnothing}} \quad [\varphi_4;g;VP_{f,\varnothing}/VP_{b,\varnothing}]^4
}{
\cfrac{\varphi_4\circ\varphi_2\circ\varphi_1;\ g(f(P));\ VP_{f,\varnothing} \quad [\varphi_3;y;NP]^3}{\varphi_3\circ\varphi_4\circ\varphi_2\circ\varphi_1;\ f(P)(y);\ S_{f,\varnothing}}
}
$$

$$\vdots$$

$$
\begin{array}{l}
\varphi_3 \circ \varphi_4 \circ \\
\quad \varphi_2 \circ \varphi_1; \\
f(P)(y); S_{f,\varnothing} \\
\overline{\lambda\varphi_3.\varphi_3 \circ \varphi_4 \circ} \quad \lceil I^3 \quad
\begin{array}{l}
\lambda\sigma_1. \\
\quad \sigma_1(\text{every} \circ \\
\quad \text{physicist}); \\
\end{array} \\
\quad \varphi_2 \circ \varphi_1; \\
\lambda y.f(P)(y); \qquad\qquad \mathbf{V_{phys}}; \\
S_{f,\varnothing}\lceil NP \qquad\qquad S_{f,\varnothing}\lceil(S_{f,\varnothing}\lceil NP)
\end{array}
$$

$$
\frac{\text{every} \circ \text{physicist} \circ \varphi_4 \circ \varphi_2 \circ \varphi_1; \mathbf{V_{phys}}(\lambda y.f(P)(y)); S_{f,\varnothing}}{}\ \lceil I^4
$$

$$
\begin{array}{ll}
\lambda\varphi_4.\text{every} \circ \text{physicist} \circ & \\
\quad \varphi_4 \circ \varphi_2 \circ \varphi_1; & \lambda\sigma_2.\sigma_2(\text{could}); \\
\lambda f.\mathbf{V_{phys}}(\lambda y.f(P)(y)); & \lambda\mathscr{F}.\Diamond\mathscr{F}(\mathrm{id}_{et}); \\
S_{f,\varnothing}\lceil(VP_{f,\varnothing}/VP_{b,\varnothing}) & S_{f,\varnothing}\lceil(S_{f,\varnothing}\lceil(VP_{f,\varnothing}/VP_{b,\varnothing}))
\end{array}
$$

$$
\frac{\text{every} \circ \text{physicist} \circ \text{could} \circ \varphi_2 \circ \varphi_1; \Diamond\mathbf{V_{phys}}(\lambda y.g(P)(y)); S_{f,\varnothing}}{}\ \lceil I^2
$$

$$
\begin{array}{ll}
\lambda\varphi_2.\text{every} \circ \text{physicist} \circ \text{could} \circ \varphi_2 \circ \varphi_1; & \lambda\sigma_3.\sigma_3(\text{not}); \\
\lambda g.\Diamond\mathbf{V_{phys}}(\lambda y.g(P)(y)); S_{f,\varnothing}\lceil(VP_{b,\varnothing}/VP_{b,\varnothing}) & \lambda\mathscr{G}.\neg\mathscr{G}(\mathrm{id}_{et}); \\
& S_{\gamma,-}\lceil(S_{\gamma,\varnothing}\lceil(VP_{b,\varnothing}/VP_{b,\varnothing}))
\end{array}
$$

$$
\frac{\text{every} \circ \text{physicist} \circ \text{could} \circ \text{not} \circ \varphi_1; \neg\Diamond\mathbf{V_{phys}}(\lambda y.g(P)(y)); S_{f,-}}{\lambda\varphi_1.\text{every} \circ \text{physicist} \circ \text{could} \circ \text{not} \circ \varphi_1; \lambda P.\neg\Diamond\mathbf{V_{phys}}(\lambda y.P(y)); S_{f,-}\lceil VP_{b,\varnothing}}\ \lceil I^1
$$

$$
\vdots
$$

$$
\begin{array}{ll}
& \lambda\varphi_2\lambda\sigma_1.\varphi_2 \circ \sigma_1(\boldsymbol{\varepsilon}); \qquad\qquad \text{vote}; \\
\lambda\varphi_1.\text{every} \circ \text{physicist} \circ \text{could} \circ \text{not} \circ \varphi_1; & \lambda\alpha\lambda P.P(\alpha); (S_{f,\beta}\lceil(S_{f,\beta}\lceil X))\lceil X \qquad \mathbf{vote}; VP_{b,\varnothing} \\
\lambda P.\neg\Diamond\mathbf{V_{phys}}(\lambda y.P(y)); S_{f,-}\lceil VP_{b,\varnothing} & \overline{\lambda\sigma_1.\text{vote} \circ \sigma_1(\boldsymbol{\varepsilon}); \lambda P.P(\mathbf{vote}); S_{f,\beta}\lceil(S_{f,\beta}\lceil VP_{b,\varnothing})}
\end{array}
$$

$$
\overline{\text{vote} \circ \text{every} \circ \text{physicist} \circ \text{could} \circ \text{not} \circ \boldsymbol{\varepsilon}; \neg\Diamond\mathbf{V_{phys}}(\lambda y.\mathbf{vote}(y)); S_{f,-}}
$$

The interaction of negation with ellipsis, illustrated in (477), is straightforward and, in contrast with the Kim and Sag (2002) account discussed above, predicts (correctly) the possibility of ellipsis following narrow-scoping negation, as shown in (476), whose importance we discuss in more detail in section 9.4:

(476) I know everyone's putting pressure on you to vote in this election, but you could always NOT.

(477)
$$
\dfrac{\left[\begin{array}{l}\varphi_2; \\ f; VP_{b,\varnothing}/VP_{b,\varnothing}\end{array}\right]^2 \left[\begin{array}{l}\varphi_1; \\ P; VP_{b,\varnothing}\end{array}\right]^1}{\varphi_2 \circ \varphi_1; f(P); VP_{b,\varnothing}} \quad \left[\begin{array}{l}\varphi_3; \\ g; \\ VP_{b,\varnothing}/VP_{b,\varnothing}\end{array}\right]^3
$$

$$
\frac{\dfrac{\varphi_3 \circ \varphi_2 \circ \varphi_1; g(f(P)); VP_{b,\varnothing}}{\varphi_3 \circ \varphi_2; \lambda P.g(f(P)); VP_{b,\varnothing}/VP_{b,\varnothing}}/I^1 \quad \left[\begin{array}{l}\sigma_0; \\ \mathscr{C}; \\ S_{b,\varnothing}\lceil(VP_{b,\varnothing}/VP_{b,\varnothing})\end{array}\right]^0}{}
$$

$$
\frac{\sigma_0(\varphi_3 \circ \varphi_2); \mathscr{C}(\lambda P.g(f(P))); S_{b,\varnothing}}{\lambda\varphi_3.\sigma_0(\varphi_3 \circ \varphi_2); \lambda g.\mathscr{C}(\lambda P.g(f(P))); S_{b,\varnothing}\lceil(VP_{b,\varnothing}/VP_{b,\varnothing})}\ \lceil I^3
$$

$$\vdots$$

$$
\frac{
\begin{array}{ll}
\lambda\varphi_3.\sigma_0(\varphi_3\circ\varphi_2); & \lambda\sigma_2.\sigma_2(\text{not}); \\
\lambda g.\mathscr{C}(\lambda P.g(f(P))); & \lambda\mathscr{G}.\neg\mathscr{G}(\text{id}_{et}); \\
\mathrm{S}_{b,\varnothing}\lceil(\mathrm{VP}_{b,\varnothing}/\mathrm{VP}_{b,\varnothing}) & \mathrm{S}_{\gamma,-}\lceil(\mathrm{S}_{\gamma,\varnothing}\lceil(\mathrm{VP}_{b,\varnothing}/\mathrm{VP}_{b,\varnothing}))
\end{array}
}{
\begin{array}{l}
\dfrac{\sigma_0(\varphi_3\circ not);\ \neg\mathscr{C}(\lambda P.(f(P)));\ \mathrm{S}_{b,-}}{\lambda\varphi_2.\sigma_0(\varphi_3\circ not);\ \lambda f.\neg\mathscr{C}(\lambda P.(f(P)));\ \mathrm{S}_{b,-}\lceil(\mathrm{VP}_{b,\varnothing}/\mathrm{VP}_{b,\varnothing})}\ \lceil\mathrm{I}^2
\end{array}
}
$$

$$
\begin{array}{l}
\lambda\sigma_1.\sigma_1(\text{could}); \\
\lambda\mathscr{F}.\Diamond\mathscr{F}(\text{id}_{et}); \\
\mathrm{S}_{f,+}\lceil(\mathrm{S}_{b,-}\lceil(\mathrm{VP}_{f,\alpha}/\mathrm{VP}_{b,\alpha}))
\end{array}
$$

$$
\frac{\sigma_0(\text{could}\circ\text{not});\ \Diamond\neg\mathscr{C}(\lambda P.P);\ \mathrm{S}_{f,+}}{\lambda\sigma_0.\sigma_0(\text{could}\circ\text{not});\ \lambda\mathscr{C}.\Diamond\neg\mathscr{C}(\text{id}_{et});\ \mathrm{S}_{f,+}\lceil(\mathrm{S}_{b,-}\lceil(\mathrm{VP}_{b,\varnothing}/\mathrm{VP}_{b,\varnothing}))}\ \lceil\mathrm{I}^0
$$

The syntactic type, prosody, and semantics provable for *could not* is thus exactly parallel in all respects to the basic properties of the lexical entries for the higher-order modals and therefore will serve as input to the ellipsis operator in exactly the same way, yielding an ellipsis version whose relation to the sign just derived will be identical to that holding between, for example, the VP ellipsis version of higher-order *could* and the lexical entry for this sign, from which the former is derived via application of the ellipsis operator and then the higher-order Geachified modal, as in (468).

9.3.5 Inversion and Higher-Order Modals

We take inversion to correspond to an alternative ordering of prosodic elements associated with a polar interrogative interpretation, the latter the effect of applying the operator "**?**" to the proposition denoted by the uninverted version.[6] To take a simple example, the correlation of this linear ordering with the specific semantics of a polar interrogative can be captured for the higher-order modal *should* as in (478):

(478) $\lambda\sigma_1.\text{should}\circ\sigma_1(\boldsymbol{\varepsilon});\ \lambda\mathscr{F}.?\Box\mathscr{F}(\text{id}_{et});\ \mathrm{S}_{f,+}\lceil(\mathrm{S}_{f,\beta}\lceil(\mathrm{VP}_{f,\alpha}/\mathrm{VP}_{b,\alpha}))$

This sign makes it possible to license (479) on the wide-scope interpretation of the modal, as in (480).

(479) Should every physicist use LaTeX?

(480)

$$\vdots$$

$$
\frac{
\begin{array}{ll}
\lambda\varphi_1.\varphi_1\circ\varphi_2\circ\text{use}\circ\text{latex}; & \lambda\sigma_2.\sigma_2(\text{every}\circ\text{physicist}); \\
\lambda y.f(\textbf{use-ltx})(y);\mathrm{S}_{f,\beta}\lceil\mathrm{NP} & \mathbf{V}_{\textbf{phys}};\mathrm{S}_{f,\beta}\lceil(\mathrm{S}_{f,\beta}\lceil\mathrm{NP})
\end{array}
}{
\begin{array}{l}
\dfrac{\text{every}\circ\text{physicist}\circ\varphi_2\circ\text{use}\circ\text{latex};}{\mathbf{V}_{\textbf{phys}}(\lambda y.f(\textbf{use-ltx})(y));\mathrm{S}_{f,\beta}} \\[6pt]
\dfrac{\lambda\varphi_2.\text{every}\circ\text{physicist}\circ\varphi_2\circ\text{use}\circ\text{latex};}{\lambda f.\mathbf{V}_{\textbf{phys}}(\lambda y.f(\textbf{use-ltx})(y));\mathrm{S}_{f,\beta}\lceil(\mathrm{VP}_{f,\alpha}/\mathrm{VP}_{b,\alpha})}
\end{array}
}
$$

with left sign:

$$
\begin{array}{l}
\lambda\sigma_1.\text{should}\circ\sigma_1(\boldsymbol{\varepsilon}); \\
\lambda\mathscr{F}.?\Box\mathscr{F}(\text{id}_{et}); \\
\mathrm{S}_{f,+}\lceil(\mathrm{S}_{f,\beta}\lceil(\mathrm{VP}_{f,\alpha}/\mathrm{VP}_{b,\alpha}))
\end{array}
$$

$$\text{should}\circ\text{every}\circ\text{physicist}\circ\boldsymbol{\varepsilon}\circ\text{use}\circ\text{latex};\ ?\Box\mathbf{V}_{\textbf{phys}}(\lambda y.\textbf{use-ltx}(y));\ \mathrm{S}_{f,+}$$

---

6. While we remain agnostic on the semantics of interrogatives, if we take ? $=\lambda p.\{p,\neg p\}$, then the interpretation will correspond to the one advocated in Karttunen (1977).

We note that here, as with the other operators we have introduced for higher-order modals, the higer-order entry in (478) can be slanted down to a sign with syntactic type $(S/VP)/NP$:

(481)

$$\cfrac{\cfrac{\cfrac{[\varphi_1; g; VP_{f,\alpha}/VP_{b,\alpha}]^1 \quad [\varphi_2; P; VP_{b,\alpha}]^2}{\varphi_1 \circ \varphi_2; g(P); VP_{f,\alpha}} \qquad [\varphi_3; z; NP]^3}{\cfrac{\varphi_3 \circ \varphi_1 \circ \varphi_2; g(P); S_{f,\alpha}}{\lambda\varphi_1.\varphi_3 \circ \varphi_1 \circ \varphi_2; g(P)(y); S_{f,\alpha}\upharpoonright(VP_{f,\alpha}/VP_{b,\alpha})}\mathord{\upharpoonright}I^1} \qquad \begin{array}{l}\lambda\sigma_1.\text{should} \circ \sigma_1(\boldsymbol{\varepsilon});\\ \lambda\mathscr{F}.?\square\mathscr{F}(\text{id}_{et});\\ S_{f,+}\upharpoonright(S_{f,\beta}\upharpoonright(VP_{f,\alpha}/VP_{b,\alpha}))\end{array}}{\cfrac{\cfrac{\text{should} \circ \varphi_3 \circ \boldsymbol{\varepsilon} \circ \varphi_2; ?\square P(y); S_{f,+}}{\text{should} \circ \varphi_3; \lambda P.?\square P(y); S_{f,+}/VP_{b,\alpha}}/I^2}{\text{should}; \lambda y \lambda P.?\square P(y); (S_{f,+}/VP_{b,\alpha})/NP}/I^3}$$

This lower-order interrogative operator will first combine with an NP to its right and subsequently with a VP to give correct readings for examples such as *Should John use LaTeX?*[7]

9.4   Comparison with a Phrase Structure–Theoretic Analysis

An alternative approach to the modal/negation scope interaction data is proposed by Kim and Sag (2002) in HPSG, whose key proposal, as already noted, is a distinction between *not* as an auxiliary complement and *not* as a VP adjunct:

(482)   a.   [$_{VP}$ modal [$_{VP}$ *not* [$_{VP}$ . . .]]]

       b.   [$_{VP}$ modal *not* [$_{VP}$ . . .]]

Kim and Sag essentially argue that *not* supports both ellipsis and extraction, motivating its analysis as a syntactic argument, and observe further that in both kinds of constructions negation scopes widely over the entire clause. On the other hand, negation can also scope narrowly, giving rise to the ambiguity of, for example, *You could not vote*, with interpretations available under both $\neg > \Diamond$ and $\Diamond > \neg$ scopings. Since only the first of these is available in, for example, . . . *but vote, you can not*, Kim and Sag apply their assumption that while dependents of heads can be extracted, head phrases themselves cannot be, in order to mandate an analysis of extracted VPs in negated contexts

---

7. We provide no analysis of negative interrogative sentences such as *Should we not tell John about the new job posting?*, which is ambiguous (though the ambiguity is apparently resolved by stress placement). The interpretation of the semantics for such examples is currently an active research issue; see, e.g., Romero and Han (2004) and Goodhue (2019) for opposing analyses of such data. Given the considerable uncertainty about the semantic action of negation in negative polar questions, we leave this particular grammatical pattern open.

such as (482a), taking the data to establish a correlation among syntactic behavior, scopal possibilities, and configurational representation that can be tidily summarized as in (483):

(483) a. VP extractability and ellipsability, wide scope for negation, and complement status for *not* are correlated.
       b. Failure of VP extraction and ellipsis, narrow scope for negation, and adjunct status for *not* are correlated.

But there is reason to believe that this correlation lacks any kind of generality. To begin with, note that with modals such as *must* and *should*, narrow scope is perfectly compatible with VP extraction and ellipsis possibilities:

(484) a. If the party wants you to not vote in this election, then vote in the election you must not.
       b. I know John wants you to vote in this election, but you really should not.

Data of this sort make it clear that if we assume Kim and Sag's configurational test for extraction and ellipsis possibilities, there is no one-to-one correlation between the "height" of *not* in the clause on the one hand and the scope of negation with respect to the clausal proposition on the other. Narrow negation scope does not necessarily entail a configuration in which *not* is an argument of the modal.

Nor is it clear that ellipsis is restricted to wide-scope negation contexts. As we have just seen, complement *not* on Kim and Sag's account can sometimes correspond to the same narrow negation that adjunct *not* is supposedly restricted to. But in the case of *can/could*, the distinction is supposed to be clear: adjunct status always corresponds to narrow-scope negation in such cases. The problem is that data such as (485), with only a narrow-scope negation reading available, is accepted by all native speakers of English we have consulted:

(485) I know everyone's putting pressure on you to vote in this election, but you could always NOT.

The presence of *always* with wide scope over the *but* clause proposition effectively privileges the narrow scope interpretation of the negation here—a major contraindication to Kim and Sag's analysis, because the *could/can* ellipsis facts are the main empirical support for the correlation of configuration with scope in English. In view of (484) and (485), it is difficult to see any hard predictions that support the configurational analysis: if narrow-scope *not* in *can/could* examples is an adverb, cases such as the latter example pretty much force the conclusion that the prohibition of adverbial remnants in VP ellipsis is a false generalization, at least as far as *not* is concerned—which then leaves no clear distributional distinction allowing us to distinguish the alleged two configurations that Kim and Sag argue are both needed. Both adverbial and complement *not* support ellipsis, and complement *not* can scope low as well as high. The same conclusion of course follows more directly if *not* is not an adverb but a complement everywhere.

It does not appear, then, that there is any robust factual basis for assuming anything other than a single combinatorics for *not*, whose narrow-scope interpretation is derivable as a theorem from its single higher-order entry, interacting with the polarity properties of the associated modal. Accordingly, the analysis we provide directly posits only a single tecto type for *not*, with alternative scoping possibilities corresponding to two different versions of the negation operator—the higher-order lexical entry and the lower-order sign derivable from it by the Hybrid TLCG proof theory.

9.5 Conclusion

It will be useful at this point to take stock of our results. Starting with the empirical motivation for higher-order modals, we have shown that the only lexical entries we need for the modals are the higher-order ones and that the analysis of VP ellipsis and pseudogapping from chapter 6 does not need to be modified in any way to license VP ellipsis and pseudogapping in examples involving higher-order, wide-scoping modals. Furthermore, a higher-order version of the negation operator *not*, of the same type (modulo the polarity features) as the higher-order modals, accounts for the idiosyncratic behavior of the modals vis-à-vis the scope of negation via the polarity-marking mechanism incorporating the analytic ideas of Iatridou and Zeijlstra (2013).

Readers familiar with the phrase structure grammar tradition may find the higher-order entry for the modal auxiliaries we have posited somewhat bewildering and unnecessarily abstract. For such readers, we would like to point out that, though seemingly abstract and complex, our proposal has at least the following three properties which we take to be highly desirable. First, it extends more straightforwardly to the puzzling (apparent) scope anomaly data in Gapping and Stripping. Second, our approach is parsimonious in that it requires only the most general form of the entries for modals and negation to be posited in the lexicon to account for their various complex scopal properties. Third, our approach is in fact closely related to the analyses of auxiliary verbs in the lexicalist tradition in that alternative signs for these auxiliary verbs that correspond to the lexically specified entries in lexicalist theories fall out as *theorems* from the higher-order ones in our setup. We take our approach to belong to the same broad tradition as other lexicalist theories, but if our analysis of auxiliaries (and other phenomena we have presented in this book) still appear somewhat alien, that may ultimately reflect different views about the appropriate level of abstraction from the empirically observable data that a theory of grammar should embody. Whatever one takes to be the right answer to this question, we believe we have at least offered an interesting enough alternative to be worth pursuing seriously.

10 On Functional Constraints on Extraction: The Status of Island Constraints

In examining the range of arguments and counterarguments for various approaches to the analysis of the grammatical patterns surveyed in previous chapters, readers will likely have been struck by the frequency with which appeal is made in the literature to supposed facts about islandhood. This is unsurprising: most analyses of coordination and ellipsis in mainstream generative grammar posit covert structure (though the details often differ considerably). Islandhood has long been regarded as the gold standard for arguments on behalf of specific configurations, based as it is on specific locality conditions that filler-gap linkages must satisfy—conditions which can be invoked as evidence for specific configurations. The critical assumption here, of course, is that islandhood is actually a reflection of purely *syntactic* conditions on locality—an assumption which has been predominant from an early stage of generative grammar research, and one shared very widely not only across phrase structural frameworks until relatively recently but also in parts of the CG research community. Thus, we find in both Combinatory Categorial Grammar (cf., e.g., Steedman 2000, 2012) and the Displacement Calculus, a version of TLCG (cf., e.g., Morrill 2010, 2017), the premise that the CG combinatory formalism must be expanded to capture island effects.

Nonetheless, the premise that island effects are entirely (or even primarily) structural in their origin has, during the past twenty-five years, been increasingly abandoned by many theorists. The significance of this general change in research practice for the approach advocated in this volume can hardly be overstated: it can now no longer be taken for granted that, for example, the null hypothesis for the appearance of island-like effects in patterns of ellipsis is the presence of covert syntactic configuration in the clause displaying such ellipsis. In the first part of this chapter, we provide an overview of the history of syntactic accounts of island effects and summarize the current controversy regarding the status of these effects in the grammar. We conclude that the alternative accounts that take island effects to be non-syntactic are more promising than the traditional syntactic view of island effects. Based on this discussion, in the second part of this chapter, we assess the validity of specific arguments made in the literature for analyses of (subtypes of) coordination and ellipsis that crucially invoke islandhood data. This critical review reveals that even if one accepts the premise that islandhood is indicative of specific phrase structural configurations, in almost all cases, such arguments are empirically defective: there is extensive counterevidence for the data that are supposed to support a specific configurational analysis. This leads us to the conclusion that the true explanations for the empirical patterns (or tendencies) first observed by the proponents of structural analyses are more likely to lie elsewhere.

10.1 The History of Syntactic Island Effects

10.1.1 Ross's Constraints: CNPC, CSC, Sentential Subject, and Left Branch Constraints

Early on in the modern history of grammatical theory, Chomsky (1964) noted data suggesting that *wh* and related extraction phenomena cannot occur in certain contexts, of the kind illustrated in (486), and proposed to account for it by what he called the A-over-A principle, given in (487).

(486) a. John discussed [your concerns relating to Mary's rash statements].
       b. *Which statements did John discuss [your concerns relating to __]?
       c. [Whose concerns relating to Mary's rash statements] did John discuss __?

(487) [I]f the phrase X of category A is embedded within a larger phrase ZXW which is also of category A, then no rule applying to the category A applies to X (but only to ZXW).

This formulation is, of course, far too general; data such as (488) show that (487) is empirically untenable:

(488) a. John came across [a remarkable new book about a nineteenth-century author].
       b. That's the author that John came across [a remarkable new book about __].

Examples such as (488b) are hardly obscure or dodgy. Nonetheless, another three years elapsed before the inadequacy of Chomsky's account was clearly demonstrated in the literature and an alternative set of proposals offered to account for a much larger range of data than had been previously considered. Ross (1967) provided the first detailed consideration of supposedly syntactic conditions on extraction phenomena, listing a number of specific phrase structure configurations prohibiting any linkage between displaced material and the gap site originally occupied by that material. These configurations became widely known, following Ross's phrasing, as *syntactic islands*.

Probably the most influential of Ross's proposed constraints was the *Complex NP Constraint* (CNPC), intended to explain the distribution of data displayed in (489)–(492).

(489) a. Mary bought a book which John wrote for MIT Press.

b. *Which publisher did Mary buy a book which John wrote for __?

(490) a. I believe Mary's promise to debug the program.

b. *Which program did you believe Mary's promise to debug __?

c. *I'll show you the theorem prover that I believed Mary's promise to debug __.

(491) a. I became aware of the rumor that John had worked for Mary.

b. *Who did you become aware of the rumor that John had worked for __?

c. *The critic who I became aware of the rumor that Mary had challenged __ to a duel entered the room.

(492) a. John is too unreliable to keep his promise to debug that theorem prover.

b. *Which theorem prover is John too unreliable to keep his promise to debug __?

On the basis of facts such as (489)–(492), Ross formulated the restriction summarized in (493), which he called the Complex NP Constraint.

(493) **Complex NP Constraint:** Nothing can be extracted out of an NP where the gap site is under S in the configuration $[_{NP} \ldots S \ldots]$.

The CNPC was frequently and enthusiastically cited in the syntactic literature; for several decades after Ross's thesis appeared, the only remaining issue seemed to be whether or not his formulation was sufficiently general. For much of the history of modern syntax, the "default" position has in fact been that it is not and that the facts motivating the CNPC can be shown to fall out from a more general condition called Subjacency, which encompasses a number of phenomena that Ross treated separately from the CNPC or did not address at all.

In contrast, the condition that Ross labeled the *Coordinate Structure Constraint* (CSC) has for the most part been regarded as a stand-alone phenomenon from the outset. It comprises two quite separate conditions:

(494) **Coordinate Structure Constraint**

a. *Conjunct Constraint:* Conjuncts may not be extracted.

b. *Element Constraint:* No element may be extracted from a proper subset of the conjuncts in a coordination.

The Conjunct Constraint was intended to account for facts like those in (495).

(495) a. I like raspberries and papayas in fruit salad.

b. *What do you like raspberries and __ in fruit salad?

c. *What do you like __ and papayas in fruit salad?

d. *What do you like __ and __ in fruit salad?

In these cases, whole constituents showing up in the pre- and/or post-conjunct particle position have been extracted, leading to markedly bad results.

What distinguishes the Conjunct Constraint from the Element Constraint is that in (495), extraction of all conjuncts does not help in the least, so far as the status of the result is concerned. Compare this pattern with the pattern illustrating the Element Constraint in (496):

(496) a. I play cards with the gang and go to night classes on alternate Thursdays.

      b. ??/*Who do you play cards with __ and go to night classes on alternate Thursdays?

      c. Who do you play cards with __ and attend lectures by __ on alternate Thursdays.

      d. Florence is the city that I visited __ last year and would like to return to __ in the near future.

      e. To whom have you presented your plans __ or shown your prospectus __?

Just as with the CNPC, we find the CSC in all extraction constructions:

(497) Visit Paris, John definitely will __ this summer and I really should __ sometime next year.

(498) a. It is easy (for us) to please John and offend Mary.

      b. John and Mary are easy (for us) to please __ and to offend __, respectively.

      c. *John is easy (for us) to please __ and offend Mary.

      d. *John is easy (for us) to please Mary and offend __.

The restriction imposed in (494b) is often referred to as the *Across The Board* (ATB) condition: a gap in a coordinate structure anywhere entails that an extraction dependency holds in *every* conjunct in the coordination, regardless of the category of the mother. In the examples of the CSC given above, the conjuncts were all VPs. But note cases such as the following:

(499) a. Who does John like (*Ann) but Mary always criticize __?   (S *and* S)

      b. What is John worried about __ and troubled by (*the tax audit)?

                                                           (AP *and* AP)

      c. Which painter did John buy a book about (*Victor Hugo) and a biography of __?   (NP *and* NP)

      d. Who did you carry messages to (*John) and from __?   (PP *and* PP)

We see in all these examples the effect that Ross aimed to capture via the ATB requirement: extraction is permitted in all of these cases as long as each conjunct hosts a gap linked to the same filler.

The third constraint Ross lists in the core chapter 4 of his dissertation is the *Sentential Subject Constraint* (SSC), which can be simply stated as follows:

(500) **Sentential Subject Constraint:** No constituent may be moved out of a clausal subject.

This condition can be illustrated via the examples in (501):

(501) a. *I know which people [s that John invited __] bother you.
     b. *Who do you suspect that [s inviting __] was a bad idea?
     c. *Who do you think that [s (for us) to invite __] would be a mistake?

Ross did not in general regard extraction from a subject as ill-formed in itself but rated all examples in which a gap appears in a subject with clausal structure as uniformly bad.

Finally, Ross posited the *Left Branch Constraint* (LBC), which had the specific intent of blocking the extraction of an NP appearing on the left branch of its mother NP— essentially, a prohibition on extracting possessor NPs as in (502).

(502) a. *Whose did you buy [NP __ book]?
     b. *John's I bought [NP __ book].
     c. *John's was too expensive to buy [NP __ book].

10.1.2 Island Constraints Following Ross (1967)

One striking aspect of how syntactic theory developed over the decades following Ross's watershed dissertation is the way in which the generalization of one of the four constraints he proposed, namely the CNPC, came to dominate the search for increasingly abstract and supposedly general principles of syntactic well-formedness. The main goal of this line of research was to link the conditions on extraction to supposedly separate grammatical domains, such as anaphora and coreference, with the SSC eventually assimilated to a subcase of the Subjacency Condition that Chomsky (1973) proposed to account for the breakdown of filler-gap connectivity in the configurations specified in the CNPC. There have also been efforts to derive the LBC as a consequence of various principles posited in later developments of transformational grammar. The CSC, in contrast, has for the most part been treated as a stand-alone restriction unconnected to more fundamental principles.

10.1.2.1 Principles and Parameters: Subjacency and weak vs. strong islands Chomsky (1973), the next major development in the theory of constraints opened up as a research area by Ross (1967), recast the CNPC in more general terms as a locality condition on movement defined with respect to a certain class of category types. In earlier work, transformations had been taken to apply in cyclic fashion in both clausal and nominal domains, whose respective maximal projections, $\bar{S}$ and NP, were therefore identified as "cyclic nodes," and it was just these nodes—an apparent natural class—which defined the locality domains for movement. Chomsky's proposed reanalysis of the CNPC is the condition in (503), which he called *Subjacency*.

(503) **Subjacency:** In the structure $[_\alpha \ldots [_X \ldots C \ldots] \ldots]$, α cyclic, no extraction rule moving a category C out of X can apply unless C is subjacent to α, that is, embedded no more than a single cyclic node below α.

(503) has the status of an analytic primitive in connection with a revision of the phrase structure of clauses in which the Comp node (which hosts words such as *that*, *for*, and *if*) is a sister to the uncomplementized clause S. Certain other conditions that Chomsky proposed in this paper imposed conditions which suggested that this Comp node could act as a gateway through the barriers to movement imposed by those conditions but was only available to *wh* phrases; these, in turn, once in Comp, could *only* move to a higher Comp node. This restriction, according to Chomsky, accounted for the fact that (504) is ill-formed, since the lack of a Comp node associated with the NP means that *who* must move from its position in the lowest Comp through the immediately dominating $\overline{S}$ and then directly across NP (both of which are taken to be cyclic nodes under the theory of the transformational cycle generally assumed at that time), violating Subjacency:

(504) *Who did he believe the claim (that) John saw ___?

As Chomsky noted with specific reference to (503), "in this way we can explain many of the examples that fall under the complex noun phrase constraint" (Chomsky 1973, 104).

But in fact, on the assumptions in Chomsky (1973), the Subjacency condition appears to mispredict dramatically, since Ross's key example (505), which he had invoked in his argument against Chomsky's earlier A-over-A constraint, is likewise incorrectly ruled out under (503):

(505) What books does the government prescribe [NP the height of [NP the lettering on [NP the covers of ___]]]?

The reasoning here is the same: *what books* must pass through three NP nodes in order to reach Comp, in clear violation of (503). While Chomsky argues that (506) supports the Subjacency condition, he acknowledges that there appears to be a conflict with cases such as (505) but says nothing about the empirical challenge to Subjacency posed by (505) beyond the observation that "I see no obvious explanation for an apparent difference in degree of acceptability."[1]

---

1. As made clear in later work by Robert Kluender (1998), discussed below, there is indeed an obvious difference between the two examples, viz., the level of referential specificity carried by the extracted *wh* phrase. Suppose we replace (506) with (i):

(506) *??What do you receive [$_{NP}$ requests for [$_{NP}$ articles about __]]?

Yet despite the fact that the empirical basis for the Subjacency condition provided in Chomsky (1973) is not just sparse but empirically dubious, it was widely accepted among theoreticians as preferable to Ross's CNPC, largely, it seems, on the basis of its greater generality and abstractness. Further wrinkles involved changes in the assumptions about which English categories embodied that same property. In particular, it was recognized that if one took S, rather than $\bar{S}$, to be the clausal bounding category, then the following configuration fell negatively under the scope of Subjacency,

(507) [$_{\bar{S}}$ wh [$_{S}$ ... [$_{\bar{S}}$ X [$_{S}$ ... __]]]]

where X's occupancy of the position under Comp has the effect of blocking the wh phrase's movement to that position en route to the matrix Comp. This is in fact the description of a class of examples exemplified in (508):

(508) a. *What did you wonder who John gave __ __?
       b. *Where did you figure out when John put the receipts __ __?

In these and similar cases, a wh phrase occupies a Comp node through which a subsequently moved wh phrase would need to pass en route to its final position in the structure.[2] The data pattern in (508) was taken to be an instance of something called a "wh island," which, by replacing $\bar{S}$ with S among the set of bounding nodes in English, was automatically reduced to just another consequence of Subjacency.

Further research on what Chomsky began to call "bounding theory" came from the work of Rizzi (1980) and others, who presented evidence that could be understood to support the variability of the nodes which count in any given language as having the bounding property with respect to Subjacency. The limited freedom of languages to determine which nodes counted as bounding nodes was historically perhaps the major influence leading to the concept of parameterization: universal grammar as a set of

---

(i) Which natural disasters do you receive requests for articles about __?

Structurally, there is no difference between (i) and (506) in relevant respects, and the lexica in the extraction domain are identical in the two cases, but (i), in marked contrast to (506), is close to impeccable. The properties of the respective extractees themselves constitute the sole difference. This shows that whatever the source of the ill-formedness in (505) and (506) might be, it cannot be an attribution of "bounding" status to NP nodes. Also, while Chomsky (1971, 1980, 1981, 1982, 1986b) repeatedly refers to the A-over-A constraint as though it were not just a viable but generally accepted hypothesis, it is plainly falsified by the data set in Ross's thesis, which includes (505). See Levine and Postal (2004) for discussion of some of the implications involved.

2. There is an alternative derivation in which the higher wh phrase moves first, passing through the lower Comp before moving to the higher one, but this would entail the wh in the lower position to replace the trace left by the first wh movement, which was generally assumed to be ruled out as a possibility in transformational grammar (though it is difficult to find a principled argument in the literature undergirding this assumption).

underspecified principles containing parameters with certain possible settings. The child then sets the value of each parameter on the basis of the positive data s/he is exposed to.

The picture of "bounding theory" that had emerged by the end of the 1970s proved relatively stable until the appearance of *Barriers* (Chomsky 1986a), in which it became considerably more complicated. In particular, the notion "barrier," which corresponded to the bounding nodes of earlier work, was no longer completely fixed in advance for the movement of any constituent, but rather depended for its status on the extraction path followed by that constituent prior to encountering the potential barrier. *Barriers* provides an intricate and in places somewhat opaque set of definitions, whose crucial content is given in the following passage (Chomsky 1986a, 14–15):

> We first define *blocking category* (BC) as in (25) and then define *barrier* in terms of BC as in (26):
>
> (25) γ is a BC for β iff γ is not L-marked and γ dominates β.
> (26) γ is a barrier for β iff (a) or (b):
>   a. γ immediately dominates δ, δ a BC for β;
>   b. γ is a BC for β, $\gamma \neq$ IP
>
> We understand γ in (25) and (26) to be a maximal projection, and we understand *immediately dominate* in (26a) to be a relation between maximal projections (so that γ immediately dominates δ in this sense even if a nonmaximal projection intervenes). In case (26a) the category γ inherits barrierhood from a BC that it dominates; in case (26b) γ is a barrier intrinsically, by virtue of its own status as a BC.

L-marking refers to the relationship of lexical selection: X L-marks Y if X is a lexical head and Y is a constituent which saturates one of X's valence requirements; IP corresponds to the early GB assumption that an Infl node was the head of the clause, so that what was written "S" in previous work was actually to be analyzed as IP, the maximal projection of Infl. The point of (26b) is that, while other blocking categories automatically count as barriers for movement, the IP node only becomes a barrier by "inheriting" barrierhood from a daughter (blocking) category.

The best way to see how Chomsky applies (25) and (26) to the characterization of islandhood is to take two contrasting examples: extraction from a subject NP and extraction from an object NP. So far as the first is concerned, since NP is not L-marked, it is a blocking category, and since all blocking categories except IP are automatically barriers, NP is also a barrier. Thus, by Chomsky's (26a), IP is also a barrier for anything originating within the subject NP. Hence any constituent originating within the subject which moves to the nearest privileged landing site for *wh* movement crosses two barriers and is therefore, under Chomsky's finer-grained characterization of Subjacency, in "2-subjacent" violation of bounding theory. An object NP, on the other hand, is L-marked by the head of its VP, so that IP does not inherit barrierhood from anything, and thus no barriers are crossed by the extraction—at least at first glance. Similarly, in the case of extraction from a relative clause attached to a nominal head, a *wh* phrase internal to that clause can move unproblematically to its Comp node; but the CP above it is both a blocking category (since it is not lexically selected) and an inherent barrier, and the NP above the CP inherits barrierhood from the latter. Hence, movement out of the relative clause crosses two barriers and therefore incurs a major bounding theory violation.

But the above scenarios omit a critical detail: the same line of reasoning appears to make *any* extraction from IP illicit for the same reason as extraction from a subject: VP is, after all, no more L-marked than its NP subject is, and hence by (25) is a blocking category for anything it dominates; hence by (26b) is a barrier for anything it dominates. But there is a special escape hatch that allows such extraction after all: the movement

(509) $[_{VP} \ldots \alpha \ldots] \rightarrow [_{VP} \alpha [_{VP} \ldots t_{\alpha} \ldots]]$

is permitted via adjunction, and since, according to a novel interpretation of domination introduced in *Barriers*, not all the "segments" of the VP containing α actually dominate it, the VP as a whole does not dominate it. Thus the only maximal projection dominating α at this point is the IP itself, which is a blocking category, but now not a barrier, and so movement of α out of IP is now permitted. Why then cannot a constituent originating under the subject NP node, or within a relative clause attached to a nominal head, adjoin to NP as its first move and so escape IP and NP in the same way? In effect, the answer is that it can't because it can't. Adjunction to VP is possible; adjunction to NP is not.

It is evident in retrospect that the whole development of the theory of islandhood in the two decades between Ross (1967) and *Barriers*, originally predicated on the need to derive Ross's descriptive characterization of island environments from more general and abstract fundamental principles, had instead culminated in an extensive set of stipulative conditions and *ad hoc* exceptions. The use of adjunction to eliminate dominance relations where such relations would otherwise block legal movements and similar add-on mechanisms are certainly far more abstract than Ross's conditions. But they do not emerge from a simple set of fundamental principles any more than his do. The theory of islandhood in *Barriers* actually becomes considerably more ramified and intricate than we can detail in the space available, but the upshot can be summarized as follows: the "murky" questions that Chomsky wished to address in *Barriers* did not receive answers in which foundational simplicity and naturalness were much in evidence. One can in fact plausibly read the ready acceptance of the Minimalist framework within a decade after the appearance of *Barriers* as a sign that few researchers within the theoretical syntax community felt much would be lost by, in effect, scrapping the elaborate superstructure of the *Barriers* framework and starting again more or less from scratch.

10.1.2.2 The Empty Category Principle (ECP) Immediately after Ross's dissertation appeared, work by David Perlmutter (1968, 214–215) pointed out yet another perplexing restriction on English extraction. Perlmutter's examples included the data in (510):

(510) a. What did he say that Laura hid __?
b. *Who did he say that __ hid the rutabaga?
c. Who did he say __ hid the rutabaga?

As (510a) shows, there is no general problem with extraction from a clause with a *that* complementizer. And there is no problem with extraction of subjects, as (510c) itself makes quite clear. The problem arises just when the filler is linked to a subject gap position following a complementizer. This phenomenon became widely known (and is still typically referred to) as the *that-trace effect* (or *that*-t effect), although it also arises when subjects following *if* and *whether* are displaced (*Who did you wonder if/whether __ would get the job?*). For a decade or more after it was discovered, the *that*-t effect was taken in much influential work to be yet another primitive condition, a kind of "surface filter" on extraction which just had to be assumed as part of the grammar of English, with no obvious deeper source.

A line of thinking which began in the early 1980s seemed to suggest, however, that such a source might well exist. The details are complex, but the general idea was that a trace cannot just appear anywhere. It has to occur in a context in which it has a particular relationship to a selecting head or, as a secondary possibility, in a configuration which *resembles* head-selection contexts in the right way. For example, in a structure such as (511), which will be part of the representation of the sentence *I wonder which book you reviewed*, the head V is in the right position, as the left sister, to be a lexical selector of an NP complement.

(511) [s [NP which book] [s you [v reviewed] [NP *t*]]]

Whether or not this selection actually takes place, the "left sister" configuration was taken to correspond to special licensing properties that made the appearance of a following trace legal. But literal sisterhood wasn't necessary. For various reasons, it was assumed at this time that the following configurations defining structural relations between a lexical head X and a selected complement YP as in (512a) were at some abstract level equivalent to the more distant relationship in (512b), characterizable as instances of a single notion of *government* under the right circumstances (with bolded text indicating the constituents in the government relation), depending on what the intervening node Z is.

(512) a. [XP ... **X YP**]
b. [XP ... **X** [Z **YP** ...]]

For example, in the case of (513a), the complement of *expect* is assumed to be an infinitive clause with an accusative subject, as in (513b), under standard transformational assumptions.

(513) a. I expected her to get the job

b. expected [$_S$ *her* [$_{VP}$ *to get the job*]]

The subject of such clauses is in a parallel relationship to YP in (512a), since in, for example, *I expected her at 9:00 a.m.*, accusative case also appears. It was understood that accusative case assignment was determined by a lexical head in a government configuration with an NP, with both cases in (512) as subspecies of that configuration.[3] The configuration in (512b) was further assumed to subsume the relationship between a moved constituent and lower traces in Spec, although in this latter case X does not have the status of a selecting head.

This last point bears in a crucial way on analyses seeking accounts of the *that*-t effect at a deeper level than the simple surface filter account assumed through the late 1970s. Such analyses started from the premise that one or the other of the configurations in (512) had to hold if YP were a trace. For example, in (514), we have the trace in a properly governed position:

(514) Who$_i$ did you expect t_i to get the job?

There is an evident problem with this approach, however: it is clear that the subject position of *finite* clauses does not satisfy the restrictions on Z in (512b). We do not, for example, get *I expected him would get the job*. Yet extraction from finite subject position, as we have seen in (510), is unproblematic as long as the complementizer *that* is not present. Hence, examples such as (514) are actually misleading; if being properly governed is necessary for traces to appear, simply being in the position of YP in (512b) must not in itself guarantee proper government.

Transformational theorists working in this early-to-mid-1980s framework, therefore, made a further assumption. In the kind of analysis of filler-gap linkage assumed, as we have seen, from Chomsky (1973) onwards a constituent in a certain position moves in a series of steps, always upward and to the left, appearing in some "protected" position on the periphery of the clause and then moving up/leftward again, leaving a trace behind. The result is a chain of movements from one protected position to a higher protected position, and the typical structure of filler-trace or trace-trace linkages along this chain is displayed in (515):

---

3. A critical aspect of this analysis was the assumption that while subjects of embedded finite clauses are "shielded" from government by an external head via an intervening clausal boundary node ($\overline{C}$), infinitival complement clauses either lose this node by deletion or never possess it in the first place. The subject of infinitival clausal complements to heads such as *expect* are therefore subject to government by those heads.

(515) $[_S XP_{i_3} [_S \ldots [_S \mathbf{t}_{i_2} \ldots [_S \mathbf{t}_{i_1} [_S \ldots \mathbf{t}_{i_0} \ldots]]]]]$

The idea is that the relation between hierarchically adjacent traces in this configuration, such as the bolded pairs $\langle \mathbf{t}_{i_{n+1}}, \mathbf{t}_{i_n} \rangle$ in (515), or between the filler and its highest trace, bears *some* relation to the configuration in (512b), enough that it can be seen, at a quite abstract level, as an instance of the same tree-geometric relation depicted in (512b). And, just as in (512b), much depends on just what intervenes between the lower trace and the structure higher up. In particular, if the "landing site" for the movement leaves the higher trace in a position where a complementizer is present, it is stipulated that the lower trace is separated from the upper trace by a barrier which nullifies the connection between the two traces, and the movement fails. If this rather elaborate story were correct, then we would have an account of why the structure in (510b) is ill-formed when *that* is present: the presence of *that* was assumed to interrupt the linkage between the filler and the trace, with the resulting configuration failing the requirement that the "proper government" relationship must hold between traces on the one hand and either the filler or a higher trace left by the filler on its upward movement path. Note that the presence of the complementizer does not block extraction from the object position, since object NPs satisfy "proper government" by being in the privileged configuration with respect to its lexical selector via (512a); thus, examples such as *Who does John think that Terrence should hire t?* are correctly licensed.[4]

But now a new problem arises: adjuncts can freely move through higher clauses to filler positions, even when a clause marked with *that* intervenes:

(516) a. When $[_S$ do you suppose $[_S$ that **t** John will leave **t** on his next trip]]?
       b. How fast $[_S$ would you say $[_S$ that **t** Mary can expect to run one hundred meters **t**]]?
       c. Tuesday, $[_S$ I don't think $[_S$ that **t** we're doing very much of anything **t**]].

In all of these cases, the movement chain of the fronted filler passes safely through a complementizer-marked clause, yet the examples are good. The reason cannot involve licensing in the structure (512), since adjuncts do not appear as selected elements. These data appear to be clear counterexamples to the "privileged configuration" explanation.

To circumvent this difficulty, transformationalists added further wrinkles to the system. One quite-often-cited proposal, suggested in Lasnik and Saito (1984, 1992), consisted of two parts: (i) the stage at which adjuncts are licensed by filler-gap chains

---

4. "Proper government" was disjunctively defined as either local selection by a lexical head in order to satisfy a valence requirement or a specific local structural configuration (so-called antecedent government). No convincing arguments were ever provided to suggest that these two distinct conditions represented any kind of natural class.

occurs later than the point at which arguments of the verb are licensed, and (ii) *that* is "edited out" for purposes of chain licensing before this later stage (but not until argument licensing has been determined). It follows that at the stage where the status of the adjunct chain is determined, the structure of (516a) will look like (517):

(517) When [$_S$ do you suppose [$_S$ ~~that~~ **t** John will [$_{VP}$ [$_{VP}$ [$_{VP}$ leave] **t**] on his next trip]]]?

At this point, although *that* is present in the phonological representation, it is no longer visible at the particular syntactic location where adjunct traces are checked in terms of whether they satisfy the privileged-configuration criterion. Various versions of this by now extraordinarily complex and only rather vaguely spelled out scenario appeared during the later 1980s and early 1990s, but the essential features of the approach sketched in this section are preserved in later variants. By this point, the excessive complexity and epicyclic quality of the principal syntactic accounts on offer to explain islandhood had become evident even to many of those approaching the problem from a transformationalist perspective.

10.1.2.3 Ross's constraints under Minimalism   The current Chomskian framework, the Minimalist Program (MP), officially inaugurated in Chomsky (1995), represents a dramatic break with the previous version of the Principles and Parameters architecture, with most components of the Government and Binding version that preceded it summarily removed from the analytic toolkit—a point that has been recognized both within and outside the Principles and Parameters research community. For example, Culicover and Jackendoff (2005, 93) note that "the MP lacks an account of most of the phenomena handled by GB/PPT [Principles and Parameters Theory] and other syntactic theories," citing on this point the following remark by Hilda Koopman (2000, 2), a prominent contributor to research in the Government and Binding framework:

> [C]ompared to the GB framework, the Minimalist Program led to relatively few new insights in our understanding of phenomena in the first half of the nineties. This is probably because it did not generate new analytical tools, and thus failed to generate novel ways of looking at well-known paradigms or expand and solve old problems, an essential ingredient for progress to be made at this point.

A showpiece example of Koopman's and Culicover and Jackendoff's point is the notion of government, which provided the crucial conceptual platform on which the *Barriers* framework rested and which was jettisoned completely in the MP. Elimination of government as an analytic concept rendered the notion of barriers and other components of that analysis unavailable. But the obvious need for a new source from which the descriptive generalizations originally proposed in Ross's thesis could be derived was largely unmet in the earlier phases of the Minimalist project; Chomsky (1995) mentions island phenomena only a handful of times, with no actual explicit specification of island environments in terms of the new framework given anywhere. A decade later, Radford's (2004) textbook, *Minimalist Syntax*, offers nothing that sheds any further light on the origins of islandhood. Much of the syntactic literature for a considerable period after the appearance of Chomsky (1995) gives the strong impression that syntacticians were simply taking for granted the islandhood of the standard stock of configurations from previous incarnations of transformational grammar, with little concern about just how these were to be characterized under Minimalist assumptions.

Probably the most serious effort to derive island constraints from Minimalist assumptions is the analysis offered in Müller (2010), which makes critical use of the notion of "phase," referring, somewhat ambiguously, to both a set of category types and a subsequence of operations in a derivation upon whose completion the resulting object is "transferred" to LF for semantic interpretation and PF for prosodic realization and becomes opaque to further syntactic operations. In particular, in categories which have phasal status, the complement of the head of such categories undergoes transfer to SpellOut, leaving only the head itself and its specifier(s) syntactically active. For example, simplifying considerably, a transitive verb V may undergo the Merge operation with a DP to yield a VP, which in turn serves as the argument to an abstract "light causative verb" v. Successive applications of Merge give rise to the structure in (518).

(518) $[_{vP}$ DP$_2$ $[_{v'}$ v $[_{VP}$ V DP $]]]$

In order to project this structure, Müller makes the innovative proposal that Minimalism incorporate the argument-saturation specification typical in categories in HPSG and CG. On this view, (518) is built up by saturating a DP argument requirement in V (notated in Müller (2010) as V$\langle$D$\rangle$); the resulting Merge is then $[_{VP}$ V DP $]$. The VP constituent so derived then saturates the VP specification of the light verb v, and finally v's last-in DP requirement is satisfied by a DP which is Merged into v's Spec position, giving rise to the structure in (518). A further derivation step adds T$\langle$vP$\rangle$, with an unsaturated vP argument requirement, and Merge then gives rise to the structure in (519).

(519) $[_{TP}$ T $[_{vP}$ DP$_2$ $[_{v'}$ v $\boxed{[_{VP}$ V DP $]}$ $]]]$

The boxed material in the last stage of the derivation represents the portion of the structure which has been transferred to the PF interface of the grammar and is no longer available for syntactic operations. Note that the saturated phasal head v and its specifier remain outside the box, notating their continued syntactic accessibility to processes dictated at higher levels of structure as the derivation proceeds. Under standard MP assumptions, this accessibility persists until the point at which the vP in (518) is itself part of a structure which is transferred to the syntactically opaque interface domains. The derivation outlined for (519) will be part of the syntactic history of an ordinary English sentence such as *John saw Mary.*

Given the fact that argument lists have been part of nontransformational frameworks from the beginning, it might seem that they add little in the way of explanatory resources that could be brought to bear on the origin of islandhood. In Minimalist analysis, however, certain additional mechanisms are available which Müller exploits for this purpose—in particular, the treatment of extraction as an instance of valence satisfaction. In many MP analyses, *wh* movement is a possibility dependent on the presence of what is commonly referred to as an EDGE feature in the specifications of the phasal head *v*. This feature, sometimes written [*wh*-P(eriphery)], will on some versions of Minimalist syntax be a freely added specification on *v*, in effect licensing an "extra" specifier position arising from the movement of the transitive object *who*. Müller adapts these features to his account of islands, treating them literally as valence specifications, displayed as an HPSG-style list, licensing "internal Merge" operations in the same way that *v*'s VP and DP argument features license ordinary syntactic structure building via "external Merge," based on material in the numeration.

Permitted cases of extraction, such as *Who did John think that Mary criticized?*, point to the *wh* word's escape from the lower VP complement to *v* at some point prior to the transference stage exhibited in (519). An edge feature must therefore be present in *v*'s valence list at that point, allowing a *wh* phrase in the object position to reMerge as the specifier to *v*—a position from which it will be syntactically accessible to subsequent reMerges, that is, movement to a still higher Spec, even after the subsequent transfer of *v*'s VP complement to the SpellOut interface.

This general approach to extraction appears in principle somewhat perverse, given the island facts (as assumed in mainstream syntactic theorizing over the past half century). The material which becomes syntactically opaque at the end of each phase is the complement to the phasal head; the specifier of that head is still syntactically active. A *wh* phrase contained in the former can in principle become trapped there via LF/PF transfer, while the same phrase contained in the specifier is still accessible to the movement-triggering features added during successive applications of Merge. In other words, the default situation is that the complements of *v* are predicted to be more likely to have island status than the specifier of *v* which becomes the subject of the sentence after raising to [Spec, T]. Thus, the phase-based approach to syntactic islands appears to fly in the face of the universally observed pattern that subjects are more difficult to extract from than complements, all other things being equal.

Müller's proposal offers, however, a detailed set of premises which are claimed to correct this anomaly and yield what has been called the Condition on Extraction Domains (CED). The CED, introduced in Huang (1982), essentially posits a unitary explanation for the putative prohibition on extraction from subjects and adjuncts based on the distinction between complements and non-complements of a selecting head. Objects and other valents of a verb are thus extractable, but dependents which do not qualify as directly selected arguments are not. The key assumptions that Müller makes, which supposedly achieve the needed result, are the following:

1. The order of valence satisfaction is strictly determined by stacks, or lists, of features borne by all heads (with later-satisfied features written to the left of any that must be saturated earlier);

2. "edge" features—*wh* phrase attractors—can be added freely to phrasal heads (which Müller takes to include all category types), as supposedly required by languages with multiple *wh* extraction to the same CP;

3. but only while these heads are still syntactically active, that is, have not had all their arguments saturated; and

4. when an "edge" feature is added to a head's list of valence features, it is added just to the right of the top of the list—that is, as *v*'s penultimate argument specification—and hence must be saturated before the head's specifier requirement.

Specifiers are then the arguments that saturate the "top" specification in this list and hence are Merged with their selecting heads as the very last step in the saturation of the latter. The result of these assumptions is that as long as the specifier argument of *v* is not saturated, a *wh*-attracting edge feature can still be legally added. The steps involved that underwrite such a derivation will then be something along the lines of (520):

(520)   a. $[_{vP} v[\langle DP \rangle] [_{VP} V \ DP \ ]] \overset{by\ 2-4}{\Longrightarrow}$
         b. $[_{vP} v[\langle \ DP, wh\text{-}P \rangle] [_{VP} V \ DP \ ]]$

This addition to the *v* head's valence list has the consequence (by 1) that before *v* can saturate its Spec position argument, some *wh* phrase α must be attracted to the left edge of *v'* to "clear" the *wh*-P feature; otherwise this uninterpretable feature will crash the derivation at LF. But where can α originate? Clearly, it cannot be internal to *v'*'s specifier, destined to be the subject of the sentence, since at the stage of the derivation depicted in (520b), that DP specifier does not yet exist and can only be Merged into the derivation *after* the edge feature added to *v* in (520b) has been saturated and eliminated from *v*'s argument list. Hence, the only way to complete the saturation process yielding *v*P is to move α from inside VP to eliminate the *wh*-P specification. But of course once this occurs, and the specifier DP is then added to form *v*P, no further edge features can be added, since now *v*'s valence list is completely saturated and *v* is inert, meaning no further edge features can be added, as per 1. Hence, nothing internal to *v*'s specifier—which as noted will surface as the subject of TP—can be moved.

   In effect, under Müller's analysis, extraction from subject position faces a kind of catch-22: by 1 no content can be instantiated in subject position till the penultimate edge feature specification has been saturated, but after that, instantiating such content in *v*'s Spec position deprives any *wh* phrase within that content of an escape hatch to the edge, since, by 3 no new edge features can be added at that point. Müller's conclusion appears to be that the only alternatives are either to add an edge feature and move material out of the VP (exclusively) or to saturate all of v's arguments and not add an edge feature, with nothing moving out. No matter which choice one makes at this point, all subjects thus wind up displaying island properties—as has been standard doctrine at every phase of transformational grammar following the appearance of Chomsky (1973).[5]

But the second option—saturate v without adding any edge features to its argument list—has, as Boeckx (2012) points out, a rather different possible outcome from the one Müller envisages. Suppose that, instead of inserting a [wh-P] feature into v, we simply saturate the DP argument of v with a constituent which happens to contain a wh phrase, call it $wh\beta$, notating this DP specifier as DP$_{...\beta...}$. Nothing in Müller's proposal blocks this move, which simply represents satisfaction of the v head's specifier valence requirement by a phrase such as *a painting of which mountain* and which by 4 will yield the structure in (521):

(521)   [$_{vP}$ DP$_{...\beta...}$ [$_{v'}$ $\boxed{v \text{ [}_{VP} \text{ V DP] }}$]]

The derivation can freely proceed as sketched earlier. It is true that movement to the edge of vP is prohibited at this point. Suppose, however, that we introduce a functional head T from the numeration, but, prior to Merging it with the vP argument on its valence list, we add an edge feature, as allowed by 2, so that the head has the form T[$\langle$DP,wh-P,vP$\rangle$], allowing it to combine first with vP, then with a filler, and finally with its own specifier DP as the last-in argument, per Müller's proposal. The result is the structure in (522):

(522)   [$_{TP}$ T$\langle$DP,wh-P$\rangle$ [$_{vP}$ DP$_{...\beta...}$ $\boxed{v \text{ [}_{VP} \text{ V DP] }}$]]

In order for the derivation to yield an acceptable input to LF, the edge feature in T must be canceled—but this can now be achieved simply by moving $wh\beta$ out of DP$_{...\beta...}$ to the left edge of the TP, yielding (523):

(523) $wh\beta$ [$_{TP}$ [$_{T'}$ T [$_{vP}$ DP$_{...t\beta...}$ [$_{v'}$ $\boxed{v \text{ [}_{VP} \text{ V DP] }}$]]]]

And now DP$_{...t\beta...}$ can itself undergo A-movement into the DP specifier position of TP:

(524) $wh\beta$ [$_{TP}$ DP$_{...t\beta...}$[$_{T'}$ T [$_{vP}$ t [$_{v'}$ $\boxed{v \text{ [}_{VP} \text{ V DP] }}$]]]]

---

5. Very few analyses in the P&P tradition acknowledge the markedly gradient nature of extraction from subjects, which Ross was well aware of, and which led him to restricted subject islandhood to clausal constituents, where the restriction on movement appeared to be more sharply defined. We return to this issue in section 10.2.

As Boeckx notes, the import of this possible line of derivation is that even assuming, as per Müller's scenario, that you can't move wh_β to [Spec,vP] (since, ex hypothesi, you haven't added an edge feature to v's argument list), you can *still* carry out unbounded extraction from the subject position by simply waiting till the next operation of Merge with an edge-argument-seeking head. In fact, exactly such a derivation must be involved in the extraction *of* subjects, which in the absence of a preceding complementizer is typically unexceptionable. It seems, then, that free instantiation of edge features on functional heads, cited by Müller as necessary to allow multiple *wh* fronting as reported in much of the literature over the past two decades, winds up making it very difficult to enforce subject islandhood.

The consequences for Müller's proposal are thus quite drastic. As Boeckx (2012, 66) points out,

> invoking the PIC [Phase Impenetrability Condition] *alone* cannot account for the Subject Condition. For that to be feasible in a PIC-based story, the external argument should be included in the transfer domain, but that would only happen if the vP *in full* were transferred upon merger of T. (emphases added)

In short, once a phase head is completely inert—that is, there are no valence or other features triggering syntactic operations left to discharge—the *whole* phase would be transferred to the interface, not just the head's complement. This at least would put complements and subjects on an equal footing, so that the final step in the derivation would then be not (522) but (525):

(525) [$_{TP}$ T⟨DP,wh-P⟩ ⟦ [$_{vP}$ DP. . .$_\beta$. . .[$_{v'}$ v [$_{VP}$ V DP]]] ⟧]

Thus, even if T contains a feature attracting a lower *wh* phrase to [T,Spec], it would not be able to reach inside the now opaque vP to a target constituent within the specifier. But this of course means that nothing else could move either. On Boeckx's scenario—in effect, a reductio of Müller's proposal—a *wh* phrase within the VP complement will move to the [Spec,vP] position, awaiting its chance to move to the Spec of TP and finally to [Spec,CP], but that chance will never come: as soon as vP is Merged with T, it becomes syntactically opaque, having undergone transfer to the prosodic interface, and anything that was within it, even in its Spec position, is now inaccessible. The rather undesirable result is the prediction that there are no extraction phenomena.

Given that in this case the cure seems to be worse than the disease, we have to conclude that this latest attempt to derive subject islandhood from general principles of the current version of the P&P framework is no more successful than previous efforts.[6] In any case, the CED only accounts for a portion of Ross's original constraints. Presumably, the supposed prohibition on extraction from relative clauses would be an instance

---

6. And it is obvious that the same is true of adjunct-internal *wh* phrases, notwithstanding Müller's (2010, 46) observation that

of Müller's adjuncts-as-specifiers analysis (see footnote 6), but the ill-formedness of extractions from complement clauses within complex NPs, for example, does not seem to receive a natural account from either the standard CED or Müller's phase-based derivation of it based on the interplay of edge features with other aspects of the already highly elaborate syntactic machinery provided by the Minimalist Program.

On the whole, then, it is difficult to see the Minimalist effort to derive island effects as natural consequences emerging from the foundations of syntactic theory as any more successful than earlier attempts to achieve that objective. Far from providing conceptual and analytic resources which make sense of the diversity (and, as has become increasingly obvious, the variability) of island effects, the current mainstream grammatical architecture appears to have given up the chief tools employed in its previous avatars to capture these effects, without providing effective replacements: specified syntactic configurations are excluded in the definition of island boundaries, even in the relativized form of the *Barriers* framework, but no plausible alternatives have been proposed and generally accepted within the research community built on Chomsky (1995) and its elaborations. Rather than subsuming Ross's descriptive characterizations of island environments under deep, natural principles, restrictions on extraction have taken on the appearance of a series of new epicycles attached to previous, already overly complex characterizations of island configurations. In the sciences generally, this sort of situation is typically taken as a warning that the research strategy leading up to it has been on the wrong path and needs urgent—and drastic—rethinking.

10.1.3   Challenges to Syntactic Islandhood

It is therefore not particularly surprising that, within the past decade and a half, a fundamental shift in perspective has become increasingly evident in syntacticians' attitudes toward constraints of the kind discussed above. This new line of thinking breaks decisively with the assumption that the prohibitions on filler-gap connectivity sketched above are syntactic in nature. It now seems clear that the three decades following the appearance of Ross's thesis have not provided anything like confirmation—or even

---

[t]he barrier status of adjuncts follows immediately if we assume that adjuncts are to be reanalyzed as last-merged specifiers of special functional projections (see Alexiadou 1997; Cinque 1999). The reasoning is then identical to that given before for subjects.

No actual argumentation is provided to motivate the assumption that adjuncts are components of "special functional projections," or to document their syntactic parallelism with other syntactic objects that are generally assumed to be specifiers; rather, the primary motivation for this treatment of adjuncts seems to be a need to provide some generality for the elaborate and otherwise special-purpose machinery proposed earlier in the paper to account for a single island environment. For a more recent Minimalist analysis of adjunction that urges an analysis in which complements and specifiers, which are introduced into a derivation by Merge, are radically distinguished from adjuncts—which are *not*—see Hunter (2015). There appears to be little or no current acceptance among Minimalists for the identification between adjuncts and specifiers that Müller's argument here depends on.

an increase in plausibility—for the position that such prohibitions, to the extent that they apply at all, arise from restrictions within the combinatoric system itself. On the more recently developed approach to the data, the unacceptable (and sometimes uninterpretable) sentences in question are syntactically well-formed. That is, nothing is *structurally* deficient about them; rather, the problems that arise are due to independent (but occasionally interacting) sources. The ill-formed examples can be shown either to violate restrictions imposed by some non-syntactic part of the grammar (e.g., prosody, semantics, and pragmatics) or to incur costs that have little to do with the grammar directly, but rather with the nature of psychological mechanisms (depending, for example, on certain kinds of memory) required to process linguistic information in real time. Such processing events are easily derailed—possibly to the point of failure—by certain kinds of interference and complexity. On this view, it is the latter set of interacting factors, rather than any kind of prohibitions on structures, which give rise to the ill-formedness previously attributed to configuration-based constraints.

10.1.3.1   Island effects via processing: Kluender (1998, 2004); Chaves (2013); Chaves and Dery (2019)   The far-reaching reassessment of islandhood just alluded to was in no small measure due to the work of Robert Kluender, whose innovation takes as its point of departure a well-known effect called *center embedding*, arising from the repetition of specific structures underlying the form of a certain kind of relative clause illustrated in (526).

(526) The man [$_S$ the host knew __] left the room.

Clearly, there is nothing wrong with this structure (the name *center embedding* comes from the fact that the relative clause is embedded after the nominal subject head and before the VP). But when this structure is iterated—that is, when the relative clause subject itself contains a center-embedded structure—things get bad very quickly. Thus, a typical paradigm illustrating the gradual decline in acceptability is displayed in (527):

(527) a. The man left the room.
       b. The man the host knew left the room.
       c. The man the host the intelligence people investigated knew left the room.
       d. The man the host the intelligence people the reporter interviewed investigated knew left the room.

(527b) is still fine, but (527c) is considerably more difficult to process without a very deliberate use of intonation to make clear the intended structure; and (527d) is still worse. Such examples were known at quite an early stage of syntactic research (see, e.g., Yngve [1960, 460], where center-embedding data are referred to as examples of "regressive structures") and became a somewhat clichéd piece of evidence that whether or not some string of words was acceptable only indirectly implicated its status as a possible output of the rules of the grammar. The assumption for many years has been that there is something about the nature of center-embedding structures which taxes the short-term memory resources available to keep track of linguistic structures. In the case of (527), these effects make it difficult for the hearer to link particular nominal structures in the string preceding the verbs to the associated gap site. The particular configuration in (527d) requires a certain correspondence pattern—crossing dependency—to hold between the nominal heads and their respective correlated verbs and gaps. Crossing dependencies are independently known to invoke processing difficulties in other domains—an often-cited example is the difficulty of interpreting patterns of crossing filler-gap linkages addressed by Fodor's (1978) Nested Dependency Condition.

All this was old news even in the 1970s. But Kluender's remarkable results during the 1990s made it clear that much of the thinking about center-embedding constructions had missed possibly the most important point: these structures could be improved significantly by certain purely lexical adjustments. A hierarchy of intelligibility is shown in (528), where we follow Kluender's (1998) usage in notating relative acceptability with inequality markers, so that X < Y indicates greater acceptability for Y as compared with X.[7]

(528) a. The woman [the man [the host knew __] brought __] left.
      b. < The woman [that man [the host knew __] brought __] left.
      c. < The woman [a man [the host knew __] brought __] left.
      d. < The woman [someone [the host knew __] brought __] left.
      e. < The woman [someone [he knew __] brought __] left.

                                                    (Kluender 1998, 254)

The improvement between the first and the last of these examples is quite striking. Yet nothing about the structure has changed. What has happened to yield this unexpected improvement?

In passing from (528a) to (528d), note the progressive reduction in the definiteness of the NP subject in the highest relative clause. *The man* conveys uniqueness more strongly than *that man*, while *a man* indicates no uniqueness at all. In (528d) we find

---

7. Kluender attributes the discovery of such examples to Thomas Bever (1970). But careful inspection of the latter source fails to reveal any data pattern along the lines of (528). Bever did note that the acceptability of center embedding is variable to some extent and reflects lexical choice, but the examples he provides have no bearing on the kind of effect reflected in the acceptability gradient in Kluender's paradigm. What is critical about that set of judgments is not only the fine-grained gradient effect Kluender notes but, most significantly, the relationship of this gradient effect to referential specificity—the same variable that, as we discuss directly, is responsible for the dramatic amelioration of island effects. It is this connection—that amelioration of a clearly processing-based effect is faithfully mirrored in the judgments of putatively syntactic island conditions—that constitutes the initial empirical basis for Kluender's breakthrough, and it appears that the crucial paradigm in (528) which establishes the linkage between the center-embedding facts and the gradience of island effects represents an original observation by Kluender himself.

a completely indefinite NP, *someone*, from which all we can infer is that an unspecified human being is being referred to. Finally, in the final example, the subject of the lower relative clause is replaced by a pronoun *he*, carrying far less information than the definite NP *the host*. Cumulatively, what has happened is that the intermediate NPs between the highest NP and the lowest gap site, into which this NP must be interpreted, have been in some sense diminished in terms of their information content, in particular, their referential specificity. This reduction has the concomitant effect, of course, of increasing the referential specificity of the filler which has to go the furthest distance to find its gap site, relative to any intermediate filler(s) occupying positions at clause boundaries along the way.

Apparently, then, the problem with center-embedded relative clauses is not structural in essence; while there are structural aspects to it, such as the location of clause boundaries in relation to where the various NPs occur, these structural factors alone do not determine the difficulty of psychologically processing such relative clauses successfully. Rather, they only create the possibility for a high degree of difficulty in that task, depending on what else is going on, and it is that "what else" that turns out to play the critical role. The determining factor seems to be the degree of difficulty that the hearer encounters in trying to link a filler to an increasingly deeply embedded gap site, when such linkage encounters processing tasks along the way that distract the parser. If these tasks cumulatively place too much demand on limited processing resources, the speaker in effect loses track of the filler in topmost position, making completion of the linkage impossible. Linkage of fillers to gap sites, in the case of center-embedded relative clauses, is thus more successful to the degree that the filler can be made more informative and its intervening NP competitors made less so.

One must bear in mind that from the outset, as already noted, the diminished acceptability/intelligibility effects in center-embedding constructions were taken to reflect facts about the mechanism by which speakers establish the relationships among parts of the sentence required for interpretation, rather than whether or not such relative clauses were sanctioned as legal by the grammar. Kluender's discoveries about the improvements in comprehensibility in these constructions were therefore altogether plausible, even expected, *if* we make certain specific assumptions. We can say in advance that the "repair" strategy exhibited in (528) makes sense on the assumption that judgments of a legal structure which is psychologically difficult to process in real time can be dramatically improved through means which have nothing to do with structural factors. Certainly the center-embedding gradient discovered by Kluender constitutes evidence for such improvement. If the same kind of gradient profile were reflected in the case of classic islandhood phenomena, then general considerations of parsimony appear to put a substantial burden of proof on advocates of a syntax-based account in which ungrammatical utterances, corresponding to structures never generated by the grammar, somehow acquire syntactically acceptable and semantically interpretable status by as-yet-unknown mechanisms. We return to this point below.

These methodological considerations have immediate relevance in the face of the data such as the following, exemplifying the amelioration effects with CNPC.

(529) a.   What do you need to find the professor [who can translate __]?
      b.   < What do you need to find a professor [who can translate __]?
      c.   < What do you need to find someone [who can translate __]?
      d.   < Which article do you need to find someone [who can translate __]?
      e.   < Which article do you need to find someone [to translate __]?

(based on Kluender [1998, ex. (12)])

Here, (529a) is a typical example of CNPC violation and, unsurprisingly, strikes the ear as extremely awkward at best. But acceptability increases gradually—and markedly—in (529b–e). Note moreover that the factors which lead to this improvement are the very same ones that yield the successful examples of center embedding in cases such as (528): acceptability gradually increases by making the intervening NPs referentially more specific ((529a–d)), and we obtain a nearly impeccable sentence (529e) by changing the finite tense to an infinitive (where the finite/nonfinite contrast is arguably a counterpart of definiteness in the verbal domain; cf. Partee 1984).

Similar patterns of improvement can be observed with many other examples as well. For example, in (530), decreasing the complexity of intervening NPs on the boundary of the lower clause (*a random assortment of tradespeople* → *anyone, friends of whom* → *whom*) leads to a distinct improvement in acceptability.

(530) a.   John, I can't think of a random assortment of tradespeople [friends of whom like __]. <<
      b.   John, I can't think of anyone [who likes __]?

Another example strongly suggesting that what's involved here is a processing-based effect is the contrast in (531).

(531) a.   Euthanasia is a topic which$_2$ I can never find anyone who$_1$ I can argue with t_1 about t_2 . <
      b.   Euthanasia is a topic$_2$ I can never find anyone$_1$ to argue with t_1 about t_2 .

Note that here, (531a) is already fairly acceptable, despite the fact that it involves a CNPC configuration. This already casts considerable doubt on the syntactic status of the CNPC. But the example can be improved still more by replacing the finite modal to an infinitive and removing the two explicit relative pronouns (*which* and *who*), as in (531b). Since (531a) is already a good (enough) example, the increased acceptability in (531b) can be nothing other than a processing effect.

In short, CNPC fits the profile not of a structural condition (blocking the licensing of word strings which violate that condition) but of a performance effect which inhibits the processing of a legal sentence (reducing its comprehensibility by interfering with the identification and retention of possible reference targets and preventing the latter from surviving long enough in the processing task to be linked to the filler).

But the explanatory reach of these discoveries extends well beyond the case of CNPC. Let's reconsider the *wh* island cases we considered earlier, where few would argue that (532) is an acceptable example.

(532) Who did you wonder what Mary said __ to __?

(533) a. Who did you wonder what you should say __ to __?
     b. Who did you wonder what to say __ to __?

(534) a. Which of the people at the party did you wonder what you should say __ to __?
     b. Which of the people at the party did you wonder what to say __ to __?

(535) a. John is someone who I never know what I should say __ to __.
     b. John is someone who I never know what to say __ to __.

Acceptability increases gradually in (533)–(535), and in each pair, the infinitive version is somewhat better than the finite clause version involving a modal. This gradual increase of acceptability is completely expected on an extragrammatical account of island effects. There are two key factors involved: pragmatic felicity (of the sort we discuss in more detail in the next subsection) and processing factors of the sort discovered by Kluender (such as referential specificity).

Note first that the content of the question is much more natural in the examples in (533) than (532) (where one can imagine contexts in which the sentence might be uttered much more easily for (533) than for (532)). The slight improvement in the infinitive version (533b) over the finite modal version (533a) can be attributed to something analogous to referential weight in the verbal domain: while the modal form is already less "definite" than simple finite past tense (where the latter is about some specific past event, whereas modal statements are about possible situations), infinitives (with no overt subjects) arguably carry still less specific content. (534) improves on (533) by making the extracted material referentially heavier, and (535), involving relativization, improves still more by eliminating any presuppositional content associated with an interrogative, which increases processing burdens (invoking extra accommodation process unless appropriate contextual background is already provided).

The acceptability of these island violation examples and the gradual effect of amelioration observed in (533)–(535) correlating with factors independent of syntactic structure seriously call into question the elaborate machinery that has standardly been posited in the syntactic literature to account for the alleged ungrammaticality of such structures and point instead to a non-syntactic treatment in terms of performance and pragmatic factors.

It is of course true that such cases were not entirely unmentioned in the mainstream generative literature, and it is instructive to consider how they were approached. Examples such as the contrast between (533b) and (534b) were recognized in, for example, Pesetsky (1987), who argued that they reflect a difference in *D-linking* ("discourse-linking") properties, with D-linking defined as a restriction of the possible answers to the question to members of some contextually salient set. D-linking was subsequently adopted in Cinque (1989) and Rizzi (1990), but as Kroch (1989) pointed out, the critical distinction underlying the notion was semantically not particularly well-founded: a supposedly non-D-linked "bare" *wh* word such as *who* in (533b) "*does* constrain answers to membership in fixed sets. The sets are only rigidly (i.e., semantically), and very broadly, rather than contextually, and more narrowly, defined" (emphasis added). More fundamentally, it is not clear why an essentially semantic/pragmatic distinction should allow any kind of exception to a purely syntactic restriction.[8]

In subsequent work, Kluender extended his processing-based account of CNPC and *wh* islands to subject islands, arriving at the conclusion that "the same general processing factors will apply in a slightly different way to subject islands to render them difficult-to-impossible to interpret" (Kluender 2004, 102). The essence of his proposal is that a subject island—necessarily already a "heavy" structure with significant referential content (since it must contain enough material to constitute a context for the extracted filler)—imposes the kind of processing costs that, without amelioration, create islandhood effects similar to those observed in relative clauses, *wh* islands, and other cases covered in Ross's (1967) thesis. Kluender presents evidence from a wide range of data sources—adult and child language production research, as well as work with elderly speakers on processing difficulties—that establish that among the various possible sites for phrasal constituents to occupy, subject position presents special parsing difficulties quite independently of whether or not its occupant contains a gap. The result is, predictably, a strongly negative assessment of subject-internal gaps. However, as Kluender (2004, 491) demonstrates, "Subject islands can in fact be made

---

8. A model that incorporates gradience in acceptability in the architecture of the grammar itself may provide a suitable framework for explicitly modeling such interactions between semantic and pragmatic factors and the combinatoric component of syntax (see, for example, Keller [1998] and the papers collected in Fanselow et al. [2006]). While such approaches seem to generally share the same motivations and goals with processing-based accounts of island constraints advocated by Kluender (1998), Michel (2014), Chaves (2013), Hofmeister and Sag (2010), and others, it is currently an open question whether/to what extent this type of gradient architecture of grammar is compatible with the processing-based accounts discussed in the present chapter (the latter of which seem to generally assume a more traditional distinction between narrow grammar [violations of whose constraints are strictly categorical] and the processing component), either at the specific level or at the more general, foundational level.

more transparent to extraction" through the same kind of techniques shown in Kluender (1998) to materially improve CNPC violations (eliminating referentially heavy subjects, or indeed any subjects at all, in the island context; changing finite [i.e., semantically definite] tensed clauses to infinitive clauses; increasing the linear distance between the gap and the filler, and so on). One observation of particular interest in Kluender's findings is that "[semantic] association of the filler with . . . the main assertion of the current sentence, i.e., the main clause predicate," as well as the gap site, typically results in significant improvement in the acceptability of extractions from subjects—a point that is taken up and developed in Chaves (2013) and Chaves and Dery (2019).

In his 2013 paper, Chaves begins by reprising the parsing model in Kluender's 2004 paper, observing that, in the face of complex subjects, "the speaker's memory resources are strained sooner in the sentence, and longer, since those resources are not available for processing the remainder of the sentence," so that "filler-gap dependencies in them are harder to maintain in working memory without additional support" (Chaves 2013, 14). But these considerations in themselves do not explain why processing gaps within subjects should become so much easier in parasitic gap constructions or why certain rather short examples (such as *What did the owner of __ sneeze), involving minimal processing burdens, are nonetheless judged severely ill-formed. Chaves's (2013, 28–29) solution hinges on the following premise:

> Given that processing complex subjects is cognitively more strenuous than processing complex objects, and that certain pragmatic conditions restrict the use of filler-gap dependencies in general, . . . speakers avoid the use of sentences with subject-internal gaps. This leads to extremely low (near zero) frequency. In turn, extremely low frequency may cause the language processor to develop a conventionalized processing heuristic: expect gaps to be in the verbal structure, not in the subject phrase. . . . This gapless subject expectation cannot be seen as a grammatical condition. Precisely because it is a parsing expectation rather than a grammatical rule, it can be dampened by the presence of prosodic, pragmatic and contextual cues that signal the correct parse.

Based on this background, Chaves documents a wide range of acceptable subject gaps, noting the effect of three factors mentioned by Kluender in distinguishing such cases from ill-formed examples: (i) prosodic cues, (ii) referential specificity, and (iii) a relevance relationship between the filler and the gap.

On this type of account, parasitic gaps enable the establishment of connectivity between the filler and the subject gap in two ways. On the one hand, the parser's expectation-based search for a nonsubject gap site—that is, one internal to the VP—is rewarded. On the other hand, as Chaves (2013, 37) puts it, "multiple gaps in close proximity . . . reactivate the same filler," strongly facilitating the backtracking necessary to link the filler to the subject gap venue.

The line of reasoning pursued by Kluender, Chaves, and a number of other theorists based on a range of experimental results thus provides a major step toward reducing island effects to the interaction of largely extragrammatical factors. Nonetheless, a number of other lines of inquiry have been pursued during the same recent phase of investigation. For example, in the processing-based accounts we have summarized above, the role of pragmatic and semantic factors in the processing-based work is largely confined to the influence of such factors in enabling or inhibiting the course of parsing in an island environment. But in other work, these factors are argued to independently contribute effects which account for the apparent islandhood of various classes of extraction prohibitions. This line of research, to which we now turn, was largely pioneered in research by Kroch (1989), highlighting the role of speech act presuppositions, pragmatically determined implicatures, and other kinds of felicity conditions on discourse that are altogether independent of syntactic configuration.

10.1.3.2 Island effects via discourse pragmatics: Kroch (1989); Kehler (2002); Kubota and Lee (2015); Culicover and Jackendoff (2005); Oshima (2007)

Kroch (2007) argued that in the case of ill-formed data such as (536), a failure of presupposition rather than any kind of syntactic condition was responsible for blocking the "long movement" of an amount-quantified NP:

(536) *How much did Bill wonder whether to pay __ for the book?

The essence of Kroch's proposal is that the question in (536) presupposes the existence of a specific dollar figure that Bill had in mind as a possible purchase price for some book and was wondering whether to pay exactly that amount for it. Kroch suggests that such a state of affairs is pragmatically very implausible, hence unlikely to occur to anyone hearing (536) as part of whatever discourse background was involved. He shows that in contexts where such presuppositions are actually part of the pragmatic context, interrogatives such as (536) become markedly better, even unexceptionable. This analysis should probably be credited for opening what has become a very active and widely accepted line of explanation for many island effects—one which takes them to be emergent phenomena, reflecting a basic conflict between the interpretation associated with extraction on the one hand and the broader semantics of the constructions from which the extraction has occurred on the other.

A particularly persuasive illustration of this line of analysis is the variety of evidence pointing to the origins of the CSC as a fatal deviation from contextual expectations not unlike the presupposition failures associated with interrogatives which Kroch posited for *wh* extraction of amount or quantity *wh* phrases. Certain coordinate structures support extractions which fail to apply to all the conjuncts in a coordinate structure. Consider, for example, the following cases:

(537) a. This is the house that I plan to dress up as a water use inspector and break into __.

    b. How many political debates can you listen to __ and not become completely
       cynical?
    c. This is the cereal that I plan to eat __ for breakfast every morning and live
       to be 100.

These data were discovered in the 1970s and '80s. See, for example, Schmerling
(1972), Goldsmith (1985), and Lakoff (1986), which offer quite different accounts of
the possibilities reflected in (537). On the one hand, Goldsmith assumed the correctness
of Ross's syntactic formulation of the CSC but proposed that examples such as those in
(537) reflect not coordination but subordination; on the other hand, Lakoff argued that
the data in (537) are acceptable because they reflect a single complex predication on the
extracted element. In Lakoff's view, the CSC could not be a purely syntactic constraint,
since it evidently can be overridden by conditions which he characterized as semantic
and hence cannot be structure-dependent; rather, it must be reformulated as a semantic
requirement that, in effect, only a unitary predicate can apply to an extracted referent,
where a condition on a propositional function being unitary is that all of its parts are in
some respect relevant. *To listen to X and not become completely cynical* denotes a unitary predicate, in Lakoff's view, because what is being predicated crucially depends on
the satisfaction of the truth conditions on both conjuncts. In contrast, (496b) displays a
propositional function comprising two conjuncts, the second of which—expressing the
fact that the hearer goes to night classes on the days when he doesn't play poker—is
irrelevant to the definition of the set of individuals with whom the hearer plays poker
on the other days. Thus, the acceptability of (537) and the unacceptability of (496b)
are said to reflect the difference between the two clauses with respect to the relevance
of the denotation expressed by the gapless conjunct vis-à-vis the propositional function
carried in the clause containing the extraction site.

   Despite the persuasiveness of Lakoff's examples—which do indeed make a syntactic
source for the CSC appear very unlikely—the concept of relevance that he calls on and
its relation to the technical notion of the predication relation are somewhat elusive,
as noted by Kehler (2002, 111). Without making this point more precise, Lakoff's
proposal as it stands faces the charge that it is devoid of predictive power. Indeed,
Kehler's (2002) own account, which links exceptions to the ATB pattern to a wide range
of other phenomena in the syntax-semantics interfaces of Gapping, ellipsis, anaphora,
and the semantics of tense, could be viewed as offering a particular line of refinement
of Lakoff's by making more explicit the role of *coherence* in determining the well-
formedness of discourse.

   The essential point of Kehler's account is that extraction out of coordinated VPs have
to obey constraints imposed by the coherence relations between the two conjoined constituents. Building on David Hume's philosophical work, Kehler identifies three basic
coherence relations: Resemblance, Contiguity, and Cause-Effect. In the case of Re-

semblance, one can identify sets of participants in two situations as bearing the same semantic roles with respect to either the same predicate (*resemblance*) or to predicates which are in some clear sense opposites. The Cause-Effect coherence relation holds between two situations where one is, roughly speaking, a necessary precursor to the other. Contiguity between situations is a relationship in which one is the occasion, pretext, or noncausal precurser to the other.

The badness of (538) (= (499a)) is then straightforward.

(538) Who does John like (*Ann) but Mary always criticize __.

Here, there is no inherent semantic relation between the two conjuncts, either in the Cause-Effect type or the Contiguity type. The use of *but* as the conjunction marker suggests a contrastive relation, which is a type of Resemblance relation. In this case, extraction out of a single conjunct is prohibited since the presence of a filler-gap linkage in one conjunct versus an absence thereof in the other conjunct breaks the "equal" status imposed on the two conjuncts by the Resemblance discourse relation. Thus, when the discourse relation is Resemblance, filler-gap relations into a coordinated structure must apply across the board.

In contrast, consider (539):

(539) This is the house that I plan to dress up as a water use inspector and break into
       __.

The specific relationship between the first and second clauses is something we might call "precursor/outcome": the implication is that a particular disguise (water use inspector) will expedite an illicit activity (a house break-in), which makes the sentence coherent as an instance of Contiguity. Unlike the Resemblance relation, Contiguity does not require the two conjuncts to have "equal" status to each other. This means that asymmetrical extraction does not violate any constraint and hence is predicted to be perfectly acceptable, which indeed is the correct prediction.

A similar account goes for cases involving the Cause-Effect relation, such as the following:

(540) This is the cereal that I plan to eat __ for breakfast every morning and live to be
       100.

Here, the underlying relation that makes the whole sequence coherent is that the habit described in the first clause is the cause which (supposedly) brings about the consequence described in the second clause. Just like the Contiguity relation, the Cause-Effect relation does not require the cause and the result to have an equal status (if anything, they are in an asymmetrical relation in that the result would never obtain without the cause). Thus, asymmetrical extraction is fine with the Cause-Effect relation too.

A useful follow-up to this last point is that any nonstructural change which alters the interpretation possibilities of a clausal discourse environment from an unequivocally parallel interpretation to a means-end, cause-effect, or some similar nonsymmetrical interpretation will allow the same structure to support non-ATB extraction. Compare, for example, the following:

(541) a. I caught a bus last week and attended a lecture this morning.

       b. ??*Which lecture did you catch a bus last week and attend __ this morning?

(542) a. I caught the bus and attended a lecture this morning.

       b. Which lecture did you catch the bus and attend __ this morning?

Suppression of the first conjunct's temporal adjunct *last week* makes it possible to plausibly construe the VP *catch the bus* as identifying an event which is something like the means to the end of attending the lecture, thus ensuring the possibility of non-ATB extraction. For a more detailed discussion of this kind of contrast in possibilities, see Kehler (2002, 129–132).

A further prediction follows. If what non-ATB extraction hinges on is (non-)parallelism in the semantic relations between the coordinated constituents, rather than the particular meaning of the coordinating particle, we would expect to see the same correlation between parallel readings and ATB extraction on the one hand and between nonparallel readings/non-ATB extractions on the other in the case of conjunct particles other than *and*. Certainly, if this pattern were restricted to *and*, one might well suppose (as does, e.g., Steedman [2012, 95], among others) that the syntactic behavior noted by Kehler is a mere idiosyncrasy of a single lexical item. However, as shown below, the patterns predicted by Kehler's account hold across all cases of syntactic coordination, regardless of which conjunct particle is chosen. We list some examples with the disjunction particle *or* and the "contrastive" conjunction particles *but*/*yet* in (543)–(546) (the slightly reduced acceptability for *yet* is possibly due to its somewhat stylized "learned" register requirements).

(543) a. John will go to Seattle this week or visit Chicago next week.   (parallel)

       b. ??*Which city will John go to Seattle this week or visit __ next week?

(544) a. Chris will have to be polite to the guests or face a stern talking-to.

                                         (nonparallel, cause-effect)

       b. John and Mary are the people that Chris will have to be polite to __ or face a stern talking-to.

(545) a. ??*What did John have __ for lunch but ate soup for dinner?   (parallel)

       b. ??*Who did John vote for __ but Mary voted for Obama?   (parallel)

(546) a. Aspirin . . . THAT'S what I went to the store but forgot to buy __!

                                             (nonparallel)

    b. What are we to make of the fact that it was this prescription medicine that John took __ but/(?)yet got sick anyway? (nonparallel)

    c. The situation arose because there were a number of problems that John vaguely knew about __ but at that point was just wandering around in his usual foggy state. (nonparallel)

The contrast here between the parallel non-ATB extractions and the nonparallel ones is striking. Again, then, we find that non-ATB extraction becomes completely acceptable when the intended reading is based on a nonparallel semantic relation between the conjuncts and that this pattern is far from restricted to coordinations with *and*. Two nice examples from actual text are the following:

(547) [He] regards the limitless abundance of language as its most important property, one that any theory of language must account for __ or be discarded.

(Campbell 1982, 183)

(548) Penitence abroad is little worth. There where we live lie the temptations we must defeat __, or perish. (Reade 1869)

We therefore have a solid basis for taking the CSC to reflect the interaction of the semantic effect of extraction as the establishment of a predication relation, with the pragmatic understanding of the basis for the relationship between the conjoined clauses. This is, again, not a configurational account but a *functional* account, based on how speakers make sense of sets of propositions rather than on phrase structure hierarchical relations. The content differs from the functional account Kluender gives for various island constraints, but what the two analyses have in common is that syntactic factors play a distinctly secondary role in these restrictions on the speaker's judgments.

    Significant support for Kehler's reinterpretation of the CSC as a semantic/pragmatic effect comes from certain analogous patterns in Japanese and Korean relative clause and *wh* question constructions presented in Kubota and Lee (2015). What distinguishes the Japanese-Korean paradigm from the English case is that, on the one hand, the syntactic relationship between the two clauses is clearly some kind of subordination, and on the other, the gaps involved not only fail to correspond to *wh* extraction but are themselves optional. That is, there is a version of the *wh* question construction in which no gap at all appears; rather, the relationship is one of construal. Yet, just as in English, the ATB requirement correlates with the parallel coherence relation, and the suspension of that requirement depends on the involvement of other coherence relations instead. See Kubota and Lee (2015) for details (showing, inter alia, that any attempt to treat the Japanese-Korean facts via a covert movement analysis encounters insuperable empirical problems and will in addition render the CSC empirically vacuous).

    Finally, we note that from time to time one encounters assertions that the counterexamples which are taken to show the nonexistence of the CSC as a syntactic effect are suspect, because they are all restricted to cases of conjoined VPs rather than full-fledged clauses. The examples in (549), displaying acceptable non-ATB extraction from conjuncts, show that this claim is empirically unfounded.[9]

(549) a. [Which guy]$_i$ did they say [$_S$ [$_S$ they would hire __$_i$] and [$_S$ that would make everything all right]]?

   b. The guy who they said they would hire and that would make everything all right was Harry.

   c. How many barrels of toxic waste did he say/do you remember he said [they had dumped __ into the inlet and the Coast Guard had done nothing about it]?

   d. Which people did Ann say that Nigel had fired __ and as a result everyone came to their defense?

Here, in each case, both the gapless clause and the clause containing the gap are under the scope of *say/said*.

The foregoing remarks all pertain to the Element Constraint, where the evidence seems extremely strong that non-syntactic factors interact to yield the ATB effects noted in the literature. But what of the Conjunct Constraint, which is far stricter, blocking *any* extraction of a complete conjunct at all? This phenomenon has occasionally been appealed to as an example of the inadequacy of functional approaches (sometimes labeled, somewhat misleadingly, as "reductionist treatments," as in, e.g., Boeckx [2012] and Ott [2014]) to islandhood; thus Boeckx (2012) cites the example in (550) as "evidence" that functional accounts cannot be the complete story of the CSC.

(550) *What does John like __ and oranges?

This assessment seems to be based on the unfounded premise that the Conjunct Constraint must have the same basis as the Element Constraint—a position for which there is neither a conceptual nor an empirical basis. It could just as well be that the Conjunct Constraint is a phonotactic phenomenon owing nothing to coherence conditions on discourse. The former possibility is in fact a plausible candidate for an explanation of the restriction illustrated in (550): Suppose, for example, that English requires all conjuncts to bear at least one nuclear stress. Such a requirement will immediately account not only for the Conjunct Constraint but the fact that conjuncts cannot consist of unstressed contracted forms:[10]

---

9. Such cases also rule out treatments of ATB counterexamples as conjunctions of a clause containing a filler-gap dependency with some other constituent type lacking such a gap.

10. This kind of prohibition is strongly reminiscent of Zwicky's (1986) discovery that the syntactic anti-pronominality of dative second objects in English, frequently invoked in the syntactic literature (see, e.g.,

(551) a. I talked to əm about safety equipment.

b. I want us and $\left\{ \begin{array}{l} \text{them} \\ \text{*əm} \end{array} \right\}$ to get along, understand?

We therefore have at least one promising candidate for a purely prosodic explanation of the Conjunct Constraint.

Still another interesting application of the line of analysis introduced by Kroch is the explanation provided in Culicover and Jackendoff (2005, 335–336) for the so-called *factive islands*, an effect alluded to (though not illustrated for extraction constructions) in Kiparsky and Kiparsky (1971), illustrated in (552).[11]

(552) a. What does Ginny think that Don bought __? >>>

b. What does Ginny regret that Don bought __?

Culicover and Jackendoff note Chomsky's "purely stipulative" syntactic treatment of this kind of difference as a possible manifestation of a syntactic difference between verbs that allow movement from S to S′. They further observe that there is an independent, purely semantic basis for the difference in well-formedness manifested in (552). Factive verbs such as *regret* presuppose the truth of the proposition expressed by their complements and therefore the existence of the event which is the clausal argument of *regret*. In the case of (552b), the use of this factive therefore creates the implicature that the event is in the common ground, so that what it was that Don bought is presumably known to both speaker and hearer. Hence, even if the hearer shares the speaker's knowledge that Ginny regrets Don's purchase of the item in question—which itself might not be the case—the fact that the speaker is querying something which by virtue of the use of the factive should be something s/he already knows the answer to (i.e., the object(s) that Don bought) makes the question distinctly anomalous.

The example in (552a) is quite different. Here, it isn't necessarily the case that Don actually bought something, only that Ginny believes that there was something Don bought, and it is perfectly possible for Ginny to hold that belief without the speaker knowing what she imagined that object to be. Hence the speaker's request for the

---

Cinque 1990; Postal 1998), is in fact explicable on the basis of what are familiar, independently needed *phonotactic* grounds; see the discussion below.

11. Szabolcsi and Zwarts (1993) offer a semantic account of factive islands as a subcase of their general theory of weak islands, where *wh* elements can only be extracted (and therefore scope wide) from contexts in which the denotation domain of the *wh* material is defined. As noted in Oshima (2007), their account has a number of analytic problems: it hinges critically, for example, on the claim that syntactic coordination of manner adverbials forms not intersections but "sums," i.e., unions, despite the fact that all semantic indications (such as entailment relations) point to the former, not the latter, analysis. They also introduce a type distinction between singleton sets and sets with larger memberships for no apparent reason other than to exclude *wh* extraction of manner predicates from contexts corresponding to non-iterable events, a point identified as a serious weakness by Schwarz and Simonenko (2018).

hearer to identify that object is pragmatically quite reasonable if there is reason for the speaker to believe the hearer to possess that knowledge.

This pragmatic account predicts that, as long as the right context is provided, acceptability of extraction out of factive islands will improve. Culicover and Jackendoff offer exactly this sort of evidence by embedding the question in a discourse context where a multiplicity of possible purchase objects is made explicit and where there is a strong implicature that the hearer has knowledge of Ginny's attitude toward these purchases that the speaker partly lacks:

(553) Yes, I KNOW that Ginny was happy about Don buying the laptop and external memory, but what I want to know is, what did she REGRET that Don bought?

Examples like (553) are, as Culicover and Jackendoff note, indeed much better than analogues along the lines of (552b).

On this account of "factive islands," the problem therefore once again arises from a question which is extremely odd given the network of background assumptions shared by the speaker and hearer. Culicover and Jackendoff show that not only island effects but a range of data exemplifying the definiteness effect, as well as certain cases of the CNPC, find natural accounts on the basis of this kind of pragmatic infelicity. A related proposal is given in Oshima (2007), which is further elaborated in Schwarz and Simonenko (2018), where the data set is somewhat expanded and refined from the Culicover and Jackendoff account; Oshima derives the decreased acceptability of manner adverbial *how* extraction from factive contexts, the absolute prohibition on *why* extraction, and the relative acceptability of spatial/temporal *wh* extraction from the basic scenario he sketches for the important minimal pair first cited in Szabolcsi and Zwarts (1993):

(554) a. (?)To whom do you know that John showed a letter?
      b. *??From whom do you know that John got a letter?

On Oshima's (2007) and Schwarz and Simonenko's (2018) approach, the ill-formedness of (554b) is essentially due to inevitable pragmatic infelicity. In a nutshell, the felicity condition on *wh* questions requires that the question has at least one true answer. At the same time, the pragmatics of question-answer exchange requires that the answer to the question be informative. And in (554b), there is no way in which these two conditions can be satisfied at the same time.

The account goes as follows. (554b) involves a non-iterable event (for any given letter, there can be only one receiving event; by contrast, with (554a), the event is iterable since one can show the same letter to different people at different occasions) under the complement of a factive predicate. This means that, due to the factive presupposition, the speaker and the hearer both know about the relevant letter-receiving event. And whoever the sender of the letter, the hearer either knows or does not know the identity of the sender. The felicity condition that there be at least one true answer to the question, jointly with the factivity the question attributes to the hearer's knowledge, requires that the hearer does actually know the identity of the sender. Assuming that the speaker is posing the question (554b) on the (usual) assumption that its felicity condition is satisfied, the speaker should also already know that the hearer knows the identity of the sender. But then, the only one answer that the hearer can give for (554b) is not informative at all with respect to what is being asked, namely, the hearer's epistemic state (which is what the *wh* question of the form "who *do you know* . . .?" is all about). Thus, whatever the discourse context, (554b) inevitably leads to infelicity, and this is why this sentence is unacceptable.

There thus appears to be a range of plausible pragmatically based research on factive islands which derives such island effects from the interaction of felicity conditions on discourse and the lexical semantics of a certain class of verbs (which properly includes those imposing a factive presupposition). This result is of course important in itself. But its broader lesson is that, as in other island effects, functional factors can induce negative judgments of acceptability that—as in the case of (554b)—are as strong as what we would expect from examples that were syntactically ungrammatical. The factive island pattern thus illustrates the explanatory potential of the discourse-based line of investigation into islandhood phenomena inaugurated in Kroch's (1989) watershed paper.

10.1.3.3   Island effects via prosody: Kandybowicz (2006, 2009)   The fate of the ECP in the twilight of the GB era represents a kind of case study of how long-held assumptions about the syntactic origins of some grammatical patterns can be drastically undermined by a few uncontroversial counterexamples and consequently abandoned in short order across much of the field. A 1993 *Linguistic Inquiry* squib by Peter Culicover (1993) sharply challenged more than a decade's reliance on the ECP to account for a wide variety of phenomena, based on its seeming indispensability in accounting for the *that*-t effect. The crucial counterexamples Culicover adduced are given in (555):

(555)   a.   Robin met the man {Op_i that/who$_i$} Leslie said that *(for all intents and purposes) t_i was the mayor of the city.

     b.   This is the tree Op_i that I said that *(just yesterday) t_i had resisted my shovel.

     c.   I asked what$_i$ Leslie said that *(in her opinion) t_i had made Robin give a book to Lee.

     d.   Leslie is the person who$_i$ I said that under no(rmal) circumstances t_i would run for president.

Such data severely jeopardize the claim that the *that*-t effect represents a failure of proper government with respect to the gap in subject position.[12] In order to preserve the ECP account of *that*-t ungrammaticality, one must assume that adverbials such as *for all intents and purposes* and *in her opinion* govern the gap in subject position. But the network of assumptions about phrase structure in the GB framework did not readily provide for a way to govern into a "canonical" position from an adjoined site. Culicover himself discusses, and rejects, various possibilities along these lines, concluding with the bleak assessment that "in view of the data discussed here it appears that the original Chomsky and Lasnik (1977) proposal for a *that*-t filter is empirically more adequate than a standard ECP-type account."

In the years following the publication of Culicover's squib, no convincing way around the difficulty based on plausible, independently motivated syntactic representations ever emerged. Inevitably, syntacticians began to suspect that the *that*-t effect is not the consequence of a dedicated syntactic principle or set of principles, but is rather a by-product of the interaction of a variety of factors, with syntax only one of the elements in the mix, and not necessarily the primary factor.

The work by Jason Kandybowicz (2006; 2009) is a good example. Kandybowicz points out a number of constructions, in addition to those noted by Culicover (1993) (and still earlier by Bresnan [1977]), which seem to at least ameliorate the severity of the effect, in certain cases quite markedly, and several other subtle aspects of the effect which point to a solution in terms of intonational properties in the relevant data. The gist of his analysis is that an empty syntactic category may not appear on the left edge of a syntactic constituent which corresponds to a phonological phrase and that, in the unacceptable cases such as (510b) (with the complementizer *that*), a complementizer falls on the wrong side of an intonational phrase boundary from a trace that immediately follows it. The effect of this prohibition is that a certain separation between *that* and the trace is necessary. This separation can be achieved in various ways, each of which contributes to the reduction of the *that*-t effect's severity. The intervening material in the kinds of data presented in Culicover's paper has the effect of moving the subject trace away from the boundary of the intonational phrase following *that* and

---

12. What is especially interesting is that data of just this sort were actually discovered a decade and a half earlier by Joan Bresnan, who mentioned them in a brief footnote in Bresnan (1977). At the time, the *that*-t effect had the status of little more than an isolated, idiosyncratic restriction, a "surface filter" as in Chomsky and Lasnik (1977). Since the effect neither followed from, nor had any deep significance for, any principles or premises taken to be fundamental at that time, Bresnan's exceptions had little theoretical resonance. By the time of Culicover's rediscovery of such examples, the status of the *that*-t phenomenon was of course quite different.

other complementizers, with the result that the syntactic and prosodic phrases are no longer in conflict.[13]

Kandybowicz backs up his argument with crosslinguistic support based on the Benue-Congo language Nupe. In Nupe, whose relative clauses behave in ways quite parallel to those in English, clausal complementizers also block extractions as in the ECP data displayed above, but there is a dedicated relative clause complementizer which can appear directly before a VP just as English *that* can in (556):

(556)   John is the kind of person that looks for trouble and then seems surprised when he finds it.

Kandybowicz demonstrates that this apparent exemption from ECP effects is predicted on his account, because in Nupe, the relative clause complementizer is *part of* the relevant phonological phrase that corresponds to the syntactic clause from which the subject has been extracted. The subject gap in the relative clause is not on the left edge of that phrase; instead, the phonology of the relative complementizer begins that phrase, and the gap follows it. Hence there is no "missing" phonological material on the left edge of the crucial phonological phrase, and the latter is well-formed. If something similar were true in the case of English relative clauses, but not *that* complements, we would get the discrepancy between the two that is at issue.

One highly suggestive fact which supports such a parallel analysis for English is that both the relative pronoun and the finite declarative complementizer with an in situ subject are pronounced in normal-paced speech with a markedly reduced vowel—[ð ət] rather than [ðæt]—suggesting that these markers have cliticized to the following word, that is, have been integrated into the phonological phrase corresponding to the clauses they mark.

(557)   a. Rocco's the guy [ðət] was here yesterday evening.

          b. I think [ðət] Rocco needs to get his story straight.

But when speakers attempt to pronounce sentences in which a subject gap in a clausal complement follows *that*, the prosody of the complementizer is typically the full [ðæt] form:

---

13. It is very tempting to speculate that there is a linkage between this proposal on the one hand and, on the other, the general approach taken by Kluender and those pursuing his research paradigm in terms of processing bottlenecks at the edges of clauses which can be ameliorated in various ways, and to see the source of the *that*-t problem in the difficulty posed by the close linkage of the complementizer and the trace for recognition of the trace *as* a gap site. It seems likely that not only the kinds of factors noted by Kluender but various others as well, including matters of prosody, play a role in expediting or inhibiting the processing mechanism's efforts to connect the filler to a site within the structure where it can receive a coherent interpretation; work along the lines sketched here ultimately is likely to lead to a general theory of filler-gap processing in which morphological, semantic, pragmatic, and prosodic factors play significant roles.

(558) *Who do you think [ðæt] likes pizza?

The contrast indicates that the marker has failed to cliticize—that is, to attach itself, as a kind of prosodic dependent—to *likes*, and so remains outside the prosodic phrase—whose leftmost element will therefore be the phonologically null gap position, and hence ruled out.

A natural first reaction to the prosodic treatment of the *that*-t effect along the lines sketched above is that something more must be involved than just "sounding wrong" in the strong negative judgments speakers form in response to *that*-t examples. But there are precedents for just such a prosodic explanation masquerading as a syntactic effect. The following kinds of data had long been taken to reflect a syntactic fact about the "second object" position associated with verbs such as *tell*, *give*, and *show*, which take two NP complements. The second of these NPs cannot be a weak (i.e., necessarily unstressed) pronoun:

(559) a. I told John the facts.

 b. *I told $\left\{ \begin{array}{l} \text{John} \\ \text{her} \end{array} \right\}$ them.

It has been assumed, for most of the history of modern syntax, that this pattern reflects a lexical property of such verbs ruling out pronouns from the second NP position (for example, Wasow [1975] cites the prohibition on weak definite pronouns in the dative object position as "well known"). A number of fairly intricate arguments have attempted to use this supposed fact about such verbs to construct claims about the nature of filler-gap dependencies. But Zwicky (1986) demonstrated that the effect in (559) had a far simpler basis. As it happens, a number of other phenomena display patterns similar to the "double object" construction exhibited in (559). What they all have in common are morpho-syntactic properties that prevent the unstressed pronoun from attaching itself phonologically to a preceding or following lexical item. They must, therefore, stand on their own as independent intonational units. Such units necessarily contain a major stress. Since the second NP in double object constructions has the status of an intonational phrase, it follows that in the normal course of things, weak definite pronouns—so called because they cannot receive normal intonational stress—will not appear in this second object position.

Zwicky's solution, which is completely consonant with standard views of intonational phrasing, eliminates what otherwise would be a very eccentric stipulative lexical restriction on a particular class of verbs. But the kind of negative judgment this prosodic violation induces is much more like what one expects from syntactic ungrammaticality. The so-called antipronominality of the dative second object position is a textbook illustration of the fact that a phonological source can have an effect indistinguishable from a syntactic failure.

10.1.3.4 Defenses of syntactic islandhood and their shortcomings The increasingly large body of evidence in favor of islandhood as an epiphenomenon of interactions among a wide range of independently attested functional factors has not gone uncontested. A range of results in experimental syntax has been offered which purportedly undermines the conclusions drawn by Kluender and other proponents of islandhood as functional in origin, as outlined in the preceding section. The major empirically driven objections to processing-based accounts of islands are given in two widely cited sources, Phillips (2006) and Sprouse et al. (2012). The thrusts of these two sources are in a sense complementary: whereas the conclusion that Phillips defends is that cognition itself, as embodied in the parser, consults the constraint pool defined by the grammar in the course of its operations, the point of Sprouse et al. (2012) is that perceptions of islandhood do not vary among subjects along the lines that processing-based accounts would lead us to expect. The findings reported in these studies seem to have been taken in some quarters as a definitive basis for maintaining the syntactic origin of islands (see, e.g., Boeckx 2012), but in fact, as more recent research has shown, there are crucial shortcomings in both of these works which make them ill-suited to serve as defenses of a syntactic view of islands. In this section we focus on what we take to be the major content of the first of these and provide our own assessment of how successful it is in rebutting the arguments for processing accounts of island effects.

Phillips (2006) reports the results of an experimental suite comprising two studies. The first of these is a kind of screening test, establishing the well-formedness of parasitic gaps and the ill-formedness of extractions from relative clauses within subject NPs, regardless of the tense of the clause. The second experiment, constituting the major contribution of the suite, uses a self-paced reading task to determine whether or not gaps are posited in the incremental parsing of extraction dependencies involving island domains, and whose methodological pivot is best explained by example. Consider the variants in (560):

(560) The school superintendent learned which high school students the proposal
$\left\{ \begin{array}{l} \text{a. to expand} \\ \text{b. that expanded} \end{array} \right\}$ drastically and innovatively upon the current curriculum
would motivate during the following semester.

Expand is optionally transitive and therefore a target for filler-gap linkage in *wh* extraction, but the semantics of the verb preclude *which high school students* as the direct object. Under an incremental processing scenario, if the parser projects a gap following *expand(ed)* which it attempts to fill with the only available *wh* NP, the incoherence of the result will force a backtracking which in effect returns the latter to storage until a semantically compatible linkage is possible. This backtracking will be reflected in a slowdown in reading times. The absence of such a slowdown might therefore be taken as an indication that the parser does not posit a gap within the subject. Phillips argues that on a strictly processing account of islandhood, the badness of unsupported filler-gap linkages into subjects entails that the parser should not be able to posit a gap within subjects under any circumstances, which would lead to the prediction that no matter what form a subject-internal "garden path" took, there should be no slowdown observed in the reading-time experiment. What actually happens is, however, quite different: while the finite version of the "spurious gap" context in (560b) indeed showed no slowdown in reading time following *expanded*, "[i]n the infinitival conditions, . . . average reading times . . . were 27 ms slower in the implausible conditions" (Phillips 2006, 812).

On the basis of these results, Phillips concluded that the parser projects gaps within subject-internal infinitival relative clauses but not their finite counterparts. This is, in Phillips's view, indirect but strong confirmation of the syntactic nature of the subject island constraint, since he saw the simplest explanation of the discrepancy as an architecture in which the parser is guided by the different statuses assigned by grammatical principles to extraction from finite and infinitive relative clauses. Thus, islandhood originates in the grammar and *determines* the behavior of the parser.

But a careful reading of Phillips's argument provides ample grounds for skepticism about his conclusion. The putative difference in acceptability between finite- and infinitive-clause-internal parasitic gaps is the indispensable empirical linchpin of his argument; if it turns out to be spurious, then obviously there would be nothing for there to be a "strictly syntactic" basis *for*. Yet at the same time that he states this difference in acceptability as an unequivocal fact, Phillips (2006, 803) acknowledges that there are clear counterexamples—the "classical examples of acceptable parasitic gaps discussed by Kayne (1983)," offering, however, no explanation for how these examples evade suppression by the grammatical filter guiding the parser.[14]

Such examples cut the ground out from under Phillips's line of reasoning; the fact that there is a subset of such examples which are uncontroversially well-formed makes it particularly difficult to maintain a syntactic constraint which suppresses their possibility. But there might still be a systematic *preference* for parasitic gaps out of infinitive contexts arising from semantic/pragmatic factors. A pointer to such factors is in fact given in Kluender (1998), as we have already noted.

Phillips's claims are, however, fundamentally undercut by the experimental results reported in Michel (2014) for *whether* islands, and most strongly and convincingly rebutted by the results reported in Chaves and Dery (2019), as discussed below. Michel (2014, 334) notes that his high-span subjects adjusted the probability of a gap down-

---

14. Phillips claims that "all of Kayne's examples . . . used relative clauses with a quantificational head NP," with further discussion of the relevance of this fact to his claims about finite clause subject extraction. In fact, it is not difficult to find examples, parallel to Kayne's in all critical respects, in which the head of the NP displays no quantification at all; see Chaves and Dery (2019) for examples.

ward when it occurred in a *whether* clause, but the experimental results still showed that an association between the filler and the gap site was posited:

> [T]he data reported in the ERP experiment indicate that both [low- and high-span] groups successfully identify the gap (P600 . . .) and associate the filler and gap (LAN . . .). . . . We simply see a difference in predictability: gaps are less predictable in *whether*-islands. Even so, when that less predictable gap is encountered, the parser still associates the filler with it, as evidenced by the post-gap LAN response in all four conditions. *Whether*-islands are unexpected, but not unprocessable.

Phillips is of course writing about subject-internal gaps and Michel about *whether* clause gaps. But on Phillips's account, a grammar-guided parser should be expected to fail to posit a gap in a *wh* island context such as a *whether* clause just as such a parse is expected to in the case of a subject-internal gap. And this prediction is strongly contraindicated by Michel's experiments: a gap site supposedly rendered unavailable to the parser because of the latter's guidance by the syntax has been shown, through extensive and careful experimental protocols, to be in fact available.[15]

The discrepancy between Phillips's earlier results and Michel's findings in his follow-up experiment naturally raises important questions about the source of this fairly dramatic divergence. Much of the answer to these questions can be inferred from the recent work reported in Chaves and Dery (2019), based on a suite of experiments probing Phillips's claims. Chaves and Dery found Phillips's conclusions wide of the mark on essentially every point, demonstrating that speakers do indeed posit and fill gaps within subject islands and that, when certain critical factors overlooked in Phillips's original experiments are taken into account in designing the stimulus examples, speakers find such data as acceptable as the uncontroversially grammatical control materials.

The difference between Phillips's finding and Chaves and Dery's basically comes down to the following factors:

- Phillips's test materials do not take into account the constructional conflict inherent in extractions from subjects. As noted repeatedly in the literature, subjects typically have the topic role of introducing old information, while extracted elements correspond to "information focus," the new or added information that is part of what is predicated *of* the topic.
- More than half of the tensed-clause embedded gaps in subject islands in Phillips's test materials were semantically anomalous in their *un*extracted variants.
- The constructional conflict is resolvable when the extracted material bears a plausible semantic/pragmatic relationship to the main predication.

---

15. This same point is reinforced by the findings reported in Chaves and Dery (2019), discussed below.

• The acceptability of subject island extractions further increases markedly with repeated exposure to such examples.

When the constructional clash noted is reduced to a minimum and the experimental subjects are exposed to several such examples, the discrepancy between normal, fully acceptable sentences and the subject island violations largely disappear. This result is documented not only for the simple extractions but for the supposedly proscribed subject parasitic gaps within tensed clauses, once the anomalous instances have been replaced by examples based on well-formed non-extraction sources.

Chaves and Dery's assessment of Phillips's study, and their own experimental results, are mirrored in the critique of the conclusions offered in Sprouse et al. about the putative support their investigation lends to the position that island effects in general reflect violations of structural constraints rather than functional factors.

The gist of Sprouse et al.'s (2012) claim is that the performance of speakers displaying a sizable range of working memory capacities show, according to certain metrics for working memory under laboratory conditions, a uniformity in processing activity with respect to island contexts which does not reflect the variation that should be expected on the basis of that range. This conclusion, they claim, runs counter to the reduction of island effects to restricted memory resources.

As noted in Michel (2014, 114), however, there are a number of problems with Sprouse et al.'s reasoning here. The most fundamental problem is that the key assumption underlying Sprouse et al.'s argument—which Michel calls the "cognitive covariation intuition" (CCVI)—is based on premises which Michel's experiments show to be empirically deficient. The CCVI is broadly stated as follows:

> [I]f island phenomena are due to working memory related processing costs . . . then individuals who have greater working memory capacities should be able to process the island violation sentences better and thus rate them as more acceptable. (Michel 2014, 105)

But as Hofmeister et al. (2013) and Michel (2014) argue, the choice of cognitive metrics that Sprouse et al. employ to test the working memory capacities of their subjects are not the right ones, testing only memory storage size and not (as in the Just and Carpenter model of working memory) active computation capacity.

Michel additionally raises a number of concerns about the statistical methods Sprouse et al. use to extract conclusions about the processing account of islands from their experimental results. Moreover, one foundational assumption they rely on—a so-called "push the limits" view that increasing processing difficulty will translate in a simple linear way into decreasing acceptability scores—is not supported by prior research on this specific correlation. In these and several other respects, Michel adduces strong evidence that the reasoning behind the Sprouse et al. (2012) conclusions was based on a number of dubious, overly simplistic premises.

In his own replication of Sprouse et al.'s experiments, Michel systematically corrects for these flaws in the experimental design: Michel's test suite uses the reading span test that Just and Carpenter themselves take to be the optimal probe for working memory, along with three others, including, crucially, the so-called memory lure diagnostic, which "provides a measure of how well participants can suppress distractors that compete with items in recent memory" (Michel 2014, 113). What emerges from Michel's much-improved test suite is the inadequacy of the Just and Carpenter model of working memory and its limitations due to storage cost. As Michel notes, his own results in themselves correspond to a trade-off between the constrained-capacity interpretations of working memory limitation on the one hand and the content-accessibility interpretation on the other, and is—along with the less-refined version of his Experiment 1 in Sprouse et al. (2012)—essentially neutral on the relationship between processing and combinatorics so far as island effects are concerned. He further notes that his own experiments do point to a relevant cognitive factor that may well be significantly implicated in island effects, having to do not with storage, as in the Just and Carpenter model, but with *processing* capacity—in particular, the ability of speakers with a higher ability to filter out distractors in real-time syntactic processing to parse long-distance dependencies. One of Michel's key points is that the relationship between processing ease and positive acceptability judgments is still too complex and poorly understood to conclude a simple linear correlation between the two.

The state of the art in the experimental syntax of islands thus, in our view, supports two conclusions which are entirely congenial to the functional view of islandhood and its origins.

- There is no evidence supporting the claim that speaker variation data in responding to island violations favor a syntactic origin for the latter. The reported facts, rather, suggest that a more fine-grained and probably more complex model of cognitive limits on processing capacity is called for.
- There is positive evidence that speakers both hypothesize and fill gaps in syntactic contexts in accordance with their probabilistically based expectations, that islandhood strongly corresponds with those expectations, and that revising them radically ameliorates islandhood effects.[16]

---

16. There is, conversely, also some reason to believe that subjects' expectations can be revised in the opposite direction, leading to perceptions of ill-formedness in constructions which other evidence suggests should be regarded as grammatical. Phillips's (2006) use of defective sources for testing subject island extractions from finite contexts is a good example; Chaves and Dery (2019, 30) observe that "because more than half of the items in the tensed condition were odd . . . it is possible that comprehenders adapted to the near-systematic oddness of the sentences in the tensed condition and simply refrained from attempting to fill gaps in that condition." Yet their results show that when the anomalous tokens are eliminated from the experimental suite, the status of the same class of examples approaches the same level of acceptability as the nonfinite relatives.

10.1.4   The Status of Syntactic Islandhood: Summing Up

The foregoing discussion has touched on only a small portion of the research on the non-syntactic sources of island effects. Nonetheless, we believe that the evidence presented to this point puts a strong burden of proof on advocates of an approach to island effects which seeks a syntactic explanation for these effects, along the lines of research in the grammatical tradition following Ross (1967) or various adaptations thereof to non-movement frameworks (e.g., Gazdar 1981; Gazdar et al. 1985; Steedman 2012; Morrill 2017). As time goes on, work along the lines described in the sources cited above, including Deane (1991), Hofmeister and Sag (2010), Gibson (2018), Culicover and Winkler (2019), and many others, has revealed a steadily widening network of independently attested extragrammatical effects sufficient to account for the classical island phenomena and other constraints that have been proposed over the past half century since Ross's thesis appeared. The comprehensive critical overview of research on islandhood during this period, Chaves and Putnam (2020), argues that upon close examination, the evidence that has accumulated against a unitary syntactically determined source of islandhood is now overwhelming.

This state of affairs has come to be recognized even by supporters of mainstream generative grammar, as attested in the following remarks in Newmeyer (2016, 207):

> The explanation of island phenomena has been a central feature of formal grammatical theory practically since its inception. However, a growing number of linguists have provided explanations for these phenomena that are not based on purely syntactic constraints. Some linguists have proposed alternative explanations that appeal to information structure or to semantic information. Others find the basis for island constraints to lie in processing: In brief, sentences that violate island constraints are difficult to parse. In the course of the last few decades, more and more formal syntacticians have concluded that an exclusively syntactic approach to islands is overly ambitious, but there is broad uncertainty about how to construct a general theory of island phenomena, or even whether a general theory is a possibility.

Against this increasingly skeptical background, we examine in the following section specific islandhood-based arguments putatively supporting the transformational analyses of coordination and ellipsis phenomena we have considered in previous chapters. We demonstrate that, consonant with the empirically problematic status of syntactic islandhood, these argument simply fail to hold up.

10.2   Islands, Coordination, and Ellipsis

The history of coordination and ellipsis analyses in mainstream generative grammar has seen frequent appeals to island effects, a fact which is hardly surprising in view of the nature of the constructions involved. In ellipsis, for example, the principal issues center on the existence of structure which has no phonological expression and is therefore only indirectly detectable. On the assumption that islands are essentially syntactic in nature, it is certainly logically possible that the effects of the deletion operation would leave any ill-formedness due to island violations unaffected, but matters are a bit more complex if, as the preceding discussion suggests, syntactic form plays only a partial or secondary role in restricting extraction possibilities. In particular, it becomes more likely that island effects in coordination and ellipsis in the literature either are spurious or can be shown to arise on the basis of independent factors not taken into account in the original sources.

In the remainder of this chapter, we revisit the movement-based analyses of coordination and ellipsis considered in previous chapters and demonstrate that the evidence based on island effects given in support of these proposals does not, in fact, stand up to closer examination. The importance of this discussion in the present context is that once the islandhood-based arguments are removed, the movement-based analyses lose perhaps the strongest basis for their validity, leaving them distinctly unfavorable in relation to the much simpler analyses that eschew covert structural representations we have already given (specific problems of these analyses that don't pertain to the issue of islandhood have already been discussed in detail in previous chapters).

10.2.1 Gapping

We begin with the island-based argument in the analysis of Gapping supposedly motivating the low VP coordination analysis. Advocates of the low VP coordination approach in one or another version have attempted to construct such an argument by invoking alleged parallelisms between syntactic island effects in extraction and in Gapping.

The unacceptability of the following examples from Johnson (2004), for example, is offered in an effort to establish the adherence of Gapping to island constraints, and hence the plausibility of the movement-based analysis (see also Toosarvandani [2013, 18] for a similar argument).

(561) a. *John wondered what to cook today and Peter ~~wondered what to cook~~ tomor-
           row.   (*Wh* Island)
       b. *John must be a fool to have married Jane, and Bill ~~must be a fool to have
           married~~ Martha.   (Adjunct Island)
       c. *I read out the order to fix the tortillas, and Mary ~~read out the order to fix~~
           beans.   (Complex NP Constraint)
       d. *Stories about Frankenstein terrified John, and ~~stories about~~ Dracula ~~terrified~~
           Peter.   (Subject Island)

However, counterexamples are easy to find. Examples such as the following, some of which are from Culicover and Jackendoff (2005), are structurally parallel to those in (561), but they seem well within the bounds of acceptability.

(562) a. [Wife of a couple discussing who decides what to cook for which meal:]
           Ok, how about this: I get to decide what to cook for LUNCH, and you, for
           DINner.   (*Wh* Island)
       b. ROBIN believes that everyone pays attention to you when you speak FRENCH,
           and LESLIE, GERMAN.
                                   (Adjunct Island [Culicover and Jackendoff 2005, 273])
       c. ROBIN knows a lot of good reasons why DOGS are good pets, and LESLIE,
           CATS.   (Complex NP Constraint [Culicover and Jackendoff 2005, 273])
       d. I don't think we need worry about John harassing us. Threats directed at ME
           would offend his *wife*, and at YOU, everyone else!   (Subject Island)

Examples like these contraindicate the supposed parallel between Gapping possibilities
and syntactic extractability (see also Repp [2009, 13] for a similar conclusion).

A note is in order here regarding speaker variability. Some readers may find the
examples in (562) not fully acceptable. While we have not done any systematic survey, we have consulted seven speakers on the status of (562a) and (562d), and the
latter was unanimously found impeccable, while the former showed some variability
in acceptability. In relation to Gapping in particular, one possible reason for speaker
variability is prosody. In all of the examples in (562), strong contrastive/parallel stress
is required on the corresponding elements in the antecedent and gapped clauses, along
with distinct but quite short pauses before the second of these elements. For example,
in (562a), *lunch* and *dinner* should be contrastively stressed, with the former receiving
high/falling pitch, and the latter, following a clipped pause between *you* and *for dinner*,
pronounced with steady mid-level pitch.

Having addressed the speaker variability issue (which may already provide part of
the answer to the following question), the next question is where the difference lies
between the (allegedly) unacceptable examples in (561) and the structurally parallel
good examples in (562). We have already provided extensive evidence to support the
position that processing, coherence, and other functionally based principles are the
source of island effects in the typical extraction contexts. It seems highly likely that
similar factors are at play in the variability exhibited by specific examples with respect
to acceptability, though we have to leave a detailed examination of this effect in the
case of Gapping for future study.

Note that there are also cases of acceptable extraction with the corresponding Gapping examples ill-formed:

(563) a. There were certain cars of which only [the windows __] were damaged in
           the explosion.   (slightly modified from Ross [1967, 242])
       b. ??The windows of the van were cracked, and of the cars, shattered.

(563a), discussed in Ross (1967) as evidence *against* a general restriction on extraction from subjects, is perfectly good. But the structurally parallel Gapping example in (563b) sounds severely degraded. This kind of example strongly suggests that the real-time interpretation of Gapping involves mechanisms that are somewhat different from those involved in filler-gap dependencies.

10.2.2 "Respective" Predication

In chapter 5, we provided a detailed analysis linking *respectively* interpretations, symmetrical predicates, and summative predicates to the effect of a single **resp** operator which, when applied to two multisets of cardinality n and a "continuation," relates the members of the two multisets in a pairwise manner with respect to the continuation, preserving the original multiset structure (so as to enable recursive applications of **resp**). This analysis involves a covert-movement-like operation, formalized via the vertical slash in Hybrid TLCG. In the literature, the interdependency between non-adjacent expressions in terms of semantic interpretation found in "respective" predication and related phenomena has sometimes been analyzed in terms of a similar nonlocal movement (or movement-like) operation (as in Barker's [2007] analysis of *same* via "parasitic scope"; cf. section 5.4.1.2) and sometimes via a chain of local operations (as in Gawron and Kehler's [2004] analysis of "respective" readings; cf. section 5.4.1.1). One might then wonder whether any empirical argument can be made for one or the other type of analysis.

There are some discussions in the literature relevant to this question, though the investigations in this domain are considerably less thorough than in other, well-studied domains such as extraction. Thus, Carlson (1987) claimed that the internal readings of *same/different* obey the same syntactic island constraints as filler-gap dependencies, but this observation was disputed by Dowty (1985) and Moltmann (1992). We concur with these latter authors. Note in particular the following cases, all of which seem to induce the internal reading for the symmetrical predicates relatively easily:

(564) a. Robin and Leslie believe that the acquisition of $\left\{ \begin{array}{l} \text{the same} \\ \text{different} \end{array} \right\}$ skill sets is crucial to success in the business world.

> (Subject Island violation on the *de re* reading)

   b. [Robin and Leslie usually agree about who's a bad singer at a karaoke party, and they both get immediately mad when such a person starts singing.] But today, something weird happened: Robin and Leslie got mad when different people started singing.   (Adjunct Island violation)

   c. The Smiths$_1$ and the Joneses$_2$ go to the same$_1$ psychiatrist and to different$_2$ psychiatrists respectively.

> (Coordinate Structure Constraint violation; Dowty 1985, 6)

Similar facts seem to hold for the "respective" reading (though so far as we can tell, examples such as (565) have not been discussed in connection with island effects in the previous literature):

(565) a. Robin and Leslie thought that studying category theory and intuitionistic logic respectively would be all that was needed for success.

(Subject Island violation)

   b. Robin and Leslie got home before the train and the bus stopped running respectively.   (Adjunct Island violation)

   c. Robin and Leslie named someone who was innocent and guilty respectively.

(Complex NP Constraint violation)

It is somewhat difficult to tell what conclusion to draw from data such as those in (564)–(565). One thing we can say is that if one takes island effects to be by-products of functional factors such as constraints on real-time processing and felicity conditions on discourse, what the above data suggest is that the processing and discourse factors which come into play in filler-gap dependencies are not the same ones which govern the interpretation of "respective" and symmetrical predicates. In the former case, island violation *does* result in reduced acceptability (but can be ameliorated via various strategies); in the latter case, island violation simply does not seem to arise to begin with, or, at least, the effects seem considerably weaker in general.[17] In any event, like the case of Gapping discussed above, a more careful investigation is needed to determine what is really going on in these data.

10.2.3 Pseudogapping

Miller (2014, 82–83) notes a variety of attested examples in which pseudogapping displays insensitivity to island restrictions (note that (566b) is a case of antecedent-contained deletion (ACD); as discussed in chapter 6, we take pseudogapping and ACD to be licensed by the same mechanism).[18]

(566) a. According to current ideas, the frothiness of space **retards the arrival of** a burst's highest-energy photons more than it does ~~retard the arrival of~~ *the lowest-energy photons.*   [Subjacency]

   b. **Bring the same kind of carry-ons** when traveling by train as you would ~~bring~~ ___ ~~when traveling~~ *by air*; you're allowed two per person.

[Adjunct Island]

---

17. Note in this connection the robustness of semantic islands, which presents yet another pattern, discussed in section 10.3.

18. Miller (2014) labels (566a) as Complex NP, but Subjacency seems more appropriate.

In order to derive these examples via movement + ellipsis, the movement operation prior to ellipsis would have to evacuate the remnant by moving it across an island.

It should be noted in this connection that, although islandhood is often invoked to argue for a movement-based analysis of ellipsis (a representative and very clear instance of this can be found in Kennedy [2003]; see chapter 8 and the discussion in the next subsection), the relationship between ellipsis and islandhood is actually much more intricate. In fact, since Ross's (1969) celebrated observation that sluicing is completely insensitive to islandhood, the literature has struggled to account for the apparent dilemma that some cases of ellipsis are (apparently) island-sensitive while others are not. One typical (and influential) explanation offered in the mainstream literature for this dilemma, a version of which can be found in Merchant (2008a), involves the "size" of the structure that undergoes ellipsis (the key idea is that as long as what's elided is "large enough," the offending island-inducing structure gets elided via the ellipsis process and thus the resultant string is well-formed).

Thus, we might conclude that, after all, pseudogapping's insensitivity to islandhood does not have any direct implication for the viability of a movement-based analysis. This is true to some extent at a general level. But there are two important points which are worth keeping in mind. First, even though island insensitivity is not a dead end for a movement-based approach, it significantly weakens the motivation for a movement-based analysis by removing a key piece of evidence for assuming covert syntactic structure. Second, the classification of island-sensitive and island-insensitive types of ellipsis should be done consistently inside movement-based approaches, and in this respect, Miller's (2014) data seem highly problematic. This is because Merchant's (2008a) classification identifies VP ellipsis as a type of ellipsis that does *not* admit island repair. Since pseudogapping is usually taken to be an instance of VP ellipsis in most mainstream approaches, this apparently poses a serious tension in the kind of structure-based account of island repair of the sort proposed by Merchant.[19]

10.2.4 Extraction Out of Ellipsis and Islandhood

The issue of islandhood is relevant in two distinct cases in Kennedy's (2003) argument for covert structural representations underlying ellipsis. We review these two cases and conclude that in neither case does the argument go through.

---

19. One might think that if the contrast between VP ellipsis and pseudogapping with respect to island repair is real, the empirical problem itself remains unaccounted for in non-movement approaches as well. This is true, but note that non-movement approaches (including ours) start from the premise that non-syntactic factors play major roles. In the case of VP ellipsis and pseudogapping, seeking explanation in independently observed differences in the discourse structural properties of the two constructions (cf., e.g., Hoeksema 2006) seems to be a promising direction.

10.2.4.1 *Wh* **extraction**   As noted above, Kennedy's argument for covert structural representations in VP ellipsis is a version of the familiar type of logic in the transformational literature invoking the island sensitivity of structure that is invisible on the surface string. The argument is crucially based on the observation that examples of the following sort are unacceptable:

(567) a. *Sterling criticized every decision that Doug was upset because Lou did.

      b. *Dogs, I understand, but cats, I don't know a single person who does.

According to Kennedy, this fact follows straightforwardly from the assumption that these examples are derived in the following manner, where the fronted *wh* phrase (or the relativization operator) is extracted from an island environment which at a later stage of derivation gets deleted via VP ellipsis. On this view, the ungrammaticality follows from the violation of island constraints in the *wh* movement involved:

(568) a. *Sterling criticized every decision that Doug was upset [$_S$ because Lou did ~~criticize *t*~~].   (Adjunct Island)

      b. *Dogs, I understand, but cats, I don't know [$_{NP}$ a single person [$_S$ who does ~~understand *t*~~]].   (Complex NP)

However, this argument is problematic since there is an alternative explanation of the unacceptability of these examples that does not make any reference to the notion of islandhood. To see this point, note that examples such as the following, in which VP ellipsis takes place in an environment in which the target clause is embedded, are at least as unacceptable as (567a):

(569)*STERLING criticized every decision (that) Doug was unhappy (that) [$_S$ LOU did ~~criticize *t*~~].

Note that in (569), unlike the examples in (567), the extraction site is not located within an island. Thus, the relevant factor here is not islandhood, but simply the level of embedding of the elided material. In fact, theorists from widely divergent approaches have noted that such embedding corresponds to semantic/pragmatic difficulties which are in themselves sufficient to guarantee that such examples are perceived as anomalous (see, e.g., Jacobson [2016] on short-answer ellipsis and Toosarvandani [2016] on Gapping). In fact, Kennedy himself had, in prior work on the identity conditions holding between antecedent and ellipsed VP (Kennedy 1994/2008), argued that examples such as (569) are ill-formed because they violate a complex set of essentially semantic requirements in which islandhood considerations have no role at all. Thus, Kennedy's own account of ACD in Kennedy (1994/2008), by unifying the patterns displayed in (567) and (569), decisively undercuts his own invocation of islandhood—and the concealed structure which it would entail—in the analysis of VP ellipsis in Kennedy (2003).

Moreover, there seems to be considerable speaker variation in the judgments on at least some of the relevant examples. For example, the judgment given to (567b) by Kennedy (2003) was disputed by our informants, according to whom the example is only somewhat awkward at worst. In fact, an even more natural example that is structurally parallel to (567b) can be constructed without too much difficulty:

(570) Life, I like to think about, but death, I don't and I don't know $\left\{ \begin{array}{l} \text{ANYONE} \\ \text{a single person} \end{array} \right\}$
       who DOES.

This strongly suggests that here, too, syntactic islandhood *per se* is orthogonal to the source of any negative judgments reported in (567b). For speakers who accept (570), the semantic parallelism between the two clauses after *but* is apparently all that is needed to make the gap in the elided VP transparent to linkage with the fronted topic. While the mechanisms involved in this effect are still far from clear, the fact that both clauses present a strong negation contrast to the first conjunct is surely a crucial factor. The pattern just described, then, can be seen as the reflection of a priming effect which speaks to a processing problem rather than a grammaticality issue *per se*.

We therefore have reason to reject the claim that islandhood is relevant for the analysis of the "extraction out of VP ellipsis" type of data (and relatedly, pseudogapping; cf. section 10.2). Rather, it appears to be some currently unknown set of factors related to the complexity of the *antecedent* that bears most critically on the possibilities for instantiating the free variable in the ellipsis operator introduced in chapter 6. This aspect of the syntax-semantics interface has not, so far as we are aware, been the focus of psycholinguistic investigation, although recent work by Kim and Runner (2018) has begun to explore the interaction of generalized conditions on discourse felicity with what they argue is a specific "structural" restriction on VP ellipsis.[20] We conjecture that a full understanding of the patterns in ellipsis is crucially dependent on future work targeting the kind of phenomena noted in this section. In particular, it is possible that the sorts of complexity noted by Kluender and others, summarized earlier, is implicated in the psycholinguistics of anaphora in ellipsis, though the specific ways in which such factors play a role are likely to differ in different types of phenomena. We leave further investigation of this issue for future work.

---

20. Kim and Runner's conclusion—that there is a specific syntactic identity condition on VP ellipsis whose violation degrades output regardless of any further deficits due to functional infelicities—is completely consonant with the analysis we provide above, at least in the rather broad terms in which it is framed. Their use of the description "structural" in this context does not, so far as we can tell, necessarily implicate facts about branching tree structure, and could instead be interpreted as restrictions on the syntactic type of the antecedent, as per the particular restriction in (330).

10.2.4.2 Attributive comparatives   Kennedy (2003), following Kennedy and Merchant (2000), takes the degraded status of examples like (571) to reflect the Left Branch Condition, formalized as a syntactic condition that is sensitive to the form of *structural* representations in the prosodic domain:

(571) John buys more expensive wine than he buys beer.

As noted in section 8.3.5, we disagree with Kennedy and Merchant on the assessment of the empirical status of data like (571). Specifically, contrary to Kennedy and Merchant (and much of the literature following it, such as Bacskai-Atkari [2014] and LaCara [2016]), we take examples such as (571) to be syntactically well-formed. While such examples are not impeccable, we have observed that they are not altogether ruled out, and much better examples can be found. For example, a substantial number of our informants report that examples such as (572) (which is structurally parallel to (571)) are simply not ill-formed at all:

(572) John writes better novels than he/Mary writes plays.

More generally, we have noted considerable speaker variability in judgments on attributive adjective subdeletion without pseudogapping. It is true that on the whole, the pseudogapped versions are more readily acceptable, but the non-elliptical versions are noticeably improved by, for example, using higher-frequency lexica (thus replacing *writes* with *composes* materially degrades (572)).

In place of Kennedy and Merchant's syntactic account, we suggest that a much simpler mechanism is at work here: a garden path effect created in large part by the fact that in the non-elliptical version of the sentence, the *than* clause is already parsable *without* the "comparative deletion" to the left of the direct object. Unlike syntactic ill-formedness, which gives rise to either-or judgments, garden path effects typically result in a much more complex set of speaker responses which often depend on non-structural factors, exactly of the sort found in the responses we have received from our informants.

Our view here is essentially in line with the "expectation-based" processing model proposed in Chaves (2013), which assumes that the parser's performance is at least in part guided by application of the rules and constraints of the grammar.[21] To articulate this non-syntactic alternative account a bit further, in languages such as English that do not allow for the option of left branch extraction for overt material, parses in which material corresponding to an NP left branch must be "imported" from elsewhere in the comparative structure will be initially overlooked by the parser, based on the lack of

---

21. Similar models of human sentence processing have been proposed in Phillips (2006) and Wagers and Phillips (2009) as well, although the specific claims about the role of grammatical constraints in the processing model that these latter works advocate have been challenged by Michel (2014).

such syntactic-semantic linkages in the simpler (and more basic) cases involving overt filler-gap linkages. Instead, the parser will compose what appear to be self-evidently well-formed sentences such as *he buys beer* in (571). But once such a parse is obtained for the *than* clause, it fails to be composable with the antecedent clause in the comparative, and this will at best force the kind of real-time backtracking that registers as diminished acceptability or even outright ill-formedness (see, e.g., Du and Yu [2012] for a computational model of processing breakdown under backtracking in garden path sentences, and Chaves [2013] for an account linking such effects to extraction possibilities).[22]

But this requirement—that the parser follow the line of least resistance, so to speak—is counteracted in exactly the class of cases in which such comparatives are unproblematic, namely, cases involving ellipsis in the *than* clauses such as (573):

(573) John buys more expensive wine than he does beer.

As already noted, what makes these examples different from their non-elliptical counterparts is that they involve an additional process of ellipsis, and there is reason to believe that this additional component has a nontrivial consequence for the real-time processing of the sentence. Recall from the discussion in chapter 8 that in pseudo-gapping clauses, obtaining a coherent interpretation critically depends on instantiating the free variable P introduced by the ellipsis operator based on discourse context. The real-time recovery of an interpretation from the antecedent clause entailed by this anaphora resolution requirement will, by its very nature, force the processor to inspect the antecedent and ellipsis clauses simultaneously, as it were, upon encountering the "transitive" auxiliary in cases such as (573). This interruption keeps the otherwise automatic default parsing routine—and the garden path effect it gives rise to—from being completed. Moreover, this ellipsis resolution process reinforces the Parallelism relation between the main clause and the *than* clause, thereby facilitating the construal of the whole sentence as a comparative construction. The extra anaphora resolution step

---

22. One might wonder why the same garden path effect does not arise in simpler comparative sentences such as the following, whose *than* clause is similarly parsable as a stand-alone sentence:

(i) Mary runs faster than John runs.

While a complete account is beyond the scope of the present work, the difference between examples like (i) and cases of attributive subdeletion such as (571) seems to follow from a relatively simple syntactic difference in the position of the gap site: in (i) (unlike (571)), at the end of parsing the *than* clause, the modifier which must be interpreted into the parse in order to yield a semantically coherent interpretation corresponds to a position in which the parser expects to find such a modifying term (as in *runs fast*). Moreover, the sentence-final position is where such a modifier is routinely interpreted in overt extraction cases, as in, e.g., *How fast did John run __?* Based on such extraction possibilities elsewhere in the language, the parser need do nothing more than identify the position following *run* as a site into which a modifier introduced earlier in the sentence can be interpreted.

triggered by ellipsis therefore circumvents the error-plus-backtracking sequence which the default parsing strategy leads to.

There is a corollary to this processing-based explanation of the improved status of pseudogapped variants of attributive comparatives: the same amelioration effect should be observed in any other possible form of the *than* clause in which the default parse routine fails to produce a well-formed stand-alone interpretation. This prediction is indeed corroborated by data involving the cognate object construction. Note first that the cognate object construction is usually not well-formed without a modifier:

(574) *John will probably die a death as a result of all this.

But as part of an attributive comparative, this specific construction is well-formed (here, small caps indicate a lower level of contrastive stress and full caps a maximum degree of contrastive stress):

(575) I feel like I'm SLEEPING a much more painful SLEEP these days than I'll eventually DIE a DEATH at the end of my life.

The default processing routine does not yield a well-formed result on its own, and it seems reasonable to suppose that the parser, in its attempt to make sense of this otherwise uninterpretable cognate object expression, is able to make early use of the contrastive parallelism supplied by the comparative construction (which can be further facilitated by appropriate intonational cues). The amelioration effect observed in (575) provides strong support for the current processing-based view over Kennedy and Merchant's syntactic account: on the latter type of approach, since (575) does not involve any deletion operation, it is predicted to be just as unacceptable as (571), and its improved acceptability remains a total mystery.[23]

---

23. Another case that shows the importance of considering plausible alternatives to syntactic accounts of speakers' judgments comes from Kennedy and Merchant's (2000) discussion of examples such as (i).

(i) John wrote a successful novel, and Bill, a play.

Kennedy and Merchant argue that this sentence has two readings, corresponding to (iia) and (iib):

(ii) a. John wrote a successful novel. Bill wrote a play.
      b. John wrote a successful novel. Bill wrote a successful play.

According to them, (iib) is a distinct reading corresponding to an LF (different from the one for (iia)) that is derived by a deletion operation (similar to the one involved in their analysis of attributive comparatives) that deletes not just the verb but also a prenominal adjective. However, the assumption that Gapping is derived by deletion directly contradicts the standard assumption about the analysis of Gapping in the Principle and Parameters approach: Johnson (2000, 2009) and Vicente (2010) have argued extensively that Gapping should *not* be analyzed via deletion. We believe that a much simpler account of the apparent ambiguity of (i) is more plausible. In our view, the two readings of (i) paraphrased in (ii) reflect vagueness (or underspecified interpretation) rather than true ambiguity. Specifically, (iia) is the only reading that the grammar licenses for (i) (which is immediately available in any standard analysis of Gapping). The sentence is of course compatible with a situation in which the speaker intends to convey (iib), especially in the right kind of

Seen in this light, the cross-linguistic evidence that Kennedy and Merchant adduce in support of their association between left branch extractability and non-elliptical attributive adjective subdeletion need have no syntactic implications at all. The observed cross-linguistic correlation would follow at least equally well from the garden path alternative account we have proposed above, in tandem with a parser guided in its search possibilities by whichever constructions are syntactically available in a language. Specifically, a parser taking into account the grammatical option of a left branch extraction can be counted on to include this possibility in how it handles the processing of the *than* clause in the comparative, rather than automatically running a default processing routine that creates a garden path effect. In other words, the parser's expectation includes the possibility of covert modification of nominal heads in attributive comparative constructions just in case the language allows for the option of overt left branch extraction (as in Polish and Czech). Thus, since the same effect is predicted just as readily on the current processing-based alternative, this additional "evidence" does not distinguish between Kennedy and Merchant's syntactic account and the present processing-based account.

10.2.5   Right-Node Raising and Islandhood

One point that deserves special attention in connection with island effects is the immunity of the shared material in RNR constructions to island effects. Examples such as (576) are fully representative of the island-exempt status of RNR:

(576)   John had the conviction that Bill was the collector who had bought __, and Mary held to the fervent belief that Ann was the dealer who had sold __, the last orange Lamborghini ever sold in North America.

The apparent gap in both conjuncts is located within a relative clause that is itself part of a definite complex NP. Note that a leftward extraction example involving (mostly) the same lexica sound distinctly less natural:

(577)   ??Which car did John have the conviction that Bill was the collector who had bought __?

The island insensitivity of RNR has long been recognized as theoretically problematic for mainstream approaches to islandhood which take RNR to be a case of rightward movement (see Wexler and Culicover [1980] for an early discussion of the troublesome issues raised by a movement analysis of RNR for syntactic theory).

context (for example, in a discussion of literary successes of one's friends), but the additional meaning that is felt to be present in such contexts is simply inferred as a conversational implicature (Relevance), presumably facilitated by the constructional property of Gapping that induces a strong Parallelism discourse relation on the two conjuncts.

One obvious line of response to the problem posed by (576)–(577) would be rejection of the movement analysis of RNR, and this line has in fact been widely taken in the literature. But in the case of approaches such as ours, matters are a bit more complex. Not only is movement (in the sense of a structure-changing operation applying at the level of configurational syntactic representations) not available in the first place in our framework, but our analysis of both extraction and RNR is based on the same "mechanism"—hypothetical reasoning—in the two families of construction (albeit involving different types of connectives). If islandhood is taken to be a syntactic effect, one might attempt to argue that this identity commits us to the position that both classes of phenomena should display a certain ill-formedness when the apparently missing material—regardless of its relative position to the "gap site"—is associated with an ostensible gap in an island context.

Such a challenge would, however, be seriously misguided. One of our core assumptions, backed by the considerable and increasing body of evidence for the essentially non-syntactic nature of island effects of the kind surveyed earlier, is that islandhood is the by-product of complex interactions among functional factors. In accord with this stance, we hold that there is indeed a crucial asymmetry between extraction and RNR, involving not the position of the "filler" material simpliciter, but rather whether the speaker/hearer encounters the gap or the filler first. Based on the arguments, evidence, and results adduced above from the work of Kluender, Michel, and Chaves, we conclude that the difference between (576) and (577) is exactly what we would expect on the assumption that islandhood is often attributable to difficulties for the parser in the course of real-time processing.

In the case of leftward extraction, the speaker is confronted with material which cannot be interpreted with respect to its immediate local context; it must be "read into" a gap which the parser expects somewhere in the upcoming material, but whose location it has no clues to. All material between the filler and the intended gap site must therefore be inspected, entailing the investment of considerable cognitive effort, particularly when distractors such as referentially "heavy" nominals are encountered along the way. Under these conditions, the parser's task is extremely challenging, and we expect it to be easily derailed as the number of subsidiary processing tasks to be gotten out of the way before the gap can be securely identified increases past a certain point. But in RNR constructions, the parser encounters the gap first. There is no difficulty identifying the context into which any missing material subsequently encountered must be supplied; that context is immediately evident at the point where some argument sought by a selecting functor type is absent. The parser is now looking for a string corresponding to some type X which has not locally combined with some other functor seeking an X argument. All that it need do is process incoming material until it encounters such an argument, in which case its search ends immediately and a complete interpretation can be composed. The problems that the parser faces in the two respective construction types are therefore of quite different orders, with RNR representing by far the simpler processing task.

Thus, we take it that the puzzle of island insensitivity of RNR in the classical literature is only an artificial puzzle, one arising out of a certain set of assumptions. These assumptions may have seemed plausible back in the 1980s, but given the more nuanced and sophisticated view of island effects in the current literature, they are difficult to maintain. Under the more plausible set of assumptions about the nature of island constraints, the insensitivity of RNR to island effects is in fact consistent with what kinds of effects arise in what kinds of syntactic constructions. While the discussion here is rather sketchy, we take this result to further corroborate the extragrammatical view on island constraints as a whole.

10.3 A Note on Semantic Islands

Our discussion up to this point has been restricted to syntactic islands, but it has been recognized for a long time that there are islands for scope-taking as well, known as *scope islands*. It is sometimes alleged that universal quantifiers are restricted to scope within the closest finite clauses containing them, but this is not true; there are sentences such as (578):

(578) John believes that everyone in this room is trying to get him fired.

There is a reading for (578) in which for it to be true and felicitous, John does not necessarily need to know that any of the people in question is actually in the room. Nonetheless, genuine semantic islandhood effects do seem to exist. Typical examples are given in (579).

(579) a. Fido has a bone that is in every corner of the house. (Rodman 1976)
       b. If every woman in this room gave birth to John, then he has a nice mother.
          (Winter 2001)

(579a) has only the strange reading according to which there is a single bone possessed by Fido that is in every corner of the house (compare: *Fido has a bone in every corner of the house*), suggesting that the universal quantifier inside a relative clause cannot scope out of the relative clause. Similarly, if the quantifier were able to scope out of the *if* clause in (579b), the sentence should have a sensible interpretation 'for every woman in the room, it is the case that if she gave birth to John, then John has a nice mother.' However, (579b) has only the nonsensical reading entertaining the possibility that John had multiple mothers giving birth to him.

One point that should be stressed before we speculate on any possible deeper sources for the anomaly in (579) is that the traditional argument which takes these data to provide evidence for the representational treatment of scope via syntactic movement at LF (see, e.g., Winter [2001, 81–84] and Ruys and Winter [2010] for relatively recent versions of this type of argument) loses much of its force given that, as abundantly documented above, so far as *syntactic* island constraints go, it is not difficult to find acceptable examples of even supposedly strong islands. Consider, for example, (580), where an acceptable violation of the Subjacency condition is contrasted with a covert-movement counterpart, for which a similar "island violation" reading seems much more difficult to obtain:

(580) a. Euthanasia is [$_{NP}$ a topic [$_S$ which I can never find [$_{NP}$ anyone [$_S$ I can argue with __ about __]]]].

     b. #John is [$_{NP}$ a reporter [$_S$ who wrote about [$_{NP}$ a prosecutor [$_S$ that claimed that everyone in this room is guilty of perjury]]]].

The intended reading for (580b) is that for every person now in the room with the speaker, some prosecutor(s) claimed that that person is guilty of perjury and John wrote a story about each such prosecutor. But this reading in unavailable. The only accessible interpretation is that John wrote a story or stories about a prosecutor who claimed that the group of people currently in the room were all guilty of perjury.

Given the robustness of (at least some of) the semantic island effects, it may appear that the only way to capture them properly would be to encode them directly within the grammar (which is possible to do in our approach, for example, by building on the work by Pogodalla and Pompigne [2012] briefly discussed in chapter 7). However, we feel that at this point such a move may still be a bit too hasty. After all, syntactic and semantic processing pertain to different components of grammar and deal with somewhat different types of abstract representations of linguistic knowledge. Thus, it would be hardly surprising if it turned out that the same type of dependency/configuration presents a much more robust processing difficulty in one domain than the other. There is some pioneering work investigating the real-time semantic processing of scope islands (see, for example, Wurmbrand 2018) in the recent literature. Hopefully, this new line of work will delineate more clearly the proper division of labor between the combinatoric and processing components regarding the treatment of the semantic island effect, along lines similar to that done for syntactic island effects in the line of work reviewed in the present chapter. We therefore regard the source of apparent scope islands as an entirely open question whose answer is likely to emerge only well in the future.

11 Bringing Back "Hierarchical Constituency": Multi-Modal Prosodic Calculus and Its Empirical Applications

Up to this point, we have assumed the associative variant of the Lambek calculus (**L**) as the underlying calculus that governs the behavior of the connectives / and \. As should already be clear by now, this effectively has the consequence of denying the significance of the notion of phrase structural constituency as a theoretically primitive notion that determines the "units" that grammatical operations or constraints directly target. We have seen in the preceding chapters that the flexibility of the combinatoric system that this architecture of grammar allows for has significant advantages in accounting for complex empirical phenomena in the domains of coordination and ellipsis.

However, if we are left with this all-or-nothing choice between either retaining or totally abandoning (the analogue of) the traditional notion of constituency, the flexibility gained by taking the latter option would be both a strength and a weakness for the purpose of accounting for a wider range of empirical phenomena. For example, the so-called complex predicate constructions are found in a variety of languages across typologically distinct language types (including Germanic, Romance, and East Asian languages such as Japanese and Korean). Roughly speaking, this is a type of phenomenon in which higher and lower verbs (most typically, in the raising and control constructions) form some sort of morpho-syntactic cluster in the "surface syntax," to the exclusion of their nominal arguments. It is unclear how verb clustering of this sort would be modeled in an architecture that totally dispenses with the traditional notion of syntactic constituency.

Since we have mostly focused on the grammar of English in this book, the fragment we have developed up to this point is not equipped with a mechanism that can handle this type of phenomenon appropriately. However, extensions of the Lambek calculus and related approaches with mechanisms for dealing with this type of complex phenomena pertaining to morpho-syntax have been proposed by various authors in the literature (Moortgat and Oehrle 1994; Kraak 1998; Baldridge 2002). In fact, the underlying architecture of Hybrid TLCG is perfectly compatible with an extension that is well suited for accounting for such additional complexities. This involves adding more structure to the prosodic component of the tripartite representation of linguistic signs, thereby modeling morpho-syntactic constituency. The resultant system can capture both the flexibility of constituency and restrictions imposed on this flexibility exhibited by such phenomena. Kubota (2010, 2014) offers a detailed demonstration of the empirical advantage of such an architecture of grammar through an analysis of two types of complex predicate constructions in Japanese that exhibit different degrees of morpho-syntactic flexibility.

While empirical evidence for the need for such an elaborate architecture of the morpho-syntactic component is limited in English, a certain puzzling pattern in RNR, known as "medial Right-Node Raising" (or "Right-Node Wrapping"; Whitman 2009; Yatabe 2012), arguably constitutes one such case. Thus, in this chapter we sketch an analysis of medial RNR in an extended fragment of our system and thereby illustrate the theoretical toolkit that is available in CG for regulating flexibility of constituency appropriately. The medial RNR data are important theoretically as well, since some authors have claimed (see, e.g., Yatabe and Tam 2019) that it poses a threat to the nonconstituent-as-constituent analysis of coordination in CG of the sort we have developed and advocated in the preceding chapters. The fact that a natural solution for this problem becomes available once we extend the morpho-syntactic component (along lines that have considerable cross-linguistic support) provides support not only for such an extension but also for the basic analysis of nonconstituent coordination as constituent coordination that we have argued for in the preceding chapters.

11.1   Some Basic Facts about Medial Right-Node Raising

Several authors (Wilder 1999; Whitman 2009; Bachrach and Katzir 2008; Yatabe 2012, 2013) have noted a class of examples that at first sight appear to pose a serious challenge to this otherwise very successful analysis of coordination in CG of the sort we have argued for in the preceding chapters. The problem is illustrated by the following example from Wilder (1999):

(581) John should [fetch] and [give ***the book*** to Mary].

In this example, the material shared between the two conjuncts appears *inside* the second conjunct, rather than to its right (as would be the case in ordinary RNR), since the indirect object *to Mary* is an argument of *give* but not of *fetch*.

Similar examples from English are given in (582) (Whitman 2009).

(582) a. I've got friends in low places, where [the whiskey drowns] and [the beer chases ***my blues*** away].

   b. The blast [upended] and [nearly slices ***an armored Chevrolet Suburban*** in half].

    c. Please move from the exit rows if you are [unwilling] or [unable *to perform the necessary actions* without injury].

    d. In the players' box was Tony Nadal, the [uncle] and [coach *of Rafael Nadal* since he started playing as a youngster].

Yatabe (2013) notes an even more vexing case from Japanese where the material shared between the two conjuncts is a discontinuous string, split in the middle by some element that belongs solely to the second conjunct.

(583) a. [Taroo-wa hidari-gawa-no manekin-ni makkuro-na], sosite [Hanako-wa
        Taro-TOP left-side-GEN figure-DAT pitch.black and Hanako-TOP
        awai pinku-iro-no *boosi-o* migi-gawa-no manekin-ni] **kabuse-ta**.
        pale pink-color-GEN hat-ACC right-side-GEN figure-DAT put-PAST
        'Taro put a pitch-black hat on the figure on the left and Hanako put a pale pink hat on the figure on the right.'

    b. [Katate-nabe-de 1-rittoru-gurai-no], sosite [sore-to heikoo-si-te tyoodo
        pan-with 1-liter-about-GEN and that-with in.parallel just
        5-rittoru-no *oyu-o* huka-nabe-de] **wakasi-masu**.
        5-liter-GEN water-ACC deep-pot-with boil-POL
        'Boil about 1ℓ of water in a pan and exactly 5ℓ of water in a pot simultaneously.'

In (583a), the left conjunct is missing both the head noun for the prenominal modifier *makkuro-na* 'pitch-black' and the sentence-final verb *kabuse-ta* 'put.' While the shared verb appears to the right of the right conjunct, the shared head noun *boosi-o* 'hat' is buried inside the second conjunct, split from the right-peripheral shared verb by a dative NP belonging solely to the right conjunct. Following Yatabe (2012), we call this type of Right-Node Raising (RNR) (encompassing both the English examples in (581)–(582) and the more complex Japanese data in (583)) *medial RNR* (MRNR). As Yatabe (2012) notes, these examples pose a serious challenge to (at least the simplest formulation of) the CG-based analysis of RNR, since the second conjunct contains within itself what would have to be "factored out" to the right of both conjuncts as the RNR'ed material in order for such an analysis to succeed.

    These facts have not been unnoticed in the CG literature. Whitman (2009) proposes an analysis for a subset of the data in (582) in terms of *wrapping* (Bach 1979). Wrapping is a mechanism proposed in the early literature of CG/Montague grammar which treats discontinuous constituency in verb-particle constructions and related phenomena via surface reordering. In a wrapping-based analysis, (584) is derived by first combining the verb and the particle to form an "underlying" constituent, and the direct object of this "complex transitive verb" is infixed right next to the verb in the surface string.

(584) The whiskey chases my blues <u>away</u>.

According to Whitman (2009), at least some of the examples in (582) can be subsumed under like-category coordination by taking into consideration this word order surface anomaly manifest in wrapping. Specifically, in (582a), the two conjuncts *the whiskey drowns* and *the beer chases away* form a coordinate structure before the shared NP is wrapped around by the verb-particle pair belonging to the second conjunct. After the shared NP is taken as an argument by the whole coordinated S/NP, surface restructuring induces the "infixation" of the direct object *my blues* between the verb and the particle of the second conjunct, just as in the simpler case of verb-particle construction in (584). Thus, Whitman's analysis reduces the apparent anomaly of (a certain subset of) MRNR to an independently motivated word order anomaly exhibited by expressions that induce the "wrapping" operation.

Thus, the key idea behind Whitman's proposal is that the apparently exceptional patterns of RNR in MRNR can be reduced to independent word order properties of the "offending" elements. Though this general idea seems essentially on the right track, attributing the word order variation to the wrapping operation specifically is too restrictive. Indeed, Whitman himself notes that his wrapping-based analysis does not extend to all of the data that he discusses. For example, (582c) is problematic since the adverbial phrase *without injury* modifies the lower verb *perform* rather than the adjective *unable*. Thus, a wrapping analysis that takes *unable without injury* to be a combinatoric unit that wraps around the infinitival VP is semantically implausible. In (582d), the *since* clause modifies the proposition that Tony Nadal is a coach of Rafael Nadal, and hence, Whitman argues, *coach since...* cannot be taken to be a discontinuous constituent that wraps around *of Rafael Nadal*. Moreover, as Yatabe (2012) notes, Whitman's approach does not extend to the more complex Japanese examples in (583), since there is no independent motivation that the word order variations in these examples are licensed by a mechanism analogous to the wrapping operation traditionally recognized in the CG literature for phenomena like verb-particle constructions.

Considerations of the above facts have led some authors (most notably, Yatabe 2012, 2013) to argue that the CG analysis of coordination is empirically inadequate and that other approaches (such as ones based on surface deletion [Yatabe 2001; Crysmann 2003; Beavers and Sag 2004; Chaves 2007] or multidominance [Bachrach and Katzir 2007, 2008]) are superior since they can accommodate such data more easily. In what follows, we offer an analysis of MRNR in an extension of Hybrid TLCG that incorporates the notion of "multi-modality" which is similar in spirit to Whitman's analysis but differs from it in specific implementational details. We argue that our approach improves over Whitman's proposal in overcoming its empirical inadequacies. We show that the MRNR pattern exemplified by the data in Japanese and English above actually falls out as an immediate consequence of the CG analysis of RNR, once the interaction between RNR and independently motivated word order properties in the respective languages is properly taken into account.

11.2 Enriching the Morpho-Syntactic Component

In this section, we sketch an extension of Hybrid TLCG along the lines worked out in detail in Kubota (2010, 2014) and Kubota and Pollard (2010), which enriches the prosodic component with the notion of "multi-modality" from the TLCG work in the 1990s (Moortgat and Oehrle 1994; Moortgat 1997). The notion of "multi-modality" (which has nothing to do with the notion of modality as understood in the semantics literature) was first introduced in CG by Dowty (1996b) (written at the end of the 1980s). Dowty sketches an architecture of syntactic theory in which the combinatoric component pertaining to predicate-argument structure and semantic composition (called "tectogrammar" following Curry [1961]) is separated from a component that deals with surface word order ("phenogrammar").[1] Building on the proposals by Morrill and Solias (1993), Morrill (1994), Moortgat and Oehrle (1994), and Bernardi (2002), Kubota (2010, 2014) and Kubota and Pollard (2010) implement this idea explicitly within TLCG by positing different "modes of composition" in the prosodic component, where these modes essentially encode different degrees of tightness of bond between morphemes (as reflected in surface word order). Below, we present a simplified fragment embodying this architecture.

Unlike in the original Lambek calculus, in a multi-modal system, prosodic representations of linguistic expressions have richer structures than strings. We call such "enriched" prosodic representations *abstract phonologies*. In abstract phonologies, morphemes are combined with one another via one of the abstract modes of composition. For example, a mode called the *scrambling mode* ($\circ.$) is posited to account for the relative free order among dependents of a verb within a local clause in Japanese. Thus, the sentence *Taroo-ga Hanako-o mi-ta* ('Taro saw Hanako') is assigned the following abstract phonology:

(585) taroo-ga $\circ.$ (hanako-o $\circ.$ mi-ta)

To capture the property of the scrambling mode, we posit the following ordering relations:

(586) Scrambling

$A \circ. (B \circ. C) \leq B \circ. (A \circ. C)$

(587) Pronunciation

$A \circ_i B \leq A \circ B$ (where $\circ_i$ is any abstract mode)

---

1. The same basic idea has been implemented in HPSG by Reape (1996) and Kathol (1995, 2000).

Here, $\leq$ is to be understood as defining the "rewritability" relation between prosodic representations such that if $A \leq B$ holds, then A can be rewritten as B—this will be formally guaranteed by the Prosodic Interface rule (592). (586) essentially says that elements combined in the scrambling mode can be reordered with each other, except for the rightmost one (corresponding to the head verb). (587) converts an abstract phonology to an actually pronounceable string (where $\circ$ designates string concatenation).

From (586) and (587), it follows that (588) holds. That is, the underlying abstract phonology (585) can be rewritten as the pronounceable string *Hanako-o Taroo-ga mita* corresponding to the OSV word order.

(588)   taroo-ga $\circ$. (hanako-o $\circ$. mi-ta)

       $\leq$ hanako-o $\circ$. (taroo-ga $\circ$. mi-ta)   (by Scrambling (586))

       $\leq$ hanako-o $\circ$ (taroo-ga $\circ$ mi-ta)   (by Pronunciation (587))

Modality specifications are encoded as part of the lexical subcategorization properties of functor expressions, as in the following lexical entry for the transitive verb *mi-ta*, in which the slashes carry specific modality specifications:

(589) mi-ta; **see**; $NP_{acc}\backslash_\cdot NP_{nom}\backslash_\cdot S$

The Introduction and Elimination rules for the slashes are modified accordingly to reflect this modality encoding on slashes. Specifically, both types of rules make sure that the modality encoded in the (used or derived) functor matches the modality employed in combining its phonology with the phonology of its argument. Thus, the Introduction and Elimination rules for the forward and backward slashes are redefined as follows:

(590) a. Forward Slash Elimination

$$\frac{a;\, \mathcal{F};\, A/_i B \quad b;\, \mathcal{G};\, B}{a \circ_i b;\, \mathcal{F}(\mathcal{G});\, A}/_i E$$

                                           b. Backward Slash Elimination

$$\frac{b;\, \mathcal{G};\, B \quad a;\, \mathcal{F};\, B\backslash_i A}{b \circ_i a;\, \mathcal{F}(\mathcal{G});\, A}\backslash_i E$$

(591) a. Forward Slash Introduction

$$\frac{\begin{array}{c} \vdots \ [\varphi;\, x;\, A]^n \ \vdots \\ \vdots \quad \vdots \quad \vdots \\ \hline b \circ_i \varphi;\, \mathcal{F};\, B \end{array}}{b;\, \lambda x.\mathcal{F};\, B/_i A}/_i I^n$$

                                           b. Backward Slash Introduction

$$\frac{\begin{array}{c} \vdots \ [\varphi;\, x;\, A]^n \ \vdots \\ \vdots \quad \vdots \quad \vdots \\ \hline \varphi \circ_i b;\, \mathcal{F};\, B \end{array}}{b;\, \lambda x.\mathcal{F};\, A\backslash_i B}\backslash_i I^n$$

Finally, the following *Prosodic-Interface (PI) rule* is posited so that syntactic derivations can make reference to the "rewriting" relation between prosodic representations:

(592) Prosodic-Interface (PI) rule

$$\frac{\varphi_0;\, \mathcal{F};\, A}{\varphi_1;\, \mathcal{F};\, A}\text{PI}$$

——where $\varphi_0 \leq \varphi_1$ holds in the prosodic calculus

The following derivation illustrates how the grammar licenses the OSV word order with the lexical entry for the transitive verb given in (589) (here and below, we omit parentheses for string phonologies since hierarchical structures are irrelevant for them):

(593)

$$\frac{\text{taroo-ga; } \mathbf{t};\, \text{NP}_{nom} \quad \dfrac{\dfrac{\text{hanako-o; } \mathbf{h};\, \text{NP}_{acc} \quad \text{mi-ta; } \mathbf{saw};\, \text{NP}_{acc}\backslash.\text{NP}_{nom}\backslash.\text{S}}{\text{hanako-o } \circ.\ \text{mi-ta; } \mathbf{saw}(\mathbf{h});\, \text{NP}_{nom}\backslash.\text{S}}\backslash.\text{E}}{\text{taroo-ga } \circ.\ (\text{hanako-o } \circ.\ \text{mi-ta}); \mathbf{saw}(\mathbf{h})(\mathbf{t});\, \text{S}}\backslash.\text{E}}{\text{hanako-o } \circ \text{taroo-ga } \circ \text{mi-ta; } \mathbf{saw}(\mathbf{h})(\mathbf{t});\, \text{S}}\text{PI}$$

Combining the verb with its two arguments via Slash Elimination yields the abstract phonology in (585). This abstract phonology is then mapped to the surface string corresponding to the OSV order via the PI rule, which in turn is licensed by the rewritability relation in (588).

As an illustration of how the Introduction/Elimination rules and the PI rule interact in the present system, (594) shows how an alternative entry for a transitive verb that "directly" licenses the OSV order is obtained from the lexically specified entry in (589).

(594)

$$\frac{[\varphi_1;x;\text{NP}_{nom}]^1 \quad \dfrac{\dfrac{\dfrac{[\varphi_2;y;\text{NP}_{acc}]^2 \quad \text{mi-ta; } \mathbf{saw};\, \text{NP}_{acc}\backslash.\text{NP}_{nom}\backslash.\text{S}}{\varphi_2 \circ.\ \text{mi-ta; } \mathbf{saw}(y);\, \text{NP}_{nom}\backslash.\text{S}}\backslash.\text{E}}{\varphi_1 \circ.\ (\varphi_2 \circ.\ \text{mi-ta}); \mathbf{saw}(y)(x);\, \text{S}}\backslash.\text{E}}{\dfrac{\varphi_2 \circ.\ (\varphi_1 \circ.\ \text{mi-ta}); \mathbf{saw}(y)(x);\, \text{S}}{\varphi_1 \circ.\ \text{mi-ta; } \lambda y.\mathbf{saw}(y)(x);\, \text{NP}_{acc}\backslash.\text{S}}\text{PI}}\backslash.\text{I}^2}{\text{mi-ta; } \lambda x \lambda y.\mathbf{saw}(y)(x);\, \text{NP}_{nom}\backslash.\text{NP}_{acc}\backslash.\text{S}}\backslash.\text{I}^1$$

After the verb is combined with its (hypothetically assumed) two arguments, the PI rule reverses the order between the subject and the object. This has the effect of reversing the order of arguments in the "derived" entry, via the successive applications of the two Introduction rules. Importantly, since the Introduction and Elimination rules preserve the modality specifications, the scrambling mode lexically encoded in the original transitive verb entry in (589) is retained in the derived entry in (594) for both arguments.

11.3 Regulating the Flexibility of Constituency

One important difference between the associative fragment assumed up to the previous chapter and the extended, multi-modal fragment we are working with in the present chapter is that hypothetical reasoning involving the forward and backward slashes is more tightly restricted in the latter. Specifically, the Introduction rules in (591) require the prosody of the hypothesized expression φ to appear at the (topmost) right or left edge of the hierarchically structured prosodic representation of the premise.[2] This has the consequence that nonstandard constituents that appear in NCC can be derived only if all of the modes of composition involved in putting together the relevant expressions are associative, thereby allowing for restructuring of the hierarchical structure. See the derivation in (599) below for a concrete demonstration on this point. Thus, we now have a way to control flexibility of constituency in the appropriate way.

Since argument clusters like *Taroo-ga Hanako-o* can be coordinated, we assume that the scrambling mode is associative, meaning that it (together with the *associative mode* $\circ_\diamond$ introduced below) satisfies the following two ordering relations:

(595) Right Association

$$A \circ_i (B \circ_j C) \leq (A \circ_i B) \circ_j C \qquad\qquad (\circ_i, \circ_j \in \{\circ., \circ_\diamond\})$$

(596) Left Association

$$(A \circ_i B) \circ_j C \leq A \circ_i (B \circ_j C) \qquad\qquad (\circ_i, \circ_j \in \{\circ., \circ_\diamond\})$$

For a reason that will become clear below, we posit a special mode of composition for coordination ($\circ_c$), called the *coordination mode*. Thus, the conjunction has the following lexical entry:

(597) sosite; $\sqcap$; $(X\backslash_c X)/_c X$

This enables an analysis of the DCC sentence in Japanese in (598) along the lines of (599) (where TV abbreviates $NP_{acc}\backslash.NP_{nom}\backslash.S$).

(598) [Taroo-ga Hanako-o],   sosite [Ziroo-ga Mitiko-o]   mi-ta.
      Taro-NOM Hanako-ACC and   Jiro-NOM Michiko-ACC see-PAST
      'Taro saw Hanako and Jiro saw Michiko.'

In (599), after the hypothetical transitive verb is combined with the two arguments it subcategorizes for, the PI rule applies to restructure the abstract phonology of the sentence so that the hypothetically assumed φ appears on the right periphery. Crucially, the restructuring is possible here since the two arguments of the verb are combined with the verb in a mode that satisfies Right Association (595). By this restructuring, Forward Slash Introduction becomes applicable to derive the string *Taroo-ga Hanako-o* in the category $S/.(NP_{acc}\backslash.NP_{nom}\backslash.S)$. The rest of the derivation just involves coordinating the derived expression with another expression of the same type and combining it with the missing transitive verb.

---

2. In the simpler, non-modalized fragment in the previous chapters, in which prosodic representations were assumed to be completely flat, the prosodic variable of the hypothesis merely had to be on the left or right periphery stringwise in order for the Introduction rules to apply.

(599)

$$\dfrac{\text{hanako-o;} \quad \left[\begin{matrix}\varphi; \\ P;\mathrm{TV}\end{matrix}\right]^1}{\text{hanako-o} \circ. \ \varphi; \quad P(\mathbf{h});\mathrm{NP}_{nom}\backslash.\mathrm{S}} \backslash.\mathrm{E}$$

$$\dfrac{\dfrac{\text{taroo-ga;} \quad \dfrac{\text{hanako-o} \circ. \ \varphi;}{P(\mathbf{h});\mathrm{NP}_{nom}\backslash.\mathrm{S}}}{\dfrac{\text{taroo-ga} \circ. \ (\text{hanako-o} \circ. \ \varphi);}{P(\mathbf{h})(\mathbf{t});\mathrm{S}}} \backslash.\mathrm{E}}{\dfrac{(\text{taroo-ga} \circ. \ \text{hanako-o}) \circ. \ \varphi;}{P(\mathbf{h})(\mathbf{t});\mathrm{S}}} \mathrm{PI}$$

For the main combined derivation:

taroo-ga; t;NP_{nom}

$$\dfrac{(\text{taroo-ga} \circ. \ \text{hanako-o}) \circ. \ \varphi;}{P(\mathbf{h})(\mathbf{t});\mathrm{S}}$$ PI

$$\dfrac{\text{taroo-ga} \circ. \ \text{hanako-o};}{\lambda P.P(\mathbf{h})(\mathbf{t});\mathrm{S}/.\mathrm{TV}}/.\mathrm{I}^1$$

sosite; ⊓;(X_cX)/_cX

$$\dfrac{\text{ziroo-ga} \circ. \ \text{mitiko-o};}{\lambda P.P(\mathbf{m})(\mathbf{j}); \ \mathrm{S}/.\mathrm{TV}}$$

$$\dfrac{\text{sosite} \circ_c (\text{ziroo-ga} \circ. \ \text{mitiko-o});}{\lambda G.G \sqcap \lambda P.P(\mathbf{m})(\mathbf{j}); \ (\mathrm{S}/.\mathrm{TV})\backslash_c(\mathrm{S}/.\mathrm{TV})} /_c\mathrm{E}$$

$$\dfrac{(\text{taroo-ga} \circ. \ \text{hanako-o}) \circ_c (\text{sosite} \circ_c (\text{ziroo-ga} \circ. \ \text{mitiko-o}));}{\lambda P.P(\mathbf{h})(\mathbf{t}) \sqcap \lambda P.P(\mathbf{m})(\mathbf{j});\mathrm{S}/.\mathrm{TV}} \backslash_c\mathrm{E}$$

mi-ta; saw; TV

$$\dfrac{((\text{taroo-ga} \circ. \ \text{hanako-o}) \circ_c (\text{sosite} \circ_c (\text{ziroo-ga} \circ. \ \text{mitiko-o}))) \circ. \ \text{mi-ta};}{\mathbf{saw}(\mathbf{h})(\mathbf{t}) \wedge \mathbf{saw}(\mathbf{m})(\mathbf{j});\mathrm{S}} /.\mathrm{E}$$

$$\dfrac{}{\text{taroo-ga} \circ \text{hanako-o} \circ \text{sosite} \circ \text{ziroo-ga} \circ \text{mitiko-o} \circ \text{mi-ta}; \ \mathbf{saw}(\mathbf{h})(\mathbf{t}) \wedge \mathbf{saw}(\mathbf{m})(\mathbf{j}); \mathrm{S}} \mathrm{PI}$$

More complex examples such as (600) are derived in essentially the same way. In (600), the prenominal modifier is left stranded in each conjunct from the RNR'ed head noun. For this example, it suffices to assume that the mode of composition employed for putting together the prenominal modifier and the head noun is also associative.

(600) [Katate-nabe-de iti-rittoru-no],   sosite [huka-nabe-de go-rittoru-no]
    pan-with   1-liter-about-GEN and deep-pot-with 5-liter-GEN
    oyu-o   wakasi-masu.
    water-ACC boil-POL
    'Boil 1 liter of water in a pan and boil 5 liters of water in a deep pot.'

But since, unlike arguments of verbs, prenominal modifiers alone do not undergo scrambling, a separate mode $\circ_\diamond$ is posited, to which only Right (595) and Left (596) Association are applicable. The analysis of RNR, then, is essentially parallel to the case of (598) in (599) (here, VP abbreviates $\mathrm{NP}_{nom}\backslash.\mathrm{S}$, and in this and other derivations below, we omit the semantics).

(601)

$$\dfrac{\text{iti-rittoru-no; NP}/_\diamond\mathrm{NP} \quad [\varphi_1;\mathrm{NP}_{acc}]^1}{\text{iti-rittoru-no} \circ_\diamond \varphi_1; \mathrm{NP}} /_\diamond\mathrm{E}$$

$$\dfrac{\dfrac{\text{iti-rittoru-no} \circ_\diamond \varphi_1; \mathrm{NP} \quad [\varphi_2;\mathrm{NP}\backslash.\mathrm{VP}]^2}{(\text{iti-rittoru-no} \circ_\diamond \varphi_1) \circ. \ \varphi_2; \mathrm{VP}}}{\backslash.\mathrm{E}}$$

katate-nabe-de; VP/.VP

$$\dfrac{\text{katate-nabe-de} \circ. \ ((\text{iti-rittoru-no} \circ_\diamond \varphi_1) \circ. \ \varphi_2); \mathrm{VP}}{/.\mathrm{E}}$$

$$\dfrac{((\text{katate-nabe-de} \circ. \ \text{iti-rittoru-no}) \circ_\diamond \varphi_1) \circ. \ \varphi_2; \mathrm{VP}}{\mathrm{PI}}$$

$$\dfrac{(\text{katate-nabe-de} \circ. \ \text{iti-rittoru-no}) \circ_\diamond \varphi_1; \mathrm{VP}/.\,(\mathrm{NP}\backslash.\mathrm{VP})}{/.\mathrm{I}^2}$$

$$\dfrac{\text{katate-nabe-de} \circ. \ \text{iti-rittoru-no}; \mathrm{VP}/.\,(\mathrm{NP}\backslash.\mathrm{VP})/_\diamond\mathrm{NP}_{acc}}{/.\mathrm{I}^1}$$

$$
\cfrac{
  \cfrac{
    \text{sosite;} \quad
    \cfrac{
      \begin{array}{c}\text{fuka-nabe-de} \circ. \\ \text{go-rittoru-no;}\end{array}
    }{}
  }{}
}{}
$$

sosite;
(X\\cX)/cX

fuka-nabe-de ∘.
go-rittoru-no;
VP/.(NP\.VP)/∘NP
———————————————— /cE

sosite ∘c (fuka-nabe-de ∘.
go-rittoru-no);
(VP/.(NP\.VP)/∘NP)\
(VP/.(NP\.VP)/∘NP)

katate-nabe-de ∘.
iti-rittoru-no;
VP/.(NP\.VP)/∘NP
—————————————————————————————————— \cE

(katate-nabe-de ∘. iti-rittoru-no) ∘c
(sosite ∘c (fuka-nabe-de ∘. go-rittoru-no));
VP/.(NP\.VP)/∘NP

mizu-o;
NP
———————————————————————————————————— /∘E

((katate-nabe-de ∘. iti-rittoru-no) ∘c
(sosite ∘ (fuka-nabe-de ∘. go-rittoru-no))) ∘◇ mizu-o;
VP/.(NP\.VP)

wakasu;
NP\.VP
——— /.E

(((katate-nabe-de ∘. iti-rittoru-no) ∘c
(sosite ∘c (fuka-nabe-de ∘. go-rittoru-no))) ∘◇ mizu-o) ∘. wakasu;
VP

Here again, the crucial step is the restructuring of the prosodic representation (shown on the fifth line of the first chunk). This restructuring enables assigning the category VP/.(NP\.VP)/∘NP to the "nonconstituent" conjuncts.

As should be clear from the above, in this multi-modal system, whether or not a particular substring of a sentence can be reanalyzed as a (nontraditional) constituent that can be coordinated depends on whether restructuring of the abstract phonology is possible. This predicts that in environments in which such restructuring is disallowed for independent reasons, NCC should be impossible. Kubota (2014, 2015) offers a detailed empirical demonstration that this architecture enables a principled account of the limited flexibility of constituency available in certain complex predicate constructions in Japanese.

11.4   Medial RNR via "Reanalysis" of Constituency

From the analysis of prenominal modifier stranding RNR in (601), it is only a small step to the medial RNR case in (583c). In fact, all we need to do is to allow for a restructuring possibility in which a substring of the whole coordinate structure corresponding to the right conjunct is "detached" from the coordinate structure and forms a unit with the RNR'ed material (after which further reordering of subconstituents takes place inside the right conjunct). For this purpose, we assume that the coordination mode allows for a restricted mode of restructuring whereby elements inside the coordinate structure are all allowed to move out of the coordinate structure. This can be achieved by recognizing the following Mixed Association rules ("mixed" in the sense that, unlike the rules introduced above, these rules involve multiple modes in the specifications of the left-hand and right-hand expressions).

(602) Mixed Right Association

$$A \circ_i (B \circ_c C) \leq (A \circ_i B) \circ_c C \qquad\qquad (\circ_i \in \{\circ_\diamond, \circ_\bullet\})$$

(603) Mixed Left Association

$$(A \circ_c B) \circ_i C \leq A \circ_c (B \circ_i C) \qquad\qquad (\circ_i \in \{\circ_\diamond, \circ_\bullet\})$$

Importantly, there are no counterparts of these rules in which the modes $\circ_i$ and $\circ_c$ are switched from each other (e.g., $A \circ_c (B \circ_i C) \leq (A \circ_c B) \circ_i C$, with $\circ_i \in \{\circ_\diamond, \circ_\bullet\}$). This effectively ensures that "extraction" out of a coordinate structure is allowed but "infixation" into a coordinate structure isn't.

With these rules in place, the prosodic representation obtained at the end of the derivation in (601) can be further restructured as follows, where, after restructuring, the right conjunct forms a unit with the RNR'ed material:

(604) (((katate-nabe-de $\circ_\bullet$ iti-rittoru-no) $\circ_c$ (sosite $\circ_c$ (fuka-nabe-de $\circ_\bullet$ go-rittoru-no)))
$\circ_\diamond$ mizu-o) $\circ_\bullet$ wakasu

$\leq$ (katate-nabe-de $\circ_\bullet$ iti-rittoru-no) $\circ_c$ (sosite $\circ_c$ (fuka-nabe-de $\circ_\bullet$ ((go-rittoru-no
$\circ_\diamond$ mizu-o) $\circ_\bullet$ wakasu))) (by Mixed Left Association (603), twice)

The string consisting of the right conjunct and the RNR'ed material is in effect "reanalyzed" as forming a full-fledged sentence by itself. Given this reanalysis, it straightforwardly follows that "co-arguments" of this reanalyzed sentence can be scrambled with each other, via the Scrambling rule (586).

(605) (katate-nabe-de $\circ_\bullet$ iti-rittoru-no) $\circ_c$ (sosite $\circ_c$ (fuka-nabe-de $\circ_\bullet$ ((go-rittoru-no
$\circ_\diamond$ mizu-o) $\circ_\bullet$ wakasu)))

$\leq$ (katate-nabe-de $\circ_\bullet$ iti-rittoru-no) $\circ_c$ (sosite $\circ_c$ ((go-rittoru-no $\circ_\diamond$ mizu-o) $\circ_\bullet$ (fuka-nabe-de $\circ_\bullet$ wakasu)))

$\leq$ katate-nabe-de $\circ$ iti-rittoru-no $\circ$ sosite $\circ$ go-rittoru-no $\circ$ mizu-o $\circ$ fuka-nabe-de
$\circ$ wakasu

We thus obtain the surface word order in (583c). The other examples in (583) can be derived analogously. In short, in the present multi-modal setup, the possibility of MRNR straightforwardly falls out from an interaction between independently motivated analyses of RNR and scrambling, once we allow for a possibility that the right conjunct is reanalyzed to form a unit with the RNR'ed material in the morpho-phonological representation.

A comparison is perhaps useful at this point with an ellipsis-based analysis of MRNR proposed by Yatabe (2012, 2013). In contrast to the "multi-modal" analysis sketched above, in which the existence of MRNR is almost an immediate prediction, the ellipsis-based analysis Yatabe advocates captures the relevant empirical pattern essentially via a stipulation: in order to accommodate the MRNR pattern, Yatabe relaxes the condition on the relevant deletion operation so that the counterpart of the deleted string in the final conjunct can be discontinuous. However, unlike our analysis, such an account leaves unexplained why the matching string in the final conjunct and not the deleted string itself can be discontinuous. It then seems reasonable to conclude that, contrary to Yatabe's claim, the existence of MRNR actually provides additional support for the analysis of NCC in CG, rather than posing a challenge for it. The general architecture of grammar of the sort sketched above in which the restructuring operation in the prosodic component interacts with syntactic derivations in the combinatoric component finds independent support from the facts pertaining to the word order possibilities in complex predicate constructions in Japanese, as shown in detail in Kubota (2010, 2014). We take it that the MRNR pattern provides further empirical support for this architecture of grammar.

11.5 Extending the Analysis to English

The present proposal extends straightforwardly to English data that Whitman (2009) identifies as being problematic for his wrapping-based approach.[3] The relevant examples are repeated in (606)–(607).[4]

---

3. For examples like (582), we take it that Whitman's (2009) wrapping-based account (which can straight-forwardly be adopted in our multi-modal setup) represents an adequate (and elegant) solution. Yatabe (2012, 2013) rejects Whitman's analysis based on an observation, originally due to Sabbagh (2014), that "right-node wrapped" quantifiers cannot scope over conjunction:

(i) a. The lieutenant will either arrest or shoot **every suspected arsonist** with his rifle. ($\vee > \forall$/* $\forall > \vee$)
     b. The lieutenant will either arrest or shoot with his rifle, **every suspected arsonist**. ($\vee > \forall$/ $\forall > \vee$)

But such a scoping pattern is possible, at least with indefinites, in examples such as the following:

(ii) Picasso designed, built, and gave **a giant sculpture** to Chicago.   (Whitman 2009)

We leave for future research to determine what principle governs the scopal interactions between quantifiers and Right-Node Wrapping.

4. Whitman (2009) additionally gives the following examples as potential problems for a wrapping-based approach to Right-Node Wrapping:

(i) a. [Mothers now cheerfully push strollers] and [kids dash] through his sculptures as if they were playgrounds.
     b. We've got information on [where else] and [what else] he's wanted for.

For (ia), it seems possible to take the sentence-final modifier to be modifying both conjuncts, in which case it is not an instance of MRNR. (ib) involves an unlike category coordination of *wh* expressions, which is known to exhibit several idiosyncrasies (see Whitman [2004] for a detailed study of this construction). Since the exact licensing condition of this *wh* coordination pattern is itself currently not very well understood, we leave an analysis of (ib) for future research.

(606) . . . the right of governments to [safeguard], [promote], and even [protect] their cultures <u>from outside competition</u>.

(607) a. Please move from the exit rows if you are [unwilling] or [unable] to perform the necessary actions <u>without injury</u>.

   b. In the players' box was Tony Nadal, the [uncle] and [coach] of Rafael Nadal <u>since he started playing as a youngster</u>.

(606) is an example in which both the first and the third (but not the second) conjuncts share a material which wraps around the direct object. This type of example is derivable in a multi-modal system by assuming a phonetically null conjunction between the first and second conjuncts (perhaps tied to the intonational break), conjoining *safeguard* and *promote and even protect* in the category $VP/(VP/_wNP)\backslash(VP/_wNP)/_wNP$ (where *w* stands for the "wrapping" mode and $(VP/_wNP)\backslash(VP/_wNP)$ is the category of *from outside competition*).[5]

For the examples in (607), there is an analytic possibility (which Whitman does not consider in detail, though he mentions in passing a related idea) according to which they essentially instantiate the same pattern as the Japanese medial RNR examples in (583). More specifically, given that there is a certain degree of freedom in word order for adverbs, it seems possible to take the examples in (607) as order variants of some ordinary RNR sentences. On this view, the word order in (607) is obtained by surface reordering of the adverb, which takes place in a "reanalyzed" constituent consisting of the right conjunct and the RNR'ed material, just as in the related Japanese examples in (583). Whitman (2009) takes surface restructuring in RNR to be possible only with expressions that combine in the wrapping mode, effectively limiting MRNR to cases where surface reordering is *obligatory* independently of RNR. This is why his approach does not extend to the examples in (607). But we do not see any reason for restricting the interaction between surface restructuring and RNR. Our suggestion here is essentially to generalize the approach due to Whitman (2009) to cases where surface restructuring is optional.

To see how this approach may work, note first that a shorter adverb such as *safely* can be placed either before or after the whole infinitival VP:

(608) a. . . . an employee is unable safely to perform a non-essential job function . . . https://law.resource.org/pub/us/case/reporter/F3/213/213.F3d.209.97-50367 .html

---

5. Phonetically null conjunction is also needed in the analysis of certain nonconstituent coordination such as the following (Beavers and Sag 2004):

(i) Jan travels to Rome tomorrow, to Paris on Friday, and will fly to Tokyo on Sunday.

   b. unable to perform a non-essential job function safely

With the expression *without injury*, as Whitman notes, the preverbal position is at best awkward.

(609) ??unable without injury to perform the necessary actions

But given the acceptability of (608a), we take the awkwardness of (609) to result from some extragrammatical factors (perhaps having something to do with disrupted prosodic alignment), and we take it that the grammar is equipped with a mechanism that derives both of the orders in (608) for (any type of) adverbial expressions modifying VPs. For this purpose, we assume that the adjective *unable* and the VP modifier *without injury* combine with the infinitive in the *reordering mode*, for which the following deducibility relation holds, as well as (both ordinary and Mixed) Left and Right Association:

(610) Reordering

   $A \circ_r (B \circ_r C) \leq A \circ_r (C \circ_r B)$

This is somewhat similar to the Japanese *Scrambling* mode, but since English is head-initial, the element that stays in situ and which serves as the "pivot," as it were, of the reordering is on the left of the elements that actually undergo reordering.

   With these assumptions, (607a) can be derived as follows:

(611)

$$\cfrac{\text{unable}; \text{Adj}/_r \text{VP}_{inf} \quad \cfrac{[\varphi; \text{VP}_{inf}]^1 \quad \text{without} \circ \text{injury}; \text{VP}_{inf} \backslash_r \text{VP}_{inf}}{\varphi \circ_r (\text{without} \circ \text{injury}); \text{VP}_{inf}} \backslash_r E}{\cfrac{\cfrac{\text{unable} \circ_r (\varphi \circ_r (\text{without} \circ \text{injury})); \text{Adj}}{(\text{unable} \circ_r (\text{without} \circ \text{injury})) \circ_r \varphi; \text{Adj}} \text{PI}}{\text{unable} \circ_r (\text{without} \circ \text{injury}); \text{Adj}/_r \text{VP}_{inf}} /_r I^1}$$

$$\vdots \qquad\qquad\qquad\qquad\qquad\qquad \vdots$$

$$\cfrac{\text{unwilling} \circ_c (\text{or} \circ_c (\text{unable} \circ_r (\text{without} \circ \text{injury}))); \text{Adj}/_r \text{VP}_{inf} \quad (\text{to} \circ \text{perform} \circ \ldots); \text{VP}_{inf}}{\cfrac{(\text{unwilling} \circ_c (\text{or} \circ_c (\text{unable} \circ_r (\text{without} \circ \text{injury})))) \circ_r (\text{to} \circ \text{perform} \circ \ldots); \text{Adj}/_r \text{VP}_{inf}}{\cfrac{\text{unwilling} \circ_c (\text{or} \circ_c (\text{unable} \circ_r ((\text{without} \circ \text{injury}) \circ_r (\text{to} \circ \text{perform} \circ \ldots)))); \text{Adj}/_r \text{VP}_{inf}}{\cfrac{\text{unwilling} \circ_c (\text{or} \circ_c (\text{unable} \circ_r ((\text{to} \circ \text{perform} \circ \ldots) \circ_r (\text{without} \circ \text{injury})))); \text{Adj}/_r \text{VP}_{inf}}{\text{unwilling} \circ \text{or} \circ \text{unable} \circ \text{to} \circ \text{perform} \circ \ldots \circ \text{without} \circ \text{injury}; \text{Adj}/_r \text{VP}_{inf}} \text{PI}} \text{PI}} \text{PI}} /_r E$$

Here, by hypothesizing an embedded infinitival VP and then reordering it to the right periphery, *unable without injury* is derived as $\text{Adj}/_r \text{VP}_{inf}$. Since this is the same category as the left conjunct *unwilling*, the two are coordinated and then combined with the argument infinitival VP. Via restructuring which "incorporates" the RNR'ed material to the right conjunct, the VP modifier *without injury* can then be put back to its sentence-final position, just as in the Japanese MRNR example in (583). In short, the grammaticality of (607a) is a predicted consequence of the relative free order of adverbs modifying VPs.

(607b) receives a similar treatment. Note first that appositive postnominal modifiers can appear with or without the definite article.

(612)   a. Tony Nadal, the coach of Rafael Nadal, . . .

       b. Tony Nadal, coach of Rafael Nadal, . . .

Given this, (607b) can be analyzed as a word order variant of the following:

(613)   . . . was Tony Nadal, [the uncle] and, [since he started playing as a youngster, coach] of Rafael Nadal

In (613), the *since* clause is reordered to the beginning of the second conjunct from its conjunct-final position. (613) can be derived as a standard case of RNR, and, via further reordering after the incorporation of the RNR'ed material to the second conjunct, the surface order in (607b) is obtained.

To summarize, just as in the Japanese examples involving scrambling discussed above, in these English examples too, the apparently problematic MRNR pattern in fact receives a straightforward analysis in a multi-modal fragment, once independently motivated factors regulating relatively flexible word order possibilities of the relevant expressions are properly taken into account.

11.6   Conclusion

Medial RNR apparently poses a quite serious challenge to the like-category constituent coordination analysis of RNR standard in CG. Moreover, the phenomenon is not limited to just one language, nor is it linked to one specific type of word order variation (such as wrapping). We have shown in this chapter that, despite these apparent challenges, MRNR in fact receives a straightforward analysis in a multi-modal variant of CG. As demonstrated above, in a multi-modal system, the existence of this pattern of RNR essentially falls out from independently motivated analyses of RNR on the one hand and of phenomena (such as scrambling in Japanese) that pertain to surface word order on the other. Moreover, this analysis leads to a more principled account of the data than an ellipsis-based alternative due to Yatabe (2012, 2013); the latter type of approach leaves unexplained why the licensor string rather than the deleted string can be discontinuous. More generally, the phenomenon of MRNR is important since it provides yet another type of evidence for the architecture of grammar embodied in multi-modal variants of CG. The analysis presented above crucially exploits the multi-modal architecture in which grammatical inferences pertaining to surface word order are interspersed with inferences pertaining to the combinatoric component of grammar.

The conclusion of the present chapter thus reinforces the general conclusion in Kubota (2014) that such an architecture of grammar is essential in capturing complex interactions between phenomena pertaining to surface word order (such as scrambling) and those pertaining to the combinatoric component (such as coordination) found in natural language.

12 Comparison with Other Variants of Categorial Grammar

In this chapter, we provide a brief comparison of our framework with other variants of CG. The presentation in chapter 2 has deliberately emphasized the similarities between Hybrid TLCG and mainstream generative syntax, but being a variant of CG, Hybrid TLCG also owes a lot to the so-called lexicalist tradition in syntactic research to which most variants of CG (especially CCG) are normally assimilated. In what follows, we try to clarify what we take to be the key similarities and differences between our approach and other major variants of CG in the current literature.

12.1 Other Variants of TLCG

Variants of TLCG can all be seen as extensions of the Lambek calculus to cope with its shortcomings in dealing with phenomena such as medial extraction and quantification. They are thus closely related to each other (for example, theorems in the Lambek calculus are also theorems in all these systems). Among these different variants, Morrill's Displacement Calculus and Barker and Shan's continuation-based calculus NL_λ are most closely related to Hybrid TLCG.

12.1.1 Multi-Modal TLCG

There is a line of work in the TLCG literature, most actively investigated back in the 1990s by researchers such as Michael Moortgat, Dick Oehrle, and Rafaella Bernardi (Moortgat and Oehrle 1994; Moortgat 1997; Bernardi 2002), which sees the underlying combinatoric component of natural language syntax as a kind of substructural logic (Restall 2000). As discussed in chapter 11, the multi-modal prosodic component of (an extended version of) Hybrid TLCG is inspired by some of the technical innovations in this line of work, but the conceptual and technical underpinnings are rather different in the two approaches. One crucial difference between Hybrid TLCG and this earlier version of TLCG is that, instead of recognizing a separate level of prosodic representation, this version of TLCG deals with various (somewhat heterogeneous) phenomena ranging from morpho-syntactic properties of verb clusters in Dutch cross-serial dependencies (Moortgat and Oehrle 1994) to technical difficulties with the Lambek calculus in view of medial extraction (Moortgat 1997) via the abstract notion of "structural control," building on the technique of mixing different kinds of logic within a single deductive system originally developed in the literature of substructural logic (Restall 2000).

To see this point, it is instructive to take a look at the analysis of medial extraction in Bernardi (2002):

(614)

$$
\cfrac{
(N\backslash N)/(S/_a NP) \vdash \atop (N\backslash N)/(S/_a NP)
\quad
\cfrac{
\cfrac{
\cfrac{
NP \vdash NP
\quad
\cfrac{
\cfrac{
(NP\backslash S)/_a NP \vdash \atop (NP\backslash S)/_a NP
\quad [\, NP \vdash NP \,]^1
}{(NP\backslash S)/_a NP \circ_a NP \vdash NP\backslash S}{}_{/_a E}
\quad
{(NP\backslash S)\backslash (NP\backslash S) \vdash \atop (NP\backslash S)\backslash (NP\backslash S)}
}{((NP\backslash S)/_a NP \circ_a NP) \circ (NP\backslash S)\backslash (NP\backslash S) \vdash NP\backslash S}{}_{\backslash E}
}{NP \circ (((NP\backslash S)/_a NP \circ_a NP) \circ (NP\backslash S)\backslash (NP\backslash S)) \vdash S}{}_{\backslash E}
}{NP \circ (((NP\backslash S)/_a NP \circ (NP\backslash S)\backslash (NP\backslash S)) \circ_a NP) \vdash S}{}_{\text{Diss}}
}{
\cfrac{
\cfrac{
(NP \circ ((NP\backslash S)/_a NP \circ (NP\backslash S)\backslash (NP\backslash S))) \circ_a NP \vdash S
}{NP \circ ((NP\backslash S)/_a NP \circ (NP\backslash S)\backslash (NP\backslash S)) \vdash S/_a NP}{}_{/_a I^1}
}{}
}{}
}{}
$$

$$\text{MixAssoc}$$

$$(N\backslash N)/(S/_a NP) \circ (NP \circ ((NP\backslash S)/_a NP \circ (NP\backslash S)\backslash (NP\backslash S))) \vdash N\backslash N \quad {}_{/E}$$

Here, the derivation is written in the sequent-style natural deduction, in which a sequent is a construct of the form $\Gamma \vdash A$ where the consequent A is a syntactic type and the antecedent Γ is a structured object consisting of possibly multiple syntactic types that are combined with one another via binary connectives (of several sorts). On the leaves of the trees, we find axioms of the form $A \vdash A$, and the sequent on the final line of the proof tree is obtained by applying the rules of logic (such as the Elimination and Introduction rules similar to the ones we have posited in previous chapters) and "structural rules," which manipulate the forms of the antecedents of the sequents that are derived.

Intuitively, what is going on in the above derivation is that an object NP that is hypothesized on the right of a transitive verb is "moved" to the right edge via the structural rules of Diss and MixAssoc in the structured antecedent on the third line from the bottom. This licenses the $/_a$I rule, withdrawing the hypothesis to create the $S/_a$NP category that is suitable as an argument to the relative pronoun. After lexical substitution, the derivation in (614) embodies, for example, a formal proof of the fact that the string *which Sara wrote __ there* is a well-formed relative clause in English containing a medial gap.

There are a couple of important points of difference between this version of TLCG and other variants of categorial grammar that should already be clear from this rather cursory exposition. First, the analysis of extraction via a series of structure rewriting operations in the abstract substructural component of the type logic is very different from the prosodic λ-abstraction analysis of extraction we have adopted in our own approach, which is due originally to Muskens (2003) and is incorporated in many contemporary variants of TLCG and related approaches (such as Hybrid TLCG and Linear Categorial Grammar—see below). Second, the exact ontological status of this "multi-modal" substructural component is somewhat unclear. As noted above, the structure-changing operations have been put to use not just for extraction in English but also for dealing with complex morpho-syntactic properties of verb clustering in Dutch cross-serial dependencies (Moortgat and Oehrle 1994) (in Hybrid TLCG, the latter type of phenomenon would be dealt with in the multi-modal prosodic component, as discussed in chapter 11). All of these are done inside a complex logic of syntactic types, where these syntactic types are taken as primitives that enter into binary composition operations of various sorts having different combinatorial possibilities. While there is nothing technically wrong with this approach, it considerably obscures the conceptual underpinnings of the system as a theory of natural language syntax. But the different ontological setup in different variants of TLCG may reflect different research goals and research practices. When the emphasis is on linguistic application (as in our approach), a clear separation of ontologically distinct components would be an important point of consideration, but when the emphasis is on studying the metalogical properties of the formal calculus, building directly on the rich literature of substructural logic and formalizing the type logic for natural language syntax literally *as* a substructural logic is certainly an attractive research strategy.

12.1.2 Displacement Calculus and NL_λ

Displacement Calculus (Morrill et al. 2011; Morrill 2010) and NL_λ (Barker and Shan 2015) are perhaps the versions of categorial grammar that are closest to Hybrid TLCG in terms of both the general architecture, analytic toolkits available in the respective approaches, and the linguistic analyses of specific phenomena formulated in each. There are, however, several nontrivial differences. Roughly speaking, Hybrid TLCG's vertical slash $\upharpoonright$ plays more or less the same role as the discontinuity connectives $\uparrow$ and $\downarrow$ in Displacement Calculus and the "continuation" slashes $/\!/$ and $\backslash\!\backslash$ and in NL_λ. Many empirical analyses of linguistic phenomena formulated in one of these variants of TLCG translate to the other two more or less straightforwardly (for example, the analyses of Gapping and symmetrical predicates in Kubota and Levine [2016a] and Kubota and Levine [2016b], whose key ideas are briefly sketched above, build on Morrill's and Barker's analyses of the respective phenomena).

One major difference between the Displacement Calculus and Hybrid TLCG on the one hand and NL_λ on the other is that the latter takes **NL**, namely, the Non-associative Lambek calculus, as the underlying calculus for the directional slashes $/$ and $\backslash$. Barker and Shan (2015) briefly comment on this property of their system, alluding to the possibility of controlling flexibility of constituency via the notion of "structural control" in Multi-Modal Type-Logical Categorial Grammar (see above). This certainly is a viable view, but no explicit extension of NL_λ along these lines currently exists. The other major difference pertains to the broader architectural design: NL_λ is technically a version of Multi-Modal TLCG, and the behaviors of the two continuation slashes $/\!\!/$ and $\backslash\!\!\backslash$ are controlled by structural rules of the sort described above.

Morrill's approach differs from ours in certain important ways in the treatment of specific linguistic phenomena. The most substantial disagreement pertains to the treatment of island constraints. Morrill consistently holds the view that major island constraints should be treated within the narrow syntax (Morrill 1994, 2010, 2017), which contrasts sharply with our own view explicated in chapter 10. See also a brief discussion about determiner gapping in chapter 3 for another point of disagreement.

12.2 Combinatory Categorial Grammar

CCG (Steedman 1996, 2000) is essentially an extension of the AB Grammar that proposes to simulate movement with a limited set of additional rules. Though there are several different variants and extensions, CCG typically consists of rules of *type raising* and *function composition*, together with function application.[1] Thus, the following represents a reasonable rule set for a simple CCG fragment (to facilitate comparison, we have written these rules in the tripartite sign format and have adopted the Lambek slash notation):[2]

(615) a. Forward Function Application

$$\frac{a; \mathcal{F}; A/B \quad b; \mathcal{G}; B}{a \circ b; \mathcal{F}(\mathcal{G}); A}\text{FA}$$

b. Backward Function Application

$$\frac{b; \mathcal{G}; B \quad a; \mathcal{F}; B\backslash A}{b \circ a; \mathcal{F}(\mathcal{G}); A}\text{FA}$$

(616) a. Forward Function Composition

$$\frac{a; \mathcal{F}; A/B \quad b; \mathcal{G}; B/C}{a \circ b; \lambda x.\mathcal{F}(\mathcal{G}(x)); A/C}\text{FC}$$

b. Backward Function Composition

$$\frac{b; \mathcal{G}; C\backslash B \quad a; \mathcal{F}; B\backslash A}{b \circ a; \lambda x.\mathcal{F}(\mathcal{G}(x)); C\backslash A}\text{FC}$$

(617) a. Forward Type Raising

$$\frac{a; \mathcal{F}; A}{a; \lambda v.v(\mathcal{F}); B/(A\backslash B)}\text{TR}$$

b. Backward Type Raising

$$\frac{a; \mathcal{F}; A}{a; \lambda v.v(\mathcal{F}); (B/A)\backslash B}\text{TR}$$

---

1. In some variants of CCG (such as Steedman [2012]), type raising is not recognized as a syntactic rule, but the effects of type raising are all lexicalized. This has certain advantages in terms of computational considerations.

2. But the fragment here is an impoverished version of CCG for an expository purpose only. A linguistically more adequate version typically involves rules of "crossed" function composition (for extraction from nonperipheral positions; cf. Steedman 1996) and the so-called substitution rules for the treatment of parasitic gaps (Steedman 1987).

As noted by Steedman (1985), with type raising and function composition, we can analyze a string of words such as *John loves* as a constituent of type S/NP:

(618)
$$\frac{\dfrac{\text{john; } \mathbf{j}; \text{NP}}{\text{john; } \lambda f.f(\mathbf{j}); \text{S}/(\text{NP}\backslash\text{S})}\text{TR} \quad \text{loves; } \mathbf{love}; (\text{NP}\backslash\text{S})/\text{NP}}{\text{john} \circ \text{loves; } \lambda x.\mathbf{love}(\mathbf{j})(x); \text{S}/\text{NP}}\text{FC}$$

Thus, in CCG, essentially the same analysis of RNR is possible as in Hybrid TLCG. The same is true for DCC, as first noted by Dowty (1988). For details, we refer the reader to Dowty (1988) and Steedman (2000). Note, however, that in CCG the derived constituents in RNR and DCC are obtained by the rules in (615)–(617) rather than via hypothetical reasoning. In fact, CCG is notable for its strong thesis of "surface compositionality," according to which the semantic interpretation of a sentence is directly obtained on the basis of the surface constituent structure assigned on the basis of a limited set of "combinatory" rules like those in (615)–(617). In particular, there is no direct analogue of vertical slash in CCG.

As far as the coverage of the basic syntactic patterns of NCC is concerned, CCG and Hybrid TLCG are more or less equivalent. But things are not so simple when we consider a wider range of data. First of all, CCG does not have a fully general analysis of the interactions between coordination and quantifier scope. An analysis of wide-scope readings of quantifiers in coordination (including RNR and DCC) in examples like (619) is straightforward in CCG (as demonstrated in (620)).

(619) (Either) the department owns, or the library has an interlibrary license to, every single book in the SLAP series.

(620)
$$\vdots$$

$$\frac{\begin{array}{ll}\text{the} \circ \text{department} \circ \text{owns} \circ \text{or} \circ \text{the} \circ \text{library} \circ \text{has} \circ \text{a} \circ \text{license} \circ \text{to;} & \text{every} \circ \text{book;} \\ \lambda x.\mathbf{own}(x)(\mathbf{d}) \vee \mathbf{has\text{-}license}(x)(\mathbf{l}); \text{S}/\text{NP} & \mathbf{V}\mathbf{book}; (\text{S}/\text{NP})\backslash\text{S}\end{array}}{\begin{array}{l}\text{the} \circ \text{department} \circ \text{owns} \circ \text{or} \circ \text{the} \circ \text{library} \circ \text{has} \circ \text{a} \circ \text{license} \circ \text{to} \circ \text{every} \circ \text{book;} \\ \mathbf{V}\mathbf{book}(\lambda x.\mathbf{own}(x)(\mathbf{d}) \vee \mathbf{has\text{-}license}(x)(\mathbf{l})); \text{S}\end{array}}\text{FA}$$

However, it is unclear how the distributive readings of quantifiers, exemplified by data such as (621) (in its $\vee > \forall$ reading), are obtained in CCG.

(621) (The department used to have a heavy requirement for candidacy. For example, I no longer remember which it was, but) back in those days, every student had to pass at least two language exams or had to write QPs in both syntax and phonology.

In CCG, coordinated VPs are unambiguously of type NP\S and the subject quantifier has category S/(NP\S). Thus, only the weaker $\forall > \vee$ reading is predicted for this sentence. The discussion of the interaction between coordination and scope in Steedman (2012, section 2.3 and chapter 10) suggests that Steedman takes the distributive readings of quantifiers in coordination to be unavailable.[3] However, we have argued in chapter 4 that distributive readings for quantifiers are in fact available for both constituent coordination and NCC by setting up the appropriate pragmatic context and pronouncing the sentence in the right prosody.

It is of course conceivable to extend the rule set of CCG so that the $\vee > \forall$ reading is obtained for (621). In particular, with the rule of *argument raising* (Hendriks 1993), one can derive the type $(S/(NP\backslash S))\backslash S$ from the lower type $NP\backslash S$ for the VP. But argument raising is usually not recognized as an admissible rule in standard CCG.[4]

This reveals one important difference between TLCG and CCG: rules such as type raising, function composition, and argument raising are all theorems that can be derived from the more basic rules of inference in the more general, logic-based setup of TLCG, including ours. Thus, unless some additional constraints are imposed, the availability of both scopal relations are predicted for sentences such as (621) in TLCG, assuming that the generalized conjunction entry for *or* can be instantiated to any arbitrarily complex category. Such a prediction does not automatically follow in CCG, since only a subset of theorems in the Lambek calculus are recognized as legal syntactic rules in CCG. Whether one takes this "limited" flexibility of CCG to be desirable seems to largely depend on one's take on the status of empirical data such as (621).

Other areas of potential difficulty for CCG include the analysis of symmetrical predicates and related expressions (chapter 5) and Gapping (chapter 3). In both of these cases, we have made crucial use of the vertical slash and proposed movement-like analyses of the scope-taking properties of the relevant expressions. Since CCG does not have a direct analog of the vertical slash, the analyses we have proposed for these phenomena do not seem to translate straightforwardly to CCG. It is of course conceivable that alternative analyses of these empirical phenomena in CCG are possible, but so far as we are aware, no concrete analysis that has comparable empirical coverage to ours has been proposed in CCG to date.[5]

---

3. See also Gärtner (2012) for some discussion about quantification and scope in CCG. The treatment of distributive readings for sentences like (621) is similarly unclear in Gärtner's (2012) approach.

4. Also, the category metavariables A and B in the type-raising schema in (617) are usually taken to be restricted in a certain way in CCG, ruling out the possibility of obtaining the same effect via type raising.

5. As far as anomalous scope in Gapping is concerned, the recent proposal in HPSG by Park et al. (2019) comes closest to a starting point for such a counter-analysis in CCG. But Park et al.'s analysis relies heavily on underspecification, and not all formal details are worked out explicitly. Thus, whether the key ideas of their analysis can be implemented in CCG is still considerably unclear.

12.3 Linear Categorial Grammar

The problem that quantification (or scope-taking more generally) poses for CCG essentially stems from the fact that the forward and backward slashes that encode directionality are not the optimal tool for characterizing the mismatch between the surface position of the quantifier and its semantic scope. In fact, as we have already noted in connection to our discussion of the vertical slash, most variants of CG, including the *Lambek calculus* (Lambek 1958), have essentially the same problem. The family of CGs that we call LCG here, which include the term-labeled calculus of Oehrle (1994), *Abstract Categorial Grammar* (de Groote 2001), *Lambda Grammar* (Muskens 2003), and *Linear Categorial Grammar* (Mihalicek and Pollard 2012), have been proposed partly in response to this empirical shortcoming of "directional" variants of CG, including the Lambek calculus.

LCG is essentially Hybrid TLCG with only $\upharpoonright$ as the syntactic connective and only $\upharpoonright$I and $\upharpoonright$E as the syntactic rules. All the lexical entries involving / and \ are rewritten using $\upharpoonright$ and specifying word order directly in the prosodic form of the lexical entries via λ-terms, as in the following lexical entry for the transitive verb *saw*:[6]

(622) $\lambda\varphi_2\lambda\varphi_1.\varphi_2 \circ \mathsf{saw} \circ \varphi_1;\ \mathbf{saw};\ \mathrm{S}\upharpoonright\mathrm{NP}\upharpoonright\mathrm{NP}$

To facilitate comparison, we present in (623) the derivation for inverse scope in LCG.

(623)

$$\dfrac{\lambda\varphi_1\lambda\varphi_2.\varphi_2 \circ \mathsf{talked} \circ \mathsf{to} \circ \varphi_1;\ \mathbf{talked\text{-}to};\ \mathrm{S}\upharpoonright\mathrm{NP}\upharpoonright\mathrm{NP} \qquad \begin{bmatrix}\varphi_1;\\ x_1;\\ \mathrm{NP}\end{bmatrix}^1}{\lambda\varphi_2.\varphi_2 \circ \mathsf{talked} \circ \mathsf{to} \circ \varphi_1;\ \mathbf{talked\text{-}to}(x_1);\ \mathrm{S}\upharpoonright\mathrm{NP}}\upharpoonright\mathrm{E}$$

$$\dfrac{\begin{bmatrix}\varphi_2;\\ x_2;\\ \mathrm{NP}\end{bmatrix}^2 \qquad \lambda\varphi_2.\varphi_2 \circ \mathsf{talked} \circ \mathsf{to} \circ \varphi_1;\ \mathbf{talked\text{-}to}(x_1);\ \mathrm{S}\upharpoonright\mathrm{NP}}{\varphi_2 \circ \mathsf{talked} \circ \mathsf{to} \circ \varphi_1;\ \mathbf{talked\text{-}to}(x_1)(x_2);\ \mathrm{S}}\upharpoonright\mathrm{E}$$

$$\dfrac{\varphi_2 \circ \mathsf{talked} \circ \mathsf{to} \circ \varphi_1;\ \mathbf{talked\text{-}to}(x_1)(x_2);\ \mathrm{S} \qquad \lambda\varphi.\varphi \circ \mathsf{yesterday};\ \mathbf{yest};\ \mathrm{S}\upharpoonright\mathrm{S}}{\varphi_2 \circ \mathsf{talked} \circ \mathsf{to} \circ \varphi_1 \circ \mathsf{yesterday};\ \mathbf{yest}(\mathbf{talked\text{-}to}(x_1)(x_2));\ \mathrm{S}}\upharpoonright\mathrm{E}$$

$$\dfrac{\varphi_2 \circ \mathsf{talked} \circ \mathsf{to} \circ \varphi_1 \circ \mathsf{yesterday};\ \mathbf{yest}(\mathbf{talked\text{-}to}(x_1)(x_2));\ \mathrm{S}}{\lambda\varphi_2.\varphi_2 \circ \mathsf{talked} \circ \mathsf{to} \circ \varphi_1 \circ \mathsf{yesterday};\ \lambda x_2.\mathbf{yest}(\mathbf{talked\text{-}to}(x_1)(x_2));\ \mathrm{S}\upharpoonright\mathrm{NP}}\upharpoonright\mathrm{I}^2$$

$$\dfrac{\lambda\sigma.\sigma(\mathsf{someone});\ \mathbf{\exists_{person}};\ \mathrm{S}\upharpoonright(\mathrm{S}\upharpoonright\mathrm{NP}) \qquad \lambda\varphi_2.\varphi_2 \circ \mathsf{talked} \circ \mathsf{to} \circ \varphi_1 \circ \mathsf{yesterday};\ \lambda x_2.\mathbf{yest}(\mathbf{talked\text{-}to}(x_1)(x_2));\ \mathrm{S}\upharpoonright\mathrm{NP}}{\mathsf{someone} \circ \mathsf{talked} \circ \mathsf{to} \circ \varphi_1 \circ \mathsf{yesterday};\ \mathbf{\exists_{person}}(\lambda x_2.\mathbf{yest}(\mathbf{talked\text{-}to}(x_1)(x_2)));\ \mathrm{S}}\upharpoonright\mathrm{E}$$

$$\dfrac{\mathsf{someone} \circ \mathsf{talked} \circ \mathsf{to} \circ \varphi_1 \circ \mathsf{yesterday};\ \mathbf{\exists_{person}}(\lambda x_2.\mathbf{yest}(\mathbf{talked\text{-}to}(x_1)(x_2)));\ \mathrm{S}}{\lambda\varphi_1.\mathsf{someone} \circ \mathsf{talked} \circ \mathsf{to} \circ \varphi_1 \circ \mathsf{yesterday};\ \lambda x_1.\mathbf{\exists_{person}}(\lambda x_2.\mathbf{yest}(\mathbf{talked\text{-}to}(x_1)(x_2)));\ \mathrm{S}\upharpoonright\mathrm{NP}}\upharpoonright\mathrm{I}^1$$

$$\dfrac{\lambda\sigma.\sigma(\mathsf{everyone});\ \mathbf{\forall_{person}};\ \mathrm{S}\upharpoonright(\mathrm{S}\upharpoonright\mathrm{NP}) \qquad \lambda\varphi_1.\mathsf{someone} \circ \mathsf{talked} \circ \mathsf{to} \circ \varphi_1 \circ \mathsf{yesterday};\ \lambda x_1.\mathbf{\exists_{person}}(\lambda x_2.\mathbf{yest}(\mathbf{talked\text{-}to}(x_1)(x_2)));\ \mathrm{S}\upharpoonright\mathrm{NP}}{\mathsf{someone} \circ \mathsf{talked} \circ \mathsf{to} \circ \mathsf{everyone} \circ \mathsf{yesterday};\ \mathbf{\forall_{person}}(\lambda x_1.\mathbf{\exists_{person}}(\lambda x_2.\mathbf{yest}(\mathbf{talked\text{-}to}(x_1)(x_2))));\ \mathrm{S}}\upharpoonright\mathrm{E}$$

6. Here, for notational consistency with other parts of the book, we adopt our notation of slashes. Since $\upharpoonright$, the only syntactic connective in LCG, is really just linear implication, $A\upharpoonright B$ in our notation is more standardly written as $B \multimap A$ in the LCG literature.

Notwithstanding the elegant analysis of scope-taking phenomena available with the use of λ-binding in the prosodic component, however, LCG has its own, quite serious empirical shortcoming: unlike CCG and Lambek calculus–based variants of CG, in which there is a very simple analysis of coordination extending straightforwardly to NCC, in LCG, coordination becomes an almost intractable problem. Since this is an important empirical issue that has not received sufficient attention in the literature (but see Muskens [2001] for a cursory remark noting but ultimately dismissing the problem), we discuss it in some detail here. A more thorough discussion addressing various partial fixes one might make in LCG, such as adding information about grammatical case (none of which generalizes properly), is found in Moot (2014) (see also Kubota 2010, section 3.2.1).

The problem can be succinctly illustrated by RNR examples such as the following:

(624) Terry hates, and Leslie likes, Robin.

Suppose we attempt to derive this example in LCG. The derivation in (625) goes through straightforwardly.

(625)

$$\cfrac{\cfrac{\lambda\varphi_1\lambda\varphi_2.\varphi_2 \circ \text{hates} \circ \varphi_1;\ \textbf{hate};\ S\!\upharpoonright\!NP\!\upharpoonright\!NP \quad [\varphi_3;x;NP]^3}{\cfrac{\lambda\varphi_2.\varphi_2 \circ \text{hates} \circ \varphi_3;\ \textbf{hate}(x);\ S\!\upharpoonright\!NP}{\text{terry} \circ \text{hates} \circ \varphi_3;\ \textbf{hate}(x)(\textbf{t});\ S}\ {}_{\upharpoonright E} \quad \text{terry};\ \textbf{t};\ NP}\ {}_{\upharpoonright E}}{\lambda\varphi_3.\text{terry} \circ \text{hates} \circ \varphi_3;\ \lambda x.\textbf{hate}(x)(\textbf{t});\ S\!\upharpoonright\!NP}\ {}_{\upharpoonright I^3}$$

A parallel derivation yields the category $S\!\upharpoonright\!NP$ for *Leslie likes*. But a complication arises at this point, since, unlike in CCG (or in the Lambek calculus), in LCG, the conjuncts do not correspond to strings; they are functional terms of type **st→st**. Thus, they cannot be directly concatenated to form the coordinated string. One might think that assigning the following type of lexical entry for the conjunction word *and* (of type **(st→st)→(st→st)→(st→st)**) would work:

(626) $\lambda\sigma_1\lambda\sigma_2\lambda\varphi.\sigma_2(\boldsymbol{\varepsilon}) \circ \text{and} \circ \sigma_1(\varphi);\ \sqcap;\ (S\!\upharpoonright\!NP)\!\upharpoonright\!(S\!\upharpoonright\!NP)\!\upharpoonright\!(S\!\upharpoonright\!NP)$

Applying this functor to the two conjuncts indeed yields the following sign for the whole coordinate structure,

(627) $\lambda\varphi.\text{terry} \circ \text{hates} \circ \boldsymbol{\varepsilon} \circ \text{and} \circ \text{leslie} \circ \text{likes} \circ \varphi;\ \lambda x.\textbf{hate}(x)(\textbf{t}) \wedge \textbf{like}(x)(\textbf{l});\ S\!\upharpoonright\!NP$

to which the object NP *Robin* can be given as an argument to complete the derivation.

This analysis, however, overgenerates in a quite serious way. To see this, note that the following can also be derived as a well-formed sign with category $S\!\upharpoonright\!NP$ in LCG via hypothetical reasoning:

(628) $\lambda\varphi_1.\varphi_1 \circ \text{likes} \circ \text{robin};\ \textbf{like}(\textbf{r})(x);\ S\!\upharpoonright\!NP$

Conjoining this with the same first conjunct *Terry hates* above yields the following expression:

(629) $\lambda\varphi.\text{terry} \circ \text{hates} \circ \boldsymbol{\varepsilon} \circ \text{and} \circ \varphi \circ \text{likes} \circ \text{robin}; \lambda x.\mathbf{hate}(x)(\mathbf{t}) \wedge \mathbf{like}(\mathbf{r})(x); S\!\upharpoonright\!NP$

By giving *Leslie* as an argument to this functor, we have an analysis for the sentence *Terry hates and Leslie likes Robin*, to which the meaning "Terry hates Leslie and Leslie likes Robin" is assigned, which is obviously wrong. The problem, of course, is that what in a directional CG would be two distinct types S/NP and NP\S are conflated as both instances of S↾NP in LCG, and therefore there is no apparent way to avoid conjoining *Terry hates* with *likes Robin*.[7]

A problem of essentially the same nature arises with even more basic cases of constituent coordination such as the following, with an even more embarrassing effect:

(630) John caught and ate the fish.

Note that, in LCG, the following two signs are interderivable (hypothesizing object and subject NPs and withdrawing them in the opposite order derives (631b) from (631a)):

(631) a. $\lambda\varphi_1\lambda\varphi_2.\varphi_2 \circ \text{ate} \circ \varphi_1; \mathbf{ate}; S\!\upharpoonright\!NP\!\upharpoonright\!NP$
    b. $\lambda\varphi_2\lambda\varphi_1.\varphi_2 \circ \text{ate} \circ \varphi_1; \lambda x\lambda y.\mathbf{ate}(y)(x); S\!\upharpoonright\!NP\!\upharpoonright\!NP$

Then, a conjunction entry in (632) for coordination of transitive verbs of type S↾NP↾NP can license (630), at the expense of predicting that the sentence is ambiguous in all of the four readings in (633).

(632) $\lambda\sigma_1\lambda\sigma_2\lambda\varphi_1\lambda\varphi_2.\varphi_2 \circ \sigma_2(\boldsymbol{\varepsilon})(\boldsymbol{\varepsilon}) \circ \text{and} \circ \sigma_1(\boldsymbol{\varepsilon})(\boldsymbol{\varepsilon}) \circ \varphi_1;$
    $\sqcap; (S\!\upharpoonright\!NP\!\upharpoonright\!NP)\!\upharpoonright\!(S\!\upharpoonright\!NP\!\upharpoonright\!NP)\!\upharpoonright\!(S\!\upharpoonright\!NP\!\upharpoonright\!NP)$

(633) a. $\mathbf{caught}(\mathbf{j})(\mathbf{the\text{-}fish}) \wedge \mathbf{ate}(\mathbf{j})(\mathbf{the\text{-}fish})$
    b. $\mathbf{caught}(\mathbf{j})(\mathbf{the\text{-}fish}) \wedge \mathbf{ate}(\mathbf{the\text{-}fish})(\mathbf{j})$
    c. $\mathbf{caught}(\mathbf{the\text{-}fish})(\mathbf{j}) \wedge \mathbf{ate}(\mathbf{j})(\mathbf{the\text{-}fish})$
    d. $\mathbf{caught}(\mathbf{the\text{-}fish})(\mathbf{j}) \wedge \mathbf{ate}(\mathbf{the\text{-}fish})(\mathbf{j})$

This issue of overgeneration in coordination has received some attention in the recent LCG literature (see, e.g., Kanazawa 2015; Pollard and Worth 2015; Worth 2016). In particular, Pollard and Worth (2015) and Worth (2016) propose to overcome this problem by encoding order sensitivity for linguistic expressions that have functional

---

7. Even though Hybrid TLCG incorporates LCG as its subsystem, the type of overgeneration in LCG in coordination discussed here does not arise in Hybrid TLCG. The problem with LCG in a nutshell is that since the system allows for only the vertical slash ↾, which does not encode linear order, one is forced to specify the conjunction category for functional expressions (such as verbs) in terms of ↾, losing control over linear order. In Hybrid TLCG (as in CCG), the conjunction category is specified in terms of directional slashes (except for the case of Gapping, which receives a different treatment due to the fact that the "gap" is medial), and conjunction entries such as (626) and (632) discussed here are not posited.

prosodies via operators called "phenominators" that make reference to fine-grained subtyping in the prosodic type system encoding directionality information. This enables simulating most of the empirical analyses of coordination developed in directional variants of CG within LCG. However, based on the results reported in Pollard and Worth (2015) and Worth (2016), it is as yet not totally clear whether a completely general characterization of the prosodic subtyping system involving phenominators can be worked out. Until such a characterization is provided, we take it that coordination poses a major empirical challenge for LCG.

13 Conclusion

Coordination and ellipsis represent two major empirical domains that have been extensively investigated in the literature of generative grammar. As should be clear by now, the complex and recalcitrant issues that are abundant in these two empirical domains constitute the touchstone for any adequate theory of the syntax-semantics interface of natural language. We hope to have convinced the reader through the detailed analyses of some of the major phenomena in these respective empirical domains that the explicit and flexible syntax-semantics interface of Hybrid TLCG offers an attractive alternative to the currently dominant phrase structure–based architecture of grammar (in the broader sense encompassing both transformational and nontransformational approaches).

The conceptual shift tied to this alternative perspective is to take the notion of "proof" (as opposed to hierarchical constituent structure) as the central guiding principle underlying the combinatoric component of syntax. At first sight, this may appear to be a rather radical move, entailing an (almost) wholesale abandonment of one of the most fundamental notions of contemporary syntactic theory. One of the points we tried to make in the present monograph is that the distance between the familiar syntactic theories and the logic-based approach we have argued for is not as large as it may initially appear, and the latter can be seen as a proper extension of (at least the core component of) the former, for the following two reasons.

First, there are certain phenomena that receive straightforward analyses only by taking the logic-based approach, such as the Gapping/auxiliary scope interaction and the interactions between various scopal expressions and nonconstituent coordination phenomena. Second, as we have noted in several places throughout the monograph, the logic-based approach often enables us to synthesize various analytic ideas that have been proposed separately whose connection to each other has so far been almost entirely overlooked in the literature. This includes the local and nonlocal analyses of respective predication, the derivability relation between the higher-order and lower-order entries of modal auxiliaries, and the anaphora-based analysis of ellipsis that is sensitive to (certain types of) syntactic information. In this sense, nothing important (at least nothing fundamentally important as a primitive "building block" for a theory of syntax) is lost by giving up the notion of phrase structural constituency. This is unsurprising, since from the logic-based perspective, the traditional architecture taking phrase structural constituency as a primitive notion is, in a sense, just an impoverished proof system that has only modus ponens (and no hypothetical reasoning) as a deductive rule. Thus, it is only natural that hidden similarities of related ideas become fully explicit by recasting them in a fully general system.

We thus hope to have convinced the reader that the logic-based architecture embodied in Hybrid TLCG (and TLCG more generally) offers an interesting alternative perspective on the basic architecture of a formal theory of natural language syntax and semantics. But even limiting our attention to English, the empirical domains we have focused on in the present monograph by no means exhaust the entire domain of study in syntactic research, and it is important to keep in mind that the success of our approach should ultimately be evaluated against a much wider range of empirical facts than we have been able to cover in the present monograph. Some of the major issues we have left out include the following:

- a detailed investigation of extraction phenomena, in particular, the treatment of multiple-gap phenomena (including "parasitic gaps" and ATB extraction)
- partially productive patterns in syntax that are not easily lexicalizable, such as phrasal idioms and "constructions" (Boas and Sag 2012; Goldberg 1995)
- aspects of compositional semantics in which the notion of inference (in the broader sense) plays a central role, such as anaphora and "projective content" (including presupposition projection) (Tonhauser et al. 2013)

These are all empirical domains that have been actively investigated in the current literature, and for this reason, we believe that exploring them in detail in future study in our approach, in comparison with alternative proposals in competing approaches, will shed further light on the nature of syntactic theory as well as on the empirical phenomena themselves.

A Formal Fragment of Hybrid TLCG

A.1 Syntactic, Semantic, and Prosodic Types

Syntactic types are defined as follows:

(634) Atomic types include (at least) NP, N, PP, and S.

(635) Directional types
  a. An atomic type is a directional type.
  b. If A and B are directional types, then (A/B) is a directional type.
  c. If A and B are directional types, then $(B \backslash A)$ is a directional type.
  d. If A and B are directional types, then $(A \vee B)$ is a directional type.
  e. If A and B are directional types, then $(A \wedge B)$ is a directional type.
  f. Nothing else is a directional type.

(636) Syntactic types
  a. A directional type is a syntactic type.
  b. If A and B are syntactic types, then $(A \upharpoonright B)$ is a syntactic type.
  c. Nothing else is a syntactic type.

We omit outermost parentheses and parentheses for a sequence of the same type of slash, assuming that $/$ and $\upharpoonright$ are left associative, and $\backslash$ right associative. Thus, S/NP/NP, NP\NP\S, and S$\upharpoonright$NP$\upharpoonright$NP are abbreviations of $((S/NP)/NP)$, $(NP \backslash (NP \backslash S))$, and $((S \upharpoonright NP) \upharpoonright NP)$, respectively.

Note that the algebra of syntactic types is *not* a free algebra generated over the set of atomic types with the three binary connectives $/$, $\backslash$, and $\upharpoonright$. Specifically, given the definitions in (634)–(636), in Hybrid TLCG, a vertical slash cannot occur "under" a directional slash. Thus, S/(S$\upharpoonright$NP) is not a well-formed syntactic type. One way to make sense of this restriction is to think of it as a "filter" on uninterpretable prosodic objects. An expression with syntactic type X/(Y$\upharpoonright$Z) would have to concatenate a string to the left of a functor of type **st→st**, but it does not make sense (at least if one takes the "meanings" of slashes literally) to "concatenate" a string to the left of a *function* from strings to strings since concatenation is an operation defined only on strings.

The functions Sem and Pros, which map syntactic types to semantic and prosodic types, can be defined as follows:

(637) a. For atomic syntactic types,
       Sem(NP) = Sem(PP) = e, Sem(S) = t, Sem(N) = $e \rightarrow t$
    b. For complex syntactic types,

$$\mathrm{Sem}(A/B) = \mathrm{Sem}(B\backslash A) = \mathrm{Sem}(A\upharpoonright B) = \mathrm{Sem}(B) \to \mathrm{Sem}(A)$$
$$\mathrm{Sem}(A \vee B) = \mathrm{Sem}(A) = \mathrm{Sem}(B)$$
$$\mathrm{Sem}(A \wedge B) = \mathrm{Sem}(A) \times \mathrm{Sem}(B)$$

(638) a. For any directional type A, $\mathrm{Pros}(A) = \mathbf{st}$ (with $\mathbf{st}$ for "strings").

  b. For any complex syntactic type $A\upharpoonright B$ involving the vertical slash $\upharpoonright$,
     $\mathrm{Pros}(A\upharpoonright B) = \mathrm{Pros}(B) \to \mathrm{Pros}(A)$.

Note in particular that, corresponding to the asymmetry between $/$, $\backslash$, and $\upharpoonright$ in the definition of syntactic types, the two types of slashes behave differently in the mapping from syntactic to prosodic types. Specifically, for the mapping from syntactic types to prosodic types, only the vertical slash $\upharpoonright$ is effectively interpreted as functional. Thus, for example, $\mathrm{Sem}(S\upharpoonright(S/NP)) = (e \to t) \to t$, whereas $\mathrm{Pros}(S\upharpoonright(S/NP)) = \mathbf{st}{\to}\mathbf{st}$.

The prosodic calculus is a λ-calculus with constants of type $\mathbf{st}$ (which includes ordinary string prosodies such as john, walks, and so on, and the empty string $\boldsymbol{\varepsilon}$) and a binary connective $\circ$ for string concatenation. In addition to beta equivalence, the following axioms hold in the prosodic calculus:

(639) a. $\boldsymbol{\varepsilon} \circ a \equiv a$ (left identity)

  b. $a \circ \boldsymbol{\varepsilon} \equiv a$ (right identity)

(640) $a \circ (b \circ c) \equiv (a \circ b) \circ c$ (associativity)

In the derivations, we omit parentheses for $\circ$ and implicitly assume associativity (except in the multi-modal fragment in chapter 11).

A.2 Sample Lexicon

(641) a. john; $\mathbf{j}$; NP

  b. mary; $\mathbf{m}$; NP

  c. walks; $\mathbf{walk}$; NP$\backslash$S

  d. loves; $\mathbf{love}$; (NP$\backslash$S)/NP

  e. $\lambda\sigma.\sigma(\text{everyone})$; $\mathbf{V_{person}}$; $S\upharpoonright(S\upharpoonright NP)$

  f. $\lambda\varphi\lambda\sigma.\sigma(\text{every} \circ \varphi)$; $\mathbf{V}$; $S\upharpoonright(S\upharpoonright NP)\upharpoonright N$

  g. $\lambda\sigma.\sigma(\text{must})$; $\lambda\mathscr{F}.\Box\mathscr{F}(\mathrm{id}_{et})$; $S\upharpoonright(S\upharpoonright(\mathrm{VP}/\mathrm{VP}))$ (where $\mathrm{id}_{et} = \lambda P_{et}.P$)

For strings in prosodic representations we use sans-serif. Semantic constants are written in **bold-face**. For prosodic variables we use Greek letters $\varphi_1, \varphi_2, \ldots$ (type $\mathbf{st}$ for string). $\sigma_1, \sigma_2, \ldots$ (type $\mathbf{st}{\to}\mathbf{st}$, $\mathbf{st}{\to}\mathbf{st}{\to}\mathbf{st}$, and so on); $\tau_1, \tau_2, \ldots$ (type $(\mathbf{st}{\to}\mathbf{st}){\to}\mathbf{st}$, and so on). For semantic variables we use roman italics $(x, y, z, p, q, \ldots, P, Q, R, \ldots)$. Calligraphic letters $(\mathcal{U}, \mathcal{V}, \mathcal{W}, \ldots)$ are invariably used for variables with polymorphic types. We use copperplate letters $(\mathscr{P}, \mathscr{Q}, \ldots)$ for higher-order variables of fixed types.

A.3 Syntactic Rules

A.3.1 Logical Rules

(642)

Connective	Introduction	Elimination

/

$$\begin{array}{c} \vdots \quad [\varphi; x; A]^n \quad \vdots \\ \vdots \quad \vdots \quad \vdots \\ \dfrac{b \circ \varphi; \mathcal{F}; B}{b; \lambda x.\mathcal{F}; B/A}/\text{I}^n \end{array}$$

$$\dfrac{a; \mathcal{F}; A/B \quad b; \mathcal{G}; B}{a \circ b; \mathcal{F}(\mathcal{G}); A}/\text{E}$$

\

$$\begin{array}{c} \vdots \quad [\varphi; x; A]^n \quad \vdots \\ \vdots \quad \vdots \quad \vdots \\ \dfrac{\varphi \circ b; \mathcal{F}; B}{b; \lambda x.\mathcal{F}; A\backslash B}\backslash\text{I}^n \end{array}$$

$$\dfrac{b; \mathcal{G}; B \quad a; \mathcal{F}; B\backslash A}{b \circ a; \mathcal{F}(\mathcal{G}); A}\backslash\text{E}$$

$\upharpoonright$

$$\begin{array}{c} \vdots \quad [\varphi; x; A]^n \quad \vdots \\ \vdots \quad \vdots \quad \vdots \\ \dfrac{b; \mathcal{F}; B}{\lambda \varphi.b; \lambda x.\mathcal{F}; B\upharpoonright A}\upharpoonright\text{I}^n \end{array}$$

$$\dfrac{a; \mathcal{F}; A\upharpoonright B \quad b; \mathcal{G}; B}{a(b); \mathcal{F}(\mathcal{G}); A}\upharpoonright\text{E}$$

All of the three slashes are linear. That is, the three connectives can bind only one occurrence of a hypothesis at a time. Note also that the prosodic labels in Hybrid TLCG are not proof terms but rather are used for the purpose of narrowing down the set of possible derivations. Specifically, the applicability of the Introduction rule for / (\) is conditioned by the presence of the variable φ at the right (left) periphery in the prosody of the premise.

In addition to the rules for the implication connectives above, we assume the following rules for the meet and join connectives:

(643) a. Left Meet Elimination

$$\dfrac{a; \mathcal{F}; A \wedge B}{a; \pi_1(\mathcal{F}); A}\wedge\text{E}_l$$

b. Right Meet Elimination

$$\dfrac{a; \mathcal{F}; A \wedge B}{a; \pi_2(\mathcal{F}); B}\wedge\text{E}_r$$

(644) a. Left Join Introduction

$$\dfrac{a; \mathcal{F}; B}{a; \mathcal{F}; A \vee B}\vee\text{I}_l$$

b. Right Join Introduction

$$\dfrac{a; \mathcal{F}; A}{a; \mathcal{F}; A \vee B}\vee\text{I}_r$$

Note that we assume that meet is semantically potent whereas join is semantically nonpotent (see Bayer [1996] for the distinction between semantically potent and nonpotent variants of meet and join).

A.3.2 Nonlogical Rule

(645) P-Interface rule

$$\frac{\varphi_0;\; \mathcal{F};\; A}{\varphi_1;\; \mathcal{F};\; A}\text{PI}$$

——where φ_0 and φ_1 are equivalent terms in the prosodic calculus

The P-Interface rule is the analogue of the structural rules in other variants of TLCG (Morrill 1994; Moortgat 1997). This rule is used for applying beta-reduction to prosodic terms obtained by function application via the $\upharpoonright$E rule. For example, a more "pedantic" and technically precise (but cumbersome) version of the quantifier scope derivation in (22) from chapter 2 would contain the following proof steps (note the step-by-step β-reduction in the prosodic component mediated by PI):

(646)

$$\frac{\begin{array}{cc}\lambda\sigma.\sigma(\text{someone}); & \lambda\varphi_2.\varphi_2\circ\text{talked}\circ\text{to}\circ\varphi_1\circ\text{yesterday};\\ \exists_{\textbf{person}};\text{S}\upharpoonright(\text{S}\upharpoonright\text{NP}) & \lambda x_2.\textbf{yest}(\textbf{talked-to}(x_1)(x_2));\text{S}\upharpoonright\text{NP}\end{array}}{\dfrac{\lambda\sigma.[\sigma(\text{someone})](\lambda\varphi_2.\varphi_2\circ\text{talked}\circ\text{to}\circ\varphi_1\circ\text{yesterday});}{\dfrac{\lambda\varphi_2.[\varphi_2\circ\text{talked}\circ\text{to}\circ\varphi_1\circ\text{yesterday}](\text{someone});}{\begin{array}{c}\text{someone}\circ\text{talked}\circ\text{to}\circ\varphi_1\circ\text{yesterday};\\ \exists_{\textbf{person}}(\lambda x_2.\textbf{yest}(\textbf{talked-to}(x_1)(x_2)));\text{S}\end{array}}\text{PI}}}\upharpoonright\text{E}$$

In practice, we omit explicitly writing the application of this rule to avoid cluttering the derivations.

One way to understand the (apparent) asymmetry between the $\upharpoonright$I rule and the $/$I and $\backslash$I rules as formulated above as to the explicit presence of λ-binding in the prosodic component in the former but not in the latter two is to think of the $/$I and $\backslash$I rules as abbreviations of the following proof steps:

(647)

$$\frac{\dfrac{[\varphi;\; x;\; A]^n}{\dfrac{b\circ\varphi;\; \mathcal{F};\; B}{\lambda_r\varphi.[b\circ\varphi](\boldsymbol{\varepsilon});\; \lambda x.\mathcal{F};\; B/A}/\text{I}^n}}{b;\; \lambda x.\mathcal{F};\; B/A}\text{PI}$$

That is, there is actually lambda binding (by "left" and "right" lambdas) in the prosody in the $/$I and $\backslash$I rules, but the functional lambda terms obtained are immediately applied to the empty string to "close off" the gap. On this view, the $/$I and $\backslash$I rules are not so different from the $\upharpoonright$I rule after all, but the key difference is that, unlike the $\upharpoonright$I rule, the $/$I and $\backslash$I rules are immediately followed by an obligatory application to the empty string, so that a string prosody rather than a functional prosody is obtained.

A.4   The Status of Syntactic Features

In the present monograph, we have assumed the following syntactic features:

(648)   a.   S:

- $\{bse, fin, pst, ger, \ldots\}$ (for "vform")
- $\{+, -, \varnothing\}pol$

b.   NP:

- $\pm p$ ("pronominal")
- $\pm wh$
- $\{nom, acc, dat\}$ (for case)
- $\{pl, sg\}$ (for number)

c.   PP:

- $\{to, from, about, \ldots\}$ (for "pform"),

d.   (for all atomic types): $\{1, 2, 3, 4, \ldots\}$ (for clause-level index, written superscript)

These features are to be thought of as playing analogous roles to syntactic features in lexicalist frameworks of syntax such as HPSG and LFG. While it is in principle possible to work out a formal theory of syntactic features and feature instantiation/unification along the lines done, for example, in HPSG, we leave the full development of a theory of syntactic features in categorial grammar for future work and instead adopt a simplistic view (described below) for the time being (for a more sophisticated approach dealing with syntactic features via subtyping within the logic itself making use of dependent types, see Morrill [1994] and Pogodalla and Pompigne [2012]).

Specifically, for the fragment in this book, we take all syntactic categories with different subscript (and superscript) notations to be distinct *atomic* categories. Formally, syntactic category notations in which the relevant features are omitted are all metavariable notations (and thus, not real syntactic categories/types) in the lexicon. The metavariable notations range over all the atomic categories that instantiate the omitted feature(s) in one way or another. For example, taking the clause-level index superscript n to range over $\{1, 2, 3\}$, the case feature to range over $\{nom, acc, dat\}$, and three binary features $\pm wh$, $\pm p$, sg/pl, NP is a metavariable notation for $3 \times 3 \times 2 \times 2 \times 2 = 72$ distinct atomic categories. This may give the misleading impression that our lexicon/grammar lacks a way to handle lexical generalizations, but this is an artificial consequence of leaving out the development of a proper theory of the lexicon for the time being. In syntactic derivations, whenever we omit feature specifications, it should be understood as an abbreviation for some appropriately specified atomic category.

Bibliography

Abbott, Barbara. 1976. Right Node Raising as a test for constituenthood. *Linguistic Inquiry* 7: 639–642.

Abeillé, Anne, Gabriela Bîlbîie, and Francois Mouret. 2014. A Romance perspective on Gapping constructions. In *Romance in Construction Grammar*, eds. H. Boas and F. Gonzálvez García, 227–265. Amsterdam: John Benjamins.

Abels, Klaus. 2018. Movement and islands. In *The Oxford handbook of ellipsis*, eds. Jeroen van Craenenbroeck and Tanja Temmerman, 389–424. Oxford: Oxford University Press.

Abels, Klaus, and Luisa Martí. 2010. A unified approach to split scope. *Natural Language Semantics* 18: 435–470.

Ades, Anthony F., and Mark J. Steedman. 1982. On the order of words. *Linguistics and Philosophy* 4 (4): 517–558.

Ajdukiewicz, Kazimierz. 1935. Die syntaktische Konnexität. In *Polish logic 1920-1939*, ed. Storrs McCall, 207–231. Oxford: Oxford University Press. Translated from *Studia Philosophica*, Vol. 1: 1–27.

Akmajian, Adrian, and Frank Heny. 1975. *An introduction to the principles of Transformational Syntax*. Cambridge, MA: MIT Press.

Alexiadou, Artemis. 1997. *Adverb placement*. Amsterdam: John Benjamins.

Alonso-Ovalle, Luis. 2006. Disjunction in alternative semantics. PhD diss, University of Massachusetts Amherst.

Bach, Emmon. 1979. Control in Montague Grammar. *Linguistic Inquiry* 10 (4): 515–531.

Bach, Emmon, and Barbara Partee. 1980. Anaphora and semantic structure. In *Papers from the parasession on pronouns and anaphora*, eds. K. J. Kreiman and A. Ojeda, 1–28. University of Chicago: Chicago Linguistic Society.

Bach, Emmon, and Barbara Partee. 1984. Quantification, pronouns, and VP anaphora. In *Truth, interpretation and information*, eds. Jeroen Groenendijk, Theo Janssen, and Martin Stokhof, 99–130. Dordrecht: Foris.

Bachrach, Asaf, and Roni Katzir. 2007. Spelling out QR. In *Proceedings of Sinn und Bedeutung 11*, ed. E. Puig-Waldmueller, 63–75. Barcelona: Universitat Pompeu Fabra.

Bachrach, Asaf, and Roni Katzir. 2008. Right-Node Raising and delayed spellout. In *Interphases: Phase-theoretic investigations of linguistic interfaces*, ed. Kleanthes K. Grohmann, 249–259. Oxford: Oxford University Press.

Bacskai-Atkari, Julia. 2014. The syntax of comparative constructions: Operators, ellipsis phenomena and functional left peripheries. PhD diss, Universitätsverlag Potsdam.

Baker, C. L. 1978. *Introduction to Generative-Transformational Grammar*. New York: Prentice-Hall.

Baldridge, Jason. 2002. Lexically specified derivational control in Combinatory Categorial Grammar. PhD diss, University of Edinburgh.

Baltin, Mark. 2000. Implications of pseudogapping for binding and the representation of information structure. Unpublished manuscript. Available at https://as.nyu.edu/content/dam/nyu-as/faculty/documents/gapping.doc.

Bar-Hillel, Yehoshua. 1953. A quasi-arithmetic notation for syntactic descriptions. *Language* 29: 47–58.

Bar-Hillel, Yehoshua, Chaim Gaifman, and Eliyahu Shamir. 1960. On categorial and phrase structure grammars. *Bulletin of the Research Council of Israel* 9F: 1–16. Also in Bar-Hillel (ed.) 1964, *Language and information*, Chapter 8 (Boston: Addison Wesley).

Barker, Chris. 2007. Parasitic scope. *Linguistics and Philosophy* 30 (4): 407–444.

Barker, Chris. 2012. The same people ordered the same dishes. In *UCLA Working Papers in Linguistics: Theories of everything*, eds. Thomas Graf, Denis Paperno, Anna Szabolcsi, and Jos Tellings, Vol. 17, 7–14. Department of Linguistics, UCLA. Available at http://phonetics.linguistics.ucla.edu/wpl/issues/wpl17/papers/02_barker.pdf.

Barker, Chris. 2013. Scopability and sluicing. *Linguistics and Philosophy* 36 (3): 187–223.

Barker, Chris, and Chung-chieh Shan. 2015. *Continuations and natural language*. Oxford: Oxford University Press.

Barros, Matthew, Patrick D. Elliott, and Gary Thoms. 2014. There is no island repair. Unpublished manuscript. Available at http://ling.auf.net/lingbuzz/002100/.

Barros, Matthew, and Luis Vicente. 2011. Right node raising requires both ellipsis and multidomination. In *University of Pennsylvania Working Papers in Linguistics*, Vol. 17. art. 2.

Bayer, Samuel. 1996. The coordination of unlike categories. *Language* 72: 579–616.

Beavers, John, and Ivan A. Sag. 2004. Coordinate ellipsis and apparent non-constituent coordination. In *Proceedings of the 11th International Conference on Head-Driven Phrase Structure Grammar*, ed. Stefan Müller, 48–69. Stanford: CSLI. Available at http://web.stanford.edu/group/cslipublications/cslipublications/HPSG/2004/.

Beck, Sigrid. 2000. The semantics of 'different': Comparison operator and relational adjective. *Linguistics and Philosophy* 23 (2): 101–139.

Beghelli, Fillipo, and Tim Stowell. 1997. Distributivity and negation: The syntax of *each* and *every*. In *Ways of scope taking*, ed. Anna Szabolcsi, 71–107. Dordrecht: Kluwer.

Bekki, Daisuke. 2006. Heikooteki-kaishaku-niokeru yoosokan-junjo-to bunmyaku-izon-sei (The order of elements and context dependence in the "respective" interpretation). In *Nihon Gengo-Gakkai Dai 132-kai Taikai Yokooshuu (Proceedings from the 132nd Meeting of the Linguistic Society of Japan)*, 47–52.

Bekki, Daisuke. 2014. Representing anaphora with dependent types. In *Logical Aspects of Computational Linguistics 2014*, eds. Nicholas Asher and Sergei Soloviev, 14–29. Heidelberg: Springer.

Bekki, Daisuke, and Koji Mineshima. 2017. Context-passing and underspecification in Dependent Type Semantics. In *Modern perspectives in type-theoretical semantics*, eds. Stergios Chatzikyriakidis and Zhaohui Luo, 11–41. Heidelberg: Springer.

Belk, Zoë, and Ad Neeleman. 2018. Multi-dominance, Right-Node Raising and coordination. Available at https://ling.auf.net/lingbuzz/003848.

Bennett, Michael. 1974. Some extensions of a Montague fragment of English. PhD diss, UCLA.

Bernardi, Raffaella. 2002. Reasoning with polarity in categorial type logic. PhD diss, University of Utrecht.

Bever, Thomas. 1970. The cognitive basis for linguistic structures. In *Cognition and language development*, ed. John R. Hayes, 279–362. New York: John Wiley and Sons.

Bloomfield, Leonard. 1933. *Language*. New York: Holt, Rinehart and Winston.

Boas, Franz. 1911. Introduction. In *The handbook of American Indian languages*, ed. Franz Boas, 1–70. Washington, DC: Bureau of American Ethnology.

Boas, Hans C., and Ivan A. Sag. 2012. *Sign-based Construction Grammar*. Stanford: CSLI.

Boeckx, Cedric. 2012. *Syntactic islands*. Cambridge: Cambridge University Press.

Bouma, Gosse, Rob Malouf, and Ivan A. Sag. 2001. Satisfying constraints on extraction and adjunction. *Natural Language and Linguistic Theory* 19 (1): 1–65.

Brame, Michael. 1976. *Conjectures and refutations in syntax and semantics*. New York: North-Holland.

Brame, Michael. 1978. *Base generated syntax*. Seattle: Noit Amrofer.

Brasoveanu, Adrian. 2011. Sentence-internal *different* as quantifier-internal anaphora. *Linguistics and Philosophy* 34 (2): 93–168.

Bresnan, Joan. 1977. Variables in the theory of transformations. In *Formal syntax*, eds. Peter W. Culicover, Thomas Wasow, and Adrian Akmajian, 157–196. New York: Academic Press.

Bresnan, Joan. 1982. The passive in lexical theory. In *The mental representation of grammatical relations*, ed. Joan Bresnan, 3–86. Cambridge, MA: MIT Press.

Bresnan, Joan, Ash Asudeh, Ida Toivonen, and Stephen Wechsler. 2016. *Lexical Functional Syntax*, 2nd ed. Hoboken, NJ: Blackwell.

Bumford, Dylan, and Chris Barker. 2013. Association with distributivity and the problem of multiple antecedents for singular *different*. *Linguistics and Philosophy* 36: 355–369.

Büring, Daniel. 2005. *Binding theory*. Cambridge: Cambridge University Press.

Campbell, Jeremy. 1982. *Grammatical man*. New York: Simon & Schuster.

Carlson, Greg N. 1987. Same and different: Some consequences for syntax and semantics. *Linguistics and Philosophy* 10 (4): 531–565.

Carpenter, Bob. 1997. *Type-logical semantics*. Cambridge, MA: MIT Press.

Champollion, Lucas. 2010. Cumulative readings of *every* do not provide evidence for events and thematic roles. In *Logic, language and meaning*, eds. M. Aloni, H. Bastiaanse, T. de Jager, and K. Schulz, 213–222. Heidelberg: Springer.

Chaves, Rui Pedro. 2005. A linearization-based approach to gapping. In *FG-MOL 2005: The 10th Conference on Formal Grammar and the 9th Meeting on Mathematics of Language*, eds. G. Jäger, P. Monachesi, G. Penn, and S. Wintner, 207–220. University of Edinburgh, Scotland. Available at https://web.stanford.edu/group/cslipublications/cslipublications/FG/2005/FGMoL05.pdf.

Chaves, Rui Pedro. 2007. Coordinate structures: Constraint-based syntax-semantics processing. PhD diss, University of Lisbon. Available at https://ubir.buffalo.edu/xmlui/handle/10477/38718.

Chaves, Rui Pedro. 2008. Linearization-based word-part ellipsis. *Linguistics and Philosophy* 31 (3): 261–307.

Chaves, Rui Pedro. 2009. Construction-based cumulation and adjunct extraction. In *Proceedings of the 16th International Conference on Head-Driven Phrase Structure Grammar*, 47–67. Stanford: CSLI. Available at http://web.stanford.edu/group/cslipublications/cslipublications/HPSG/2009/.

Chaves, Rui. 2012. Conjunction, cumulation and respectively readings. *Journal of Linguistics* 48 (2): 297–344.

Chaves, Rui. 2013. An expectation-based account of subject islands and parasitism. *Journal of Linguistics* 49: 285–327.

Chaves, Rui P. 2014. On the disunity of right-node raising phenomena: Extraposition, ellipsis, and deletion. *Language* 90 (4): 834–886.

Chaves, Rui, and Jeruen E. Dery. 2019. Frequency effects in subject islands. *Journal of Linguistics* 55: 475–521.

Chaves, Rui P., and Michael T. Putnam. 2020. *Unbounded dependency constructions: Theoretical and experimental perspectives*. Oxford: Oxford University Press.

Chomsky, Noam. 1957. *Syntactic structures*. The Hague: Mouton.

Chomsky, Noam. 1964. *Current issues in linguistic theory*. The Hague: Mouton.

Chomsky, Noam. 1971. *Problems of knowledge and freedom*. New York: Random House.

Chomsky, Noam. 1973. Conditions on transformations. In *A festschrift for Morris Halle*, eds. Stephen A. Anderson and Paul Kiparsky, 232–286. New York: Holt, Rinehart and Winston.

Chomsky, Noam. 1980. On binding. *Linguistic Inquiry* 11: 1–46.

Chomsky, Noam. 1981. *Lectures on government and binding*. Dordrecht: Foris.

Chomsky, Noam. 1982. *The generative enterprise*. Dordrecht: Foris.

Chomsky, Noam. 1986a. *Barriers*. Cambridge, MA: MIT Press.

Chomsky, Noam. 1986b. Changing perspectives on knowledge and use of language. In *The representation of knowledge and belief*, eds. Myles Brand and Robert M. Harnish, 1–58. Tucson: University of Arizona Press.

Chomsky, Noam. 1995. *The Minimalist Program*. Cambridge, MA: MIT Press.

Chomsky, Noam, and Howard Lasnik. 1977. Filters and control. *Linguistic Inquiry* 8: 425–504.

Chung, Sandra. 2013. Syntactic identity in sluicing: How much, and why. *Linguistic Inquiry* 44 (1): 1–44.

Cinque, Guglielmo. 1989. "Long" *wh*-movement and referentiality. Talk given at the Second Princeton Workshop on Comparative Grammar, Princeton University.

Cinque, Guglielmo. 1990. *Types of A'-dependencies*. Cambridge, MA: MIT Press.

Cinque, Guglielmo. 1999. *Adverbs and functional heads*. Oxford: Oxford University Press.

Cipollone, Domenic. 2001. Morphologically complex predicates in Japanese and what they tell us about grammar architecture. In *Ohio State University Working Papers in Linguistics*, eds. Michael W. Daniels, David Dowty, Anna Feldman, and Vanessa Metcalf, Vol. 56, 1–52. Ohio State University: Department of Linguistics. Available at https://linguistics.osu.edu/sites/default /files/osu_wpl_56_sm.pdf.

Cohen, J. M. 1967. The equivalence of two concepts of categorial grammar. *Information and Control* 10: 475–484.

Cooper, Robin. 1979. The interpretation of pronouns. In *Selections from the Third Groningen Round Table*, eds. Frank Heny and Helmut S. Schnelle. Vol. 10 of *Syntax and semantics*, 61–92. New York: Academic Press.

Cooper, Robin. 1983. *Quantification and syntactic theory*. Vol. 21 of *Synthese language library*. Dordrecht: Reidel.

Copestake, Ann, Dan Flickinger, Carl Pollard, and Ivan A. Sag. 2005. Minimal Recursion Semantics: An introduction. *Research on Language and Computation* 4 (3): 281–332.

Coppock, Elizabeth. 2001. Gapping: In defense of deletion. In *Proceedings of the Chicago Linguistic Society 37*, eds. Mary Andronis, Christopher Ball, Heidi Elston, and Sylvain Neuvel, 133–147. University of Chicago: Chicago Linguistic Society.

Cresswell, Max J. 1976. The semantics of degree. In *Montague Grammar*, ed. Barbara H. Partee, 261–292. New York: Academic Press.

Crysmann, Berthold. 2003. An asymmetric theory of peripheral sharing in HPSG: Conjunction reduction and coordination of unlikes. In *Proceedings of Formal Grammar 2003*, eds. Gerhard Jäger, Paola Monachesi, Gerald Penn, and Shuly Wintner, 47–62. Available at https://web .stanford.edu/group/cslipublications/cslipublications/FG/2003/.

Culicover, Peter. 1999. *Syntactic nuts: Hard cases, syntactic theory and language acquisition*. Oxford: Oxford University Press.

Culicover, Peter W. 1993. Evidence against ECP accounts of the *that*-t effect. *Linguistic Inquiry* 24: 557–561.

Culicover, Peter W., and Ray Jackendoff. 2005. *Simpler syntax*. Oxford: Oxford University Press.

Culicover, Peter, and Susanne Winkler. 2019. Parasitic gaps aren't parasitic, or, the case of the uninvited guest. Unpublished manuscript.

Curry, Haskell B. 1961. Some logical aspects of grammatical structure. In *Structure of language and its mathematical aspects*, ed. Roman Jakobson. Vol. 12 of *Symposia on applied mathematics*, 56–68. Providence: American Mathematical Society.

Dalrymple, Mary. 2001. *Lexical Functional Grammar*. Vol. 34 of *Syntax and semantics*. New York: Academic Press.

Dalrymple, Mary, Makoto Kanazawa, Yookyung Kim, Sam Mchombo, and Stanley Peters. 1998. Reciprocal expressions and the concept of reciprocity. *Linguistics and Philosophy* 21 (2): 159–210.

Dalrymple, Mary, Stuart M. Shieber, and Fernando C. N. Pereira. 1991. Ellipsis and higher-order unification. *Linguistics and Philosophy* 14 (4): 399–452.

Deane, Paul. 1991. Limits to attention: A cognitive theory of island phenomena. *Cognitive Linguistics* 2 (1): 1–63.

de Groote, Philippe. 2001. Towards abstract categorial grammars. In *Association for Computational Linguistics, 39th Annual Meeting and 10th Conference of the European Chapter*, 148–155. Association for Computational Linguistics. Available at https://www.aclweb.org/anthology/P01-1033.pdf.

Dotlacil, Jakub. 2010. Anaphora and distributivity. PhD diss, Utrecht University.

Dougherty, Ray C. 1970. A grammar of coördinate conjoined structures, I. *Language* 46 (4): 850–898.

Dougherty, Ray C. 1971. A grammar of coördinate conjoined structures, II. *Language* 47 (2): 298–339.

Dowty, David. 1982. Grammatical relations and Montague Grammar. In *The nature of syntactic representation*, eds. Pauline Jacobson and Geoffrey K. Pullum, 79–130. Dordrecht: Reidel.

Dowty, David. 1985. A unified indexical analysis of same and different: A response to Stump and Carlson. Unpublished manuscript. Columbus: Ohio State University.

Dowty, David. 1987. Collective predicates, distributive predicates, and *all*. In *Proceedings of the 1986 Eastern States Conference on Linguistics (ESCOL)*, eds. Fred Marshall, Ann Miller, and Zheng sheng Zhang, 97–115. Columbus: Ohio State University.

Dowty, David. 1988. Type raising, functional composition, and non-constituent conjunction. In *Categorial grammars and natural language structures*, eds. Richard T. Oehrle, Emmon Bach, and Deirdre Wheeler, 153–197. Dordrecht: Reidel.

Dowty, David. 1994. The role of negative polarity and concord marking in natural language reasoning. In *Proceedings of SALT 4*, eds. Mandy Harvey and Lynn Santelmann, 114–144. Ithaca, NY: Cornell University. Available at http://journals.linguisticsociety.org/proceedings/index.php/SALT/issue/view/105.

Dowty, David. 1996a. Non-constituent coordination, wrapping, and multimodal categorial grammars. Expanded draft of Aug. 1996 paper from International Congress of Logic, Methodology, and Philosophy of Science in M. L. Dalla Chiara et al. (eds.) 1997, *Structures and norms in science*, 347-368, Dordrecht: Springer.

Dowty, David R. 1996b. Toward a minimalist theory of syntactic structure. In *Discontinuous constituency*, eds. Harry Bunt and Arthur van Horck. Vol. 6 of *Natural language processing*, 11–62. Berlin: de Gruyter.

Dowty, David. 2007. Compositionality as an empirical problem. In *Direct compositionality*, eds. Chris Barker and Pauline Jacobson, 23–101. Oxford: Oxford University Press.

Du, Jiali, and Pingfang Yu. 2012. Predicting garden path sentences based on natural language understanding systems. *International Journal of Advanced Computer Science and Applications* 3 (11): 1–6.

Eggert, Randall. 2000. Grammaticality and context with respect to *and . . .* and *or . . .* respectively. In *Proceedings of the Thirty-Sixth Annual Meeting of the Chicago Linguistics Society*, 93–107. University of Chicago: Chicago Linguistic Society.

Elbourne, Paul. 2008. Ellipsis sites as definite descriptions. *Linguistic Inquiry* 39 (2): 191–220.

Engdahl, Elisabet. 1985. Parasitic gaps, resumptive pronouns, and subject extractions. *Linguistics* 23: 3–44.

Fanselow, Gisbert, Caroline Féry, Matthias Schlesewsky, and Ralf Vogel, eds. 2006. *Gradience in grammar: Generative perspectives*. Oxford: Oxford University Press.

Fodor, Janet Dean. 1978. Parsing strategies and constraints on transformations. *Linguistic Inquiry* 9 (3): 427–473.

Frazier, Michael, David Potter, and Masaya Yoshida. 2012. Pseudo noun phrase coordination. In *Proceedings of WCCFL 30*, 142–152. Somerville, MA: Cascadilla Press.

Gärtner, Hans-Martin. 2012. Function composition and the linear local modeling of extended neg-scope. In *Local modelling of non-local dependencies in syntax*, eds. Artemis Alexiadou, Tibor Kiss, and Gereon Müller, 337–352. Berlin: de Gruyter.

Gawron, Jean Mark, and Andrew Kehler. 2002. The semantics of the adjective *respective*. In *Proceedings of WCCFL 21*, 85–98. Somerville, MA: Cascadilla Press.

Gawron, Jean Mark, and Andrew Kehler. 2004. The semantics of respective readings, conjunction, and filler-gap dependencies. *Linguistics and Philosophy* 27 (2): 169–207.

Gazdar, Gerald. 1981. Unbounded dependencies and coordinate structure. *Linguistic Inquiry* 12: 155–184.

Gazdar, Gerald, Ewan Klein, Geoffrey K. Pullum, and Ivan A. Sag. 1985. *Generalized Phrase Structure Grammar*. Cambridge, MA: Harvard University Press.

Gazdar, Gerald, Geoffrey Pullum, and Ivan Sag. 1982. Auxiliaries and related phenomena in a restrictive theory of grammar. *Language* 58: 591–638.

Gengel, Kristen. 2013. *Pseudogapping and ellipsis*. Oxford: Oxford University Press.

Gibson, Edward. 2018. Why are syntactic "island" structures complex? Complex syntax only? Or because of their complex meanings? Available at http://thescienceoflanguage.com/2018 /09/17/why-are-syntactic-island-structures-complex-complex-syntax-only-or-because-of-their -complex-meanings/.

Ginzburg, Jonathan, and Ivan A. Sag. 2000. *Interrogative investigations: The form, meaning, and use of English interrogatives*. Stanford: CSLI.

Goldberg, Adele E. 1995. *Constructions: A Construction Grammar approach to argument structure*. Chicago: University of Chicago Press.

Goldsmith, John A. 1985. A principled exception to the Coordinate Structure Constraint. In *CLS 21 Part 1: Papers from the general session*, 133–143. University of Chicago: Chicago Linguistic Society.

Goodhue, Daniel. 2019. High negation questions and epistemic bias. In *Proceedings of Sinn und Bedeutung 23*, eds. M. Teresa Espinal, Elena Castroviejo, Manuel Leonetti, Louise McNally, and Cristina Real-Puigdollers Vol. 1, 469–485, Universitat autonoma de Barcelona. Available at https://ojs.ub.uni-konstanz.de/sub/index.php/sub/issue/view/25.

Haïk, Isabelle. 1987. Bound VPs that need to be. *Linguistics and Philosophy* 10 (4): 503–530.

Hardt, Daniel. 1993. Verb phrase ellipsis: Form, meaning, and processing. PhD diss, University of Pennsylvania.

Hardt, Daniel. 1999. Dynamic interpretation of verb phrase ellipsis. *Linguistics and Philosophy* 22: 187–221.

Harris, Zellig. 1946. From morpheme to utterance. *Language* 22: 161–183.

Harris, Zellig. 1951. *Methods in structural linguistics*. Chicago: University of Chicago Press.

Hellan, Lars. 1981. *Towards an integrated analysis of comparatives*. Tübingen: Narr.

Hendriks, Herman. 1993. Studied flexibility. PhD diss, University of Amsterdam.

Hendriks, Petra. 1995a. Comparatives and categorial grammar. PhD diss, University of Groningen.

Hendriks, Petra. 1995b. Ellipsis and multimodal categorial type logic. In *Formal Grammar: Proceedings of the Conference of the European Summer School in Logic, Language and Information, Barcelona, 1995*, eds. Glyn V. Morrill and Richard T. Oehrle, 107–122.

Hepple, Mark. 1990. The grammar and processing of order and dependency: A categorial approach. PhD diss, University of Edinburgh.

Hoeksema, Jack. 2006. Pseudogapping: Its syntactic analysis and cumulative effects on its acceptability. *Research on Language and Computation* 4 (4): 335–352.

Hofmeister, Philip. 2010. A linearization account of *either . . . or* constructions. *Natural Language and Linguistic Theory* 28: 275–314.

Hofmeister, Philip, Inbal Arnon, T. Florian Jaeger, Ivan Sag, and Neal Snider. 2013. The source ambiguity problem: Distinguishing the effects of grammar and processing on acceptability judgments. *Language and Cognitive Processes* 28: 48–87.

Hofmeister, Philip, and Ivan A. Sag. 2010. Cognitive constraints and island effects. *Language* 86 (2): 366–415.

Houser, Michael J. 2010. The syntax and semantics of *do so* anaphora. PhD diss, University of California, Berkeley.

Howard, William A. 1969. The formulae-as-types notion of construction. In Jonathan P. Seldin and J. Roger Hindley (eds.) 1980, *To H. B. Curry: Essays on combinatory logic, lambda calculus, and formalism*, 479–490 (New York: Academic Press).

Huang, C. T. James. 1982. Logical relations in Chinese and the theory of grammar. PhD diss, MIT.

Huang, C. T. James. 1993. Reconstruction and the structure of VP: Some theoretical consequences. *Linguistic Inquiry* 24 (1): 103–138.

Huddleston, Rodney, Geoffrey K. Pullum, and Peter Peterson. 2002. Relative clause constructions and unbounded dependencies. In *The Cambridge grammar of the English language*, eds. Rodney Huddleston and Geoffrey K. Pullum, 1031–1096. Cambridge: Cambridge University Press.

Hudson, Richard A. 1976. Conjunction Reduction, Gapping and Right-node Raising. *Language* 52 (3): 535–562.

Hunter, Tim. 2015. Deconstructing Merge and Move to make room for adjunction. *Syntax* 18 (3): 266–319.

Hyemes, Dell, and John H. Fought. 1981. *American Structuralism*. The Hague: Mouton.

Iatridou, Sabine, and Hedde Zeijlstra. 2013. Negation, polarity and deontic modals. *Linguistic Inquiry* 44: 529–568.

Jackendoff, Ray. 1977. *X-bar syntax: A study of phrase structure*. Cambridge, MA: MIT Press.

Jackendoff, Ray S. 1971. Gapping and related rules. *Linguistic Inquiry* 2 (1): 21–35.

Jacobs, Joachim. 1980. Lexical decomposition in Montague Grammar. *Theoretical Linguistics* 7: 121–136.

Jacobs, Roderick A., and Peter S. Rosenbaum. 1968. *English Transformational Grammar*. Waltham, MA: Blaisdell.

Jacobson, Pauline. 1992. Antecedent Contained Deletion in a variable-free semantics. In *Proceedings of SALT 2*, eds. Chris Barker and David Dowty, 193–213. Department of Linguistics, Ohio State University. Available at https://journals.linguisticsociety.org/proceedings/index.php /SALT/issue/view/81.

Jacobson, Pauline. 1998. Antecedent Contained Deletion and pied-piping: Evidence for a variable-free semantics. In *Proceedings of SALT 8*, eds. Devon Strolovitch and Aaron Lawson, 74–91. Ithaca, NY: Cornell University. Available at https://journals.linguisticsociety.org /proceedings/index.php/SALT/issue/view/101.

Jacobson, Pauline. 2007. Direct compositionality and variable-free semantics: The case of "Principle B" effects. In *Direct compositionality*, eds. Chris Barker and Pauline Jacobson, 191–236. Oxford: Oxford University Press.

Jacobson, Pauline. 2008. Direct compositionality and variable-free semantics: The case of Antecedent Contained Deletion. In *Topics in ellipsis*, ed. Kyle Johnson, 30–68. Cambridge: Cambridge University Press.

Jacobson, Pauline. 2009. Do representations matter or do meanings matter?: The case of antecedent containment. In *Theory and evidence in semantics*, eds. Erhard Hinrichs and John Nerbonne, 81–107. Stanford: CSLI.

Jacobson, Pauline. 2016. The short answer: Implications for direct compositionality (and vice versa). *Language* 92 (2): 331–375.

Jacobson, Pauline. 2019. Ellipsis in categorial grammar. In *The Oxford handbook of ellipsis*, eds. Jeroen van Craenenbroeck and Tanja Temmerman, 122–141. Oxford: Oxford University Press.

Jäger, Gerhard. 2005. *Anaphora and Type-Logical Grammar*. Berlin: Springer.

Jayaseelan, K. A. 1990. Incomplete VP deletion and Gapping. *Linguistic Analysis* 20: 64–81.

Johnson, Kyle. 2000. Few dogs eat Whiskas or cats Alpo. In *University of Massachusetts Occasional Papers*, eds. Kiyomi Kusumoto and Elisabeth Villalta, Vol. 23, 47–60. University of Massachusetts Amherst: GLSA.

Johnson, Kyle. 2001. What VP ellipsis can do, and what it can't, but not why. In *The handbook of contemporary syntactic theory*, eds. Mark Baltin and Chris Collins, 439–479. Oxford: Blackwell.

Johnson, Kyle. 2004. In search of the English middle field. Unpublished manuscript. Available at http://people.umass.edu/kbj/homepage/Content/middle_field.pdf.

Johnson, Kyle. 2009. Gapping is not (VP-) ellipsis. *Linguistic Inquiry* 40 (2): 289–328.

Joos, Martin, ed. 1957. *Readings in linguistics*. Chicago: University of Chicago Press.

Kamp, Hans. 1975. Two theories of adjectives. In *Formal semantics of natural language*, ed. Edward Keenan, 123–155. Cambridge: Cambridge University Press.

Kanazawa, Makoto. 2015. Syntactic features for regular constraints and an approximation of directional slashes in Abstract Categorial Grammars. In *Proceedings for ESSLLI 2015 Workshop "Empirical Advances in Categorial Grammar"*, eds. Yusuke Kubota and Robert Levine, 34–70. University of Tsukuba and Ohio State University. Available at https://www2.ninjal.ac.jp/kubota /papers/procCG2015.pdf.

Kandybowicz, Jason. 2006. Comp-trace effects explained away. In *Proceedings of WCCFL 25*, 220–228. Somerville, MA: Cascadilla Press.

Kandybowicz, Jason. 2009. Embracing edges: Syntactic and phono-syntactic edge sensitivity in Nupe. *Natural Language and Linguistic Theory* 27 (2): 305–344.

Karttunen, Lauri. 1977. Syntax and semantics of questions. *Linguistics and Philosophy* 1 (1): 3–44.

Kathol, Andreas. 1995. Linearization-based German syntax. PhD diss, Ohio State University.

Kathol, Andreas. 2000. *Linear syntax*. Oxford: Oxford University Press.

Kay, Paul. 1989. Contextual operators: *Respective, respectively,* and *vice versa*. In *Proceedings of BLS 15*, 181–192. Berkeley, CA: Berkeley Linguistic Society. Available at https://journals .linguisticsociety.org/proceedings/index.php/BLS/article/view/3359.

Kayne, Richard. 1983. Connectedness. *Linguistic Inquiry* 14: 223–249.

Kehler, Andrew. 2002. *Coherence, reference, and the theory of grammar*. Stanford: CSLI.

Keller, Frank. 1998. Gradient grammaticality as an effect of selective constraint re-ranking. In *Papers from the 34th Meeting of the Chicago Linguistic Society, vol. 2*, eds. M. C. Gruber, D. Higgins, K. S. Olson, and T. Wysocki, 95–109. University of Chicago: Chicago Linguistic Society.

Kennedy, Christopher. 1994/2008. Argument contained ellipsis, Linguistics Research Center Report LRC-94–03, University of California, Santa Cruz. Reprinted in Kyle Johnson (ed.) 2008, *Topics in Ellipsis*, 95–131. Cambridge: Cambridge University Press.

Kennedy, Christopher. 2003. Ellipsis and syntactic representation. In *The interfaces: Deriving and interpreting omitted structures*, eds. Kerstin Schwabe and Susanne Winkler, 29–53. Amsterdam: John Benjamins.

Kennedy, Christopher. 2005. Comparatives, semantics of, 2nd ed. In *Encyclopedia of language and linguistics*, 690–694. Oxford: Elsevier.

Kennedy, Christopher, and Jason Merchant. 2000. Attributive comparative deletion. *Natural Language and Linguistic Theory* 18 (1): 89–146.

Kennedy, Christopher, and Jason Stanley. 2008. What an average semantics needs. In *Proceedings of SALT 18*, eds. Tova Friedman and Satoshi Ito, 465–482. Ithaca, NY: Cornell University. Available at https://journals.linguisticsociety.org/proceedings/index.php/SALT/issue/view/91.

Kertz, Laura. 2010. Ellipsis reconsidered. PhD diss, University of California, San Diego.

Kertz, Laura. 2013. Verb phrase ellipsis: The view from information structure. *Language* 89 (3): 390–428.

Kim, Christina S., and Jeffrey T. Runner. 2018. The division of labor in explanations of verb phrase ellipsis. *Linguistics and Philosophy* 41 (1): 41–85.

Kim, Jong-Bok, and Ivan Sag. 2002. Negation without head movement. *Natural Language and Linguistic Theory* 20: 339–412.

Kiparsky, Paul, and Carol Kiparsky. 1971. Fact. In *Semantics: An interdisciplinary reader in philosophy, linguistics, and psychology*, eds. Danny D. Steinberg and Leon A. Jacobovits, 345–369. Cambridge: Cambridge University Press.

Klein, Ewan, and Ivan Sag. 1985. Type-driven translation. *Linguistics and Philosophy* 8 (2): 163–201.

Kluender, Robert. 1998. On the distinction between strong and weak islands: A processing perspective. In *The limits of syntax*, eds. Peter Culicover and Louise McNally. Vol. 29 of *Syntax and semantics*, 241–279. San Diego: Academic Press.

Kluender, Robert. 2004. Are subject islands subject to a processing account? In *Proceedings of WCCFL 23*, 101–125. Somerville, MA: Cascadilla Press.

Koopman, Hilda. 2000. *The syntax of specifiers and heads*. London: Routledge.

Kraak, Esther. 1998. A deductive account of French object clitics. In *Complex predicates in nonderivational syntax*, eds. Erhard W. Hinrichs, Andreas Kathol, and Tsuneko Nakazawa. Vol. 30 of *Syntax and semantics*, 271–312. San Diego: Academic Press.

Kratzer, Angelika. 2007. On the plurality of verbs. In *Event structures in linguistic form and interpretation*, eds. Johannes Dölling, Tatjana Heyde-Zybatow, and Martin Schäfer, 269–300. Berlin: de Gruyter.

Krifka, Manfred. 1990. Boolean and non-boolean "and". In *Papers from the Second Symposium on Logic and Language*, eds. L. Kálmán and L. Polos, 161–188. Budapest: Akadémiai Kiadó.

Kroch, Anthony. 1989. Amount quantification, referentiality, and long *wh*-movement. Unpublished manuscript: University of Pennsylvania. Available at https://repository.upenn.edu/pwpl /vol5/iss2/3/.

Kubota, Yusuke. 2007. The scope interpretation of complex predicates in Japanese: A unified lexicalist analysis. *Journal of Linguistics* 43 (3): 489–530.

Kubota, Yusuke. 2010. (In)flexibility of constituency in Japanese in Multi-Modal Categorial Grammar with Structured Phonology. PhD diss, Ohio State University.

Kubota, Yusuke. 2014. The logic of complex predicates: A deductive synthesis of "argument sharing" and "verb raising." *Natural Language and Linguistic Theory* 32 (4): 1145–1204.

Kubota, Yusuke. 2015. Nonconstituent coordination in Japanese as constituent coordination: An analysis in Hybrid Type-Logical Categorial Grammar. *Linguistic Inquiry* 46 (1): 1–42.

Kubota, Yusuke, and Carl Pollard. 2010. Phonological interpretation into preordered algebras. In *The Mathematics of Language: 10th and 11th Biennial Conference*, eds. Christian Ebert, Gerhard Jäger, and Jens Michaelis, 200–209. Berlin: Springer.

Kubota, Yusuke, and Jungmee Lee. 2015. The Coordinate Structure Constraint as a discourse-oriented principle: Further evidence from Japanese and Korean. *Language* 91 (3): 642–675.

Kubota, Yusuke, and Robert Levine. 2012. Gapping as like-category coordination. In *Logical Aspects of Computational Linguistics 2012*, eds. Denis Béchet and Alexander Dikovsky, 135–150. Heidelberg: Springer.

Kubota, Yusuke, and Robert Levine. 2013a. Coordination in Hybrid Type-Logical Categorial Grammar. In *OSU Working Papers in Linguistics*, Vol. 60, 21–50. Ohio State University: Department of Linguistics.

Kubota, Yusuke, and Robert Levine. 2013b. Determiner gapping as higher-order discontinuous constituency. In *Proceedings of Formal Grammar 2012 and 2013*, eds. Glyn Morrill and Mark-Jan Nederhof, 225–241. Heidelberg: Springer.

Kubota, Yusuke, and Robert Levine. 2014a. Pseudogapping as pseudo-VP ellipsis. In *Logical Aspects of Computational Linguistics 2014*, eds. Nicholas Asher and Sergei Soloviev, 122–137. Heidelberg: Springer.

Kubota, Yusuke, and Robert Levine. 2014b. Unifying local and nonlocal modelling of respective and symmetrical predicates. In *Proceedings of Formal Grammar 2014*, eds. Glyn Morrill, Reinhard Muskens, Rainer Osswald, and Frank Richter, 104–120. Heidelberg: Springer.

Kubota, Yusuke, and Robert Levine. 2015. Against ellipsis: Arguments for the direct licensing of "non-canonical" coordinations. *Linguistics and Philosophy* 38 (6): 521–576.

Kubota, Yusuke, and Robert Levine. 2016a. Gapping as hypothetical reasoning. *Natural Language and Linguistic Theory* 34 (1): 107–156.

Kubota, Yusuke, and Robert Levine. 2016b. The syntax-semantics interface of "respective" predication: A unified analysis in Hybrid Type-Logical Categorial Grammar. *Natural Language and Linguistic Theory* 34 (3): 911–973.

Kubota, Yusuke, and Robert Levine. 2017. Pseudogapping as pseudo-VP ellipsis. *Linguistic Inquiry* 48 (2): 213–257.

Kubota, Yusuke, Koji Mineshima, Robert Levine, and Daisuke Bekki. 2019. Underspecification and interpretive parallelism in Dependent Type Semantics. In *Proceedings of the IWCS 2019 Workshop on Computing Semantics with Types, Frames and Related Structures*, 1–9. Gothenburg, Sweden: Association for Computational Linguistics. Available at https://www.aclweb.org/anthology/W19-1001.

Kuno, Susumu. 1973. *The structure of the Japanese language*. Cambridge, MA: MIT Press.

Kuno, Susumu. 1976. Gapping: A functional analysis. *Linguistic Inquiry* 7: 300–318.

Kuno, Susumu. 1981. The syntax of comparative clauses. In *Chicago Linguistic Society*, eds. Roberta Hendrick, Carrie Masek, and Miller Mary Frances, Vol. 17, 136–155. Chicago: University of Chicago.

LaCara, Nicholas J. 2016. Anaphora, inversion and focus. PhD diss, University of Massachusetts Amherst.

Lakoff, George. 1986. Frame semantic control of the Coordinate Structure Constraint. In *CLS 22 Part 2: Papers from the parasession on pragmatics and grammatical theory*, eds. Anne M. Farley, Peter T. Farley, and Karl-Erik McCullough, 152–167. University of Chicago: Chicago Linguistic Society.

Lambek, Joachim. 1958. The mathematics of sentence structure. *American Mathematical Monthly* 65 (3): 154–170.

Landman, Fred. 1989. Groups, I & II. *Linguistics and Philosophy* 12: 559–605, 723–744.

Landman, Fred. 2000. *Events and plurality*. Dordrecht: Kluwer.

Lasersohn, Peter. 1988. A semantics for groups and events. PhD diss, Ohio State University.

Lasersohn, Peter. 1992. Generalized conjunction and temporal modification. *Linguistics and Philosophy* 15 (4): 381–410.

Lasnik, Howard. 1999. Pseudogapping puzzles. In *Fragments: Studies in ellipsis and gapping*, eds. Shalom Lappin and Elabbas Benmamoun, 141–174. Oxford: Oxford University Press.

Lasnik, Howard, and Mamuru Saito. 1984. On the nature of proper government. *Linguistic Inquiry* 15: 235–289.

Lasnik, Howard, and Mamuru Saito. 1992. *Move α*. Cambridge, MA: MIT Press.

Levin, Nancy S. 1979. Main verb ellipsis in spoken English. PhD diss, Ohio State University. Available at https://linguistics.osu.edu/sites/default/files/workingpapers/osu_wpl_24.pdf.

Levin, Nancy S., and Ellen F. Prince. 1986. Gapping and causal implicature. *Papers in Linguistics* 19: 351–364.

Levine, Robert. 2011. Linearization and its discontents. In *Proceedings of the 18th International Conference on Head-Driven Phrase Structure Grammar*, ed. Stefan Müller, 126–146. Stanford: CSLI. Available at http://web.stanford.edu/group/cslipublications/cslipublications/HPSG/2011/.

Levine, Robert. 2013. The modal need VP gap (non)anomaly. In *Beyond "any" and "ever": New perspectives on negative polarity sensitivity*, eds. Eva Csipak, Regine Eckardt, Mingya Liu, and Manfred Sailer, 241–265. Berlin: de Gruyter.

Levine, Robert D., and Ivan Sag. 2003. Wh-nonmovement. *Gengo Kenkyu: Journal of the Linguistic Society of Japan* 123: 171–219. Available at https://www.jstage.jst.go.jp/article/gengo1939/2003/123/2003_123_171/_pdf/-char/en.

Levine, Robert D., and Paul Postal. 2004. A corrupted linguistics. In *The anti-Chomsky reader*, eds. Peter Collier and David Horowitz, 203–231. San Francisco: Encounter Books.

Levine, Robert D., and Thomas E. Hukari. 2006. *The unity of unbounded dependency constructions*. Stanford: CSLI.

Lin, Vivian. 2000. Determiner sharing. In *Proceedings of the WCCFL 19*, eds. R. Billerey and B. D. Lillenhaugen, 274–287. Somerville, MA: Cascadilla Press.

Lin, Vivian. 2001. A way to undo A movement. In *Proceedings of WCCFL 20*, eds. Karine Megerdoomian and Leora Anne Bar-el, 358–371. Somerville, MA: Cascadilla Press.

Lin, Vivian. 2002. Coordination and sharing at the interfaces. PhD diss, MIT.

Link, Godehard. 1983. The logical analysis of plurals and mass terms: A lattice-theoretical approach. In *Meaning, use, and interpretation of language*, eds. Rainer Bäuerle, Christoph Schwarze, and Arnim von Stechow, 302–323. Berlin: de Gruyter.

Martin, Scott. 2013. The dynamics of sense and implicature. PhD diss, Ohio State University.

Martin, Scott, and Carl Pollard. 2014. A dynamic categorial grammar. In *Proceedings of Formal Grammar 2014*, eds. Glyn Morrill, Reinhard Muskens, Rainer Osswald, and Frank Richter, 138–154. Heidelberg: Springer.

Martin-Löf, Per. 1984. *Intuitionistic type theory*. Naples, Italy: Bibliopolis.

Matsumoto, Yoshiko. 1997. *Noun-modifying constructions in Japanese: A Frame Semantics approach*. Amsterdam: John Benjamins.

Matthewson, Lisa. 2001. Quantification and the nature of crosslinguistic variation. *Natural Language Semantics* 9 (2): 145–189.

Maxwell, John T., and Christopher D. Manning. 1996. A theory of non-constituent coordination based on finite-state rules. In *Proceedings of the LFG '96 Conference*, eds. Miriam Butt and Tracy Holloway King. Stanford: CSLI. Available at http://web.stanford.edu/group /cslipublications/cslipublications/LFG/LFG1-1996/.

McCawley, James D. 1993. Gapping with shared operators. In *Proceedings of Berkeley Linguistics Society 19*, ed. David A. Peterson, 245–253. Berkeley: University of California, Berkeley. Available at https://journals.linguisticsociety.org/proceedings/index.php/BLS/article/view /1507.

McCawley, James D. 1998. *The syntactic phenomena of English*, 2nd ed. Chicago: University of Chicago Press.

McCloskey, James. 1979. *Transformational syntax and model-theoretic semantics*. Dordrecht: Reidel.

Merchant, Jason. 2001. *The syntax of silence*. Oxford: Oxford University Press.

Merchant, Jason. 2004. Fragments and ellipsis. *Linguistics and Philosophy* 27 (6): 661–738.

Merchant, Jason. 2008a. An asymmetry in voice mismatches in VP-ellipsis and pseudogapping. *Linguistic Inquiry* 39 (1): 169–179.

Merchant, Jason. 2008b. Variable island repair under ellipsis. In *Topics in ellipsis*, ed. Kyle Johnson, 132–153. Cambridge: Cambridge University Press.

Merchant, Jason. 2015. On ineffable predicates: Bilingual Greek-English code-switching under ellipsis. *Lingua* 166: 199–213.

Merchant, Jason. 2019. Ellipsis: A survey of analytical approaches. In *The Oxford handbook of ellipsis*, eds. Jeroen van Craenenbroeck and Tanja Temmerman, 19–45. Oxford: Oxford University Press.

Michel, Daniel. 2014. Individual cognitive measures and working memory accounts of syntactic island phenomena. PhD diss, University of California, San Diego.

Mihalicek, Vedrana. 2012. Serbo-Croatian word order: A logical approach. PhD diss, Ohio State University.

Mihalicek, Vedrana, and Carl Pollard. 2012. Distinguishing phenogrammar from tectogrammar simplifies the analysis of interrogatives. In *Formal Grammar 2010/2011*, eds. Philippe de Groote and Mark-Jan Nederhof, 130–145. Heidelberg: Springer.

Miller, Philip. 1990. Pseudogapping and *do so* substitution. In *Proceedings of CLS 26*, Vol. 1, 293–305. University of Chicago: Chicago Linguistic Society.

Miller, Philip. 1991. Clitics and constituents in phrase structure grammar. PhD diss, University of Utrecht.

Miller, Philip. 2014. A corpus study of pseudogapping and its theoretical consequences. In *Empirical issues in syntax and semantics*, ed. Christopher Piñón, Vol. 10, 73–90. Available at http://www.cssp.cnrs.fr/eiss10/eiss10_miller.pdf.

Miller, Philip, and Geoffrey K. Pullum. 2013. Exophoric VP ellipsis. In *The core and the periphery: Data-driven perspectives on syntax inspired by Ivan A. Sag*, eds. Philip Hofmeister and Elisabeth Norcliffe, 5–32. Stanford: CSLI.

Moltmann, Frederike. 1992. Reciprocals and *same/different*: Towards a semantic analysis. *Linguistics and Philosophy* 15 (4): 411–462.

Montague, Richard. 1973. The proper treatment of quantification in ordinary English. In *Approaches to natural language: Proceedings of the 1970 Stanford Workshop on Grammar and Semantics*, eds. Jaakko Hintikka, Julius M. E. Moravcsik, and Patrick Suppes, 221–242. Dordrecht: Reidel.

Moortgat, Michael. 1988. *Categorial investigations: Logical and linguistic aspects of the Lambek calculus*. Dordrecht: Foris.

Moortgat, Michael. 1990. The quantification calculus. In *Theory of flexible interpretation: Esprit DYANA deliverable R.1.2.A*, eds. Herman Hendriks and Michael Moortgat. Institute for Language, Logic and Information, University of Amsterdam.

Moortgat, Michael. 1997. Categorial type logics. In *Handbook of logic and language*, eds. Johan van Benthem and Alice ter Meulen, 93–177. Amsterdam: Elsevier.

Moortgat, Michael. 2014. Typelogical grammar. In *The Stanford encyclopedia of philosophy (spring 2014 ed.)*, ed. Edward N. Zalta. Stanford University. Available at https://plato.stanford.edu/archives/spr2014/entries/typelogical-grammar/.

Moortgat, Michael, and Richard T. Oehrle. 1994. Adjacency, dependence, and order. In *Proceedings of the Ninth Amsterdam Colloquium*, eds. Paul Dekker and Martin Stokhof, 447–466. Universiteit van Amsterdam: Instituut voor Taal, Logica, en Informatica.

Moot, Richard. 2014. Hybrid Type-Logical Grammars, first-order linear logic and the descriptive inadequacy of Lambda grammars. Unpublished manuscript: Laboratoire Bordelais de Recherche en Informatique.

Moot, Richard, and Christian Retoré. 2012. *The logic of categorial grammars: A deductive account of natural language syntax and semantics*. Heidelberg: Springer.

Moot, Richard, and Symon Jory Stevens-Guille. 2019. Proof-theoretic aspects of Hybrid Type-Logical Grammars. In *Formal Grammar, 24th international conference, FG 2019*, 84–100. Heidelberg: Springer.

Morrill, Glyn. 1994. *Type Logical Grammar: Categorial logic of signs*. Dordrecht: Kluwer.

Morrill, Glyn. 2010. *Categorial grammar: Logical syntax, semantics, and processing*. Oxford: Oxford University Press.

Morrill, Glyn. 2017. Grammar logicised: Relativisation. *Linguistics and Philosophy* 40 (2): 119–163.

Morrill, Glyn, and Josep-Maria Merenciano. 1996. Generalizing discontinuity. *Traitement Automatique des Langues* 27 (2): 119–143.

Morrill, Glyn, and Oriol Valentín. 2017. A reply to Kubota and Levine on gapping. *Natural Language and Linguistic Theory* 35 (1): 257–270.

Morrill, Glyn, Oriol Valentín, and Mario Fadda. 2011. The displacement calculus. *Journal of Logic, Language and Information* 20 (1): 1–48.

Morrill, Glyn, and Teresa Solias. 1993. Tuples, discontinuity, and gapping in categorial grammar. In *Proceedings of the Sixth Conference on European Chapter of the Association for Computational Linguistics*, 287–296. Morristown, NJ: Association for Computational Linguistics. Available at https://www.aclweb.org/anthology/E93-1034/.

Mouret, Francois. 2006. A phrase structure approach to argument cluster coordination. In *Proceedings of the 13th International Conference on Head-Driven Phrase Structure Grammar*, ed. Stefan Müller, 247–267. Stanford: CSLI. Available at http://web.stanford.edu/group/cslipublications/cslipublications/HPSG/2006/.

Mukai, Emi. 2003. On verbless conjunction in Japanese. In *Proceedings of NELS 33*, eds. Makoto Kadowaki and Shigeto Kawahara, 205–224. University of Massachusetts Amherst: GLSA.

Müller, Gereon. 2010. On deriving CED effects from the PIC. *Linguistic Inquiry* 41 (1): 35–82.

Muskens, Reinhard. 2001. Categorial Grammar and Lexical-Functional Grammar. In *Proceedings of the LFG '01 Conference*, eds. Miriam Butt and Tracy Holloway King. University of Hong Kong. Available at http://web.stanford.edu/group/cslipublications/cslipublications/LFG/6/lfg01.html.

Muskens, Reinhard. 2003. Language, lambdas, and logic. In *Resource sensitivity in binding and anaphora*, eds. Geert-Jan Kruijff and Richard Oehrle, 23–54. Dordrecht: Kluwer.

Muskens, Reinhard. 2007. Separating syntax and combinatorics in categorial grammar. *Research on Language and Computation* 5 (3): 267–285.

Nakamura, Taichi. 2013. Semantic identity and deletion. *English Linguistics* 30 (2): 643–658. Available at https://www.jstage.jst.go.jp/article/elsj/30/2/30_643/_article.

Newmeyer, Frederick J. 2016. Nonsyntactic explanations of island constraints. *Annual Review of Linguistics* 2: 187–210.

Nida, Eugene. 1949. *Morphology: The descriptive analysis of words*. Ann Arbor: University of Michigan Press.

Nykiel, Joanna. 2013. Clefts and preposition omission under sluicing. *Lingua* 123: 74–117.

Oehrle, Richard T. 1971. On Gapping. Unpublished manuscript: MIT.

Oehrle, Richard T. 1987. Boolean properties in the analysis of gapping. In *Syntax and semantics: Discontinuous constituency*, eds. Geoffrey J. Huck and Almerindo E. Ojeda, Vol. 20, 203–240. New York: Academic Press.

Oehrle, Richard T. 1994. Term-labeled categorial type systems. *Linguistics and Philosophy* 17 (6): 633–678.

Oehrle, Richard. 1995. Some three-dimensional systems of labelled deduction. *Logic Journal of the IGPL* 3 (2–3): 429–448.

Oehrle, Richard. 1996. Austinian pluralities. In *Language, logic, and computation*, eds. Jeremy Seligman and Dag Westerståhl, 433–441. Stanford: CSLI.

Okada, Sadayuki. 1999. On the function and distribution of the modifiers *respective* and *respectively*. *Linguistics* 37 (5): 871–903.

Oshima, David Y. 2007. On factive islands: Pragmatic anomaly vs. pragmatic infelicity. In *New Frontiers in Artificial Intelligence: Joint JSAI 2006 Workshop Post-Proceedings*, eds. Takashi Washio, Ken Satoh, Hideaki Terada, and Akihiro Inokuchi, 147–161. Heidelberg: Springer.

Ott, Dennis. 2014. Review of Cedric Boeckx, *Syntactic islands* (Cambridge University Press, 2012). *Language* 90 (1): 287–291.

Park, Sang-Hee, Jean-Pierre Koenig, and Rui P. Chaves. 2019. A semantic underspecification-based analysis of scope ambiguities in Gapping. In *Proceedings of Sinn und Bedeutung 23*, eds. M. Teresa Espinal, Elena Castroviejo, Manuel Leonetti, Louise McNally, and Cristina Real-Puigdollers Vol. 2, 237–251, Universitat autonoma de Barcelona. Available at https://ojs.ub.uni -konstanz.de/sub/index.php/sub/issue/view/26.

Partee, Barbara Hall. 1970. Negation, conjunction, and quantifiers: Syntax vs. semantics *Foundations of Language* 6: 153–165.

Partee, Barbara. 1984. Nominal and temporal anaphora. *Linguistics and Philosophy* 7: 243–286.

Partee, Barbara, and Mats Rooth. 1983. Generalized conjunction and type ambiguity. In *Meaning, use, and interpretation of language*, eds. Rainer Bäuerle, Christoph Schwarze, and Arnim von Stechow, 361–383. Berlin: de Gruyter.

Penka, Doris. 2011. *Negative indefinites*. Oxford: Oxford University Press.

Pentus, Mati. 1993. Lambek grammars are context free. In *Proceedings of the 8th Annual IEEE Symposium on Logic in Computer Science*, 429–433. Montreal, Canada: IEEE Computer Society Press.

Percival, W. Keith. 2018. On the historical source of immediate-constituent analysis. Available at http://people.ku.edu/~percival/ICanalysis.html. Originally published in James D. McCawley (ed.) 1976, *Notes from the linguistic underground, Syntax and semantics, Vol. 7*, 229–242 (New York: Academic Press).

Perlmutter, David. 1968. Deep and surface structure constraints in syntax. PhD diss, MIT.

Pesetsky, David. 1987. *Wh*-in-situ: Movement and unselective binding. In *The representation of (in)definiteness*, eds. Eric J. Reuland and Alice ter Meulen, 98–129. Cambridge, MA: MIT Press.

Phillips, Colin. 1996. Order and structure. PhD diss, MIT.

Phillips, Colin. 2006. The real-time status of island constraints. *Language* 82: 795–823.

Pickering, Martin. 1993. Direct association and sentence processing: A reply to Gorrell and to Gibson and Hickok. *Language and Cognitive Processes* 8: 163–196.

Pickering, Martin, and Guy Barry. 1991. Sentence processing without empty categories. *Language and Cognitive Processes* 6: 229–264.

Pogodalla, Sylvain, and Florent Pompigne. 2012. Controlling extraction in Abstract Categorial Grammars. In *Formal Grammar 2010/2011*, eds. Philippe de Groote and Mark-Jan Nederhof, 162–177. Heidelberg: Springer.

Pollard, Carl J. 1988. Categorial grammar and phrase structure grammar: An excursion on the syntax-semantics frontier. In *Categorial grammars and natural language structures*, eds. Richard T. Oehrle, Emmon Bach, and Dierdre Wheeler, 391–415. Dordrecht: Reidel.

Pollard, Carl. 2013. Linear Categorial Grammar. Unpublished manuscript. Lecture notes at ESS-LLI 2013.

Pollard, Carl. 2014. What numerical determiners mean: A non-ambiguity analysis. Talk presented at the Workshop on Semantics of Cardinals, Ohio State University.

Pollard, Carl, and Chris Worth. 2015. Coordination in linear categorial grammar with phenogrammatical subtyping. In *Proceedings for ESSLLI 2015 Workshop "Empirical Advances in Categorial Grammar"*, eds. Yusuke Kubota and Robert Levine, 162–182. University of Tsukuba and Ohio State University. Available at https://www2.ninjal.ac.jp/kubota/papers/procCG2015.pdf.

Pollard, Carl, and E. Allyn Smith. 2012. A unified analysis of *the same*, phrasal comparatives and superlatives. In *Proceedings of SALT 22*, 307–325. eLanguage. Available at https://journals.linguisticsociety.org/proceedings/index.php/SALT/issue/view/87.

Pollard, Carl, and Ivan Sag. 1983. Reflexives and reciprocals in English: An alternative to the binding theory. In *Proceedings of the Second West Coast Conference on Formal Linguistics*, 189–203. Stanford: Department of Linguistics, Stanford University.

Pollard, Carl, and Ivan A. Sag. 1992. Anaphors in English and the scope of binding theory. *Linguistic Inquiry* 23 (2): 261–303.

Pollard, Carl, and Ivan A. Sag. 1994. *Head-Driven Phrase Structure Grammar. Studies in contemporary linguistics*. Chicago: University of Chicago Press.

Post, Emil. 1943. Formal reductions of the general combinatory decision problem. *American Journal of Mathematics* 65: 197–215.

Post, Emil. 1947. Recursive unsolvability of a problem of Thue. *Journal of Symbolic Logic* 12: 1–11.

Postal, Paul M. 1971. *Cross-over phenomena*. New York: Holt, Rinehart and Winston.

Postal, Paul M. 1993. Parasitic gaps and the across-the-board phenomenon. *Linguistic Inquiry* 24 (4): 735–754.

Postal, Paul M. 1998. *Three investigations of extraction*. Cambridge, MA: MIT Press.

Postal, Paul M. 2004. *Skeptical linguistic essays*. Oxford: Oxford University Press.

Potter, David, Michael Frazier, and Masaya Yoshida. 2017. A two-source hypothesis for Gapping. *Natural Language and Linguistic Theory* 35: 1123–1160.

Pullum, Geoffrey K. 1985. *Such That* clauses and the context-freeness of English. *Linguistic Inquiry* 16: 291–298.

Pullum, Geoffrey K. 2011. On the mathematical foundations of *Syntactic Structures*. *Journal of Logic, Language and Information* 20: 277–296.

Pullum, Geoffrey K., and Gerald Gazdar. 1982. Natural languages and context-free languages. *Linguistics and Philosophy* 4: 471–504.

Puthawala, Daniel. 2018. Stripping isn't so mysterious, or anomalous scope, either. In *Formal Grammar 2018*, eds. Annie Foret, Greg Kobele, and Sylvain Pogodalla, 102–120. Heidelberg: Springer.

Radford, Andrew. 1981. *Transformational Syntax: A student's guide to Chomsky's Extended Standard Theory*. Cambridge: Cambridge University Press.

Radford, Andrew. 2004. *Minimalist syntax*. Cambridge: Cambridge University Press.

Ranta, Aarne. 1994. *Type-theoretical grammar*. Oxford: Oxford University Press.

Reade, Charles. 1869. *The cloister and the hearth*. Boston: Fields, Osgood & Co.

Reape, Mike. 1996. Getting things in order. In *Discontinuous constituency*, eds. Harry Bunt and Arthur van Horck. Vol. 6 of *Natural language processing*, 209–253. Berlin: de Gruyter.

Reinhart, Tanya, and Eric Reuland. 1993. Reflexivity. *Linguistic Inquiry* 24 (4): 657–720.

Repp, Sophie. 2009. *Negation in Gapping*. Oxford: Oxford University Press.

Restall, Greg. 2000. *An introduction to substructural logics*. London: Routledge.

Richter, Frank, and Jan-Philipp Soehn. 2006. Braucht niemanden zu scheren: A survey of NPI licensing in German. In *Proceedings of the 13th International Conference on Head-Driven Phrase Structure Grammar*, ed. Stefan Müller, 421–440. Stanford: CSLI. Available at http://web.stanford.edu/group/cslipublications/cslipublications/HPSG/2006/.

Richter, Frank, and Manfred Sailer. 2004. Basic concepts of Lexical Resource Semantics. In *ESSLLI 2003: Course material I*, eds. Arnold Beckmann and Norbert Preining. Vol. 5 of *Collegium logicum*, 87–143. Vienna, Austria: Kurt Gödel Society Wien.

Rizzi, Luigi. 1980. Violations of the *Wh*-Island constraint and the Subjacency Condition. *Journal of Italian Linguistics* 5: 157–195.

Rizzi, Luigi. 1990. *Relativized minimality*. Cambridge, MA: MIT Press.

Rodman, Robert. 1976. Scope phenomena, "movement transformations", and relative clauses. In *Montague Grammar*, ed. Barbara Partee, 165–176. New York: Academic Press.

Rodrigues, Cilene, Andrew Nevins, and Luis Vicente. 2009. Cleaving the interactions between sluicing and preposition stranding. In *Romance Languages and Linguistic Theory 2006*, eds. Torck and W. Leo Wetzels. 245–270. Amsterdam, John Benjamins.

Romero, Maribel, and Chung-Hye Han. 2004. On negative *yes/no* questions. *Linguistics and Philosophy* 27: 609–658.

Rooth, Mats. 1985. Association with focus. PhD diss, University of Massachusetts Amherst.

Ross, John Robert. 1967. Constraints on variables in syntax. PhD diss, MIT. Reproduced by the Indiana University Linguistics Club.

Ross, John Robert. 1969. Guess who? In *Chicago Linguistic Society*, eds. Robert I. Binnick, Alice Davison, Georgia M. Green, and Jerry L. Morgan, 252–286. University of Chicago: Chicago Linguistic Society.

Ross, John Robert. 1970. Gapping and the order of constituents. In *Progress in linguistics*, eds. Manfred Bierwisch and Karl E. Heidolph, 249–259. The Hague: Mouton.

Ruys, Eddy, and Yoad Winter. 2010. Quantifier scope in formal linguistics. In *Handbook of philosophical logic*, eds. Dov Gabbay and Franz Guenthner, Vol. 16, 159–225. Amsterdam: John Benjamins.

Sabbagh, Joseph. 2007. Ordering and linearizing rightward movement. *Natural Language and Linguistic Theory* 25: 349–401.

Sabbagh, Joseph. 2014. Right-Node Raising. *Language and Linguistic Compass* 8 (1): 24–35.

Safir, Kenneth. 2004. *The syntax of anaphora*. Oxford: Oxford University Press.

Sag, Ivan. 1976. Deletion and Logical Form. PhD diss, MIT.

Sag, Ivan A. 1997. English relative clause constructions. *Journal of Linguistics* 33 (2): 431–484.

Sag, Ivan A. 2012. Sign-based Construction Grammar: An informal synopsis. In *Sign-based Construction Grammar*, eds. Hans C. Boas and Ivan A. Sag, 1–51. Stanford: CSLI Publications.

Sag, Ivan A., Gerald Gazdar, Thomas Wasow, and Steven Weisler. 1985. Coordination and how to distinguish categories. *Natural Language and Linguistic Theory* 3 (2): 117–171.

Sag, Ivan, and Joanna Nykiel. 2011. Remarks on sluicing. In *Proceedings of the 18th International Conference on Head-Driven Phrase Structure Grammar*, ed. Stefan Müller, 188–208. Stanford: CSLI. Available at http://web.stanford.edu/group/cslipublications/cslipublications /HPSG/2011/.

Sag, Ivan, Rui P. Chaves, Anne Abeillé, Bruno Estigarribia, Frank Van Eynde, Dan Flickinger, Paul Kay, Laura Michaelis, Stefan Müller, Geoffrey Pullum, and Thomas Wasow. 2020. Lessons from the English auxiliary system. *Journal of Linguistics* 56: 87–155.

Sailor, Craig, and Gary Thoms. 2014. On the non-existence of non-constituent coordination and non-constituent ellipsis. In *Proceedings of WCCFL 31*, 361–370. Somerville, MA: Cascadilla Press.

Sauerland, Uli. 1998. The meaning of chains. PhD diss, MIT.

Scha, Remko. 1981. Distributive, collective and cumulative quantification. In *Formal methods in the study of language*, eds. Jeroen Groenendijk, Theo Janssen, and Martin Stokhof, 483–512. Amsterdam: Universiteit Amsterdam, Mathematical Center.

Schachter, Paul. 1978. English propredicates. *Linguistic Analysis* 4 (3): 187–224.

Schein, Barry. 1993. *Plurals and events*. Cambridge, MA: MIT Press.

Schmerling, Susan. 1972. Apparent counterexamples to the Coordinate Structure Constraint: A canonical conspiracy. *Studies in Linguistic Sciences* 2 (1): 91–104.

Schwarz, Bernhard, and Alexandra Simonenko. 2018. Factive islands and meaning-driven unacceptability. *Natural Language Semantics* 26: 253–279.

Schwarzschild, Roger. 1996. *Pluralities*. Dordrecht: Kluwer.

Shimada, Masaharu. 1999. VP-ellipsis and parasitic gaps. *English Linguistics* 16: 145–151. Available at https://www.jstage.jst.go.jp/article/elsj1984/16/1/16_1_145/_article.

Siegel, Muffy A. 1987. Compositionality, case, and the scope of auxiliaries. *Linguistics and Philosophy* 10 (1): 53–75.

Siegel, Muffy E. A. 1984. Gapping and interpretation. *Linguistic Inquiry* 15 (3): 523–530.

Sprouse, Jon, Matt Wagers, and Colin Phillips. 2012. A test of the relation between working memory and syntactic island effects. *Language* 88: 82–123.

Steedman, Mark. 1985. Dependency and coordination in the grammar of Dutch and English. *Language* 61 (3): 523–568.

Steedman, Mark. 1987. Combinatory grammars and parasitic gaps. *Natural Language and Linguistic Theory* 5 (3): 403–439.

Steedman, Mark. 1990. Gapping as constituent coordination. *Linguistics and Philosophy* 13 (2): 207–263.

Steedman, Mark. 1996. *Surface structure and interpretation*. Cambridge, MA: MIT Press.

Steedman, Mark. 2000. *The syntactic process*. Cambridge, MA: MIT Press.

Steedman, Mark. 2012. *Taking scope*. Cambridge, MA: MIT Press.

Szabolcsi, Anna. 1992. Combinatory grammar and projection from the lexicon. In *Lexical matters*, eds. Ivan A. Sag and Anna Szabolcsi. Vol. 24 of *CSLI Lecture Notes*, 241–268. Stanford: CSLI.

Szabolcsi, Anna. 1997. Strategies for scope taking. In *Ways of scope taking*, ed. Anna Szabolcsi, 109–154. Dordrecht: Kluwer.

Szabolcsi, Anna. 2004. Positive polarity - negative polarity. *Natural Language and Linguistic Theory* 22: 409–452.

Szabolcsi, Anna, and Bill Haddican. 2004. Conjunction meets negation: A study in cross-linguistic variation. *Journal of Semantics* 21 (3): 219–249.

Szabolcsi, Anna, and Frans Zwarts. 1993. Weak islands and an algebraic semantics for scope taking. *Natural Language Semantics* 1 (3): 235–284.

Takahashi, Shoichi. 2004. Pseudogapping and cyclic linearization. In *Proceedings of NELS 34*, eds. Keir Moulton and Matthew Wolf, 571–585. University of Massachusetts Amherst: GLSA.

Tanaka, Hidekazu. 2011. Voice mismatch and syntactic identity. *Linguistic Inquiry* 42 (3): 470–490.

Thoms, Gary. 2016. Short answers in Scottish Gaelic and their theoretical implications. *Natural Language and Linguistic Theory* 34 (1): 351–391.

Tonhauser, Judith, David Beaver, Craige Roberts, and Mandy Simons. 2013. Toward a taxonomy of projective content. *Language* 89 (1): 66–109.

Toosarvandani, Maziar. 2013. Gapping is low coordination (plus VP-ellipsis): A reply to Johnson. Unpublished manuscript: MIT.

Toosarvandani, Maziar. 2016. Embedding the antecedent in gapping: Low coordination and the role of parallelism. *Linguistic Inquiry* 47 (2): 381–390.

van Benthem, Johan. 1988a. The Lambek calculus. In *Categorial grammars and natural language structures*, eds. Richard T. Oehrle, Emmon Bach, and Dierdre Wheeler. Vol. 32 of *Studies in linguistics and philosophy*, 35–68. Dordrecht: Reidel.

van Benthem, Johan. 1988b. The semantics of variety in categorial grammar. In *Categorial grammar*, eds. Wojciech Buszkowski, Witold Marciszewski, and Johan van Benthem, 37–55. Amsterdam: John Benjamins.

Vicente, Luis. 2010. A note on the movement analysis of gapping. *Linguistic Inquiry* 41 (3): 509–517.

von Stechow, Arnim. 1984. Comparing semantic theories of comparison. *Journal of Semantics* 3: 1–77.

Wagers, Matthew W., and Colin Phillips. 2009. Multiple dependencies and the role of the grammar in real-time comprehension. *Journal of Linguistics* 45 (2): 395–433.

Ward, Gregory, and Andrew Kehler. 2005. Syntactic form and discourse accessibility. In *Anaphora processing: Linguistic, cognitive, and computational modelling*, eds. António Branco, Tony McEnery, and Ruslan Mitkov, 365–384. Amsterdam: John Benjamins.

Wasow, Thomas. 1975. Anaphoric pronouns and bound variables. *Language* 51: 368–383.

Wells, Rulon. 1947. Immediate constituents. *Language* 23: 81–117.

Wexler, Kenneth, and Peter Culicover. 1980. *Formal principles of language acquisition*. Cambridge, MA: MIT Press.

Whitman, Neal. 2004. *Category neutrality: A type-logical investigation*. London: Routledge.

Whitman, Neal. 2009. Right-node wrapping: Multimodal categorial grammar and the "friends in low places" coordination. In *Theory and evidence in semantics*, eds. Erhard Hinrichs and John Nerbonne, 235–256. Stanford: CSLI.

Wilder, Chris. 1999. Right Node Raising and the LCA. In *WCCFL 18 Proceedings*, eds. Sonya Bird, Andrew Carnie, Jason D. Haugen, and Peter Norquest, 586–598. Somerville, MA: Cascadilla Press.

Winkler, Susanne. 2005. *Ellipsis and focus in Generative Grammar*. Berlin: de Gruyter.

Winter, Yoad. 1995. Syncategorematic conjunction and structured meanings. In *Proceedings of SALT 5*, eds. Mandy Simons and Teresa Galloway, 387–404. Ithaca, NY: CLC Publications. Available at https://journals.linguisticsociety.org/proceedings/index.php/SALT/issue/view/104.

Winter, Yoad. 2001. *Flexibility principles in boolean semantics*. Cambridge, MA: MIT Press.

Worth, Chris. 2014. The phenogrammar of coordination. In *Proceedings of the EACL 2014 Workshop on Type Theory and Natural Language Semantics (TTNLS)*, 28–36. Gothenburg, Sweden: Association for Computational Linguistics. Available at http://www.aclweb.org/anthology/W14-1404.

Worth, Christopher. 2016. English coordination in linear categorial grammar. PhD diss, Ohio State University.

Wundt, Wilhelm. 1900. *Völkerpsychologie: Eine Untersuchung der Entwicklungsgesetze von Sprache, Mythus und Sitte*, Vol. I. Leipzig: Wilhelm Engelmann.

Wurmbrand, Susanne. 2018. The cost of raising quantifiers. *Glossa* 3 (1): 1–40.

Yatabe, Shûichi. 2001. The syntax and semantics of left-node raising in Japanese. In *Proceedings of the 7th International Conference on Head-Driven Phrase Structure Grammar*, eds. Dan Flickinger and Andreas Kathol, 325–344. Stanford: CSLI. Available at http://web.stanford.edu/group/cslipublications/cslipublications/HPSG/2000/.

Yatabe, Shûichi. 2012. Comparison of the ellipsis-based theory of non-constituent coordination with its alternatives. In *Proceedings of the 19th International Conference on Head-Driven Phrase Structure Grammar*, ed. Stefan Müller, 453–473. Stanford: CSLI. Available at http://web.stanford.edu/group/cslipublications/cslipublications/HPSG/2012/.

Yatabe, Shûichi. 2013. Hi-kooseiso tooi-setsuzoku ni kansuru ku-koozoo bunpoo ni motozuku bunseki no yuui-sei o shimesu saranaru shooko (Additional evidence for the superiority of the PSG-based account of non-constituent coordination). In *Nihon Gengo-Gakkai Dai 147-kai Taikai Yokooshuu (Proceedings of the 147th Meeting of the Linguistic Society of Japan)*, 272–277. Linguistic Society of Japan.

Yatabe, Shûichi, and Wai Lok Tam. 2019. In defense of an HPSG-based theory of non-constituent coordination: A reply to Kubota and Levine. *Linguistics and Philosophy* in press.

Yngve, Victor H. 1960. A model and an hypothesis for language structure. *Proceedings of the American Philosophical Society* 104 (5): 444–466.

Yoon, Jae-Hak. 1993. Different semantics for different syntax: Relative clauses in Korean. In *Papers in syntax*, eds. Andreas Kathol and Carl J. Pollard. Vol. 42 of *Ohio State University Working Papers in Linguistics*, 199–226. Ohio State University: Department of Linguistics. Available at https://linguistics.osu.edu/sites/default/files/workingpapers/osu_wpl_42.pdf.

Yoshida, Masaya, Honglei Wang, and David Potter. 2012. Remarks on "gapping" in DP. *Linguistic Inquiry* 43 (5): 475–494.

Yoshida, Masaya, Tim Hunter, and Michael Frazier. 2015. Parasitic gaps licensed by elided syntactic structure. *Natural Language and Linguistic Theory* 33 (4): 1439–1471.

Zaenen, Annie. 1983. On syntactic binding. *Linguistic Inquiry* 14 (3): 469–504.

Zaenen, Annie, and Lauri Karttunen. 1984. Morphological non-distinctiveness and coordination. In *Proceedings of the First Eastern States Conference on Linguistics*, eds. Gloria Alvarez, Belinda Brodie, and Terry McCoy, 309–320. Columbus: Ohio State University.

Zielonka, Wojciech. 1978. A direct proof of the equivalence of free categorial grammars and simple phrase structure grammars. *Studia Logica* 37: 41–57.

Zwicky, Arnold. 1986. The unaccented pronoun constraint in English. In *Interfaces*. Vol. 32 of *Ohio State University Working Papers in Linguistics*, 100–113. Ohio State University: Department of Linguistics. Available at https://linguistics.osu.edu/sites/default/files/workingpapers/osu_wpl_32.pdf.

Author Index

Subject Index